Eighth Edition

DEATH, SOCIETY, and HUMAN EXPERIENCE

Robert J. Kastenbaum

Arizona State University

PEARSON

Boston • New York • San Francisco
Mexico City • Montreal • Toronto • London • Madrid • Munich • Paris
Hong Kong • Singapore • Tokyo • Cape Town • Sydney

Senior Editor: Jeff Lasser
Editorial Assistant: Andrea Christie
Marketing Manager: Krista Groshong
Production Administrator: Marissa Falco
Electronic Composition: Omegatype Typography, Inc.
Composition and Prepress Buyer: Linda Cox
Manufacturing Buyer: JoAnne Sweeney
Cover Administrator: Kristina Mose-Libon
Photo Researcher: PoYee Oster
Editorial-Production Service: Matrix Productions, Inc.

For related titles and support materials, visit our online catalog at www.ablongman.com

Library of Congress Cataloging-in-Publication Data

Kastenbaum, Robert.
    Death, society, and human experience / Robert J. Kastenbaum.—8th ed.
        p. cm.
    Includes bibliographical references and index.
    ISBN 0-205-38193-6 (pbk.)
        1. Death—Psychological aspects.   2. Death—Social aspects.   I. Title.

    BF789.D4K36 2004
    306.9—dc21

                                                    2003052293

Photo Credits: Frontispiece: © Tom Tingle/The Arizona Republic. 9-12-2001. Used with permission. Permission does not imply endorsement; xx, 8, AP/Wide World Photos; 10, © Reuters NewMedia Inc./CORBIS; 18, © Scala/Art Resource, NY; 30, © Tom & Lee Ann McCarthy/CORBIS; 37, © Lynn Johnston Productions, Inc./Distributed by United Feature Syndicate, Inc.; 40, Dreyfuss/Monkmeyer; 44, © Bettmann/CORBIS; 51, © Giraudon/Art Resource, NY; 64, North Wind Picture Archives; 68, DILBERT reprinted by permission of United Feature Syndicate, Inc.; 78, © Hulton Archive/Getty Images;

Credits are continued on p. 537.

Printed in the United States of America

10 9 8 7 6 5 4 3 2 1   RRD-VA   08 07 06 05 04 03

Death, Society, and Human Experience

Yvonne Quinn takes care of her prized pet, Amoeba, a sparrow she saved three years ago. She thinks the bird is attracted to her blue nail polish.

For Cynthia

and for those

you have loved...

CONTENTS

3   WHAT IS DEATH?   45

What does death mean?

4   THE DEATH SYSTEM   79

5   DYING   *113*

Transition from life

10 EUTHANASIA, ASSISTED DEATH, ABORTION, AND THE RIGHT TO DIE 275

11 DEATH IN THE WORLD OF CHILDHOOD 307

12   BEREAVEMENT, GRIEF, AND MOURNING   347

13   THE FUNERAL PROCESS   387

14   DO WE SURVIVE DEATH?   *427*

15   HOW CAN WE HELP?   *465*

The promise of death education and counseling

16   GOOD LIFE, GOOD DEATH?   *485*

Trying to make sense of it all

PREFACE

Approximately 6,000 Americans died on September 10, 2001. Another 6,000 died on September 12. The "same" 6,000 also died September 11, the day of the terrorist attack on America—not the same people, of course, but the average number of those who die of any and all causes every day of the year. The jogger who collapsed with a massive myocardial infarction, the long-term sufferer with chronic obstructive pulmonary disease who just could not draw another breath, the driver who had persuaded himself that he could handle his alcohol, and the woman who could still remember the names of all her grandchildren but could not coax another day's life from her worn body—all these people and more end their lives without making a ripple in society at large.

The sudden, unexpected, and traumatic deaths of September 11, 2001, made more than a ripple. There were many reasons for this intense response, as will be discussed in Chapter 1. Nevertheless, it is striking how much we can be affected by some deaths while at the same time averting our attention from the universal exit procession of all mortals. Are some deaths more important than others? If so, would this mean that some lives are more important, or is it the circumstance of death that makes the difference? Perhaps there is still another explanation: We prefer not to notice dying, death, and grief unless it forces itself on us. Woody Allen probably spoke for more than a few others when he cracked that "I'm not afraid to die. I just don't want to be there when it happens."

In this book, we consider dramatic and violent forms of death, the kind that go by such names as homicide, suicide, terrorism, accident, and disaster. However, we will not allow these events to lull us into believing that death mostly happens to other people in other places when something goes very much wrong. We sort of know better, even if we try to keep ourselves from knowing we know. We also know that it is useful to give some thought to the road ahead and how we might prepare for the journey. There will be surprises enough, even so, but perhaps fewer occasions on which we find ourselves at a loss to cope.

The first business of life is to stay alive. Ask the blades of grass that struggle up to the sunlight through the hard surfaces of a city street. Ask our resourceful adversaries, the virus and the microorganism, which continue to reinvent themselves whenever we launch a new pharmacological assault. Ask the child of a devastated homeland who has already experienced massive loss, stress, and deprivation but has determined to survive it all and does. Ask nurses, paramedics, and physicians who have seen people make remarkable recoveries, seemingly because they had such a strong will to live. Ask firefighters why they risk their own lives to save people they have never met.

Even at its most resourceful and most fortunate, though, life does not succeed indefinitely in its first business of staying alive. That is a pretty good reason for having books and courses focused on dying, death, and grief. For many years, society featured the strategy of ignoring death and practically everything connected with it, including the dying and the grieving person. Unfortunately, the rule of silence created more problems than it solved. There was little comfort for the dying or grieving person and little counseling for the troubled mind of the suicidal person. Inadequate communication contributed to tense and conflictful relationships. Health care professionals had their own share of misery: responsible for care of the "incurable" (as dying people often were known) but not prepared to deal with mortality in their own thoughts and feelings.

Many people participated in the systematic avoidance of death and paid the price in anxiety, burdensome defenses, and hard knocks from a reality that would not let itself be ignored when the defenses failed. Others trembled or brooded alone, haunted by death-related anxieties that isolated them because these feelings scared off their friends. Still others challenged death by risky actions; these episodes turned passive anxiety into active thrills but, too often, resulted in serious injury or death. Few had the opportunity to reflect on dying and death with the help of a sensitive instructor and knowledge-based writings. There was at first a lot of resistance to what has now become known as death education. By now, however, many people recognize that *thanatology*—the study of life, with death left in—can be one of the most valuable projects for a student of any age.

This book is intended to contribute to your understanding of your relationship with death both as an individual and as a member of society. For example, you will learn

- How our thoughts and feelings about death develop from childhood and how we struggle with anxiety and denial toward a more mature and effective view of death.
- What very different ideas and meanings have been associated with death throughout the centuries.
- How and why the ideas of "death" and "dead" have become unsettled in our own time.

- How dying people are perceived and treated in our society, and what can be done to provide the best possible care.
- What choices and decisions we have about the way we are treated at the end of our lives.
- How people respond to the sorrow and anxiety of grief and the challenge of moving on with their lives.
- Why the funeral and memorialization process is still with us today after so many centuries.
- Who is most at risk for suicide and who is most likely to become either a killer or a victim of homicide.
- What is happening in the continuing controversy over physician-assisted death.
- What the evidence tells us and what is left to our own judgment and intuition about near-death experiences and reincarnation as proof of survival of death.
- How we can help others cope with their death encounters.

These and many other topics are presented as interactions between the individual and society. It is true that we live and die as individuals. However, it is also true that we live and die within a particular society during a particular time in world history. Preoccupation with our thoughts and feelings as individuals could lead us to lose sight of the larger picture in which social dynamics so often influence the timing, mode, and experience of dying as well as our basic interpretations of life and death.

We draw on the best available scholarship and research as well as on the words of people who have found themselves in the middle of death-related situations. Often, we will note the limitations of current knowledge and offer alternative interpretations. It is our intention to present information clearly, but without undue simplification.

I welcome you personally to this book and to the course to which this book may contribute. When I first taught a course on death approximately 40 years ago, there were few death educators, counselors, and researchers addressing these issues. Today, both the cadre of death educators and their knowledge base have expanded considerably. Take advantage of your instructor's expertise: Do not hesitate to ask questions and share your experiences. Explore the ever-growing literature on the human encounter with mortality: Discover what observers from many different perspectives can offer to us. Now join me in one of humankind's oldest—and newest—voyages of discovery.

NEW FOR THE EIGHTH EDITION

The Eighth Edition begins with a new chapter that describes and discusses the terrorist attacks on America. I do not leave this disturbing topic at the close of this chapter. Implications and reverberations are traced in several other chapters.

Other topics that receive new or expanded treatment include abortion, human sacrifice, and extinction. The new multiple-perspective approach to dying and terminal care intro-

duced in the Seventh Edition is presented in more detail at the suggestion of instructors and students. Dame Cicely Saunders, founder of the international hospice movement, has kindly consented to discuss her own views in a new interview. Throughout the book, I have updated wherever significant new information or developments have emerged.

The structure of the book was revised slightly for the Seventh Edition, seems to have worked, and so has been left alone except for the addition of the new introductory chapter.

I appreciate the comments offered by the reviewers: Lois M. Easterday, Onondaga Community College; Lewis P. Gravis, Sampson Community College; James R. Johnson, Albuquerque TVU Community College; J. Alan Kee, Amarillo College; and Daniel Leviton, University of Maryland. It was also good to hear from other instructors and readers who had useful suggestions. I hope you will find this book helpful in your explorations of death, society, and human experience.

The skeletal remains of a WTC tower continue to stand as a memorial to the victims.

chapter 1

SEPTEMBER 11, 2001,
AND THE AMERICAN DEATH SYSTEM

It did happen, right? It's not something I'm going to close my eyes and open again and I'm going to see the tower again? It's not there.
—Dennis Tadia, Captain, New York Fire Department

I couldn't wait to get down there again. I thought we're going to have plenty of people trapped there for sure and we've got to get them out.
—Tom Spinard, New York Fire Department

Hey, Chief! We've got another body over here. Where's that body bag?
—Unidentified voice from Ground Zero rescue and recovery operation

You have two 110-story buildings. You don't find a desk, a chair, a phone, a computer. The biggest piece of a phone I found was half a keypad. The buildings are dust. How are we supposed to find people?
—Joe Casaliggii, New York Fire Department

SHANKSVILLE, Pa.—So many out-of-towners have been wandering through this tiny village in search of the United Flight 93 crash site that residents have formed a corps of volunteers to lead them to the barren hilltop and makeshift memorial.
—Charles Sheehan, March 11, 2002

September 11, 2001 (9/11/01) might have been the longest day in the history of the United States. It is not over yet. Although that day properly belongs to the past, it also shadows the present and moves with us into the future. Al-most immediately, this date was experienced as a great divide between past and future. Survivors, first responders, and witnesses quickly realized that things would never again be the same (Libaw & Goldman, 2002). Like the December 7,

1941, attack on Pearl Harbor and a very few other events in American history, 9/11/01 punctured the assumption that life as we knew it would just go on and on. The impact of the Pearl Harbor attack on American attitudes should not be underestimated, but the events of 9/11/01 appear to be making an even more profound effect. The casualties were mostly civilians, the destruction occurred on the mainland, the skyline of a great city was altered, and, perhaps most compelling, millions of people could see the events as they occurred on their television sets.

Smoke continued to rise from the World Trade Center (WTC) disaster site (Ground Zero) for 6 months, and body recovery efforts persisted long after hope of rescuing a live victim had vanished. The attack was also repeated in video reports on a daily basis. Many viewers were unable to resist watching the repeats at the same time that they felt a growing resentment toward the media (i.e., "They're going to keep showing the buildings collapsing! What good does that do?").

Time has passed, but the shock, sorrow, fear, outrage, and other more complex responses continue to affect the nation. The physical destruction is complete, the death certificates issued. It is clear, however, that as individuals and a nation we are still trying to come to terms with this long and harrowing day.

This book begins with 9/11/01 because of the tragic deaths and the powerful and pervasive effect on our lives. How could the losses and the pain be ignored? There are questions to consider and lessons to learn. We are not likely to come up with the same answers or draw the same lessons. The events are still so close to us and the situation still complex and subject to change. Nevertheless, it is useful to explore the relationship between what Daniel Leviton (1995; Chapter 16 interview) calls "horrendous death" and our everyday style of life in which thoughts of mortality seldom break through the surface and even more rarely linger. We will find it useful to apply the *death system* concept to explore the connections between the habits and expectations of everyday life and the impact of sudden disaster. This chapter focuses on one dark day in American history, but it also introduces the larger issues that bear on our personal relationships to life and death.

The events of 9/11/01 are described, followed by immediate and later responses and some relevant history. We will see that the response has continued to evolve not only with the emergence of new information and misinformation but also as people have had time to absorb and reflect on the impact.

THE TERRORIST ATTACKS OF SEPTEMBER 11, 2001

We start with basics of the attacks and then briefly sample the reports of survivors, first responders, the media, and the public.

The WTC Attacks

The sky was already streaming with commercial jets on the morning of September 11, 2001. Among the scheduled flights were four jets that departed from three major airports within a 15-minute span (7:59–8:14 a.m. eastern time). American Airlines (AA) Flight 11 left Boston with 81 passengers and 11 crew, headed for Los Angeles. United Airlines (UAL) Flight 93 departed from Newark with 38 passengers and 7 crew en route to San Francisco. AA Flight 77 left Dulles with 58 passengers and 6 crew bound for Los Angeles. UAL Flight 175 headed from Boston to Los Angeles with 56 passengers and 9 crew. All 266 people aboard these jets would be dead within 2 hours.

The twin towers of the WTC were sharply defined under a clear early autumn sky. Eyewitnesses in New York City would later recall that it felt like a magnificent day to be in Manhattan. The first of the four doomed flights to depart was also the first to strike a target. AA Flight 11 struck the north tower at 8:45 a.m. The south tower was hit by UAL Flight 175 16 minutes later. Slightly less than 1 hour later, AA Flight 77 crashed into a section of the Pentagon. UAL 93, the fourth hijacked jet, had the White House as its primary target. Passengers aboard this flight learned of the previous assaults and resisted their captors. Although all aboard this flight perished, there were no casualties on the ground because the plane fell to Earth in a field near the village of Shanksville, approximately 80 miles southeast of Pittsburgh.

Impact and First Responses

The events of that morning were experienced from at least three perspectives: people caught inside the towers, witnesses, and first responders attempting to cope with the catastrophe. These personal experiences would be supplemented later by investigations into the ways in which the buildings both failed to resist the impact.

Michael A. Trinidad, a telecommunications accountant, placed a call to say good-bye to Monique Ferrer, his friend and former wife. "'What good-bye?' I asked him. 'Are you going anywhere?' He replied, 'I love you, and I love the kids. I am not going to make it out.'" Trinidad then asked to speak to her husband: "Michael asked my husband to be his children's father and love them for him" ("Report Reveals Communication Breakdown," 2002, p. 503). Ferrer had not yet learned of the disaster: AA Flight 11 had crashed into Trinidad's place of employment, the north tower, only a few moments before. There were other communications of this kind after the impacts. Many workers and visitors had a little time left, time enough to recognize the danger and contact people dear to them. Some survived, but many others perished. It was a situation few people would have anticipated for the end of their lives: healthy, located in a familiar environment, but suddenly confronted with their imminent deaths.

Reports suggest that there were a variety of responses to the crisis. People who judged they had no chance of escape used their last minutes to attempt to contact loved ones. Others decided to vacate the building by whatever means were available at the moment, elevator or stairs. Scattered reports indicate that there was a sense of danger but also a confidence that one could make it out safely. Many people did not know just what had happened or how serious it might be. What occupants knew and when depended much on their location: north or south tower and above or below the point of impact. As it turned out, the chance of survival was almost completely determined by location. There also seemed to be conflicting advice in circulation: "Stay where we are and we will be rescued" versus "get out as soon as we can." Those who were in a position to com-

prehend the crisis often came to the assistance of others who had blanked out and were slow to move. There is little or no information to indicate that occupants died because of their own inability to deal with the situation. Most either had a chance or did not, depending on their location at impact and the type and amount of destruction that stood between themselves and safe exit. The fragmentary reports of both survivors and witnesses indicate some occupants responded in a calm and orderly way, whereas others panicked. It is likely that responses were strongly affected by the particular circumstances that people encountered at their location.

The most horrifying response will never be forgotten by witnesses. Desperate people became bodies hurtling to the ground. Trapped above the point of impact, an unknown number of people leaped to their deaths rather than perish in flame and smoke. Even firefighters who had experienced many previous disasters were overwhelmed by the sight and sound of bodies hitting the pavement. Many first responders felt devastated that they could not rescue these people, and few witnesses could say that they might not have also taken the same way out if trapped in such an overwhelming situation.

People who happened to be in the area at that time became witnesses to the unexpected catastrophe. There was panic among some of the first witnesses as well as people rushing from the buildings. These responses were not inappropriate: Even the survivors and witnesses were still in danger. The following are a few of the reports, as collected by NewYorkMetro.com ("The Longest Week," 2002):

- It was so fast. It was so loud. I just came out of the Fulton Street subway when I heard this terrifying explosion. I looked up and saw smoke surrounding the World Trade Center. People started running. There was mass hysteria.
- I saw dozens of people jumping to their deaths from the 80th floor. Bodies were landing on nearby rooftops and on the plaza.
- There were throngs of people all looking up. All those people were crushed when the second building came down. I ran for four blocks and stopped just past Chambers and sat down. But

the cloud kept coming. I got up and started to run. I saw a fireman who was totally traumatized. He and another fireman were holding hands when one of the buildings collapsed. And then all he was holding was the hand.

A student in a sixth-grade classroom across the river saw that one of the twin towers was on fire. The scene was in full view: The teacher said,

- I called down to the office and told the secretary, who didn't believe me. She said, "How do you know?" and I said, "We're watching it— Tell the principal." I told the class I was sure many people had died and that we needed to close our eyes and be silent for a moment. I gave them the date and the time and said that this was a day that they would never forget.

This chapter opened with the words of members of the New York City Fire Department who had rushed to the scene (excerpted from the powerful CBS documentary, *9-11*, 2002). The units that first arrived were very familiar with the WTC and its towers. They knew they would be up against a major disaster as soon as the call came in: "Right then and there I knew it. This was going to be the worst day of my life." This apprehension proved more than justified. Among the hazards and difficulties they faced were the following:

- The cause of the disaster was at first unclear to the firefighters as well as others in the WTC area. Not until the second tower was struck could they be sure they were dealing with a terrorist attack rather than an accident. This immediately raised the concern that additional attacks would occur.
- Communication was limited throughout the ordeal. For example, it would be a while before firefighters in the first tower would learn that the other tower had been hit. Even more disorienting was the loss of contact among firefighters within the same building as communication equipment failed. This disruption of communication affected decision making by the commanders, who did not have the latest information and could not readily direct the firefighters who were moving throughout the burning and crumbling building.
- Senior fire department officers on the scene lost their lives when large pieces of debris collapsed

on them. Remaining and incoming officers had to establish a new command center and start to operate in the midst of the turbulent scene.

- The elevator system broke down after a few minutes. This meant that firefighters, each carrying 60 pounds of equipment, had to climb 78 floors before they could even start to deal with the primary disaster scene. Even under less hazardous conditions, it takes approximately 1 minute to climb one set of stairs. In this situation, exhausted firemen still had a long way to go as they ascended as quickly as possible. For many of these first responders, every step upward took them that much closer to their own deaths. A woman on the 83rd floor reports, "I was thinking we were doomed because there were so many people on the stairs and it wasn't moving. Dozens and dozens of firefighters were running past us, telling us to stay calm and keep moving. I remember looking into their eyes, thinking how brave they were" ("The Longest Week," 2002).
- Events occurred in an unpredictable and unprecedented swirl of confusion and threat. There was little time to make and carry out decisions and no way of knowing either the full extent of the damage or what might happen next. For example, a perilous search for a possible safe exit had to be made when orders to evacuate the tower finally reached some of the firefighters. Smoke, dust, heat, sink holes, and flaming debris were among the hazards for rescue and survival.

Dissolving Reality, Chaos, and Order

The WTC attacks had a profound impact on all the senses, including the sense of reality. Familiar reality lost its defined boundaries and dissolved for people on the scene. The disaster continued to unfold before their eyes. They were disoriented by sounds of destruction, sounds of panic, and the eerie sound of silence. The ground trembled and vibrated under their feet. Fast-moving clouds of thick dust and choking smoke invaded their lungs while obscuring vision. The blue sky as well as the landmark towers had vanished, and the thriving business center was becoming a vast and charred scene of desolation.

The physical impact was accompanied by the urgent need to understand what was taking place. Obviously, the people on the scene were in the midst of a life-threatening disaster, but it was difficult to take effective action while feeling stunned and confused (Gorski, 2002). A "normal" emergency most often occurs within a relatively stable environment. The community is still present and functioning, for example, when a few people are in peril from a motor vehicle accident or a fire. People often can respond quickly and vigorously when it is an emergency-within-everyday reality situation. Even then, it might take a little while to realize what is happening. Soon, the "fight-or-flight" impulse asserts itself. One might attempt either to escape or to somehow cope with the threat. Circumstances play a significant role in which impulse becomes dominant. People may seek safety for themselves or accept further risk by trying to rescue others. These basic options were kept on hold at the WTC for many people on the scene because it was so difficult to comprehend what was happening and, therefore, what should and could be done. Many witnesses, including media reporters on the scene, would later report that the catastrophic events seemed like something from a movie with lavish special effects. In fact, if they had seen anything like this before, it was in some "shake-and-bake" disaster film.

The prompt arrival of professional firefighters, paramedics, and police brought a new element to the scene. Here were people who were trained and experienced in dealing with emergencies. They had their skills, their equipment, and their practiced teamwork. The contest now was order versus chaos. Could society's response system cope with chaos unleashed on such a large and intense scale? In this instance, the first responders helped to save the lives of many people who had not been killed at or soon after impact. There was no way, though, to save those still trapped at the highest floors, nor to bring all of their fellow responders back to safety.

This valiant rescue effort would earn worldwide respect and admiration. Less obvious, but perhaps even more consequential, was the implication for society's general sense of security. Chaos had won. Thousands had died. The towers had fallen. Death—raw, unpredictable, unfair death—

could still break loose in a society that had established so many levels of physical, symbolic, and ritualistic protections against mortal danger. We were not supposed to die young, violently, and in public, especially in a place where international commerce flourished. Our society's apparent victories over death anxiety had been snatched away in one morning of terror and a long wave of grief and stress that continues to this day.

During those first hours, millions of other people throughout the world could not help but watch events that they also found so difficult to believe. Along with everything else, the WTC disaster became part of the lifelong memories of a great many people who were not physically on the scene. Those who visited the scene even months later reported that the enormity of the destruction was far beyond what they could comprehend from television. People would feel compelled to visit Ground Zero to somehow test and come to terms with the reality.

Pentagon Attack and Shanksville Crash

The two other terrorist attacks of 9/11/01 were just as deadly to jetliner passengers and crew—all died. These disasters did receive much attention but have remained somewhat in the shadow of the New York attack, with its larger number of deaths on the ground and its devastation of the WTC. (Table 1.1 presents the death toll from all three sites. Note that there might still be changes in the WTC total as the verification process continues.)

The Pentagon may or may not have been the primary target for the hijackers of AA Flight 77. Many analysts have concluded that the hijackers could not find the White House and decided instead to attack another objective symbolic of

TABLE 1-1

Deaths from the Terrorist Attacks of 9/11/01

	WTC	*Pentagon*	*Shanksville*
Jetliner	92	65	64
Ground	2,801	184	0
Total	2,893	249	64

American power. There was some good fortune in that the wing of the building struck by the plane was being remodeled and had fewer occupants than usual. This was a military target, and the terrorists might have been regarded as having declared war through a sneak attack, but the slaughter of thousands of civilians (including foreign visitors) in New York had already eliminated the possibility of considering 9/11/01 to have any kind of legitimacy.

It was a painful and desperate scene on the ground after the first impact of the hit as smoke and flames engulfed Pentagon employees. There were heroes here as well as at the WTC (Cannon, 2002):

> Staff Sgt. Christopher Braman sprinted three times into the black, burning building to look for survivors. He found a burned woman struggling so hard to breathe that she clapped her hands to be heard. He saw another woman whose clothes had been ripped off by the explosion's force. He saw a beam of light that turned out to be a man on fire. Braman saved a handful of people in those first horrifying moments, but he didn't stop there. For the next few days, with Ben-Gay shoved up his nose to block the smell of death, he recovered the bodies—or body parts—of 63 people. "I found them doing their jobs. I found someone with a phone melted to his head. People died with honor."

The attack did not interrupt Pentagon operations, the physical damage was soon repaired, new safety and security measures were put into place, and the victims were honored with a national memorial service. Many lives were permanently changed, though, by disabilities, the loss of family and friends, and memories of the traumatic event.

The fate of UA Flight 93 differed in two significant ways from the other hijacked airliners (Levine, 2002). Modern communication technology—telephones in the sky—made it possible for some passengers and crew to learn of the two earlier attacks. Their courage and concern for others was the other factor. Assaulting the hijackers, they prevented the airliner from completing its mission of destroying another major target and killing many more people on the ground. The jet fell to Earth instead in an open area that had once been a strip-mining field. There were no homes or businesses to be destroyed (had the crash occurred a few moments later it might have hit a school).

This disaster will long be remembered for the poignancy of the last telephone conversations between several passengers and a family member and the quick thinking and resolve with which they responded against the hijackers. People in neighboring communities offered their own spontaneous memorialization with flowers, religious symbols, and other objects (see Chapter 12).

RESPONDING TO THE LOSS AND TRAUMA

Smoke would continue to rise from Ground Zero for months after the attack. Rescue and recovery efforts were covered by the international media on a daily basis. Other major events often fall from media and public attention in a short time, but 9/11/01 was still happening, with the ruins of the WTC as its persistent reminder.

It is probable that the continuing attention to Ground Zero was motivated by more than its obvious "newsworthiness." There was a need to comprehend what had happened. We would have to view the scene again and again to make both the emotional and the intellectual connections. Thanatologist Avery D. Weisman (1974) identified the process of *realization* that must occur before a superficial recognition of a critical situation can fully register on us. Millions repeatedly viewed the smoking ruins and laboring workers with decreasing expectation of witnessing a rescue. Why subject ourselves to such a grim scene? "Because we needed to make it real to ourselves before moving on with life" is probably at least part of the answer.

Much else had happened and was still happening while the smoke continued to rise from Ground Zero. It is useful to remind ourselves of some of the major developments:

1. *Doctors and nurses without patients.* Health care professionals responded swiftly to the disaster. Doctors and nurses rushed to hospitals and clinics. Equipment, supplies, and ambulances all were placed on the ready and the call went out for immediate blood donations. The health care system

had demonstrated its ability to overcome bureaucratic tangles and make its resources quickly available during a crisis. But where were the patients? Doctors and nurses were standing by as the minutes and then the hours passed. Gradually, the almost unbelievable situation became clear: Those directly affected by the attack were beyond medical assistance. There were first responders with injuries and respiratory problems, and a few people had incurred minor injuries while leaving the towers. The lack of survivors, though, seemed to merge with the silence at Ground Zero: All those active, lively people had vanished in just a few minutes.

2. *From rescue to recovery.* Firefighters and other trained professionals had continued to arrive at the WTC. Like the doctors and nurses, they expected to save people. It would take them longer to discover that very few, if any, remained to be rescued. Workers in the construction industry also arrived with their heavy and specialized equipment in the hope of rescuing people trapped in the debris. There was no way of knowing if rescue was still possible or even where it would be most useful to explore. There would be much exhausting labor and frustration before the strongly motivated volunteers (including firefighters looking for lost comrades) were forced to conclude that there were no lives to be saved, no successes to reward their efforts.

Giving up the rescue effort was a public action that confirmed private doubts and seemed to close the door on lingering hope. (Some family members and friends would continue to harbor the hope for a miracle.) There was another important objective to achieve, however: recovering and identifying the victims. Not long ago, the topics of dying, death, grief, and mourning were generally avoided in the United States and many other developed nations (see Chapters 2, 4, and 15). Today, there are more people who are willing to deal with and bring understanding to these challenges. This heightened awareness was evident in the recovery effort. Many people recognized that the affected families could not put their lives back together until they had a sense of closure, which would include being able to have a funeral and memorial service for the person they had lost. The firefighters seemed to feel as strongly for the comrades who had not returned

from the WTC; together, they had been a kind of family. There was also a special need to honor those who died while trying to help others. The men and women searching through the debris (and putting themselves at risk while doing so) developed their own on-the-spot rituals when a body was found. All in the vicinity would pause in their work, kneel, and observe a moment of silence. Then—back to work.

The recovery process was nearly as stressful as the rescue effort. Much hard work would be performed without finding a body. Furthermore, many of the remains were in the form of shattered body parts. This was a disturbing sight and also increased the difficulty of attempting to identify the remains. It was both disappointment and horror to have so little left of a person. Eventually, it would become painfully clear that bodies of some of the victims would probably never be found. A memorial service was held for families who were left without the physical remains of their loved ones, and this experience might have been of some help in enabling them to cope with the loss and move on with their lives.

3. *Remembering individuals.* Memorial services and media coverage were exceptional in their recognition of individuals who lost their lives at all of the attack sites (*U.S. News & Word Report,* 2000). The high number of fatalities dominated national response at first. Soon, though, attention focused on the individuality of the victims. Newspapers, magazines, and television made efforts to find photographs and relate information about the victims and their families. Large-scale memorial services in New York City and the nation's capital also devoted time to remembering the victims by name. It would have been easier perhaps to respond primarily to the mass loss of life, but the care taken to remember individuals probably served as one of the first steps in the long process of healing.

4. *Sharing in the sorrow.* A wave of compassion arose not only throughout the United States but also from many people in many other nations. It is probable that this sense of sharing in the sorrow was enhanced by the fact that many people elsewhere had visited New York City or knew people who lived and worked there. New York City has long been an international destination, and its disaster could be felt by many people far beyond the

A woman is overcome with a sense of devastation as she inspects photographs of people missing after the WTC attack in New York City. "Missing" meant there still was hope, but also intense anxiety.

five boroughs. Saturated and continuous television coverage also brought the disaster home to viewers throughout the world. It may also be that the sorrow of bereaved family members resonated with the personal experiences of viewers who had undergone other ordeals in their own lives. Whatever the reasons, much of the world shared the sorrow in the weeks immediately following 9/11/01.

5. *More religious, more patriotic.* Soon after the disaster, there was a perceptible increase in overt religiosity and patriotism. Churches reported higher attendance, and person-in-the-street interviews found many people who said they had rekindled an interest in religion that had become dormant. The search for understanding, strength, and protection as well as the comfort of being with other people during the postdisaster crisis all

seemed to contribute to the heightened expression of both religion and patriotism. This large-scale emotional response to a large-scale disaster brings to mind the terror management theory of death anxiety discussed in Chapter 2.

6. *Heroes among us.* The United States has often been criticized as a society that allows itself to be dazzled and infatuated by "celebrities" while giving little attention to people who make significant contributions in many other walks of life. The events of 9/11/01 transformed this situation. The courage and determination of rescue workers impressed and inspired the public. Although new in our own time, this admiration for people who risk their own lives to save others was once strongly established: The volunteer firefighters, racing to the emergency call at any moment, were the heroes of both small towns and large cities from co-

lonial times to the early twentieth century. A new generation now realized that there are "real-life" heroes among us.

The first phase of response was marked by sorrow and pain but also by a sense of national unity and compassion. It could also be described as a feeling-oriented and self-reflective phase. Many people experienced vicarious grief (Chapter 12), sorrowing for other people's sorrow. There was concern about the stress and trauma experienced by bereaved family members, especially the possible impact on children. When New York City Mayor Rudolph Giuliani mentioned that these events had forced him to think about his own mortality, it is probable that many others agreed: Perhaps it was time to reflect on our own lives with a renewed awareness of death in mind.

WAR AGAINST TERRORISM

Feeling orientation and personal reflection did not long remain the dominant national response. Military rhetoric and the call to arms for a war against terrorism soon became official policy. There would be aggressive measures to punish and defeat the terrorists and protective measures to safeguard against further attacks. International cooperation would be sought to identify and uproot terrorist organizations. Airport security would be tightened. Attempts would be made to seal the borders against terrorist infiltrators. Flight instruction programs would be monitored. Later, smallpox vaccine would be acquired in case of a bioterrorism attack and a variety of other measures either proposed or put into practice to reduce casualties. Congress would vote to establish a new cabinet level Department of Homeland Security. Funding priorities would shift to deal with the terrorism issue. Government agencies would be granted additional powers to conduct investigations, detain suspects, and even use lethal force when deemed necessary.

The attack on al-Qaida and Taliban forces in Afghanistan was the most evident and dramatic example of the turnabout in response to 9/11/01. It was preceded and accompanied by televised press conferences with the secretary of defense and military officers. There were still human interest stories about victims and their families, but primary attention had been refocused on military plans and activities. The enemy was not well known to the public, so experts (Bergen, 2001; Carr, 2002; Goodson, 2001) offered background information and interpretation. Although questions were raised about details of the declared war on terrorism, public support was united behind the military effort.

The war against terrorism can be understood in terms of its national security and political objectives. Another important facet has been generally overlooked but needs to be mentioned here: The military stance quickly took precedence over the feelings orientation and self-reflection in the wake of 9/11/01. This was a transformation from "passive victim" to "aggressive crusader against injustice." Preparation for action with a more or less definite objective became the implicitly approved alternative to the more subjective quest for meaning and emotional recovery. People (including first responders) who had lost family members and friends in the terrorist attacks would continue to struggle with the emotional impact and the recovery process. The general public, though, was being invited to set aside the daunting inner challenge of feelings and reflections and become part of a united national effort against the external threat of terrorism (Kastenbaum, 2002)

STRESS, CRITICISM, AND "RETURN TO NORMAL"

Studies have shown that people often come together to offer support during and immediately after a large-scale disaster (Weaver, 2002). The altruistic impulse is demonstrated in risk-taking rescues and a generous outpouring of time, effort, supplies, housing, and personal comforting. Public response to 9/11/01 was certainly an example of this kind of response. However, studies also show that the compassion, altruism, and unity start to fade within a relatively short time. Some people continue to help, but most others return to their usual patterns of life, looking after their own obligations and interests, and engaging in a variety of conflicts and disputes that had been interrupted by the need to become good samaritans. This phase of public response also occurred within a few months of the terrorist attacks.

Sorrow, compassion and a surge of heightened patriotism united the nation after the September 11, 2001, terrorist attacks.

Church attendance declined to its previous level (Rose, 2002), and at least one pastor was fired because he held a 9/11/01 memorial service open to all denominations (Cooperman, 2002). American flags were less frequently displayed. Baseball games were played without the singing of "God Bless America." An early proposal to establish 9/11/01 as an official national day or mourning was tabled for lack of support ("9-11," 2002), and there was negligible increase in public interest in news of the world ("Survey," 2002).

There was no doubt that people were still affected by the attacks, some very much so. However, there was also little doubt that life in the United States was trying very hard to return to normal. This shift was strongly supported by government and the business community. "If we don't get back on our feet, the terrorists will have won!" was a rallying cry.

The spirit of national unity continued with respect to overcoming terrorist threats, honoring the victims, and admiring the courageous first responders. The national mood, however, now allowed criticisms to be expressed, and with increasing intensity. Few aspects were spared controversy. Bereaved families organized in protest against the bureaucracy that had been established to provide death benefits. Not only did the process seem unnecessarily slow and complicated but also the bureaucracy was accused of making the judgment that some lives had been worth more than others. Recovery workers had a brief dispute with the city of New York. A statue depicting the body of a person who leaped from a WTC tower was fiercely rejected, and the fate of another work of art is in doubt (Gaskell, 2002):

> A statue based on the famous photograph of the flag-raising at the World Trade Center site is being criticized because the three white firefighters in the picture have been transformed into one white, one black, and one Hispanic. Some firefighters and their families say the 19-foot bronze is political correctness run amok, and an attempt to rewrite history.

The most extensive controversies have swirled around the possibility that the attacks might have been prevented or the casualties significantly reduced (McClan, 2002). There was a practical side to these investigations and accusations. Further acts of terrorism might be prevented if gaps and failures could be identified. However, there was also a psychological need at work: finding somebody or something to blame.

One major focus of controversy was the design and construction of the WTC towers. As a child of New York returning to visit the city, I treated myself to an open-air bus tour. The guide proudly informed us that the terrorists who had planted a bomb in the WTC garage in 1993 had no chance of destroying the massive structures because they were rooted deeply and firmly into the earth. That was a few months before 9/11/01. The tour guide was not the only person who believed the towers could withstand practically any disaster. Obviously, all the safeguards were not enough. How safe were the towers? What had gone so terribly wrong? Barter (2001) noted,

> The design of the WTC saved thousands of lives by standing for well over an hour after the planes crashed into its twin towers, say structural engi-

neers. But the towers' ultimate collapse was inevitable, as the steel cores inside them reached temperatures of 800°C—raising questions as to why hundreds of rescue workers were sent into the doomed buildings to their deaths.

The experts who contributed to this report judged that the structures held up amazingly well, thereby saving many lives, but that nothing that exists could have withstood the extremely high temperature from a large quantity of aviation fuel. The intense heat could be resisted for only a limited time. The force of the crashing jets would not have brought the buildings down, but one steel floor melted after another and collapse became inevitable as an estimated 100,000 tons of weight fell from the upper floors alone. Despite this defense, others have argued that the structure provided too limited a pathway of escape. An official government report (Glanz & Lipton, 2002) later noted that the temperatures had actually risen as high as 2,000°C and generated heat equivalent to the energy output of a nuclear power plant. It was not surprising that fireproofing, sprinkler systems, and water supply for the hoses failed under such blazing heat.

Criticism of the decisions made by firefighter officials has been somewhat muted because it is recognized that they were functioning under extremely difficult conditions and that, in fact, captains and commanders were among those who died in or near the towers. The CBS documentary ("9-11," 2002) shows firefighter officials trying desperately to learn what was happening inside the towers and frustrated because they could not reach their teams as the communication radio system failed. It was later reported that police and fire commanders had not communicated with each other during the crisis, and that a warning of imminent building collapse by a police helicopter was relayed to police officers but not to most firefighters ("Report Reveals Communication Breakdown," 2002).

Firefighters, communication specialists, architects, and others concerned with safety issues have been studying the disaster to draw useful lessons for the future. Our own lessons might well include being aware that criticisms and accusations are very likely to follow the altruistic phase of a disaster response. (The WTC attack also gave rise to many unsubstantiated speculations that, fortunately, have been pretty much set aside [Vendantam, 2002]).

Warnings Not Heeded

The most intense controversy became public with disclosures that government agencies apparently had neglected signals of the impending attacks and had therefore missed the opportunity to prevent them. At first, there were allegations that "Phoenix FBI agents attempting to investigate terrorism were hamstrung for years by top bureau officials in the valley despite abundant evidence of Middle Eastern extremists, according to a letter sent to FBI agents by a longtime special agent" (Krikorian & Connell, 2002).

There was a particular concern that flight training schools in Arizona might have been used by people planning terrorist actions, but this investigation was given the lowest priority. It soon turned out that other signs of possible terrorist action seemed to have been neglected at the highest levels of government. Detailed articles and books described proceedings in which terrorist warnings were given little consideration and possible interventions neglected (Benjamin & Simon, 2002; Hanson, 2002; Elliott, 2002). A congressional panel probed the attack and blamed the intelligence network for many failures, including reluctance to share vital information with each other (Yaukey, 2002). A shortage of personnel was one of the main points of defense offered by intelligence agencies.

Whether or not 9/11/01 could have been avoided by more vigilant counterterrorism work is a question beyond the scope and competence of this book. It is relevant to note, however, that public confidence in the ability of the government to protect against sudden and violent death was shaken. Not only the attacks but also the apparent shortcomings of the nation's security system contributed to a heightened sense of vulnerability. Were "death anxiety" as simple to measure as pulse rate, we would probably have found a notable increase after both the attacks and the revelations.

Stress and Distress

Painful reverberations from 9/11/01 have continued in the lives of many people. Those affected

include family and friends of the attack victims, including firefighters, but also the grappler operators who excavated debris during the Ground Zero cleanup and were not emotionally prepared to discover unearthed bodies (Kugler, 2002). The ripple effect, though, goes beyond people who were so close to the disaster. Postdisaster stress was documented in Oklahoma City several years after the bombing (Sprang, 1999), and similar responses to other large-scale disasters throughout the world have also been observed. Researchers went to work quickly, aware that the 9/11/01 terrorist attacks might have widespread effects. They were right.

The nonprofit RAND group conducted a national survey that found a broad increase in stress-related symptoms among most Americans immediately after the terrorist attacks (Schuster et al., 2001). Their findings included the following:

- Nine of 10 adults reported at least one stress-related symptom.
- Nearly half the adults reported one or more "substantial" symptoms of stress (i.e., a disorder that interfered significantly with their lives).
- Nearly half the children were worried about their own or their loved ones' safety, and one in three were experiencing stress symptoms.

Children who watched the most television had more stress symptoms, but there was also reason to believe that the information provided by news coverage also helped children as well as adults to understand and cope with the situation.

These findings were based on responses from the general population. Mental health experts noted that people with preexisting psychiatric vulnerabilities were at a heightened risk for a severe stress response after the attacks (Panda & Weiden, 2001). People without a previous psychiatric vulnerability were also likely to be at risk for posttraumatic stress disorder (Stephenson, 2001; see also Chapter 12) if they had witnessed the disaster first hand (e.g., seeing people leap from a tower or discovering a mutilated body).

Particular attention was given to increased risk for depression and suicidality (Salmon & Sun, 2001). The first known suicide occurred 3 months after the attack when the widow of a WTC victim shot herself. It is difficult to determine how many other suicides might have occurred as a result of this disaster, but experts fear that the number is substantial and not necessarily limited to the period immediately after the attack. Mental health experts and public and private agencies cooperated following the Oklahoma City bombing to offer counseling and support to bereaved family members. There was a similar response in New York City, with the media doing its part to inform people about the availability of grief support services and encourage their utilization. Psychological and social support for traumatic grief was no longer regarded as a sign of weakness or mental illness. New York schoolchildren were considered to be at "extreme risk" from anxiety-related disorders associated with the attacks (Bauder, 2002).

Did 9/11/01 also have effects on physical well-being? Yes, at least for people who were in the vicinity of the WTC. Six months after the attack, workers reported substantial rates of physical symptoms, especially problems with breathing and irritation of mucous membranes (Bernard et al., 2002). A new term came into existence: World Trade Center cough (Prezant et al., 2002). The cough was a symptom of severe respiratory symptoms that required medical leave of at least 4 weeks. Even a brief exposure to the smoke and dust at Ground Zero was enough to jeopardize the health and imperil the life expectancy of previously healthy people (Scanlin, 2002).

Depression and sustained high levels of anxiety are stressful on body, mind, and interpersonal relationships. It is possible that stress and distress as a result of the 9/11/01 attacks could undermine both the quality and the length of life for many people, even if no reliable statistics can ever be compiled because of the complexity of the connections (Silver et al., 2002). For example, accident researchers report that since the attacks, more people have been driving while drowsy because they decided against air travel, contributing to motor vehicle accidents (Brody, 2002). Those who have increased their use of alcohol as a result of the stress are also at a higher risk for involvement in accidents.

Abrupt changes in the economy are also likely to be stressful. Thriving businesses in the WTC vicinity suffered significant losses, and some had to lay off employees or even shut their doors. The economic impact was much broader, however. Airlines and the hotel industry, for example, lost many customers and were forced to reduce their services and payroll (Alexander & Alexander, 2002). Many people lost their jobs and also their health insurance coverage. Families that had been financially secure found themselves in debt, and some even became homeless. The stock market wavered and fell (although not entirely as a result of the terrorist attacks).

Governmental assistance programs were overloaded with their increased responsibilities and had to find their way through numerous bureaucratic tangles. The public responded generously to calls for charitable donations: Within a month, the astounding amount of $1.4 billion had been raised to help the families of victims and rebuild. Unfortunately, the Red Cross and some other charitable organizations soon came under critical attack for allegedly misdirecting or poorly administering the funds. On and on went the long wave of economic instability in the wake of the terrorist attacks. Financial stress and uncertainty affected many lives and may have had a significant, if indirect, role in many deaths.

Anxiety about the prospect of further attacks also became a condition of American life. Government officials repeatedly warned that additional attacks were a certainty but could not say precisely where or when, although alerts were issued from time to time. It was also difficult to comprehend that there are people with such hatred toward the United States that they would carry out suicidal attacks to kill people they had never met. The national self-image has been one of promoting freedom and assisting those in need. Attempts have been made to provide profiles of the new enemy. For example, Thomas Friedman (2002) analyzed Muslim extremists in Europe who have played a major role in terrorist activities:

> When these young Muslim men in Europe turn to religion, and to Islam, it becomes the sole source of meaning in their lives, and they see it, and feel it, as being under attack every day all around them...besieged by the liberation of women, who no longer obey any of the traditional social rules...and by the promotion of consumerism and materialism—all of which they believe is driven primarily by America. They see America as the most lethal weapon destroying their religious universe...or the universe they

would like to build. And that is why they transform America into the ultimate evil. (p. 336)

Perhaps these explanations are adequate, perhaps not. It is clear, however, that the world seems less predictable, friendly, and safe since 9/11/01, and death less under control.

TERRORIST ATTACKS AND THE DEATH SYSTEM

Approximately 6,000 people die every day in the United States. Thousands of other people thereby lose somebody who was vital to their lives. Almost all these deaths and grieving experiences receive little general attention. Death is a crucial event for individuals and their families, but it is routine for society. In fact, death is so firmly rooted in social structure and process that some thoughtful people believe that our communal lives are organized primarily around the challenge of coping with mortality (see Chapter 2). We do not have to go that far, though, to recognize that much of society is influenced by death and vice versa.

The *death system* concept has proven useful in tracing and comprehending the complex relationships between society and death, with special attention to fear of death and denial of that fear. The death system is discussed in detail in Chapter 4. It is useful here, though, to examine briefly some aspects of the 9/11/01 disaster from the death system perspective. *The death system can be defined as the interpersonal, sociocultural, and symbolic network through which an individual's relationship to mortality is mediated by his or her society.* There is a continuing loop between the ways in which we live and the ways in which we die. In practice, it is often difficult to determine which came first— for example, a social taboo against discussing death that may have heightened death anxiety, or frightening experiences with death that may have bred the taboo in the first place. All societies have a death system. The components of this system are people, places, times, objects, and symbols. At this point, we are more interested in the functions of the death system, as given in Table 1.2, along with concise annotations regarding the terrorist attacks.

The death system within American society operates with much less general notice in everyday life and death. For example, a person learns he or she has a medical condition that could become life-threatening. This warning might be sufficient to cause general changes in the person's health management, and death remains a somewhat dis-

TABLE 1-2

Functions of the Death System and 9/11/01

Function	Comment
Warning and predicting	Warnings not evaluated, given priority, and followed-up effectively; attacks come essentially as surprise.
Preventing	Failed to prevent deaths on airliners. Failed to prevent loss of life on ground, but design features of WTC towers and courageous actions by first responders reduced the number of casualties.
Caring for the dying	Direct casualties either died on the scene or escaped without life-threatening injuries.
Disposing of the dead	Exceptionally long and arduous efforts required to recover bodies of victims, and identified remains not found for all believed to have died at WTC.
Social consolidation after death	Delay and stress in grief recovery for bereaved families because so many bodies not found or identified; the cities attacked and the nation as a whole responded strongly and compassionately.
Making sense of death	Major issue immediately after trauma of unexpected attacks; at least temporary stimulus to personal reflections on life and death.
Killing	Shift to killing (war on terrorism) orientation after being victimized by an external death system.

tant prospect. There might be the need, however, to introduce specific medical interventions to prevent death, if possible. At a certain point, it might be determined that the person is terminally ill, thereby raising questions and options about the type of care that would be most desired and suitable with death in the near future. Another whole set of considerations comes into focus when decisions are made about after-death actions (regarding burial or cremation, the role of religion in memorial services, etc.). Family, friends, and colleagues at work will have their own emotional and practical adjustments to make as their lives go on in the absence of a person who had been important to them. There may be either little or profound concern for making sense of death, depending on circumstances (e.g., the death of an adult with a known physical condition that has gradually declined over the years is likely to raise fewer disturbing emotional and philosophical issues than the death of a child. The killing function of the death system ordinarily would not be applicable to an expected "trajectory" of death (Chapter 5), being much more conspicuous in suicide, murder, war, or death by negligence.

The terrorist attacks of 9/11/01 differed in almost every way from the everyday operation of our society's death system. Death came without warning: there was no time to prepare and little to respond. A significant part of the usual sequence was eliminated for most victims and families: There was no opportunity to care for the dying and affirm love and support. The opportunity to dispose of the dead in a timely and acceptable way was denied to many families because of the horrific circumstances at Ground Zero. On the positive side, the family survivors were not alone in their grief as the nation mourned with them. Social consolidation after death similarly was a challenge for the entire nation. Making sense of death remains a continuing challenge because our assumption that a familiar world is a safe world was shown to be mistaken and for other psychological, philosophical, and religious reasons. Killing, often an overlooked facet of the death system, claimed prominence. We were forcefully reminded of the potential for violence within both individuals and their societies.

Table 1.2 presents the major functions of the death system neatly. The reality is not nearly so simple, of course. Making smallpox vaccine available in the event of a bioterrorism attack, for example, was an appropriate strengthening of the prevention function but also reintroduces the risks associated with the vaccinations. As another example, frequent announcements of terrorism alerts demonstrate a more active warning-predicting function but can also both raise stress levels and induce a sense of indifference when warnings continue in the absence of further attacks. The functions can interact and sometimes contradict each other in many ways, and changes in one function can affect others. At the least, we might want to remind ourselves that in coping with danger, our personal concerns, vulnerabilities, attitudes, and resources are mediated through complex and shifting societal patterns.

SUMMARY

The terrorist attacks of September 11, 2001, took many lives and affected the way that many people feel about themselves and the world. We first revisited the basic events centering around the airliner crashes at the WTC, the Pentagon, and a field in Shanksville, Pennsylvania. Detailed attention was given to the chaos at the WTC as employees and visitors in the twin towers became victims and a legion of firefighters and police rushed in with the hope of rescuing them. The overwhelming chaos cannot be described in words alone, but we learned something of the disaster from people who experienced it first hand. All that was familiar seemed to have dissolved in just a few minutes and become surreal, almost beyond imagination.

Media coverage, both immediate and continuing, ensured that the nation and the world would witness the events. For months, perhaps the most familiar image on television was smoke continuing to rise from Ground Zero as workers shifted from a rescue to a recovery mission. Looking for survivors and then for bodies was an extended and stressful operation, while families held on to hope that their missing person might be found alive. Many memorial services were held, with special attention given to the individuality of those who had lost their lives in airliners or on the ground. The public responded with compassion and generosity, donating blood, money, and work. Amid the sorrow and pain was a renewed sense of national unity and the resolve to recover from the attack. The early response also included heightened expressions of patriotism and religiousity, along with reflections about the meaning of life and death.

The pattern of response shifted dramatically in less than 1 month as the government announced a war on terrorism and mobilized to take action against terrorists in Afghanistan and elsewhere. Feeling-oriented responses, such as grief and self-reflection, became overshadowed by rhetoric and action to destroy the terrorist threat. Patriotism and religiousity declined to their previous levels, as did public interest in world events. Criticisms and divisiveness developed with, for example, the FBI blamed for failing to follow-up on warning signs.

Studies discovered physical ailments (e.g., World Trade Center cough) among people directly exposed to the attacks and also evidence that throughout the nation many other people were suffering stress symptoms linked to 9/11/01. Depression and suicidality were among the problems noted. Parents and teachers were informed that children could be at special risk for anxiety and other stress responses. We concluded with a brief preview of the death system concept and explored a few of the ways it operated before, during, and after the terrorist attacks.

REFERENCES

Alexander, D. C., & Alexander, Y. (2002). *Terrorism and business. The impact of September 11, 2001.* Ardsley, NY: Transnational.

Barter, S. (2001, September 13). *How the World Trade Center fell.* www.news.bbc.co.uk/hi/english/world/americas.

Bauder, D. (2002, August 20). *NBC seeks psychiatric help on 9/11 coverage.* New York: Associated Press.

Benjamin, D., & Simon, S. (2002). *The age of sacred terror.* New York: Random House.

Bergen, P. (2001). *Holy war, Inc.* New York: Free Press.

Bernard, B. P., Baron, S. L., Mueller, C. A., Driscoll, R. J., Tapp, L. C., Wallingford, K. M., & Tepper, A. L. (2002). Impact of September 11 attacks on workers in the vicinity of the World Trade Center. [Special issue]. *Monthly Mortality & Morbidity Report, 51,* 8–10.

Brody, J. E. (2002, January 17). Driving while drowsy on rise. Traffic safety experts struggle to find solutions. *The Arizona Republic,* B-1.

Cannon, A. (2002, November 11). Soldiering On. *U.S. News and World Report,* 42–46.

Carr, C. (2002). *The lessons of terror.* New York: Random House.

Cooperman, A. (2002, July 7). Lutherans suspend pastor over service. Post-9/11 interfaith gathering at issue. *The Washington Post* as carried by *The Arizona Republic,* A3.

Elliott, M. (2002, August 12). Special report: The secret history. *Time,* 29–43.

Friedman, T. L. (2002). *Longitudes and attitudes. Exploring the world after September 11.* New York: Farrar Straus Giroux.

Gaskell, S. (2002, January 11). *Conflict unfurled at "Ground Zero."* New York: Associated Press.

Glanz, J., & Lipton, E. (2001, March 29). Weaknesses cited in twin towers' collapse. *The New York Times,* A-1.

Goodson, L. P. (2001). *Afghanistan's endless war. State failure, regional politics, and the rise of the Taliban.* Seattle: University of Washington Press.

Gorski, T. (2002). *After 9/11: Stress and coping across America.* www.tgorski.com/Terrorism/PTSD.

Hanson, V. D. (2002). *An autumn of war. What America learned from September 11 and the war on terrorism.* New York: Random House.

Kastenbaum, R. (2002). Terrorists attacks on America. In R. Kastenbaum (Ed.), *Macmillan encyclopedia of death and dying* (Vol. 2, pp. 881–885). New York: Macmillan.

Krikorian, G., & Connell, R. (2002, May 5). Phoenix FBI stonewalled. Ex-agent: Bosses stalled terror probe. *The Arizona Republic,* A1, A8.

Kugler, S. (2002, September 11). *Silence to be foremost at ceremonies.* New York: Associated Press.

Leviton, D. (1995). Horrendous Death. Linking Thanatology and Public Health (pp. 185–213). In J. Kauffman (Ed.), *Awareness of Mortality.* Amityville, NY: Baywood Publications Company.

Libaw, L., & Goldman, M. C. (2002, September 12). *Unspeakable horror. Eyewitness accounts of N.Y. Attacks.* abc.NEWS.com

The longest week. (2002, August 11). NewYorkMetro.com.

McClam, E. (2002, December 23). *Whistle-blowers get "Time" honor.* New York: Associated Press.

9-11 [video documentary]. (2002). New York: CBS.

One year after 9-11. A Nation Changed. [Commemorative issue]. (2002, November 11). *U.S. News and World Report.*

Panda, A. U., and Weiden, M. (2001). Trauma and disaster in psychiatrically vulnerable populations. *Journal of Psychiatric Practice, 7,* 426–431.

Poll: Support for 9/11 holiday slips. (2002, September, 2). CNNnews.com.

Prezant, D. J., Weiden, M., Banauch, G. I., McGuinness, G., Rom, W. N., Aldrich, T. K., & Kelly, K. J. (2002). Cough and bronchial responsiveness in firefighters at the World Trade Center site. *New England Journal of Medicine, 347,* 806–815.

Report reveals communication breakdown in New York attacks. (2002, July 2). *The New York Times,* A–4.

Rose, J. (2002, September 4). From fear to reality. A year after 9/11, a look at America's predictions of change. *The Arizona Republic,* B1.

Salmon, J. L., & Sun, L. H. (2001, December 19). Victims at risk again. Counselors scramble to avert depression, suicides after Sept. 11. *The Washington Post,* A01.

Scanlon, P. D. (2002). World Trade Center cough—A lingering legacy and a cautionary tale. *New England Journal of Medicine, 347,* 804–805.

Schuster, M. A., Stein, B. D., Jaycox, L. H., Collins, R. L., Marshall, G. N., Elliott, M. N., Zhou, A. J., Kanouse, D. E., Morrison, J. L., & Berry, S. H. (2001). A national survey of stress reactions after the September 11 attacks. *New England Journal of Medicine, 345,* 1507–1512.

Silver, R. C., Holman, E. A., McIntosh, D. N., Poulin, M., & Gil-Rivas, V. (2002). Nationwide national study of psychological responses to September 11. *Journal of the American Medical Association, 288,* 2118–2183.

Sprang, G. (1999). Post-disaster stress following the Oklahoma City bombing. *Journal of Interpersonal Violence, 14,* 161–175.

Stephenson, J. (2001). Medical, mental health communities mobilize to cope with terror's psychological aftermath. *Journal of the American Medical Association, 286,* 1823–1825.

Survey: Foreign news still foreign. No perk in U.S. interest after Sept. 11. (2002, June 10). Mesa, AZ: Tribune Wire Services.

Vendantam, S. (2002, January 4). Legends of the fall: September 11 myths abound. *The Washington Post,* A03.

Weaver, J. D. (2002). Disasters. In R. Kastenbaum (Ed.), *Macmillan encyclopedia of death and dying.* (Vol. 1, pp. 231–240). New York: Macmillan.

Weisman, A. (1974). *The realization of death.* New York: Jason Aronson.

Yaukey, J. (2002, December 12). Sept. 11 panel blasts U.S. intelligence. *The Arizona Republic,* A19.

GLOSSARY

Bereavement: The loss of a person close to us by death.

Ground Zero: Name given to New York City's World Trade Center area after the 9/11/01 attack.

Horrendous death: A painful, humiliating, undignified death produced by hostile and/or immoral human behavior (see also Chapter 16).

Thanatologist: A person who studies, teaches, or offers helping services with respect to death-related situations (see also Chapters 4 and 15).

In Edvard Munch's (1896) *Death in the Sick Room,* some family members turn away and sink into their private grief while others offer comfort.

chapter 2

AS WE THINK ABOUT DEATH

In the land of the Uttarakurus grows the magic Jambu tree, whose fruit has the property of conferring immunity from illness and old age, and, by means of this fruit, they lengthen their lives to a thousand years or even, in some accounts, to eleven thousand years.... Among other things, their realm includes landscapes of precious stones and trees from whose branches grow beautiful maidens.
—Gerald J. Gruman (2003, p. 33)

Estimates of self-immolations in Afghanistan are hard to come by, especially in the largely lawless northern and southern regions. Doctors at the Herart Public Hospital said they had received more than 100 female burn cases this year, with most of the women dying soon after arrival.... Some female deaths may be ascribed to suicide in order to cover up for "honor killings"— when women deemed to have "dishonored" their family are killed—or to dowry deaths—when brides are burned for not bringing adequate dowries into their in-laws' households.
—Leela Jacinto (2002)

I never try to reason, to bargain, or to make sense of the why. I have no arguments with men or gods. I take the children on as they are from the time of the first connection and work on ways to make living a little better. It continues to amaze me that a "little" better can make such a huge difference. Reflections of the dying are etched in one's memory like on stone. Parents remember the way in which their child died throughout their entire lifetime.
—Gerri Frager (1996, p. 41)

Life is supposed to go on. And on. Yes, there is death, but not here, not now. We wake to a familiar world each day. We splash water on the same face we rinsed yesterday. We go through our familiar routines. We talk with people whose faces are familiar to us. We see the streets and buildings we have seen many times before. It is so comforting—this ongoingness of daily life. Why disturb this pattern? Why think of death?

• Through the centuries, most people died before what we now would consider to be midlife. Many, in fact, did not survive childhood. Perhaps this is one reason why the folklore and legends of ancient times are filled with stories about fortunate people who lived so long that one hardly needed to think about death. The Uttarkurus were supposed to live in the far north of India, but similar tales flourished in Greek, Persian, Teutonic, Hindu, and Japanese lore, among others. One of the oldest Hebrew legends speaks of the River of Immortality, which some scholars believe provided the background for Christ being identified with the Fountain of Life. The idea that there are refreshing waters in a faraway place that can extend life and perhaps also renew youth was still credible enough to fund Ponce de Leon's expedition to Florida. Fear of dying could be attributed to the prevailing short life expectancy, but the relatively few prosperous and powerful elders also sought ways to postpone death. If only we could do something about death, we would not have to be thinking about it so often.

• Young women, even girls as young as 11, have set themselves on fire, choosing an extremely painful death to a life enslaved to a man they did not want to marry. These events are still occurring in regions of Afghanistan and perhaps in other areas where females are still treated as disposable property. Some of these deaths are finally coming to general attention, as when Shakiba, a 19-year-old Afghan woman, was interviewed by television from the hospital bed in which she would soon die. Shakiba was sold by her family to become a man's second wife. "My family was selling me and I didn't know what else to do." Most of the self-immolations have been women be-

tween 14 and 20 years of age who were desperately trying to escape marriages to older men. The daughters were being married off for a "bride price" intended to help the rest of the family survive. However, families have also been accused of killing daughters for being uncooperative or having violated their rigid sexist code of conduct. Not only death but also death in youth, and not only death in youth but also death preceded by intense suffering—this was chosen over a kind of life that seemed even worse.

The preference for death over life takes other forms as well. For example, many families today have fading photographs of relatives who died years ago of pneumonia, tuberculosis, cholera, typhoid, scarlet fever, infantile paralysis, and other widespread diseases. These people wanted to live. One hoped to survive the diseases that threatened children and young adults. One hoped for the chance to realize personal dreams for a good life. Again, however, expectations have changed. There are now increasing demands for release from life when the quality of that life has been reduced by painful or incapacitating illness. Death, once the problem, is being regarded as the answer by a growing number of people.

• Perhaps there is no more stressful and painful situation than being with a dying child. There is added stress for physicians and nurses when they find that all their skills cannot save the child's life. Gerri Frager was a nurse before she became a doctor. She calls on both perspectives as well as her own sense of values as she tries to comfort dying children and their families. There is no way that people such as Dr. Frager can hold fast to the illusion that anybody, even the youngest child, is safe from the threat of death.

In this chapter, we begin our exploration of thoughts, knowledge, attitudes, and feelings about death. Although our focus is on the United States, we also consider dying, death, grief, and suicide in other societies. It is not enough, though, to attend only to the way other people think about death; therefore, this chapter also provides the opportunity to take stock of our own thoughts, knowledge, attitudes, and feelings.

NOT THINKING ABOUT DEATH: A FAILED EXPERIMENT

We have tried not thinking about death. The educational system cooperated. Millions of us completed our school days without being exposed to substantial readings and discussions about dying, death, grief, and suicide. Who would have taught us, anyway? Our teachers were products of the same "never say die" society. Making it through college did not add anything to our store of knowledge or our ability to cope with death-related circumstances. Death did surface occasionally as a number or event remote from our own experiences. *X* many gunmen popped each other off in a famous shootout. Some king or other died and somebody else grabbed the throne on a date we might need to remember for the exam.

Those who persevered until they had a graduate degree received only further lessons in death avoidance. Nurses, physicians, psychologists, social workers, and others who would be relied on to provide human services were not expected to understand their own death-related feelings and attitudes, let alone anybody else's. During these long years, even clergy often felt unprepared to cope with the death-related situations they would face. Few of their instructors had mastered the art of ministering to the dying.

The media also cooperated. Nobody died. Nobody had cancer. Instead, people would "pass away" after a "long illness." Deaths associated with crime and violence received lavish attention, then as now, but silence had settled over the everyday death of everyday people. When a movie script called for a deathbed scene, Hollywood would offer a sentimental and sanitized version. A typical example occurs in *Till the Clouds Go By* (1946), a film that purported to be the biography of songwriter Jerome Kern. The dying friend tries to communicate his realization that this will be the last time they see each other, but Kern's character obeys the Hollywood dictum that deception is the best policy: Even mature adults cannot face the reality of death, so it is best to play "let's pretend." As a result, the friends never actually "connect," never offer significant words of parting to each other. A physician then enters the room and nods gravely to the friend, who immediately departs. Another mortal lesson from Hollywood: The moment of death belongs to the doctor, not to the dying person and the bereaved. Audiences today see this scene as shallow and deceptive. One student spoke for many others in complaining, "It was as phony as can be—what a terrible way to end a relationship!"

Not thinking about death was pretty much a failure. People continued to die, and how they died became an increasing source of concern. Survivors continued to grieve, often feeling a lack of understanding and support from others. Suicide rates doubled and then tripled among the young, and remained exceptionally high among older adults. Scattered voices warned us that in attempting to evade the reality of death, we were falsifying the totality of our lives. Who were we kidding? Neither an individual nor a society could face its challenges wisely without coming to terms with mortality.

It is still difficult to think about death, especially when our own lives and relationships are involved. Nevertheless, the days of enforced silence and frantic evasion seem to be over. There is an increasing readiness to listen and communicate.

Listening and Communicating

"Doctor, I want to die. Will you help me?" This question is the title of an influential article by Timothy E. Quill (1993). He advised that

> Dying patients need more than prescriptions for narcotics or referrals to hospice programs from their physicians. They need a personal guide and counselor through the dying process—someone who will unflinchingly help them face both the medical and the personal aspects of dying, whether it goes smoothly or it takes the physician into unfamiliar, untested ground. Dying patients do not have the luxury of choosing not to undertake the journey, or of separating their person from their disease. Physicians' commitment not to abandon their patients is of paramount importance. (p. 872)

Statements of this kind are becoming increasingly common. More physicians are now listening and communicating. There is now the expectation of dialogue between patient and physician. Patients and family members feel more empowered to express their concerns, needs, and wishes. Physicians feel more compelled to take these concerns, needs, and wishes into account.

Some people have a ready-made answer that dismisses open discussion of death: "There's nothing to think about. When you're number's up, it's up." This idea goes back a long way. It is part of that general view of life known as *fatalism*. Outcomes are determined in advance. There is really nothing we can do to affect the outcomes so, to quote a well-known philosopher, *"What—me worry?"* Fatalism is a way of excusing ourselves for our perceived lack of ability to predict and control events. There is something to be said for respecting the limits of human knowledge and efficacy. However, there is also something to be said for doing what we can to reduce suffering and risk within our limits. The person who is quick to introduce a fatalistic statement is often attempting to end the discussion before it really begins. It is what communication experts call a "silencer."

Fatalistic attitudes in today's world are perhaps more dangerous than ever. As we will see, many deaths in the United States can be attributed to lifestyle. Our attitudes, choices, and actions contribute to many other deaths across the entire life span. Ironically, it is the belief that there is no use in thinking about death and taking life-protective measures that increases the probability of an avoidable death.

YOUR SELF-INVENTORY OF ATTITUDES, BELIEFS, AND FEELINGS

We have touched briefly on a few of the death-related questions and beliefs that are current in our society. Perhaps some of your own thoughts and feelings have come to mind. One of the most beneficial things you can do for yourself at this point is to take stock of your present experiences, attitudes, beliefs, and feelings. This will not only give you a personal data baseline but also contribute further to your appreciation of the ways in which other people view death.

Before reading further, please begin sampling your personal experiences with death by completing Self-Inventories 1–4. It is in your own interest to complete these exercises in a frank and serious manner. As a personal bonus, try to notice what thoughts and feelings come to mind as you answer these questions. Which questions make you angry? Which questions would you prefer not to answer? Which questions seem foolish or make you want to laugh? Observing your own responses is part of the self-monitoring process that has been found invaluable by many of the people who work systematically with death-related issues.

Each of the inventories takes a distinctive perspective. We begin with your knowledge base, sampling the information you have acquired regarding various facets of death. This is followed by exploring your attitudes and beliefs. We then move on to your personal experiences with death. Finally, we examine the feelings that are stirred in you by dying, death, and grief. Our total view of death is composed of knowledge, attitudes, experiences, and feelings—and that is it useful to identify each of these components accurately. For example, if I fail to distinguish between my personal feelings and my actual knowledge of a death-related topic, I thereby reduce my ability to make wise decisions and take effective actions.

Please complete the Self-Inventories now.

INVENTORY #1:
MY KNOWLEDGE BASE

Fill in the blanks or select alternative answers as accurately as you can. If you are not sure of the answer, offer your best guess.

1. How many deaths are there in the United States each year? ____

2. The leading cause of death for the population in general is _____.

3. A person born in the United States a century ago had an average life expectancy (ALE) of about _____ years.

INVENTORY #1:
(continued)

4. A person born in the United States today has an ALE of about ____ years.

5. People who live in the continent of _____ have the lowest ALE.

6. Throughout the world, who has the higher ALE, females or males? _____

7. There is a new entry among the 10 leading causes of death in the United States. This is _____.

8. Motor vehicle accidents have been the leading cause of fatal injuries for many years. What is the second leading cause? _____

9. A seriously ill person is in the hospital and not expected to recover. How much time is this person likely to spend alone each 24-hour day? _____

10. Homicide rates in the United States have been consistently highest in

    New England _____
    Mountain states _____
    Southern states _____
    West north central states _____

11. The nation with the highest homicide rate in the world is _____.

12. A suicide attempt is most likely to result in death when made by a

    Young adult _____ Middle-aged adult _____
    Elderly adult _____

13. Cryonic suspension is a technique that is intended to preserve a body in a hypothermic (low-temperature) state until a cure is discovered for the condition from which that person suffered.

    How many people have actually been placed in cryonic suspension? _____

    Efforts have been made to revive how many of these people? _____

    With what results? _____

14. What is plastination, and why is it of interest to us here? _____

15. The living will was an early example of an _____.

16. _____ is the first and so far the only state to legalize physician-assisted death under specified conditions.

17. Palliative care most often has relief from _____ as its top priority.

18. "PTSD" is a term that has been heard with increasing frequency in recent years. What is it? _____

19. What was placed inside the chest of a royal Egyptian mummy and why? _____

20. In the United States, cremation is now chosen by about one person in _____.

21. In recent years, belief in an afterlife in the United States has:

    Decreased _____ Remained steady _____
    Increased _____

22. Near-death experience reports have several key elements in common With G-LOC. What is G-LOC? _____

23. Why have the "Harvard criteria" been so influential? _____

24. Jack Kevorkian "assisted" in the death of more than 100 people. How many of these people were terminally ill? _____

25. "Periodic mass extinctions" have totally eliminated many species and taken a tremendous toll of life. The three most recent mass die-offs are thought to have been caused by _____

    Answers to self-inventory questions are provided later in this chapter. Please don't peek!

INVENTORY #2:
MY ATTITUDES AND BELIEFS

Select the answer that most accurately represents your belief.

1. I believe in some form of life after death:

   Yes, definitely _____
   Yes, but not quite sure _____
   No, but not quite sure _____
   No, definitely _____

2. I believe that you die when your number comes up: It is in the hands of fate:

   Yes, definitely _____
   Yes, but not quite sure _____
   No, but not quite sure _____
   No, definitely _____

3. I believe that taking one's own life is:

   Never justified _____
   Justified when terminally ill _____
   Justified whenever life no longer seems
      worth living _____

4. I believe that taking another person's life is:

   Never justified _____
   Justified in defense of your own life _____
   Justified when that person has committed a
      terrible crime _____

5. I believe that dying people should be:

   Told the truth about their condition _____
   Kept hopeful by sparing them the facts _____
   Depends on the person and
      the circumstances _____

6. In thinking about my own old age, I would prefer:

   To die before I grow old _____
   To live as long as I can _____
   To discover what challenges and opportuni-
      ties old age will bring _____

7. The possibility of nuclear weapon warfare or accidents that might destroy much of life on Earth has been of:

   no concern _____   little concern _____
   some concern _____   major concern _____
   to me.

8. The possibility of environmental catastrophes that might destroy much of life on Earth has been of:

   no concern _____   little concern _____
   some concern _____   major concern _____
   to me.

9. Drivers and passengers should be required to wear seat belts:

   Yes, agree _____   Tend to agree _____
   Tend to disagree _____   No, disagree _____

10. The availability of handguns should be more tightly controlled to reduce accidental and impulsive shootings.

    Yes, agree _____   Tend to agree _____
    Tend to disagree _____   No, disagree _____

11. A person has been taken to the emergency room (ER) with internal bleeding that is likely to prove fatal. This person is 82 years of age and has an Alzheimer-type dementia. What type of response would you recommend from the ER staff?

    Comfort only _____
    Limited attempt at rescue _____
    All-out attempt at rescue _____

12. You have been taken to the ER with internal bleeding that is likely to prove fatal. You are now 82 years of age and have an Alzheimer-type dementia. What type of response would you hope you receive from the ER staff?

    Comfort only _____
    Limited attempt at rescue _____
    All-out attempt as rescue _____

13. Another round of chemotherapy has failed for a woman with advanced breast cancer. The doctor suggests a new round of experimental therapy. She replies, "I wish I were dead." What do you think should be done and why?

    _____

    _____

INVENTORY #3:
MY EXPERIENCES WITH DEATH

Fill in the blanks or select the most accurate alternative answers.

1. A. I have had an animal companion who died: Yes _____ No _____

   B. How I felt when my pet died can be described by words such as:

   _____, _____, and _____.

2. The following people in my life have died:

   Person   *How Long Ago?*

   A. _____

   B. _____

   C. _____

   D. _____

   E. _____

3. The death that affected me the most at the time was _____.

4. How I felt when this person died can be described by words such as: _____, _____, and _____.

5. This death was especially significant to me because _____

   _____

   _____.

6. In all the circumstances surrounding this person's death, including what happened afterward, my most positive memory is of:

   _____.

7. My most disturbing memory is of: _____

   _____.

8. I have conversed with dying people:

   Never _____ One person _____
   Several people _____ Many people _____

9. I have provided care for a dying person:

   Never _____ One person _____
   Several people _____ Many people _____

10. I have known a person who attempted suicide:

    Not to my knowledge _____
    One person _____ Several people _____

11. I have known a person who committed suicide:

    Not to my knowledge _____
    One person _____ Several people _____

12. I have known a person who died in an accident:

    Not to my knowledge _____
    One person _____ Several people _____

13. I have known a person who was murdered:

    Not to my knowledge _____
    One person _____ Several people _____

14. I have known a person who died of AIDS-related disease:

    Not to my knowledge _____
    One person _____ Several people _____

15. I know a person who has tested positive for the AIDS virus:

    Not to my knowledge _____
    One person _____ Several people _____

SELF-INVENTORY #4:
MY FEELINGS

Select the answer that most closely represents your feelings.

1. I would feel comfortable in developing an intimate conversation with a dying person.

   Yes, agree _____ Tend to agree _____
   Tend to disagree _____ No, disagree _____

2. I would hesitate to touch someone who was dying.

   Yes, agree _____ Tend to agree _____
   Tend to disagree _____ No, disagree _____

3. My hands would tremble when I was talking to a dying person.

   Yes, agree _____ Tend to agree _____
   Tend to disagree _____ No, disagree _____

4. I would have more difficulty in talking if the dying person was about my age.

   Yes, agree _____ Tend to agree _____
   Tend to disagree _____ No, disagree _____

5. I would avoid talking about death and dying with a person who was terminally ill.

   Yes, agree _____ Tend to agree _____
   Tend to disagree _____ No, disagree _____

6. I would avoid talking with a dying person if possible.

   Yes, agree _____ Tend to agree _____
   Tend to disagree _____ No, disagree _____

7. I have had moments of anxiety in which I think of my own death:

   Never _____ Once _____
   Several times _____ Often _____

8. I fear that I will die too soon:

   Yes, agree _____ Tend to agree _____
   Tend to disagree _____ No, disagree _____

9. I have no fear of death as such:

   Yes, agree _____ Tend to agree _____
   Tend to disagree _____ No, disagree _____

10. I have no fears associated with dying:

    Yes, agree _____ Tend to agree _____
    Tend to disagree _____ No, disagree _____

11. I feel good when I think about life after death:

    Yes, agree _____ Tend to agree _____
    Tend to disagree _____ No, disagree _____

12. I am anxious about the possible death of somebody I love:

    Yes, definitely _____ Tend to agree _____
    Tend to disagree _____ No, disagree _____

13. I am grieving over somebody who has already died:

    Yes, definitely _____ Tend to agree _____
    Tend to disagree _____ No, disagree _____

14. I have a hard time taking death seriously: It feels remote to me, not really connected to my own life:

    Yes, definitely _____ Tend to agree _____
    Tend to disagree _____ No, disagree _____

15. I have some strong, even urgent feelings regarding death these days.

    Yes, definitely _____ Tend to agree _____
    Tend to disagree _____ No, disagree _____

Note. Questions 1–6 are part of a scale introduced by Hayslip (1986/1987).

SOME ANSWERS—AND THE QUESTIONS THEY RAISE

Knowledge Base

Here are the answers to Self-Inventory #1:

1. Well over 2 million people die in the United States each year. The most recent data (2000) document 2,404,624 deaths (Chapter 4).
2. Heart disease continues to be the leading cause of death in the United States (Chapter 4).
3. A person born in the United States early in the 20th century had an ALE of less than 50 years (Chapter 4).
4. A person born in the United States today has an ALE of approximately 77 years (Chapter 4).
5. People who live in Africa have the lowest ALE (54 years) (Chapter 4).
6. Females outlive males almost everywhere throughout the world (Chapter 4).
7. Alzheimer's disease has become the eighth leading cause of death in the United States, an unfortunate consequence of the aging of the population and the limited success in preventing or treating this condition (Chapter 4).
8. Falls (mostly among elderly people) are the second most common type of injury fatality in the United States (Chapter 4).
9. Seriously and terminally ill people were alone almost 19 hours a day according to a recent hospital study (Chapter 5).
10. Homicide rates have been consistently the highest in southern states (Chapter 9).
11. The United States has the highest homicide rate in the world (Chapter 9).
12. Elderly adults are the most likely to die from a suicide attempt (Chapter 8).
13. Fewer than 100 human bodies have been placed in cryonic suspension worldwide, and no known attempts have been made to resuscitate (Chapter 7).
14. Plastination transforms flesh into a kind of stone glass. It has recently been introduced into the cryonic process and is also used to create learning materials for medical students (Chapter 7).
15. The living will was an early example of an advance directive, a document that conveys a person's instructions or wishes for management at the end of life (Chapter 7).
16. Oregon is currently the only state to have legalized a form of physician-assisted death (Chapter 10).
17. Relief from pain is most often the top priority for palliative care or hospice programs. Relief from other symptoms is also provided as much as possible (Chapter 6).
18. Posttraumatic stress syndrome is a disabling form of grief that is related to overwhelming experiences, such as warfare and disaster (Chapter 12).
19. The royal physicians replaced the heart with a scarab, a carved stone that represented the dung beetle whose mysterious work of helping to bring life back from death was regarded as intrinsic to the great cycle of being (Chapter 12).
20. About one person in four in the United States now chooses cremation. There is much variation within the United States and among nations (Chapter 12).
21. Several studies have found that belief in an afterlife has increased in the United States in recent years (Chapter 14).
22. G-LOC is a sudden loss of normal consciousness that is experienced by pilots under acceleration stress. Tunnel vision and bright lights are among the perceptual changes that resemble near-death experience reports (Chapter 14).
23. The Harvard criteria have been applied to determine whether a nonresponsive person should be considered brain dead (Chapter 3).
24. Less than one-third of the patients whose lives Kevorkian helped to end were actually terminally ill at the time (Chapter 10).
25. Scientists now believe that asteroids were responsible for the three most recent mass die-offs or extinctions (Chapter 16).

Attitudes, Experiences, Beliefs, and Feelings

We do not live by facts alone. It is now time to explore the attitudes, experiences, beliefs, and feelings that we bring to our encounters with death.

Attitudes refer to our action tendencies. I am ready to act or I am not ready to act. I am ready to approach or to avoid this situation. *Beliefs* refer to our relatively stable and broad interpretations of the world and our place in it. Fatalism, already mentioned, is one type of belief. *Feelings* provide us with qualitative information on our total sense of being—a "status report." I feel safe or endangered. I feel happy or sorrowful. I feel aroused or lethargic. Two people may hold identical beliefs and attitudes but differ greatly in their feelings. On Inventory 2, question 10, for example, these two people may answer, "Yes, agree: The availability of handguns should be more tightly controlled to reduce accidental and impulsive shootings." However, one of these people may have relatively little feeling attached to this view. Perhaps he or she thinks that it is risky to have a lot of handguns around on general principles. The other person might be the widow of a physician who was shot to death by an emotionally disturbed person who did not even know him. Her feelings could hardly be more intense. (This is a real person, the former owner of a home my wife and I purchased. Incredible as it may seem, the young widow became the recipient of death threats because she spoke up in favor of gun control.)

Personal *experience* influences our attitudes, beliefs, and feelings. For example, people who have had near-death experiences while in a life-threatening situation often develop a different perspective on both life and death (Chapter 14). A paramedic who has responded to 1,000 motor vehicle accidents is likely to have a stronger attitude and more intense feelings when he or she notices children without seat belts in a car. A person who has never suffered the death of a loved one may be more impatient with a bereaved colleague who does not seem to "snap back" right away.

The most significant experiential difference is between people who had a personally significant death and those for whom death has remained a distant topic or even just a word. Death stopped being just a word for a graduate student of social work when both her parents were killed in an automobile accident. She could not go on with her own life until she fully *realized* their deaths as well as her own mortality: "Before all this happened, it was just a word to me, death. I could hear death. I could say death. Really, though, it was just a word. Now it's like something under my own skin, if you know what I mean." Simply

knowing intellectually that people die was not enough; she now had to connect death with life in a very personal way.

This challenge is ours as well. If we have experienced a death that "got" to us—whether the death of a person or an animal companion—then we are also more likely to realize what other people have been going through. This is one of the most powerful dynamics at work in community support groups. Organizations such as Compassionate Friends and Widow-to-Widow provide understanding and emotional support for bereaved persons from those who have already experienced the sorrow and stress of loss. New support groups continue to be formed to help people with specific types of death-related stress (e.g., for parents whose child has been killed by a drunk driver or for persons with AIDS).

However, there are limits to the value of experience. Just because a person has had a particular kind of loss experience does not necessarily mean that this person also has the ability to support others. Furthermore, some people have proven helpful to the dying, the grieving, and the suicidal even if they have not had very similar experiences in their lives. The basic point to consider is whether at this point in your life you are "part of the club" that has experienced death in an undeniably personal and significant way, or whether you still have something of an outsider's perspective.

Some people have an inner relationship with death that goes beyond basic realization. A person's thoughts, attitudes, and feelings may be *dominated* by death-related experiences. The sense of being dominated or haunted by death can emerge from one critical experience or from a cluster of experiences. Perhaps you have mourned the deaths of so many people that you could not even list them in the space provided. Perhaps several people died unexpectedly at the same time. Perhaps you are still responding strongly to the death of one person who had been at the center of your life. The question of whether or not your life is being highly influenced, even dominated, by death-related experiences cannot be answered by examining a simple list. We would need to appreciate what these people meant to you and what lingers in your mind regarding the deaths, the funeral, and the memorialization process. Furthermore, we would need to examine your own involvement in the situation. For example, people who have provided direct personal care for a dying friend or relative have a different set of experiences than those who did not. Perhaps you have a clear and powerful memory of your last visits with a person who was a very important part of your life. On the other hand, perhaps you were thousands of miles away when this person died and had no opportunity to be with your loved one. We may be very influenced by *how* a person has died as well as by the fact of death. A death by suicide, for example, has often been considered tainted, resulting in additional stress and social isolation for the family survivors.

These are but a few of the ways in which our past experiences with death are likely to influence us in the future. Paramedics who have rushed to many accident scenes and other emergencies are likely to respond differently to the next death-related situation they encounter than people who have never seen death and dying up close. If we do not respond in the same way when we encounter a death-related situation, then it is probably not really the "same" situation for each of us.

How Does State of Mind Affect Death-Related Behavior?

Much remains to be learned about the link between what goes on in our minds and how we actually behave in death-related situations. The following are a few studies that have addressed specific aspects of this question:

- *The living will: Why most of the living won't.*
  The document known as the *living will* has been available since 1968 for people who want to limit the type of medical interventions that would be carried out if they should be close to death and at that point unable to express their wishes (see Chapter 7). Although this document was designed to meet the growing public expression of interest in controlling end-of-life decisions, most people did not choose to use it. Why? VandeCreek and Frankowski (1996) found that most people had not thought much about their own death and also considered that their last days were a long way off. The authors concluded that "completing living wills connotes personal death, and this appears to be a

substantial barrier to completing the document" (p. 80). Avoidance of death thoughts was therefore closely associated with letting a significant opportunity go by to influence their situation when the last days do come.

- *Should I sign an organ donation card?*
  All states, as well as the District of Columbia, have enacted some version of the Uniform Anatomical Gift Act (Robbins, 1990). Despite the widespread availability of this option (in association with the driver's license), relatively few people sign and carry organ donor cards. Personal attitudes play a major role in this decision. The studies show that nondonors tend to be more anxious about death. Furthermore, they often had the specific fear of being declared dead prematurely. Robbins found that nondonors were also more uneasy about their physical condition in general. Additionally, there was a relationship between willingness to donate organs and the sense of *self-efficacy:* People who think of themselves as effective and self-reliant are more likely to sign the donation cards. Whether or not one is willing to donate organs to save another person's life seems closely related to the individual's general attitude and personal fears and anxieties.

- *Stepping off the curb.*
  Is there a relationship between state of mind and risk-taking behavior in everyday life? Laura Briscoe and I (1975) observed 125 people as they crossed a busy street between the Detroit Art Institute and Wayne State University. There were equal numbers of street-crossers in five risk categories. People classified as Type A, the safest pedestrians, stood at the curb until the light changed in their favor, scanned traffic in both directions, entered the crosswalk, moved briskly across the street, and checked out traffic from the opposite direction lanes before reaching the halfway point. At the opposite extreme were Type E pedestrians, who crossed in the middle of the block, stepping out from between parked cars with the traffic lights against them, and they did not look at traffic in either direction (miraculously, all 25 in this study did survive their crossings). All street-crossers were interviewed when they reached the other side. The observed street-

Crossing a street is one of the every day actions that can be made more or less risky by our patterns of thought and behavior.

crossing behavior was closely related to the individual's general attitudes toward risk taking. For example, the high-risk pedestrians also classified themselves as high-risk drivers and judged that they put their lives in jeopardy approximately 16% of the time during an average week, compared with only 2% for Type A crossers. The Type E crossers were four times more likely than the Type A crossers to have contemplated or attempted suicide. They also reported a higher level of frustration with life. Within the limits of this study, it was clear that

a person's general attitudes and feelings can be expressed in behavior choices that either increase or decrease the probability of death.

HUMANS ARE MORTAL: BUT WHAT DOES THAT HAVE TO DO WITH ME?

Our attitudes toward life and death are challenged when a person close to us dies. In *The Death of Ivan Ilych*, Leo Tolstoy (1886/1960) provides an insightful portrait of the complexities, confusions, and urgencies that may afflict a survivor as well as the dying person. Consider just one passage from a novel that has lost none of its pertinence and power during the past century:

> The thought of the sufferings of the man he had known so intimately, first as a schoolmate, and later as a grown-up colleague, suddenly struck Peter Ivanovich with horror.... "Three days of frightful suffering, then death! Why, that might suddenly, at any moment, happen to me," he thought, and for a moment felt terrified. But—he himself did not know how—the customary reflection at once occurred to him, that this *had* happened to Ivan Ilych and not to him.... After which reflection Peter Ivanovich felt reassured, and began to ask with interest about the details of Ivan Ilych's death, as though death were an accident natural to Ivan Ilych, but certainly not to himself. (pp. 101–102).

Peter Ivanovich is a responsible adult who presumably knows that death is both inevitable and universal, sparing nobody. Yet we catch him, with Tolstoy's help, playing a desperate game of evasion. Consider some of the elements in Peter Ivanovich's response:

1. He already knows of Ivan Ilych's death; otherwise, he would not have been participating in an obligatory paying of respects. However, it is only on viewing the corpse that the realization of death strikes him. There is a powerful difference between intellectual knowledge and emotional impact or realization. For one alarming moment, Peter feels that he himself is vulnerable.
2. Peter Ivanovich immediately becomes concerned for Peter Ivanovich. His feelings do not center on the man who has lost his life or the woman who has lost her husband.
3. He cannot admit that his outer line of defenses has been penetrated, that his personal anxieties have been triggered. He is supposed to show concern for others, not let them see his own distress. Furthermore, he hopes to leave this house of death with the confidence that death has, in fact, been left behind.
4. Peter Ivanovich's basic evasive technique is the effort to *differentiate* himself from Ivan

Ilych. Yes, some people really do die, but not people like him. The proof was in the fact that Peter was the vertical and mobile man, whereas Ivan (that luckless, inferior specimen) was horizontal and immobile. We witness Peter Ivanovich, then, stretching and tormenting his logic in the hope of arriving at an anxiety-reducing conclusion.

5. Once Peter Ivanovich has quelled his momentary panic, he is able to discuss Ivan Ilych's death. Even so, he is more interested in factual details than in feelings and meanings. He has started to rebuild the barriers between himself and death. Whatever he learns about how his friend died will strengthen this barrier: All that was true of Ivan obviously is not applicable to him.

ANXIETY, DENIAL, AND ACCEPTANCE: THREE CORE CONCEPTS

Three concepts that are central to understanding death attitudes are interwoven through the previous excerpt from Tolstoy's masterpiece. Peter Ivanovich felt tense, distressed, and apprehensive. *Death anxiety* is the term most often applied to such responses. Anxiety is a condition that seeks its own relief. To reduce the painful tension, a person might try many different actions—taking drugs or alcohol, for example, or fleeing from the situation. One form of avoiding death anxiety has received most of the attention: *denial*. This is a response that rejects certain key features of reality in the attempt to avoid or reduce anxiety. "If I acknowledge '*X*' I will feel devastated—so '*X*' is not there." Peter Ivanovich denies the basic fact that he is as mortal as Ivan Ilych in order to distance himself from the death.

Many writers have urged that we should *accept* death. This advice sounds positive and appealing. However, people are not always clear about what they mean by acceptance: For example, how does it differ from resignation or depression? Precisely what should we accept and on whose authority? What is it that makes acceptance the most desirable response? In Tolstoy's novel, Ivan Ilych eventually achieves a sense of acceptance, but Peter Ivanovich seems to be as self-deceived and befuddled as ever.

Anxiety, denial, and acceptance are not the only death attitudes that we encounter, although most research has concentrated on these concepts. Depression and a sense of loss are often experienced by people when death is in prospect. Although sorrow and anxiety have much in common, neither can be reduced to the other. Sorrow is oriented toward the past, and anxiety is oriented toward the future. Still another strategy is to identify with death: Some people attempt to reduce their own death anxieties by joining forces with death, killing others, whether in reality or in games and fantasies. How much harm have people done to each other when they have tried to control their own anxiety by becoming instruments of death?

THEORIES AND STUDIES OF DEATH ANXIETY

We should know something about death anxiety by now because it is the most frequently studied topic by academic researchers (Neimeyer, 1994). The most popular instrument has been Donald Templer's (1970) *Death Anxiety Scale,* which consists of 15 true/false items, such as the following:

"I am very much afraid to die."

"The sight of a dead body is horrifying to me."

Respondents receive a total score based on the number of answers that are keyed in the direction of anxiety. Another often used instrument is the Collett–Lester scale (Lester, 1994), which has the advantage of providing separate scores for "death of self," "death of others," "dying of self," and "dying of others." Self-report instruments such as these have the advantage of brevity, convenience, and simple quantitative results. What we actually learn from them, however, is limited by a number of problems, as I have addressed in more detail elsewhere (Kastenbaum, 2000a). The most significant difficulties with death anxiety scales are as follows:

1. Little is learned about the respondent's overall attitude structure or belief system; therefore, death anxiety is taken out of context and difficult to interpret.
2. Low scores on death anxiety scales are especially difficult to interpret. Do they mean low

anxiety or high denial? The scales provide no way to make the distinction.
3. How high is high anxiety, and what is a "normal" level? The fact that an individual's score is higher than most others' does not by itself demonstrate that it is "too high"—too high for what? Little has been learned about the level of death anxiety that is most useful and adaptive in various situations.
4. Respondents are often selected opportunistically. College students continue to be over represented (are you pleased to be so popular?), and members of ethnic and racial minorities continue to be underrepresented.
5. The typical study is a one-shot affair. How the same respondents might express their attitude at another time or in another situation is seldom explored.
6. No link is established between attitude and behavior. The findings do not tell us how people with low, average, or high scores will cope with real-life situations that involve dying, death, or grief.

Despite the limitations of most death anxiety studies, some findings have been obtained repeatedly and are worth attention.

MAJOR FINDINGS FROM SELF-REPORTS OF DEATH ANXIETY

Several patterns have emerged from self-report studies of death anxiety as we will now see.

How Much Do We Fear Death?

Self-report studies consistently find a low to moderate level of death anxiety. This is consistent with responses to a Gallup poll ("Fear of Dying," 1991) in which three out of four adults declared that they did not fear death. Should we take these results at face value? Or should we suspect that most people are in the habit of suppressing their anxieties, trying to convince themselves and others that death holds no terror? The self-report studies do not provide information that would enable us to decide between these competing answers. However we interpret the results, it appears that most people do not consider themselves to be very anxious about death as they go about their everyday lives.

I am inclined to believe that the self-report instruments measure death anxiety only when the scores are very high: when the respondent is in a genuine state of alarm. If we really want to identify death anxiety, then we may have to do what we should have been doing all along—make direct observations of emotional response and behavior in death-related situations.

Are There Gender Differences in Death Anxiety?

Women tend to have higher death anxiety scores on self-report scales. This finding has come out of many studies. Does this mean that women tend to be too anxious? Probably not. There is evidence that women are more comfortable than men in dealing openly with their thoughts and feelings on many emotionally intense subjects.

Over the years, I have observed that women almost always outnumber men decisively in seminars and workshops that deal with dying, death, and grief. I have met many more women than men in hospice and other caregiving situations (see Chapter 6). If this is anxiety, perhaps we should be grateful for it since relatively few "low death anxiety" men have responded to these challenges. In any event, research findings reveal a gender difference but do not demonstrate that women are too anxious. A study by Deborah Witt Sherman (1996–1997) found that most nurses reported a higher level of death anxiety than the general population but also accepted death as an integral part of life. As one nurse said, "Death is quiet and peaceful, but something I would not like to face at the present time" (p. 130). Level of death anxiety tells us something, but not everything, about the way a person interprets and responds to death-related situations.

Are There Age Differences in Death Anxiety?

It is often assumed that anxiety increases as the distance between ourselves and death decreases. If this assumption is correct, then elderly adults might be expected to express a higher level of death anxiety. Not so. Self-report studies show either no age differences or somewhat lower death anxiety for elders. Again, this type of study does not tell us whether the lower scores represent greater acceptance or more effective denial.

Death anxiety tends to be relatively high in adolescence and early adulthood. There is a decrease as one's life becomes more settled and predictable. Death anxiety is apt to rise again in later middle age, perhaps occasioned by the death of friends and family and signs of one's own aging. After this rise, there is a decline to a new low in death anxiety for people in their 70s. This life course pattern of death anxiety needs to be confirmed by studies that follow the same people throughout their lives. Almost all the available studies are cross-sectional—different people at different ages. More information is also needed regarding the particular sources of death anxiety at various points in the life course. An adolescent may fear sudden violent death, for example, whereas a parent might fear primarily for his or her children's welfare if he or she dies. Thurson and Powell (1994) found that adolescents tend to have strong death-related fears of decomposition, immobility, uncertainty, pain, helplessness, and isolation. In contrast, elderly adults were more likely to be concerned about loss of control, dependency, and an afterlife.

Is Death Anxiety Related to Mental Health and Illness?

Death anxiety that is high enough to be disabling is a problem at any age and may warrant the attention of professional caregivers. Generally, self-reported death anxiety is somewhat higher in people with diagnosed psychiatric conditions. Furthermore, it is not uncommon for mental health workers to observe panic reactions centering around death fears on the part of their clients. The usual interpretation is that death anxiety rushes to the surface when a person's "ego defenses" are weakened and can no longer inhibit the impulses, fears, and fantasies that are ordinarily suppressed.

We should bear in mind, however, that death concern is not limited to people who are emotionally disturbed, nor to any one particular type of person. For example, it is not unusual for people to experience an upsurge of death anxiety when they realize how close they have come to being killed in a motor vehicle accident. The sudden, unexpected death of another person can also heighten one's own concern. Situations in which people feel alone and unprotected can also arouse a passing sense of separation anxiety, which for most purposes is indistinguishable from death anxiety.

There are both reasons to be anxious about death and reasons to keep our anxiety within bounds. People with a sound mental health status have learned to avoid the extremes of too much anxiety and too heavy a reliance on defenses against anxiety.

Does Religious Belief Lower or Raise Death Anxiety?

The influence of religion in death anxiety has been a subject of controversy for many years. Bronislaw Malinowski (1948), a notable anthropologist, interpreted his observations as demonstrating that religion has the basic function of reducing the individual's intense fear of death. That is really what religion is all about. A fellow anthropologist, A. R. Radcliffe-Brown (1952), came to the opposite conclusion: Religion gives rise to fear of evil spirits, punishment, torment, and hell. Both sets of observations are most directly based on pre-literate societies and therefore beg the question of whether or not religion serves the same function in societies at a higher level of general development.

There are marked differences in the substance of religious belief from one society to another. In many tribal societies, death is believed to be followed by a life similar to the one that has just been concluded. One may be anxious about the journey through death from one life to another, but the outcome is neither annihilation nor some frightening new state of being. In contrast, spirit possession is a major component in some religions, so interactions between the living and the dead are vital concerns. Fear of the dead may be more intense than fear of death, as J. G. Frazer (1933/1966) observed in his review of numerous anthropological reports. Precisely what it is that a particular person most fears about death may depend much on the substance of his or her belief system. One person may fear eternal damnation, whereas another may be obedient to taboos against contact with a dead body.

Studies of the relationship between death anxiety and religion have not discerned a clear pattern (Kastenbaum, 2000a). There is some indication that people with a strong religious faith have a lower level of death anxiety, but even this finding is not firmly supported. Religion seems to enter into our death orientations in a complex manner. From a practical perspective, we would probably be more effective by learning how religion and death are associated for a particular person or family rather than beginning with a general assumption about the connection.

THEORETICAL PERSPECTIVES ON DEATH ANXIETY

There are two classic theories of death anxiety, and they could hardly be more opposed to each other.

Early Psychoanalytic Theory

Sigmund Freud (1913/1953) reasoned that we could not really be anxious about death:

> Our own death is indeed quite unimaginable, and whenever we make the attempt to imagine it we can perceive that we really survive as spectators.... At bottom nobody believes in his own death, or to put the same thing in a different way, in the unconscious everyone of us is convinced of his own immortality. (p. 304)

Our "unconscious system" does not respond to the passage of time, so the end of personal time through death would not register. Again, on the unconscious level we do not have the concept of negation, so there is no death that can erase life. Furthermore, we have not actually experienced death. In Freud's view, when we express death anxiety it is only a cover story that conceals the real fear. For many years, psychoanalysts spoke of *thanatophobia* as the expressed fear of death that serves as a disguise for the actual source of discomfort. Their mission was to dig, dig, dig until unearthing the underlying fear.

What, then, do we fear, if it is not death? Freud's answer was not exactly his finest moment: Thanatophobia derives from the castration anxiety experienced during the normal abnormal psychosexual development. Boy loves mother and fears that father will cut him down to size. Freud's description of the Oedipus complex has enjoyed a flourishing career in fiction, drama, and popular psychology but does not succeed here. There are numerous flaws in this explanation. For example, if people have not been dead before, it is also the case that very few have been castrated so, to use Freud's own reasoning, how could they be afraid of this calamity? Castration anxiety is even more of a stretch when applied to females. The assertion that girls feel they have already been castrated because they do not have what boys have deserves all the ridicule it has reaped.

However, Freud's castration–death anxiety theory could be interpreted more generously. He admitted to making up stories as a way of getting new ideas across. In this case, Freud might well have been suggesting that the source of death anxiety is the fear of losing value, love, and security by being less than a whole person. People who feel they are losing or have lost their sense of security in the world might well experience this generalized confusion and fear as death anxiety. This is an interpretation that does ring true with clinical observations. People who feel they cannot control the frightening things that are happening (or might happen) to them often do experience an upsurge in death anxiety (Kastenbaum, 2000b).

The bottom line for the early psychoanalytic position is clear, even if the explanation is open to question: Way down deep, we cannot comprehend our own annihilation; therefore, our anxieties can only seem to be about death.

The Existential Challenge

The *existential* position takes the opposite approach. Awareness of our mortality is *the* basic source of anxiety. Our fears take many specific forms but can be traced back to our sense of vulnerability to death. A leading advocate of this view was Ernest Becker (1973). He argues that death anxiety is at the root of severe psychopathology, such as *schizophrenia*. The schizophrenic person suffers because he or she does not have enough insulation from the fear of death. If we are not devastated by death anxiety it is because society works so hard to protect us from the realization of personal mortality.

Society's primary function is to help us all pretend that life will continue to go on and on. This is accomplished by a belief system that is supported with rituals and other practices that produce a sense of coherence, predictability, and meaning. We feel that we are part of something bigger, more powerful, and more durable than ourselves. Monumental edifices contribute to the illusion of invulnerability. From this standpoint, the destruction of the World Trade Center (WTC) towers would be thought to have had a profound unsettling effect on all of us, allowing our death anxiety to break through the cracks in society's protective posture.

Becker's writings have stimulated the development of *terror management theory* (Tomer, 2002), which suggests that we try to control our death anxiety by socially sanctioned evasions and fantasies. If we believe as we are supposed to believe and behave as we are supposed to behave, then we will be safe from death. There are two facets to this strategy: Keep up our own self-esteem, and become an integral part of an entity greater than ourselves. It can be seen immediately that religious belief and practice could go a long way to meeting this need. Religious faith and authority, however, are vulnerable to internal conflict and external threats. Faith can be undermined by disasters that overtake society (e.g., virulent epidemics and famine) as well as by radically changing circumstances (e.g., the rise of science and technology). Furthermore, if becomes very difficult to control death anxiety if a person has become almost completely dependent on religious and other social institutions that are losing their grip.

Recent studies have tended to support terror management theory. For example, people with higher self-esteem expressed less need to protect themselves against the breakthrough of death anxiety by relying on a culturally endorsed belief system (Harmon-Jones et al., 1997). Helping to strengthen a person's self-esteem also seems to decrease death anxiety. There may be potential in the idea that we can find protection against death anxiety either by increasing our self-esteem or by investing heavily in reassuring sociocultural constructions of life and death. Other studies have found that people tend to become more defensive when reminded of their mortality and then try to control their anxiety by focusing on the worldviews from which they draw comfort (Tomer, 2002).

Another promising theoretical approach has been offered by Tomer and Eliason (1996), who emphasize the regrets that people may have about what they have accomplished in life and what yet remains to be accomplished. According to this view, we are more likely to experience a high level of death anxiety if we perceive ourselves as not having made good use of the years through which we have already traveled. This anxiety is intensified when we also judge that we will not live long enough to accomplish our goals in the future. Death anxiety is therefore a function of past and future regrets. Is this death anxiety or anxiety about having an incomplete life? Either way, the effect is the same. We are not as likely to stew about the quality of our lives if we view death as still being a safe distance away. When the prospect of personal death comes into sharp focus, however, we may become acutely concerned about all that we have not accomplished and all that we will not accomplish.

Additionally, anxiety may be either increased or decreased by our interpretation of the meaning of death. As discussed in Chapter 3, there are many possible interpretations of death, and each may have distinct implications for anxiety arousal or reduction. The "regrets" theory of death anxiety perhaps places too much emphasis on "accomplishments" as distinguished from relationships and other sources of strength and satisfaction. Nevertheless, one can only welcome a new approach that might perhaps lead to new understanding.

Edge Theory

Neither the Freudian nor the existential position on death anxiety have been established by the available research. Both theories make assumptions that are difficult to subject to empirical investigation. How can we know with any degree of certainty what the "unconscious system" knows or does not know (even if we accept the reality of unconscious processes)? How can we prove all anxieties have their root in the fear of nonbeing? Why is it that most people do not report a high and disabling level of death anxiety but also do not completely deny such feelings?

The typical report of a moderate level of death anxiety supports neither the psychoanalytic nor the existential positions. There are many useful observations in the writings of insightful psychoanalysts and existentialists (including existential psychoanalysts). However, we might have to devise theories that are closer to testable propositions if we wish to have a well-supported model of death anxiety. Fortunately, both the terror management and the regrets theory are starting to receive research attention.

There is room for other theories as well. I have proposed an *edge theory* that distinguishes between our everyday low level of death anxiety and the alert and alarmed state that is aroused when we encounter danger (Kastenbaum, 2000a). The experience of death anxiety is the self-awareness side of a complex organismic response to danger. We feel ourselves to be at the very edge of the safe and known, perhaps just one step away from disaster. Edge theory emphasizes our survival and adaptation functions—the ability to detect sources of potential harm both through built-in biomechanisms and through the development of cognitive and social skills. There is no need to be anxious all the time; in fact, this would be an exhausting and ineffective way to function. However, there are dangerous situations in this world, and we might save our own or somebody else's life by moving quickly to an emergency footing when confronted by a significant threat.

The first responders to the WTC attacks showed a remarkable blend of alarm and control. They neither ignored nor faltered in the face of an overwhelming threat to life. Most of us do not have their training and experience to cope with emergent disasters, but we can hone our own danger response systems to provide enough anxiety to provoke our attention but also exercise enough control and balance to see the situation through.

ACCEPTING AND DENYING DEATH

We now focus on death-related feelings, attitudes, and actions within our everyday lives.

Sitting in his favorite chair after dinner, the man suddenly went pale. He felt severe pain in his chest and had to gasp for breath. His wife was by his side in a moment. "What's wrong? Oh! I'll get the doctor, the hospital." The man struggled for control and waved his hand feebly in a dismissive gesture. "It's nothing—really.... I'll just lie down till it goes away."

This scene, with variations, has been repeated often enough to become well recognized by professional caregivers. The concept of denial may come to mind when a person has delayed seeking diagnosis and treatment for a life-threatening condition. Accepting the reality of serious illness might help to extend that person's life. Both denial and acceptance show their true power in real-life situations such as the one just sketched rather than in self-report questionnaires.

Types and Contexts of Acceptance and Denial

"Acceptance" and "denial" are used in a variety of ways, and sometimes their meanings become so blurred that they mislead more than they help. From a psychiatric standpoint, denial is regarded as a primitive defense. Denial rejects the existence of threat. This strategy may be effective for a short period of time and in situations in which there is an overwhelming threat. However, denial becomes increasingly ineffective when prolonged or used repeatedly: We do not survive long in this world when we ignore crucial

aspects of reality. Denial is most often found among people who are suffering from a psychotic reaction or as any person's first response to crisis and catastrophe.

Denial in this fundamental sense is not usually part of our everyday repertoire of coping strategies. However, we do engage in a number of behaviors that appear more or less like denial. There has been a widespread tendency to speak of all forms of resistance or evasive action as though they were denial. "Oh, she's just in denial!" By using this term as a buzz word, we often come to glib and premature conclusions. Usually, the person is not "denying" in the psychiatric sense of the term: a primitive and ineffective mechanism. Rather, the person is more likely to be coping with a difficult situation in the most resourceful way he or she can discover at the moment. This will become clearer as we distinguish among several process, all of which can be mistaken for denial (Box 2-1):

1. *Selective attention.* Imagine a situation in which many stimuli and events are competing for our attention. We cannot give equal attention to everything that is going on. A person who has never been in a hospital before, for example, might find many new, interesting, and challenging things to observe. These may seem more vivid and perceptually real than something as abstract as the diagnosis and prognosis that eventually will

For Better or For Worse® by Lynn Johnston

BOX 2-1
DENIAL AND DENIAL-LIKE RESPONSES TO DEATH

- *Selective attention*
  "I will feel less anxious if I don't allow myself to notice some things."

- *Selective response*
  "It would be better if I did not let others know how I feel right now."

- *Compartmentalizing*
  "One subtracted from one will not be zero as long as I keep these two numbers separate from each other."

- *Deception*
  "I will deliberately mislead you in order to reduce your anxiety and mine."

- *Resistance*
  "Of course I know that my life is in danger—but I'm not going to give in to it anyway."

- *Denial*
  "A touch of indigestion, that's all."

---

be made. This often happens with children. The individual is not "in denial" but simply directing his or her attention to whatever seems most salient in the immediate situation.

2. *Selective response.* A person exhibiting this behavior may have significant thoughts and feelings about death. However, he or she has judged that this is not the time or place to express them. "I'm not going to open up to this young doctor who looks more scared than I am," the person may think, or "there is nothing effective I can do about the situation at this moment, so I will talk about something else, or just keep quiet." The person may also decide that "there is something very important I must accomplish while I still have the opportunity, and it must take priority over dealing with my death as such." Therefore, the person who may seem to be denying his or her death might actually be working very hard at completing tasks in full awareness that time is running out.

3. *Compartmentalizing.* The individual is aware of being in a life-threatening situation, and the individual also responds to some aspects of this situation. However, something is missing: the connection between one aspect of the situation and another. For example, the person may know that the prognosis is poor. This is an accurate perception: No denial is involved. The person may also be co-

operating with treatment and discussing the situation rationally (adaptive response and still no denial). However, this same individual may be making future plans that involve travel or vigorous exercise, as if expecting to be around and in good health for years to come. In compartmentalizing, much of the dying and death reality is acknowledged, but the person stops just short of *realizing* the situation. All the pieces are there, but the individual resists putting them together to complete the whole picture.

4. *Deception.* People sometimes deliberately give false information to others. This takes place in dying and death situations, too. When people are telling each other lies (for whatever purpose), it makes sense to acknowledge this deceptive action for what it is and not confuse the issue with the buzzword denial.

5. *Resistance.* People who are in stressful situations may recognize their danger but decide not to "give in" to it. Some people in war-torn Bosnia, for example, decided to go about their daily rounds of shopping and visiting even though these activities increased vulnerability to snipers. These people were not denying the death risk. Rather, they had resolved to defy the war and keep their spirits up by not becoming prisoners to fear. A person who has been diagnosed with an incurable medical condition might become an-

gry instead of anxious. "I'll show them!" Sometimes, as we all know, a person with an apparently terminal condition does recover. There is a significant difference between the person who cannot accept the reality of his or her jeopardy and the person who comprehends the reality but decides to fight for life as long as possible.

6. *Denial* (the real thing). This is the basic defensive process that was defined earlier. The individual is not just selecting among possible perceptions and responses, limiting the logical connections between one phenomenon and the other, or engaging in conscious deception. Rather, the self appears to be totally organized against recognizing death-laden reality. Such an orientation can be bizarre and may accompany a psychotic reaction. It does not have to be that extreme, however. We can sometimes detect the existence of a true denial process that weaves in and out of other, more sophisticated ways of coping.

Temporary denial responses can be experienced by anybody who is under extreme stress. Denial responses are often seen in the wake of overwhelming catastrophes. For example, a woman was discovered intently sweeping the floor of her home after a tornado had passed through the city; the floor was practically all that was left of her home. Another woman was so debilitated by her long illness that she could no longer take nourishment by mouth or carry out other basic activities of everyday life. She had participated actively in decisions about her impending death: cremation, a simple memorial service, gifts to her church's youth program in lieu of flowers, and so forth. One morning, though, she astonished her visitors by showing them a set of travel brochures and her new sunglasses. She spoke of feeling so much better and eager as can be to take a long-delayed vacation. Two days later she was dead.

The Interpersonal Side of Acceptance and Denial

Each person in a dying and death situation influences and is influenced by others. The process

of acceptance and denial, therefore, is both interpersonal and *intrapsychic.* Change the interpersonal dynamics, and the dynamics of acceptance/denial are also likely to change. Furthermore, both the immediate situation and the historical background must be considered. One man may come from an ethnic background that treats dying and death in a straightforward manner (e.g., Amish). However, suppose that person finds himself dealing with a medical establishment in which death is still a high-anxiety taboo topic: Here is a potential death accepter trapped among the deniers. The reverse also happens. Consider a woman who grew up learning how to deny death, especially the deeper emotions associated with death. Suppose she becomes a patient in a more liberated health care establishment in which the staff is relentless in practicing its belief that we must be open and sharing with each other. Here, the denier is confronted by the accepters. We need to be aware of the forces operating in the present situation and the individual's previous life pattern in order to understand what is taking place between the dying person and the caregiver.

Weisman (1972) observed that a person does not usually deny everything about death to everybody. More often, a selective process is involved. We must go beyond the question, "Is this person denying death?" It is more useful to ask instead, "What aspects of dying or death are being shared with what other people, under what circumstances, and why?" The same questions could be asked about acceptance—a person might "deny" with one friend and "accept" with another. Apparent denial on the part of the patient may derive from a lack of responsive people in the environment.

A related point has to do with the *function* of so-called denial. Weisman (1972) noted that the purpose of denial is not simply to avoid a danger but to prevent loss of a significant relationship. All the adaptive processes that have been described here might be used to help the other person feel comfortable enough to maintain a vitally needed relationship. The individual faced with death may have to struggle as much with the other person's anxiety as with his or her own. Instead of placing the negative label of denial on these adaptive efforts, we might instead

Amish communities, unlike mainstream American culture, have traditionally regarded and accepted death as a natural part of their lives.

appreciate the care and sensitivity with which they are carried out.

Anxiety, Denial, and Acceptance: How Should We Respond?

Anxiety is an uncomfortable and, at times, almost unbearable condition. It is no wonder that anxiety has a bad reputation. However, small, sharp jolts of anxiety can alert us to danger: "Something's wrong here, what?" It can also prepare us for action: "I've been on stage a thousand times and been a bundle of nerves a thousand times—but that's just how I want to feel before the curtain goes up!"

The response strategies of acceptance and denial likewise are not necessarily good or bad. We must examine the contexts in which these pro-

cesses are used and the purposes they serve. For example, a person might be making a desperate stand against catastrophe. He or she has been forced to fall back on a primitive defense process that rejects important aspects of reality. This person definitely needs help.

On the other hand, the person may not be denying so much as selectively perceiving, linking, and responding to what is taking place. This pattern of coping with difficult reality may have its evasive aspects at certain times with certain people, but there is method, judgment, and purpose at work. Even flashes of pure denial may contribute to overall adaptation, such as when challenges come too swiftly, last too long, or are too overwhelming to meet in other ways. Later, the individual may find another way to deal with the same challenge, once the first impact has been partially deflected and partially absorbed. In every instance, we would want to understand the situation and identify the type of response.

I suggest that we proceed with the following set of premises:

1. Most of us have both acceptance and denial-type strategies available for coping with stressful situations. These strategies may operate within or outside our clear awareness, and one strategy or the other may dominate at various times.

2. States of total acceptance and total denial of death do occur, but they usually occur only in extreme circumstances: when the individual is letting go of life after achieving a sense of completion and having struggled as long as struggling seemed worthwhile, or when the individual is resisting the first onslaught of catastrophic reality.

3. Much of what is loosely spoken of as denial can be understood more adequately as adaptive processes through which the person responds selectively to various aspects of a difficult situation.

4. The individual's pattern of adaptation should be considered within the context of the acceptance and denial that characterize the larger interpersonal network of which he or she is a part.

5. Acceptance and denial can be evaluated only when we are in a position to understand what the person is trying to accomplish and what he or she is up against.

The instructor of our Monday evening Tai 'chi class does not slight the preparation phase. Sifu Dale Snow persuades us to reduce the body tension accumulated during the day and adopt a relaxed posture, knees slightly bent, arms dangling. Then, in a blend of Eastern wisdom and Western shootouts, he suggests that we remain in relaxed alertness, like a gunfighter who might be called on to draw at any moment. This might not be bad advice for dealing with our response system for possible life-threatening situations. Whatever reduces our everyday stress level is likely to improve our ability to detect and respond to actual threats. A relaxed attitude is also more likely to free us to discover opportunities for adventure, creativity, and more rewarding relationships. Despite their differences, all the theories mentioned here are in agreement that feeling at peace with ourselves and secure (but not overconfident) in our abilities can reduce death anxiety without compromising our ability to cope with threats.

In the Shade of the Jambu Tree

This chapter opened with a brief visit to the exotic land of the Uttarakurus, where the magic Jambu tree grows and people live 1,000 or, perhaps, 11,000 years. Sounds good—especially if we want to keep the thought of death as distant as possible. Attempts to remove the sting from the prospect of death have also stimulated more than beguiling legends. Influential worldviews have been formed around the core issue of what should be done with death. A significant example is Taoism, a major philosophical–religious system that developed in ancient and medieval China and continues to contribute to world thought and culture. Our eyes see a diversity of forms and activities as well as a relentless process of change. It is up to our minds to comprehend what cannot be so easily perceived: the basic unity of nature. *Tao* (pronounced "dow") is translated as The Way. It is the force that both moves and unites all that exists. We may be in the habit of separating mind from matter, for example, but both are in the flow of the tao.

What we call life and what we call death are also facets of the tao. The same reality underlies both. This sense of an affinity or communion between life and death is part of the Taoist answer to death. There is also a more activist dimension, though. Life can be prolonged by drawing on the power of the tao. In practical terms, this philosophy led to exercise, diet, and use of natural substances (such as herbs) that were thought to strengthen health and preserve life. Present-day fitness regimes were prefigured in Taoist philosophy and practice.

Chemistry, biology, pharmacology, metallurgy, and other sciences and technologies also were given impetus by taoist philosophy (Gruman, in press). Nature has secrets that might be divined by patient study and a moment of inspired observation. We can live longer and better and therefore keep the simmering pot of death anxiety from boiling over. Chinese alchemy devoted much attention to life prolongation, and this also became one of the prime goals of alchemy when it developed in Western culture (transforming base into precious metals was also an ardent pursuit, but a life free from death anxiety was the true gold standard).

Thinking of life, we are also at least implicitly thinking of death. Thinking of death, we are attracted to the idea of a life that somehow flourishes, continues, and renews despite a universe that seems to have other plans. Perhaps each of us can find our own comfort zone in which life can be enjoyed while death is given its due.

SUMMARY

Life is supposed to go on. Why pause to think of death? We remind ourselves of some ways in which death breaks through into our awareness, including catastrophic accidents, acts of terrorism and violence, the vulnerability of children, and the limitations of even our state-of-the-art health care system. Not thinking about death has been a failed experiment. Listening and communicating are far more helpful approaches. You monitored your own knowledge, attitudes, beliefs, and feelings about death in a series of self-inventories. These exercises have provided you with a stronger base for looking at the way other people think about death and how state of mind can affect death-related behavior.

The dynamics of accepting and denying death were explored with the help of characters in Leo Tolstoy's probing novel, *The Death of Ivan Ilych*. We then carefully examined the core concepts of anxiety, denial, and acceptance. Freudian and existential theory offer competing ideas about death anxiety and its place in our lives. Recent theoretical approaches and empirical studies provide further information but also raise questions that have not yet been answered adequately. One of the most consistent findings is that people generally report a low to moderate level of death anxiety, with women having somewhat higher scores. We also saw that denial of death is a term that is often used too loosely. Some responses that are misinterpreted as denial are better understood as selective attention, selective response, compartmentalizing, deception, or resistance. Attention was also given to the kinds of interactions we have with each other in death-related situations, and some suggestions were offered. The ancient philosophical–religious system of Taoism provides an influential example of thinking about life and death as unified in the reality underlying all that exists.

REFERENCES

Becker, E. (1973). *The denial of death.* New York: Free Press.

Fear of dying. (1991). Washington, DC: Gallup Poll.

Frager, G. (1996). Bearing witness. In C. K. Cassel (Ed.), *Caring for the dying. Identification and promotion of physician competency* (p. 41). Washington, DC: American Board of Internal Medicine.

Frazer, J. G. (1966). *The fear of the dead in primitive religion.* New York: Biblo & Tannen. (Original work published 1933)

Freud, S. (1953). Thoughts for the times on war and death. In *Collected works* (Vol. 4, pp. 288–317). London: Hogarth. (Original work published 1913)

Gruman, G. J. (in press). *A history of ideas about the prolongation of life.* New York: Springer.

Harmon-Jones, E., Simon, L., Greenberg, J., Pyszczynski, T., Solomon, S., & McGregor, H. (1997). Terror management theory and self-esteem: Evidence that increased self-esteem reduces mortality salience effects. *Journal of Personality and Social Psychology, 73,* 24–31.

Hayslip, B. (1986–1987). The measurement of communication apprehension regarding the terminally ill. *Omega, Journal of Death and Dying, 17,* 251–261.

Jacinto, L. (2002, December 11). *Death by fire. Forced marriages are driving some women to self-immolation.* abcNEWS.com

Kastenbaum, R. (2000a). *The psychology of death* (3rd ed.). New York: Springer.

Kastenbaum, R. (2000b). Counseling the elderly dying patient. In V. Molinari (Ed.), *Professional psychology in long term care.* New York: Hatherleigh. (pp. 201–226).

Kastenbaum, R. (2002c). Cryonic suspension. In R. Kastenbaum (Ed.), *Macmillan encyclopedia of death and dying* (Vol. 1, pp. 192–195). New York: Macmillan.

Kastenbaum, R., & Briscoe, L. (1975). The street corner. A laboratory for the study of life-threatening behavior. *Omega, Journal of Death and Dying, 7,* 351–359.

Lester, D. (1994). The Collett-Lester Fear of Death Scale. In R. A. Neimeyer (Ed.), *Death anxiety handbook* (pp. 45–60). Washington, DC: Francis & Taylor.

Malinowski, B. (1948). *Magic, science, and religion and other essays.* Garden City, NJ: Doubleday.

Quill, T. E. (1993). *Death and dignity.* New York: Free Press.

Radcliffe-Brown, A. R. (1952). *Structure and function in primitive society.* New York: Free Press.

Robbins, R. A. (1990). Signing an organ donor card: Psychological factors. *Death Studies, 14,* 219–230.

Sherman, D. W. (1996–1997). Correlates of death anxiety in nurses who provide AIDS care. *Omega, Journal of Death and Dying, 34,* 117–138.

Tomer, A. (2002). Terror management theory. In R. Kastenbaum (Ed.), *Macmillan encyclopedia of death and dying* (Vol. 2, pp. 885–887). New York: Macmillan.

Tomer, A., & Eliason, G. (1996). Toward a comprehensive model of death anxiety. *Death Studies, 20,* 343–366.

Templer, D. I. (1970). The construction and validation of a death anxiety scale. *Journal of General Psychology, 82,* 165–177.

Thurson, J. S., & Powell, F. C. (1994). A revised death anxiety scale. In R. A. Neimeyer (Ed.), *Death anxiety handbook* (pp. 31–44). Washington, DC: Taylor & Francis.

Tolstoy, L. (1960). *The death of Ivan Ilych.* New York: New American Library. (Original work published 1886).

VandeCreek, L., & Frankowski, D. (1996). Barriers that predict resistance to completing a living will. *Death Studies, 20,* 73–82.

Weisman, A. D. (1972). *On dying and denying.* New York: Behavioral Publications.

GLOSSARY

Anatomical Gift Act: A law that permits people to designate their bodily organs for transplantation to another person upon their own death.

Coroner: A physician who functions on behalf of a governmental agency to regulate and, when necessary, investigate the condition of human corpses. The same functions may be carried out by a physician with the title of medical examiner.

Death Anxiety: Emotional distress and insecurity aroused by encounters with dead bodies, grieving people, or other reminders of mortality, including one's own thoughts.

Denial: An extreme response in which one attempts to cope with danger or loss by ignoring important features of reality.

Edge Theory: An approach that emphasizes the survival function of death-related anxiety.

Existentialism: A philosophical position that emphasizes people's responsibilities for their own lives and deaths.

Fatalism: The belief that future events have already been determined; therefore, one is powerless to affect the future.

Hospice: (1) A program of care devoted to providing comfort to terminally ill people through a team approach with participation by family members. (2) A facility in which such care is provided.

Intrapsychic: Events that occur within a person's mind (e.g., thoughts, images, feelings, memories, and dreams).

Living Will: A document that instructs medical personnel on the individual's wishes should a situation arise in which that person cannot communicate directly. It almost always involves the request for limiting the type of medical interventions. The living will is one of a class of documents known as advance directives.

Schizophrenia: A form of mental and perhaps biomedical illness in which a person is out of contact with reality and emotionally alienated from others.

Self-Efficacy: The ability of a person to act competently in meeting needs and pursuing goals.

Taoism: An ancient and still influential Chinese philosophical–religious system that views life and death as linked in a fundamental reality that underlies the apparent diversity, change, and disorder of the observable world.

Thanatophobia: Fear of death.

Terror Management Theory: A theory based on the proposition that many of our sociocultural beliefs, symbols, and practices are intended to reduce our sense of vulnerability and helplessness.

Ironically, Dr. Victor Frankenstein's name was transferred by popular usage to the flawed creature he addressed as "Abhorred monster! Fiend! Wretched devil!" Basil Rathborne is the arrogant scientist here and Boris Karloff his monster in the famous 1931 film version.

chapter 3

WHAT IS DEATH?

What Does Death Mean?

I collected the instruments of life around me, that I might infuse a spark of being into the lifeless thing that lay at my feet. It was already one in the morning; the rain pattered dismally against the panes, and my candle was nearly burnt out, when, by the glimmer of the half-extinguished light, I saw the dull yellow eye of the creature open; it breathed hard, and convulsive motion agitated its limbs.
—Victor Frankenstein, in Mary Shelley's *Frankenstein* (1818/1977, p. 72)

I carefully noted the simulated positions of seventeen different kinds of insects belonging to different genera, both poor and first-rate shammers. Afterwards I procured naturally dead specimens of some of these insects…others I killed with camphor by a slow easy death; the result was that in no instance was the attitude exactly the same, and in several instances the attitudes of the feigners and of the really dead were as unlike as they could possibly be.
—Charles Darwin's notebook as quoted by Carrington and Meader (1921)

The EEG is flat and there is a complete absence of spontaneous respiration.
—From the Harvard Critera (1968)

Even though a person may be "dead" because his heart stops working, some muscle, skin and bone cells may live on for many days. So, while the entire person as a functioning organism is dead, parts of the biologic organism live on for varying periods of time. The amount of time these cells and tissues live depends on their ability to survive without oxygen and other nutrients, and with an increasing amount of metabolic waste products building up within them…. Then when is a person dead?
—Kenneth V. Iserson, M.D. (2001, p. 3)

Death is not to be ruled by the mere lifting of life support until it is certain that the soul has departed the body.
—Dr. Bakr Abu Zaid (2002, p. 3)

Then, when lust hath conceived, it bringeth forth sin; and Sin, when it is finished, bringeth forth death.
—New Testament, James: 1:15

So death, the most terrifying of ills, is nothing to us, since so long as we exist, death is not with us, but when death comes, then we do not exist. It does not then concern either the living or the dead, since for the former it is not and the latter are no more.
—Epicurus, third century B.C.

Death? It's a change of clothes. That's all!
—Interview respondent

Death, I see him as very patient and very polite. He waits for each of us some place, just around a corner or even at the foot of our bed. I think of him as being there all the time, but only when we can see him is he there for us. He doesn't have to say anything and neither do we. We know what he's here for and he knows we know.
—Respondent in a study of death personification

COMPETING IDEAS ABOUT THE NATURE AND MEANING OF DEATH

All these people were speaking of death, but not in the same way. In mainstream Western tradition, we have become accustomed to thinking of death as the end of life—or something that begins *after* the end of life. We are also inclined to an either/or way of thinking: *Either* we are alive *or* we are dead. Two other views continue to thrive, although in an uneasy relationship: Death is the implacable enemy of life, or it is the portal through which one enters a higher form of existence. Those of us who were brought up within the Judeo-Christian tradition may have difficulty in realizing that life and death are regarded quite

differently by many other people. In Hindu philosophy, for example, birth, death, rebirth, and, again, death are linked in a constantly recurring cycle (Hopkins, 1992). We are born to die, but we die to be reborn.

Not everybody agrees with the ideas about death most familiar in Western society, and what we mean by "death" becomes of practical importance when we communicate with others who might have a different conception. Reflecting on ideas about death also becomes important when we draw on them in making life decisions. We begin, then, by examining competing ideas about the nature and meaning of death. We ask: What is this *death* that one person "accepts" and another person "denies?" That one person seeks and another person avoids? That one person cannot stop thinking about and another person believes is hardly worth thinking about?

Not only do individuals differ in their attitudes and feelings but also the same person may differ in his or her attitudes and feelings from situation to situation, such as when I noticed that the starboard engine of the ancient DC-3 had burst into flame. "Death" was no longer a word for scholarly contemplation but the vivid prospect of a rapid plunge into the green hills of West Virginia. Years later as pretty much an inert lump on an intensive care unit (ICU) ward, I felt death to be already with me, rather slow and casual about its work, and somehow not very interesting (Kastenbaum, in press). Many survivors of near-death experiences have reported an enduring change in their conceptions of death and life alike (Chapter 14). There are practical consequences to the fact that death can mean different things to different people or to the same person at different times. If you and I hold varying assumptions about the nature of death, then we may also take different courses of action at decisive moments.

We return now to the opening quotations to become more familiar with the variety of ways in which death has been conceived.

DEATH AS OBSERVED, PROCLAIMED, AND IMAGINED

Both Victor Frankenstein and his monster were created by an 18-year-old woman whose own life had been born through death. Mary Shelley's mother was an independent thinker who wrote powerfully about the rights of women 200 years ago. That Mary Wollstonecraft died in childbirth is thought to have had an enduring effect on the daughter, who would later marry poet Percy Shelley and go on to a creative, adventuresome, but tragedy-marked life. The Frankenstein story did not come out of thin air, then. In addition to her own curiosity about death, Mary Shelley came of age at a time when "galvanic" (electrical) experiments were a conspicuous part of the new scientific enterprise, doctors were procuring corpses by suspicious means to improve the quality of medical education and knowledge, and reports were circulating about people having been buried alive (Bondeson, 2001).

Her novel brought the growing excitement and fears into sharp focus. Perhaps the dead could be reanimated: That would mean death is not necessarily permanent and irreversible. Perhaps the age of the "modern Prometheus" was about to rise. Just as Prometheus pilfered fire from the gods as a gift to humans, so a Victor Frankenstein might harness lightning to the alarming project of creating life. Mary Shelley knew very well, however, that Prometheus suffered a terrible punishment for his disobedience, and such punishment was also part of the novel and its many stage and film adaptations. Frankenstein's creation turned out to be painfully and pitifully flawed—a warning to all scientists of the future, reaching to the gene splitters and cloners of today. Attitudes toward death and the dead became more complex with the introduction of Frankenstein as well as Bram Stoker's *Dracula* (1975) and many other works that dared to test the boundaries.

Unlike Victor Frankenstein, Charles Darwin was a real scientist and on his way to transforming our understanding of life on earth, water, and sky. When not making discoveries ashore, he conducted many small experiments aboard his ship, *The Beagle*. In the experiments described previously, Darwin could distinguish clearly between insects that were either looking or actually dead. *Thanatomimesis* is the simulation of death, often to avoid being killed (Kastenbaum, 2002a), although it is also used in children's play to master death-related anxiety (see Chapter 11). His observations contribute to the unsettling realization that the dead may be only apparently so (Bondeson, 2001). The fact that he saw no harm in experimentally ending lives "by a slow easy death" perhaps has little significance because his victims were insects, but soon scientists would be "sacrificing" animals of many species, and physicians on the Nazi payroll would be conducting lethal experiments on humans. Mary Shelley's concern about scientific adventuring on the borderlands of life and death would also be the concern of subsequent generations.

The Harvard Medical School faculty, which established criteria for death in 1968, sent no lightning bolts into recycled corpse material and camphorized no unfortunate spiders. They did have an apparatus to rely on, though—the electroencephalogram (EEG). They did develop an influential definition of death that seemed to replace speculation with objective assessment. Perhaps that should have been the end of the story, but death has not remained quite so easily defined.

Medical Professor Kenneth V. Iserson does his part to keep us off balance by discussing death not as a sudden and massive event but as a complex process that takes place over time. Even as the physician signs a death certificate there may still be biologic activity ongoing throughout the body. Tradition, society, and science have decided on the criteria for pronouncing death, but nature does not entirely agree (Pernick, 1988).

Islam does not agree either. A thousand years ago, the most learned and effective physicians were in Islamic lands, writing treatises that guided other European doctors for centuries to come. Dr. Bakr Abu Zaid is well aware of current practices in the definition of death and life support systems. Nevertheless, he cautions against taking a purely materialistic or objective approach. According to Islamic teachings, death is certain and final only when the soul has left the body. Neither Dr. Zaid nor Islam are alone in this belief. The people of many societies have long believed that death is marked by the separation of soul from body. One would surely want to pay attention to EEG and other observations of a faltering body, but one would also have to be sensitive to the less tangible event of soul/body separation.

We enter still other realms of death perspectives when we open books of ancient philosophy or the *New Testament.* In the third century B.C., *Epicurus* offered a philosophy that has influenced many people from ancient times to the present. (A good way to become familiar with this view is to read *On the Nature of Things,* the narrative poem in which Lucretius articulates many of Epicurus' ideas.) Epicurus, agreeing with another philosopher, Democritus, argued that the universe is composed of atoms in motion, and that our own actions—indeed, our innermost thoughts and feelings—are shaped by the pattern of past events. We live and die in a materialistic universe. What, then, is death? It is really not much of anything—simply one more event in a long sequence of events that have no intrinsic meaning or value. We never actually experience death,

and the fact of death does not violate any contract we might imagine that the gods have cosigned with us.

How, then, should one live, Epicurus? The wise person will appreciate life and maintain a sense of balance and proportion. We are not major players in a great cosmic drama. We just happen to be here for a while and then again become part of the vapor from which we arose. A depressing view? Not for Epicurus, at least. He formed a community known as The Garden in which like-minded people—women as well as men, poor as well as rich, and slaves as well as free citizens—lived in equality and friendship (this community endured for approximately 500 years). He has offered a model for harmonious living within a universe that does not seem to care about either our lives or our deaths, but most people have preferred a version in which the universe is rule abiding and purposeful and in which human lives and deaths do count for something. The Christian version has met this need for many people for many years.

The New Testament tells the story of Christ's life and teachings. The story is told somewhat differently from one gospel to the next, and a bewildering variety of interpretations have been offered by preachers and Biblical scholars. It is not surprising that the Christian message regarding death can be read as simple or complex, depending on the reader's preference. The quotation from James delivers one facet of this message. Lust—sexual feeling, thought, and activity—is intimately associated with death. Before the emergence of Christianity, other religions in the ancient world emphasized a connection between withering away and fertility. Life was regenerated through death. Careful observance of rituals might persuade the gods to allow crops to succeed and babies to thrive. Sacrifices (animal or human) could also help matters—a little death here and there as payment for life.

The Christian version was different, however: It was specified that sexuality is sinful and carries the death penalty. The person who is responsive to this facet of the Christian message may find it difficult to think about sexuality without also thinking about death. Within this frame of reference, virginity and abstinence have theological resonances. Suicide and martyrdom, especially in earlier eras, were viewed by some Christians as appropriate alternatives to sexual indulgence. Not only the "deathification of sex" but also the "sexualization of death" have been consequences of the concept put forth in the gospel of James and other passages in the New Testament. A passionate and mystical union with God became an increasingly dominant theme in the version of Christianity that became known to the world through the interpretations of *Paul the Convert* (Segall, 1990). At the same time, sexual union between two humans and their bonds of attachment were seen as less spiritual and worthy. Long before celibacy became a requirement for priests, there was a strong advocacy for choosing religious devotion over sexual relationships. Not all Christians favor this intertwining view of death and sexuality, but it is undeniably an influential part of the tradition.

The man who said death is "a change of clothes. That's all!" identifies himself with the New Age movement (although the individuals themselves sometimes reject this term). In this view, life is a journey through multiple lives. Death is not an ending; it is a transition, a door through which one passes on the way to the next life. This conception clearly differs from the others. Unlike Epicurus and other atomists, life and death are purposeful—there is a point to it all, and a progression. Unlike the New Testament view, death is not a punishment for sexuality or for anything else. A flat EEG is not impressive because the life and death of the spirit are not seen as by-products of brain activity. In this view, there is some commonality with Islam and other religious traditions that believe in a soul principle that is not entirely dependent on the physical body. This is clearly a robust idea because it has gathered renewed support in our age of rampant biotechnology.

Death becomes less abstract when represented as a person. The college student who envisioned death as "very patient and very polite" was stepping away from the more common American view of death as an enemy whose presence should be denied as long as possible. Instead, she pictured death as a kind of watchful companion who knows and respects us throughout our lives and who we should not be surprised to see when the time comes.

Death as Symbolic Construction

Some contemporary scholars view death as a *symbolic construction.* What is death? An idea, a concept. Something our minds have constructed from our experiences, our guesswork, our needs, and our ignorance. Death is therefore subject to the same rules and limitations as any other concept. This does not mean that death is unreal or fictitious. Death is a concept we need because it has so many important referents, associations, and consequences. Water is also a concept. We look at ice, snow, mist, rain, standing pools, and flowing streams and write the formula H_2O on the board and call them all water, even though the forms seem so different. Water is not simply something that presents itself to our eyes, but a useful concept. When we try to determine the difference between "alive" and "dead" and to define death we are dealing with symbolic constructions. We are working with the words, concepts, and ways of thinking that are available to us in a particular society at a particular time.

What are the moral and practical implications of the symbolic construction view of death? We are left with the feeling that dead and death are concepts that are still under construction—still subject to question, challenge, and revision. For example, I have often had to sort out my own observations and feelings when at the bedside of an unresponsive person who has been given little or no hope of recovery. If I judge that this person is dead (as a person), then I would not have much reason to attempt communication. If I judge, however, that I cannot really know this person's state of being with any assurance, then I might well choose to attempt to communicate as best I can. Symbolic constructions of death may lead us either to increased or to reduced interactions.

Some of the most influential constructions of death in our society come from movies and television. The average person today is less likely to have direct, unfiltered encounters with dying and death than in the past. At the same time, we are frequently exposed to depictions of dying and death in the movies. Schultz and Huet (2000/2001) examined popular and award films. Trained observers categorized the number and type of death events, including the responses of others to the deaths. Most deaths were presented in a sensational and violent manner. Seldom were we shown anything resembling the actual course of dying and death that is experienced by most people in our society. Encouragingly, perhaps, films that had received awards for special merit were much more likely to include expressions of sorrow and sadness. Gender differences were striking. Male characters were six times more likely to instigate death, and female characters were twice as likely to be the victims. The authors conclude that "in American film, death is distorted into a sensational stream of violent attacks by males, with fear, injury, further aggression, and the absence of normal grief reactions as the most common response."

What, then, would a person think who knew death only from the movies? Death must be the result of anger and brutal assault by men, mostly against women. Furthermore, people usually don't spend a lot of time feeling sad—they're too busy getting ready to get even. We will see in Chapter 12 that it takes a while for children to understand that death is not just intentional or accidental but will befall everybody in one way or another. The child's attempt to understand the nature and meaning of death is certainly not assisted by the aggressive and violent constructions of death in popular movies.

The ideas about death that we have sampled have recently taken on a more urgent aspect. Is this person "dead enough" to have organs removed and transplanted to save another person's life? To have the life support system removed? The ancient question, *What is death?* has been joined by an even more pressing concern: *When is dead?* We turn now to biomedical approaches to answering these related questions.

BIOMEDICAL APPROACHES TO THE DEFINITION OF DEATH

Death is "certified" thousands of times every day by physicians. The physician meets society's need for verifying that one of its members has been lost. This verification is a signal to the survivors that they have to begin the process of reorganizing their lives around the fact of this loss. It is also a signal to society that many arrangements are to be altered; for example, insurance benefits are to be paid, the deceased will not be expected to vote at the next election, and this individual death will become part of mortality statistics. To perform these functions for society in a consistent and rational way, the physician must have an answer to the *"when* is dead?" question that takes the practical form: *"Under what conditions should a person be considered dead?"*

Traditional Determination of Death

The most common signs of death have been lack of respiration, pulse, and heartbeat as well as failure to respond to stimuli, such as light, movement, and pain. Lowered body temperature and stiffness are other characteristics that are expected to appear, followed later by bloating and signs of decomposition. In the past, a competent physician usually had no need for the equipment available today. Simple tests, carefully performed, would make it clear whether or not life had fled. In many instances, the physician and family could also take some time before making burial arrangements, thereby allowing more opportunity for a possible spontaneous revival of function.

Nevertheless, life-threatening errors could be made on occasion. Victims of drowning and lightning, for example, would sometimes be taken for dead, when in fact their vital functions had only been suspended. Those who suffered a stroke, epileptic seizure, or diabetic coma might also be pronounced dead instead of receiving treatment. The same fate could befall a person gifted in the once popular art of hysterical fainting. The possibility that people might be pronounced dead while still alive was an unsettling one, and Edgar Allan Poe seized on this fear for some of his most popular writings. One of my favorite articles from the past was published in the land where, popular mythology has it, the undead have been most active. Writing in the *Transylvanian Journal of Medicine* in 1835, Dr. Nathan Shrock reports that his own uncle had almost been buried alive until, at the last minute, he showed faint signs of life. Shrock then leads the reader through all of the traditional signs of death and shows how almost all of them, even the lack of moist breath on a mirror held in front of the nose and mouth, can be misleading.

Mark Twain (1883/1972) gave his own version of the possibility of unexpected resuscitation, calculated to horrify or amuse, depending on the reader's mind-set. He claimed to have visited a municipal "dead house" in Munich:

Around a finger of each of these fifty still forms, both great and small, was a ring; and from the ring a wire led to the ceiling, and thence to a bell in a watch-room yonder, where, day and night, a watchman sits always alert and ready to spring to the aid of any of that pallid company who, waking out of death, shall make a movement—for any, even the slightest movement will twitch the wire and rings that fearful bell. I imagined myself a death-sentinel, drowsing there alone, far into the dragging watches of some wailing, gusty night, and having in a twinkling all my body stricken to quivering jelly by the sudden clamor of that awful summons! (p. 189)

A very different kind of observer devoted himself to exploring the what and when of death some years later (Kastenbaum, 2000). A pathologist working in a Detroit hospital instructed nurses to call him when a patient's death was imminent. He wanted to be there at the moment of death or as close to that as possible. The physician's name did not become well known for some time, but Jack Kevorkian was already drawn to the mysterious transition between life and death. Kevorkian was one of the few physicians in our time who wrote about the status of the eye at death. He believed the condition of the eye provided the most reliable basis for determining whether or not the person was dead (and, if

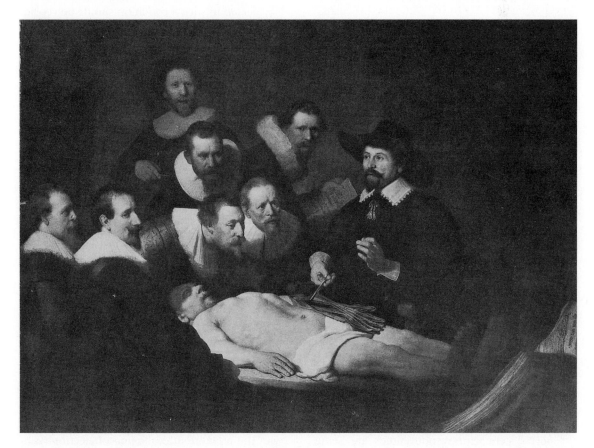

The Anatomy Lesson of Dr. Nicholus Tulp (Rembrandt, 1632)

dead, for how long). He reported his observations with 51 consecutive cases (1957) and discussed his method and overall findings in a later paper (1961). Specifically, he found that the status of the eye at death included (a) segmentation and interruption of blood circulation, (b) a haziness of the cornea, and (c) the appearance of homogeneity and paleness. Kevorkian urged other physicians to do as he had been doing—examining the patient's eyes with the use of an opthalmoscope. Few took up his suggestion. Health care providers as well as the general public were not ready to look death in the face. Most people, even now, prefer to construct death from a safer, less harrowing distance. Medical advances and a growing set of rules and regulations have since transformed the realm in which only Kevorkian and a few others dared explore in the past. There may not be just one way of being dead anymore.

Ways of "Being Dead"

Medical advances have made it possible to maintain the body of a nonresponsive individual in a vegetative state for an indefinite period of time—weeks, months, even years. The heart continues to beat and the respiratory system continues to exchange its gases. Reflex responses may also be elicited. The person, however, no longer seems to be "at home." In such circumstances, we may hesitate to evoke either category, *alive* or *dead*. Eventually, though, somebody may have to make a decision, and this decision will require a definition of "deadness," if not of death. Consider the following brief examples, each dependent on a firm definition of death:

1. Family members and the attending physician agree that the life support system should be withdrawn because the patient is unresponsive and has no apparent chance to recover. Would "pulling the plug" constitute murder? Or is the *person* already dead? If we cannot murder the dead, is it nevertheless a crime of some sort because vegetative functions could have continued indefinitely?
2. Another patient is also comatose and unresponsive, but vegetative processes continue even in the absence of an elaborate life support system. (Intravenous fluids are being given, but there is no ventilator to maintain respiration.) Elsewhere in the hospital, an organ transplant team is urgently seeking a kidney that might keep somebody else alive for many years. The needed kidney could be liberated by ruling that the comatose patient is dead. The organ must be removed while the host body is still relatively intact if it is to have its best chance to function in the other patient. Removal of the kidney is a procedure that will probably be fatal for the comatose patient. Would this operation be an act of murder or some other crime that we do not yet have a name for? Or is it a desirable procedure because it might help one person and cannot harm another because he or she is actually dead?
3. The vegetative functioning of a comatose, nonresponsive woman is being maintained by elaborate life-prolonging procedures. If a person in such a condition should be considered dead, then this is a dead woman. However, there is a living fetus within. The fetus will not survive unless society decides to keep the woman's vegetative processes intact until it has become more viable. Does this mean that society is keeping a dead person alive? And does it mean that society knowingly kills that dead person in order to deliver a baby who has a fighting chance to survive?

Either the similarities or the differences among these conditions could be emphasized. How vital is the distinction between cessation of bodily processes and loss of the person *as* a person? What difference, if any, is there between the "deadness" of a body that continues to function on a vegetative level with or without an elaborate life support system? Who or what is it that no longer lives—perhaps still a person but not the *same* person?

Brain Death and the Harvard Criteria

By the 1950s it was recognized that some unresponsive patients were "beyond coma"; that is, no electrophysiological activities could be detected from the brain. Postmortem examinations revealed extensive destruction of brain tissue consistent with the premortem evaluation of electrophysiological activity. This condition came to be known as

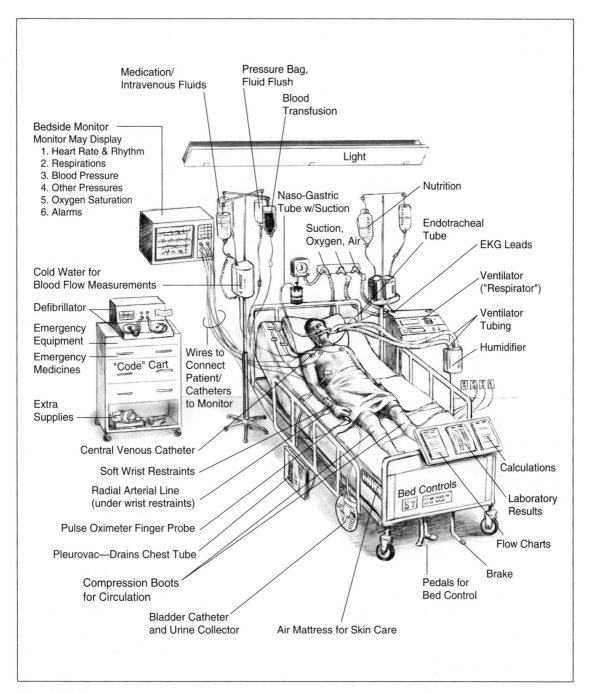

FIGURE 3.1

A comotose patient lies in a critical care unit room. The diagram represents the types of equipment that may be seen there. While equipment may vary in appearance at different hospitals, its function to monitor and support remains the same.

respirator brain. The implication was clear: Some patients who were connected to ventilators had lost their brain function irreversibly and therefore should be considered dead.

At first the concept of brain death served mainly to help physicians decide that additional medical procedures would be of no benefit to the patient. Soon, however, the new concept was being used in a new and controversial way (McCullagh, 1993):

> As the original intention of recognizing brain death was to spare patients from treatment that was likely to be futile and burdensome, it appears paradoxical that a diagnosis of brain death has, more recently, become a guarantee that a full range of such treatment will be imposed, provided the individual is suitable as an organ source and accessible to facilities for transportation.... There have been some radical modifications of previous practice. Undoubtedly, the most striking of these has been the adoption of the practice of undertaking organ removal from beating-heart donors rather than waiting upon the cessation of effective pumping of blood by the heart. (p. 9)

Here was certainly a remarkable change in the construction of deadness. The heart is still beating—in fact, physicians make sure the heart is still beating—but the patient is dead or dead enough to be classified as an appropriate organ donor. Biomedical advances had led us into a twilight zone in which ethical standards and value priorities seem elusive and ambiguous.

There was also increasing pressure on those who had to make the brain death diagnosis. Both the health care and the justice systems felt the need for guidance. About a decade later, a committee of Harvard Medical School faculty issued its opinion (Ad Hoc Committee, 1968). Since that time, the Harvard Criteria for determination of brain death have served as the primary guide. The first three criteria would have come as no surprise to physicians of an early generation. It is the last two criteria, dependent on technological advances, that introduce a new consideration.

The Harvard Criteria

1. *Unreceptive and unresponsive.* No awareness is shown for external stimuli or inner need.

The unresponsiveness is complete even when ordinarily painful stimuli are applied.
2. *No movements and no breathing.* There is a complete absence of spontaneous respiration and all other spontaneous muscular movement.
3. *No reflexes.* The usual reflexes that can be elicited in a neurophysiological examination are absent (e.g., when a light is shined in the eye, the pupil does not constrict).
4. *A flat EEG.* Electrodes attached to the scalp elicit a printout of electrical activity from the living brain. These are popularly known as brain waves. The respirator brain does not provide the usual pattern of peaks and valleys. Instead, the moving stylus records essentially a flat line. This is taken to demonstrate the lack of electrophysiological activity.
5. *No circulation to or within the brain.* Without the oxygen and nutrition provided through blood circulation, brain functioning will soon terminate.

The first three criteria, the traditional ones, usually serve the purpose. The Harvard report was not intended to require the use of the EEG in all cases—only those in which a question remains and the traditional criteria may not be sufficiently reliable. It was recommended that in such situations the tests of brain functioning should be repeated approximately 24 hours later.

The Harvard report provides useful guidelines and has found widespread application. However, the definition of death and its ramifications were still a source of concern and a presidential commission produced its own monograph, *Defining Death* (President's Commission, 1981). The commission concluded,

> The "Harvard criteria" have been found to be quite reliable. Indeed, no case has yet been found that met these criteria and regained any brain functions despite continuation of respirator support. Criticisms of the criteria have been of five kinds. First, the phrase, "irreversible coma" is misleading as applied to the cases at hand. "Coma" is a condition of a living person, and a body without any brain function is dead, and thus *beyond* any coma. Second, the writers of these criteria did not realize that the spinal cord reflexes actually persist or return quite

commonly after the brain has completely and permanently ceased functioning. Third, "unreceptivity" is not amenable to testing in an unresponsive body without consciousness. Next, the need adequately to test brainstem reflexes, especially apnea, and to exclude drug and metabolic intoxication as possible causes of the coma, are not made sufficiently explicit and precise. Finally, although all individuals that meet "Harvard criteria" are dead (irreversible cessation of all functions of the entire brain), there are many other individuals who are dead but do not maintain circulation long enough to have a 24-hour observation period. (p. 25)

Perhaps you have noticed something odd in this otherwise straightforward passage. It speaks of individuals who are "dead but do not maintain circulation long enough to have a 24-hour observation period." This quirky turn of thought alerts us again to the contemporary breakdown of the old, comfortably secure concept of *dead.* The presidential commission here seems to be rebuking some dead individuals for not maintaining their circulation. It may not yet have become a patriotic duty for the dead to make themselves available for all possible testing. Nevertheless, the message conveyed here is that there are echelons among the dead—some appear to be "deader" than others. This is surely a departure from the usual conception of *dead* and *death* in Western society, although it would not have raised eyebrows in some other cultures.

Whole-Brain or Neocortical Death?

There is still controversy with regard to brain death. Brain death can refer to any of the following conditions:

- *Whole-brain death* is the irreversible destruction of all neural structures within the intracranial cavity. This includes both hemispheres and all tissue from the top (cerebral cortex) to the bottom (cerebellum and brainstem).
- *Cerebral death* is the irreversible destruction of both cerebral hemispheres, excluding the lower centers in the cerebellum and brainstem.
- *Neocortical death* is the irreversible destruction of neural tissue in the cerebral cortex—the most highly differentiated brain cells, consid-

ered to be of critical importance for intellectual functioning.

Whole-brain death is the most frequently used biomedical definition today and the one that appears most often in regulatory documents. It is a conservative definition; the certification of death is delayed as long as there is observable functioning in any subsystem of the brain. Some advocates of this view suggest that the lack of neocortical functioning might be caused by dysfunction in lower centers, such as the reticular formation in the medulla and midbrain. If this is true in some cases, then the absence of consciousness and electrical activity of the neocortex could represent a potentially reversible situation.

What is the situation today? Possibilities of error have been sharply reduced by the health care system's use of the more conservative, whole-brain definition of death. McCullagh (1993) concludes that "There do not appear to have been any adequately authenticated incidents in which subjects meeting all the criteria of brain death have been recovered." Unfortunately, though, there is a tendency to blur the distinction between "cannot recover" and "already dead." The nonresponsive person whose minimal brain activity and overall physical status indicate "cannot recover" may nevertheless still be alive. There are a great many people who have physical problems that cannot be reversed, but they are still among the living and deserve to be so recognized.

Cautions and criticisms are still being voiced by some physicians, neuroscientists, and ethicists. Philosopher Peter Singer (1994), for example, expresses concern that the brain death criteria might be subverted to declare some people dead for political, racist, or other unethical reasons. Another caution has been raised with respect to the length of time a person can remain in the brain dead condition. Not long ago, it was thought that brain death could not continue beyond approximately 2 weeks because general collapse of body systems would soon occur. In fact, many articles and books insisted on this brief duration as an established fact. Subsequent experience has led to a revision of this view. The most striking instances have involved pregnant women who suffered traumas that resulted in brain death. These women

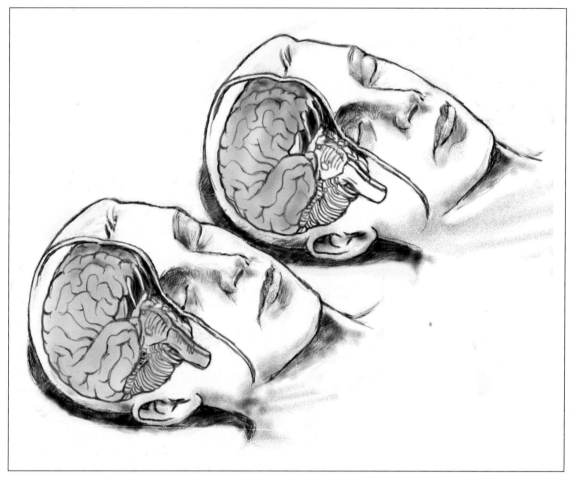

FIGURE 3.2
Neocortical death (top) involves loss of the higher brain functions. Whole-brain death (bottom) includes also the loss of function in subcortical structures that are vital for survival.

would not recover, but the unborn infants might still have a chance for life. Placed on a life support system, some pregnant women have been maintained for more than 2 months after suffering brain death, thereby providing additional crucial time for development and survival of their infants. Furthermore, some people have remained brain dead on life support systems for as long as 14 years (Truog, 1997). This prompts the question of how dead they really were.

The critics do not deny the value of brain death criteria in some circumstances, but they do suggest that we should not rely exclusively on brain functioning as a definitive indication of death. Physician Paul A. Byrne (2001) notes,

> There is a unity or a oneness to every living human being. Each one has a body structure which is a composite of many organs...grouped together as a system to carry out certain functions.... There is an interdependence of organs and systems. No one organ or system is in charge of all other organs and systems. The body, as well as the organs and systems, have certain environmental requirements in order to carry out their functions. A change in the environment can result in nonfunc-

tion. Nonfunction means idle and says nothing about the cause of nonfunction. (p. 4)

A specific concern has been raised about possible misinterpretations in either direction. There is a possibility of making an inaccurate diagnosis of brain death in infants and children younger than age 5 because of differences between their neural status and that of adults (Koszer & Moshe, 2001).

Brain death might therefore be considered a symbolic construction in which certain features of the individual's medical condition have been combined into a significant and useful concept—but still a concept that is subject to various interpretations and cautions.

Event Versus State

We create some of our own difficulties by using the same word for two different but related ideas. Death is sometimes treated as an event—that is, something that occurs in a specific way and at a specific time and place. When it is death as event that concerns us, it is often possible to be factual and precise. ("This is the room where the victim was found. There is the blunt instrument. The clock was toppled over and still shows the exact moment that this dastardly act was committed!")

Quite different is our use of the same word in referring to the state that *follows* the event. Life has ceased (death as event). What happens from now on? The answer to this question is much less accessible to ordinary sources of information. Some interpretations of death as state follow, including a challenging new construction that is still under construction.

WHAT DOES DEATH MEAN?

Let's take an example before systematically examining the meanings that are summarized in Table 3-1.

The soloist in Bach's haunting Cantata No. 53 sings

Schlage doch, gewunschte Stunde,
brich doch an gewunschter Tag!
Strike, oh strike, awaited hour,
approach thou happy day!

The hour that is awaited eventually will be displayed on the face of an ordinary clock. It be-

TABLE 3-1
Meanings That Have Been Given to Death

- Death is an enfeebled form of life.
- Death is a continuation of life.
- Death is perpetual development.
- Death is waiting.
- Death is cycling and recycling.
- Death is nothing.
- Death is virtual and therefore not really death after all.

longs to public, shared, or mortal time. The hour and day of death will be entered into the community's vital statistics. What the devout singer anticipates, however, is entry into a new realm of being in which the time changes of terrestrial life no longer apply. The survivors will continue to measure their own lives by clock and calendar. They may remember that the deceased has been dead for 6 months, 5 years, and so on, but this conventional manner of marking time has no bearing on the deceased. She will have entered heaven. The death event will have cleaved her from the community's shared time framework at the same instant that it transports her to eternity. The hour that strikes refers to death as event; the heavenly blessing that follows refers to death as state.

This, however, is only one interpretation of death as a state. Let us now consider other meanings that have been attributed to death.

INTERPRETATIONS OF THE DEATH STATE

The following are competing interpretations of the death state that have long been influential, and a new interpretation that has been emerging in our society and deserves consideration is also presented.

Enfeebled Life

Young children often think of death as a less vigorous form of life. The people who "live" in the cemetery don't get hungry, except once in a while. The dead are tired, sad, bored, and don't have much to do. A 3-year-old girl was saving her comic books for her grandmother, worried that she might have forgotten to take her bifocals with her to the grave.

The little child of today who offers this interpretation is in a sense carrying forward the belief system common in Mesopotamia thousands of years ago. The deceased person is gradually submerged into the underworld. There, he or she is transformed into a repulsive and pitiable creature one might expect to find today in a horror movie. The mightiest ruler and the fairest maiden lose all power, all beauty. The dead become equal in their abysmally low estate.

The decremental model of the death state ruled throughout much of the ancient world. Abandonment, depletion, and endless misery were the lot of all mortals, with the possible exception of mighty rulers and those of very special merit. The idea that the death state can be influenced by pious belief or moral conduct had not yet taken firm hold.

Continuation

Passage from life on Earth has sometimes been interpreted as a transition to more of the same. This notion might seem odd today. We are accustomed to concepts of the afterlife that involve a profound change, a transformation. Because death seems extraordinary, it must also lead to something extraordinary. However, a number of tribal societies have viewed the death state as one that has much in common with life as usual. One hunts, fishes, plays, makes love, becomes involved in jealousies and conflicts, and so forth. Life remains a hazardous journey, even after death. In fact, life after death even includes the risk of death. The individual faces challenges and crises just as before, including the possibility of a final annihilation. For example, the Dayak of Borneo believed that the soul returns to Earth after its seventh death and there enters a mushroom or fruit near the village. This returned soul invades the body of a woman who chances to eat the morsel, and one is therefore reborn. One may be less fortunate, however. A buffalo, deer, or monkey might find this delicacy first, and the soul will then be reborn as an animal, losing its human identity in the process.

Perpetual Development

Suppose that the universe is not completely determined, that all of existence is en route to making something else of itself. Suppose further that what we make of our lives is part of this universal process. What might be the death state in such a flowing, changing universe?

The answers to this question do not come from the ancient people of Mesopotamia or tribespeople maintaining their traditional customs against the encroachment of technology. Instead, the answers come from the prophets and philosophers of evolution, individual thinkers who either anticipated or built on Darwin's discoveries in fashioning a radically different view of life and its place in the universe. For example, philosophers Samuel Alexander (1920) and Lloyd Morgan (1923) went beyond Darwin with their suggestions that evolution applied not only to species but also to the universe as a whole. Life itself is an emergent quality from a universe that continues to transform itself. Mind is a further quality that has emerged from life. In Alexander's words, the universe is in the process of "flowering into deity": God is still being created. In this view, the relationship between life and death also continues to evolve. The basic law is continued development both for individual minds and for the universe at large.

One of the most striking conceptions was offered by a man who also made enduring contributions to scientific methodology. In 1836, Gustav Theodor Fechner (1836/1977) proposed a model of the death state as perpetual development. Death is a kind of birth into a freer mode of existence in which continued spiritual growth may occur. Precisely what the death state *is* or *means* to the individual depends on the stage of spiritual development that has been attained up to the moment of the death event. In Fechner's view, the death state not only varies among different people but also is subject to change as the entire universe continues to evolve. In a sense, then, the death state provides everyone with at least the opportunity to become more alive than ever.

Do these ideas seem merely quaint? Evolutionary biology (Gilbert, 1997; Kaufmann, 1993) and chaos theory (Hall, 1991; Ruelle, 1991) focus on the premise that one cannot entirely predict the future state of a system from knowledge of its starting point. In other words, change is real (or reality is change). Biological systems are subject to change within the larger system we call the universe, which is itself subject to change. Why should what we call life and death be the exceptions to the apparent changingness of the universe at large?

Waiting

What happens after the death event? We wait!

In Western society, this waiting period is often regarded as having three phases. It begins with a period of suspended animation in which the person is presumed to exist in a sleep-like state. This is followed by a dramatic Day of Judgment. Finally, the soul proceeds to its ultimate destination or condition. "The sleeper awakens," receives judgment, and takes his or her place either for "eternity" or "for all times" (concepts that often are treated as though functionally equivalent, although philosophers hold them to be sharply different).

These three phases may be given different priorities by particular individuals and societies. Some Christians, for example, emphasize the taking-a-good-long-rest phase. Others focus attention on the critical moment of judgment. Still others contemplate that ultimate phase when sorrows and anxieties will have passed away, when the just are rewarded and everlasting radiance and peace prevail. Some believers have embellished this phase by predicting that their own redemption will be accompanied by the punishment of unbelievers and other enemies. In ancient Egypt, in contrast, the act of judgment was thought to occur rather promptly after the death event. More emphasis was placed on the phases of judgment and final disposition than on the preceding sleep-like state of suspended animation.

I have characterized this general conception of the death state as *waiting* in order to emphasize its implications for time, tension, and striving. A tension exists between the death event and the end state. The dead may seem to be at rest, but it is actually a time for watchful waiting. Judgment and final disposition are still to come.

Furthermore, the sense of waiting hovers on both sides of the grave. The aged and the critically ill are sometimes regarded as waiting for death. In this view, death is not simply the cessation of life but a kind of force, perhaps a kind of deliverance as well. From a broader perspective, all the living, healthy though they may be, are only "putting in time" until they too move through the event into the state of death. The waiting is not over until all souls have perished and then awakened for judgment and final disposition. Not everybody shares this view of death. However, it has been around long enough in Western society to influence almost everybody. Perhaps some of our daily tension derives from this apprehension that our success, failure, or fate will not be determined until the end of the end…beyond death.

For the thoughtful Christian, the situation could be even more complex and perhaps ambiguous. In examining *Life and Death in the New Testament*, Leon-Dufour (1986) notes that the man who most forcefully interpreted Jesus' message himself wavered between radically different alternatives. Paul at first conceived that the Kingdom of Heaven would not open its gates until the end of time (i.e., when the last generation of life on Earth had perished). Later, he expressed the belief that one would experience the gratifications of eternal life immediately after death. Paul conceived of death both as a welcome release and as a catastrophic event. However one chooses to interpret the interpretations, the concept of waiting both for death and for the final outcome of death may have more influence on us than we usually realize.

Cycling and Recycling

One of the most traditional and popular conceptions of the death state is also one of the most radical. It is simply this: death comes and goes, wending in and out of life. This view is often expressed by children. After a person has been dead for a while, he or she will probably get up again and go home. Sure, the bird was dead Friday, but maybe its been dead long enough.

Some adults also have regarded death as a temporary condition that alternates with life and that represents a stage of transition between one form of life and another. Death has been seen, for example, as just one position on a constantly revolving wheel, the great wheel of life and death.

(We may forgive ourselves if the "Bankrupt" space on "The Wheel of Fortune" television show comes to mind—it is not a bad analogy at all!)

In his classic *The Wheel of Death* (1971), Philip Kapleau points out that the wheel is one of the core symbols of Buddhism. Another important symbol is a flame passing from lamp to candle. This indicates a rebirth that continues an ongoing process, not the simple transference of a substance. Kapleau also reminds us of the *phoenix,* "a

FIGURE 3.3
After consuming itself in fire, the mythical phoenix rises from the ashes to a new life.

mythical bird of great beauty who lived for five hundred years in the desert. It immolated itself on a funeral pyre and then rose from its own ashes in the freshness of youth, living another cycle of years" (p. viii). The phoenix represents both death and regeneration. Some funeral rituals also encourage the regeneration or recycling of life through death (Block & Parry, 1996).

Kapleau (1971) argues that the cyclical view of life and death is more rational than many people in Western society are willing to grant:

> The assertion that nothing precedes birth or follows death is largely taken for granted in the West, but however widely believed, it is still absurd from a Buddhist viewpoint. Such an assertion rests on the blind assumption—in its own way an act of faith—that life, of all things in the universe, operates in a vacuum. (p. xvii)

Kapleau's comparison between the states of prebirth and postdeath also makes me think of the all-too-bright 10-year-old who attended one of my classes with his mother. At the end of the class I asked him if there were anything he would like to say. He replied, "Just a little question. I mean, what are we *before* life and where are we or is it only nothing and would that be the same nothing we are after life or a different kind of nothing and...." As you will not be surprised to learn, I have since grown more cautious in asking 10-year-olds for their questions!

The recycling of life through the death state was an article of faith for many peoples in the past. This idea has regained popularity in recent years in the United States as one of the core beliefs of the Aquarian or "New Age" movement (Ferguson, 1987). The following is a typical statement: "Death is simply a transition from one life to another. We all live many lives."

Nothing

Perhaps we are deceiving ourselves when we imagine death to be any kind of state at all. This self-deception can be encouraged by the failure to distinguish between dying and death. Dying *is* something. However we define the term dying, there are significant bodily changes, and these changes have consequences for thought, feeling, and social interaction. The *death event* is also

something: the final cessation of life processes. But is death a *state?* One might think instead of death as total absence: absence of life, absence of process, absence of qualities. The more we say about death, the more we deceive ourselves and use language to falsify. Even when I say, "This person is dead," I may be slyly contradicting myself. This person *is?* No, the whole point is that this person is not. Our language forms lead us repeatedly into subtle affirmations of being even when we are trying to acknowledge nonbeing.

The concept of death as nothing is repugnant to many people. It is believed to be much too barren and devoid of hope. Furthermore, it is difficult to cope with the concept of nothing. Calling it *nothingness* is a useless exercise that essentially reifies a reification, making a *bigger somethingness* out of *nothing.* We know little, if anything, about nothing. Our minds do not know what to do with themselves unless there is a little something to work with. Yet the difference between even *a little something* and the concept of *nothing* is enormous. Furthermore, we tend to become anxious when faced with formlessness and with experiences that do not fit into our usual fixed categories of thought.

Sometimes people attempt to deal with this anxiety by calling death a "void" or a "great emptiness." It seems reassuring to give things a name: Perhaps giving nothing a name can be helpful, too. Unfortunately, even terms such as void tend to obscure the recognition of death as a nonstate. We have to watch ourselves carefully: how resourcefully we construct images that are intended to conceal the possibility of *nothing.*

Few people seem to care for the definition of death as nonstate, and fewer still exercise the mental rigor it would require to adhere consistently to this view. However, as much as we ignore or reject *nothing,* it refuses to vanish into, well, nothingness.

Virtual, Therefore Not Death

Many of us have become involved with people who are not exactly either here or there. We also see, hear, and interact with beings, scenes, and events that never were nor will be. *Virtual reality* first came to general attention through audio-video devices that delivered impressions so vivid and lifelike that our brains are tempted to suppose them real. There is already an abundance of practical and recreational applications. With a menu and a virtual hand, one can design a safer highway or an earthquake-resistant building. We can also teach and learn scientific concepts in "immersive virtual worlds," such as NewtonWorld, MaxwellWorld, and Pauling World (vrinfo@gmu.edu). Virtual reality is opening new opportunities for learning, experiencing, achieving, and escaping.

What does all this have to do with death? What, if anything, is the problem? It has already become cliché to intermix living people with the deceased in movies or television commercials. We already have "virtual cemeteries" on the Internet in which not the bodies and not exactly the souls but something of the deceased reside. No, not where they reside—*where the dead can be accessed.* The more we become accustomed to remote interactions, the less our senses and feelings are guided by the breath and presence of real people who really live and can really die. The more we become engrossed in virtual reality, the greater may be the temptation to view death as also something that is without dimension and place. Virtual reality has the compelling characteristic of being everywhere and nowhere at the same time. It can also be shuttled back and forth between existence and nonexistence at our pleasure. The virtual universe can go dark at our command and return in all its glory whenever we choose to access it again. The engrossing but distant and sanitary world of virtual reality is not as messy as real life and death. It offers the illusion of control without asking very much of us in return. Perhaps, ever increasingly, it will become an alternative for spiritual approaches to life and death. How freely these images float; how they move and morph and sport! What a model for out-of-the-body experiences and for all our attempts to transcend the limits of our physical being!

Virtual death is perhaps the natural accompaniment to the virtual life that has so rapidly entered our culture, a life that cannot truly die because it was never truly alive. Here, then, is a new modality to accommodate our desires to transform death into something safer, less disturbing, less consequential, and less personal. People sometimes regard the images on television and movie screens as more real than the people and events in their own lives. Virtual reality may result in a quantum leap in the tendency to see both life and death as somewhere else.

Implications of the Ways in Which We Interpret Death

How we interpret the state of death can influence our thoughts, feelings, and actions. A person may refuse to touch or approach a corpse, even though it is that of a much beloved individual. The ancient Babylonians, Egyptians, and Hebrews revered and attempted to comfort their aged. But who among them would want to be contaminated by a body that was beyond the pale of life? Elaborate decontamination rituals were prescribed for those who inadvertently or by necessity had touched a corpse:

> Whoever touches the dead body of anyone will be unclean for seven days. He must purify himself with water on the third day and on the seventh day.… Whoever touches the dead body of anyone and fails to purify himself…must be cut off from Israel. (Old Testament: Num. 19)

The people of ancient times and distant lands were not alone in shunning the dead. Religious rituals and individual behavior patterns that are prevalent today also have as their purpose the avoidance of contact with what is thought to be the alien and contaminating aura of the human corpse.

In contrast, death might be regarded as a tranquil state. This would be the case if death is waiting, and waiting is a restful sleep. The emphasis might be on the first phase of death after life: a serene period of restful repose. However, the prospect of waiting would be anything but tranquil for the person who is attuned to the moment of judgment instead of the interlude between death event and final state. Two terminally ill people who are equally firm in their religious convictions might differ in their specific anticipations of death and therefore in their mood and behavior. A terminally ill person who believes that death is simply a passage to his or her next reincarnation may be less concerned about the moment of judgment than either of the foregoing people and more interested in what is to come than the life that one is leaving.

These are but a few implications of the ways in which we interpret death as a state. Because of the difficulties that are encountered in trying to interpret death as any kind of state, humankind has often used a supplementary approach—comparing death to conditions with which we have more direct knowledge.

CONDITIONS THAT RESEMBLE DEATH

We can liken death to something else, or we can liken something else to death. Exploring death analogies will not only help in continuing the task of defining death but also lead us into several problem areas that deserve further attention.

Inorganic and Unresponsive

Fire, lightning, whirlpools, floods, earthquakes, and other natural phenomena have always impressed humankind. However, we can also be impressed by an apparent *lack* of activity in the world. This perception may contribute to a sense of comforting stability. Gaze at those everlasting mountains! They were here in the days of our ancestors and will continue to tower above our children's children! At other times, however, inert surroundings may elicit a sense of deadness. "Stone cold dead in the marketplace" is one old phrase. The parallel with the stiff form of a cadaver is obvious. "Stone cold" reinforces the deadness of the dead.

The hard, unyielding surface of a rock contrasts with our vulnerable flesh and sensitive feelings that can be wounded so easily. A person exposed to stress and danger may envy the durability of the rock. When we hear that somebody has "stonewalled it" in a difficult situation, we understand that he or she attempted self-protection through a shield of unresponsiveness, emulating the lifeless character of the rock. Stone as a representation of death is also familiar to us through a succession of mythological unfortunates who were transformed from flesh and blood into insensate rock by incident or unwise action—a glimpse of Medusa's terrifying visage on one of

her "bad hair days" or that fatal backward glance made by Orpheus upon leaving Hades.

We live in an invented as well as a natural world. The motor has died. Perhaps a "dead" battery is at fault. We age, and our machines wear out. Ancestors who lived close to the rhythms of Earth had fire and stone to inspire their representations of life and death. We have added the mechanical and electronic apparatus, from windmill to computer and beyond. For example, stand at the bedside of a critically ill person who is connected to an external support system with multiple lifelines. Interpret the situation. Is this a living person? Or is it a set of machines functioning? Or can the situation best be understood as an integrated *psychobioelectromechanical* process in which the human and nonhuman components have merged to form a special system of their own? While you are considering this situation, it ends. The monitor reveals a flatline: Life activity has ceased. But *what* has ended? Do we say the machines failed or the body, or—?

Today, the machine is more than a casual analogy to human life. Many have come to view the termination of human life as a mechanical failure. When we liken death to the hard, cold unresponsiveness of a stone we usually recognize that we are dealing in an evocative figure of speech. However, the distinction between analogy and fact is easy to blur. Failure of the machine can be seen as the failure of the machine that is the person as well. "Pulling the plug" is a revealing phrase that bridges analogy and fact. But the fact is that the machine is far from an adequate representation of the person.

Sleep and Altered States of Consciousness

Sleep has long served as another natural analogy to death. The ancient Greeks pictured sleep (*Hypnos*) as twin brother to death (*Thanatos*). Sleep and death remain entwined in cultural traditions. Orthodox Jews, for example, thank God for restoring them to life again on arising from sleep in the morning.

Some people today still replace the words "death" or "dead" with "sleep" when they want to speak in a less threatening way, such as to children. However, when children are told that a deceased person is "only sleeping," we may question what message is intended and what message is coming across. Does the parent intend just to soften the impact of death somewhat or actually to lie to the child and deny that a death has occurred? The young child is not likely to have a firm grasp on the distinction between sleep and death. The analogy, therefore, may register as reality. Late in the evening the child is told, "Go to sleep!" Earlier the same day this child may have been told by the same parent that grandmother is asleep, or that death is a long sleep. It should not be a surprise if the child has difficulty falling asleep that night. Children do have nightmares in which death-related themes are prominent.

Adults as well as children may experience insomnia when death has intruded in their lives. While working in a geriatric hospital, for example, experience taught me to expect insomnia and other nocturnal disturbances on any ward where a patient had died unexpectedly. An aged man or woman might speak matter-of-factly about the death and seem not to have been personally affected but then awaken in terror and confusion that night, seeking a living face and a comforting word.

Whether used wisely or foolishly, however, sleep remains one of the most universal and easily communicated analogies to death. Myth and fairy tale abound in characters who, believed dead, are actually in a deep, enchanted sleep. Snow White and Sleeping Beauty are perhaps the examples best known to children.

Altered states of consciousness occurring in sleep or resembling sleep have also been used as analogies to death. People may dream they are dead and feel frozen, immobilized, or powerless to act. Consider the following dream report from a client in counseling who was experiencing several types of situational stress:

My dream was going along OK, for a dream. Then it was suddenly not my dream. It was something that was happening, and I couldn't do anything about whatever it was. I couldn't move anything. Not my hand, not one finger. The more I thought about it the worse it got. The harder I tried to move, the worse, it got. I was in a panic,

Briar Rose and Sleeping Beauty are among the classic folk tales in which a woman remains in a prolonged slumber resembling death until rescued by a handsome young man.

frozen in a panic. My heart was pounding like mad and I still couldn't do anything. I remember thinking, "Yeah, maybe I'm dead in my grave and this is just what it's like, thinking you can do something, you should do something, but you can't."

Drug- and alcohol-induced states of mind are also sometimes likened to death, whether as a joyful or a terrifying "trip." The now rarely employed technique of insulin coma therapy was known to generate terrifying deathlike experiences.

Normal sleep differs from the altered states of consciousness that can result from disease, trauma, drugs, alcohol, or other special circumstances. The coma of the seriously ill person, for example, is not likely to represent the same psychobiological state as normal sleep. The temporary loss of consciousness in some epileptic seizures has occasionally been interpreted as a deathlike state, but, again, the status of the brain during these episodes differs markedly from both normal sleep and cerebral death.

Beings Who Resemble or Represent Death

In Homer's epic, *Ulysses* ties himself to the mast of his ship to protect himself from an unusual peril. Enormous birdlike creatures with the heads of women menace him and his crew. Some are perched on a rock, trying to lure them with sweet song; others are circling near the vessel. The hybrid bird-person has been a compelling figure in art and mythology for many centuries. Not all winged creatures are associated with death, but such imagery is very common. In post-Homeric Greek times, *sirens* were distinguished from *harpies*. Both were rather nasty creatures. Sirens brought death, and harpies had the special knack of obliterating memory. Death, then, might come with or without loss of memory, as represented by two different fabulous beings.

The winged hybrid at other times was depicted as a soul bird. This represented the spirit leaving the body at the time of death, suggesting resurrection. Later, the bird-people were joined by a variety of fish-people, many of whom are also associated with death. The hybrid death-beings are usually portrayed as females. Some historians hold that among ancient peoples there was a tendency for peaceful death to be represented in masculine terms, whereas painful and violent death came through female agents. This characterization hardly seems fair: Consider how many people have died violently in man-made wars and how many have been comforted in their last days by women. The *Muses,* arriving later in history than the sirens and harpies, were females who were depicted in a more kindly light. The Muses would sing at funerals and guide departed souls on their journeys through the underworld. (Some also devoted themselves to inspiring artists, writers, and musicians in their creative ventures.)

Orpheus was a being fabulous for his powers rather than his appearance. A master musician, Orpheus represented power over death. He could not only liberate his beloved Eurydice from Hades through his song but also bring rocks and trees to life. Orpheus is one of many personified symbols of resurrection that the human mind has created through the centuries.

The *skeleton* has also enjoyed a long career as a deathly being. Examples can be found from many sources in the ancient world. Artifacts from the buried city of Pompeii include a rather modern-looking depiction of a skeleton boxed inside a black border, suggesting a symbolic depiction of death. The skeleton flourished particularly in medieval Europe, appearing in numerous works of art from approximately the 13th through the 15th centuries. We see the skeleton, for example, bearing a scythe on its shoulder and confronting young men, with the world behind them and hell gaping open underneath. This depiction appears on the title page of one of many books of the time titled *Ars Moriendi* (*The Art of Dying*). The skeleton is also a prominent figure in van Eyck's rendering of *The Last Judgment.*

The animate skeleton did not simply pose for pictures. It danced. One whirl with this dancer was enough for any mortal. Images of the Dance of Death flourished during the 14th and 15th centuries when the effects of the bubonic plague (the "Black Death") were keenly felt. Skeletal death was a quiet, almost sedate dancer; such was its power that extreme movements were not required.

We have not entirely forgotten this representation of death even today. The skeleton still dangles from many a door on Halloween, and the image of skull and crossbones appears on bottles containing poisonous substances, in highway safety brochures, and in old Erroll Flyn pirate films. The skeleton is especially conspicuous on the Day of the Dead, celebrated in Mexico and in Mexican American communities in the United States. The living and the dead greet each other and renew old acquaintances on this day. Special religious services are held in private homes, churches, and graveyards, and skull-shaped candies are among the delicacies of the day (perhaps not what the pious had in mind when singing "Come sweet death").

These are but a few of the shapes resembling and representing death that have formed themselves in the human mind. The next shape to consider is the human form itself.

DEATH AS A PERSON

The field glitters in the intense sunlight. In the field a solitary worker is attempting to harvest the crop with his scythe. This worker is

> a vague figure fighting like a devil in the midst of the heat to get to the end of his task—I see in him the image of death, in the sense that humanity might be the wheat he is reaping. So it is—if you like—the opposite to that sower I tried to do before. But there's nothing sad in this death; it goes its way in broad daylight with a sun flooding everything with a light of pure gold. (as quoted in Gottlieb, 1959, p. 161)

This was Vincent Van Gogh's own interpretation of his painting. Many other artists have also chosen to present death in the form of a person or person-like figure. Death has also had a starring role in movies. In two of death's most notable film appearances, we find him as a somber man in a monk's robe in Ingmar Bergman's *The Seventh Seal* and as Mr. Brink in Paul Osborne's *On Borrowed Time*. A determined knight delays the death monk's victory in a chess match, and an elderly man captures Mr. Brink in a tree. Nobody can be taken by death while these serious games are in progress.

It is not only the artist and the film maker who have created compelling images of personified death. Personifications of death take many forms and can be found throughout the spectrum of human expressive activity from ancient times to the present (Aries, 1981; Tamm, 1996). For example, children's games through the centuries often have involved the participation of a character who represents death. Hide-and-seek is a game that has thrilled children the world over, possibly because the child who is "It" can be understood as a stand-in for Death who will catch the unwary. The child who is tagged can later enjoy taking a turn as the impersonator of Death (Opie & Opie, 1969).

Personifications can help individuals and societies to cope with death by (a) objectifying an abstract concept that is difficult to grasp with the mind alone; (b) expressing feelings that are diffi-

cult to put into words; (c) serving as a coin of communication among people who otherwise would hesitate to share their death-related thoughts and feelings; (d) absorbing some of the shock, pain, anger, and fear that are experienced as a result of traumatic events; and (e) providing symbols that can be reshaped over and over again to stimulate emotional healing and cognitive integration.

How We Personified Death: 1971

Studies of death personification can tell us something useful about the ways in which both the individual and society are interpreting death. We are now in a position to compare young adults' personifications of death over two points in time: 1971 and 1996.

Four types of personification were offered most frequently by participants in the first (1971) study. The *macabre* personification vividly depicted ugly, menacing, vicious, and repulsive characters. One undergraduate replied,

> I see Death as something I don't want to see at all. He or she—I guess it's a he, but I'm not sure—has jagged, sharp features. Everything about how he looks is sharp and threatening, his bony fingers with something like claws on the end of all of them, even a sharp nose, long, sharp teeth, and eyes that seem as though they can tear and penetrate right into you. Yet all this sharpness is almost covered over by…hair, bloody, matted hair.

A young nurse had difficulty in personifying death at first and then said

> I can imagine him, Death, being nearby. It makes me feel trembly and weak, so I don't want to take a good look at him. No look at him could be good, anyhow, if you know what I mean. I feel his presence more than actually see him. I think he would be strong, unbelievably strong, and powerful. It could make your heart sink if you really had to look at him. But if he wanted you, there wouldn't be anything you could do about it.

Macabre personifications sometimes included outright physical deterioration. It was common for the respondents to express emotional reactions to their own images; for example, "When I look at this person—don't think it isn't possible—

a shivering and nausea overwhelms me." The macabre personification often was seen as an old person and almost always as a terrifying being who is the sworn enemy of life. The relationship between age and personification is not so simple, however, as the next image reveals.

The *gentle comforter* could hardly be more different. Although usually pictured as an aged person, there was little physical and no psychological resemblance to Mr. Macabre. The gentle comforter was the personification of serenity and welcome. People who gave this kind of personification generally were those who also found the task easiest and least threatening to do. The following typical example is from a registered nurse:

A fairly old man with long white hair and a long beard. A man who would resemble a biblical figure with a long robe which is clean but shabby. He would have very strong features and despite his age would appear to have strength. His eyes would be very penetrating and his hands would be large.

Death would be calm, soothing, and comforting. His voice would be of an alluring nature and, although kind, would hold the tone of the mysterious. Therefore, in general, he would be kind and understanding and yet be very firm and sure of his actions and attitudes.

Although often seen as an aged person, the gentle comforter could also be seen as a younger individual, most often a male. Respondents were not always clear as to whether this was a male or female being. In general, this personification seems to represent a powerful force quietly employed in a kindly way.

The *gay deceiver* is an image of death that is usually seen as a young and appealing or fascinating individual. (The term does not refer to a homosexual orientation: "gay deceiver" was applied to this form of death personification before "gay" became widely used as a synonym for male homosexuality.) The personification can be either male or female, often with sexual allure. The gay deceiver tends to be an elegant, knowing, worldly person who can guide one into a tempting adventure. However, "one could not trust him. He would be elusive in his manners, hypocritical, a liar, persuasive. Death would first gain your confidence. Then you would learn who he really is, and it would be too late."

One young woman described death in the following manner:

She is beautiful, but in a strange way. Dark eyes and long dark hair, but her skin is pale. She is slender and she is sophisticated looking.... I imagine her beckoning me to come with her. She will take me to a new circle of people and places, a lot fancier, more exotic than what I have in my own life. I feel sort of flattered that she would want my company, and I sort of want to go with her, to discover what I may have been missing.... But I am scared, too. How will this evening end?

The gay deceiver is unique for its mixture of allure, excitement, and danger. Death remains the outcome, but at least the getting there is interesting.

The *automaton* does not look like anything special. He is undistinguished in appearance. One might pass him on the street and not really notice him. The automaton tends to be dressed conservatively. There are no striking mannerisms. If there is any distinctive quality at all, it is a sort of matter-of-fact blandness, a blank expression. This "ordinariness" is an important facet of his personality and meaning. One woman, for example, characterized him as

having no feeling of emotion about his job— either positive or negative. He simply does his job. He doesn't think about what he is doing, and there is no way to reason with him. There is no way to stop him or change his mind. When you look into his eyes you do not see a person. You see only death.

The automaton, then, appears in human guise but lacks human qualities. He does not lure, comfort, or terrify; he just goes about his business as might any bored but competent functionary. It has always seemed to me that there is something rather modern about this depersonalized personification: Does he represent a quality of alienation in mass society?

Respondents were most likely to see death as "a gentle, well-meaning sort of person." The "grim, terrifying" image was the least frequently selected. Death was usually personified as a relatively old person. Masculine personifications were given much more frequently than feminine. In more recent samples, the percentage of feminine personifications has increased across all categories. Masculine representations continue to remain most common, however.

How We Personify Death Today

Much has changed in our society since the 1971 study. For example, there are now many death education courses, grief counselors, peer support groups, and hospice care programs, as well as a raging controversy regarding physician-assisted death. There are also larger societal changes, such as the reduction of nuclear war menace, the increase in terrorism, transformations in electronic communication, and continued progress in the empowerment of women. Have our personifications of death also changed in some way?

Kastenbaum and Herman (1997) found that

- Death is still represented predominately as a male, but there is a sharp increase in female personifications from female respondents.
- Men and women now differ more in the type of personality they attribute to death. Women continue to favor the image of death as the gentle comforter. Men, however, now most often describe death as a "cold and remote" person. Men were also more likely than women to see death as "grim and terrifying." More than

three fourths of men but slightly less than half of women viewed death as either cold or grim.

- There is still a tendency for the gentle comforter to be viewed as an elderly person, but this is no longer true of the other personifications.

There is an additional finding that is not easily explained—perhaps you would like to help us with it. After completing the death personification items, respondents were asked to identify Jack Kevorkian. Most correctly reported that he is the physician who "puts people out of their misery" and who always seems to be in court defending his right to do so.

We wondered if Dr. Kevorkian's central role in the public controversy on physician-assisted death might have produced a new or modified personification, one that might be modeled after him. The answer was clear. Nobody mentioned Dr. Kevorkian as a person who comes to mind when they think about their death personifications. Some respondents named people in their own lives (e.g., a kind but stern grandfather), and some named other public figures, usually actors or actresses. Despite his name and face recognition and his media image as "Doctor Death," Kevorkian has not influenced death personifications. Perhaps our personifications come from deeper levels of the mind, as discussed by Jung (1959) and Neumann (1971), and therefore cannot easily be moved aside by passing faces and events. Perhaps there are other reasons. What do you think? Why are young men in the current

DILBERT

BY SCOTT ADAMS

generation more likely to have negative images of personified death than were those a quarter of a century ago, while young women continue to believe that death is gentle and comforting?

CONDITIONS THAT DEATH RESEMBLES

"That was an awfully dead party," we might say, just as actors might remark when the final curtain drops, "Whew! What a dead house tonight!" Or we say about a particular individual: "He has no life in him, just going through the motions" or "Look how tired she is—she's dead on her feet!"

These are examples of using death or dead as metaphors to describe other things. Here are some other ways in which deadness serves as an instructive way of acknowledging certain aspects of life.

Social Death

You are with other people but nobody is paying attention to you. You might as well not be there at all.

Social death must be defined situationally. It is read by observing how a person is treated by others. The individuals may be animated enough. They may even be desperately seeking interaction. Despite their readiness for recognition and contact, they are being disconfirmed and excluded. The concept of social death recognizes that when we die in the eyes of others, we may become somewhat less of a person.

Social death can be seen in the following ways:

- A person has violated one of the taboos of the group. As a result, he or she is "cut dead." This could be the West Point cadet who is given the silent treatment or the child who married somebody of the "wrong" religion, race, or socioeconomic echelon.
- A member of the tribe violates a taboo and is ritualistically expelled, a symbolic execution. In a bone-pointing ceremony, the tribal community certifies one of its errant members as dead. This public ritual does not harm a hair on the offender's head but has the effect of terminating his or her life as a group member. Property that once belonged to this person may be redis-

tributed and the name discarded or assigned to somebody else after it has become decontaminated. Parallel processes sometimes occur in mainstream Western society: When an agency supervisor was dismissed on the basis of sexual harassment charges, a corporate official issued a command to all the agency employees: This man's name was never to be mentioned again. Here was bone pointing, minus the bone. The law may also strip a person of the rights of citizenship, and the church may excommunicate.

- There is a real or apparent change in an individual that results in the loss of "live person status." I have observed this phenomenon all too often in facilities for the impaired and vulnerable aged. The social transformation of living person into custodial object can occur in modern facilities with cheerful decor as well as in grim and physically deteriorating institutions. Even the old person who lives independently in the community can be victim of the socially dead treatment (e.g., being passed over while trying to get the attention of a store clerk or being placed at the bottom of medical or educational priorities).

Exclusionary actions may also operate against people who have developed feared diseases such as AIDS or who make others uncomfortable because of scars or physical infirmities. A person whose face has been severely burned in an accident, for example, may discover that others avert their eyes and keep a greater distance.

- The dying person may be treated as though already dead. An elaborate pattern of aversive and person-denying behavior may be generated around a living person whose demise is anticipated. This pattern is likely to include little or no eye contact, reluctance to touch, and talking to others in the presence of the person as though he or she were not there. What makes this kind of situation even more unfortunate is that the person taken for dead may still be very much alive, alert, and capable of meaningful interaction.

Phenomenological Death

Concentrate now on what is taking place *inside* the person. Regardless of society's attitudes and actions, is the individual alive to himself or herself?

There are two types of *phenomenological death.* First, *part of the person may die in the mind of the surviving or observing self.* Partial death can range in personal significance from the trivial to the profound. Two examples follow:

- A young man undergoes surgery that saves his life but results in the loss of the capacity to father children. In his own mind, one part of his total self has died. He will never be a parent. Although much else about his own self remains alive to me, there is now the mental and emotional challenge of working through the loss of one of his most valued potential roles and sources of satisfaction.
- A young athlete is physically fit by most standards. However, she has suffered an injury in athletic competition that is disabling enough to end her career. She is a runner with bad knees. She was an accomplished athlete both in her mind and in the minds of others. Now she has to remake her identity while still mourning privately for the athlete who has perished.

The essence of phenomenological death in this first sense is that there is a surviving self who recognizes the loss of one or more components of the total self: "I am still here, but I am not the person I once was or might have become." There is an element of mourning for the lost aspect of the self.

The other type of phenomenological death is quite different. Here, *the total self takes on a deadened tone.* The person does not experience life as freshly or intensely as in the past. Pleasures do not really please. Even pain may fail to break through the feeling of dulled indifference.

Feeling dead to yourself is a quality of experience that can shade into depersonalization: "I have no body" or "This body is not mine." Some psychotic people present themselves as though they were dead. This can be either in the sense that they have actually died or through the impression that they do not relate to their own bodies and biographies as though they belong to living persons. This may be accompanied by a depersonalized attitude toward other people as well. The person may be mute, slow moving, and given to maintaining a rigid posture for pro-tracted periods (as in the catatonic form of schizophrenia).

The sense of inner deadness or fading out is sometimes experienced with the use of alcohol or other drugs. It can also accompany other alterations in bodily state. Whatever the cause, the circumstances, or the outcome, we must recognize a state of mind in which the person becomes as dead to himself or herself.

People sometimes choose pain over sedation to avoid the sense of being dead to themselves (Baider, 1975):

> Mrs. A. was a 62-year-old Puerto Rican who constantly refused to take any medicine, even when in great pain. Her rationale was similar to other Puerto Rican patients (with far advanced cancer) I met. Doctors don't know as much as they think they do about the person's body. Each body has a soul, and if the doctor cannot see the soul, then he cannot see the body. "I know, I know that my family does not want that I suffer...but suffering is part of life...and without it you are not a man. No medicine can help with any pain...or, sometimes it could help putting all your body asleep ...like a baby...*and then it takes away my pain...but it also takes away all that I feel and see. If I could feel the pain I can also feel my body...and then I know I am still alive. (p. 378)*

One person, perhaps in good physical health, reduces his or her sense of aliveness in an effort to avoid emotional pain. Another person, perhaps in extremely poor health, accepts intense physical pain as a link to life. These differences in our relationship to phenomenological aliveness and deadness are but two of the variations that must be acknowledged as we continue our exploration into the human encounter with death.

DEATH AS AN AGENT OF PERSONAL, POLITICAL, AND SOCIAL CHANGE

The meanings of death can often be encountered in public as well as personal life. How we interpret death can serve either to support the *status quo* or to hasten political and social change. Following are a few examples.

The Great Leveler

Since ancient times the people of the world have been sorting each other out by class, caste, sex, race, geography—by just about any imaginable criterion. This process of setting some people above others on some basis other than ability and achievement occurs within as well as between groups. For example, the latest wave of immigrants from "the old country" often were looked down on by those who had made the same transition a little earlier. Those who have themselves been victims of discrimination on the basis of religious or racial identities have sometimes discriminated against people within their own groups (e.g., as "too orthodox," "too liberal," or looking too much like or too much different from those in the mainstream). How far does the urge to discriminate go? Does it at least end with death?

On the eve of his execution in 1672, Peter Patrix (1910) wrote the following lines in his dungeon cell:

I dreamt that, buried in my fellow clay,
Close by a common beggar's side I lay.
And, as so mean a neighbor shock'd my pride,
Thus, like a corpse of quality, I cried,
"Away, thou scoundrel! Henceforth touch me not;
More manners learn, and at a distance rot!"
"Thou scoundrel!" in a louder tone, cried he,
"Proud lump of dirt! I scorn thy word and thee.
We're equal now, I'll not an inch resign;
This is my dunghill, as the next is thine." (p. 292)

Yes, death has often been used in an ironic and forceful manner to support the cause of equal worth and rights during life. If death has equal power over the mighty and the lowly—but we have Shakespeare to say this for us in a speech he gives to *King Richard II:*

Within the hollow crown
That rounds the mortal temples of a king
Keeps Death his court; and there the antick sits,
Mocking his state, and grinning at his pomp;
Allows him a breath, a little scene,
To monarchize, be fear'd, and kill with looks;
Infusing him with self and vain conceit—
As if this flesh, which walls about his life,
Were brass impregnable; and humor'd thus,
Comes at the last, and with a little pin

Bores through his castle wall, and—farewell king!
(III:2)

This speech probably did not increase the comfort level of crowned heads the world over. With no weapon other than his pen, Shakespeare advanced the cause of a society in which the living as well as the dead might regard each other as people with certain inalienable rights.

Works of art commissioned during medieval times often displayed the theme of death as the great leveler. Gallant knights and beauteous maidens are interrupted on their journeys by death, often in the form of a skeleton. Skulls stare sightlessly from tables, shelves, and nearly hidden corners of the room as scholars ponder their books or marriage rites are performed. In such ways did the elite remind themselves that pride and triumph are fragile commodities.

The enormous toll of lives taken by the bubonic plague during its several major visitations temporarily unseated both the aristocracy and the church. Death did not seem impressed with the powers-that-be on Earth. Peasants observed how royalty and church officials either fell prey to the disease or scurried away, unable to exercise any control. The first clumsy revolutions were attempted, and a few reforms were achieved (only to be lost when the power establishment had recovered itself). Many years later, a new and more equitable social order would take hold. As the winds of social change swept through Europe, death the leveler had a distinctive role, embolding the common person to resist the established system. Peter Patrix would have liked that.

The Great Validator

Society can also use death to measure the value of its deceased members. Funereal splendor is an obvious way of using death to demonstrate the worth of the individual—and his or her survivors. A midwestern funeral director expressed the situation as he sees it:

I do what you want me to do. You come in here and say you want simple arrangements, and that is exactly what I will provide. You know what you want, and I am here to meet your needs.... But let me tell you why I sell some of the more expensive items—it's because the people themselves want it that way! They are not satisfied until they feel they are getting the best funeral for their loved one that they can afford. If everybody wanted bare-minimum funerals, that is what we would be providing. When you see a big, a magnificent funeral, you are seeing what the family felt it truly must have.

Interestingly, the tradition of a "big funeral" in which no expense is spared has its roots in early American tradition. In colonial days, families sometimes spent to the verge of poverty to publicly validate both their worth and that of the deceased. Religious leaders such as Cotton Mathers decried the lavish funerals much as critics do today, but many of his brethren remained intent on proving their piety and worth by funereal displays.

The opportunity for survivors to affirm their own worth through the funeral process (Chapter 13) has been seized upon throughout the centuries. The heroine in a Greek tragedy risks her own life by arranging for the proper burial of her outcast brother. Committees meet in closed session to decide whether a deceased person is distinguished enough to deserve burial in sacred soil. The legendary cowboy simply implores, "Bury me not on the lone prairie."

We have found that obituary notices in Boston and New York newspapers give more space and more often use photographs in reporting the deaths of men compared to women (Kastenbaum, Peyton, & Kastenbaum, 1977). Studies by other researchers in other regions of the United States confirmed this finding (Moremen, 2002), and the same pattern has been discovered in the United Kingdom. Bytheway and Johnson (1996) also found that most of the obituaries were written by men. It will be difficult to convince anybody that both sexes are equally valued by society as long as their deaths are treated in such a differential manner.

Death Unites/Separates

Death radically alters our relationships with others. It can be seen either as the ultimate act of separation or as the opportunity to rejoin others who have gone before us. Occasionally, death has even been seen as a way of bringing friends and foes together. Alexander Pope wrote in the 17th century

The grave united, where even the great find rest
And blended lie the oppressor and oppressed.

Two centuries later, a British soldier and poet imagined his own death in battle—an event that soon thereafter actually happened to him as World War I neared its end. Wilfred Owen (1918/1959) conveyed a fervent antiwar sentiment as he wrote of unity through death. The poem concludes with this poignant stanza

I am the enemy you killed, my friend.
I knew you in this dark, for so you frowned
Yesterday through me as you jabbed and killed.
I parried; but my hands were loath and cold.
Let us sleep now.

The despairing or dying person may yearn to become united with God. This hope has been expressed in many hymns and carols. Typical is the following verse included in a popular collection from 1844, *The Original Sacred Heart*:

Northfield

How long, dear Savior, O how long
    Shall this bright hour delay?
Fly swift around, ye wheels of time,
    And bring the promised day.

This promise, however, was not without its threatening aspect. The gravestone marker for Miss Polly Coombes of Bellingham, Massachusetts (dated 1785), takes a somber and challenging tone:

READER ATTEND: THIS STATE
    WILL SOON BE THINE
BE THOU IN YOUTHFUL HEALTH
    OR IN DECLINE
PREPARE TO MEET THY GOD

The prospect of arriving at a secure, homelike heaven could be tempered, then, by doubts as to whether one was prepared for the judgment of God. Some people have lived in terror of that moment.

Perhaps the most common form of the union-through-death theme is the wish to be with loved ones who are "on the other side." An old woman dreams that she has become a little girl once again and is being welcomed by her father. A boy wrestles privately with thoughts of suicide so that he can join the big brother he misses so much. The survivor of a random, drive-by shooting consoles herself with the expectation of being reunited some day.

Although some of us may find comfort in the prospect of reunion with loved ones through death, the more obvious consequence is separation. The familiar face of someone who has died is not to be seen again. One has lost a treasured companion, and the pain of separation can be overwhelming.

"I felt like part of me had been pulled apart. Like I wasn't a whole person any more. And then I went numb. Like I was in shock, with loss of blood, just like I had lost an arm or a leg or worse." This is the way a young woman felt when she learned that her husband had been killed in Vietnam. He had been alive to his loved ones until the message came, although in objective fact he had been dead for an indeterminate time. The moment that his wife learned of their final separation is the moment when the death event occurred for her. The moment we as survivors feel the shock and anguish of separation may be the most significant moment of death. The shock and pain of sudden loss was experienced again by thousands of Americans after the terrorist attacks of September 11, 2001. Family and friends of terrorist victims had some comfort in knowing that the nation shared in their grief: Those bereaved by the Vietnam war had much less support because the war had been opposed by many people.

This sense of separation can occur in advance of the actual death and can linger long afterward. For example, some families undergo the extreme stress of facing the probable death of their living children while still suffering from the loss of one or more who have already died (Atkin, 1974):

> The family were still grieving Ann's death when Roy began to exhibit symptoms of the same disease.... Adam has a similar form of the same illness.... "We know it all now—we shall be left with nothing—no children—nothing." (p. 66)

Children also experience the sorrow of separation from each other even if they do not fully understand the concept of death:

> He had lost one sibling and was facing the experience a second time. His sister, in the latter stages of her illness, seemed unaware and unresponsive. Yet her little brother seemed to evoke some faint recognition. She appeared to smile with her eyes—a last window into the darkness. He said: "I don't mind if you don't talk to me. It's lonely without you. I can talk to you." He prattled on about his rabbit, his cars, and his wish to have a party on his birthday. (p. 69)

The difficulty in understanding death coupled with the strong need to continue the relationship can lead both children and adults to behave at times as though final separation had not really taken place (see Chapters 8 and 11). The deceased person may still be spoken of in the present tense ("Jimmy only likes smooth peanut butter"), and interaction patterns may seem to include the expectation that he or she has only been temporarily detained.

The Ultimate Problem or the Ultimate Solution?

Death is sometimes regarded as either the ultimate problem or the ultimate solution. As individuals or as a society, we may even hold both views at the same time.

A dark jest made the rounds in the aftermath of the French Revolution. "Come and see the wonderful new machine—a miracle! One treatment by the good Dr. Guillotine and—phoof!— never again a headache!" The Guillotine brothers were actually appalled by public executions and suggested the device as a replacement for slower and more painful methods. But why have public executions in the first place? Are there no other ways to resolve conflicts and protect the legitimate interests of society?

Death as ultimate solution has been applied on a mass level as well (Chapter 9). Hitler's "final solution of the Jewish problem" translated into the genocidal murder of more than 6 million men, women, and children. Unfortunately, the attempt to solve a problem by killing others neither started nor ended with the Holocaust. People who were once fellow citizens of Yugoslavia or the Soviet Union are not yet done shedding each other's blood and engaging in atrocities. Angola, Burundi, Haiti, Somalia, The Sudan—these names are only a partial listing of nations from which reports of mass violence continue to reach us. Never mind history: We need only read today's news.

Students of death, society, and human experience tend to focus on the death of individuals and the grief of their survivors. It is important, however, to look beyond our personal lives and sorrows from time to time and recognize the large-scale destructive forces through which people bring threat, disruption, and death to each other. We consider what Daniel Leviton (1991) calls *horrendous death*—genocide, environment degradation, and man-made starvation—in Chapter 16.

Opposing this theme is the conviction that death, far from being the final solution, is humankind's worst enemy and most profound problem. Death may be seen as the ultimate problem because it ends our opportunity to achieve. This is certainly a threat in a society in which the need to achieve has been a dominant motive: "I can't die just yet—I have so much to do!"

Death may also be seen as the ultimate problem because it closes the theater of inner experience. We will have no more thoughts, no more feelings. Consciousness and awareness will be extinguished. Still again, death may be seen as the ultimate problem because it defies understanding. Faith may take the place of understanding for some people, but others will be anxious and frustrated because the prospect of nonexistence seems to be beyond the penetrating powers of human intellect. "Last words" are sometimes given special attention in the hope that those who are closest to the mystery might also be closer to the answer and somehow able to impart this answer to us. Unfortunately, this logic is questionable (Kastenbaum, 1993, 2002b). We can learn much from the strength and resourcefulness of many people as they cope with the dying process, but they do not necessarily understand death any better than the rest of us. (The Zen Buddhists, however, have a tradition of pithy last words and "graceful exit"; Blackman, 1997.)

The Ultimate Meaningless Event

Random, senseless death might be regarded as the ultimate meaningless event. A young man fires an automatic weapon into a group of people working out in a health and fitness facility. A pregnant woman is fatally wounded by a gunman in a passing car. A person who will later be described as a "disgruntled former employee" returns to the workplace and fires at everybody who happens to be there. A retired man with a grudge against a homeowners' association blasts away at neighbors enjoying themselves at a community activities center.

The family, friends, and colleagues of these victims suffer not only the grief of loss but also the shock and confusion that accompany an event that is outside one's normal frame of reference. We can understand why violent death might occur in the course of criminal activities or dysfunctional relationships. Some deaths, however, appear to make no sense at all, especially those in which the killer did not know the victim or have anything palpable to gain from the act of murder.

Fatal accidents can also raise the question of meaninglessness. A man survives many hazardous battle situations but is killed by a neighbor backing her car out of the driveway. An infant is left unattended for a few minutes and drowns in a bathtub that contained only a few inches of water. Two children are playing quietly on a sidewalk near the school when a van swerves over the curb, strikes them dead, and then plows into another group of people. In tragedies of this kind, we can learn the specific reasons for the accident (e.g., the driver of the van had been impaired by the prescription drugs he had taken, ignoring cautions against operating a motor vehicle). However, the "why" of the death is not as easily answered. The consequences of a few minutes of inattention or a disregard for safety precautions seem so tremendously out of proportion to the "little" error that was involved. As with the victims of random killings, accidental deaths may seem to violate our basic expectations about life. This is not the way things are supposed to happen—not the way that lives are supposed to end.

Most people are reluctant to conclude that there is no answer. It is difficult to accept the proposition that a death could be meaningless because this implies that life, too, might not be part of a meaningful, rational, and coherent universal pattern. Perhaps we are misled at times by faith in rationality. There has to be a good explanation for everything, even death. Everything has to make sense; everything (even *nothing*) has to be logical.

But—maybe not!

SUMMARY

There are many competing answers to the following related questions: What is death? What does death mean? Epicurus (third century B.C.) held that the universe consisted fundamentally of atoms in motion without any guiding principle or purpose. In this indifferent universe, neither life nor death had any special meaning. Christianity entered with a powerful message of hope—a sanctified life after death—but also with the complications of death as punishment for sin. For people who are often described as New Agers, death is not meaningless, punishment, or salvation. It is simply one of the way stations in a long, perhaps infinite, spiritual journey across many lives. Fantasy (Victor Frankenstein) and actual (Charles Darwin) scientists of the past explored the uncertain boundaries between life and death, and this endeavor continues to flourish today. The competing ideas about death can be seen as symbolic constructions, drawn from our experiences, our needs, and our guesswork. It would be difficult to do without a concept of death, but it seems almost as difficult to agree on the specifics.

Currently, in our society there are two very different sources of death constructions: the visual media (films and television) and biomedical practice and research. Death is constructed mainly as the result of male violence in movies. The biomedical approach is more complex and tends to focus on the following question: When (under what conditions) is a person dead? The traditional methods for determining death have occasionally proven unreliable. The development of life support systems and organ transplant procedures has created more situations in which questions can arise. The Harvard criteria for determining brain death were introduced as guidelines, although questions remain, especially concerning the condition known as brain death.

Several interpretations of the death state were examined in detail in this chapter. The traditional interpretations are death as enfeebled state, continuation of life, perpetual development, waiting, cycling and recycling, and nothing. We also considered an emerging new interpretation: death as virtual and, therefore, not really death at all. We also explored conditions that resemble death, including inorganic and unresponsive objects, sleep and altered states of consciousness, and beings who resemble or seem to personify death. The most commonly given death personifications were identified and discussed. There are also conditions that death resembles, such as social and phenomenological death.

Death has often served as an agent of personal, political, and social change. It has taken the form of the great validator that measures the social value of deceased people. However, death has also been seen as either uniting or separating people, representing the ultimate problem, the ultimate solution, or the ultimate meaningless event.

REFERENCES

Ad Hoc Committee of the Harvard Medical School to Examine the Definition of Brain Death. (1968). A definition of irreversible coma. *Journal of the American Medical Association, 205,* 337–340.

Alexander, S. (1920). *Space, time, and deity* (Vols. 1–2). London: Macmillan.

Atkin, M. (1974). The "doomed family": Observations on the lives of parents and children facing repeated child mortality. In L. Burton (Ed.), *Care of the child facing death.* Boston: Routledge & Kegan Paul.

Aries, P. (1981). *The hour of our death.* New York: Knopf.

Baider, L. (1975). Private experience and public expectations on the cancer ward. *Omega, Journal of Death and Dying, 6,* 373–382.

Blackman, S. (1997). *Graceful exits: how great beings die: death stories of Tibetan, Hindu and Zen masters.* New York: Weatherhill.

Block, M., & Parry, J. (Eds.). (1996). *Death and the regeneration of life.* Cambridge, UK: Cambridge University Press.

Bondeson, J. (2001). *Buried alive.* New York: Norton.

Byrne, P. A. (2001). Understanding brain death. www.vitalsignsministries.org.

Bytheway, B., & Johnson, J. (1996). Valuing lives? Obituaries and the life course. *Mortality, 1,* 219–234.

Carrington, H., & Meader, J. R. (1921). *Death, its causes and phenomena.* New York: Dodd, Mead & Co.

Fechner, G. T. (1977). *The little book of life after death.* New York: Arno. (Original work published 1836)

Ferguson, M. (1987). *The Aquarian conspiracy: Personal and social transformation in the 1980s* (Rev. ed.). Los Angeles: Tarcher.

Gilbert, S. F. (1997). *Developmental biology.* Sunderland, MA: Sinauer.

Gottlieb, C. (1959). Modern art and death. In H. Feifel (Ed.), *The meaning of death* (pp. 157–188). New York: McGraw-Hill.

Hall, N. (Ed.). (1991). *Exploring chaos. A guide to the new science of disorder.* New York: Norton.

Hopkins, T. (1992). Hindu views of life and afterlife. In H. Obayashi (Ed.), *Death and afterlife: Perspectives on world religions* (pp. 98–122). New York: Praeger.

Iserson, K. V. (2001). *Death to dust.* Tucson: Galen Press, Ltd.

Jung, C. G. (1959). *Four archetypes.* Princeton, NJ: Princeton University Press.

Kapleau, P. (1971). *The wheel of death.* New York: Harper & Row.

Kastenbaum, R. (1993). Last words. *The Monist, An International Journal of General Philosophical Inquiry, 76,* 270–290.

Kastenbaum, R. (2000). Looking death in the eye: Another challenge from Doctor Kevorkian. In K. K. Kalman (Ed.), *Right to die versus sacredness of life* (pp. 279–286). Amityville, NY: Baywood.

Kastenbaum, R. (2002a). Thanatomimesis. In R. Kastenbaum (Ed.), *Macmillan encyclopedia of death and dying* (Vol. 2, p. 888). New York: Macmillan.

Kastenbaum, R. (2002b). Last words. In R. Kastenbaum (Ed.), *Macmillan Encyclopedia of Death and Dying.* Volume 2, pp. 515–518. New York: Macmillan.

Kastenbaum, R. (in press). *On our way: the final passage through life and death.* Berkeley: University of California Press.

Kastenbaum, R., & Herman, C. (1997). Death personification in the Kevorkian era. *Death Studies, 21,* 115–130.

Kastenbaum, R., Peyton, S., & Kastenbaum, B. (1977). Sex discrimination after death. *Omega, Journal of Death and Dying, 6,* 33–44.

Kaufmann, S. A. (1993). *The origins of order. Self-organization and selection in evolution.* New York: Oxford University Press.

Kevorkian, J. (1957). Rapid and accurate opthalmoscopic determination of circulatory arrest. *Journal of the American Medical Association, 164,* 1660–1662.

Kevorkian, J. (1961). The eye in death. *CIBA Clinical Symposia, 13,* 51–62.

Koszer, S., & Moshe, S. L. (2001). *Brain death in children.* www.medicine.cm/neuro/topic491.htm.

Leon-Dufour, X. (1986). *Life and death in the New Testament.* New York: Harper & Row.

Leviton, D. (Ed.). (1991). *Horrendous death, health, and well-being.* New York: Hemisphere.

McCullagh, P. (1993). *Brain Dead, Brain Absent, Brain Donors.* New York: Wiley.

Moremen, R. D. (2002). Gender discrimination after death. In R. Kastenbaum (Ed.), *Macmillan encyclopedia of death and dying* (Vol. 1, pp. 311–314). New York: Macmillan.

Morgan, L. (1923). *Emergent evolution.* London: Williams & Norgate.

Neumann, E. (1971). *The origins and history of consciousness.* Princeton, NJ: Princeton University Press.

Opie, I., & Opie, P. (1969). *Children's games in street and playground.* London: Oxford University Press.

Owen, W. (1959). Strange meeting. In E. Blunden (Ed.), *The poems of Wilfred Owen.* New York: New Directions. (Original work published 1918)

Patrix, P. (1910). In F. P. Weber (Ed.), *Aspects of death and correlated aspects of life in art, epigram, and poetry.* London: Lewis.

Pernick, M. S. (1988). Back from the grave: Recurring controversies over defining and diagnosing death in history. In R. M. Zaner (Ed.), *Death: Beyond whole-brain criteria* (pp. 17–74). Boston: Kluwer.

President's Commission for the Study of Ethical Problems in Medicine and Biomedical and Behavioral Research (1981). *Defining death: Medical, legal, and ethical issues in the determination of death.* Washington, DC: U.S. Government Printing Office.

Ruelle, D. (1991). *Change and chaos.* Princeton, NJ: Princeton University Press.

Schultz, N. W., & Huet, L. M. (2000/2001). Sensational! Violent! Popular! Death in American movies. *Omega, Journal of Death and Dying, 42,* 137–150.

ScienceSpace (no date). vrinfo@gmu.edu.

Segall, A. (1990). *Paul the convert.* New Haven, CT: Yale University Press.

Shelley, M. (1977). *Frankenstein, or the modern prometheus.* In L. Wolf (Ed.), *The annotated Frankenstein.* New York: Potter. (Original work published 1818)

Shrock, N. M. (1835). On the signs that distinguish real from apparent death. *Transylvanian Journal of Medicine, 13,* 210–220.

Singer, P. (1994). *Rethinking life and death: The collapse of our traditional ethics.* New York: St. Martin's.

Stoker, B. (1975). *Dracula.* In L. Wolf (Ed.), *The annotated Dracula.* New York: Potter.

Tamm, M. E. (1996). Personification of life and death among Swedish health care professionals. *Death Studies, 20,* 1–22.

Truog, R. (1997). Is it time to abandon brain death? *Hastings Center Report, 27,* 29–31.

Twain, M. (1972). *Life on the Mississippi.* Norwalk, CT: Heritage. (Original work published 1883)

Zaid, B. A. (2002). The Islamic ruling on brain death and life support. TheModernReligion.com/misc/hh/brain-death.html.

GLOSSARY

Brain Death: A condition in which vegetative processes of the body may continue, although the capacity for thought, experience, and behavior has been destroyed.

Coma, Comatose: A state of nonresponsiveness to the environment that is associated with impairment to brain functioning but that is not identical to brain death and is sometimes reversible.

EEG: The electroencephalogram is a sequence of ink tracings on paper that record the electrical activity of the brain in several of its regions.

Intravenous Fluids: Liquids that are introduced directly into the veins to restore metabolic balance and provide nutrition, avoid dehydration, or serve other medical goals.

Martydom: The heroic sacrifice of one's life for a cause or a faith.

Respirator Brain: Physical destruction of the brain as observed in postmortem (after-death) examinations.

Vegetative State: The persistence of vital body functions over a period of weeks, months, or even years despite the individual's lack of responsiveness (often maintained through the use of a ventilator and/or other life-support devices, but may also exist spontaneously).

Virtual Reality: Computer-generated scenes, beings, and events that simulate actual or possible versions of the world.

Elvis Presley was an electrifying performer during his foreshortened life and has continued to generate an enormous income since his death.

chapter 4

THE DEATH SYSTEM

Everybody needs to die in 2010 if they don't want to pay estate tax.
—Larry Dace, certified public accountant

Elvis Presley, the King of Rock 'n' Roll, on Monday, was crowned top-earning dead celebrity of the past 12 months, according to a list compiled by Forbes.com, the Web site of the popular business magazine, Forbes.
—Netscape, August 13, 2002

I watch Fellers creep around the pond, his beard dripping, his burly form crouched over his waders, a net in his hand and a flashlight in his mouth. Taking care not to let the frog see his moon shadow, Fellers inches forward, pauses, inches closer—and then whips the net down in a splash. It comes up full of slimy stuff that he pulls out, a handful at a time, until he reaches the frog at the bottom.
—W. Wayt Gibbs (2002)

In the early 1990s the Parsis started to notice that there were fewer birds at the tower. At first they assumed that the vultures had simply gone elsewhere.... But researchers in other parts of India began to observe a similar condition...about forty vulture deaths in a colony in Keoladeo National Park.... Many of the vultures had exhibited a strange behavior before dying, hanging their heads so low that their beaks nearly touched their bellies.
—Stephen Bodio (2001)

As more people move to more hazard-prone areas, "catastrophes, the really big ones, are getting larger," said Dennis Meleti, director of the National Hazards Research and Applications Information in Boulder, Colorado. Disasters are a growing problem. Seven of the nation's 10 costliest have struck in the last decade.
—Seth Borenstein (1999)

Seven newborn boys, six of whom were black, were injected with radioactive iodide in the early 1950s at a hospital in Memphis, Tenn., as part of a study funded by the federal government…it was one of at least five done around the country on a total of 235 newborns and older infants.
—Scripps Howard (1993)

Simon was the family angel. He was handsome. He was perfect. Everybody loved him. Of course, he got more attention than I did, but you couldn't get angry at him. Then he died. It was diphtheria. Most people today don't even know that word. Diphtheria was just terrible. My mother's sister died about the same time after delivering her second baby. That baby died, too, or was born dead, I don't know which. Ellie came down with rheumatic fever. She made it to her 15th birthday, and couldn't even blow out the candle; that's a fact. The graveyard kept filling up with family. When I was about 10 or so, I remember coming back from the graveyard and thinking: "Why, there are as many of us here at home." Maybe that's why I've always felt at home at graveyards.
—A man of 93, reflecting on his childhood

Each of these statements reveals something about our death system. The death system might be viewed as the negative or shadow image of our society. Everything that makes a collection of individuals into a society and keeps that society going has implications for our relationship to death. We previewed the death system in the opening chapter with a focus on the terrorist attacks on America. In this chapter, we examine the death system more systematically. First, however, we will take the following examples as our introduction.

- "Nothing is certain except death and taxes" has been a familiar bromide for many years. There are, in fact, many links between the two. One specific example was brought to my attention by the accountant who noticed my eyes had glazed over as we went through forms and numbers. With the mere hint of a smile, Dace pointed out that a new law would provide the maximum benefits to pass on to survivors in the Year 2010. A conscientious family person should do his or her best to die in that year to take advantage of this one-time opportunity. The law was due to expire after that one golden year. Even without this example, though, it would not be difficult to identify many ways in which a death has significant financial implications throughout society—and in tribal groups as well as large industrialized nations (Middleton, 1996).

- Dead, Elvis Presley still makes way more money each year than most hard-working people earn in a lifetime (www.forbes.com). Elvis' $37 million in 2002 was followed by other equally deceased luminaries: "Peanuts" cartoonist Charles Schulz ($28 million), Beatle John Lennon ($20 million), racecar driver Dale Earnhardt ($20 million), and "Dr. Seuss" (Theodore Geisel; $19 million). Some people have been so valued by society that they continue to flourish in economy as well as memory. Elvis is remarkable for having such a successful afterlife in society through a variety of modalities, from images on black velvet to a legion of look-alikes, and from sales of his recordings and videos to admissions and sales at his own museum. Although there are unique features about Elvis adoration, it is not that unusual for what a person has created to become more esteemed after his or her death. Vincent Van Gogh's paintings, for example, could have been purchased for the cost of dinner and a bottle of inexpensive wine while the artist lived. Although the social memories of some people fade almost instantly upon their deaths, others become even more treasured. How and why these choices are made is a provocative topic that could tell us much about the way in which society uses, abuses, or dismisses its dead.

- Frogs and vultures. We think of these creatures as belonging to the natural order of things. They do not have Social Security numbers and e-mail addresses or pay taxes (at least not yet). Nevertheless, they are very much a part of the death system in every nation where they flick their tongues for flying insects or keep watch for carrion. The connection has turned lethal in recent years. Many ponds where the lusty songs of frogs were a sure sign of spring have gone silent. Grossly deformed frogs have also turned up in great numbers, and some species seem to have disappeared from their habitats.

  Meanwhile, vultures, those large and awesome scavengers, have also been dropping to their own deaths in alarming numbers. Why "alarming"? For centuries in India vultures have been relied on to strip the corpses of humans as well as animals. Tibetan Buddhists have also assigned vultures a key role in "sky burial" (Bodio, 2001):

  > Although the Parsis continue to stack their dead within the towers (their religion, Zoroastrianism, forbids them to contaminate earth, fire, or water with their corpses), the bodies remain unmolested except by the gradual effects of the elements. (p. 26)

  Furthermore, with vultures now in short supply, India's sacred cattle—living and dying on the streets—are being left to rot because Hindus are forbidden to touch these corpses. The remains of other dead animals will also remain longer. Outbreaks of tuberculosis, anthrax, and other diseases can occur in these circumstances, and the situation could also spread to Africa.

  Two elements are especially significant in the frog and vulture die-off: the most probable cause—pesticides, especially DDT; and religious attitudes and practices that have enhanced the role of vultures. The possible impact of frog extinction is less obvious but perhaps even more significant in the long term because it could be part of a much broader pattern of endangerment to many biological species, a cascading process with effects of unknown breadth and magnitude.

  There is even a philosophical issue here if we care to think about it: What should we make of the deaths of the creatures who seem to have been designed by nature to assist the dead into new life-forms?

- Where we choose to live may seem to have little relationship to the prospect of death. We make our decision based on the attractiveness of the region, career opportunities, proximity of friends and family, and other reasons that have a lot to do with how we prefer to live and not much to do with thoughts of death. Specialists in disaster and catastrophe, however, continue to compile facts that demonstrate an increased risk to life as more and more of us move into hazardous environments. Earthquakes, the most lethal type of natural disaster (Chapter 8), can take a much greater toll as larger numbers of people crowd into a hazardous area. Life decisions have had major consequences for death in the past as well. For example, conditions for the spread of contagious disease were markedly increased as people started to crowd into cities. The point here is not that we should stay away from attractive places but simply that many of the decisions we make as part of our lives do affect our chances for death whether or not we happen to be aware of the connections. Our society's pattern of beliefs and practices has much to do with the choices we make and, therefore, with the ever-shifting potentials for risk.

Vultures await their next assignment as part of nature's program of recycling life through death. Pesticides are threatening the lives of vultures in India, arousing public health concerns as well as disrupting the established order of life-death transition.

- The act of injecting newborn infants with radioactive iodide as part of a government-funded study met with severe criticism by physicians and ethicists as soon as the facts became public (after nearly 40 years of silence). John Gofman, a leading expert on the dangers of low-level radiation, stated that this experiment increased the risk of cancer for these children: "It's like saying, 'We're going to visit cancer on some of you—not necessarily all of you—but we have increased the risk individually and some of you will get it.' It's not a nice thing to do with children" (Scripps Howard, 1993). The fact that this was an official government project exposes still another type of conflict within our society's death system. The government is supposed to be a mechanism through which we can protect ourselves against threats to life and security—and here was the government playing an active role in increasing the probability of illness and death, and for newborns! The Memphis study was further disturbing in its revelation that "liberty and justice for all" may not have been applied to infants of color. Racism in life prepares for racism in death.
- The man of 93 is part of a disappearing generation that remembers when childhood was a time of ever-present risk for disabling illness and death. The local cemetery was an extension of the neighborhood where so many promising and cherished family members now resided. Dramatic changes in longevity and life expectation are usually expressed in statistics, but we do not want to forget that advances in public health are really about giving individuals the opportunity to survive well into their adult years.

These are but a few of the conflicts and complications that are found in any society's death system. Perhaps we should make things simpler for ourselves—why don't we just get rid of death?

A WORLD WITHOUT DEATH

Suppose that the world is just as we know it with one exception: *Death is no longer inevitable.* Disease and aging have been conquered. Let us also suppose that air and water pollution have been much reduced through new technologies.

Take a few minutes to consider the implications and consequences. What will happen? How will people respond to this situation individually and as a society? How will the quality of life change?

Think first of the effects of the "no death" scenario on the world at large. Write down the changes you think would be likely to happen in the left side of Box 4-1.

Think next of how the no death scenario would influence your own life. Describe some of the major ways the no death situation would be likely to influence you on the right side of Box 4-1. After you have completed this thought exercise, please continue and see how your prophecies compare with those most often made by other students in classes such as this one.

None of us can know for sure what would actually happen if this hypothetical situation became reality. Nevertheless, many plausible and interesting predictions can be offered. Compare your ideas with those that follow, as given by other students who have completed this exercise.

General Consequences

- Overcrowding would lead to infringements on privacy, mobility, and other individual liberties. "Space would be incredibly precious." "People would develop new mental and physical habits to keep others at an emotional distance." "Turf mentality would be all-powerful."

"After a while, nobody would feel comfortable being alone even if you could be." "I don't see how people could still be individuals."

- Stringent birth control would be enforced. This control would be an exercise of power and prestige. "It will all depend on what the elite want people bred for." "If basketball coaches get control, they'd want to breed for 7-foot centers." "Every group of crackpots and bigots would try to use selective birth control to exterminate the kind of people they don't happen to like."

- New laws would be needed because relationships between people will have changed so much. "Inheritance might not mean anything any more. The younger generation couldn't expect anything from the older generation unless we cooked up new laws." "I think that babies with genetic or with birth defects might not be allowed to survive because there would be room for so few babies when adults are not dying off."

- Society would become very conservative and slow to change its ways. "Old people would outnumber young people so much that anything new would hardly have a chance." "The world wouldn't really have a future. There'd only be a terrific bias to keep things as they are or even to roll things back to the past."

- The economic structure of society would change greatly in ways that are difficult to predict. "Life insurance—who would need it? And then, what would happen to that whole industry?" "People wouldn't have to put

---

BOX 4-1
GENERAL AND PERSONAL CONSEQUENCES OF A WORLD WITHOUT DEATH

Consequences for the World	*Consequences for Me*
_____	_____

money away for their funerals. In fact, there would be hardly any money to be made on the dead." "Doctors might not make as much money because there wouldn't be all this fear of death. But maybe they'd make even more money with plastic surgery and fancy ways to try to keep people looking young. Who knows?"

- Moral beliefs and priorities might change in many ways. "That would be just about the end of marriage, and maybe of divorce, too. People would think, hey, what's the point of being married to just one person forever and ever. Everybody'd either screw around a lot with everybody else or maybe just get tired of it after a couple of thousand years and play video games instead."

- Death would take on a different aspect. "Religion is mostly getting people to shape up or go to Hell. If we're not going to die, then who's going to listen and what's going to happen to religion?" "Death has always been the enemy. Now it might be the biggest friend ever. We might hire people to kill us in some really decisive way, like blowing us to pieces. I think I would buy shares in the Mafia. Or maybe governments would arrange special wars only for the purpose of getting a lot of people killed." "I really don't think we can do without death psychologically. Society would find some way to make death possible, and this would be considered the right thing, not an evil thing."

Personal Consequences

- We would plan and organize our lives differently. "I don't know if I would have the same ambitions and make any progress on them. As it is now, about the only way I get anything done is when a deadline is staring me in the face, which happens all the time in my classes. If there's all the time in the world, there wouldn't be any pressure, and I might not ever get anything done." "I would just give up trying to plan ahead. There would be just too much ahead, so much that it would be very hard to comprehend." "I'd be really afraid of making some terrible mistake in what I do, because the consequences could follow me I guess forever, for centuries anyhow."

- We would be free from the fear of death. "If I found out that there really and truly wasn't going to be any more death, I would feel light and free for the first time and I could really enjoy life. I hope I'm not kidding myself either, but even the thought of a no-death world makes me feel wonderfully free." "My brother's got himself almost killed at least three times. He's into being a macho risk-taker. I'm a lot more careful. I would probably take more chances with my life, and do some more exciting things, because it really wouldn't be taking such a chance, would it? I wonder what my brother would do?"

- Our personal relationships would extend indefinitely, creating new opportunities and new challenges. "It's a crazy idea, but I like it. The people I care about would always be with me." "I find it hard to think of becoming an old person and being an old person right along with my parents and grandparents. Would I still feel like a child. What would become of generations if we all spent most of our lives being old together?"

- Our ideas about the purpose and meaning of life might change. "It would be a hard idea to get used to, especially with all that I have always believed as a Christian. I would want to keep my beliefs—I would have to—but it might make some difference, there not being natural death and therefore not being eternity and heaven. Or would there still be? It could be confusing." "I have to wonder what value anything would have anymore. Maybe the only thing I would value is how to fill all that time, how to fill all that time."

A world without death would differ in many ways from the world we know today. You may have thought of some consequences that go beyond those presented here, and the list certainly could be extended. The main point is that many of our individual and societal patterns of functioning are connected with death in one way or another. Death is never the only factor involved. Life insurance, for example, depends also on the profit motive, and the profit motive in turn arises from complex ideological and social conditions. However, as respondents have often observed, no death means no life insurance. Take as another example the relationship some respondents have predicted between the elimination of death and the establishment of stringent birth control measures. "If nobody dies, then nobody can get born."

Individual implications of our relationship to death cannot easily be separated from the general consequences. Consider, for example, those who fear they would lose their drive for accomplishment if time were endless. This is a personal matter, but it is connected with a cultural ethos in which the achievement motive is highly valued. Social philosophers have argued that one of the most powerful driving forces in Western society is the need to achieve a kind of salvation through achievement. We accumulate material goods and acquire status to demonstrate that we should be among the blessed. A bumper sticker that had its day in the sun once advised us that "The winner is the one who dies with the most toys."

Lessen the need to achieve and acquire and we begin to have a different relationship to time and death. The work and achievement-oriented lifestyle has been increasingly challenged by enthusiasm for a leisure lifestyle. Being a very diligent worker now may earn a person the sobriquet of "workaholic." Notice, though, that many devotees of the leisure lifestyle actually "work religiously" on their hobbies. Members of the baby boom generation sometimes work very hard at play as the early signs of aging and the shadow of mortality arise. A colleague of the baby boom generation may have spoken for many others when he confided to me, "If I work any harder at playing and staying young, I'll be old before my time and kill myself for sure." Then he was off jogging again under simmering Arizona skies.

This no-death thought experiment raises many questions that require us to think of society as well as the individual. The death system concept, touched on earlier, provides a way of doing so. We now start thinking more systematically about the death system.

BASIC CHARACTERISTICS OF THE DEATH SYSTEM

Understandably, we often focus on our own personal situations when they cross paths with death. How serious is *my* health problem? What should *I* say to my neighbor whose child was killed in an automobile accident yesterday? Would *I* be better off dead than old? All these individual confrontations, however, take place within a dynamic society. It is true that we live and die as individuals, but it is also true that we are linked with each other by language, expectations, customs, and needs. In this section, we shift our focus to the ways in which our confrontations with death are systematically influenced by our participation in society.

The concept of the death system invites our attention to interconnections, to the subtle network of relationships and meanings through which one sphere of action influences another. We have already considered one powerful example in the terrorist attack on America (Chapter 1) and touched in this chapter on connections between death and tax regulations, the financial afterlife of celebrities, the confluence of pesticides and religious practices on the fate of frogs and vultures, choice of residence and disaster risk, racism and medical child abuse, and lives either foreshortened or protected by public health measures. There are many more examples than can be considered in this book, but we can heighten our awareness of these connections and interactions between individual lives and a society's death system. We face death alone in one sense, but in another and equally valid sense, we face death as part of a society whose expectations, rules, motives, and symbols influence our individual encounters. This will become clearer as we turn our attention to the components and functions of the death system.

Components of the Death System

The death system is made up of people, places, times, objects, and symbols, as noted in Chapter 1.

People

All people are potential components of the death system. Tomorrow, I might be called on suddenly to use the techniques I learned in a cardiopulmonary resuscitation course, or somebody else may be called on to use his or her skills on me. (I hope we have both learned well!) Most of us phase in and out of the death system as circumstances dictate. Some of us, though, such as people working in the funeral and memorial industry, serve as core participants. Their entire identity, including how they are perceived by others, is often strongly influenced by their profession.

One funeral director described the typical situation with which members of this trade must contend: "When I walk into a room, Death walks in with me. That is how people react to me." The fact that many of us find it difficult to think of a funeral director as a normal and distinct individual testifies to his or her embeddedness in the death system.

The agent who sells life insurance is also very much a part of the death system. The same may be said for all the clerks, adjusters, marketing people, and executives. The members of the custodial staff who clean up the high-rise offices of MegaMoolah Insurance Company late in the evening are unlikely to reflect on their role in the death system, but their paychecks have their origin in somebody's decision to make a financial investment in anticipation of death. The premiums we pay to guarantee death benefits are part of a complex network of investments. The death money may be used to create new jobs or abolish old ones, support a local business or challenge it with a competitor, and so on.

The florist is also part of the death system. "Floral tributes" help flower growers and merchants stay in business. The lawyer who draws up wills and living trusts is another person. This is one of the few situations in which a healthy adult is likely to sit down and discuss personal death-related issues. Even so, many lawyers report that their clients usually prefer to delay making a will or living trust as long as possible because of the obvious connection with death.

People working in a variety of occupations earn their livelihoods, in whole or part, from services they perform in connection with death. A consumer movement that encourages less elaborate and costly funerals will affect the funeral director, the florist, the cemetery association, and so on. A trend toward merged families with "his, her, and our" children might complicate the inheritance process. The availability of life care retirement communities could reduce the amount of money that can be passed along to children and therefore also reduce the importance of will making. A change in one facet of our social or economic life can show up as pressure or opportunity elsewhere. Our relationship to death can be caught up in these changes.

Other people associated with the death system may not come so readily to mind. Think, for example, of the big truck you saw pull up behind a supermarket the other day. It was filled with case after case of pet food. Every can in every case depicts a contented dog or cat, whereas the inside contains some type of meat product. All that meat, of course, came from what once were living creatures. The truck driver, the person who shelves the cans, the assistant store manager who makes sure they are priced correctly, and the clerk at the checkout register are but a few of the people who participate in the death system through their processing of pet food. Those who raise, those who slaughter, and those who process a variety of living animals to become food for pets also should be included. The people in the canning factory should be included, as should the accountants, executives, and advertising agency. The cat that meows so convincingly for its favorite brand on television is also part of the death system, as is the cat at home that, unimpressed by the advertising programs, sniffs disdainfully at the food dish, turns up his or her tail, and walks away with an offended air. As purchasers of this product, are we not all part of this complex network as well, a network that requires the death of animals to feed other animals?

Still unmentioned are the health professions and the clergy, all of whom have important roles in the death system. It would not do to leave out the scientists who are designing lethal weapons or tinkering with both life and death with cloning techniques. Now that Dolly the Sheep has arrived, (and, sadly departed) should we also clone the extinct Tasmanian tiger (Tinkler, 2002) to keep it company, or perhaps rescue the wooly mammoth from the dead as a theme park feature ("Wildlife Park," 2002)? Trying to create new forms of life or reversing extinction are on the cutting edge of science today, although imagined in the past (as with *Frankenstein*, Chapter 3). What other occupations have an important bearing on death and might not even exist otherwise? This open list is in your hands to extend as you like.

At any moment, you or I might become drawn actively into the death system through a variety

Dolly, left, became the most celebrated sheep since Mary's little lamb. Although regarded as a successful clone, Dolly aged rapidly and succumbed to a variety of medical problems. The first successfully cloned kitten, right, was given the clever name, cc (carbon copy). Like Dolly, cc enjoyed the companionship of a motherly surrogate. She was doing well at the most recent report.

of paths. A friend unexpectedly reveals that she has a fatal illness. We are in an automobile accident in which somebody dies. A funeral procession interrupts our cruise down the street. Perhaps it is the insurance agent gently inquiring if we have made adequate provisions for the education of our children. The points of entry are numerous and, of course, when we exit, we are all part of the death system.

Places

Certain places have become identified with death. The cemetery and the funeral home are obvious examples. There are other places whose associations with death depend on the ideas and experiences we carry with us. Today, people come and go from the hospital all the time. It is the place where babies are born, where routine surgical procedures are performed, where accident victims are treated, where clinics are avail-

able for outpatient care, and so on. It is also the place where people die sometimes, but it is only one facet of the modern medical center. People with long memories, however, give a different perspective. A spry woman of 93 explained:

> The doctors would say, "We're taking you to the hospital, Mike." And Mike he would directly close his eyes and turn his face to the wall. Then the doctor would say, "Now, now Mike. Don't take on like that. We're going to make you well at the hospital." And Mike he wouldn't say a word. But when the doctor walked out the room, Mike he would say, "I'm a dead man." Everybody knew it. You went to the hospital to die.... And even to walk by the hospital, you would shudder right down to your shoes. And you'd walk a little faster.

In a modern hospital, death is often granted its small, isolated territory in return for promising to stay within those bounds. Here, the patients with the most severe life-threatening conditions reside. However, any room on any unit can become a death place when a patient unexpectedly "goes sour." It can take months before the ward feels safe again. In the meantime, you can see a variety of decontamination rituals as those associated with the ward attempt to rid the environment of its newly acquired "deathness." Similar measures have been taken in private homes as well: A bed may be given away because it is the one in which Uncle Otto "expired," and its continued presence somehow keeps the unwelcome aura of deathness in the household atmosphere.

Historical battlefields have been thought of as death places for centuries, as have the royal murders in the Tower of London, that grim edifice by the banks of the Thames. The Ford Theater in Washington, DC is remembered mostly as the place where Lincoln was assassinated. A pathway in the woods may be spoken of in hushed tones by the schoolchildren who discovered a human corpse while on a nature walk. Even a familiar house across the street can be a death place in the minds of neighbors who now feel uncomfortable as they pass by. Once a place has become associated with death, we no longer think and feel the same way about it. We have but to think of Oklahoma City and New York City, where people perished and buildings collapsed as a result of domestic and foreign terrorism. The people of Oklahoma City may never forget how a major downtown building suddenly became a place of death.

Times

Death also has its times or occasions. Memorial Day, for example, is a regularly occurring time set aside in the United States to honor those who have fallen in defense of the nation. In some tribal societies, 1 or more days are devoted to communal mourning that honors all who have died during the preceding year. (Simpler burial rituals are held immediately after the deaths.) The Days of the Dead in Mexican tradition can startle the unprepared visitor who expects death observances to be somber and restrained. The public carnival atmosphere suggests an easy familiarity with the dead, and the visitor might not be aware of the more reflective and somber rituals that are conducted at the family level. Many societies have established periodic occasions when death is

granted dominance over everybody's thoughts and feelings. Just as we might grant death its own space in return for death not invading ours, so we might set aside special times for death, hoping that death will not steal the time of our lives.

Prayers for the dead are offered on regular occasions, for example, by Jewish and Japanese Americans who are keeping the faith, and Catholics celebrate Mass. December 29 is observed in honor of the Sioux annihilated by the Seventh Cavalry at Wounded Knee, South Dakota, in 1890. Anniversaries of the disasters in Waco, Texas, Oklahoma City, and the three sites of the September 11, 2001, terrorist attacks are observed by many of those who were affected. Some of us also acknowledge a death time that has deep personal significance that may not be shared by others. This can take the form of a valuable spiritual reflection but also what psychiatrists call an anniversary reaction in which the survivor falls ill, behaves erratically, or suffers an "accident."

The clock and the calendar treat each passing moment, each passing day with equal disinterest. For the individual and for society, however, certain times seem to fall under the particular auspices of death, and we tend to treat these times in a special manner.

Objects

Death has its objects and things as well as its people, places, and times. The hearse and the death certificate are among the conspicuous objects in the American death system. Death notices have their own separate section in the daily newspaper. The noose, the gallows, and the electric chair are also among our more obvious images of death. The unexpected telegram often arouses concern. The spraying device that "kills bugs dead" is an object in our society's death system; the same may be said of the nuclear devices that we aimed at potential enemies for years while they aimed their nuclear devices back at us.

Objects whose intended uses have little to do with death may produce lethal effects through accidents or misuse. Both the automobile and the cigarette have been spoken of as instruments of death, although they were conceived as positive additions to the quality of life. Alcoholic beverages and other pharmacological substances have also been viewed as instruments of death, al-

Once family, always family. The Mexican Day of the Dead affirms respect and affection for those who have departed.

though, again, not intended for such a purpose. Things such as people, places, and times can be recruited into the death system, and when this happens their meanings are transformed, even though the objects themselves remain the same.

Symbols

Language and other symbols play a major role in death systems. In Western culture the black armband tells a story. Funeral directors generally provide limousines for the funeral procession and garb themselves in similar colors. Not all societies symbolize death with dark colors, but we soon learn to recognize those particular colors and other symbols meant to convey death-related messages in a given society or subculture. In some neighborhoods, closing all the shutters has been a traditional signal of a death within, although this practice continues to fade. Administration of the priestly ritual for the sick is often related to the prospect of death (although technically it is not regarded by the Catholic Church as "last rites," despite this common attribution given to the ceremony).

Death symbols tell us something about a culture's attitudes toward death. The choice of music is one example (Kastenbaum, in press). Slow, solemn music intoned on an organ suggests a different orientation from a simple folk song with guitar accompaniment and is also different from a brass band strutting down the street playing "When the Saints Go Marching in." When gang members decided to organize the funeral for a slain member, they included a rap song written in his memory (Holveck, 1991). In contrast, when Queen Mother Elizabeth died in her 101st year (Associated Press, 2002, April 10).

> Slow drumbeats punctuated the shrill bagpipe lament of nearly 200 regimental musicians. Soldiers of the Royal Horse Artillery in gold-trimmed black tunics rode six black horses pulling a gun carriage that bore the coffin.

That soldiers and a gun carriage should be so integral to the funeral services also tells us something about a society's associations with death.

The words we use and those we refrain from using also reveal much about the nature of the culture's death system. For many years in our society, people "passed on," "expired," or "went to their reward." I have noticed a decrease in euphemisms and an increase in antisentimental expressions in recent years, such as "She OD'd" (overdosed) or "He croaked." Both the euphemistic and the dysphemistic approach serve to keep a distance between the speaker and the raw reality of death. Currently, health care professionals prefer the objectivistic "terminally ill" to the still uncomfortably emotional "dying."

Although today more people discuss death openly, we still tend to code the topic with indirect, symbolic, and sometimes downright evasive language. I know of one major hospital system, for example, in which a deceased patient is still spoken of as having been transferred to "Tower Nine." There are eight towers or units in this hospital: The ninth is not of this world. Notice with what linguistic garments people clothe their communications about dying and death, and you will also be observing something important about their underlying attitudes.

FUNCTIONS OF THE DEATH SYSTEM

We have surveyed the components of the death system. Next, we will become acquainted with seven of its major functions.

Warnings and Predictions

A core function of society is to protect its members. All societies issue warnings and predictions intended to stave off threats to life. These warnings and predictions can be based on folk customs, science, pseudoscience, organized religion, or individual revelation. The threats that are forecast may be accurate, exaggerated, or completely imaginary. Also, society may choose either to respond to or ignore the alarms. Cassandra's plea to destroy the horse that the Greeks left as a gift at the gates of Troy is a classic example of a warning unheeded and its disastrous consequences. The congressional investigation of the FBI and CIA responses to warnings of a terrorist attack is a recent example (Yaukey, 2002).

Often, it is difficult to determine which warnings should be taken seriously. A central problem for our times is how to navigate between the extremes of constant hypervigilance and smug neglect. How much of our attention should be devoted to the recently surfaced threats posed by terrorism and how much by the continuing problem of air and water pollution? To the possible effects of overhead high-voltage wires? To radon, asbestos, and lead in our homes and workplaces? Are we tempting death if we dine in a sushi bar or drive across one of the nation's many bridges that are considered to be hazardous?

"Small-craft warning" and "tornado watch" are familiar phrases in some areas of the United States. In Arizona, we hear occasional "flash flood" warnings: It is not easy to imagine that a dry ravine might suddenly resound to the roar of a vigorous current of water. We expect to be advised of impending floods, blizzards, dust storms, and avalanche conditions. There are frequent announcements of possible hazards associated with consumer goods and services. Evaluating and responding to all these warnings would seem to be a full-time job.

The death system provides warnings and predictions to specific individuals as well as to larger units of society. The physician may hesitate before interpreting a laboratory report for us. The mechanic may fix us with a hard look: "Your car is an accident ready to happen."

Hearing that there is a threat to our well-being does not end the story. We must still decide what we are going to do about this communication. Mr. Macho Guy and Ms. Lucky Goose might well ignore all the warnings, as might those who live life by the numbers and figure that there is nothing they can do when their own number comes up.

Preventing Death

All death systems have techniques and strategies that are intended to prevent death. In Western society, we tend to think of health professionals, firefighters, policemen, and researchers striving for cures or safety improvements. One of the great accomplishments of the past few generations has been the control of contagious diseases that once took a high toll, especially among the very young and the very old. Efforts are still being made to prevent other causes of death, such as cancer and heart disease, and to minimize hardships associated with aging.

The treatment of acute and emergent conditions has attracted the most interest. Specialists and advanced equipment are rushed to the bedside of a person suffering from a condition that almost surely would have been fatal in the past. Surgery has become increasingly sophisticated and successful. The number of pharmacological treatments also continues to expand.

Hard-won medical victories create rising expectations. As one physician with more than 40 years of experience explained,

> People don't want much these days. All they expect is to live forever and, well, maybe to be young forever, too.... I guess it's our fault for knocking off typhoid, scarlet fever, diphtheria, tuberculosis and whatever. They expect us to cure everything now. I guess we almost expect it, too.

We seem to enjoy the idea of "making war" on death and disease. Perhaps this image suits us because it is active and easy to grasp. There are problems with this conception, however. The "war against death" is often conducted in a selective manner: more vigorously on behalf of certain favored subpopulations and less vigorously on behalf of others. This selectivity follows society's general paths of discrimination and unequal opportunity. Whatever makes some people appear to have high social value in general makes them more favored candidates for death-prevention efforts. "If you are going to have a heart attack, make sure you are wearing a good suit and are in the right part of town—also, try to be young and white!" Cynical comments of this type unfortunately retain a core of truth even today, as disclosure of the radioactive iodide studies has reminded us. For example, poor women in the United States are still less likely to be diagnosed and treated for breast cancer and are therefore more likely to die from this ailment (Associated Press, 2002, April 3). People without health insurance have been found less likely to receive prevention services and, perhaps as a consequence, to have a death rate almost double that of insured people (Franks, Clancy, & Gold, 1993).

It could also be said that the war against death also includes a war against ourselves because many lives now end as a result of lifestyle practices and decisions, for example, tobacco and alcohol use as well as through HIV-AIDS transmission.

Caring for the Dying

A staff member in one of the world's most sophisticated medical research centers was describing her work to me in a completely professional manner. Suddenly, tears of sorrow and frustration intruded as she tried to explain what happens when the decision is made to shift from "cure" to "comfort" care:

> Sometimes the point comes when the doctors decide that's it. There's nothing we can do—or should do—all the cards have been played, and there's just no way we can really hope to arrest the illness. The brakes screech! We all have to come to a full and sudden stop. We may have been doing everything in the world to keep this

DEATH'S DISPENSARY.

OPEN TO THE POOR, GRATIS, BY PERMISSION OF THE PARISH.

The discovery that a polluted water pump in an impoverished area of London was the source of a cholera epidemic was one of the incidents that led to intensified demand for public health reforms from the middle of the 19th century onward.

person alive for months and now we have to stop all that and change what we do, but it is a lot harder to change how we feel about the patient and ourselves, about what we're doing. I don't think human thoughts and feelings were made for such sudden stops and starts!

Fortunately, the transition between trying to prevent death and providing care to a dying person is not always this drastic. Prevention and comforting can be encompassed within the same philosophy and carried out by the same people in many situations. Patients and their families may play an active part in the decision making, and health care providers may function as a team (e.g., hospice care; Chapter 5).

How can the various health professionals (each with distinctive skills, points of view, and needs), the family, and the life-threatened person work together harmoniously if some of them persist in the objective of prevention while others believe that comfort and relief should take precedence? Should prevention of death continue to be the overriding goal until the very end, or are there circumstances in which the emphasis should shift to comfort?

Advocates of both positions can be found in the ranks of all those associated with terminal care. There are physicians who take quite literally the never-say-die orientation: So long as life has any chance, it is the physician's responsibility to do all within his or her power to support this chance. Other physicians more readily accommodate their efforts to the signs of impending and inexorable death. This attitude seems to be more in keeping with earlier medical practices when the physician had fewer options to work with and was inclined to view himself or herself as Nature's assistant. There is reason to believe, however, that the United States is working seriously toward a revision of its philosophy and practice for caring for the dying (Chapters 5 and 6).

Disposing of the Dead

"Disposing of the dead" is a heartless-sounding phrase, but it refers to a task that all societies must perform. At the very minimum, there is a need to dispose of the physical remains. Seldom, however, is a society content with the minimum. The funeral and memorialization process (Chapter 13) tells much about the overall stability and cohesiveness of a culture as well as what that society makes of death.

The following are a few examples from American society:

- A minister dies unexpectedly. His wife and children are stunned, then griefstricken. Forced to think of funeral arrangements, they find themselves in perfect agreement. He had been a family-oriented person who preferred the simple, the intimate, the natural. The funeral, then, should be without ostentation. Only the family and a few special friends should be involved. However, this plan offends the congregation. A small, simple, private commemoration would fail to symbolize the deceased's significant place in the community. It would, in effect, diminish the status of the congregation itself. The congregation would also be deprived of this opportunity to express its respect for the departed spiritual leader. No, it just would not be right to let this death pass without a conspicuous public ceremony. The power of the many prevailed in this instance. The disposal of this man's body and the accompanying ritual became a public event. It was a "beautiful" funeral, with participation from community leaders as well as the congregation.

How did the family feel? They reacted as though not only the husband and father had been taken away from them but also his death. What they experienced deeply as private loss and grief had become a public exhibit. Yet the community felt that it, too, had strong rights and needs. Just as much of this man's life had been devoted to the public sphere, so his death should be shared. This is one of many examples that could be given of the contest between private and public "ownership" of the deceased. Some death systems emphasize one side, some the other, but the private versus public dialectic seems to be present in all of them.

- Two young men are pushing a gurney through the corridors of a large modern hospital. This action has been planned to take as little time as possible and to attract little or no attention from others. Soon they have reached the service elevator and the door closes behind them.

The casual observer will have noticed only an empty stretcher. A more sophisticated observer will know or guess that this is a false-bottomed device that is designed expressly for disguised transportation of the dead. A society whose health care establishment goes out of its way to wrap a cloak of invisibility around the dead is telling us something about its fundamental attitudes toward the meaning of life. Do we think of the dead as fearful, disgusting, or dirty? Are we as afraid of being "contaminated" as members of any preliterate society? Such questions arise when we observe avoidance-of-the-corpse rituals even within the corridors of the modern hospital system.

- The old man has died. Family converge from everywhere. There is a problem, however. The oldest generation, including the widow, expect a strictly traditional observation of the death. All the time-honored rituals must be observed. The younger generations, however, are more Americanized and consider the old way too formal, too consuming of time and money, and generally not to their liking. The funeral director is caught squarely in the middle. The death of a respected family patriarch, then, threatens to bring a bitter intergenerational conflict to the surface.

Our death system undergoes change with every new generation. Since three- and four-generation families are becoming increasingly common in the United States, we face the challenge of understanding each other's viewpoints when dealing with body disposal and other death-related decisions. Whatever improves intergenerational communication and understanding will help our death system to function in a more harmonious and effective manner.

- The rain and floods that devastated large areas of the United States, in the summer of 1993 created problems for the dead as well as the living. In Hardin, Mississippi, flood waters churned through the local cemetery. This burial ground had been used for approximately 200 years and was a core of the community's history. Hundreds of bodies were unearthed from their graves. Despite the pressing need to deal with flood recovery, the community showed no less concern for making things right with the dead. They did all they could to identify the corpses and return them to their designated burial places. Anthropologists, pathologists, and other outside experts offered their assistance. Eventually, approximately 100 bodies were identified; the others, still anonymous, were provided with caskets and given a mass burial. Members of the community spoke of their relief in helping their loved ones "rest in peace."

Our diverse American society includes subgroups whose lifestyles are distinctive. The Amish way of life and death provides an instructive example of alternative approaches (Bryer, 1977; Hostetler, 1993; Kraybill, 1989). There are approximately 80,000 Amish people in the United States, descendants of Swiss Anabaptists who were persecuted for their beliefs until granted refuge and religious liberty by William Penn in 1727. The Amish maintain a family-oriented society that emphasizes religious values, a simple agrarian lifestyle, separation from the non-Amish world, and a strong doctrine of mutual assistance. Marital separation and divorce are not sanctioned. The infirm and the mentally ill are looked after in the community rather than in institutions. The Amish people function "at the same unhurried pace as...their forefathers, using horses instead of automobiles, windmills instead of electricity, and facing death with the same religious tenets and steadfast faith of their fathers" (Bryer, 1977, p. 256).

The Amish way of life and death is clearly expressed in behavior associated with body disposal. The deceased is dressed in white garments by family members (Bryer, 1977):

It is only at her death that an Amish woman wears a white dress with the cape and apron which were put away by her for the occasion of her death. This is an example of the lifelong preparation for the facing of death, as sanctioned by Amish society. The wearing of all white clothes signifies the high ceremonial emphasis on the death event as the final rite of passage into a new and better life. (p. 171)

The funeral is very much a home-oriented event. A large room is cleared for the simple wooden coffin and the hundreds of friends, neighbors, and relatives who will soon fill it. The coffin is placed in the center of the room; there are no adornments to distract from the basic fact of death. The funeral service is held in the house or barn, a practice of the Amish for many generations. Neighbors dig the grave and all watch in silent prayer as the coffin is lowered and the grave filled with earth. Other families see to it that the mourners are fed. The Amish response to death is very much in keeping with the Amish way of life. This is expressed, for example, by the old woman who carefully washes, starches, and irons her own funeral clothing so it will be ready when the time comes. A death may occasion grief and lead to hardships for an Amish family like any others, but many of the doubts, tensions, and conflicts that have become commonplace in the larger death system seem to be absent for these people, who have developed and perpetuated a distinctive lifestyle of their own.

Social Consolidation after Death

Death does not merely subtract an individual from society. It can also challenge society's ability to survive. In relatively small societies, the impact of every death challenges the integrity of the entire group. In a mass society this challenge usually becomes obvious only when death unexpectedly strikes down a powerful leader.

The terrorist attacks of September 11, 2001, had the short-term effect of bringing people together in grief, compassion, and determination. The continuing effect is more complex and ongoing. Social consolidation, once achieved, does not necessarily endure, at least not in its initial form. For example, the government moved quickly to approve financial compensation for families of World Trade Center (WTC) victims. More than 1 year later, though, this program was subjected to fierce criticism: Few survivors had actually received benefits, and the application process seems unduly complicated and,

perhaps most disturbing, appears to regard some victims as deserving of more financial benefits than others (LeSure, 2002; Ridley, 2002). The government's mathematical formula has been roundly criticized as treating some lives as more valuable than others, thereby increasing the emotional pain of many survivors. Whatever the merits and flaws in this plan, social consolidation after the WTC deaths was seriously disrupted.

Before the terrorist attacks, there were the assassinations of John F. Kennedy, Martin Luther King Jr., and Robert Kennedy, which exemplified the types of death that shake even the largest and most powerful nations. Each of these men represented political power as well as something on a more personal and emotional level to millions of others. The manner of their deaths intensified the impact. The sudden, unexpected death of a significant person makes ordinary people feel vulnerable. Furthermore, each of these deaths was not only sudden but also violent, and not only violent but also intentional. People were shaken by the realization that even the most powerful among us were vulnerable.

One major function of the death system, then, is to meet the challenges posed to the individual and the group by loss of a member. This challenge may be of broad scope, as in a terrorist attack or the violent death of a powerful leader, or it can be as silent and personal as a death in the family:

The realtor's illness didn't appear serious, but he died a day after entering the hospital, even before testing could be completed. From that point on the family hardly seemed to be a family anymore. They went their own ways, found things to do that kept them from being home at the same time, and seldom took a meal together. At first the 16-year-old son appeared to be the least affected. He continued his usual routines, although he did spend even more time behind the closed door of his room. Within a few months, though, it was obvious that the young man was really not doing so well after all. Most of the time he barely spoke, but then he would explode in anger without known reason and stalk away. An observant teacher noticed that the only time he mentioned his father he used the present tense, as though he were still alive.

This is an example of the temporary failure of social consolidation after a death. The family had fragmented, and relatives, friends, and neighbors had also failed to provide useful support. For contrast, consider again the Amish. Consistent with their general orientations toward life and death, the Amish provide direct and long-term support to those whose lives have been disrupted by the death of a loved one. It is not a case of many people coming by to express sympathy for a short period and subsequently disappearing; instead, vital functions in the home may be taken over for months by relatives or friends until the family can get back on its feet.

Social consolidation after death is vital if the survivors are to continue as confident and competent members of the culture. Therese Rando (1993), a specialist in grief therapy, observes that a lack of social support can undermine the mourner in all areas of readjustment. Most obviously, the survivor needs emotional support in the form of consolation, encouragement, and empathy. However, support is also needed in the form of practical assistance and information.

> If others do not support reality testing and provide feedback, it will be difficult for the mourner to alter emotions, cognitions, expectations, and behaviors. Similarly, problems may arise from a lack of instrumental or practical assistance to manage tasks necessary for daily living or for readjusting to the death. (p. 432).

Coping with the loss and getting on with life are facilitated when the death system proves willing and able to lend its support to the bereaved person. The failure of social consolidation after death can contribute to many years of sorrow and stress on the part of the survivors.

Making Sense of Death

Our efforts to explain death to each other represent another important function of the death system. Some explanations are handed down from generation to generation in the form of philosophical statements, poetry, and commen-

taries on holy scriptures. There are also famous last words and scenes that have been attributed (and often misattributed) to heroes, leaders, and other celebrated people of the past. Authentic last words seldom meet the listener's need to discover or affirm a coherent meaning of death (Kastenbaum, 1993a, 2002a).

Still other explanations are passed along informally within a particular subculture or family or through successive cohorts in the military service or schools of nursing or medicine. "This is what we say and this is what we think and this is what we do." Nurses, physicians, clergy, funeral directors, insurance agents, and terrorists are socialized to express the attitudes and explanations of death that come with the trade.

Laconic statements such as "Nobody lives forever!" hardly qualify as explanations. However, much of our discourse on the subject of death is on this superficial level. Such statements might reduce the anxiety of the person who makes them through bridging what would otherwise be a tense and awkward silence. Perhaps hearing any words at all on the subject also has some value to the recipient.

I spent several days in a hospital waiting area unobtrusively listening to conversations among visitors to terminally ill friends and relatives. The conversation was usually on other matters, and most of the death-oriented talk was limited to clichés. The visitors seldom, if ever, seemed to say anything new or thought provoking to each other. Nevertheless, there was some comfort taken and some comfort given in exchanging words.

Consider the alternative. Not to have words spoken might confirm the fear that death is unspeakable and, therefore, perhaps unthinkable as well. We would feel more helpless and alienated than ever. When we can at least go through the motions of exchanging words in this difficult situation, then we are showing the ability to function under stress. We are trying to make sense of death, and this mental and emotional activity helps keep us going.

At other times, however, we are not searching for just any words about death. We are looking for the most cogent and powerful understanding possible. The kind of explanation is related to the particular questions in mind. A child, a young adult, and an aged adult might have different questions as well as different ways of evaluating possible answers. So, too, a person deeply rooted in Asian tradition and one with equally strong roots in the Western world are likely to differ in their approaches.

Making sense of death becomes an especially high-priority activity for us when our security is shattered by a death that comes to us in a circumstance (e.g., murder, accident, and suicide) or time (e.g., childhood) that undermines the way in which we interpret the world. Most of us can easily call on the range of explanations that are available to us within our particular death systems. It is more challenging, however, to examine the credentials of these various explanations and more challenging still to work toward our own explanations.

Killing

All death systems have another major function: killing. This function is carried out in many ways. Capital punishment is an obvious example. It has been practiced by many but not all cultures, with widely varying criteria for the conditions under which a person should be put to death. In recent years, there has been a general trend in Western nations to eliminate capital punishment. Ordinarily, only a few people have their lives ended by this mode, although there have been times and circumstances in which execution became a salient mode of death (e.g., the procession to the guillotine in the aftermath of the French Revolution). English criminal law, on which much of our own legal system is founded, made death the punishment for an astonishing array of offenses. In practice, however, relatively few were actually executed. Capital punishment conveys a mighty theme even when it is responsible for few deaths: *This same society that on many occasions functions to protect and prolong life will on certain occasions act on behalf of death.* Capital punishment is as susceptible to local circumstances and general social forces as any other function of the death system. Recent U.S. Supreme Court rulings have required states to review their rules and practices regarding cap-

ital punishment, and the possibility of reversing convictions on the basis of DNA evidence has also strengthened arguments against applying the death sentence.

Individual states have varied both in the crimes that are punishable by death and in the methods of execution. Hanging, once a common form of execution, is legal now only as an option in Montana and Washington. The firing squad, a dramatic remnant from the past, is still on the books in Idaho and Utah. There is no capital punishment at all in the District of Columbia, American Somoa, Guam, Puerto Rico, and the Virgin Islands, nor in the states of Alaska, Hawaii, Iowa, Maine, Massachusetts, Michigan, Minnesota, North Dakota, Rhode Island, Vermont, West Virginia, and Wyoming. Some states have abolished capital punishment while their neighboring state has not (e.g., North Dakota and South Dakota). Additionally, there are differences in the types of crime that are punishable by death. In Missouri, for example, capital punishment applies to those who commit murder in the hijacking of public conveyances or who murder employees of correctional facilities. Maryland has a concise rule: Subject to the death penalty are those who commit "first degree murder, either premeditated or during the commission of a felony." In contrast, Alabama lists "murder during kidnapping, robbery, rape, sodomy, burglary, sexual assault or arson; murder of peace officer, correctional officers, or public official; murder while under a life sentence; contract murder; murder by a defendant with a previous murder conviction; murder of a witness to a crime."

The death penalty is only the most obvious example of the death system exercising the function of a killer. Reference has already been made to the people who participate in the pet food industry. This component of the death system broadens even further when those who raise, slaughter, process, and consume "meat-bearing" animals are included. Even the casual fisherperson kills ("drowning worms," as they say), whether or not a fish is landed for the family table. Any culture that is not thoroughly vegetarian is involved to some extent in killing for food. (And isn't pulling a turnip up by its roots also a form of killing?)

Living creatures may be killed for other reasons as well. The quest for fur and feathers has brought several species to the edge of extinction. The belief that the horn of the rhinoceros can bestow sexual powers has led to the profitable slaughter of many a beast. Hunting may be pursued as an exercise in skill, a proof of manhood, or just an excuse to be outdoors. There are also consequences when hunting is restricted or banned. The Inuits native to Canada were forced to abandon their long tradition of seal hunting and have since experienced significant difficulties as a society even though they have received some benefits in compensation: Their way of life has been undermined. It is probable that all societies have many adjustments to make when they decide to alter the killing function in their death systems.

Two forms of killing deserve special attention: warfare and sacrifice.

War as a Function of Society

Warfare has brought death to millions throughout the centuries, although death has often been a consequence rather than the primary goal. Our propensity for slaughtering each other raises fundamental questions about human nature. Are we killers at heart? Is there a deep-rooted aggressive instinct that must find expression in bloody triumphs? Does war arise from situational pressures that could be reduced by improved knowledge, skills, and social organization? Does the commandment "Thou shalt not kill" express our real moral position, or is it undermined by a more basic conviction that we have the right to take the lives of others?

War has often been considered the natural state of affairs. It was taken for granted that one group would raid another's lands to steal the cattle and other valuables, and that the other group would retaliate as opportunities arose. Much of the routine fighting would take the form of raids and skirmishes. Killing and being killed were possible outcomes but not necessarily the main objectives. It was so much easier if we could surprise and scatter the enemy in order to loot at our leisure and return unharmed. However, there would also be raids of reprisal in which a previous death on one side would have to be avenged by killing somebody on the other side.

War also held true as a normal fact of life for the most sophisticated civilizations. The ancient Greek city-states were following the examples of their own gods when they took the field to sack and subdue another people. Had not their own deities triumphed over the Titans after the most awesome battles? Rome sent its legions on missions of conquest, and its successors, the Holy Roman Empire and the Byzantine Empire, both excelled in the military arts. Their holy men generally affirmed that deadly force was a right, indeed, a responsibility of the state. When the devout Thomas More introduced the concept of Utopia (1516) many centuries later, he also affirmed the legitimacy of war and its attendant taking of life: The Utopian must simply go about the business of killing in a thoughtful and cost-effective manner.

By the 18th century, a great philosopher, Immanuel Kant (1795/1932), had become convinced that *perpetual peace* was an absolute necessity and could be achieved by international organization and cooperation. Years later, however, Karl von Clausewitz (1832/1989) could still persuade many that the capacity to make war is vital to the success of any nation. The psychological dimensions of war were examined in a memorable correspondence between Albert Einstein and Sigmund Freud (1933). The physicist believed that the most critical problem facing humanity was not the nature of the physical universe but our own propensity for violence. The psychoanalyst agreed that an aggressive instinct did exist and was not likely to be rooted out of our nature. We might, however, learn to love the other in ourselves and ourselves in the other person—in other words, to experience and respect our common humanity. Having survived "the war to end all wars," Freud believed that civilization had at least one chance left to channel its aggressive tendencies to more constructive use. Alas, a few years later he was an old man dying in a foreign land (England) because the unthinkable second world war had already flamed out from his own country to engulf the world. The physicist who had feared so deeply for our ability to survive our own warlike nature would soon be known as godfather of the nuclear bomb.

We can find examples that seem to prove almost any theory of war and human violence. Religious faith, for example, can be seen to provide visions of universal human kinship and perpetual harmony or incitement for the most relentless and pitiless slaughter. War has taken the aspect of a rational instrument of state policy but also of a catastrophe we blunder into from time to time for any number of trivial reasons. No simple answer encompasses all the themes, motives, and events that have issued from warfare.

A Deadly Species

We have become ever more a deadly species as we have become more "civilized." The invention of the standing army, for example, made it possible to wage war in any season and extend the duration of the hostilities. The application of assembly-line tactics for raising livestock ensures that astounding numbers of chickens are hatched each day (17 million is one estimate) and rapidly moved along from egg to fast-food sandwich without ever having seen a barnyard. Improved technology has made it possible to conduct night warfare against each other and, as a spinoff, increase the hunter's advantage over his prey. Killing on behalf of society or one of its special interest groups is a function of the death system that thrives on organizational expertise.

The systematization of killing by the state can be seen in the careful specification of precisely how executions are to be conducted in relationship to the crime. Consider the following verdict passed on a 13th-century Englishman (cited in Jankofsky, 1979, p. 49):

Hugh Dispenser the Younger…you are found as a thief, and therefore shall be hanged; and are found as a traitor, and therefore shall be drawn and quartered; and for that you have been outlawed by the king, and…returned to the court without warrant, you shall be beheaded and for that you abetted and procured discord between the king and queen, and others of the realm, you shall be embowelled, and your bowels burnt. Withdraw traitor, tyrant and so go take your judgment, attained wicked traitor.

This example of "overkill" was not a random emotional outburst but a deliberate attempt to strengthen those in power. A respected individual who had taken the wrong (losing) side in a conflict or who was a member of the aristocracy might simply have his head severed. As a special privilege, the head of the executed might not be placed on a spike of the city gates. Capital punishment, then, could either inflict agony and heap disgrace on the condemned or be content with taking life but not reputation.

Killing by the death system—or, to put it another way, society turned killer—can take more subtle forms, and it is these forms that actually result in more deaths than capital punishment. Infant mortality in the United States, for example, has consistently been higher in families who live below the poverty level. Nonwhite subpopulations have an exceptionally higher risk, with respiratory illnesses being the most frequent cause of death. Excessive risk of death follows impoverished and socially disadvantaged people throughout their lives. For example, toxic waste dumps are often located in areas whose residents are people who are already at greater than average risk for death because of poverty and discrimination. Whether or not the term *kill* is used, the outcome of systematic deprivation may be premature death.

The United States is a society in which acts of lethal violence occur with remarkable frequency in entertainments such as films and television programs. It is also a society whose homicide rates are remarkably high when compared with other nations (see Chapter 9). However, nevertheless it is also a society that has been remarkably generous to individuals and nations in their times of crisis. For example, Arizona continues to struggle with the issue of providing dialysis treatments for undocumented Mexican immigrants who would soon die without this service. These people do not have the rights of U.S. citizens nor do they pay taxes, and dialysis is a costly medical item for a state with a major budget crisis (Johnson, 2002; Searer, 2002). So far,

Animal and human sacrifice were practiced throughout many world cultures both before and after the biblical period. Caravaggio (1603) portrays the *Sacrifice of Isaac* as described in the Old Testament.

the state of Arizona has continued funding, but the future is by no means certain. Should we try by all means to prevent a death (or, at least, extend a life)? This kind of question arises repeatedly from many sources, and our answers have been inconsistent.

Sacrifice: Killing for Life

Seldom if ever does a single function of the death system operate by itself. Sacrifice is a major example of several functions coming together with both death and life the intended outcomes.

Blood sacrifice has been an integral part of many world societies for about as long as histori-

cal record can tell us. Ancient sites in Asia, Europe, North Africa, and South America have provided evidence of human sacrifice (Benson & Cook, 2001; Carrasco, 1999; Davies, 1981; Eliade, 1978; Green, 2001). Sacrifice was intended to persuade the gods to favor their people and projects. Often, it was part of rituals to encourage fertile crops and/or protect against disaster. Sometimes the sacrifices were in the service of expeditions for conquest, war, or trade. Food, drink, objects, and animals were commonly dedicated to the gods, but human sacrifice was the most compelling offering.

Each society had its own distinctive configuration of beliefs and circumstances that provided the context for sacrifice. Nevertheless, at the core was a connection between the people's conception of the ruling powers of the universe and the belief that life can be traded for life if this transaction is mediated by death. Give the gods the vibrant lives they seek and in return they may award continued life to society.

One of the most disturbing facets of human sacrifice was also one of the more common: the ritual murder of children. Skeletal remains of sacrificed children have been found enclosed within gates, walls, fortresses, and other structures. Child sacrifice is specified in Judeo-Christian history as well. The Book of Kings tells us that when Joshua destroyed Jericho he made an ominous prophecy. The man who dares to rebuild that city "shall lay the foundation stones thereof upon the body of his first born and in his youngest son shall he set up the gates thereof." This is precisely what happened, according to scriptures, when Heil sacrificed his oldest and youngest sons as he rebuilt Jericho. A central episode in religious history is Abraham's preparation to obey god by sacrificing his son, Isaac (who, at the last moment, is replaced by an animal). Less often discussed is the fate of Jeptha's daughter. Jeptha asked God for victory in battle, vowing that he would sacrifice the first living creature he saw when returning home. Upon his victorious return, Jeptha was greeted by his daughter. His daughter (whose name is not mentioned) became a burnt offering to God: No last minute reprieve here.

Inca and Aztec rituals centered on the sacrifice of a great many people; new findings continue to be discovered (notably in Peru and northern Argentina). Young females were frequently the victims in Inca ceremonies; Aztec practices required such a large supply that their warriors were kept busy bringing back captives. Drinking the blood and eating the flesh of sacrificial victims was thought to transfer the vital energies of one person to another. The heart and other choice offerings were dedicated to the gods. In other cultures, such as ancient China and Egypt, family, government officials, and household servants were entombed along with a deceased royal personage of the first rank, the better to continue their service and companionship in the next life.

Human sacrifice has diminished considerably through the centuries. Human victims were largely replaced by animals and, then, often, by symbols, such as the small figurines placed in the later Egyptian tombs. How recently human sacrifices have been conducted and by whom is a matter of controversy. It is possible that occasional murder/sacrifices are still occurring at the hands of deranged people rather than established societies (Kastenbaum, 2002b).

Carolyn Marvin and David Ingle (1999) stirred another controversy with their analysis of patriotism. They suggest that totem-thinking still occurs in contemporary society, with national flags playing a significant role in both representing and licensing blood sacrifices through war. Their analysis and conclusions are almost certain to be repugnant to people who view patriotism as a pure and positive value, but they may nevertheless stimulate some thoughtful reflection and discussion.

HOW OUR DEATH SYSTEM HAS BEEN CHANGING, AND THE "DEATHNIKS" WHO ARE MAKING A DIFFERENCE

We have completed an overview of the death system, with particular attention to the United States. Now we ask where this system has been and where it is going. We begin with the kind of people who have emerged as counselors, educators, researchers, and change agents in the death system.

Changing Ways of Life, Changing Ways of Death

A thorough analysis of changes in death systems through the centuries would require an intensive rereading of world history. We would find a strong connection between ways of life and ways of death in every culture in every epoch. (For useful examples, see Arìes, 1981; Eire, 1995; Huizinga, 1926/1996; Laungani, 1996.) Here we use a more narrow focus. First, we will identify one of the main influences on death systems throughout history—the ways in which people died. Then, we see how the deathniks

TABLE 4-1
Modes of Dying and the Images of Death They Have Encouraged

Condition	Markers and Signifiers
The Black Death	Agony, disfiguration, partial decomposition while still alive, putrefaction >*human vanity and pride, punished and abandoned by God*
Syphilis	Facial disfiguration, dementia, moral degradation >*wages of sin.*
Tuberculosis	Death steals our breath; blood flows from our bodies, which increasingly become skeletonized >*curse of the cities and factories, but also romantic exit for beautiful, brilliant, doomed youth.*
Live burial	Imagined and occasionally actual fate of some who fainted, seized, or otherwise lost consciousness >*terror of life in death.*
Cancer	Pain, anxiety, body damage and distortion >*insidious attack by an enemy from within.*
Persistent vegetative state	Profound helplessness, inability to think or act on one's own behalf>*terror of death in life.*
AIDS	Symptoms and stigma of many of the earlier forms of catastrophic dying—blood and body fluid related, disfiguration, dementia, skeletonization, respiratory distress, plus linkage with taboo sexuality >*death embraces the most frightening experiences and outcomes that have ever haunted the imagination.*

Source: Kastenbaum (1993b, pp. 84–85).

and thanatology (the study of death) have emerged and contributed to the current death system.

Many societies have been dominated by a particular image of death. Their systems for interpreting and coping with death have centered around these images. But where do the images come from? One very important source is of interest to us here: Images of death are strongly influenced by the ways in which people die. Specifically, dominant sociocultural images of death are likely to be shaped by the types of catastrophic dying with which a society has become intimately familiar. Table 4-1 presents some of the major forms of catastrophic dying that have been known to human societies through the centuries, along with the markers and signifiers associated with each (Kastenbaum, 1993b).

It becomes easier to understand why people thought of death in a particular way when we understand the types of dying that were salient in their experiences. For example, tuberculosis was a real and present source of anxiety from the 19th century through the early part of the 20th century. People who felt helpless as loved ones lost their vitality, suffered, became emaciated, and died also had reason to fear that they might

have the same fate as a result of a disease that is more readily contagious than AIDS. The avoidance of death that became so entrenched in our culture was certainly influenced by experiences with people who died the harrowing death of a tuberculosis victim. We have already touched on one of the forms of dying that is making an impact on our current death system—the persistent vegetative state (Chapter 3). Our feelings and ideas about death are often influenced by what we know or think we know about how people die. As one or another mode of dying becomes more prominent in society, the death system is likely to change in response. Similarly, as sociocultural conditions change, the types of death that are most prominent are also likely to change. There may be no logical connection between how people die and what death means. Nevertheless, we are all likely to be influenced by the circumstances that surround death. Yesterday, the death systems of most societies were organized around the prospect of death at an early age as a result of contagious diseases and infections. Today, deaths related to lifestyle (smoking, drinking, murder, suicide, motor vehicle accidents, etc.) and to conditions associated with advanced age have become salient. Tomorrow?

The Beginnings of Death Education, Research, and Counseling

As noted in Chapter 1, the death system in the United States (and many other nations) was once devoted to avoiding even the thought of death. This situation started to change after World War II. The reality of violent death could not easily be denied, nor the loss and grief experienced by survivors. Reflective people also wondered anew about this strange race known as *Homo sapien* that periodically devotes its resources and passions to killing each other. People of religious faith were hard-pressed to discover purpose, redeeming value, and God's love and mercy in a slaughterhouse world. From the devastating experience of war and its lingering aftereffects there arose insistent questions about the meaning life, death, and personal responsibility. Increasingly more thinkers came to the conclusion that one had to come to terms with death in order to live a coherent and positive life.

There was also an increasing awareness of the private sorrows that had been experienced by many people. These included not only those who had lost loved ones in the war but also a great many others who had to remain silent about their griefs because there were so few who were willing and able to listen. Mental health specialists started to recognize that unresolved grief was a major factor in some of the behavioral and emotional problems that came to their attention.

Meanwhile, another massive problem was also working its way to the surface. Biomedical advances had led to some effective measures for reducing the risk of death. Many people who would have died quickly of virulent diseases and uncontrolled infections made prompt recoveries with the newly developed antibiotics and other "wonder drugs." However, these biomedical advances had achieved only limited results with other life-threatening conditions, such as many types of cancer and progressive neurological disorders. More people were therefore being maintained in the borderlands between life and death. These people often suffered physical pain, social isolation, and despair. The state of the art in medicine could not restore health but could keep people alive in stressful circumstances. Some health care professionals and some members of the general public became distressed and outraged by this situation. Why should people be made to suffer in this way, especially in a society that considers itself humane and technologically competent?

These were some of the issues that forced themselves into public and professional awareness. Instrumental in this movement were people from various backgrounds who broke through the taboo against acknowledging death. There were few if any "experts" in death half a century ago (although there were people with skills in specific areas, such as the funeral director). The people who taught the first classes on dying and death had never taken such courses themselves. The people who provided counseling to dying or grieving people had never received professional training for these services. The people who designed and conducted the first research projects likewise had to develop their own methods, theories, and databases. Included among these people were anthropologists, clergy, nurses, physicians, psychologists, sociologists, and social workers. Many had to overcome deeply entrenched resistances before they could offer educational or therapeutic services or gain entry for research. These pioneers of thanatology were hardy people, however, and soon made themselves understood and welcome in many quarters. Some described themselves as thanatologists (from the Greek *thanatos*, meaning death); some smiled and accepted the appellation deathnik. Mostly, they were not concerned about titles, nor did they believe that a whole new profession had to be created. Instead, the mission was, and still is, to bring concern for the human encounter with mortality into the awareness of caregivers, educators, and researchers within existing disciplines. The "nurse-thanatologist," for example, must first be a knowledgeable and skillful nurse. Few workers in this field would claim that the mission has been fully accomplished, but there is a growing cadre of people with expertise to give a hand. We will discuss death educators and counselors in later chapters and will continue to share useful contributions from researchers throughout the book.

CAUSES OF DEATH: YESTERDAY, TODAY, AND TOMORROW

A child born in 1900 had a life expectancy of approximately 47 years, a little more if a female, but considerably less (approximately 33 years) if "Black and other." By the middle of the 20th century, life expectancy had increased about another 20 years for people of all racial backgrounds. Children born in developed nations in 2001 have a life expectancy of 75 years: In the United States, it is 76.9 years. It is estimated that the youngest females will outlive their male peers by more than 5 years in the United States, and by 7 years in developed nations worldwide. Life expectancy in developed nations has also been increasing for people at age 50, 60, 70, 80, or 90. Unfortunately, fewer people survive into their later adult years in less developed nations, as documented in Table 4-2. The outlook could worsen even further in less developed nations if HIV-AIDS continues to spread, not only claiming lives directly but also contributing to the breakdown of societal and family functioning. Obviously, conditions of life have much to do with length of life. In succeeding chapters, we consider the dying process in general, and some of the specific ways in which death occurs, including suicide, accidents, disaster, murder, war, and terrorism.

BASIC TERMS AND CONCEPTS

Several terms and concepts are used frequently in presenting mortality data. Mortality refers to deaths, as distinguished from morbidity, which refers to illness. The following are several other key terms and concepts:

Life expectancy: The estimated number of years remaining in a person's life at a particular time (e.g., birth). This is an average for the population under consideration. It is useful to keep in mind that half of this population is expected to live longer and half is expected to live shorter lives than the mythical "average person."

Longevity: The average number of years between birth and death. This statistic is based on lives that have ended, as distinguished from life expectancy, an estimate of years yet to be lived. There is another meaning of this term for geneticists and other people who are concerned with the maximum possible life span: longevity as the upper limit for survival for a particular species.

Cause of death: This determination is made by a physician and recorded on the death certificate. There are three general categories: degenerative biological conditions, disease, and socioenvironmental (such as accident, suicide, and murder). In practice, these categories may overlap, and the completeness and accuracy of cause-of-death information are subject to question.

Mortality rate: (also known as *death rate*): This is a measure of the proportion of people who have died within a particular time period to the number of people in the population. The mortality rate is calculated on the basis of number of deaths either per 1,000 individuals or per 100,000 individuals within a 1-year period unless otherwise specified. (Unfortunately, both 1,000 and 100,000 are used in various statistical reports: We must be careful!) It is important not to confuse the mortality rate with

TABLE 4-2

Life Expectancy at Birth in World Regions (2001)

	Years		
Region	*All*	*Females*	*Males*
Africa	54	55	52
Asia	67	68	65
Latin America (and Carribean)	71	74	68
Europe	74	78	74
North America	77	80	74
Developed nations	75	79	72
Less developed nations	64	66	63
World	67	69	65

Source: World Health Organization, Population Reference Bureau.

a percentage. For example, in 2000, the mortality rate for motor vehicle accidents in the United States was 15.2. This does *not* mean that 15.2% of the population died in motor vehicle accidents in that year—that would be death on a catastrophic scale. It means that in a population of approximately 250 million, there were 41,804 deaths from this cause; which is still alarming but very different from the toll that would have been exacted from a *percentage* of 15.2.

Crude death rate (CDR): A measure that does not control for age. It is simply the total number of deaths divided by the number of people in a population. Much of the data on deaths are in the form of CDR, the easiest and least expensive kind of information to obtain. It is also the easiest kind of information to misinterpret. The number of deaths in a population is affected by the age structure. The United States today, for example, has a much higher proportion of elderly (i.e., long-lived) people today than was the case at the turn of the century.

Age-standardized mortality rate (ASMR): The ASMR does make adjustments for age. When data are presented in this form we can make more reliable comparisons between the death rates of various populations or even the same nation at different times. Developing nations, for example, often have a higher proportion of younger people because fewer reach the advanced adult years. Their death rate from cancer is likely to be lower, but mainly because many die of other causes first.

For the United States, census data provide the most comprehensive and accurate information on causes and rates of death. These data age somewhat in the 10 years between census reports; therefore, various techniques have been devised to provide useful estimates for the intervening years. These reports take some time to compile, so the most recent data available often date back approximately 2 years.

With this background information in mind, we can now examine changing patterns of mortality.

Death Learns to Wait: The Increase in Life Expectancy and Longevity

It has become easier to keep thoughts of death out of conscious awareness as death has loosened its grip on the young. In contrast, the aged man quoted at the beginning of this chapter had death etched in his mind in childhood as he lamented the short life of his brother, Simon. The people who reached the middle and late adult years were the survivors; most carried with them the memories of people they had loved and lost. Statistics are only statistics. Nevertheless, they help us to understand the conditions of life and how these conditions have influenced our thoughts, feelings, and behaviors regarding death.

Infants and children were at much greater risk for death in the past. Childbearing also brought a serious risk to mothers that would have to be measured not only by deaths that were directly related to pregnancy and delivery but also by those related to lingering health problems that shortened their lives. Unlike the general mortality rate, the infant mortality rate in the United States has continued to decline markedly in the past half century (Table 4-3).

The most recent data reveal the lowest infant mortality rate in U.S. history. Nations that are still struggling to establish effective human service programs for their citizens and/or have been

TABLE 4-3

Infant Mortality Rate, United States, 1940–1997

Year	Death rate per 1,000 live births
1940	47.0
1950	29.2
1960	26.0
1970	20.0
1980	12.6
1990	8.0
2000	6.9

Sources: National Center for Health Statistics and the U.S. Bureau of the Census.

ravaged by famine, political unrest, or internal violence have much higher infant mortality rates. In Bangladesh and Pakistan, for example, the infant mortality rate has exceeded 100 in recent years. Infant mortality rates are lowest in Japan (4), Finland (5), The Netherlands (6), Norway (6), and Sweden (6).

Leading Causes of Death in the United States Today

There have been changes not only in the death rate but also in the most common causes. In 1900, pneumonia and influenza (considered together) and tuberculosis were the two leading causes of death, almost equal in their toll. The third most common cause of death at this time was a set of intestinal illnesses in which diarrhea and enteritis were frequent symptoms. Twenty years later, these intestinal maladies had vanished from the list of major causes of death and have never returned. Pneumonia/influenza still topped the list: In fact, the nation and much of the world were still trying to recover from a devastating epidemic of influenza. Tuberculosis was still a major threat to life, but its death toll had declined markedly (from 194.4 to 113.1 per 100,000 between 1900 and 1920).

By 1940, heart disease had become the leading cause of death in the United States, and so it has remained. Why? Fewer people are dying young of infectious diseases. This means that more people are living long enough to develop physical problems in various organ systems, with many of these problems having an impact on the functioning of the heart and the entire cardiovascular system. Additionally, changes in the diet, activity, and stress patterns put more people at risk for heart problems—a risk that in recent years is being reduced by increased attention to diet and exercise. Cancer is another condition to which people become more vulnerable with increasing adult age. By 1940, cancer had become the second most common cause of death in the United States, and this also remains true today. The emergence of cancer cannot be attributed entirely to the "graying" of the population, however. For example, the use of tobacco products is linked to lung cancer as well as a variety of other life-threatening conditions. Lung cancer is the number one cause of cancer deaths. Approximately 100,000 men and more than 60,000 women die of lung cancer each year. Cancer death rates have been reduced by an estimated 60% for children since 1950, with slighter declines for young and middle-aged adults. The death rate has increased somewhat for older adults and is increasing markedly for African American males for reasons not yet determined.

In general, the pathway from health to death has lengthened for many people. Biographies, memoirs, and novels written 100 or more years ago often depict people going through intense life or death crises. The person would either die or pull through within a matter of days, and there was not much the physician could do in most cases, except to join in the prayers. In our own times, people often live for years with a life-threatening condition (see Chapter 5). The protracted and uncertain course of heart disease and cancer has even unsettled the way in which we speak of the at-risk person. Is this woman "dying" if, in fact, she operates a business from her home and continues to do much of the child care? Is this man "terminally ill" if he gets by with just a little assistance here and there and still enjoys a rewarding family life? Both people are afflicted with the condition that will probably be cited eventually as cause of death. Although it is likely that their lives are being shortened, they do not function from day to day as terminally ill or dying persons. Essentially, they are people who are trying to make the best of their lives in difficult circumstances.

We may also think of people in their late 80s or 90s who are alert and active yet frail. These people are also not terminally ill or dying, and it would be inappropriate to apply these terms to them. They, too, are trying to make the best of each day for as long as they can. We need to develop a new vocabulary and new concepts for describing the slow procession from vigorous life to death. A simple dying/not dying distinction is not very useful in a society in which so many people move through life resourcefully despite a variety of stresses and constraints.

Changes in causes of death and mortality rates have many implications for how we interpret and respond to people who are at particular

TABLE 4-4
Leading Causes of Death: 2000

Cause	Rate	No. of deaths
1. Heart disease	257.9	709,894
2. Cancer	200.5	551,833
3. Cerebrovascular[a]	60.3	166,028
4. COPD[b]	44.9	123,550
5. Accidents	34.0	93,592
6. Diabetes mellitus	24.9	68,662
7. Pneumonia, flu	24.3	67,024
8. Alzheimer's disease	17.8	49,044
9. Kidney disease	13.7	37,672
10. Septicemia	11.5	31,613
All causes	873.6	2,404,624

Source: National Center for Health Statistics.

[a]"Stroke" and related conditions.

[b]Chronic obstructive pulmonary disease.

risk for their lives. With these considerations in mind, we now examine the most recent data on major causes of death in the United States (Table 4-4).

Alzheimer's disease has become one of the 10 leading causes of death for the first time as the population continues to age. Several major causes have declined in age-adjusted rates: heart disease, cancer stroke, chronic liver disease, diabetes, homicide, suicide, and accident fatalities.

This overall picture does not identify what may be major causes of death at one age level but not another. For example, although HIV-AIDS is no longer on the list of 10 major general causes of death in the United States, it is among the leading causes for people between the ages of 14 and 64 and is at its peak as the fifth leading cause for those between ages 25 and 44.

Causes of Death in the Future?

As always, there are uncertainties about the future. Nevertheless, there is considerable concern among public health experts about the possibility of an increasing risk of death from infectious and contagious diseases. The trend has been toward decreased risks of death from these sources throughout much of the world. To some extent, the health care establishment and the public have relaxed (e.g., fewer parents have been making sure that their children receive inoculations against contagious diseases). Tuberculosis, however, has already shown signs of making a comeback, often in association with AIDS among people with weakened immune systems. It may be time now to "unrelax."

Additionally, diseases can now spread rapidly throughout the world so that an illness once restricted to a small and isolated area can enter the mainstream. Some public health authorities believe that the organism responsible for AIDS has had this kind of history. An alarming example of another possible epidemic has been receiving close scrutiny by physicians and researchers throughout the world. The Ebola virus, spread by blood, saliva, and feces, was first discovered in 1976 when there was a lethal outbreak in a small community in Zaire. This virus is fast-working, deadly, and without a definitive form of treatment. It reappeared in Zaire in 1995 in another brief and contained episode, but there are fears that there might be a "next time" in which the virus spreads to large population centers. Recently, the West Nile virus emerged and became a global threat, followed by SARS, a viral respiratory infection of high lethality.

Another prospect has public health authorities very much concerned: Antibiotics that have been so valuable in subduing infections are starting to lose their effectiveness. Some viruses and other microorganisms have developed resistance to the most frequently used antibiotics. The unwise use of antibiotics for minor ailments and the public's more than occasional failure to use them as directed may also be responsible for the loss of effectiveness. Perhaps we will be lucky. However, perhaps the *evolution of infectious disease* (Ewald, 1994) and *emerging viruses* (Morse, 1993) will result in a catastrophic increase in death rates.

To date, there have already been bioterrorism alarms that focus on the dangers of anthrax and smallpox (Preston, 2003), diseases with a lethal history that have been controlled by medical research and public health practices but that could

Thousands have created and millions have viewed quilts to honor the memory of those who died of AIDS.

be unleashed again by those who identify with the killing rather than the preventing and healing functions of the death system.

SUMMARY

Everything that makes a collection of individuals into a society and keeps that society going has implications for our relationship to death, as we have seen through many examples. At first, we tried to imagine a world without death. This helped us to freshen our perspective on the world in which we do live as mortals and the death system in which we participate. We may think of the death system as the interpersonal, sociophysical, and symbolic network through which an individual's relationship to mortality is mediated by his or her society. The death system of any society can be analyzed in terms of its components and functions. The components include people, places, times, objects, and symbols (including language) that have special death-related meanings. The functions include warnings and predictions, preventing death, caring for the dying, disposing of the dead, social consolidation after death, making sense of death, and killing. Each of these functions was illustrated with key examples that often revealed conflicts, biases, and strains in society (e.g., unequal protection from life-threatening conditions, the influence of lifestyle on vulnerability to death, war, and blood sacrifice). A brief historical review showed how various modes of dying (e.g., the Black Death, syphilis, and tuberculosis) have influenced society's images of death. We also became familiar with the beginnings of death education, research, and counseling.

Leading causes of death were examined after we solidified our knowledge of terms such as mortality and morbidity and the various ways in which mortality (death) rates are reported. We saw that the general mortality rate in the United States decreased throughout the 20th century, accompanied, as we would expect, by increases in longevity. Infant mortality rate is now at its lowest level in U.S. history, although it is not the lowest in the world. The 10 leading causes of death were identified (heart disease is still No. 1)—and current trends noted, such as the sharp decline in AIDS-related deaths in the past few years. New risks to life may be on the horizon, however, as several examples indicated.

REFERENCES

Ariès, P. (1981). *The hour of our death.* New York: Knopf.

Associated Press. (2002, April 3). Poor called more likely to die of breast cancer. *The Arizona Republic,* B1.

Associated Press. (2002, April 10). Thousands pay solemn respects to Queen Mother. *The Arizona Republic,* A1.

Benson, E. P., & Cook, A. G. (2001). *Ritual sacrifice in ancient Peru: New discoveries and interpretations.* Austin: University of Texas Press.

Bodio, S. (2001, September). India's disappearing vultures. *The Atlantic Monthly, 288,* 25–27.

Borenstein, S. (1999, May 11). Study urges disaster management. *The Arizona Republic,* p. A10.

Bryer, K. B. (1977). The Amish way of death. *American Psychologist, 12,* 167–174.

Carrasco, D. L. (1999). *City of sacrifice: The Aztec empire and the role of violence in civilization.* Boston: Beacon.

Clausewitz, K. V. (1984). *On war.* Princeton, NJ: Princeton University Press. (Original work published 1832)

Davies, N. (1981). *Human sacrifice in history and today.* New York: Morrow.

Einstein, A., & Freud, S. (1933). Why war? In C. James & S. Grachen (Eds.), *Collected papers of Sigmund Freud* (Vol. 4, pp. 273–287). London: Hogarth.

Eire, C. M. N. (1995). *From Madrid to Purgatory: The art and craft of dying in sixteenth-century Spain.* Cambridge, UK: Cambridge University Press.

Eliade, M. (1978). *A History of religious ideas.* Chicago: University of Chicago Press.

Ewald, P. W. (1994). *Evolution of infectious disease.* New York: Oxford University Press.

Franks, P., Clancy, C. M., & Gold, M. R. (1993). Health insurance and mortality. *Journal of the American Medical Association, 270,* 737–741.

Gibbs, W. W. (2002). *On cemetery pond.* www.sciam.com.

Green, M. A. (2001). *Dying for the gods: Human sacrifice in Iron Age and Roman Europe.* Charleston, SC: Tempus.

Holveck, J. (1991). *Grief reactions within the adolescent gang system* (Project paper). Tempe: Arizona State University, Department of Communication.

Hostetler, J. A. (1993). *Amish society.* (4th ed.). Baltimore: Johns Hopkins University Press.

Huizinga, J. (1996). *The autumn of the middle ages* (Corrected version). Chicago: University of Chicago Press. (Original work published 1926)

Jankofsky, K. (1979). Public execution in England in the late middle ages: The indignity and dignity of death. *Omega, Journal of Death and Dying, 10,* 433–458.

Jayes, R. L., et al. (1993). Do-not-resuscitate orders in intensive care units. *Journal of the American Medical Association, 270,* 2213–2217.

Johnson, E. (2002, July 6). Clock ticks for dialysis funding for immigrants. *The Arizona Republic,* B1, B2.

Kant, I. (1932). *Perpetual peace.* Los Angeles: U.S. Library Associates. (Original work published 1795).

Kastenbaum, R. (1993a). Last words. *The Monist, an International Quarterly Journal of General Philosophical Inquiry, 76,* 270–290.

Kastenbaum, R. (1993b). Reconstructing death in postmodern society. *Omega, Journal of Death and Dying, 27,* 75–89.

Kastenbaum, R. (2002a). Last words. In R. Kastenbaum (Ed.), *Macmillan encyclopedia of death and dying* (Vol. 2, pp. 515–518). New York: Macmillan.

Kastenbaum, R. (2002b). Sacrifice. In R. Kastenbaum (Ed.), *Macmillan encyclopedia of death and dying* (Vol. 1, pp. 733–737). New York: Macmillan.

Kastenbaum, R. (in press). Arise, ye more than dead!" Culture, music, and death. In C. D. Bryant (Ed.), *Handbook of thanatology.* Thousand Oaks, CA: Sage.

Kraybill, D. B. (1989). *The riddle of Amish culture.* Baltimore: Johns Hopkins University Press.

Laungani, P. (1996). Death and bereavement in India and England: A comparative analysis. *Mortality, 1,* 191–212.

LeSure, E. (2002, September 17). *WTC firm poses objections to victim compensation fund plan.* New York: Associated Press.

Marvin, C., & Ingle, D. W. (1999). *Blood sacrifice and the nation. Totem rituals and the American flag.* Cambridge, UK: Cambridge University Press.

Middleton, J. (1996). Lugbarra death. In M. Block & J. Parry (Eds.), *Death and the regeneration of life.* Cambridge, UK: Cambridge University Press.

Morse, S. S. (Ed.). (1993). *Emerging viruses.* New York: Oxford University Press.

Preston, R. (2003). *The demon in the freezer.* New York: Random House.

Rando, T. A. (1993). *Treatment of complicated mourning.* Champaign, IL: Research Press.

Ridley, A. (2002, December 11). WTC victims: What's a life worth? *Time Online Edition* (www.time.com/time/nation).

Scripps Howard. (1993, December 22). *Babies in U.S. study got radioactive shots.*

Searer, K. (2002, June 9). Death's door. Immigrants on dialysis face uncertain future. *The Arizona Republic,* B1, 2.

Smith, C. (1999, August 8). Now you can go out with bang. Ashes in fireworks give bright send-off. *Santa Rosa Press Democrat,* p. A26.

Wildlife park to add mammoth attraction. (2002, August 21). www.cnn.com/2002/TECH/8/21/clone.mammoth.

Yaukey, J. (2002, December 12). Sept. 11 panel blasts U.S. intelligence. *The Arizona Republic,* A19.

GLOSSARY

Age-Standardized Death Rate: A *mortality rate* in which age is statistically removed as a source of possible misinterpretation.

Capital Punishment: Execution carried out by the legal system in accordance with the death penalty.

Cardiovascular Resuscitation (CPR): The process of reestablishing respiration and heart action by opening the airway, performing rescue breathing, and compressing the chest, as required by the circumstances.

Cerebrovascular Accidents (CVA): Commonly known as stroke. Primary effects on speech and voluntary movement. Can be fatal.

Cohort: The name given to a set of people who were born at the same time (birth cohort) or entered a particular situation at the same time (e.g., students entering college in 2000).

COPD: Chronic obstructive pulmonary disease. Includes emphysema and chronic bronchitis, both of which progressively create "air hunger" (dypsnea).

Crude Death Rate: Not corrected for age (see mortality rate)

Life Expectancy: Estimated length of time between a specified point (e.g., birth) and death.

Death System: The interpersonal, sociophysical, and symbolic network through which society mediates the individual's relationship to mortality.

Excessive Death Rate: A measure of the extent to which the death rate of a particular population is higher than the rate that would have been expected for the population as a whole.

Longevity: Number of years between birth and death.

Microbial Agents: Bacteria and viruses.

Morbidity: Illness.

Mortality: Death. Also the condition of being vulnerable to death.

Mortality Rate: Proportion of people in a particular population who die within 1 year, based on the number of deaths per 1,000 or 100,000. Also known as death rate.

Pathologists: Physicians who specialize in examination and study of corpses (cadavers).

Radioactive Iodide: A substance used in diagnosing and treating disorders of the thyroid gland.

Thanatology: The study of death and death-related phenomena.

The deathbed scene of George Washington (1791) is attended by pulse-taking physicians rather than the angels and priests that were often depicted in the demise of celebrated people in earlier times.

chapter **5**

DYING

Transition from Life

When a person looks at you and says, "I'm going to die," they usually do die. That's what my experience has been. Somehow they know that their life is going to pass. What I found is going to help them the most is to be in there with them. From a medical perspective, we've always been taught to save everybody—get in there, resuscitate everyone. It's not always going to save them. Sometimes you're the last person they're talking to. What I've learned is: Get that family member, get that husband, get the wife, get the daughter, get the grandson, whoever that significant person who's waiting in that waiting room so anxiously, get them in there. So their last few breaths or conversation can be with that family member—not with someone who doesn't really know them.
—Noreen Levison (as quoted in Terkel, 2001, p. 42)

On average, patients spent 18 hours, 39 minutes per day alone. These seriously ill patients with poor prognoses spent most of their time in the hospital alone. Staff visits were frequent but brief.... Patients with advanced dementia and minority patients appear to have less bedside contact.
—Daniel P. Sulmasy (2002, p. 389)

You looked full of life, full of mischief, of energy, of playfulness, and laughter that Easter weekend during which your parents had to make the excruciating decision of whether to attempt another treatment or to attend as best as possible to your comfort. They opted for the former. From the admission to the hospital and the development, that very same day, of a benign infection following the introduction of the catheter to start yet another bout of chemotherapy, you were never well again. You died 5 weeks later.
—Dembour (1998/1999, p. 194)

My father died in his ninety-third year. He was alert, comfortable, and still very much himself. What he said most often to everybody was, "Thank you, thank you, thank you."
—Yohei Sasakawa, private communication (1996)

Patients in the study experienced considerable pain during most of their final 3 days of life. Communication between physicians and patients was poor.... Physicians misunderstood patients' preferences regarding cardiopulmonary resuscitation (CPR) in 80% of the cases. Furthermore, physicians did not implement patients' refusals of interventions.
—"Improving Care" (1995, p. 1635)

Whatever we do—people still die.
—Shigeaki Hinohara (1996)

All these observations have to do with what most physicians call terminal illness and what the rest of us call dying. Hinohara, at age 87 one of the world's most distinguished physicians, has a wealth of personal and professional experiences to draw on. He quietly reminds us that it may not be wise to overestimate what can be accomplished in preventing death, especially if this leads to the neglect of humane care for dying people. Not all health care professionals have made their peace with the inevitability of death. Emergency room nurse Noreen Levison had to overcome the pressured expectation that every life can be saved before she could find a way to be of significant help to people she had just met who were soon to inhale their last breath.

Sulmasy's study (2002) set off a new wave of comment, much of it defensive, when he reported that seriously and terminally ill hospitalized patients spend almost all their time alone. This was hardly news, however, to people who were familiar with hospital interaction patterns, and it was, in fact, one of the uncomfortable facts that inspired the hospice/palliative care movement (Chapter 6). Note that frequent brief visits by nurses and specialists are usually intended to

monitor the patient's condition and the equipment that is in use: 2 or 3 minutes can be sufficient to carry out this mission. This leaves unanswered, though, the question of what other needs the patient might have other than basic physical care.

The editorial in the *Journal of the American Medical Association* ("Improving Care," 1995) was commenting on an earlier and much more extensive study that found there are still "substantial shortcomings" in the care of seriously ill hospitalized patients, including those with a terminal illness (SUPPORT, 1995). The study and its accompanying editorial represent the continuing efforts of the medical establishment to improve the quality of life for seriously ill and dying patients. Should we be surprised that the medical profession is still struggling with the issue of providing compassionate care to dying people a century after this need was clearly identified by Sir William Osler, one of the most respected practitioners of his time? (Golden, 1997/1998).

Sasakawa is the executive director of a major philanthropic organization that has a special interest in quality of life issues. His late father, founder of the organization, lived and died peacefully after a life of significant achievement and service. Such examples demonstrate that death does not have to be regarded as failure on the part of either physician or patient.

In contrast, Isaline was a 2-year-old whose life ended too soon. Neither her parents nor the medical team could bring themselves to regard her as terminally ill. The health care system did everything it could to keep her alive and therefore did little to provide comfort in her last days. Isaline is one of many people, young and old, who cannot easily be classified as terminally ill but who face significant threats to their lives.

In this chapter, we consider dying not as an abstraction but as an experience that takes many forms depending on the nature and management of the illness, the social support system available, and the unique person whose life is in jeopardy. Perhaps we should remind ourselves at the outset that how and when we die are influenced by societal practices as well as physical disorders. For example, it has been found that hospitalized patients are more likely to die when either an understaffed nursing (Aiken, Clarke, Sloane, Sochalski, & Silber, 2002) or medical (Pronovost et al., 2002) service is trying to cope with excessive demands on its time and energy. We can see at once that staff members have less opportunity to be at the bedside when time pressure is intense, thereby contributing to the long periods of loneliness for seriously ill patients. Why do hospitals often have fewer nurses and physicians available than called for by the situation? To answer this question, we would need to delve systematically into the economics of health care and other facets of our society—in other words, into the way the American death system works. We will also be touching on some of the ways in which personal as well as societal lifestyles affect the timing and manner of our lives. For example, negative emotions have been found to endanger health by undermining or overwhelming our immune systems (Kiecolt-Glaser, McGuire, Robles, & Glaser, 2002). If negative emotions are part of our daily experiences, we are more likely to encounter life-threatening experiences and more likely to lose that battle. It is unlikely that we can understanding dying by focusing only on dying: We must also consider the total pattern and meaning of the life that is coming to an end.

DYING AS TRANSITION

Dying is one of many transitions that we experience in our lives. This means that we can call on what we already know from other new experiences and transitional situations. For example, most of us have already experienced our first day of school, our first date, our first solo ride behind the wheel of a car, and our first day on the job. Many of us have moved on to such other memorable transitions as the first time we have held our baby or discovered our first gray hair.

We all experience transitions in our lives. Some may have been long awaited ("At last, I'm old enough for a driver's license!"). Some may have been dreaded ("Do I actually have to support myself now?"). Many transitions are tinged with ambivalence ("I'm kinda ready to get married, sort of, but sort of not"). The transition from life is unique because the separation is so complete and so final. However, the dying process does have aspects in common with other types of transition: There are interactions that can either be upsetting or comforting, communications that can either inform or confuse, and self-evaluations that can either undermine or strengthen one's sense of identity. It follows that the transition from life is unique for every individual. No two people bring the same thoughts, feelings, accomplishments, and illness-related experiences. Furthermore, no two people have the same set of human relationships. The quality of life during the final illness depends much on the quality of the individual's relationships with others and the availability of those who are most capable of providing comfort and support.

As we develop an overview of the dying process, attention is given first to the basic question of what dying is and when it begins. Next, we examine some of the different "trajectories" or forms the dying process can take. The challenge of distinguishing between terminal illness and "at risk" is considered, with particular attention to hemophilia. The challenge of communicating well throughout the dying process is then explored, including attention to the problems reported in the *Journal of the American Medical Association* study. The influences of age, gender, interpersonal relationships, disease, treatment, management, and environment are considered.

This is followed by an exploration of stage theory and other models of the dying process, including a new multiple perspective approach that identifies important parallels between dying and other experiences with which most of us are more familiar. We conclude with attention to the vigorous effort to improve care of the dying that is being brought to national attention by a nonprofit organization, Last Acts.

This is a good time to pause and consider dying from a very personal perspective. I suggest that you give your attention now to the thought exercise outlined in Box 5-1. Why not try this exercise right now? It has proven helpful to other people who were also starting to study dying and terminal care. The questions raised in this exercise are taken up later in the text, and your instructor will have other observations to add.

WHAT IS DYING AND WHEN DOES IT BEGIN?

Individual and Interpersonal Responses

What is dying? When does it begin? The knowledge that "I am dying" introduces many changes in the individual's view of self and world.

A New England artist (Lesses, 1982/1983) who was terminally ill described the comfortable familiarity of her home:

I live with an oak coffee table
beside my bed where

my silver-framed clock ticks hard
through the night
like my cat when she purrs.

However, this sense of comfort could not disguise the fact that her life had changed decisively:

I hate every morning
hating it
with my stomach jumping
before I've had a chance to think
of anything I awake non-thinking and I am
like a small animal backed into the corner
of a cage to escape from the hand clutching,
reaching through the wire door
I feel the power of the hand's grasp
and fear it
without knowing what the power is.

Other terminally ill people have different experiences to report, but the feeling that "How I live now is not as I lived before" is difficult to escape. The lives of close friends and relatives are also affected, and their responses in turn affect the terminally ill person. Consider Greg, a college student I remember well through the years. Greg lived more than 2 years with the knowledge that he would probably die in the near future. He suffered from a form of leukemia that was unusually puzzling to his physicians. Greg recognized that the disease was his central problem, but often he was more concerned about the ways in which other people related to him:

I have had to develop almost a whole new set of friends. My good old buddies just felt awfully un-

---

BOX 5-1
YOUR DEATHBED SCENE

A Thought Exercise

They are planning a movie about your life. This film is intended to be as faithful as possible to the facts. Help them plan the deathbed scene. Describe the ending of your life in as much detail as you can, based on what you expect is most likely to happen. It would be best if this description is complete enough to help locate the setting, the time, who else might be on the scene, and anything else that is needed. (Yes, of course, they are giving you lots of money for your cooperation, but you are in control of planning this scene according to your best guess at what the future will bring.)

Please use a separate sheet of paper for this exercise.

comfortable around me. They couldn't be themselves anymore. I realized they'd be relieved if I would just sort of drift away from them.

What seemed to disturb Greg's friends most was the discrepancy and ambiguity. Greg was a powerfully built young man who had been healthy and vigorous for most of his life. His sturdy appearance made it difficult to accept that he was in the grip of a life-threatening disease. None of the "good old buddies" could relate to both facts: that Greg looked healthy and functioned well and that he was also terminally ill. Most of his friends and family chose to relate only to the healthy Greg:

> I guess it was my own fault. If I wanted to make things easier for everybody, I could have just shut up about my condition. But I didn't think I had to. I mean, you talk about important things with your best friends, don't you? I didn't go on and on about it. When something new happened, or I started feeling shaky about it, I would say something. Oh, man—They just couldn't handle it!

Greg posed a problem for his friends as well as his physicians. He touched on his illness often enough to make it difficult for his friends to ignore it, but often he looked well enough. When he had an acute episode, he would be in the hospital. Afterward he would keep to himself for a while. "I didn't like to show my face around when I felt rotten," he said. This pattern crossed his friends' expectations. Everybody knew that a dying person looks different, so Greg should have looked different. Similarly, it was assumed that dying was the last thing a dying person would want to talk about. A young man might be expected to be especially keen to preserve his "macho" image by concealing any signs of pain, weakness, or fear. Greg was a deviant, then, in behaving as a dying young man should not.

In contrast, Matilda D. was depleted by many years of illness and seemed too frail to survive much longer (Kastenbaum, Barber, Wilson, Ryder, & Hathaway, 1981). She was admitted to a geriatric hospital at age 86 suffering from painfully advanced rheumatoid arthritis, anemia, and difficulty in taking and utilizing nutrition. Attentive nursing care enabled her to remain relatively stable for several months, but Matilda's condition gradually worsened. Most of her time was spent sleeping or lying on her bed in considerable discomfort. At this point she was regarded as "failing" but not dying. This distinction was meaningful to staff members because it indicated to them what pattern of care would be most appropriate. They did not face the ambiguity with which Greg's friends and the significant others in the chemotherapy study had to contend. Furthermore, the staff (and Matilda's daughter, her only visitor from the community) also expected that dying and death would soon follow. This again contrasts with Greg and the chemotherapy patients for whom there was some hope of recovery or remission.

Matilda was officially considered a dying person when her lungs started to fill with fluid and her general condition weakened. The next "proper" action was to relocate Matilda to the intensive care unit (ICU). Although some patients were treated successfully for a medical crisis in the ICU, it also served as the tacitly approved exit ward. Matilda's status change to a dying person meant that she would be moved to a death place. (When a facility has an agreed on "death place," then it is possible to maintain the illusion that death will not visit elsewhere.) Her new status could also be seen in an altered pattern of staff interactions. Basic care was still provided in a conscientious, professional manner, but the contacts were now briefer and more mechanical. The subtle change from a living to a dying person had taken place in the perceptions and actions of staff members. The certainty of her death made it easier for staff to shift their patterns.

Fortunately, Matilda's life did not end with the isolation and dehumanization that might have been suggested by this description. We had started a therapeutic companion program to help provide residents with a core relationship through which they might regain their sense of personhood and control. Andrea George had formed a close relationship with Matilda just before the failing and dying sequences. There was time to discover some of Matilda's distinctive personal qualities and values. Her therapeutic companion and her daughter continued to relate to Matilda as a distinctive human being even when the old woman could no longer respond in words. Matilda's favorite music was sung and played to her, and she died literally in touch with two people for whom she remained a distinctive and valued person.

We treat people differently when they are perceived as dying. When Lester (1992/1993) replicated a study conducted in the mid-1960s, he found that undergraduates still prefer to keep a large social distance between themselves and people who are dying of cancer, in pain, or suicidal. People dying of AIDS-related complications were subject to even more vehement exclusionary attitudes than terminally ill people in general. Personal background and education can affect our perception of the dying person as well. Although most registered nurses have accepting attitudes toward people with AIDS, negative attitudes were found among nursing assistants and licensed practical nurses who had less education and less preparation for working with terminally ill people (Demmer, 1999).

Both the classification of a person as "dying" and the particular modality of death influence our willingness to associate with that person. For example, nurses took a significantly longer time before going to the bedside of a dying patient compared with other patients. The nurses were surprised and upset when they learned of their differential pattern of response and decided to make a special effort to respond promptly to terminally ill patients. After a few weeks, however, the original pattern reinstated itself (LeShan, 1982). As much as they wanted to treat all patients equally, the nurses could not avoid being influenced by society's fear of contact with dying people.

Onset of the Dying Process: Alternative Perspectives

When dying begins depends on our frame of reference. The proposition that *we die from the moment we are born* could be useful in developing a personal philosophy of life, but it encourages evasion. Often, this "We are always dying" perspective is simply a way of reducing our own discomfort and anxiety. It is also questionable as a direct statement of fact. It is true that there is a continual sequence of death among the cells that

comprise our bodies. The outer layer of the skin, for example, is composed of dead cells that are replaced in turn by other dead cells. Certain forms of tissue death are programmed to occur at particular times in psychobiological development. The loss of the umbilical cord after birth is one of the clearest examples of a biological structure phasing itself out after its function has been served. Nevertheless, it would be misleading to insist that the normal turnover of cells and the atrophy of unnecessary structures constitute a process of dying for the organism as a whole. Should the term dying be used so loosely, we would simply have to find a new term to represent the very different processes observed when life actually is in jeopardy.

A more challenging concept has been with us for many years. Three centuries ago, Jeremy Taylor, chaplain to King Charles I of England, likened aging to a form of terminal illness (Taylor, 1651/1977). The concept of *aging as dying* has more impact than the proposition that dying begins with life. It is also interesting to consider Taylor's suggestion that aging might be regarded as slow dying and dying as fast aging. However, elderly people cannot be described as dying without ignoring the vigor and vitality that many continue to express at an advanced age. It is also difficult to equate dying with aging when we examine the details. For example, a young person may die because of a specific bodily failure (e.g., an unexpected drug reaction or heart failure) even though he or she was otherwise in good health and did not resemble an aged person at all.

Dying usually begins as a psychosocial event. Organ systems fail, but it is in the realm of personal and social life that dying occurs. We construct the idea of dying from many experiences, communications, and related concepts. Let us now consider some of the contexts in which the onset of dying is discovered or certified:

1. *Dying begins when the facts are recognized.* The physician's office is visited by people with varying types of concern for their health. Included are essentially healthy people who have been convinced for years that they are dying and the person who has come in for a routine checkup (the latter may be the one who actually has a life-

The stress of anxious waiting is a common experience in medical facilities.

threatening illness that is about to be discovered). Perhaps, then, the dying process begins when the physician observes it. However, the physician in turn is likely to rely on clinical and laboratory diagnostic procedures. From this perspective, the dying process begins when the physician has obtained and analyzed enough information to make such a judgment. The physician might suspect that the patient has been on a "terminal trajectory" for some time before the diagnostic evaluation was established. However, this had not been "official" dying; it is only now that the person is considered a dying patient.

2. *Dying begins when the facts are communicated.* There is a major difference between the physician's prognosis and the patient's awareness. Perhaps, then, it would make more sense to date the onset of the dying process from the moment at which the physician informs the patient. The ac-

tual situation is even more complicated. There is likely to be an interval between the physician's determination of the prognosis and the time when it is shared with the patient. Physicians seldom break the news at the same instant they reach their conclusions. There may be a delay of days, weeks, or even months before the physician tells the patient what has been found. Furthermore, sometimes the physician never does tell the patient. Therefore, we cannot entirely depend on the physician's communication as the definitive starting point of the process from the patient's standpoint. However, even when the physician does share the findings with the patient, can this be taken firmly as the onset of the dying process? Not necessarily: The patient must be ready and able to understand the prognosis.

3. *Dying begins when the patient realizes or accept the facts.* More than one nurse has returned from

the bedside of a patient almost bursting with anger at the physician. "Why hasn't he leveled with this patient? This man is dying, and nobody has told him what's going on!" At times, this concern is well justified. The physician has not provided the terminally ill patient with a clear statement of the condition. At other times, however, the patient's apparent lack of knowledge cannot be laid at the physician's doorstep. The patient was told but "didn't stay told." Somehow the patient was able to forget or misinterpret the central facts, or perhaps the physician said one thing with words and something else with facial expression and tone of voice.

The physician's communication can be subtle or direct, couched in clear language or technical jargon. After an interaction with the physician, the patient may either have a clear understanding or be left in a state of uncertainty and confusion. There can be another time lag, then, between communication and realization of terminal illness.

For examples of poor and competent physician–patient communication, see Box 5-2.

Communication may fail because the patient has lost the ability to process information and understand concepts adequately. There are many situations in which it is not easy to determine how much the patient does understand. My colleagues and I found that many aged patients who appeared to be completely unresponsive were capable of responding when approached with patience and touch-enhanced communication (Kastenbaum, 1992). Jansson, Norberg, Sandman, Athlin, and Asplund (1992/1993) used videotapes to demonstrate that communication is possible with terminally ill people even when they are suffering from Alzheimer's disease, if caregivers are attentive to nonverbal as well as verbal responses. These patients may not be able to understand that they are dying but nevertheless be appreciative of compassionate human contact. Ann Hurley and Ladislav Volicer (2002) strongly urge that family and other caregivers of

---

BOX 5-2
"BREAKING THE BAD NEWS": PHYSICIAN–PATIENT COMMUNICATION

How Not To	*A Better Way*
Give the bad news right away and get it over with.	√ Take the time to establish a relationship with the patient and family.
Give all facts at one time.	√ Share a fact, see how the patient responds, and wait until one fact has been "digested" before going on.
Impress patients and family with your medical knowledge.	√ Keep it simple. Don't "snow" them with details unless they ask for more details.
Tell the diagnosis, then move on.	√ Take the time to discover what this diagnosis means to the patient; explain and educate.
End the session after you have told all.	√ Allow pauses, breathing spaces so patient/family can ask questions.
Make sure you have broken through denial.	√ Respect what may seem like denial; the message will be heard when the patient is ready.
Stretch the truth if necessary to cheer up the patient.	√ Do not say anything that is not true; this destroys trust and sets up later anger and sorrow.
Make it clear that there is nothing more we can do for the patient.	√ Make it clear that you will be with the patient all the way and respond to his or her needs and desires.

people with Alzheimer's prepare them to cope with the progression of the disease in the early stages, including ways of asking for help in understanding when needed.

A person is not dying to himself or herself until the situation has been realized and personalized. In this sense, the dying process cannot be dated from the medical prognosis or from the act of official communication, if there is one. We must be aware of the individual's thoughts and feelings. This can lead to disagreement as to whether or not a person knows. For example, a terminally ill person may talk about a minor symptom. This may lead me to assume that the patient is not aware of the more critical situation that threatens life. However, someone else may notice that the patient slips into the past tense when talking about family and occupational life, suggesting an absence of projection into the future. We come to different conclusions based on different observations. Perhaps I did not make that additional observation because I wanted to believe that the patient was unaware of her terminal prognosis.

Disagreements may also arise because the terminally ill person, like anybody else, behaves differently depending on the situation. A different attitude toward the illness may be expressed to a member of the immediate family than to a physician, a colleague, or a stranger. Most of the health care staff may be under the impression that the patient does not know, but one nurse may realize that the patient is keenly aware of the situation and has selected that nurse as the person with whom to share his or her innermost thoughts and feelings.

Additionally, the person's own estimation may shift from time to time. "Middle knowledge" (Weisman, 1993) is an awareness that floats from one level of consciousness to another. The individual suspects or senses what is taking place but is hesitant to put these thoughts into clear focus. Depending on our relationship with the person and the situation in which we are interacting together, we might come away either with or without the impression that the patient sees himself or herself as dying.

4. *Dying begins when nothing more can be done to preserve life.* This is a pragmatic definition that has important consequences for the care of very ill people. The physician may not have classified the person as dying despite the diagnostic signs because avenues of treatment remain open. "I haven't tried all possible combinations of drugs," the physician may reason, or "Building the patient up with transfusions might make her a better candidate for another surgical procedure." Perhaps this patient could be one of the rare survivors. This often happens when the medical and nursing staff has an exceptionally strong motivation to keep the patient alive (e.g., a child or a person of their own age and background). (This reluctance to define a patient as dying can stand in the way of discussing the possibility of hospice care, see Chapter 6.) Furthermore, the family physician may have a different opinion from the specialist, and one specialist may have a different opinion from another. Some members of the medical team may decline to think of the patient as terminally ill as long as there is one more procedure that might be tried.

The judgment that a person is dying could be considered premature if it discourages actions that might have lead to recovery. As late as the 18th century in a city as sophisticated as London, special efforts had to be made to persuade the establishment that victims of drowning could be restored by prompt treatment. In contrast, we might conclude that the classification of a person as dying has been delayed too long if painful and socially isolating treatments are continued beyond reasonable hope of success and therefore prevent the person from living his or her final days as he or she might have chosen. *When* to shift from "prevention of death" to "care of the dying" and how to accomplish this shift in an effective and humane manner are questions that hinge in part on our definition of dying.

TRAJECTORIES OF DYING: FROM BEGINNING TO END

We have been exploring the onset of the dying process as interpreted by the various people involved. Chapter 6 examines in detail the hospice approach, with its emphasis on the home and family. Here, the emphasis is on the most common pathways to death—those that conclude in a health care facility.

A series of pioneering studies by Barney Glaser and Anselm Strauss (1966, 1968) observed interactions with dying people in six medical facilities in the San Francisco area. Keep in mind that field researchers do not have the responsibility for patient care that occupies the energies of the hospital staff. Furthermore, the researchers are not the husbands, wives, or children of a dying patient, nor are they terminally ill themselves. This emotional distance gives field researchers a limited but unique perspective.

The San Francisco research team organized many of their observations according to the concept of *trajectories of dying*. All dying processes take time; all have a certain shape through time. For one person, the trajectory could be represented as a straight downward line. For somebody else, it might be represented more accurately as slowly fluctuating, going down, leveling off, declining again, climbing a little, and so on.

Certainty and Time

Staff members must answer two questions about every patient whose life is in jeopardy: "Will this patient die?" and "If so, when?" These are the questions of *certainty* and *time*. The questions are important because the attitudes and actions of the health care staff are based largely on what they take to be the answers. It is easier for the staff to organize around the patients when the answers are clear. Like other bureaucratic organizations, hospitals rely heavily on standard operating procedures. It is uncomfortable when a patient's condition does not lend itself to straightforward expectations, such as "This man will recover" or "This woman will die, but not for some time."

The time framework can vary a great deal. In the emergency room, the staff's initial uncertainty can change to certainty in just a few minutes. The fate of a premature baby may be determined in a few hours or a few days, but the outlook for a cancer patient may remain indeterminate for months.

Together, certainty and time yield four types of death expectation:

1. Certain death at a known time
2. Certain death at an unknown time
3. Uncertain death but a known time when certainty will be established
4. Uncertain death and an unknown time when the question will be resolved

The Glaser–Strauss research team found that staff interaction with patients is closely related to the expectations they have formed about time and certainty of death. These expectations are important even when they do not prove to have been correct because they form the basis for interactions among staff members as well as with patients and their families. Especially important are situations in which staff expectations change. One of the examples given is that of a physician's decision to discontinue blood transfusions. The nurses may reject this hint and continue to do everything in their power to give the patient another chance. This sequence has significant implications no matter who (physician or nurse) has made the more accurate assessment of the patient's condition. The subtle pattern of communication among staff in such a case affects everybody (Glaser & Strauss, 1968):

> Since the doctor had said nothing official, even nurses who believe the patient is dying can still give him an outside chance and stand ready to save him. They remain constantly alert to counterclues. "Everybody is simply waiting," said one nurse. If the doctor had indicated that the patient would die within the day, nurses would have ceased their efforts to save him, concentrating instead on giving comfort to the last, with no undue prolonging of life. (p. 11)

It is possible, then, for one member of the treatment team to come to a conclusion but still leave room for others to follow an alternative course. In the instance cited, the physician did not carelessly forget to instruct the nurses to alter their approach. By putting nothing into words, the physician allowed a little leeway for others to continue their efforts to maintain life against the odds. The physician, then, had decided that the *prevention* function of the death system could not be achieved but offered the nurses some maneuvering room to maintain the possibility of a reprieve while devoting most of their efforts to the *caring and comforting* function.

We can increase our awareness of the varying patterns of communication that accompany the

Isabel Espinoza has been on dialysis since her kidneys failed. She is not a U.S. citizen and faced termination of her life-prolonging treatment because of budget problems in the Arizona health-care system. The state did continue to fund her treatment, but economic issues continue to influence the care of life-threatened people throughout the nation.

dying process by considering three of the dying trajectories identified by the Glaser–Strauss research team: lingering trajectory, expected quick trajectory, and unexpected quick trajectory.

The Lingering Trajectory

The caregivers display a characteristic pattern when a patient's life is slowly fading. Seldom is there a dramatic rescue scene. The staff tries to keep the patient comfortable but is inclined to believe that it has already done "all that we can," and that the patient has "earned" death after a long downhill process. It would be unusual, for example, to find a team of specialists rushing into the geriatric ward to perform heroic measures. A

quiet fading away seems to be both expected and accepted by the staff as a fit conclusion to the lingering trajectory.

Perhaps the death that terminates a lingering trajectory is more acceptable because the person was considered *socially dead* (Sweeting & Gilhooly, 1991/1992). Some patients (almost always the more responsive) tend to be considered more alive than others. Staff members also become attached to some patients more than others through the months. For every patient who has somehow attracted the special attention and sympathy of staff members, however, there are others whose distinctive human qualities have not been perceived by staff or affirmed by friends and relatives. More people on the lingering trajectory are aware of their social death than might be realized. "You're as good as dead when they put you behind the fence. That's why they went and put up the fence!" This observation was made to me by the resident of a large geriatric facility that, in fact, had recently been fenced off from the community. "Life's on that side. We're on the other." From what I was starting to see, he was filing an accurate report.

Patients on a lingering trajectory seldom have much control over the management of their condition. Visits from family members generally fall off sharply when the lingering trajectory has become established. The slowly dying person seldom speaks of final things to family and friends—or to anybody. Staff members tend to assume that the patient also moves rather gently toward death (Glaser & Strauss, 1968):

> These patients drift out of the world, sometimes almost like imperceptibly melting snowflakes. The organization of work emphasizes comfort care and custodial routine, and is complemented by a sentimental order emphasizing patience and inevitability. (p. 64)

However, the picture is not always so tranquil. Occasionally, there is a patient, family member, or staff member who does not accept the impending death. Glaser and Strauss also noticed incidents in which a next of kin would upset the staff by showing "too much emotion" after the patient died. Perhaps strong reactions to a patient's death challenged the staff's assumption that the social loss of a "lingerer" did not amount to much.

The patience of family and/or staff may be strained when a patient fails to die on schedule. My first experience with this phenomenon occurred many years ago when the daughter of an aged patient strode angrily back from his ward and complained, "They said he was on the death list, so I came here as soon as I could. And there he was—you can see for yourself! Sitting up in bed and playing cards. And winning!" There had been a misunderstanding. A member of the hospice staff had informed the daughter that her father was on the "D.L.," a term that actually means "danger list." Nevertheless, the main problem was that the daughter did have reason

to believe that her father was close to death and had organized her emotions accordingly. After a few minutes of cooling off, she made it clear that she did not really want her father dead, but that it was difficult to keep thinking of him as all but dead and waiting "for the other shoe to drop."

The lingering trajectory has the advantage of giving both the patient and the family time—time to grow accustomed to the idea of dying, to make plans, to work through old conflicts and misunderstandings, to review the kind of life that has been lived, and so on. However, this trajectory can also have the disadvantage of attenuating relationships and creating situations in which the person is perceived as not quite alive and yet not securely dead. The lingering trajectory is not the image of dying that usually seizes the imagination of the media and the public; however, it is becoming the most typical pattern in Western society, especially in nursing care facilities.

The Expected Quick Trajectory

Time is truly of the essence when a patient is perceived as being on an expected quick trajectory. The staff organizes itself to make the most effective use of the time that remains on the side of life. This contrasts vividly with the leisurely pattern of care and staff organization that surrounds the patient on a lingering trajectory. Staff definitions of the situation can change rapidly; for example, "He is out of immediate danger but probably will not survive very long" changes to "I think he has passed the crisis point and has a real chance of pulling through."

Several types of expected quick trajectories were observed, each accompanied by a different pattern of interaction with the staff. In a *pointed trajectory,* the patients are exposed to very risky procedures, that might either save their lives or result in death. In this situation, the staff often has enough time in advance to organize itself properly. The patient may also have the opportunity to exercise some control and options (e.g., share precious minutes with a loved one and see that certain personal matters are acted on). In contrast, *the danger-period trajectory* requires more watching and waiting. The question is whether or not the patient will be able to survive a stressful experience, such as high-risk surgery or a major heart attack. The patient may be unconscious or only partially aware of the surroundings compared with the alert state of a patient with a pointed trajectory. The danger period can vary from hours to days. This is the type of situation in which the family may remain at bedside or in the corridor, with doctors, nurses, and monitoring devices maintaining their vigilance.

The *crisis trajectory* imposes still another condition on the patient and everybody else. The patient is not in acute danger at the moment, but his or her life might suddenly be threatened at any time. The tension will persist until the patient's condition improves enough so that he or she is out of danger or until the crisis actually arrives and rescue efforts can be made.

Different from all these is the *will-probably-die trajectory*. The staff believes that nothing effective can be done. The aim is to keep the patient as comfortable as possible and wait for the end to come, usually within hours or days. In recent years, there has been an increase in administrative pressure to move will-probably-die patients to units or facilities that require less expensive resources: "Open this bed for somebody who really needs it!" People who are not quite ready to die are perceived as just taking up expensive space in a cure-oriented medical center.

Problems also arise in connection with the expected quick trajectory. For example, the family is likely to be close by the patient and their presence confronts the staff with increased demands for interaction and communication. What should those people in the waiting room be told? Who should tell them? Is this the time to prepare them for the bad news, or can it be postponed a little longer? Should all the family be told at once, or is there one person who should be relied on to grasp the situation first? The staff must somehow come to terms with the needs of the family while still carrying out treatment. This situation challenges the staff's stamina, judgment, and communication skills. In my experience, however, the presence of the family can also be helpful to the staff and, more important, to the patient as well. The presence of a familiar and supportive person can make a powerful difference to a person for whom death seems to be in near prospect.

The most salient features of the expected quick trajectory are time urgency; intense organization of treatment efforts; rapidly shifting expectations; and volatile, sensitive staff–family interactions. In the midst of this pressure, errors can be made. For example, as Glaser and Strauss observed, there may be attempts to save a patient from a disease he or she does not have. A person may arrive at the hospital in critical condition with no medical history available to guide the staff. The pressure of time may then force medical personnel to proceed on the basis of educated guess rather than secure knowledge. Imagine the pressure faced by the staff when they have to cope with several expected quick trajectories while also caring for patients with different needs.

Whether or not there is a chance to save the patient's life sometimes depends on the resources of a particular hospital or even a particular ward at a particular time. The lack of an oxygen tank or a kidney machine can make the difference between the will-probably-die trajectory and one with more hope. Ask around in your area: Where would health care professionals prefer to be taken if they were in a serious accident or had some other type of medical emergency? They will probably identify significant differences in equipment and staffing that could make a life-or-death difference. The perceived social value of the endangered person can also be the difference between an all-out rescue attempt and a do-nothing orientation. This is especially apt to happen when the medical team has pressing decisions to make about who will receive emergency treatment first or be given the benefit of life-support apparatus that is in short supply. "When a patient is not 'worth' having a chance," say Glaser and Strauss (1968), "he may in effect be given none" (p. 72).

The definition of dying that we construct, then, is no less critical at the end than the beginning. Furthermore, social stereotypes that hold that one person is more important than another (whether on the basis of age, sex, race, occupation, economic status, or whatever) can play a decisive role in the death system when quick decisions must be made about priority and extent of life-sustaining effort.

The Unexpected Quick Trajectory

The significance of the interpersonal setting in which dying takes place is emphasized again by the *unexpected quick trajectory*. The experienced emergency room team adjusts quickly to situations that might immobilize most other people. However, the appearance of the unexpected quick trajectory in other areas of the same hospital can spark a crisis. On these wards, there is less preparation for emergency, and personnel may experience a "blow up" (Glaser & Strauss, 1968, p. 121). Perhaps Weisman's concept of middle knowledge should be applied to personnel as well as to terminally ill patients. The staff in nonemergency areas knows but does not believe that a life-or-death situation might arise at any moment. In this sense, something really does blow up when a patient unexpectedly enters a crisis phase on the "wrong" ward—the staff's security-giving myth of an orderly and manageable universe.

Some unexpected deaths are more disturbing than others. The "medically interesting case" is one of the most common examples. The staff is more likely to be taken aback and regret the death of a patient who presented unusual features to them. Personnel also tend to be affected more by the death of a patient whose life they had tried especially hard to save. This is not the same as mourning the loss of a patient as a person. Glaser and Strauss report that it is the "poor physician who tried so hard" who receives the sympathy of other staff members rather than the patient. The patient may have never seemed like an individual human being to the staff during intensive life-saving efforts. The patient who dies for the wrong reasons also dismays and alarms the staff. Treatment may have been focused on one critical aspect of the patient's condition while death was approaching through a different route.

The staff's need to shield itself against surprise is a major theme that runs through observations of the unexpected quick trajectory. Everybody in a life-threatening situation has a need to exercise control—professional staff as well as patient and family. This need often leads both to an *illusion of control* and to persistent efforts to maintain the illusion. Patients have reported how hard they have sometimes worked to help the doctors give the impression they have everything under control (Kastenbaum, 1978). Unfortunately, the well-practiced and institutionally supported defenses of the physician or nurse may become dangerously exaggerated or suddenly give way when reality punctures the illusion.

The hospital can precipitate an unexpected quick trajectory. Glaser and Strauss observed confusion in the mobilization of treatment resources, the turning of attention away from other patients to concentrate on an urgent case, accidents attributable to carelessness or poor safety practices, and a variety of problems that can arise when a hospital is understaffed. As we have already seen, such problems still occur regularly two decades after publication of their pioneering studies.

The combination of time pressure and surprise can lead to what Glaser and Strauss term *institutional evasions*. There is not enough time to make the moves that are officially required in the situation, so available staff members must improvise a response or use an alternative approach that could expose them to reprimand or even legal action. For example, there may not be time to bring a physician to the bedside. If nurses carry out the potentially life-saving procedures without direct medical supervision, then they will have exposed themselves to the possibility of criticism and liability action. However, if they do not act promptly, the patient may die before the physician arrives. Evasions of institutional rules may be minor or substantial. The institution may choose either to notice or to carefully ignore the infractions. One extra source of tension within the unexpected quick trajectory is the conflict between doing what seems to be best for the patient without delay and abiding strictly by the regulations.

Life-or-Death Emergencies

There is another type of "quick trajectory" that can occur any time, any place. A person in good health may suddenly become victim of an automobile accident, a small child may fall into a swimming pool, an "unloaded gun" may discharge, a restaurant patron may choke, or a person with a history of heart disease may suffer another attack. These are just a few of the emergency situations that can result in death.

Several types of problems are more likely to arise when there is a life-or-death emergency in a community setting compared with a health care facility:

- Panic: "What's happening? What should we do?"
- Inappropriate action: "Let's get him on his feet."
- Misinterpreting the situation: "Stop whining and go back to bed!"
- Minimizing the danger: "I don't need a doctor. It's just a little indigestion."
- Preoccupied by own concerns: "I'd better clean this place up before I call anybody."

There have been many examples of prompt and competent response from family members, neighbors, colleagues, and passersby. For example, a man in his 80s had the presence of mind and the skill to perform cardiac pulmonary resuscitation (CPR) on a toddler who had fallen into a pool—a frequent occurrence in Arizona. This child recovered, but many have died or suffered permanent injury. Errors and poor decisions can also be made within health care settings, but the risk is greater in most community settings. A camper's friends, for example, may think they are doing the right thing by carrying out a snake bite remedy that has been passed along for generations when they should be rushing him to a poison control center instead.

The emergency medical technician and the paramedic are often called on when life-endangering situations arise in the community. Trained to provide society's front-line response to emergent health crises, these men and women may have more encounters with disaster in 2 or 3 days than most people do in a lifetime. Relatively little attention has been given to their experiences by researchers and educators. Dale Gladden recalls one of his first experiences as a paramedic (Kastenbaum, 1993–1994, pp. 6–7):

It was at a (community fraternal club). There was a dance going on—lots of loud music, dim lights. No one dancing. Everyone was just standing around. An elderly man had collapsed.... Communication was bad. We would give medicine, then call a physician on the phone and tell him

the situation and what we had done. The man had gone into ventricular fibrillation. I intubated him, and the RN with me tried to get an IV (intravenous) in him—It was hard for her because of the bad lighting. He was a diabetic. IV was hooked up and we started defibrillation. There was that smell of burning hair associated with defib machines. We got a pulse and blood pressure back. Got an ambulance. The man was breathing fine so I took the tube out and we transported him to the hospital. He survived and was very thankful to me.

This man almost certainly would have died without the prompt and skilled intervention. Sometimes, however, no amount of skill and effort can prevent death, and it is not unusual for the paramedic to discover that there are one or more people already dead on the scene. Even though the paramedic knows that a person is beyond resuscitation, it may be necessary to carry out CPR and other procedures in order to conform with regulations. At such times, the paramedic is likely to feel—as Gladden did after responding to another call—that it is wrong "to go through all this trouble for a dead person, why not let her be at peace? I had lots of questions why we went through the whole routine when she was already dead."

Another odd situation can arise when a person dies suddenly in a community setting. Although paramedics or nurses on the scene may know that the person is dead, the legal declaration of death may not be made until the body has been transported to a medical facility. This means that some of the deaths that are reported as having occurred in a hospital actually occurred elsewhere. Hospital physicians simply confirmed the emergency room team's assessment that the patient was beyond resuscitation.

An important change is taking place throughout the nation with respect to the options available to paramedics and emergency technicians (EMTs). In many communities, emergency response personnel are now following "Field Termination of Resuscitation Guidelines" that enable them to forego useless procedures when it is obvious that the person has no chance of survival. Just such an incident was reported soon after the new provisions were approved in Mesa, Arizona. A chronically ill 90-year-old woman refused breakfast one morning, sat in her favorite chair, and stopped breathing. Her son later commented that "We didn't know what to do. She wanted to die at home. We wanted to handle it as quietly as we could." The paramedics who came to the home honored the family's wishes. Instead of performing unwanted and ineffective resuscitation procedures, they stayed to talk with the family and help them deal with their first wave of grief and in making arrangements for disposition of the body. The Mesa paramedics receive training in the basics of grief support—certainly a good idea for police officers as well and all people who may be called on when a death occurs.

In some jurisdictions, it is possible for people to complete a medical care directive that forbids resuscitation measures (this is sometimes known as the "orange card"). Where this law applies, paramedics and EMTs can refrain from performing resuscitation procedures without exposing themselves to legal risk. What is the law in your state and community? Your local department of health, hospital, or medical association can answer this question for you.

HEALTHY PEOPLE WHO ARE AT RISK: HEMOPHILIA

Many people are not ill but are at special risk for a life-threatening episode. Hemophilia is the example considered here. This condition arises from a defect in the blood coagulation process. The person may be otherwise healthy and vigorous but is in danger when bleeding occurs, whether through an external wound or internal dysfunction. The bleeding could continue until death without medical intervention. Not all such situations can be predicted and avoided, however, so there is always the possibility of a bleeding incident.

There are more than 15,000 individuals with hemophilia in the United States (and additional people with other types of bleeding disorders). Two types of hemophilia are known; both are inherited as X-linked recessive disorders. Jonathan C. Goldsmith (2001) explains:

This generally means that women carry the trait and men have the clinical disorder. The most famous carrier of hemophilia was Queen Victoria of Great Britain whose carrier daughters spread the

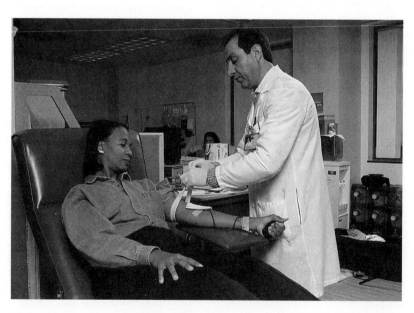

Giving blood is a way of helping to save the lives of people with hemophilia, accident victims, and surgical patients.

disorder to royal families in Germany, Spain, and Russia.... All daughters of affected men will be carriers of the gene for hemophilia. (p. 2)

The risk of serious or fatal complications of hemophilia can be reduced through early diagnosis, precautions (such as soft, cushioned helmets for preschool children), drug therapy, and the use of safe plasma transfusions. People with hemophilia become at exceptional risk when blood products are contaminated. The nation's public health establishment (including the Red Cross) was slow to respond to the dangers of HIV contamination, leading to AIDS infections among people with hemophilia who depend on blood product transfusions. Any pathological agent that contaminates the blood supply places people with hemophilia at a special risk for their lives. The warning and prevention functions of our society's death system must be ever alert to prevent catastrophes of this kind.

It is also clear that health care professionals, teachers, counselors, and others who serve the public should be aware of the special challenges that people with hemophilia face. All of us who are concerned about the fragility of life and the ever-present risk of death should learn more about the perspectives of individuals and families who must cope with hemophilia and other bleeding disorders. A logical place to start is the National Hemophilia Foundation (800-42-HANDI; http://www.hemophilia.org).

GUARDED FEELINGS, SUBTLE COMMUNICATIONS

Most of us do not say everything on our minds to whomever we happen to be with in every situation. We will speak more openly with those we have learned to trust and who demonstrate understanding and good will. Furthermore, we take the other person's state of mind into account: Should we alarm somebody who is already anxious or who has a difficult task to perform that requires complete concentration? Precisely how should we get a message across? Should we be as quick and direct about it as possible? Or should we work our way up, starting with something relatively neutral and gradually get to the point? Or must we lay out thoughts and feelings as though

making a formal presentation? How we communicate with another person depends on our own personality style, who that other person is, and what is at stake in the immediate situation.

Difficulties in Communication

We should not be surprised to find that feelings may be guarded and communications subtle among people faced with the prospect of death. One might conclude, erroneously, that the dying person either does not know what is happening or is unwilling to discuss it. Often, clear communication has been made very difficult. For example, while working in a geriatric hospital I found that personnel usually responded to patients' direct communications about death in a manner that quickly ended the interaction. The odds were about three to one against the staff member being willing to listen to what the patient had to say. Giving false reassurance ("Oh, you'll outlive me, Charlie!"), changing the subject, and a variety of other evasive responses were more common than an openness to what the dying person really wanted to communicate.

This attitude is still prevalent in many places. Aged patients on a lingering trajectory are frequently treated as though socially dead and are therefore denied even the opportunity to die as a person. I have heard staff members make remarks such as the following in the presence of the patients (Kastenbaum, 1984):

"This one, she can't talk. She doesn't know what you are saying."

"You should have seen her when she first came here, but look at her now!"

"The poor thing would be better off going in her sleep." (p. 6)

These remarks were not only degrading but also erroneous. There was independent evidence that these patients, although vulnerable and failing, could hear and understood what was being said over their (socially) dead bodies. One example that I will always remember occurred during an inspection of an extended care facility. This facility (operated by a state agency) had been under court orders to improve both its physical plant and its treatment program. The whistle had already been blown, time had been provided to improve care, and my visit as a consultant for the federal government was expected. However, there was no evidence of improvement. Part of the explanation was that "these people (the patients) don't understand anything anyhow."

I asked the staff to show me the most impaired, uncomprehending patient on the ward. This request seemed to throw them into confusion, so I walked to the farthest corner of this large, dark, and filthy ward. An old, pale, scrunched-up woman was lying in bed, her hair tangled and untended, her body smelling of neglect. The charge nurse assured me that their patients were beyond being worth the effort. I asked for the patient's name and some information about her background. Did she have a husband, children, visitors? What had been her interests, activities, and achievements before she came here? All the staff knew was her name, the fact that her husband or somebody visited once in a great while, that she could not speak or understand anything, and that she probably did not have long to live.

I stood by the woman's bed, took her hand, and spoke to her, using the small bits of information I had been given. In less than 1 minute, she had painfully faced around and squeezed my hand in return. In another few minutes she was speaking and moaning. I could not make out all the words, but there was no mistaking that she knew somebody was trying to communicate with her and that she had the need and the ability (although limited) to respond. She was still there as a person. The staff noted this interaction and retreated from it. However, at the end of the inspection visit the charge nurse turned to me and muttered, "If you're going to write anything about this, I'd better tell you that this is not the patient I told you it was. *I mixed the patients up* somehow. That was Mrs.____, not Mrs._____."

This story is not told to criticize nurses or geriatric facilities in general. The situation on this particular unit was the outcome of systematic neglect of the frail elderly and of those who try to provide care for them. Having their own sense of horror to contend with, the staff responded by erasing the patients' individuality and humanity. In the extreme circumstances I have mentioned, this woman had almost no op-

portunity to communicate to anybody about anything. Whatever she might be feeling about life and death would remain unknown. It is not simply that we often have difficulty communicating about "mortal matters": There are many people close to death who are deprived of the opportunity for normal social interaction of any kind. And how unnecessary!

Doctor–Patient Communication: The SUPPORT Study

The effective physician must do more than diagnose, prescribe, and treat: There must also be a bond of trust with the patient. A large and influential study demonstrated that problems in the communication process contribute greatly to shortcomings in the treatment of seriously and terminally ill hospitalized patients. This major project is known by the acronym SUPPORT: Study to Understand Prognoses and Preferences for Outcomes and Risks of Treatment (SUPPORT, 1995).

The SUPPORT project was intended to help physicians make better decisions about end-of-life issues and to prevent "a mechanically supported, painful, and prolonged process of dying." A major research effort was mounted:

- More than 9,000 adult patients with life-threatening diseases in five teaching hospitals
- A 2-year observational study for approximately half of the patients
- Followed by a 2-year intervention phase for the other patients during which attempts were made to improve communication and care

The observational phase examined the process of decision making and patient outcomes through extensive review of case records and interviews with patients and their surrogates as well as the senior physicians involved. Major shortcomings were documented (Box 5-3).

The observation study found that physician–patient communication was unreliable and ineffective. The blunt truth was that physicians often showed little interest in the patients' own preferences and little inclination to honor them. This nonresponsiveness to the wishes of seriously and terminally ill patients worked almost exclusively

---

BOX 5-3

THE SUPPORT STUDY OF SERIOUSLY AND TERMINALLY ILL HOSPITALIZED PATIENTS: MAJOR FINDINGS

I. The Observation Study

1. Half of the patients who died during the course of the study had moderate or severe pain during their final 3 days of life.

2. Physicians often used jargon that the patient did not understand when talking about cardiopulmonary resuscitation (CPR) and often (41%) never even discussed this subject with their patients.

3. In 80% of the cases, physicians misunderstood what the patients wanted with respect to the use of CPR.

4. Physicians often did not follow the patients' stated preference to avoid the use of CPR: In approximately 50% of cases, the physician did not write a do-not-resuscitate order.

II. The Intervention Study

1. There was no increase in discussions between physicians and patients.

2. Physicians often continued to disregard patients' preferences to have CPR withheld even when these preferences were known to them.

3. There was no improvement in pain control.

4. Computer projections of the patients' prognoses were no more accurate than those made by the attending physicians.

5. Much of the patient information generated during the intervention phase failed to reach the physicians because of various communication problems.

---

in one direction. If the patient did not want to have CPR used, physicians often continued the plan to use this procedure despite the patients' stated preference. However, if the patient did want to have CPR used, physicians did not counter this preference by excluding CPR. Pain control was also ineffective. The outcome was that many patients were exposed to unrelieved pain and aggressive treatment, and many also spent at least 10 days on life support equipment in the ICU. This is an alarmingly poor showing for hospitals and physicians two decades after the hospice movement, with its palliative care approach, started to prove its worth in the United States (see Chapter 6).

The intervention phase of the study attempted to improve this situation by providing the physicians with more information about their patients' preferences as well as their physical status. Nurses with special training were an important part of this phase, making multiple contacts with patient,

family, physician, and hospital staff. These nurses encouraged attention to pain control and to better physician–patient communication to contribute to better decisions in planning the course of treatment. Unfortunately, these interventions did not work. Communication remained flawed; physician preferences for aggressive treatment were not modified in light of patients' preferences, and pain control was as poor as before.

The findings were disturbing enough to prompt an immediate editorial response from the *Journal of the American Medical Association* ("Improving Care," 1995). The anonymous editorial writer urged other physicians:

Don't project our concept of a good death onto patients.... Respect for patient autonomy means that physicians must allow informed patients to determine what value they place on such a chance of survival and what risks they are willing to undergo. (p. 1635)

Fortunately, this research portrait of a medical system unresponsive to the values and wishes of terminally ill patients served as a wake-up call and has led to a variety of educational efforts and service reevaluations.

Improving Communication

Communication is everybody's responsibility, whether physician, nurse, patient, family member, or friend. Whatever improves self-respect, reduces fear, and encourages open communication in general is likely to have a positive impact on death-related communication as well. Here are a few suggestions:

First, *be alert to symbolic and indirect communications,* as illustrated by the following examples:

1. *Sharing dreams.* People may prepare themselves for their final separation through dreamwork before conscious thoughts and direct interpersonal communications occur. Dreams reported by terminally ill cancer patients have been found to differ from those of healthy older people (Coolidge & Fish, 1983/1984). Among these differences was a greater frequency of death content in dreams, but it was usually somebody else who was seen as dead. The dreamer often attempted to discover the identity of this person:

> I dreamt of a funeral and in the funeral was a little girl going to be buried. In her coffin I couldn't get to her so I tried to open it to see who it was and it was one of my daughters. Little Antonette. She was lying on her side and the lid was falling in the coffin.... I went to fix the lid.... I kept on doing things that would upset the coffin. I felt like a criminal that didn't belong there. (p. 3)

Listening to each other's dreams can be a valuable way to supplement and enrich interpersonal communication for people who are comfortable with their own dream lives. It is not essential that the patient or the listener come up with the "right" interpretation of these dreams. Simply being able to share these inner experiences with another person can provide an additional supportive line of communication.

2. *Symbolic language.* Although dreams provide a treasury of symbolic language and actions, such characteristics can also appear in everyday speech. The following is an example that came to our attention during a research project in a geriatric hospital (Weisman & Kastenbaum, 1968).

The 75-year-old former stonemason had lost some of the vigor he had shown earlier in his hospital stay, but otherwise appeared to be in stable condition and doing well. One morning he asked for directions to a cemetery near his former home. Although he made the direct statement that he was expecting the undertaker, this was not taken up by the staff as a clue to impending death. It was just a statement that didn't make much sense. The next day, he told several people that his boss (going back many years, in reality) had called for him: He was supposed to help dig graves for eight people. The delusion now became persistent. He insisted on staying around the ward so he could be available to the people who would come to take him back to the cemetery.

Two days before he died, the patient had several teeth extracted (a procedure that was seen as having little risk because of his good condition). He then told staff that it was time to call his sisters—about whom he had never before said a word. His death came as a surprise to the staff although, apparently, not to himself. Cause of death was determined to be cerebral thrombosis. Despite all the clues this man had given, no notice had been taken. His "crazy talk" seemed even less crazy when a subsequent review indicated that the old stonemason had outlived seven siblings—his reference to digging a grave for eight people no longer seemed so arbitrary.

After a number of experiences such as this one, both our clinical and research staffs markedly improved their ability to identify patients whose death was more imminent than might have been expected and learned to pay close attention to what was said, whether in direct or symbolic language.

3. *Leave-taking actions.* Deeds as well as words can help to express the needs and intentions of people who are close to the end of their lives. My colleagues and I in both institutional and community settings have observed such behaviors as sorting through possessions and giving some away; creating the occasion for one last interac-

tion of a familiar kind, such as playing checkers or going fishing together; and terminating mutual obligations and expectations (e.g., "Thanks for the loan of the bowling ball. I won't be needing it anymore").

Most people who are aware of their terminal illness do hope to have the opportunity to bid farewell to the important people in their lives, but not necessarily all in the same way (Kelleher, 1990). It is wise to take our cue from the dying person rather than impose a particular kind of farewell scene than happens to appeal to us.

As shown in the three examples, increasing our awareness of dreams, symbolic language, and leave-taking actions can make it easier for the dying person to convey messages that might not lend themselves as well to direct verbal expression. It also gives us more opportunity to express our own thoughts and feelings in return.

Second, *help to make competent and effective behavior possible.* Illness, fatigue, and reduced mobility make it difficult to continue functioning as a competent person. This is true whether or not the individual is suffering from a terminal condition. The progressive nature of terminal illness, however, tends to increase the individual's dependency on others and limits the range of spontaneous action. The person attempting to cope with terminal illness often retains a strong need to be competent, effective, and useful to others. Family, friends, and other caregivers cannot only improve communication but also help to support the dying person's sense of self-esteem by striking a balance between meeting the realistic needs associated with dependency and creating an environment in which the person can continue to exercise some initiative and control.

Timely and appropriate support is needed, not a total takeover of the dying person's life. Attentive listening and observing are required to match the style, level, and intensity of care with the individual's physical condition and psychosocial needs. By accomplishing one side of the communication process—listening and observing—it becomes more probable that the patient can maintain a core of competent and effective behavior and continue to communicate needs and attention.

Third, *recognize that the dying person sets the pace and the agenda.* There is no schedule that has to be met, no set of tasks that the dying person must accomplish—unless the dying person has a schedule and a set of tasks of his or her own. This is no time for the listener to impose his or her own set of needs or to expect the dying person to behave in accordance with any preconceived idea of just what it is that a dying person is supposed to do. Although the patient will usually introduce thoughts concerned with dying and death, there are individual differences regarding when and how this topic is brought up. For example, during a particular interaction the patient may choose to say nothing about death. This does not necessarily mean that the patient is "denying" or is "behind schedule." It may be that the patient is hoping for a little "vacation" from this overwhelming topic, or that other matters require attention. Furthermore, on close listening and reflection, it may become evident that the conversation had a lot to do with how the person feels in prospect of death without having ever to mention death per se. One terminally ill person might choose to discuss specific death-related issues (e.g., reviewing funeral plans or the distribution of property), but another might choose to discuss feelings and relationships. I have known many dying people who had not much left to say about death because they had already had all the time they needed to settle their thoughts and communicate their concerns and desires. These people still had need for supportive everyday communication but did not need to be reminded that they were dying.

Fourth, *do not confuse the dying person's values and goals with our own.* Communication can be distorted or broken off when others project their own needs on the dying person. We have already seen that substituting our needs and values for the patients' is a major problem in the medical care of dying people. Requiring the dying person to move along from one "stage" to another also imposes an unnecessary and unrealistic burden on everybody in the situation. A similar, or greater, stress may be introduced if we insist that the patient give up "denial." As noted earlier (Chapter 2), denial has become an overused and often misused term. There are many reasons why a person might not acknowledge his or her terminal condition at a particular time and to a particular individual. Furthermore, denial-like behaviors may be useful strategies. Connor's (1992) research with terminally ill cancer patients found confirmation that the supposed "deniers" were downplaying the seriousness of their illness because this strategy was helping them to maintain their most significant interpersonal relationships. Connor makes the important point that some people have had a dysfunctional lifestyle for many years and continue to make excessive use of denial-like behaviors in their terminal illness. Other people have functioned well until confronted with the loss, stress, and uncertainties associated with a life-threatening illness. To say that a person is denying seldom tells us all that would be useful to understand and may, in fact, misrepresent the situation.

INDIVIDUALITY AND UNIVERSALITY IN THE EXPERIENCE OF DYING

Does everybody die in the same way? If so, then it should be possible to discover general laws or regularities on which care and management can be based. Or does everybody die in an unique way, depending on many different factors? We are more likely to be good observers and useful caregivers if we understand the specifics of each situation. This can be exemplified by a survey of some of the factors that influence the nature and experience of dying. The discussion begins with respect for both universal factors and individual dimensions of dying.

Factors That Influence the Experience of Dying

The following factors are discussed here: age; gender; interpersonal relationships; and disease, treatment, and environmental context.

Age

Age by itself is an empty variable that exercises no direct influence. Nevertheless, chronological age serves as an index for a variety of factors that can make a significant different throughout life, including the process of dying.

- *Comprehension of dying and death.* Our intellectual grasp of death is related both to the level of development we have achieved and to our life experiences (see Chapter 11). At one extreme is the young child who is keenly sensitive to separation but who may not yet comprehend the finality and irreversibility of death. At the other extreme is an aged adult who not only recognizes the central facts of death but also has seen many close friends and relations die through the years. The "same" experience will be different for people with varying life histories and cognitive structures.

- *Opportunity to exercise control over the situation.* Children have fewer enfranchised rites than adults in general. Even the "natural death" acts passed by state legislatures do not strengthen the child's position as a participant in decision making. The traumatic experiences of young Marie (see Chapter 6) provide one example of a serious problem that has yet to be effectively addressed.

- *Perception and treatment by others.* Perceived social value differs with age. Elderly patients are often victimized by the assumptions that (a) they are ready to die and (b) nobody would miss them much. Both professional caregivers and the general public tend to act on these assumptions without first inquiring about their accuracy. For example, doctors are much more likely to withhold resuscitation efforts in patients older than age 75, even though they are likely to force CPR on younger patients who would prefer not to have CPR (SUPPORT, 1995).

It is all too easy to mistake a depressive reaction for a terminal course. Many circumstances can lead to depression among elderly adults, including the fatigue and depletion associated with medical conditions that have not been effectively treated. Expertise in assessing and treating depression is required, along with the independence of mind to break free of the "ready to die" stereotype and carefully examine each individual's situation. Unfortunately, every day there are depressed elderly men and women whose chances for survival as well as a renewed quality of life are diminished by society's inclination to view older adults as ready for the grave.

Misperceptions often occur at the other extreme of the age range as well. For example, there remains a stubborn belief among some physicians that infants do not experience pain to any appreciable extent. Bone marrow samples are taken, needles are inserted into the spine, and burn dressings are changed without adequate analgesia. A life-threatened infant may undergo very painful procedures repeatedly. Although this attitude is gradually changing, it may be difficult to eliminate because the belief that infants do not experience pain serves anxiety-reduction purposes for physicians and nurses who are responsible for their treatment.

Gender

A man with cancer of the prostate may be concerned with the threat of becoming impotent as well as with the risk to his life (although, in practice, timely diagnosis and treatment can sharply reduce both risks). Cervical cancer may disturb a woman not only because of the life risk but also because one of the treatment possibilities, hysterectomy, would leave her unable to become pregnant. Both the man and the woman may be troubled about the future of their intimate relationships even if the threat to their lives is lifted.

Some people interpret physical trauma affecting their sexual organs as punishment for real or imagined transgressions. Others become preoccupied with their physical condition in a way that interferes with affectionate and sexual relationships. "I'm no good anymore" may be a self-tormenting thought for either the man or the woman, each experiencing this in his or her own way. These are not the only types of reactions that people express to cancer of the reproductive system; these simply illustrate some of the many possible interactions between sex role and disease.

When a woman is faced with a life-threatening illness, she is likely to have concerns about the integrity and well-being of her family. Will the children eat well? Can her husband manage the household? What most troubles the woman/wife/mother may be the fate of her family as much or even more than her own.

The man/husband/father in the traditional family is likely to have distinctive concerns of his own. Has the illness destroyed his career prospects? Will he lose his job or his chance for advancement even if he makes a good recovery? Has he provided well enough for his family in case he does not pull through? Is he, in effect, a "good man" and a "real man" if he cannot continue to work and bring in the money? There may be a crisis in self-esteem if he is confined to hospital or home for a protracted time, away from the work situations that support his sense of identity.

Gender differences are important from the standpoint of professional caregivers as well as the patient. Direct care to the dying person is usually provided by women—often nurses, licensed practical nurses, or aides. Responsibility for the total care plan, however, is often in the hands of a male physician. The physician may be more time conscious and achievement oriented—characteristics that favor survival of the rigors of medical training. He may therefore be more persistent in cure-oriented treatments but also quicker to withdraw when death is in prospect. The nurse may be more sensitive to the patient's relationship with significant people in his or her life and less apt to regard impending death as a failure.

Changing patterns of sex roles in Western society can appear in adaptation to terminal illness. When one marital partner is disabled, the other may have more experience in the ailing one's sphere of responsibility and be better able to maintain the integrity of the family. It is more likely now than in past years, for example, that the wife is also a wage earner and familiar with financial management. Similarly, the husband of today may have had more time with the children and more responsibility for running the household than in the past. Furthermore, the healthy one may be more attuned to the needs and concerns of the sick partner because there has been more commonality in their experiences. It is likely that there will be many other effects of changing sex roles on the management of terminal illness. For example, as more women enter or reenter the workforce, the number of people available to serve as volunteers and informal helpers may decline.

Interpersonal Relationships

It is difficult to overestimate the importance of interpersonal relationships in the terminal phase of life. Clinical experience has supported the findings of an influential early study (Weisman & Worden, 1975): Among hospitalized patients who were likely to die within a few months, those who maintained active and mutually responsive relationships survived longer than those with poor social relationships. The patients who died rapidly also tended to have fewer friends, more distant relationships with their families, and more ambivalent relationships with colleagues and associates. They became more depressed as treatment failed. The investigators noted that the patients with poor relationships often expressed the wish to die, but that this did not represent an actual acceptance of death: It was a product of their frustration and disappointment with life. Weisman and Worden (1976) later found that the terminally ill patients who were experiencing the most distress also were those with the most interpersonal difficulties. Not only the length of survival but also the quality of life were associated with the kind of interpersonal relationship enjoyed or suffered by the patient.

There are situations in which the family needs the most support. For example, an elderly man on a lingering trajectory toward death was at home and under the care of his wife, with assistance from other family members. Mr. Tchinsky was in a semicomatose state not suffering either physical or emotional distress. His wife, however, was struggling with anxiety and guilt. In actuality, Mrs. Tchinsky was a loving and attentive caregiver, but she had difficulty in controlling the leakage from his colostomy bag. This relatively small problem was the source of great distress because to Mrs. Tchinsky it meant that she was failing her husband in his time of need. A visiting nurse identified and responded tactfully and effectively to this problem. Within a short time, Mrs. Tchinsky was again secure in her role as loving wife and caregiver, and the rest of the family was also relieved. This intervention did not involve the application of either high technology or counseling: A caring family just needed a little timely help to fulfill its obligations toward the dying man (Kastenbaum & Thuell, 1995). Elliott J. Rosen's *Families Facing Death* (1998) is a useful source on the role of home and family.

Where and How We Die— From the Abstract to the Particular

We die in a particular place that contributes to our comfort, misery, or both. Similarly, the particular kind of services we receive have a significant effect on our experience. Discussions of the dying process sometimes become so abstract and generalized that we neglect the specific medical problems involved. Think, for example, of the difference between a person whose likely cause of death will be kidney failure and its complications and a person suffering impairment of respiratory function (perhaps a coal or uranium miner). The person with kidney failure may fade away as waste products accumulate in the body. Over time, he or she may become more lethargic and less able to sustain attention and intention. There may be intermittent periods of better functioning when the patient seems more like his or her old self. The final hours or days may be spent in a comatose condition.

In contrast, a degenerative respiratory condition is likely to produce more alarming symptoms and experiences. Perhaps you have seen a person with advanced emphysema struggle for breath. An episode of acute respiratory failure is frightening to the individual and likely to arouse the anxiety of those around him. Once a person has experienced this kind of distress, it is difficult to avoid apprehension about future episodes.

Some conditions are accompanied by persistent pain and discomfort unless very carefully managed. Other conditions can reach peaks of agony that test the limits both of the individual and the state of medical comfort giving. Nausea, weakness, and a generalized sense of ill-being may be more dominant than pain for some terminally ill people. It is difficult to be serene when wracked by vomiting or diarrhea. (For other pathways and symptoms, see Lipman, Jackson, and Tyler, 2000, and Nuland, 1994). However, the friend, relative, caregiver, and researcher should appreciate that the particular person is not dying in an abstract sense: There is a unique set of conditions, and these conditions are continuing to change over time. Furthermore, different types of treatment may be carried out for the same condition, depending on characteristics of the patient and the hospital. As we consider theoretical models of the dying process, it is useful to keep in mind that death comes down to the individual in particular and therefore cannot be completely comprehended within any abstract perspective.

THEORETICAL MODELS OF THE DYING PROCESS

People have hesitated to interact with dying people for many reasons, including lack of a coherent and useful perspective. Here, we consider several approaches that have become available (Corr, Doka, & Kastenbaum, 1999).

Do We Die in Stages?

Two stage models of the dying process have been especially influential, although seldom to the same people. There is a basic similarity between these theories: Both regard dying as a sequence of psychological or spiritual stages. The differences are also substantial, however.

A Buddhist Perspective

Buddhists have long been aware of individual differences in the way people die. Some people are killed instantly in an accident; others slowly decline and outlive their mental powers. In such situations, there is no opportunity to progress through the stages. Furthermore, some people are anxious and beset by emotional conflict as death nears. For these people also, the transition from life to death is not likely to proceed through the stages of spiritual enlightenment. His Holiness, Tenzin Glyatso, the 14th Dalai Lama, states that Buddhism does not assert that all people move through the stages as they die (Gyatos, 1985). One must have sufficient time and be in a state of mind that is conducive to spiritual development. Those who have developed spiritual discipline throughout their lives are more likely to experience the entire cycle of stages.

For Buddhists, the relationship between mind and body is quite complex, involving "coarse," "subtle," and "very subtle" connections. At death, the coarse connections between mind and body are severed, but the very subtle connections continue. There is also a broad philosophical conception that is characteristic of Buddhism and that becomes especially significant as death approaches. As the Dalai Lama expresses it, "when you are able to keep impermanence in mind—seeing that the very nature of things is that they disintegrate—most likely you will not be greatly shocked by death when it actually comes" (p. 170).

There are eight stages in the Buddhist journey toward death. Perhaps our first surprise is that these stages occur in ordinary life as well. "In more subtle form, the eight transpire each time one goes in or out of sleep or dream, sneezes, faints, or has an orgasm" (Gyatos, 1985, p. 98). Only the sensitive and disciplined person is aware of these subtle forms of dying that occur in everyday life.

The fundamental changes that occur as one moves from the first to the final stage of dying are as follows:

Stage 1. Eyesight dims, but one begins to have mirage-like visions.

Stage 2. Hearing diminishes. There is a new internal vision: of smoke.

Stage 3. The sense of smell disappears, and there is now an internal vision that is "likened to fireflies in smoke." The dying person is no longer mindful of other people.

Stage 4. Sensation is lost from the tongue and the body. The dying person is no longer mindful of his or her own concerns. Breathing ceases. (At this point the person would be considered dead by a Western physician but not so to a Buddhist.)

Stage 5. This is the first of the pure visionary stages. White moonlight is perceived.

Stage 6. The person experiences visions of red sunlight.

Stage 7. The person experiences visions of darkness, faints, and then awakens into the final stage.

Stage 8. The clear light of death appears. This unique state of consciousness persists until death.

FIGURE 5.1
Through the ages, Buddhists have studied the stages of dying, culminating in the clear light of death.

The Buddhist stages all focus on the experiential state or phenomenology of the dying person and are divided equally into those that occur while the person is still alive by ordinary standards and those that occur when the person would appear to be dead to most observers.

This model of dying served as a guide to Buddhists for many centuries before the current death-awareness movement arose in Western society. (There is also a less elaborate stage theory of dying within the Islamic tradition [Kramer, 1988].) We now turn to the stage theory that has become most familiar to readers in the Americas and Western Europe.

Kübler-Ross: The Five Stages

Five stages of dying were introduced by Elizabeth Kübler-Ross in her book *On Death and Dying* (1969). These stages are said to begin when the individual becomes aware of his or her terminal condition. The stages are presented as normal, or nonpathological, ways of responding to the prospect of death and the miseries of dying. The patient begins with a stage known as denial and moves through the remaining stages of anger, bargaining, depression, and acceptance. Some people do not make it all the way to acceptance. Progress may become arrested at any stage along the way; furthermore, there can be some slipping back and forth between stages, and each individual has a distinctive tempo of movement through the stages. This conceptualization emphasizes a universal process that allows for a certain amount of individual variation.

Stage 1. Denial is the first response to the bad news. "No, not me, it can't be true!" is the typical feeling that is communicated. The denial stage is fueled by anxiety and usually runs its course in a short time. It could also be described as a "state of shock from which he recuperates gradually" (Kübler-Ross, 1969, p. 37).

Stage 2. Anger wells up and may boil over after the initial shock and denial response has passed. "Why me?" is the characteristic feeling at this time. Rage and resentment can be expressed in many directions—God not excluded. The patient is likely to become more difficult to relate to at this time because of the struggle with frustration and fury.

Stage 3. Bargaining is said to be the middle stage. The dying person attempts to make some kind of deal with fate. He or she may ask for an extension of life, just long enough, for example, to see a child graduate from high school or get married. The bargaining process may go on between the patient and caregivers, friends, or family or with God.

Stage 4. Depression eventually follows as the person experiences increasing weakness, discomfort, and physical deterioration. The person can see that he or she is not getting better. The symptoms are too obvious to ignore. Along with stress, strain, and feelings of guilt and unworthiness, there may be explicit fear of dying at this stage. The person becomes less responsive and his or her thoughts and feelings are pervaded by a sense of great loss.

Stage 5. Acceptance, the final stage, represents the end of the struggle. The patient is letting

go. Despite the name, it is not necessarily a happy or blissful state. "It is almost void of feelings. It is as if the pain had gone, the struggle is over, and there comes a time for 'the final rest before the long journey' as one patient phrased it" (Kübler-Ross, 1969, p. 100).

Interwoven through all five stages is the strand of hope. Realistic acknowledgment of impending death may suddenly give way to hope for a miraculous recovery. Hope flickers now and then throughout the entire sequence. In addition to describing these stages, Kübler-Ross indicates some of the typical problems that arise at each point and suggests ways of approaching them. She emphasizes, for example, the need to understand and tolerate the patient's anger during the second stage rather than to retaliate and punish him or her for it.

Evaluating the Stage Theory

We first consider shortcomings of the stage theory followed by observations that are more supportive.

First, *the existence of the stages as such has not been demonstrated.* Although more than three decades have passed since this model was introduced, there is no clear evidence for the establishment of stages in general, for the stages being five in number, or for the stages to be those specified or to be aligned in the sequence specified. Dying people sometimes do use denial, become angry, try to bargain with fate, or lapse into depression or a depleted, beyond-the-struggle way of being. However, the reality of these moods or response sets has nothing necessarily to do with stages. Dying people have many other moods and responses as well, including expressions of the *need to control* what is happening and to *preserve a continuity* between themselves and those who survive them. For a particular person at a particular moment, any of these needs may take highest priority. Kübler-Ross did not provide the kind of clear definitions of the stages that lend themselves to research, and results from the few studies that have examined facets of stage theory have not supported this model.

Second, *no evidence has been presented that people actually do move from Stage 1 through Stage 5.*

Brief clinical descriptions of various patients are given in the Kübler-Ross book as examples of the stages. However, evidence that the same person passed through all the stages was not offered then and has not been offered more than three decades later. One might as well offer snapshots of five different people in five different moods as proof that these moods occur in a particular sequence. The theory won acceptance and continues to have its adherents despite the lack of data. This casual attitude regarding the factual basis of a theory suggests that it meets social or emotional needs rather than scientific criteria.

Third, *the limitations of the method have not been acknowledged.* The conclusion that there are five stages in the terminal process was based on psychiatric-type interviews conducted by one person and interpreted by the same person. This is a reasonable way to gather information, gain insight, and develop hypotheses to be tested within the structure of a formal research project—a potentially useful beginning. However, the research effort never moved past this beginning, and its inherent flaws and limitations were never transcended. The step from observation to interpretation is a critical one, but neither the basic observations nor the process of interpretation have been checked against the judgment of other qualified people. Furthermore, what the dying person says and does in the presence of a psychiatrist is only a small and highly selective sample of his or her behavior. The nurse who cares regularly for the patient's physical functioning often sees important aspects of the personality that do not appear in an interview, and the same may be said of the physician in charge and family members and friends. Behavioral studies might reveal a different perspective, as might a diary kept by the patient.

In other words, one valuable but limited source of information about the experiences and needs of the dying patient has taken the place of extensive, multilevel, cross-validated approaches. Conclusions have been widely accepted without concern for the obvious limitations of the methodology used for obtaining and analyzing the data. This would not be an acceptable practice in any other area of research and it is not sound practice here.

Fourth, *the line is blurred between description and prescription.* Stage theories in general often fail to distinguish clearly between what happens and what should happen. Kübler-Ross cautioned against trying to rush a person through the stages. However, this impulse can often be observed among caregivers or family members who are acquainted with the basic idea of the stages. People may draw the implication that the patient should be moving "on schedule" from denial right through to acceptance, and that it is a mark of failure for everyone concerned if the timing is off. This expectation adds unnecessary pressure to the situation and enshrines the image of acceptance as the universally desired outcome of the dying person's ordeal. The concept of universal stages lends itself to misuse by those who find their tasks simplified and anxieties reduced through a standardized approach to the dying person. Moller (1996) concludes that Kübler-Ross presented her own preferences for an ideal death as though she were reporting validated facts: "Kübler-Ross and those practitioners who accept her ideal of 'the good death' have become travel agents for the dying, offering therapeutic intervention to a singular destination: tranquil, peaceful death" (p. 51). Moller is also critical of Kübler-Ross's insistence that people should make themselves ready for death rather than resisting or bargaining.

Fifth, *the totality of the person's life is neglected in favor of the supposed stages of dying.* The supposed universality of the stages sometimes leads to the dying person being treated as a kind of specimen moving along predetermined paths rather than as a complete human being with a distinctive identity. However, each dying person is male or female, of one ethnic background or another, and at a particular point in his or her life. The nature of the disease, its symptoms, and its treatment can all have a profound effect on what the dying person experiences. Perhaps most important, who the person is deserves prime consideration in this situation as in any other. Even if the stage theory were clarified and proved, it is unlikely that it would account for nearly as much of the dying person's experience as has been widely assumed. *We take the entire course of our lives with us into the final months and weeks.* Emphasis on the hypothetical stages of reaction to terminal illness tends to drain away individuality or at least our perception of it.

Finally, *the resources, pressures, and characteristics of the immediate environment can also make a tremendous difference.* There are still medical environments in which almost everybody denies death almost all of the time. When the terminally ill person denies, it may be an attempt to conform to the implicit social rules of the situation rather than a manifestation of either individual personality or the hypothetical sequence of stages. Why waste one's depleted energies by fighting the system? The same terminally ill person might respond quite differently in a community hospital, a major medical center, an Amish community, or a hospice program. Environmental dynamics, mostly neglected in stage theory, have much to do with the experiences and responses of terminally ill people.

Nevertheless, Kübler-Ross did much to awaken society's sensitivity to the needs of the dying person. Accepting the stage theory is not essential for appreciation of her many useful observations and insights. Some of the practical problems that have arisen in the wake of Kübler-Ross's presentations should be attributed to their hasty and uncritical application by others.

There is a facet of Kübler-Ross's original presentation (1969) that deserves more attention by theorists and practitioners. Her first book and some of her subsequent writings and lectures might prove of more value for their report of *communicational interactions* than as evidence for a fixed set of stages. It is useful to learn what terminally ill people said and how they responded. Problems arise when these communications are taken as evidence for an assumed intrinsic state of the individual. The communications are more convincing as communications *between* people rather than as proof of stages *within* a person with a life-threatening condition.

In summary, the need for a guide to the plight of the dying person, and the need to keep our own anxieties under control, led to a premature acceptance of the Kübler-Ross conceptualization as well as to simplistic and overly rigid uses of her observations. These range from the dismissal of a patient's legitimate complaints about poor treatment as "Just what you would expect in Stage 2" to the assumption that further research

is not really important because the stages tell all. At the very least, however, the timely and charismatic presentations of Kübler-Ross have done much to heighten awareness of dying people and their needs, making it possible for the dialogue to begin.

A Developmental Coping Model of the Dying Process

Charles A. Corr (1993) has taken all these factors into consideration with the intention of helping caregivers, researchers, and educators move beyond the flaws and limitations of the stage theory. He believes that "an adequate model for coping with dying will need to be as agile, malleable, and dynamic as is the behavior of each individual." (p. 77). The model must encompass the fact that people may try certain coping strategies only to reject them firmly or may pursue several strategies at the same time, even if they are not compatible. Furthermore, people will differ in the tasks and needs that are important to them as well as their methods of coping. The model must respect individuality as well as universality, and it must offer practical guidelines for caregivers. It is not enough to simply identify a coping process and give it a name.

Corr (1993) identifies four challenges that dying people encounter: the physical (satisfying body needs and reducing stress), the psychological (feeling secure, in control, and still having a life to live), the social (keeping valued attachments to other individuals and to groups and causes), and the spiritual (finding or affirming meaning and having a sense of connectedness, transcendence, and hope). We face challenges throughout our lives, so we can draw on what we have already learned and achieved when we must cope with the challenges of the dying process.

Above all, Corr (1993) advocates greater *empowerment* for the dying person and for those who are intimately involved in caregiving. With open communication and trusting relationships, we might feel less need for simple theories of the dying process. It is also a useful approach for recognizing that the dying person remains a living person who is attempting to cope as resourcefully as possible with challenges and stresses and for including the full range of factors that influence the experience and course of the dying process.

The Dying Person's Own Reality as the Model

Another emerging approach focuses on the patient's own reality. The emphasis here shifts from the observer's frame of reference, away from stage or developmental tasks that an outsider might find useful to make sense of the dying process. Instead, the challenge is to learn how dying people interpret their own situation. In this view, there may be as many theoretical models of dying as there are dying people. Debbie Messer Zlatin (1995) found that terminally ill people had a variety of different life themes to share. She also observed that there are important differences between people who do and who do not have integrated life themes to call on as they face the stress of the dying process.

An example is provided through the journal kept by a distinguished researcher during the last weeks of his life (Kastenbaum, 1995/1996). William McDougall was a British-born physician who became one of the most eminent researchers of the early 20th century. He was a founder of the field of social psychology and an influential thinker in several other areas of scholarly activity. His terminal illness was a painful ordeal, occurring in 1938, years before palliative care techniques became widely available. The last weeks of his life centered on this confrontation between relief of pain and his determination to exercise his willpower as long as possible. The essence of McDougall's own theoretical model of dying can be drawn from the pages of his journal. When his pain was at its most intense, the exercise of his intellect was also at its most inspired. He could avoid becoming what he perceived as a passive and defeated victim as long as he could maintain his intellectual effort against pain.

McDougall's intellectual approach to the dying process is quite at odds with the current emphasis on emotions, relationships, and peaceful acceptance, and it does not follow any standard list of "developmental tasks" that might be assigned to a dying person. Instead, McDougall continued to be McDougall—even more so—as he called on all his knowledge and skills to integrate dying and death into his overall view of self and world. A person who decided to treat McDougall from an outsider's perspective would very likely fail to understand and, thus, respond usefully to this man's distinctive interpretation of the dying process.

This individual-centered approach by no means takes attention away from all the contextual influences on the dying process (e.g., how the symptoms are being married and what kind of interpersonal support is available). It does remind us, however, that each person is an unique center of value and reality. Recent collections of patients' narratives of their own experiences (Barnard et al., 2000; Lawton, 2000) offer further hints of the variety of perspectives that people bring to the end of their lives. Whatever other theoretical approach one might favor, it does make sense to learn what we can about the dying person's own implicit theory of what is happening and what it means.

A Multiple Perspective Approach

Is it possible that we might focus so much on what is unique about dying that we do not give enough attention to what dying shares with many other human experiences? I could not help but notice that much of what the dying person experiences has its counterpart in other situations. This suggests that the more clearly we recognize the similarities, the more we can draw on knowledge of these other phenomena to help us understand and support the dying person. A new multiple perspective approach asks us first to identify these other processes one at a time and then to gradually put them together to form both a more comprehensive and a more detailed understanding of the dying person's situation. The central fact that the person is terminally ill would then be added to complete the picture (Kastenbaum, 2000).

Seventeen partial models of the dying process are identified in Box 5-4. By "partial model," I mean that each offers a framework for observing and responding to one aspect of the dying person's situation. Which of these partial models would be most useful for understanding what a

---

BOX 5-4
PARTIAL MODELS OF THE DYING PERSON'S SITUATION

Model	*Brief Description*
1. Restricted activity	I can do less and less.
2. Limited energy	I must conserve what is left of my strength.
3. Damaged body image	I do not look and feel as I should.
4. Contagion	You act like you would catch something bad from me.
5. Disempowerment	I have lost the ability to influence you.
6. Attributional incompetency	You think I cannot do anything right.
7. Ineffectuance	I cannot make things happen the way I want them to.
8. Stress response overload	My defenses have become so intense that they are causing problems of their own.
9. Time anxiety	I fear it is too late to do all I must do.
10. Performance anxiety	How am I doing? How do you think I am doing?
11. Loss and separation	I am losing contact with everything that is most important to me.
12. Disengagement	I feel like withdrawing from interactions and responsibilities.
13. Journey	I am going some place I have never been before.
14. Closing the book	I am doing everything for the last time; it will soon be over.
15. Endangered relationship	I fear I am losing your love and respect.
16. Struggling brain	My mind is not working as it should; the world is slipping away from me.
17. Storying	I must come up with the best possible story of all that has happened, is happening, will happen.

---

particular person is experiencing will depend on that particular person and his or her situation.

It would be unusual to go through life without experiencing some of these situations, perhaps repeatedly. A person with a progressively life-threatening condition is almost certain to have many of these sources of concern, in addition to concerns that are associated specifically with the prospect of death. Perhaps we have not yet had to confront our own probably-will-die-soon situation, but we probably do know something about most of the other conditions identified among the partial models. We can draw on our own life experiences and observations to help us understand and respond effectively to what a dying person is experiencing. We will be careful, of course, to avoid assuming that the other person must be interpreting the situation the same way we did. Here, brief comments regarding a few of the partial models are presented. Draw on your own observations and reflections to go beyond what space permits us to present here (see also Kastenbaum, 2000).

1. *The restricted activity model.* We are likely to become frustrated, angry, and depressed when circumstances prevent us from doing what we usually do and from what we feel very much needs doing. Some people become tense and agitated when confined to bed for just a few days. Some people in perfect physical health either stew or feel helpless when their activities are restricted by external circumstances (such as bad weather, bureaucratic delay, or insufficient funds). Part of the tension and frustration experienced by dying people can be attributed to restricted activity. Everything we know and everything we can devise to help people deal with a restricted activity situation could relieve some of the dying person's stress.

2. *The damaged or altered body image model.* You have never been upset because the mirror suggests you might be too thin or too heavy. You have never had a bad hair day. You will certainly not be concerned when your hair begins to silver and wrinkles and age spots appear. Certainly you felt just as good about yourself as ever when you had that runny nose or outbreak of zits. Many of the rest of us, though, do respond with concern when our body no longer looks the same. Our anxiety tends to increase further when our body no longer performs the same. We may experience anything from mild to severe distress as we experience both visual and biological feedback that suggests we are not now as we were. The dying person is subject to prolonged and ever-intensifying feedback that is hurtful to self-image and confidence. What do we know about coping with distorted and altered body image? What can we do to help? These are among the constructive questions we could set our minds to when we want to be helpful to a dying person.

3. *The disempowerment model.* Other people are now making all the decisions. You are pretty much out of the loop. Life is going along without you. Once you were at the center of things; now you are a disenfranchised outsider, not really abused but not really taken seriously as a real player either. People experience disempowerment in many situations. The one-hit pop singer, the executive whose leverage disappeared during the latest corporate reorganization and the wife who has become a widow and lost much of her social status along with her husband. Some people are relieved to relinquish positions of power in the family, community, and workplace, but others feel rejected, abandoned, and bitter. There is often a period of doubt and seeking regarding one's own identity: "Who am I now, and am I worth anything?" Many dying people experience disempowerment in various forms. If we can heighten our awareness of this phenomenon, we put ourselves in a better position to be helpful.

4. *The time anxiety model.* Will you ever get it done in time? How can you write all those term papers and prepare for all those exams with so little time left? Schedules and deadlines are ever present in the lives of many people. It is not unusual to face several sets of schedules and deadlines at the same time as personal, family, social, and work demands converge on us. Everything seems to be moving too fast, and we feel tense and irritable as we look for some way out of the dilemma. The situation is intensified when we have too little time to accomplish something that is of great importance to us. Dying people sometimes find themselves in precisely this situation. They may have such crucial end-of-life issues as making financial arrangements to benefit the family or rescuing an intimate relationship that had come apart. We might be more helpful if we recognized that a dying person might be struggling with a foreshortened future and pressing needs to accomplish some things.

5. *The journey model.* The idea of journey is embedded in most if not all world cultures (Cole, 1992). Galen, Aristotle, and other voices from ancient times described the life course as a journey from one age or stage to the next. Christian theologians spoke of "spiritual ages," and in our own time Erik H. Erikson's (1950) "Eight Ages of

Man" is among the more influential updatings of the journey idea. Rituals have long been closely associated with journeys. It is risky to leave our current situation and venture forth. The real and symbolic distance between where we are and where we are going is full of danger. Ritual protects. Anybody who has ever moved into a new relationship, new job, or new community has probably experienced something of the anxiety that can be associated with even a positive change. Dying people are in transition from the world they have known (Kastenbaum, in press). Some of their thoughts and feelings might well be understood in these terms. Are there forms of ritual that would be meaningful and supportive to the person on the final journey?

There is still another step to take in a multiple perspective approach to the dying person's situation: taking into account the specific medical condition and its management. Nausea and constipation, for example, are more common in some conditions than others (Lipman et al., 2000) and can increase the intensity of many of the problems already identified. A spiritual approach can be another step beyond what has been discussed here but can also benefit from close attention to the situational and medical factors involved.

Your Deathbed Scene

Perhaps you attempted the deathbed scene exercise suggested in Box 5-1. The following is some information on how other people participating in death-related classes have depicted their own deaths (Kastenbaum & Normand, 1990). The typical respondent

- Expected to die in old age
- At home
- Quickly
- With the companionship of loved ones
- While remaining alert and
- Not experiencing pain or any other symptoms

What was the most common alternative response? Those who did not expect to die in the manner summarized previously instead viewed themselves as perishing in an accident, usually on the highway and while they were still young. In fact, those who thought their lives would end in a fatal accident tended to expect these accidents to occur in the near future. Almost all thought they would be alert and experience no pain or other symptoms as they neared death, whether death happened at home in old age or on the road in youth.

These deathbed scene expectations by mostly young college students will take on more meaning when we continue our exploration of the dying process in Chapter 6 with the focus on hospice care. You can enhance the personal meaning of the next chapter by pausing to answer the questions raised in Box 5-5.

Last Acts: How Do People Die in America Today?

That too many people die in pain, isolation, and despair has been known for a long time by those close to the situation. The palliative care movement developed in response to this need. However, the medical establishment and society in general, especially elected officials and other decision makers, have been slow to address this issue. Last Acts, a nonprofit organization composed of human service providers and other concerned citizens, has been making a significant impact.

A national survey commissioned by Last Acts (2002) found that Americans judge that end-of-life care is inadequate and should be improved. This critical judgment was made by people of all racial/ethnic backgrounds, education levels, ages, places of residence, and of both genders. Most of the respondents reported having lost a family member or friend during the past 5 years, and their low ratings of end-of-life care were similar to those of people who had not been recently bereaved.

There was an obvious disconnect between the way in which most Americans wanted their lives to end and what usually did happen. For example, 7 of 10 people said they would prefer to die at home, surrounded by family and friends, but more than 7 in 10 died in a hospital. There is also a disconnect between the hospice/palliative care philosophy and what occurs in medical training and facilities. Six of 10 physicians still have not received formal training for end-of-life care, and few U.S. hospitals have programs designed to support and comfort terminally ill people. Improved care for dying people is still somewhere between vision and reality. (For specific information on the quality of terminal care in your state, check the Last Acts Web site: www.lastacts.org/bettterend.)

SUMMARY

Dying, the transition from life, is unique because the separation is so complete and so final. However, the dying process has much in common with other types of transition with which we are all familiar: interactions that can be either disturbing or comforting, communications that can either inform or confuse, and self-evaluations that can either undermine or strengthen one's sense of identity and value. This chapter therefore considers dying as part of our total life experience while at the same time attending to what is distinctive about living with terminal illness. You were given the opportunity to imagine your own deathbed scene before we turned to the fundamental questions: What is dying and when does it begin? How we answer these questions is consequential because a person is often treated very differently by others when defined as dying or terminally ill. Several competing alternatives

were identified. Dying might be said to begin when (a) the physician draws this conclusion, (b) the physician informs the patient, (c) the patient accepts this conclusion, or (d) nothing more can be done to preserve life.

The transition from life to death can take one of several different trajectories, as described by Glaser and Strauss. We gave particular attention to the lingering trajectory, the expected quick trajectory, and the unexpected quick trajectory. Hospital staff usually feel differently about and respond differently to people who are on different trajectories. Awareness of these differences can help us to provide more effective support to patients, family, and staff. Familiar terms, such as healthy, dying, and terminally ill, do not apply to all individuals. We examined hemophilia as an example of a life-threatening condition in people who are healthy and vigorous yet go through their lives with greater risk.

Some people end their lives in social isolation because of inadequate communication with others. We identify some of the problems involved, including the special issues that arise in doctor–patient communication. A major hospital-based study (SUPPORT) has documented continuing gaps in communication between many physicians and their terminally ill patients. The physician's inability or unwillingness to listen to the patient's statements often leaves the patient with uncontrolled pain and violates the patient's preferences for end-of-life man-

---

BOX 5-5
A THOUGHT EXERCISE

The following questions were included in the National Hospice Demonstration Study (in a slightly different form). In Chapter 6, you will learn how terminally ill people responded to these questions and some of the implications for hospice care.

Now imagine yourself nearing the end of your life, and give the answers that best describe your own thoughts and feelings. Write your answers on a separate piece of paper.

1. Describe the last 3 days of your life as you would like them to be. Include whatever aspects of the situation seem to be of greatest importance.

2. What will be your greatest sources of strength and support during these last days of your life?

agement. Suggestions were made for improving communication with dying family members and friends.

We reminded ourselves that dying is both a universal and an individual experience. Age, gender, interpersonal relationships, and the nature of the disease, its treatment, and the environmental setting were considered as influences on the individual's experience of dying.

Theoretical models of the dying process include two stage theories that have originated in markedly different contexts: the ancient Buddhist conception and the clinical observations made by Kübler-Ross. The eight-stage Buddhist model is intimately related to that religion's view of the ever-changing and disintegrating process we call everyday life. The last four of these stages are said to occur past the point at which a physician would have certified death. The Kübler-Ross model consists of a sequence of responses that moves through denial, anger, bargaining, depression, and acceptance. Individuals do not always proceed through all the stages in either of these models. The Kübler-Ross stage theory was carefully evaluated. Attention was also given to three recent theoretical approaches: a developmental coping model; accepting the dying person's own reality as the model; and a multiple perspective model in which many different physical, personal, and interpersonal processes are considered separately and then brought together. We concluded by revisiting the deathbed scene you created and by inviting you to consider further questions about how you might feel in the last days of your life. In conclusion, we noted that how Americans would prefer to end their lives is still not the way that most lives do end: The campaign to improve care of dying people has a ways to go.

REFERENCES

Aiken, L. H., Clarke, S. P., Sloane, D. M., Sochalski, J., & Silber, J. H. (2002). Hospital nurse staffing and patient mortality, nurse burnout, and job dissatisfaction. *Journal of the American Medical Association, 288,* 1987–1993.

Barnard, D. (2000). *Crossing over: Narratives of palliative care.* New York: Oxford University Press.

Cole, T. R. (1992). *The journey of life.* Cambridge, UK: Cambridge University Press.

Connor, S. R. (1992). Denial in terminal illness: To intervene or not to intervene. *Hospice Journal, 8,* 1–15.

Coolidge, F. L., & Fish, C. E. (1983/1984). Dreams of the dying. *Omega, Journal of Death and Dying, 14,* 1–8.

Corr, C. A. (1993). Coping with dying: Lessons that we should and should not learn from the work of Elisabeth Kübler-Ross. *Death Studies, 17,* 69–84.

Corr, C. C., Doka, K. J., & Kastenbaum, R. (1999). Dying and its interpreters: A review of selected literature and some comments on the state of the field. *Omega, Journal of Death and Dying, 39,* 239–261.

Dembour, M.-B. (1998/1999). The conscious death of a two-year-old: Beautiful and unbearable. *Omega, Journal of Death and Dying, 38,* 187–200.

Demmer, C. (1999). AIDS attitudes and attitudes toward caring for dying patients. *Death Studies, 23,* 433–442.

Erikson, E. H. (1950). *Childhood and society.* New York: Norton.

Glaser, B. G., & Strauss, A. (1966). *Awareness of dying.* Chicago: Aldine.

Glaser, B. G., & Strauss, A. (1968). *Time for dying.* Chicago: Aldine.

Golden, R. L. (1997/1998). Sir William Osler: Humanistic thanatologist. *Omega, Journal of Death and Dying, 36,* 241–258.

Goldsmith, J. C. (2001). *About hemophilia.* New York: The Hemophilia Foundation.

Gyatos, Tenzin, the 14th Dali Lama. (1985). *Kindness, clarity, and insight* (J. Hopkins, Trans.). Ithaca, NY: Snow Lions.

Hinohara, S. (1996). Comments. In *QOL in medicine and nursing international conference.* Tokyo: Life Planning Center.

Hurley, A. C., & Volicer, L. (2002). Alzheimer's disease. "It's okay, mama, if you want to go, it's okay." *Journal of the American Medical Association, 288,* 2324–2331.

Improving care near the end of life: Why is it so hard? [Editorial]. (1995). *Journal of the American Medical Association, 274,* 1634–1636.

Jansson, L., Norberg, A., Sandman, P.-O., Athlin, E., & Asplund, K. (1992/1993). Interpreting facial expressions in patients in the terminal stage of Alzheimer disease. *Omega, Journal of Death and Dying, 26,* 309–324.

Kastenbaum, R. (1978). In control. In C. A. Garfield (Ed.), *Psychosocial care of the dying patient* (pp. 227–244). New York: McGraw-Hill.

Kastenbaum, R. (1984). The changing role of the physician with the terminally ill elderly. In I. Rossman (Ed.), *Clinical geriatrics* (3rd ed., pp. 618–620). New York: Lippincott.

Kastenbaum, R. (1993). Gender as a shaping force in adult development and aging. In R. Kastenbaum (Ed.), *The encyclopedia of adult development* (pp. 165–170). Phoenix: Oryx.

Kastenbaum, R. (1993/1994). Dale Gladden: An Omega Interview. *Omega, Journal of Death and Dying, 28,* 1–16.

Kastenbaum, R. (1995/1996). "How far can an intellectual effort diminish pain?" William McDougall's journal as a model for facing death. *Omega, Journal of Death and Dying, 32,* 123–164.

Kastenbaum, R. (2000). *The psychology of death* (3rd ed.). New York: Springer.

Kastenbaum, R. (in press). *On our way: The final passage through life and death.* Berkeley: University of California Press.

Kastenbaum, R., Barber, T., Wilson, S., Ryder, B., & Hathaway, L. (1981). *Old, sick, and helpless.* Cambridge, MA: Ballinger.

Kastenbaum, R., & Normand, C. (1990). Deathbed scenes as expected by the young and experienced by the old. *Death Studies, 14,* 201–218.

Kastenbaum, R., & Thuell, S. (1995). Cookies baking, coffee brewing: Toward a contextual theory of dying. *Omega, Journal of Death and Dying, 31,* 175–188.

Kelleher, A. (1990). *Dying of cancer. The final year of life.* London: Harwood.

Kiecolt-Glaser, J. K., McGuire, L., Robles, T. F., & Glaser, R. (2002). Emotions, morbidity, and mortality: New perspectives from psychoneuroimmunology. *Annual Review of Psychology, 53,* 83–107.

Kramer, K. (1988). *The sacred art of dying.* New York: Paulist Press.

Kübler-Ross, E. (1969). *On death and dying.* New York: Macmillan.

Lawton, J. (2000). *The dying process. Patients' experiences of palliative care.* London: Routledge.

LeShan, L. (1982). In M. N. Bowels, E. N. Jackson, J. A. Knight, & L. LeShan (Eds.), *Counseling the dying* (pp. 6–7). New York: Nelson.

Lesses, K. (1982/1983). How I live now. *Omega, Journal of Death and Dying, 13,* 75–78.

Lester, D. (1992/1993). The stigma against dying and suicidal patients: A replication of Richard Kalish's study twenty-five years later. *Omega, Journal of Death and Dying, 26,* 71–76.

Lipman, A. G., Jackson, K. C., & Tyler, L. S. (2000). *Evidence based symptom control in palliative care.* New York: Haworth.

Moller, D. W. (1996). *Confronting death. Values, institutions, & human mortality.* New York: Oxford University Press.

Nuland, S. B. (1994). *How we die.* New York: Knopf.

Provonost, P. J., Angus, D. C., Dorman, T., Robinson, K. A., Dremsizov, T. T., & Young, T. L. (2002). Physician staffing patterns and clinical outcomes in critically ill patients. *Journal of the American Medical Association, 288,* 2151–2162.

Rosen, E. J. (1998). *Families facing death.* San Francisco: Jossey-Bass.

Sulmasy, D. P. (2002). I was sick and you came to visit me: Time spent at the bedsides of seriously ill patients with poor prognoses. *American Journal of Medicine, 111,* 385–389.

SUPPORT (1995). A controlled trial to improve care for seriously ill hospitalized patients. *Journal of the American Medical Association, 274,* 1591–1599.

Sweeting, H. N., & Gilhooly, M. L. M. (1991/1992). Doctor, am I dead? A review of social death in modern societies. *Omega, Journal of Death and Dying, 24,* 251–270.

Taylor, J. (1977). *Holy dying.* New York: Arno. (Original work published 1651)

Turkel, S. (2001). *Will the circle be unbroken?* New York: New Press.

Weisman, A. D. (1993). Avery D. Weisman: An Omega interview. *Omega, Journal of Death and Dying, 27,* 97–104.

Weisman, A. D., & Kastenbaum, R. (1968). *The psychological autopsy: A study of the terminal phase of life.* New York: Behavioral Publications.

Weisman, A. D., & Worden, J. W. (1975). Psychosocial analysis of cancer deaths. *Omega, Journal of Death and Dying, 6,* 61–65.

Weisman, A. D., & Worden, J. W. (1976). The existential plight in cancer. Significance of the first 100 days. *International Journal of Psychiatry in Medicine, 7,* 1–16.

Zlatin, D. M. (1995). Life themes: A method to understand terminal illness. *Omega, Journal of Death and Dying, 31,* 189–206.

GLOSSARY

Cardiopulmonary Resuscitation (CPR): Massage, injection, or electrical stimulation intended to restore heart and breath.

Colostomy Bag: A container for the collection of feces, attached to an abdominal opening following a surgical procedure on the bowel.

Danger List (D.L.): A classification used by some health care systems to indicate that a patient is at risk for death.

Euthanasia: Originally: painless and peaceful dying. Currently: ending a person's life to avoid continued or increased suffering.

Hemophilia: A genetically linked defect that interferes with the coagulation of blood and therefore can result in excessive bleeding.

Institutional Evasions: Techniques used by staff members to bypass the rules in order to get through a difficult situation.

Middle Knowledge: A state of mind in which the person has some awareness of death but shifts from time to time in acknowledging and expressing this awareness.

"Orange Card": A legal document in which a person renounces the use of CPR and other emergency procedures.

Stage Theory: Holds that the phenomena in question occur in a fixed sequence of qualitatively different forms.

Surrogate: A person who acts in the place of another person who is not available or unable to respond.

Trajectories of Dying: The distinctive patterns through time that can be taken by the dying process, for example, a long fading away (lingering trajectory) or unexpected (quick trajectory).

It is a woman who provides care for disabled and life-threatened men in this 13th-century illustration, and it is still most often women who serve at the bedside of terminally ill people.

chapter 6

THE HOSPICE APPROACH TO TERMINAL CARE

Dr. Singer had prepared her for the symptoms that were to come: "You are now in the terminal phase, first the bowel, then your stomach gets hard like a rock, you have nausea and your stomach is not able to process food anymore." He prescribed morphine for her pain, but Mrs. Legendre was reluctant to take it. She was like many patients with advanced cancer who resist taking pain medication as a way of staving off the reality that their disease has progressed. To take the medication was to admit that the pain was getting worse. To admit that the pain was getting worse was to admit that the cancer was getting worse. And to admit the cancer was getting worse was to begin to look into the face of death.
—Anna Towers (2000, p. 81)

I told her gently that it was part of the disease progress, and that all she could do was to keep her mum comfortable. She burst into tears and ran into the kitchen. I followed her but when I put my arms around her, she pushed me angrily away. I stood back helpless, as she shed her silent tears. When she stopped crying, I asked her if she would like to talk about it, but she just shrugged her shoulders. "It's all so hopeless," was all she said, and then she changed the subject.
—McGrath, Yates, Clinton, and Hart (1999, p. 25)

At Gates' home, the living room that was a flurry of activity just 6 days ago is now empty and quiet. (Nurse Jeanne) Fabricius sits with Gates at a kitchen table as the recent widow recounts the story of her husband's death. "Her compassion for me was amazing," Gates said as her eyes filled with tears. "She gave me the tools I needed to care for him, but the first thing she did was to give me a hug. She was not there just as a nurse, but as a friend. I will never forget that."
—Heather Stringer (2002, p. 18)

Louise was 77 at the time she died. She was tiny, no more than 5 feet tall. She had a cart in which during the day she kept four suitcases. Every night she brought the cart with her and took the cases one by one up a series of steps to the shelter. She would set up a foldout chair and table that served as her "dining room," and open her can of tuna, or maybe sardines... whatever little snack she had, as she waited for the shelter to open. Every morning she would pack the four bags down to her cart and spend her day walking the streets of the city.
—Wright, Jones, and Wright (1999, p. 240.)

Desperate refugees flooded the nation by the hundreds of thousands. Hospitals and rehabilitation centers were overwhelmed by the number of wounded people. The mass media was filled with reports of killing, torture, and extreme suffering physically, emotionally, socially, and spiritually. The question was raised: Does it make any sense to speak about "dying with dignity" amid so many terrible and extremely humiliating deaths? Is it realistic to speak about dying decently in a country where so many persons now cannot live decently?"
—Anica Jusic, MD (1997, p. 126), founder of the first palliative care unit in Croatia just before his country was invaded by the Serbian/ Yugoslav army.

Each year, an estimated 600,000 Americans receive what is known as hospice or palliative care at the end of their lives. We might say this is "only" a little more than one out of four terminally ill people, or we can say that this is a remarkable development, considering that hospice care was almost unknown in the United States until the 1970s. Perhaps we should simply say that hospice was always intended as an option for the care and comfort of dying people and their families—a new choice to consider.

The hospice approach has become an international model and beacon of hope for terminally ill people and their families. A snapshot of hospice care in action would show us an intact and loving family that is providing support for the terminally ill person with guidance and assistance from nursing and medical personnel and com-

munity volunteers. The scene would probably be at the dying person's own home, although it might also take place in a residential setting. We would assume the patient to be a well-integrated, mentally competent person and, of course, the community to be peaceful, orderly, and well functioning.

We have started this chapter, however, by reminding ourselves that this idyllic picture does not always hold true. Many kinds of people die under many kinds of conditions. Mrs. Legendre's resistance to accepting the seriousness of her condition deprived her of adequate pain medication and other services that could have been offered by a palliative care program. Like the family members of many other terminally ill patients, her husband was devastated by her suffering but was unable to persuade her to accept pain relief.

The nurse who was rebuffed by the angry and resistant daughter had come up against the fact that family members are not always ready to deal with the loss and do not always have the ability to communicate openly on emotional issues. In contrast, Mrs. Gates was making her way through bereavement and grief because her family had accepted hospice care that offered compassion as well as skill. More challenging was Louise's situation. She was a mentally ill widow who had suffered years of abuse from her husband and had little or no contact with her other family members. The staff members of the shelter for the homeless had few resources and little or no legal standing as they tried to care for her during her final illness and tried to arrange a dignified funeral and memorial service. Even more challenging was the situation confronting the new Croatian Society for Hospice/Palliative Care in the midst of the deprivations and devastations of war. Nevertheless, the caregivers did help some people to die "decently," and the society is continuing its work today. The world is not perfect—not for the living, not for the dying, and not for those who provide care. Yet the hospice approach itself was created by imperfect people within this imperfect world.

In this chapter, we describe the origins and nature of hospice care for terminally ill people. We also consider both the potential of the hospice movement and the difficulties that limit and threaten its distinctive role in society. It will be important to understand not only the workings of hospice programs but also the ways in which they are affected by their host communities and national cultures.

We begin where hospice began: in the compassionate vision of those who were moved by the suffering and despair of dying people long before the advent of the modern health care system. This historical background provides the foundation for understanding hospice today and tomorrow.

HOSPICE: A NEW FLOWERING FROM ANCIENT ROOTS

Temples of healing ministered to the psychological and physical ailments of the Greeks. The priests and other healers recognized that health and illness involved more than physical condition: One must consider the whole person. The temples of healing were designed to please, soothe, and encourage the anxious and ailing people who journeyed to them. Music as well as medicine were part of the healing program. Every effort was made to restore the patients through an appealing physical environment, therapeutic conversation, positive imagery, bathing, massage, and walks in the countryside.

Imperial Rome established hospitals for military personnel. You would recognize something of the modern bureaucratic style of organization in these early hospitals, just as you would recognize the resonance between the holistic approach offered in the temples and the approach taken by modern hospice programs. However, neither the temple nor the hospital were designed for the care of the dying person. Health care providers, then as now, were more interested in working with people who were thought to have a chance of recovery.

There is no reason to doubt that some compassionate people did provide comfort to the dying as best they could. It is likely that the earliest examples of hospice-type care did not leave documentary traces for the historian. Perhaps in the *ha-rem* of a Byzantine ruler there were women with special skill and sensitivity in caring for the dying. Perhaps some wealthy families in Syria or Athens saw to it that the poor were treated well in their last days of life. The documentary trail becomes clearer with the advent of the Christian era. Public infirmaries (*nosocomeia*) were established in Greek-speaking areas of Christianity during the 4th century. These facilities provided care for people dying of epidemics as well as patients who were likely to recover. Roman emperor Julian, an opponent of the upstart Christian movement, acknowledged that these hospices had made a very favorable impression on everybody "owing to the humanity evinced by Christians toward outsiders" (Phipps, 1988). Julian resolved to establish his own hospice in every city, but his own death aborted this plan.

The hospice movement spread to western Europe at the end of the 4th century through the influence of Fabiola, a wealthy Roman widow who had been inspired by the care for the sick that she had witnessed in monasteries in the Holy Land (Phipps, 1988). Fabiola brought this concept with her to Italy, not only supporting hospices financially but also serving as a nurse. St. Jerome knew Fabiola and honored her contributions, writing that "Often too she washed away the matter discharged from wounds which others, even though men, could not bear to behold.... She gave food with her own hand and even when a patient was but a breathing corpse she would moisten his lips with liquid" (cited in Phipps, p. 93). And so Fabiola, a woman who lived and died approximately 1600 years ago, may have given an enduring gift to humankind that in our own time has been renewed as the modern hospice program.

A type of hospice became well established in the 5th century. The term derives from the Latin *hospitium,* which has also given us such words as host and hostess. The medieval hospice was usually a house in which people in need could find food, shelter, and other comforts under Christian auspices. Care of the homeless dying was but one function of the medieval hospice, which most commonly served those undertaking the arduous pilgrimage to the Holy Land. Travelers who were fatigued, ill, or dying would find welcome. Certain religious orders became especially known for their hospice care. Established by Benedictine monks in the 6th century, the Monte Cassino monastery was one of the most noted hospices. Unfortunately, this historic shelter was destroyed during World War II in a misguided military operation. Throughout the medieval period the hospice functioned as one of the purest expressions of Christian piety: Here the hungry were fed, the thirsty given water, the naked clothed, the homeless sheltered, and the sick provided care and comfort. Medical treatment was minimal, which was probably just as well considering how ineffective or even dangerous most "remedies" were at that time.

Unfortunately, something went very wrong between the time that the early hospices flourished and the beginning of the modern hospice movement. During the intervening centuries the original hospice tradition clung to life in only a few scattered facilities. Phipps (1988) suggests that hospices became an innocent casualty of the Protestant Reformation and then were replaced by state-run institutions with different types of personnel and philosophies. Whatever the reasons, the religiously oriented hospice and its mission of mercy for the dying faded away, although the spark was kept alive in a few places. Bureaucracy and technology-oriented medicine took over. The newly emerging systems of health care evaded dying people, who were now seen as disquieting reminders that "to all things there is a season."

The renewed hospice approach occurred in the 19th century. Again, the leaders were women who recognized the need to provide more compassionate and effective care for people at the end of their lives. Jeanne Garnier inspired other young widows to establish L'Association des Dames du Calvaire in Lyon, France, in 1842. Her influence spread to several other cities that established organizations that now provide the modern version of hospice care (Clark, 2000). Another major step forward was Mary Aikenhead's establishment of St. Vincent's Hospital in London. In her memory, Our Lady's Hospice for the Dying started in 1879 at a nearby convent. By 1905, a similar facility had been established in London: St. Joseph's Hospital introduced improvements in pain relief and general medical care. The worldwide hospice movement today owes much to the compassionate and strongly motivated women who created such caregiving institutions despite their initial lack of financial resources and political influence. For some time, however, these programs remained small and isolated as industrial and technological development continued to transform society. They were also deeply embedded in religious belief systems and church practices (Humphreys, 2001).

The hospice movement took its next major step when a medical officer at St. Joseph's Hospice introduced improvements in pain control for dying people. Dr. Cicely Saunders subsequently became the founder of St. Christopher's Hospice in London, which has served as an inspiration and model for many others. Starting out as a student of philosophy, politics, and economics, Saunders enrolled in a nurse training program during World War II. A back injury made it difficult for her to continue as a nurse, so she became a social worker and then a physician. This triple perspective on caregiving liberated Saunders from seeing the dying person from the limitations of any one health provider standpoint. Her vision of hospice care has always emphasized contributions and interactions from people of diverse backgrounds.

I asked Dame Saunders about the circumstances that led to her introduction of modern hospice care. The inspiration provided by two people was especially important. Lillian Pipkin, a Salvation Army matron, had taught her the basics of pain management for terminally ill patients, which she was then able to apply for the first time herself at St. Joseph's and, subsequently, St. Christopher's. Pipkin was also a role model for Saunders in understanding and communicating with dying patients. The other person was David Tasma, a dying man who (Saunders, 1993)

> needed not only symptom relief, but also the time, space, and atmosphere in which to come to his own terms with his life. At this point, David was feeling that his life had been unfulfilled and perhaps meaningless. Something emerged during our long conversations that not only sparked the inspiration for hospice but also made possible his own quiet peace.... David had made a personal peace with the God of his forefathers before he died, and he left me with the assurance that he had found his answers—and with the belief that all our caring must give total freedom to others to make their own way into meaning." (p. 264)

Tasma also contributed his small legacy to Saunders for what would become the hospice project.

What was the first response of physicians and nurses to Saunders innovations? Would they be dubious and resistant? Saunders (1993) stated,

> I was therefore soon able to demonstrate to an increasing number of visitors that dying patients could be alert, as well as free from pain, and very able to do the teaching themselves. Without this opportunity, I do not think the modern hospice movement would have been established and I am everlastingly grateful to the patients and Sisters of St. Joseph's who, together with David Tasma and the patients of St. Luke's, I see as the true founders. (p. 264)

These personal reflections are valuable for what they tell us about the spirit in which the hospice movement was conceived:

- From Fabiola onward, women have been the prime movers in attempting to improve the care of dying people.
- Unique personal interactions and relationships have been crucial to the development of hospice. Both in its origins with Dame Saunders and with its later introductions to other nations, hospice has grown from the efforts of a few highly motivated individuals rather than as part of a formal plan hatched by bureaucratic committees.
- The stereotype that doctors "know better" than their patients has been reversed in hospice philosophy. All care providers are invited to learn from the people who really know what it feels like to cope with the physical and psychological stresses of dying: the patients themselves.
- Although hospice leaders are often people with strong religious belief, the emphasis is on giving "total freedom to others to make their own way into meaning." This was evident at the start in the interaction between a Christian physician (Saunders) and her Jewish patient (Tasma).

By the early 1970s, it was clear that hospice care was a promising alternative to the "never-say-die," high-tech, impersonal approach increasingly dominant in Western medicine. Many questions and problems remained, however, including the establishment of standards of care and the challenge of establishing hospices in other nations, including the United States.

STANDARDS OF CARE FOR THE TERMINALLY ILL

The International Work Group on Death and Dying, which included Dr. Saunders and other pioneers, saw the need to develop guidelines for the further development of hospice care. The task force decided first to give expression to the implicit assumptions that governed the care of the terminally ill. As you read the following list, remember that these were not the standards that the task force intended to recommend; rather, it was our way of identifying the hidden standards that governed the way in which terminally ill people were then treated.

The items on the following list were seen as the typical pattern of a "good" or "successful" death from the perspective of the facility in which a terminally ill person spent his or her final days of life.

Hidden or Implicit Standards of Care

1. The successful death is quiet and uneventful. The death slips by with as little notice as possible; nobody is disturbed.
2. Few people are on the scene. There is, in effect, no scene. Staff is spared the discomfort of interacting with family and other visitors whose needs might upset the well-routined equilibrium.
3. Leave-taking behavior is at a minimum: no awkward, painful, or emotional good-byes to raise the staff's anxiety level.
4. The physician does not have to involve himself or herself intimately in terminal care, especially as the end approaches.
5. The staff makes few technical errors throughout the terminal care process and few mistakes in medical etiquette.
6. Attention is focused on the body during the care-giving process. Little effort is wasted on the unique personality of the terminally ill individual.
7. The patient expresses gratitude for the excellent care received.
8. The person dies at the right time; that is, after the full range of medical interventions have been tried and before the onset of a long period of lingering.
9. After the patient's death, the family expresses gratitude for the excellent care received.
10. The staff is able to conclude that "we did everything we could for this patient."
11. Physical remains of the patient are made available to the hospital for clinical, research, or administrative purposes (via autopsy permission or organ donations).
12. A memorial (financial) gift is made to the hospital in the name of the deceased.
13. The cost of the terminal care process is determined to have been low or moderate; that is, money was not wasted on a person whose life was beyond saving or, more important, the hospital came out ahead after expenses were compared with reimbursements.

The task force proposed a very different set of standards.

Proposed Standards Recommended by the International Task Force

- *Patients, family, and staff all have legitimate needs and interests.*
- *The terminally ill person's preferences and lifestyle must be taken into account in all decision making.*

These were the basic guidelines from which the others were generated. The first proposition was intended to promote honest interactions and reduce conflicts. Recognition that everybody in the situation is human and has legitimate needs and interests provides a realistic starting point for care. The second proposition suggests that treatment should not be overly standardized. The specific standards follow.

Patient-Oriented Standards

1. *Remission of symptoms is a treatment goal.* Even if it is expected that the person will die within hours or days, efforts should be continued to maintain functional capacity and relieve pain and anguish. A dying person should not be made to endure thirst, for example, or gasp for breath when a change of position might afford relief.
2. *Pain control is a treatment goal.* Uncontrolled pain not only intensifies the anguish of dying but also disturbs interpersonal relationships and can lead to demoralization. The patient's ability to maintain psychological equilibrium is severely tested by pain.
3. *The patient's intentions will be respected as one of the main determinants of the total pattern of care.* This does not mean that every expressed wish of the patient will automatically be granted. The rights and responsibilities of family, staff, and society as represented by the

Hospice care offers a more personal and comforting approach to helping terminally ill people.

legal system must also be taken into account. The point is the willingness of family and health care providers to take seriously any document through which patients express their own wishes. (See Chapter 7 for a discussion of advance directives.)

4. *The patient should have a sense of basic security and protection in his or her environment.* This standard is met when dying people feel they can depend on the caregivers to perform their functions and maintain effective communication. Patients should feel safe. They should not have to live in apprehension of unexpected diagnostic or treatment procedures, brusque interactions, or a breakdown in medication and meal routines.

5. *Opportunities should be provided for leave-takings with the people most important to the patient.* This requires flexibility in visiting hours and rules for admitting visitors (e.g., children were often excluded). There should also be a good place to sit, privacy, and freedom from interruption. The patient should also have the opportunity to take leave of other patients and staff members if desired.

6. *Opportunities should be provided for experiencing the final moments in a way that is meaningful to the patient.* For example, patients should be afforded the opportunity to listen to music or poetry of their choice. Physical contact should be made possible if desired, unless there is some major contraindication (e.g., a highly contagious disease). This certainly includes a dying person being held in the arms of a loved one if this is what they both want.

Family-Oriented Standards

1. *Families should have the opportunity to discuss dying, death, and related emotional needs with the staff.* It is not acceptable for the staff to disregard requests for information or expressions of the need to share feelings.
2. *Families should have the opportunity for privacy with the dying person both while living and immediately after death.* This might include participation of close kin and friends in dressing the corpse and accompanying it to the funeral home, or it might include simply being alone with the dead spouse, sibling, or parent for an hour or so without interruption by staff.

Staff-Oriented Standards

1. *Caregivers should have adequate time to form and maintain personal relationships with the patient.* This is not a priority in most medical facilities, so it would require developing a new attitude toward the needs and utilization of personnel. Hospital scheduling practices seldom make it possible for a nurse or other staff member to maintain a steady relationship with a patient. There is still a pressing need for hospitals to schedule around the needs of the patients, especially those who are most vulnerable.
2. *A mutual support network should exist among the staff.* Care for the terminally ill can become an emotionally depleting experience, especially in high death rate situations. A medical facility in which staff are given little opportunity to discuss experiences and share feelings about their work with the terminally ill would be seen as deficient, regardless of the facility's competence in other respects.

ESTABLISHMENT OF HOSPICE PROGRAMS IN THE UNITED STATES

From Guidelines to Operational Programs

The standards proposed by the international task force became well established in the hospice movement, incorporated later in the Medicare reimbursement option and the guidelines of the National Hospice and Palliative Care Organization.

The hospice movement, though, did not simply materialize from definitions. Although hospice principles had found a way into several existing health care systems, it was the establishment of the Connecticut Hospice in New Haven in 1974 that marked the first full-service program of its type in the United States. Like St. Christopher's, the Connecticut Hospice provides both inpatient and home care services. Unlike St. Christopher's, however, the New Haven program started with home care and later added an inpatient facility when the National Cancer Institute agreed to provide startup support. The founders of the Connecticut Hospice had to solve many organizational and financial problems that have also confronted most of the other programs that followed. The goals and methods of hospice care were often misunderstood; many physicians were reluctant to participate in the new approach, and reliable sources of funding were difficult to find. It is a tribute to hospice leaders throughout the United States and to the flexibility of health care agencies that significant progress was made despite all the obstacles.

Today, the Connecticut Hospice is far from alone. There are now more than 2,000 hospice/palliative care organizations in the United States and Canada. Hospice organizations take several forms in North America and may even use different titles (e.g., palliative care unit is the term more frequently used in Canada). Some hospices are hospital based; others are free standing. St. Christopher's was created as an independent organization, and this has set the pattern for most other hospices in Britain. In the United States, economic considerations have favored the hospital-based approach, perhaps because surplus hospital beds existed at the time that hospice care was introduced. Either type of hospice can provide sensitive and high-quality service.

Full-Service and Partial-Service Hospices

Important differences exist in the spectrum of services that are offered by particular hospice organizations. At one extreme are programs that limit themselves primarily to home visits. A volunteer may provide companionship to the at-home patient for a few hours so the patient's family can attend to other needs and responsibilities. The hospice may also provide welcome assistance in a variety of ways, such as helping to obtain health-related supplies and equipment.

It is the more comprehensive, professional, and systematic type of hospice service that has won the support of the federal government. The National Hospice Reimbursement Act of 1983 established a Medicare Hospice Benefit that provides support for the full-service and fully accountable hospice. In return for financial support, a hospice must agree to

- Ensure continuity of care and professional management at all times, whether the patient is at home, in a hospital, or in a respite care setting.
- Establish and maintain a detailed plan of care for each patient.
- Evaluate quality of care and correct any problems that are identified.
- Provide an interdisciplinary team that includes a physician, registered nurse, social worker, and pastoral or counselor.
- Comply with licensing regulations in its state and locality.
- Maintain clinical records for each individual receiving hospice care.
- Provide all the core services required by the individual and any additional services that might be needed (e.g., physical therapy and speech-language rehabilitation).
- Guarantee that essential services are available around-the-clock every day.
- Operate an in-service training program to maintain and improve the skills of staff and volunteers.

The Medicare Hospice Benefit applies only when all three of the following conditions are met (Miller & Mike, 1995):

1. The patient's physician and the hospice medical director certify that a patient has a life expectancy of 6 months or less.

2. The patient chooses to receive care from a hospice as an alternative to basic Medicare coverage.
3. Care is provided by a hospice program certified by Medicare.

Is it really a good idea to set a specific "expected to die" date that the physician must certify? Many physicians have been distressed by this requirement. Jack D. Gordon, chief executive officer of the Hospice Foundation of America (info@hospicefoundation.org), notes that the 6-month decision was made without input from physicians and was a bureaucratic cost-control measure that had no grounding in the actual needs of terminally ill patients. It is widely believed among health care professionals that the 6-month provision has deterred some physicians from recommending the hospice option and influenced others to wait until the patient is only a few weeks or even a few days from death. Physicians are also understandably reluctant to "certify" time of death in advance because it seems too much like imposing a death sentence and people with the "same" condition may survive for different lengths of time.

All hospices have expenses that are not reimbursed by the federal program. It is for good reason that hospices conduct fund-raising programs and events and depend on community generosity to maintain their services.

THE HOSPICE IN ACTION

"Should we choose hospice or traditional care?" is a key question. We will be in a better position to consider this question after exploring just what it is that hospice does. The following are a few examples of how a hospice actually works.

Entering St. Christopher's

The first example is an observation I had the opportunity to make during a visit to St. Christopher's. Word was received that a person was arriving for admission. A station wagon had just pulled up to an entrance facing the hospice's attractive garden plaza. The patient-to-be was a frail, emaciated woman who looked to be in her

60s. She was accompanied by a younger man. Dr. Saunders and the woman greeted each other as sunlight propitiously broke through the cloudy London skies. The woman smiled and said, "Well, I finally made it!" On her face there was the mark of physical ordeal but no indication of anxiety, anger, depression, or confusion.

The patient was immediately introduced to the nurse who would be responsible for much of her care and who then assisted her to what would be her own bed (which had been transported by elevator to the ground entrance). Just a few minutes later while touring the hospice we saw this woman again. She was already settled into her own place, sipping tea with the man who had driven her to the hospice. As it turned out, he was her husband. The debilitating effects of advanced cancer had given her an aged and emaciated appearance.

This simple incident tells us something about the aims and techniques of the hospice. The patient and her family had already been well acquainted with the hospice before time of admission. Consequently, there was a sense of having made the next logical stop on her journey through life rather than a jarring transition from home to an impersonal institution. Much of St. Christopher's effort is devoted to its home care program. With the guidance of hospice personnel, some families are able to provide high-quality care to their terminally ill members throughout the course of the illness. Patient and family know that the inpatient facility is available when and if they need it.

A hospice can be thought of more aptly as a process and as a spirit of mutual concern rather than as a place. The sociophysical environment of the hospice or palliative care facility is designed for life as well as death. For example, staff recognized the importance of the first few minutes of the admission process. Efficiency was improved by having the patient's own bed ready to meet her. Many other up-to-date techniques are used throughout St. Christopher's when these are seen as beneficial to patient care. Perhaps more important was the affirmation of human contact by both the medical director and the nurse. The prompt welcoming of the husband through the tea service further signified the hospice's interest in encouraging the maintenance of interpersonal relationships and comforting habits.

The philosophy of care encompasses the entire family unit. Many family members not only visit with their own kin but also befriend other patients. This greatly reduces the likelihood of social isolation for the patient and the sense of helplessness for the family. It does raise the possibility, however, that the family might spend so much time and effort at the inpatient facility that they neglect their own needs. To place a friendly limit on family involvement, St. Christopher's established a weekly "family's day off." This allows the family a brief vacation without any sense of guilt. At the end of this day I finally noticed what was missing among the residents of St. Christopher's: anxiety, shame, or despair. They did not have much life left to them, but their dignity and security were intact.

Mother's Last Moments: A Daughter's Experience

Another example comes from an American hospice program and expresses the viewpoint of a young adult daughter of a woman who had been terminally ill for several months after a lifetime of good health. The woman was being cared for at home during what proved to be the final phase of her illness.

The next day I woke up and went in to see my mother. I noticed the difference immediately. She had this rattle in her throat. She kept trying to talk, but all her words were garbled by the mucus in her throat.... And I called the doctor and he gave me a good idea of what was happening. It was very hard for me to believe that she was so close ["to death" were the words implied but not spoken by the daughter]. She looked so calm and serene. In her room and among all her things. She looked really OK. She didn't look like she was in distress. *She looked like she was just glowing.* And my sister came over. She brought over a tape made by a priest on death and dying. We put it on and we let my mother listen to it; isn't that awful? And it was talking about acceptance of death and it seemed to be quite appropriate at the time. And then my sister went to the movies and I stayed around with Emma [a housekeeper employed by the family to help out at this time]. And my sister had left a picture of her little boy so my mother could see him. And it was just as if everything was in preparation.

I got out her makeup and lotion and started to make her up. Put lotion all over her skin. She knew what I was doing, because she held out her arm like this, and moved a little here and there to make it easier to make her up. But I was afraid in touching her body. She was so frail, I was afraid her skin might break if I touched her too hard to hug her. Before this time, she hadn't wanted to be touched, because it hurt. But now it didn't seem to hurt her at all; her pain had diminished. I put blush on her face…and lipstick on…and I brushed her hair.

And then I explained to her that I was going out for a cup of tea, because Emma said, "Why don't you go out—you deserve a break. It's good for you to go out." Okay, after I finished making her up, I told her I was going out for a cup of tea and I would be right back.

As I bent down to hug her, she—her body—I don't know how to describe it: She opened her mouth as I was holding her, and blood came out. And I thought at first, "What's wrong, what's happening?" And Emma said, "It's okay, It's nothing. She's fine. She'll be okay." But it was hard for me to let go of her. A part of me felt like "that was it," but, oh, no, it couldn't have happened. When I looked at her again, she looked—beautiful. She was glowing. She looked so smooth. She was just—beautiful. It was the only time I saw her look so beautiful during her whole illness.

And when I came back the hearse was in front of our house. And I said, "Oh, no! You're not going to take my mother away!" And my father was there and the people who were supposed to be there; the things that were supposed to happen… I resented it all. "They're not going to go into the room. I'm going into the room first!" I wanted to touch her. I wanted to be alone with her. I went in and closed the door. And I touched her all over, and took her all in. And then I realized, I realized …she had gone without a struggle. *It was really right, it was all right, you know?* She looked very good. She looked as if it was right. It wasn't painful. It was the right time, and she was ready to go.

This is part of just one person's experience with death. The other family members also responded in their own distinctive ways to the situation. The father, for example, did much planning and managing—his way of coping with the impending loss. It would have been much more difficult for all the family members as well as the terminally ill woman to have responded like the distinctive people they were had they been constricted by a traditional hospital situation.

There were other positive features as well. This woman died free of pain and suffering. She felt safe. The final impression that "it was right" helped the daughter integrate her mother's death into her own ongoing life. She would not have to live with regret, self-recrimination, or anger about her own actions. Would she have felt comfortable applying lotion and makeup to her mother if they had been in a hospital? Would this even have been permitted? Would she have been allowed to stay to the very end or been shooed away by hospital staff? Would she have been allowed to return for a few minutes of privacy with her mother after death?

The Hospice of Miami was an important source of support, but there was strength in the family—the feelings that members of an intact and affectionate family had for each other. This does not mean, however, that the relationship between hospice and family was smooth at all times. The family at first had some resistance to the hospice's approach because it confronted them with the realization that they would soon lose the mother/wife to death.

The experience reported here was not "successful" if the aim of terminal care is to keep everybody's feelings under control and maneuver the death event through with minimal impact. The daughter's life had changed at the moment she first learned of her mother's terminal illness some months before. The circumstances of her mother's death and dying influenced her so much that she selected a career in the human services so she can provide care and comfort to others.

Dying from Two Worlds

Barbara had lived an active and useful life in two worlds. She was deeply rooted in her Native

American culture and also a distinguished university faculty member. This strong and vibrant woman was diagnosed with ovarian cancer at the age of 46 and within a few years would lose the battle for her life (Staton, Shuy, & Byock, 2001). Her many friends as well as her family were resolved to help her end her days in a way that would respect both her traditions and her unique personality. During most of her final illness, Barbara received care either at her home or at her sister Irene's home. She would go to Missoula's Hospice House when needed.

One day Barbara stopped eating and drinking. She now had a faraway look in her eyes. Irene asked her, "Have you started your journey to the other side?" Barbara replied with a smile "so big. And I told her, 'I'm here with you. I'm not going to leave you. You don't have anything to be afraid of. I want to thank you for this opportunity to see through your eyes to the other side.'" The sisters shared Native American traditional beliefs in which ancestors would come to escort them to the other side but also drew comfort from the Bible, which Irene read to her near the end (Staton et al., 2001):

> I always read her the Psalms—Psalm 23—and then I would burn smudge for her. I hung my eagle fan above her head because our belief is that's the dream world. And that when you lay down to rest, that eagle spirit is going to help you to have good dreams. (p. 276).

From the hospice's first contact with Barbara through the memorial services there was a natural meld of Native American culture with Christian tradition and modern palliative care techniques. No religious spokesperson on either side demanded a pure or exclusionary approach. The Bible and the eagle feather, the hospice, and the home were meaningfully related through the life of Barbara and her friends.

Adult Respite Care

Hospice programs usually provide care at the patient's home and in medical care facilities, as needed. A third alternative is becoming increasingly important. Adult respite care offers an intermediate placement. At some point in the course of a terminal illness, the patient may feel more comfortable in a respite care setting than either at home or in a hospital. For example, Walter, a robust businessman with "never a sick day in his life," had to admit that he could not shake off an uncharacteristic feeling of fatigue and discomfort. When finally persuaded by his family to see a doctor, he learned that he had an advanced and incurable cancer.

Once it was clear that there was no realistic hope for recovery, the family agreed to select the hospice alternative. Walter's condition was stabilized for several weeks. He took advantage of this time to work out a satisfactory business deal with his partner, say his good-byes to old friends, and immerse himself in the daily life of his very supportive family. His functional capacity then declined sharply. With great tact, Walter suggested that he be given "a few days off" until he recovered his strength. In retrospect, the family and the hospice nurse realized that he had wanted to relieve the unremitting pressure on his family—and that he sensed his death was imminent.

At his suggestion, Walter was taken to a respite care center, housed in a comfortable home-like setting. He thanked his wife and son and gently ordered them to take good care of each other and the rest of the family until he perked up a little and could come home. Approximately an hour later, the hospice nurse came by to see how he was doing. "I can go now," he smiled, "and so can you." He died peacefully within a few minutes.

In this instance, the respite care center did not have to offer any special services. What Walter needed was a way of establishing a little distance between himself and his loving family at the very end of his life. It is not unusual for a dying person to feel that he or she has accomplished all that there is to accomplish in "taking care of business" and expressing one's feelings to the people who most matter. The availability of an adult respite care center can give family members a valuable relief from constant responsibility, even though this may be for only a few days. These brief "vacations" can be useful to the terminally ill person as well as the family. As one woman confided within a week of her death, "I try my best to keep their spirits up, but it's getting harder and harder. I don't like to be alone either, but at least when

I'm alone I don't have to perform." A few days with considerate and expert caregivers who are not part of one's interpersonal network can liberate the dying person from investing the limited available energy in meeting the needs and expectations of others.

HOSPICE-INSPIRED CARE FOR A VARIETY OF PEOPLE

Most hospice patients have been adults with end-stage cancer or progressive neurological conditions, most often amyotropic lateral sclerosis (known in the United States as Lou Gehrig's disease). From the start of the modern hospice movement there has been interest in providing care for other people as well. Here, we consider the promising work that has been done to achieve this goal.

Hospice-Inspired Care for Children

Consider this description of an episode in the life of Marie, "a ghostlike 7-year-old" who had already undergone three unsuccessful kidney transplants from cadavers and was being kept on dialysis treatment until a fourth transplantable organ could be located (Meagher & Leff, 1989/1990):

As Marie sat on the child-life worker's lap, she ground her teeth with great intensity and anxiously shifted the position of her blood pressure cuff. She incessantly scratched and picked at the gauze pads which guarded her old abdominal wounds. "My tummy hurts! My tummy hurts!" she announced, in hope that she would be permitted a day off. After Marie's blood pressure was read, she reenacted the procedure, detail by detail, with the child-life worker. Marie methodically placed the cuff on the child-worker's arm, pumped forcefully, and, stethoscope in hand, engagingly admonished her to be still and not to cry. Satisfied with her work, Marie carefully folded the cuff and put it away. She took the child-life worker's hand and hesitantly hobbled toward the scale where she was weighed.

When the preparations for dialysis were over, reality robbed Marie of her tenuous control over her experience. Her dialysis rituals could no longer protect her, and her fear was apparent in

her eyes. As the staff placed Marie's papoose, or restraint, under her back, she frantically pleaded, "Have to make pee-pee...Mommy coming?... Bleeding! Give me something to put me to sleep!" Three adults wrestled with Marie as in panic she squirmed and fought to release herself from the papoose. Marie's right hand, the only part of her body free of restraint, blindly gripped the child-life worker's fingers.... Marie's mother would not be waiting for her after the ordeal had ended. Sedatives would not be used to ease the passage of time. (p. 178)

This was a typical experience in Marie's life. She suffered physical and emotional pain throughout her final hospital stay, during which she was, to all purposes, abandoned by her family because they could no longer tolerate the stress themselves. Astoundingly, the medical staff systematically denied Marie the partial relief she might have experienced from pain-killing medication. Instead, they attempted to deceive her by pretending to inject medications into her tubing. Why? So that she would not become a drug addict!

Marie experienced the torment of pain and abandonment in addition to the ravages of her disease. Her caregivers were not evil or unfeeling people, but they were working within the framework of aggressive, cure-oriented medicine. This "pull out all the stops" approach often reaches its peak of intensity when the patient is a child. The death of a child is an exceptionally powerful blow and violates our expectations in a society in which so many people survive into advanced adult years. Sometimes this approach is successful; more often the child dies anyway but experiences more suffering and less comfort than would have been provided if a hospice-inspired program of care had been selected.

It is very difficult in the case of a child to say "Let her go with love and comfort" as long as there seems to be any chance at all to prolong her life. This is probably the main reason that hospice care for dying children has not become more common. The decision to select hospice care involves recognition of impending death, a recognition that is usually avoided by family and caregivers as long as possible (and even a little longer).

Ida Martinson, a nurse who has played a significant role in the development of palliative care programs for children, observes (as quoted in Kastenbaum, 1995) that

> there is a greater sense of urgency for the health care professional to respond quicker when it is a child that is dying. Perhaps parents believe they are managing, and then suddenly panic and need advice or help quicker than, say, the wife or husband who is caring for a dying spouse. Symptom control is the basic need for both groups. Explaining the signs and symptoms and how dying occurs are essential for both groups as well. I still find nurses who do not believe they could work as well with families who have a dying child in contrast to a dying adult. I really believe they *can* function as well. (p. 257)

Children's Hospice International (CHI) has taken a leadership role in advocating state-of-the-art palliative care for terminally ill patients and educating other professionals. It is largely through their efforts that almost all hospice programs in the United States are now open to accepting children as patients. CHI can be contacted at 800-24-CHILD, chiorg@aol.com, and 901 N. Pitt Street, Suite 230, Alexandria, VA 22314. There is also a growing advocacy for including children in discussions about hospice and other medical care situations (Hinds, Bradshaw, Oakes, & Pritchard, 2002). At the least, this shows respect for the child and reduces a sense of exclusion at isolation, but such discussions can also result in useful and insightful comments by the child and reduce family tension.

Home care can be arranged for many terminally ill children. The opportunity to stay at home may be even more important for children than adults, avoiding the anxiety of separation. Parents can continue to be parents to their ailing child. To carry out their demanding responsibilities, however, parents need assistance from knowledgeable health care providers who also have the communication skills to deal resourcefully with this difficult situation. The program of care might be furnished either by a hospice organization or by other agencies and individuals whose approach might be called hospice inspired.

Careful decisions must be made based on the unique realities of each situation.

Hospice Care for People with AIDS

A person whose HIV infection has converted to an active case of AIDS encounters many of the same sources of stress as does any person afflicted with any terminal illness. These include the progressive loss of functions; pain, fatigue, and other symptoms; disruption and potential loss of interpersonal relationships; and a future in which hopes, plans, and ambitions become replaced by the prospect of death. Hospice care is also as applicable to people terminally ill with AIDS as it is to people with other life-threatening conditions. Palliative care and effective management often reduce the stress level and maintain a higher degree of comfort and individual lifestyle during the final phase of the illness.

There have been barriers, however, to hospice care for persons with AIDS, including the following:

- Willingness of the community to support hospice operations through volunteer services and fundraising if hospice programs accept AIDS patients
- Willingness of hospice staff and administrators to provide services to AIDS patients
- Willingness of AIDS patients to select the hospice option and willingness of their families to serve as participating caregivers
- Willingness of the health care system to make whatever adjustments might be necessary in admission and management of AIDS patients

Hospice programs did make an extra effort and took on extra risk when they made themselves available to AIDS patients. There was at first the risk that volunteers and other forms of community support would fall away if AIDS patients were accepted. By and large, though, the community maintained its support, although troubled by the association between AIDS and a promiscuous lifestyle. More accustomed to helping patients with terminal cancer, hospice programs had to devise new procedures for dealing with AIDS, a complex condition with many symptoms to treat and difficult treatment decisions to make. As time went on, almost all hospice programs reported that people with AIDS were receiving their full range of palliative care and support services.

HIV/AIDS remains a significant cause of illness and death in the United States and throughout much of the world. There have been changes, however, since the illness was officially recognized in 1981. It still occurs most frequently among male homosexuals but has also become prevalent among drug users of both sexes and an increasing threat in unprotected heterosexual contacts (Centers for Disease Control, 2001). Few people seem to be aware that women of childbearing age have become at greater risk. Understandably, there has been a primary emphasis on prevention and treatment. Unfortunately, obvious ways of preventing the spread of HIV/AIDS have been applied only sporadically. Many people at risk ignore or reject the opportunity for HIV testing, for example, and programs to eliminate sharing of contaminated needles by drug addicts have run into intense political opposition. Durham (2002, p. 203) succinctly concludes that "homophobia, poverty, homelessness, racism, lack of education, and lack of access to health care greatly influence testing, treatment, and prevention strategies."

Another change is the extended length of survival between HIV infection and death from AIDS-related complications. More people with HIV now live for years without symptoms. New drugs have made important contributions to this development. This development, however, does not alter the fact that AIDS remains a lethal condition. People with AIDS are still vulnerable to a general collapse of body functions and invasive infections as they approach death. Palliative care by highly skilled caregivers can do much to relieve the suffering. Some people with HIV/AIDS are reluctant to enter hospice care because they either hold out hope for remission or have been denying the severity of their illness. There is a zone of uncertainty about individual prognosis with HIV/AIDS, so people may differ in how they evaluate the situations as well as change their outlooks from time to time.

Despite these and other difficulties, there is evidence that hospice programs are responding to the needs of terminally ill AIDS patients. There are both positive and negative reports from hospice surveys (Cox, 1998). A positive is that terminally ill young women with AIDS are turning to hospice care in increasing numbers. This is especially important because women of childbearing age are the fastest growing group that is likely to contract AIDS, and some already have children. Hospice care can often manage their complex physical and emotional needs more adequately than traditional medical practice and do more for the children as well. A negative is that Hispanics and African Americans with AIDS seldom make use of hospice programs. This is troubling because it is unlikely that they are receiving the full range of palliative care and supportive services elsewhere.

Hospice Care for Nursing Home Residents

Dame Cicely Saunders has long been concerned with the welfare of frail and vulnerable elderly people. She and her colleagues have provided residential care to elders on the St. Christopher's Hospice campus for many years. It is clear that hospice-inspired dedication to the physical, social, and spiritual well-being of terminally ill people would be beneficial to residents of geriatric facilities as well, but it is not clear how such programs could be established and maintained, given limitations in funding and human resources. During the past half century there has been heightened concern for institutionalized elders. Conditions have improved overall, and there are some facilities in which staff skill and devotion are at the highest level. There is still a conspicuous gap, however, between the multiple resources that converge to help a dying person over a relatively short period of time and the resources available to help an institutionalized elder who may still have years to live.

There are encouraging indications that hospice-inspired care is becoming more available to institutionalized elders during the final phases of their lives. More skilled care facilities are now providing adequate pain relief to their terminally ill residents and consideration is being given to the special needs of terminally ill people in palliative care settings (Volicer & Bloom-Charette, 1999; Volicer & Hurley, 1998). It should not be forgotten, though, that many nursing facility residents are alert and capable of expressing their needs and desires. It is a continuing challenge and there are increasing expectations for long-term care facilities to provide not only palliative services but also *quality* palliative services to their residents.

Hospice-Inspired Care for Prisoners, the Homeless, and the Impoverished?

Timely and quality health care is not equally available to all people. The United States and many other nations are still struggling with the challenge of providing health care to all who are in need while constrained by financial and other considerations. Hospice leaders strongly advocate helping terminally ill people no matter what their social or financial status. Only slowly and gradually is society starting to respond to this challenge. Canadian bioethicist David J. Roy (1999) places the problem before us:

> How do the poorest of the poor die? Do we really want to know? That knowledge could be very disturbing, loaded as it might well be with imperatives for action. It could also be accusatory knowledge if those of us "in the know" do nothing to mobilize lethargic ministries, governments, health care institutions, and professional schools to develop and organize the services the poorest of the poor need, to have a chance of dying well. But the imperatives cannot stop there. It would be humanly and socially grotesque if our passion for the poor stopped at helping them to die well. If the end of this century is question period time, the question of how the poor both live and die has to be raised clearly, loudly, and persistently. (p. 3)

Research has confirmed the impression that terminally ill people who live in extreme poverty also die with more pain and suffering (Daneault & Labadie, 1999). The person who has not become or remained securely integrated in society is likely not only to die at an earlier age but also to die with less medical and social support. This group includes individuals who have ethnic and language backgrounds that are not part of the mainstream as well as those who have become isolated and nearly invisible because of their poverty. The researchers call for a greater awareness of the needs of impoverished terminally ill people on the part of the health care system.

Prisoners are also at excess risk for inadequate palliative care during their terminal illness. There are more than 1.5 million people imprisoned in the United States, and more deaths are occurring in prison than ever before because of longer sentences, the general aging of the population, and the high rate of HIV infection among inmates. More than 3,000 prison inmate deaths occurred in 1994, the last year for which definitive data are available (Maull, 1998). Approximately 3 of every 10 prison deaths are HIV-related. This means that the terminally ill person experiences a fairly long period of decline and is vulnerable to pain, nausea, delirium, and respiratory symptoms. Hospice-inspired care would be very much welcome in these circumstances.

Fortunately, the American Correctional Association and many prison systems are working to improve the situation. The prison setting is not what the founders of hospice care envisioned; it is certainly not a warm, open, and family-oriented environment. Nevertheless, a variety of efforts is being made to bring hospice-type palliative care into the institution or to provide compassionate release into hospice programs in the community.

We have already touched on the plight of people who depend on shelters for the homeless. Life is difficult enough for them. Facing death is often more difficult than it needs to be. Up to this point, few communities have given attention to providing end-of-life comfort and care to homeless people.

Hospice Care on the International Scene

Humane and effective care for dying people is a universal challenge. This challenge has been met to some extent by the development of palliative care programs in the United Kingdom that served as the model for hospice programs in the

United States, Canada, and several European nations. The future of hospice care, however, is taking shape in many other nations whose culture and living conditions differ markedly from those in which hospice first took root. For the broader view of hospice care and a useful perspective on our own situation, it is useful to examine the international scene. The information presented here comes from an international survey of hospice programs (Wilson & Kastenbaum, 1997) and from a few of the many reports received from individual hospices. We find that

- Hospice programs are growing rapidly throughout much of the world.
- The programs vary greatly in the size and characteristics of their catchment areas. Some hospices serve small populations in a sprawling rural areas with difficult road access, few telephones, and limited health care facilities. Other hospices serve a large but compact population in a technologically developed urban area. What works well for one hospice organization may not be feasible for another.
- Throughout the world, the largest number of hospice patients are in the 60–79 age group, with only approximately one patient in nine younger than the age of 40. Men and women are using hospice services more or less equally, with some local variations.
- Home care is the type of service most often received by hospice clients in every world region—often in nations or areas in which there had been no previous home care services of any type.
- All world cultures are proving to have traditional strengths that can contribute to the success of a palliative care program. Traditional cultures may at first resist hospice services, but reports indicate that love and concern for dying members of the family eventually bring forth a warm and caring response.
- The early phases of hospice development invariably encounter resistance from some medical practitioners and governmental officials as well as a public that has long avoided open discussion of the "taboo" topics of dying and death. The United States has not been alone in its reluctance to deal with death; similar responses have been reported by hospice pioneers in Africa, Asia, the Near and Middle East, and South America.
- Pain relief remains the central objective of palliative care, no matter how the program is structured or what cultural group it serves. Most hospice programs throughout the world have had to work strenuously to persuade physicians and law makers that it is possible to relieve the suffering of terminally ill people without creating drug addicts or causing premature death. Unfortunately, there is still considerable resistance to effective pain relief from people uninformed about the actual facts of palliative care.
- Education of the general public, human service professionals, and governmental decision makers has been recognized as a high priority by hospice programs throughout the world. Palliative care requires a host society that is able to integrate dying and death into its conception of the life course.

Hospice programs can be developed even within societies experiencing severe stress and deprivation. Croatia and Zimbabwe, for example, were subjected to widespread violence and social disorganization, and Poland was under an oppressive Communist regime, but effective hospice programs emerged in these countries nevertheless.

RELIEF OF PAIN AND SUFFERING

The alleviation of pain and suffering is the primary goal of palliative care programs. Although there is consensus on this goal, it is difficult to assess the level of pain, and, therefore, the level of relief from pain, because the experience is private or subjective. We can observe a person's body language and often we can ask a person about his or her experience of pain, but the "measurement" of pain remains one of the most elusive problems for all health care providers and researchers. There is not an exact science of measuring pain or pain relief, and this limitation should be kept in mind in whatever context we are attempting to evaluate the control of pain.

Why Pain Must Be Controlled

Why is pain control so important? The reasons are not difficult to identify:

- Pain is, by definition, a stressful experience.
- Pain reduces the ability to give attention to other matters, thereby isolating the sufferer and reducing his or her opportunity to reflect, interact, and accomplish.
- Pain can intensify other symptoms, such as weight loss, insomnia, pressure sores, and nausea.
- Fear and anticipation of pain can also be demoralizing. "Will the pain return?" "Will it get worse?" "Will I be able to endure it?"
- Pain contributes much to anxiety about the dying process. There are people who assume that dying is "all pain" and pain is unavoidable. This expectation can cause emotional distress, impaired communication, and, in some instances, suicide ("I'd kill myself first!").

Temperature, pulse, respiration, and blood pressure are the four vital signs that physicians and nurses throughout the world have been monitoring for many years. Now there is a fifth vital sign: *pain.* The hospice movement has made pain control a major priority in terminal care. In addition, many health care providers are now trying to determine the level of pain experienced by patients with any medical condition. Although not yet universally practiced, the establishment of pain as the fifth vital sign is a remarkable contribution from hospice.

Much of the hospice success in pain control derives from superior knowledge of available medications and their optimal use. However, part of the success must be attributed to the hospice philosophy: People should be as pain-free as possible as the end of life approaches to allow them the opportunity to complete projects, engage in leave-takings, or just to find some enjoyment and meaning in each remaining day. Hospice staff do not expect dying patients and their families to endure pain as long as possible until forced to "beg" for relief.

The hospice team is particularly expert in helping people cope with unremitting pain. Traditionally, the medical profession has given more attention to relief of short-term or acute pain.

This approach is often inappropriate and ineffective when applied to a terminally ill cancer patient. Hospice practice and research have demonstrated that most people can receive significant relief from pain throughout the dying process. There are exceptions; therefore, clinicians and researchers are continuing to search for improved techniques. Many of the failures in pain relief, however, are failures to apply knowledge that has already become available (Levy, 1988). For example, one study found that a sample of hospital-based nurses and physicians did not have the correct facts about some important facets of pain relief in terminally ill people even though they held generally favorable attitudes toward hospice (Kinzel, Askew, & Goldbole, 1992):

> Only 35% of nurses and 56% of physicians recognized that the total dose of narcotic to provide equivalent pain relief would be less with a regular dosing schedule than on an as-needed basis in this (a palliative care) setting. Only 10% of nurses and 38% of physicians were able to correctly order four narcotic analgesics according to potency. None of the physicians or nurses correctly identified "more than 960 milligrams" as the correct response on a multiple choice question regarding the maximum safe dose of morphine sulfate that can be given orally over 24 hours. (p. 88)

Physicians have reported that they do not have adequate education and training in providing relief from pain (Miller, Miller, & Single, 1997). This deficiency continues to be reconfirmed by additional studies. Sloan, Donnelly, Schwartz, and Sloan (1997) presented common clinical symptoms of a patient with advanced cancer to 33 resident physicians. Many of these doctors proved unable to manage the symptoms. Two of the specific findings are particularly noteworthy: They did not prescribe adequate medication to relieve the acute suffering of dispense (difficulties in breathing), and they tried to treat lack of appetite by forced feedings. Patients with advanced cancer under the care of these physicians would have suffered the anxiety of dypsnea without relief because of the widespread fear in the medical profession that opioids, the drug of choice for this problem, would turn the patients into addicts. Inflicting forced feeding on a person with advanced cancer would add another torment without providing real benefit. One other finding also should be mentioned: Physicians with more experience were no more competent than those with less experience. Basically, physicians who were not skilled in managing pain and other symptoms were the models for younger physicians.

Findings such as these suggest that medical and nursing schools have not been providing adequate, up-to-date information on the most effective use of pain-relieving medications for terminally ill patients, nor have their graduates kept themselves current on this topic through continuing education. This picture becomes more disappointing, perhaps even alarming, when another of Kinzel and colleague's (1992) results is considered: "Ninety-two percent of nurses and 88% of physicians felt very or mostly competent in their ability to provide technically competent care to terminally ill patients." To the extent that this pattern of findings is representative, then, it appears as though the typical hospital-based physician and nurse have a level of confidence that is not supported by their actual knowledge of the effects of specific pain medication regimes for terminally ill people. Professional as well as public education about hospice procedures obviously remains a high priority.

Effective pain management requires more than a textbook knowledge of drug effects (especially since some of the textbooks are out of compliance with clinical experience). The needs and pain tolerance of the particular individual must be considered, and the course of treatment must be subject to prompt review whenever problems occur.

Knowledgeable caregivers acquaint themselves with the family's needs and concerns and show them how they can be part of the pain relief effort. Another key to alleviating pain in terminally ill patients is to reduce the mental distress that is associated with illness, dependency, loss of function, and concern about the future. The personality and mental state of the patient and the interpersonal setting in which he or she is located can either increase or decrease sensitivity to pain. Some people have difficulty with the concept that pain can be all too real and at the same time related to one's mental and emotional state. Turk and Feldman (1992) suggest that

psychological factors *may modify the perception of pain and augment the experience of pain.* This is not the same as suggesting that psychological factors *cause* the pain. Nor is it to suggest that the pain reported is only imagined. Furthermore, we are not advocating that noninvasive approaches should be used in place of medical and surgical procedures. Rather, it is the intention to sensitize health care and especially hospice workers to the importance of considering the role of psychological factors in pain and to alert them to a set of strategies that may be useful to complement the usual pharmacological and surgical modalities already in their armormentorium. (p. 3)

Specific suggestions for relieving pain without surgery or drugs have included massage; application of heat, cold, menthol, and electrical nerve stimulation to the skin; careful positioning and exercising; hypnosis; guided imagery, and even aroma therapy. Most of these techniques can be used safely by informed caregivers and provide comfort without producing stress or side effects.

Perhaps the next time we hear of a person seeking physician-assisted suicide we should think immediately of noninvasive pain alleviation techniques and respite care programs as alternatives.

Many, but not all, terminally ill people suffer pain. Hospice specialists report as many as half of terminally people are free from pain. Note, however, that a person may be free of pain at some phases of the illness but experience pain at another time. Hospice programs have proven effective in controlling pain for most patients they serve. In the most typical situation, both pain and the fear of pain are substantially reduced soon after hospice care begins. A significant achievement of the hospice movement has been to encourage effective pain relief in the traditional medical context as well as in palliative care programs, although the latter are able to offer a broader spectrum of care and comfort services to dying people and their families.

Palliative care experts Jane M. Ingham and Kathleen M. Foley (1998) conclude that "despite the extensive body of knowledge available regarding cancer pain assessment and management, it often remains untreated, thereby diminishing the quality of patient care at the end of life" (p. 89).

Other Symptoms and Problems

Pain is not the only problem that can beset a dying person. Other types of symptoms may include

- Nausea
- Vomiting
- Dypsnea (respiratory difficulties)
- Pressure sores
- Insomnia
- Incontinence
- Weakness
- Fatigue
- Confusion
- Depression

Effective care requires attention to the prevention or alleviation of all these problems. With the active participation of a family caregiver as well as the hospice professional staff and volunteers, it is often possible to relieve these symptoms—for a while. Despite the best care, however, the terminally ill person is likely to become weaker and more fatigued as the end approaches. It will also become increasingly difficult for the dying person to move about. Hospice patients are less likely to be restricted to their beds until death is very close, but eventual decline must be expected. Findings from the landmark National Hospice Study (Mor, Greer, & Kastenbaum, 1988) indicate that the social quality of life remained high for hospice patients during their final weeks and days compared with that of patients receiving traditional medical care. Despite the inescapable fact of continued physical deterioration, patients receiving hospice care maintained their intimate relationships and avoided the social isolation that has sometimes befallen the dying person. However, the data also suggested that the personality and values of the person before becoming terminally ill also had a major influence on experiences during the last weeks of life. The difference

between hospice and traditional types of care sometimes seemed to be less important than individual differences in personality and the social support system. This finding can serve as a useful reminder that people as well as treatment approaches differ markedly.

There is evidence that hospice patients were able to experience a situation close to their own preferences (given, of course, the severe problems associated with rapidly failing health). Recall the questions raised at the end of Chapter 5. You were asked first to describe the last 3 days of your life as you would like them to be. This question, suggested by Beatrice Kastenbaum, was included in the NHDS. The following types of answers were most common (in order of frequency):

- I want certain people to be here with me.
- I want to be physically able to do things.
- I want to feel at peace.
- I want to be free from pain.
- I want the last 3 days of my life to be like any other days.

The support offered by hospice care makes it possible for many patients to be at home and enjoy the company of the "certain people" who mean the most to them. Similarly, with the advice and support of hospice volunteers and staff, the patient could still control some activities of daily life. Remaining in their environment provided a context for feeling at peace and having each day keep something of the feeling of a comforting routine. The patients' goals and the goals of hospice care were identical.

It is interesting to note some of the *least* frequently mentioned wishes for the last 3 days of life. Only approximately 1 person in 20 cared about "completing a task" or being "mentally alert." Even fewer hoped to "accept death," and fewer still wanted to "know when death is imminent, "to be able to bear pain," or "live until a certain time or event." This collection of low-incidence items includes many of the most dramatic wishes that are sometimes attributed to the dying person. By far the greatest number of terminally ill people simply wanted the comfort of familiar faces and the ability to continue to do a little for themselves and have a sense of peaceful routine. The goal of accepting death philosophically or demonstrating the ability to tolerate pain was seldom stated.

There is much in these findings that invites reflection. We might simply note that (a) what most people wanted was no more and no different from what hospice care tries to achieve, and (b) it is wiser to learn from each individual what really matters than to attribute motives and themes picked up elsewhere. The question on sources of strength was also included in the NHDS survey. Following are the most frequent responses given by a subsample of NHDS patients:

- Supportive family or friends
- Religion
- Being needed
- Confidence in self
- Satisfied with the help received

There appears to be a good match in general between what terminally ill cancer patients hope for (apart from recovery) and what hospice care is designed to achieve by its philosophy and method.

Marjorie C. Dobratz (1995) observes that the dying person's quality of life depends much on the social support that has been available to that person. This connection has been well established by her studies and those of other investigators. It has become apparent that one of the most important components of this social support is "how dying persons perceive their emotional and cognitive well-being." Dying people are most likely to experience their lives as meaningful and to adapt well to the challenges they face when they feel that others truly care for them. Dobratz further notes that when liberated from pain, hospice patients often show a remarkably capacity to retain their self-esteem. Competent management of pain enhanced by loving attention from both family and hospice caregivers is helping many a terminally ill person to find meaning and value in every day of life.

Your Deathbed Scene, Revisited

Think about the personal deathbed scene you imagined while reading Chapter 5. Now that you

have read more about the dying process and terminal care, it might be instructive to review your own expectations. If your deathbed scene was similar to those of most students, you portrayed a rather sanitized image that does not have much in common with the way that most people actually die. This is true particularly with respect to pain and other symptoms. Most dying people have pain—although it may be controlled by competent physicians and nurses—and most dying people have a variety of other symptoms as well.

In contrast, most college students portray themselves as dying without pain and without other symptoms (Kastenbaum & Normand, 1990). What does this discrepancy mean? At the least, it means that even those self-selected people who have chosen to enroll in a death-focused class have unrealistic ideas about their physical condition at the end of life. What else might this discrepancy mean? I leave this question to your own reflections.

In some respects, the typical deathbed scene expected by college students has some relationship to the actual deathbed scenes experienced by many people who have received hospice care: Death occurs at an advanced age by a person who is at home, companioned by family and other loved ones. However, although many college students have made a point of indicating that they wanted to and actually *would* "go quickly," most people actually die over a longer period of time. Some terminally ill people do "slip away quietly" in their sleep, but this passage has usually been preceded by months of declining health and increased functional limitations. Realistically, most of us will live for some time with our final illness, and so will our loved ones. Each person must make his or her own decision about the desirable balance between wishful fantasy and reality.

ACCESS TO HOSPICE CARE AND THE DECISION-MAKING PROCESS

Suppose a person has learned enough and is ready to make the choice between traditional medical management and hospice care for the terminal phase of life. The following are three useful questions to consider:

1. *How certain is the prognosis?* Those who decide to seek hospice care have become convinced that they have only a few months (or less) to live. Usually these people have "been through the mill" in diagnostic and treatment procedures. In choosing hospice, they are expressing a preference for the highest possible quality of life rather than continued efforts to prolong life that would be doomed to failure. However, some people are not in the position to make this choice. Either there is still reason to hope that recovery or remission will occur or it is difficult to predict how long they have to live with their terminal condition. Certainty of death within the near future is a difficult forecast to cope with, yet it does provide a firm basis for decision making. The person who could live 1 month or several years with a life-threatening condition may not be in a position to enter a hospice program, nor may the person who still has a "fighting chance" to recover.

2. *Does the course of this terminal illness lend itself to existing forms of hospice care?* Hospice programs have developed primarily around the needs associated with patients with incurable cancer and those afflicted with progressive neuromuscular conditions such as amyotropic lateral sclerosis (Lou Gehrig's disease). There has always been a willingness to help people with other conditions as well. However, the more that the nature and course of a terminal illness differ from the patterns associated with cancer, the more questions must be raised about the match between hospice resources and the individual's needs. Two types of conditions are especially likely to raise this question: (a) conditions in which a person might either live quite awhile or die suddenly and (b) conditions that involve extensive precautions against infection—either of or by the patient. Each hospice establishes its own scope of services, and most hospices attempt to expand this scope as demands arise. It would be wise to examine carefully the abilities of local hospice organizations to meet the needs of a person whose terminal illness is not cancer related or neuromuscular.

3. *Is the family situation conducive to hospice care?* The basic hospice model involves a dying person, that person's family and home, and the services provided by professional and volunteer caregivers. Ideally, there is an intact family that wants the dying person to be at home as much as possible and whose members are ready and willing to participate in the daily care. That each hospice patient must have a primary family caregiver (e.g., spouse or child) has become a requirement in the federal regulatory and funding system. There are a growing number of exceptions, however, and regulatory agencies appear to be a little more flexible in this regard. Hospices, neighbors, and others can sometimes be very creative in coming up with a primary caregiver and a home environment. One cannot count on these exceptions, however. In deciding about hospice care, attention must certainly be given to the availability and readiness of family support.

Gaining access to a hospice program does not have to be difficult. The easiest path is for patients who are eligible for Medicare (Part A) hospital insurance. The patient's physician and the hospice medical director (unfortunately) will be required to certify that the patient has a life expectancy of 6 months or less. When this certification has been made, the patient signs a statement that expresses his or her selection of hospice care for the terminal illness. This special hospice Medicare benefit will then replace the standard Medicare benefit. From the patient's standpoint, the coverage is quite extensive. The services of physicians, nurses, home health aide, homemaker, and pastoral counselor are all covered, as are rentals of medical equipment and medications. Generally, at-home expenses are fully covered, but there may be some expenses associated with in-hospital stays. (The hospice may provide services for which it does not receive full reimbursement, but that is another story.)

Access to hospice can be more difficult if a patient does not have a primary physician with whom a strong trusting relationship has been established or is not eligible for Medicare hospital benefits. These and other possible obstacles often can be overcome after discussion with a hospice director or social worker. It is useful to allow some time to explore the situation, have one's questions answered, and find solutions to any problems that might stand in the way of access. The most common barriers to hospice service (McNeilly & Hillary, 1997) include

- Physicians' difficulty with hospice admission criteria, reluctance to lose control of their patients, and, in some cases, restrictions on the number of pain control prescriptions they are allowed to write.
- Insufficient family cooperation with hospice. As one nurse commented, "Many times, the patient is ready for hospice and the family is not."
- Inadequate communication between managed care health staff and terminally ill patients and their families. As expressed by another hospice nurse,

> Doctors don't take the time to discuss with patients and families. This is particularly true for the county system and HMOs. Patients have seen so many doctors, they don't have a particular doctor. They feel so trashed, because they feel like they've been bumped from person to person, and now they have to choose hospice.

- Late referral of patients to hospice care. This is a persistent problem not only in the United States but also throughout most of the world. Patients are sometimes referred to hospice when they have only a few days to live, thereby severely restricting the ability of palliative care providers to help them.

A special article in the prestigious *New England Journal of Medicine* provided major documentation for the pattern of (too) late referral of terminally ill patients to hospice care programs. Physicians Nicholas Christakis and Jose Escarce (1996) analyzed information available for 6,451 hospice patients. They found that approximately 1 patient in 6 died within 7 days of enrollment, and approximately 3 in 10 died within 14 days. The median length of survival after enrollment was 36 days. (There were substantial differences by specific type of terminal condition; for example, those with kidney failure had the shortest

average survival time [17 days], and those with chronic obstructive pulmonary disease had the longest [76.5 days].) Survival after hospice admission was approximately 10% shorter for men compared with women. Enrolling patients in hospice care when they have but a few days left to live deprives them of the care and quality of life they might have experienced with a more timely introduction to hospice.

DAME CICELY SAUNDERS' REFLECTIONS ON HOSPICE

The founder of the international hospice movement is a continuing inspiration to palliative care programs worldwide. Dame Cicely Saunders agreed to respond to some personal questions about her own experiences as a way of inviting you to continue your interest in this ongoing project.

Q: *How do you get used to death and to losing people you have cared for—and then having to do it all over again the next day*

A: An auxiliary nurse who has worked in St. Christopher's told me recently, "You miss some people a lot but next day there is a new patient and family to get to know and help." Both of us, and everyone else I have talked with, have mentioned "team" or "community" as a major positive as well as the continued learning of new ways to help. Above all, the patients remain the inspiration. Meeting people of great maturity facing life's end with endurance, humanity, and faith in various forms is a great encouragement.

Q: *How do hospice caregivers renew their own spirits? What do you do in your own life to keep going? What are your sources of strength and commitment?*

A: For myself, my Christian commitment, together with constant learning, reading, and traveling to other teams/units have been forms of renewal. I also have a great support system of friends and colleagues. A physiotherapist [after 30 years of working in the field] says, "We know we cannot cure our patients but we can still maximize their remaining potential...the patients keep me sane and focused. We are pioneers in an unexplored field." My colleagues all

Dame Cicely Saunders, nurse and physician, is the founder of the international hospice movement.

have an indefatigable capacity for new thinking and developing together as a team.

Q: *Women provide direct care to terminally ill people in the United States far more often than men....*

A: The preponderance of women in the field seems to be common around the world. But some men have made invaluable contributions to caring. Many have a spiritual dimension as a basis for their commitment.

Q: *Hospice/palliative care has demonstrated that pain and other symptoms often can be controlled with attentive and well-informed care. Nevertheless, we continue to hear of patients who are not provided with this level of care....*

A: Only a few countries consider this to be a medical specialty. We have established a research foundation for the enormous challenge ahead. This will make it easier for other doctors to "change gear." I believe this is less of a problem in the United Kingdom than the United States.

Q: *Two situations are often highly stressful both to caregivers and family—the patient who has no realistic hope of survival but wants to keep fighting, and the family who insists on having "everything done," although there is really nothing effective yet to be done....*

A: This is not such a desperate dilemma. Patients who want to go on fighting are likely to return to their oncologist, who will advise and counsel. Otherwise, really skilled listening and discussion with the palliative care specialist may resolve a situation. We find most people will gradually learn to let go. Cultural differences require explanation and understanding. Families likewise need careful communication from the first contact. Once trust is established these problems can be approached if and when the time comes.

Q: *What is the "worst" death you have come across, and what made it so?*

A: A patient refused all pain control on principle and died slowly and painfully over several weeks. The doctors and nurses anguished over this. When he was semiconscious and groaning, the psychiatrist maintained he was not suffering from any psychiatric symptoms and was competent to make that choice. It was felt ethically correct to respect the patient's decision, although the nurses were most unhappy and the team was split.

Q: *How does a "good death" affect the family survivors and the health care providers?*

A: I think my husband [aged 93] achieved a good death. After many years of caring as he went from one life-threatening illness to another, we had to accept his statement that "I have done what I had to do in my life and now I am ready to die." But when he was desperately breathless with a chest infection he asked me, "Can't you help me to die?" I said, "It will be in God's time" and he then replied, "I agree." A few days later the breathlessness passed and he had two peaceful weeks, still alert and gradually less talkative, except for flirting with the nurses! On the last afternoon, two of his former art pupils visited him. One wrote to me afterwards. "He seemed very peaceful but as if he was in touch with something beyond where we were." He slipped away just before I returned from home that night, but that was all right for me too, because I knew he was not alone.

Q: *Dr. Kevorkian....*

A: What Dr. Kevorkian did seemed to me to be totally unprofessional and careless of true human compassion and skill.

Q: *The international hospice movement has come a very long way in a short time. What can we all do to help the hospice philosophy fulfill its potential?*

A: We need people to conduct more research into palliative care for people dying of other diseases, more research, more skills development, more education of health care professionals outside of hospice specialists, and more understanding of the values and commitment of developing countries.

Many people have discovered a way to become active in the hospice movement by serving as volunteers. Interested? See Box 6-1.

SUMMARY

Hospice care is intended to provide comfort, relief, and a sense of security for terminally ill people and their families. It differs from traditional

BOX 6-1
SHOULD I BECOME A HOSPICE VOLUNTEER? A DIALOGUE

- **Does my local hospice need volunteers?**
  Probably so. A hospice usually has a director of volunteers and will welcome your call.

- **What should I expect when I meet the director of volunteers?**
  A friendly but "professional" interview. The hospice has responsibility for exercising good judgment in the selection of volunteers.

- **You mean they might not accept me?**
  This is a possibility. Has someone very close to you died recently? Many hospices ask people who have had a recent bereavement to wait a while before becoming a volunteer. Or the interviewer may judge that you have a disorganized lifestyle.

- **—Hey, I'm going to get organized, starting tomorrow!**
  Fine! But the volunteer director will need to be convinced that you are a person who keeps appointments and does what needs to be done in a reliable manner. And should you come across like a person who needs to impose your own religious beliefs on others—or use hospice in the service of your own fantasies and problems—then you might receive a polite but firm refusal.

- **That won't happen to me. I'm taking this great class on death and dying, and reading this really terrific textbook. So after I'm accepted as a volunteer, will they give me some guidance and supervision?**
  Definitely. You will be asked to attend a series of training sessions before you are activated as a volunteer. Most people find this to be a valuable learning experience. You will receive guidance and supervision all the way along the line, and you will always have somebody to call if problems arise.

- **What kind of things would I do as a volunteer?**
  There are many possibilities. You might be a companion for a patient in his or her home for a few hours so that others in the household have the opportunity to shop or take care of business. You might drive the patient to an appointment or to visit an old friend. You might help the patient write letters. You might help prepare a meal when family or friends visit. You might help the patient or a family member complete a special project. At times you might just "be there." A hospice volunteer can wind up doing many different things, depending on the needs of the individual families (Willis, 1989). Some volunteers devote themselves to keeping the hospice system going, rather than working with patients. They do office work, fund-raising, and other things that do not necessarily involve direct patient or family contact.

- **What are the other volunteers like?**
  I have been fortunate enough to know many hospice volunteers. As a rule, they are bright, mature, and neighborly people who have been rather successful in life. Many feel that through hospice they can give something back to other people. Some are health care professionals who believe strongly in the hospice philosophy.

- **Like nurses and medical social workers?**
  Yes, some volunteers are well-qualified professionals. Some have been very successful in other lines of work but are new to health and social care. You will find other students as well—looking for an opportunity to help others while acquiring valuable personal experience.

- **Anything else I should know?**
  Before you contact hospice, reflect on your own motivation: a passing curiosity or a firm resolve to help others? Will you be available to serve as a volunteer after you complete the course? Even though hospice may ask you to give only a few hours of your time per week, people will be counting on you to come through. If you have further questions at this time, you might ask your local hospice to put you into contact with several of their experienced volunteers.

- **See you at the hospice office!**
  Go easy on those donuts.

medical management in several important ways: (a) the staff expertise in the control of pain and other symptoms; (b) care is centered around the situation, needs, and desires of the particular dying person and family; and (c) family members and volunteers are included as part of the caregiving system. The hospice approach to terminal care has its roots in shelter houses established in the 4th century for the comfort of pilgrims, the ill, and the dying. After a period of neglect, hospice activity started again in the late 19th century and took its modern form with the establishment of St. Christopher's Hospice (London) in 1967. Connecticut Hospice (New Haven) was the first such program in the United States (1974). More than 2,000 hospice programs are now in operation in the United States. Standards of care for hospice programs include not only the well-being of the patient but also that of the family and staff. Adult respite programs can provide a useful temporary alternative to hospital and home care. Case histories provide some idea of how hospice care is offered and its benefits for dying persons and their families.

Hospice programs have usually served adults with advanced cancer or progressive neurological dysfunction. We examined several other applications of hospice philosophy and practice: for children, people with AIDS, nursing home residents, prisoners, the homeless, and the impoverished. We also learned that hospice programs are developing rapidly throughout the world, finding welcome in nations with very different cultural and religious patterns.

Research and clinical experience indicate that hospice care often does prevent and relieve suffering. Pain relief is most often the highest priority. The gradual acceptance of pain as the fifth vital sign in health care contacts with all patients is one of the remarkable achievements of the hospice movement. Unfortunately, what has been discovered about effective pain relief in palliative programs has not always been applied by physicians operating outside of the hospice framework. Many physicians are still inadequately trained to provide effective pain relief for dying people, and many still have unrealistic anxieties about turning a person into a drug addict through the administration of morphine

and related medications. Hospice care providers also understand that the relief of suffering requires relief of the mental distress that can be associated with illness, dependency, loss of function, and concern about the future. There is now a renewed call for the government to become more supportive of palliative care for dying persons.

After considering questions that arise in making the hospice decision, we were given benefit of an interview with international hospice movement pioneer Dame Cicely Saunders. We concluded with a brief revisit to your imagined deathbed scene and then explored the volunteer's role in hospice care.

REFERENCES

Centers for Disease Control and Prevention. (2001). *HIV/AIDS surveillance supplemental report, 2000.* Rockville, MD: Author.

Christakis, N. A., & Escarce, J. J. (1996). Survival of Medicare patients after enrollment in hospice programs. *New England Journal of Medicine, 335,* 172–178.

Clark, D. (2000). Palliative care history: A ritual process. *European Journal of Palliative Care, 7,* 50–55.

Cox, C. (1998). Hospice care for persons with AIDS: Findings from a national study. *Hospice Journal, 13,* 21–34.

Daneault, S., & Labadie J. F. (1999). Terminal HIV disease and extreme poverty: A review of 307 home care files. *Journal of Palliative Care, 15,* 6–12.

Dobratz, M. C. (1995). Analysis of variables that impact psychological adaptation in home hospice patients. *Hospice Journal, 10,* 75–88.

Durham, J. D. (2002). AIDS. In R. Kastenbaum (Ed.), *Macmillan encyclopedia of death and dying* (Vol. 1, pp. 16–24). New York: Macmillan.

Hinds, P. S., Bradshaw, G., Oakes, L. L., & Pritchard, M. (2002). Children and their rights in life and death situations. In R. Kastenbaum (Ed.), *Macmillan encyclopedia of death and dying* (Vol. 1, pp. 139–147). New York: Macmillan.

Humphreys, C. (2001). "Waiting for the last summons": The establishment of the first hospices in England 1878–1914. *Mortality, 6,* 146–166.

Ingham, J. M., & Foley, K. L. (1998). Pain and the barriers to its relief at the end of life: A lesson for improving the end of life health care. *Hospice Journal, 13,* 89–100.

Jusic, A. (1997). Palliative medicine's first steps in Croatia. In C. Saunders & R. Kastenbaum (Eds.), *Hospice care on the international scene* (pp. 125-129). New York: Springer.

Kastenbaum, R. (1995). Children's hospice. An Omega interview with Ida M. Martinson. *Omega, Journal of Death and Dying, 31*, 253–262.

Kastenbaum, R., & Normand, C. (1990). Deathbed scenes as expected by the young and experienced by the old. *Death Studies, 14*, 201–218.

Kinzel, T., Askew, M., & Goldbole, K. (1992). Palliative care: Attitudes and knowledge of hospital-based nurses and physicians. *Loss, Grief & Care, 6*, 85–95.

Levy, M. H. (1988). Pain control research in terminal care. *Omega, Journal of Death and Dying, 18*, 265–280.

Maull, F. W. (1998). Issues in prison hospices: Toward a model for the delivery of hospice care in a correctional setting. *Hospice Journal, 13*, 57–82.

McGrath, P., Yates, P., Clinton, M., & Hart, G. (1999). "What should I say?" Qualitative findings on dilemmas in palliative care nursing. *Hospice Journal, 14*, 17–34.

McNeilly, D. P., & Hillary, K. (1997). The hospice decision: Psychosocial facilitators and barriers. *Omega, Journal of Death and Dying, 35*, 193–218.

Meagher, D. K., & Leff, P. T. (1989/1990). In Marie's memory: The rights of the child with life-threatening or terminal illness. *Omega, Journal of Death and Dying, 20*, 177–191.

Miller, K. E., Miller, M. M., & Single, N. (1997). Barriers to hospice care: Family physicians' perceptions. *Hospice Journal, 12*, 29–42.

Miller, P. J., & Mike, P. B. (1995). The Medicare Hospice Benefit: Ten years of federal policy for the terminally ill. *Death Studies, 19*, 531–542.

Mor, V., Greer, D., & Kastenbaum, R. (1988). *The hospice experiment*. Baltimore: Johns Hopkins University Press.

Phipps, W. E. (1988). The origin of hospices/hospitals. *Death Studies, 12*, 91–100.

Roy, D. J. (1999). Palliative care Canada 1999—A question period. *Journal of Palliative Care, 15*, 3–5.

Saunders, C. (1993). Dame Cicely Saunders: An Omega interview. *Omega, Journal of Death & Dying, 27*, 263–270.

Sloan, P. A., Donnelly, M. B., Schwartz, R. W., & Sloan, D. A. (1997). Residents' management of the symptoms associated with terminal cancer. *Hospice Journal, 3*, 5–16.

Staton, J., Shuy, R., & Byock, I. (2001). *A few months to live. Different paths to life's end*. Washington, DC: Georgetown University Press.

Stringer, H. (2002, November 4). Circle of life. *NurseWeek* (www.nurseweek.com).

Tower, A. (2000). Frances Legendre. The price of a death of one's own. In D. Barnard, A. Towers, P. Boston & Y. Lambrinidou (Eds.), *Crossing over. Narratives of palliative care* (pp. 79–96). New York: Oxford University Press.

Turk, D. C., & Feldman, C. S. (Eds.) (1992). *Noninvasive approaches to pain management in the terminally ill*. New York: Haworth.

Voicer, L., & Bloom-Charette, L. (1999). *Enhancing the quality of life in advanced dementia*. Philadelphia: Taylor & Francis.

Voicer, L., & Hurley, A. C. (1998). *Hospice care for patients with advanced progressive dementia*. New York: Springer.

Willis, J. (1989). Hospice volunteers. In R. Kastenbaum & B. K. Kastenbaum (Eds.), *Encyclopedia of death* (pp. 147–149). Phoenix: Onyx Press.

Wilson, M., & Kastenbaum, R. (1997). Worldwide developments in hospice care: Survey results. In C. Saunders & R. Kastenbaum (Eds.), *Hospice care on the international scene*. New York: Springer.

Wilson, M., & Kastenbaum, R. (1997), Worldwide developments in hospice care: Survey results (pp. 21–40). In C. Saunders & R. Kastenbaum (Eds.), *Hospice care on the international scene*. New York: Springer.

Wright, K. D., Jones, A., & Wright, S. E. (1999). Dying homeless but not alone: Social support roles of staff members in homeless shelters. *Illness, Crisis, & Loss, 7*, 233–251.

GLOSSARY

Amyotropic Lateral Sclerosis: An incurable neuromuscular disorder in which there is a progression of weakness and paralysis until vital functions are inoperative. Also known as Lou Gehrig's disease after the New York Yankee Hall of Fame first baseman.

Catchment Area: The geographical region served by a health care agency.

Hospice: (1) A program of care devoted to providing comfort to terminally ill people through a team approach with participation by family members. (2) A facility in which such care is provided.

Medicare Hospice Benefit: A federal reimbursement program that enables eligible people to select hospice care as an alternative to traditional medical management during their terminal illness.

National Hospice Study: A major project (1982–1983) that compared traditional and hospice care for terminally ill people in the United States. The Medicare Hospice Benefit was established as a result of this study.

Palliative Care: Health services intended to reduce pain and other symptoms to protect the patient's quality of life.

Remission: The disappearance or relief of symptoms.

Symptom: An observable sign of dysfunction and/or distress (e.g., pain, and fever).

Terminal Illness: Defined in the Medicare Hospice Benefit as an illness that is expected to end in death within 6 months or less. In other contexts, the specific definition of terminal illness is open to discussion and controversy.

Vital Signs: Body functions that are routinely assessed by physicians and nurses. Traditionally, these included temperature, pulse, respiration, and blood pressure; now, they also include patient's experience of pain.

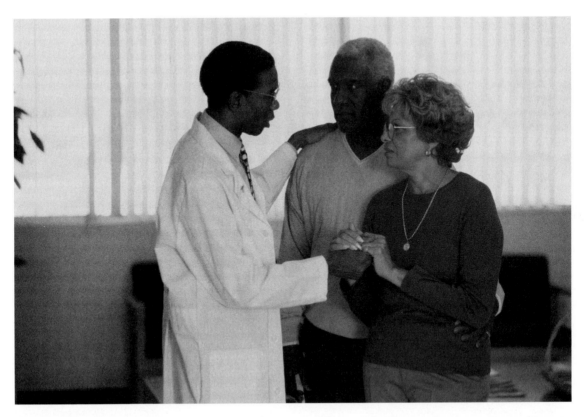

The hospice movement has encouraged more physicians to listen to family members' concerns and answer their questions.

chapter 7

END-OF-LIFE ISSUES AND DECISIONS

Ask me what I'm fixing for supper tonight, I can't tell you. So, what kind of party I'm planning to throw for the end of my life—go away!
—A woman talking back to a television program

I haven't decided anything. I haven't even decided if I should decide because, well, who knows what will happen when it happens and anyhow I'm not a doctor, and anyhow…and anyhow…{In your work, do you help other people make decisions?} That's different! [laughing]. Other people's decisions are not the problem!
—A graduate student in social work

After 2 years of nursing home care, Millie Morrisey developed pneumonia and respiratory distress. As had been its custom, the nursing home staff called an ambulance. Documentation of preferences—which included foregoing antibiotics, mechanical ventilation, and tube feeding—were neither sought nor readily accessible in her chart. The hospital quickly admitted her to the ICU, initiated antibiotics and mechanical ventilation, and used physical restraints so that she would not dislodge the tubes and lines to which she was connected. She mostly did not seem to understand what was happening and was agitated and tearful.
—Marilyn J. Field and Christine K. Cassel (1997, pp. 93–94).

FROM DESCRIPTION TO DECISION-MAKING

I don't know what we're having for supper tonight, either, but supper will probably happen. Death certainly will. Perhaps we should think some about end-of-life issues and decisions. We have prepared ourselves by observing how hospice care (Chapter 6) is attempting to provide safe conduct through the dying process (Chapter 5). Each day, many people face the decision either to continue with cure-oriented treatment or choose symptom relief and comfort care. This end-of-life decision, like the others considered in this chapter, depends much on the adequacy of communication among health care professionals, terminally ill patients, and their families. Another type of end-of-life decision is considered in Chapter 10. Physician-assisted death, also known as assisted suicide, raises legal, medical, and ethical issues that require special examination. Here, we concentrate on a broad range of basic end-of-life decisions that we are likely to encounter either directly or indirectly, including the unusual option of cryonic suspension and the challenge of organ donation.

We begin with a brief inquiry into the idea of planning for the end of our lives. This is followed by a reflection on our own ideas and feelings as we trace the development of advance directives for controlling care during a terminal illness.

WHO SHOULD PARTICIPATE IN END-OF-LIFE DECISIONS?

There has been a turnabout in public attitudes toward end-of-life decision making. The idea that we should have the "final say" in our own lives did not gather force until our society started a renewed dialogue about dying and death, stimulated by the increasingly widespread application of life-support systems and the emergence of the hospice care movement. Furthermore, the idea of patient self-determination had to overcome the habit of leaving such matters to the medical system. Those who did want to have a say had little backing from the legislatures, the courts, and the weight of professional and public opinion.

Today, there is much more opportunity for us to express our wishes. Informed consent is an established principle. A variety of advance directives are available. However, are people being offered the option of increased control over the last days of their lives or being confronted with unsettling and confusing choices?

The woman who admits she is not much for everyday planning might nevertheless decide that she would rather not have some unpleasant surprises further down the road. The graduate student who confesses, "I haven't decided any-

thing," had her reasons, at least three of them. She recognized that *we have limited control over the future.* We might be deceiving ourselves if we believed that making specific plans would somehow guarantee that events would occur in just that way. Many others have found that their best laid plans were voided by the odd jolts and bumps of life. She also recognized that *we might not know enough to make realistic decisions* about technical matters that are not within our own compass of information. The third reason had more to do with her own personality and current situation ("Other people's decisions are not the problem"). She is among those *people who try to avoid making decisions as long as they can.* A self-described procrastinator when it comes to making decisions, she was also caught up in the demands of her professional education and felt she could spare little time and energy for anything that she felt she could put off until later.

Some people find decision making stressful. Others characteristically make and unmake decisions with their minds in a revolving-door mode. Furthermore, the increased emphasis on individual autonomy is difficult for people who are accustomed to relying on others or making decisions through processing with family or friends. The idea that all individuals should make decisions for themselves has a lot of appeal in societies that laud individual personality and achievement. Not everybody shares this view, however, as Koenig (1997) notes:

> Innovations in health care ethics that emphasize advance care planning for death or a patient's "right" to limit or withdraw unwanted therapy appear to presuppose a particular patient. This ideal patient has the following characteristics: (1) a clear understanding of the illness, prognosis, and treatment options that is shared with members of the health care team; (2) a temporal orientation to the future and desire to maintain "control" into that future; (3) the perception of freedom of choice; (4) willingness to discuss the prospect of death and dying openly; (5) a balance between fatalism and belief in human agency that follows the latter; (6) a religious orientation that minimizes the likelihood of divine intervention (or other "miracles"); and (7) an as-

sumption that the individual, rather than the family or other social group, is the appropriate decision-maker. (p. 370)

There are many world cultures in which the family is clearly the center of life. Furthermore, respect for the past may be no less important than what one achieves in the future. This way of life may be accompanied by the deeply held belief that people can do little to alter their fate: It is in the hands of the gods. The "ideal" patient, then, probably does not live within the kind of ethnic and religious heritage that has been relied on by most of the earth's people through the centuries. An overemphasis on individual decision making runs the risk of making "deviates" or "failures" of a great many people who are simply moving along a well-trodden pathway as did many generations before them.

Does this mean that we should not encourage individual participation in end-of-life decision making? Not at all. It does suggest that we are most helpful when we are attentive and responsive to individual differences, whether founded on personality or ethnic/religious background. It would be unfortunate if terminally ill people were forced into either/or situations: Make your decision now, or we will make it for you! Patients do not have to make decisions in a way that is unfamiliar or unduly stressful for them. Human service providers can learn how the patients interpret their situations and help them to navigate through the perils of terminal illness in ways that are both effective in preserving comfort and function and consistent with their own lifelong beliefs and practices.

Suppose, though, that we *are* people who are interested in having our own wishes expressed and honored. How would we go about it? We would become familiar with the opportunities afforded by advance directives.

THE LIVING WILL AND ITS IMPACT

Advance directives are instructions for actions to be taken in the future if certain events occur and if we are not able to speak for ourselves at the time. The living will (LW) (Box 7-1) was the first advance directive to receive general attention in the United States. It was introduced in 1968 by a nonprofit organization that was ahead of its time in educating the public and professionals about end-of-life options. (Then known as the Euthanasia Educational Council, it was later renamed Concern for Dying.)

People were encouraged to add other specific statements between the introductory text and the signature, although few did. The LW played a valuable role in stimulating both public and professional awareness of death-related issues. People started to examine their own thoughts, feelings, and assumptions. Communication increased between individuals and their families, physicians, nurses, ministers, and lawyers. "What do you think of the living will?" "What do they mean by 'heroic measures?'" Questions such as these made it easier to open up dialogues on death and dying with the important people in our lives. Over the years, there has been increasing public acceptance of the LW in principle, although at most approximately one person in five has actually completed the document.

The LW, however, does not necessarily accomplish everything that everybody might desire. For example, it does not include provisions for assisted death. Some supporters of the LW advocate and some reject assisted death. One sentence in the standard living will does walk the boundary: "I do, however, ask that medication be mercifully administered to me to alleviate suffering even though this may shorten my remaining life." This statement is counterbalanced by the qualification, "I want the wishes and directions here expressed carried out *to the extent permitted by law.*" The LW instructs medical personnel to withhold or withdraw life-support measures for a person who has lapsed into a vegetative condition: It does not authorize assisted death.

A serious difficulty with the LW is its ambiguity. Suppose that you are a physician. The patient you are attending to at this moment has previously entrusted you with a signed and witnessed copy of her living will. She is dying. She is also in physical and emotional distress. "I want to die," she tells you. It had been your intention to control her pain with morphine. A heavier

---

BOX 7-1
THE LIVING WILL

My Living Will

To My Family, My Physician, My Lawyer, and All Others Whom It May Concern

Death is as much a reality as birth, growth, maturity, and old age. If the time comes when I can no longer take part in decisions for my own future, let this statement stand as an expression of my wishes and directions, while I am still of sound mind.

If at such a time the situation should arise in which there is no reasonable expectation of my recovery from extreme physical or mental disability, I direct that I be allowed to die and not be kept alive by medications, artificial means, or "heroic measures." I do, however, ask that medication be mercifully administered to me to alleviate suffering even though this may shorten my remaining life.

This statement is made after careful consideration and is in accordance with my strong convictions and beliefs. I want the wishes and directions here expressed carried out to the extent permitted by law. Insofar as they are not legally enforceable, I hope that those to whom this Will is addressed will regard themselves as morally bound by these provisions.

DURABLE POWER OF ATTORNEY
(optional)

I hereby designate _____ to serve as my attorney-in-fact for the purpose of making medical treatment decisions. This power of attorney shall remain effective in the event that I become incompetent or otherwise unable to make such decisions for myself.

Signed _____

Optional Notarization: Date _____

"Sworn and subscribed to Witness _____

before me this _____ day of _____ 20_____"

Witness Address _____

Notary Seal Address _____

(Optional). My Living Will is registered with Concern for Dying (No. _____).

---

dose would not only relieve her pain but also hasten an easy death. Would you feel justified in prescribing a lethal dose because it is consistent with the advance directive ("even though this may shorten my remaining life")? Would you feel that you were dishonoring your profession or even committing murder? Even physicians who were much in sympathy with the patient's request might feel uncertain about the legal and ethical implications of withholding procedures that might extend life. The LW also may be in-terpreted differently in different areas of the country, where there are varying definitions of life-sustaining treatment. Care providers may also differ in providing or withdrawing hydration and nutrition. The standard LW does not address questions of this specificity. The LW, valuable instrument that it is, did not answer all the questions for us, and, indeed, raised new questions.

Furthermore, the fact that a person had completed a LW did not guarantee that it would come to the attention of physicians and other health care personnel when it really counted. Having a document registered by the office of a New York-based organization did not necessarily mean that a physician in Pocatello, Idaho, or a paramedic in Nashville, Tennessee, would have this information readily available. Newer types of advance directives have attempted to provide more specific guidance to care providers and integrate the information more securely in health care systems.

RIGHT-TO-DIE DECISIONS THAT WE CAN MAKE

The LW stirred up interest, hope, and anxiety. As we will see in Chapter 10, troubling questions arose about both the right to refuse treatment and the kind of evidence that should be required as proof of the person's intentions. The right to refuse treatment gained support as courts upheld the principle of informed consent, which requires that *in all situations* patients receive adequate information about the nature of the procedures and the potential risks as well as benefits. It was no longer a process limited to life-threatened or terminally ill individuals.

We consider now some of the major developments that owe much to the LW but go well beyond. This includes the opportunity to review our own feelings and beliefs.

From Living Will to Patients' Self-Determination Act

State legislatures hesitated for a while but then complied with the public's request to have a legal foundation placed under the LW declaration. Starting with California in 1976, every state passed a "natural death act" (also known as "death with dignity" and "living will acts"). Two significant transfers of power from the state to the individual are embodied in these measures:

• The law recognizes a mentally competent adult's right to refuse life-support procedures (such as machines to assist respiration and circulation).

• Individuals are entitled to select a representative who will see that their instructions are carried out if the individual is not able to do so. A patient who can no longer speak, for example, should be able to count on his or her appointed health care agent to safeguard the terms of the advance directive.

Even these significant laws, however, did not guarantee that the intentions would be respected in practice. Part of the problem can be traced to the health care system's previous unfamiliarity with such documents. Physicians and hospital administrators were not accustomed to having their patients tell them what they could and could not do. There was also the problem of integrating the LW or other directive into the health care communication system. Where should the document be located? How many copies should be made? How can the individual be sure that anybody will actually look at his or her LW when the time comes? These problems were especially common in the early days of the LW and are still encountered today.

Another persistent problem has been the lack of clarity and detail in the LW. As shown in Box 7-1, the LW uses a standard text. It is now well recognized among health care professionals that advance directives would be more effective with the introduction of more specific language. It would remain difficult for us to make informed specific decisions, though, unless we are somewhat familiar with medical terminology and processes. Whatever the decision we reach, we will probably know ourselves better and be in a better position to help family and friends who may also be considering this option.

We can begin by responding to the questions presented in Table 7-1. These questions explore our readiness to consider and discuss end-of-life issues in general.

These questions go well beyond specific instructions for care during the terminal phase of life. Here, we are trying to place our entire lives and relationships in perspective. A document is only a document. The LW takes on authentic meaning when it is based on our thoughtful assessment of our lives as individuals and as companions to others.

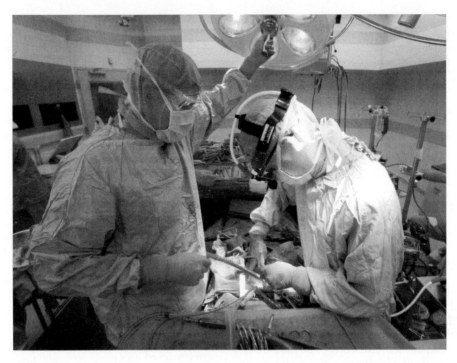

Open heart surgery is one of the many options that was not available until recent years. When should all possible treatments be tried, and when should attention turn instead to comfort care?

In prefacing *The Rules and Exercises of Holy Dying* (1655/1977), Jeremy Taylor observed that

> it is a great art to die well, and to be learned by men in health, by them that can discourse and consider, by whose understanding and acts of reason are not abated with fear or pains: and as the greatest part of death is passed by the preceding years of our life, so also in those years are the greatest preparations to it. (pp. iv–v)

Taylor's advice is perhaps even more relevant today because the options for technological prolongation of life have so greatly increased and, as we have seen, the legal and moral dimensions have also become more complex.

We are ready now for Table 7-2, which presents several of the key decision points that should be specified in a LW or other advance directive if we want to convey specific instructions to health care providers.

Notice that the first three requests in Table 7-2 differ in important respects. Unfortunately, these differences are not made clear in the usual LW document. It might be stressful to think our way through each of these decision points, but doing so will reduce the stress and ambiguity for the health care service providers who we depend on to honor our requests. Stated bluntly, we need to take responsibility for making and communicating our own decisions in the clearest possible manner if we expect others to take responsibility for respecting these decisions.

Informed Consent and the Patient's Self-Determination Act

The LW is an optional document. We can avoid even thinking about it if we so choose. Until December 1, 1991, both health care providers and the general public could follow their own

TABLE 7-1

My Readiness to Explore and Discuss Personal End-of-Life Issues

Yes	No	
___	___	1. I feel ready to consider all the issues that are related to the end of my life.
___	___	2. I intend to discuss at least some of these issues thoroughly with at least one other person whose views matter to me.
___	___	3. I intend to require of my physicians that they provide me with all the information I need to guide my decision making in a prompt, comprehensive, and honest manner.
___	___	4. I intend to select or create a document that communicates my preferences regarding treatment during the terminal phase of life.
___	___	5. I intend to designate a person to represent my preferences and interests in the event that I become incapacitated.
___	___	6. I intend to review and, if appropriate, modify my will and other legal instruments to ensure that they represent my final wishes in an effective way.
___	___	7. I intend to review my most significant relationships and take whatever steps are needed to resolve lingering problems and to renew and strengthen mutual ties.
___	___	8. I intend to do all that is possible to provide the opportunity for meaningful leave-taking interactions with the people in my life.
___	___	9. I intend to convey my preferences regarding burial/cremation and funeral services to those who will be responsible for making the arrangements.
___	___	10. I intend to review and reflect on what is of most importance to me in life and to devote much of my remaining time and energies to these core values.

tendencies, either to confront or to ignore the right-to-refuse-treatment issue. The situation changed dramatically when the Patient Self-Determination Act (PSDA) took effect. This is a federal law. It affects all health care agencies that receive any federal funding—in practice, it affects virtually all health care agencies. It affects all of us who seek treatment through a hospital or other health care agency.

The PSDA introduced the requirement that patients be given information on their rights to accept or refuse treatment. Patients were given two additional rights: the right to complete LW-type advance directives and to designate a person who

TABLE 7-2

Advance Directive Requests

Yes	No	
___	___	1. I want all life-sustaining treatments to be discontinued if I become terminally ill and permanently incompetent.
___	___	2. I want all life-sustaining treatments to be discontinued if I become permanently unconscious, whether terminally ill or not.
___	___	3. I want all life-sustaining treatments to be discontinued if I become unconscious and have very little chance of ever recovering consciousness or avoiding permanent brain injury.
___	___	4. I want to be kept alive if I become gravely ill and have only a slight chance of recovery (5% or less) and would probably require weeks or months of further treatment
___	___	5. I want to have fluids and nutrition discontinued if other life-support measures are discontinued.

would ensure that this document is respected if they were unable to act in their own behalf. In legal terms, the designated person would have *power of attorney* for health decisions (but would not have to be an attorney).

The PSDA is a forward-looking law that attempts to empower all of us in coping with life-and-death contingencies. It embodies the principle of *informed consent,* the court-established right to refuse treatment. In deciding whether or not to exercise this right, we must have adequate information on the nature of the proposed treatment, its probabilities of success, and possible side effects. We also need to be informed about other treatment (or no-treatment) options and their probable outcomes. It is also an intention of the PSDA to stimulate thought and discussion. We are encouraged to review our attitudes and options, clarify our values, and communicate with each other regarding end-of-life issues. Health care agencies are encouraged to improve their sensitivity to the needs and desires of the individual and to become more familiar with the value issues inherent in end-of-life issues.

Informed consent has proven to be a complex issue rather than a simple procedure to be carried out in a routine manner. For example, patients with a life-threatening condition may fluctuate between clear and clouded mental states. When and how informed consent is requested can make a major difference. Physicians also differ in how much they believe a patient should know. There is sometimes a fear that patients will reject the only treatment that might help them because of anxiety aroused through informed consent. Guidelines require physicians to present the possible benefits and risks in language that can be easily understood by the patient, but this is a process that can be more or less successful. Two points are clear, though: Emergency life-or-death procedures can be an exception to informed consent, and the development of a trusting and mutually respectful relationship between physician and patient/family should be a high priority.

Those of us who choose to make an advance directive will also want to specify a person who can support the enforcement of our wishes should we be unable to do so. This person is given a *durable power of attorney for health care.* The specified individual does not have to be a lawyer; it could be any person we believe we can count on to represent our views effectively should the occasion arise. The existence of an advance directive and the appointment of a person with the durable power of attorney for health care make it much easier for the health care system to honor do-not-resuscitate or other requests to place limits on medical interventions. These measures demonstrate that we made our decision in a planful manner while mentally competent. It avoids the difficult situation in which people are unable to express their wishes as a result of massive impairment. For example, Karen Ann Quinlan (Chapter 10) may have once told a friend that she would not want to be maintained in a persistent vegetative state, but there was no documentation that the courts or health care providers could rely on. In such instances, there is the issue of *substituted judgment.* What would this person tell us if this person were able to express his or her wishes? Establishing a substituted judgment decision that meets the approval of family, health care providers, and the court is a challenging, conflictful, and sometimes unsuccessful process. The PSDA offers a more direct approach and one that should result in treatment decisions that respect the patient's values and wishes.

Unfortunately, the PSDA goals have not been achieved. Factors include the lack of penalty for health care providers who fail to honor advance directives and inadequate supervision and communication of the advance directive process within the medical system. Also, the proposed program was not funded by Congress, and advance directives have often continued to be too vague and ambiguous.

There is no evidence that health care agencies have expended much effort in educating their own staff members. PSDA is too often regarded as one more burdensome regulation with which agencies must comply. Most hospitals call on the admitting clerk to ask the patient, "Do you have a living will? Do you have a durable power of attorney for health care?" The admitting clerk is not usually a person who has been selected on the basis of superior communication skills, awareness of cultural diversity, and in-depth knowledge of end-of-life issues. The clerk asks questions and fills out forms all day long. The last thing that the hard-working clerk wants is a lengthy philosophical and emotional discussion with an anxious patient and his or her family. Basically, the clerk just wants to get these questions out of the way and move on. For the patient, this interaction is also likely to be unrewarding, even puzzling and disturbing. Many people have not previously discussed these issues with their next of kin. Some have no idea what all of this means and would rather not know. The point of admission to a hospital or long-term care facility is often a time of heightened fear and tension. Communication with strangers can be especially difficult.

Researchers (Miles, Koepp, & Weber, 1996), note that most health care professionals do not have advance directives for themselves. Furthermore,

a trusted person to receive and interpret the advance directive, and not simple self-assertion alone, is the foundation of most advance directives.... Most people hedge advance treatment preferences or otherwise express insight into the difficulty of precisely formulating an advance treatment preference.... Many people, especially elderly persons, would rather trust a proxy than express a preference. (p. 1063)

FIVE WISHES: A NEW ADVANCE DIRECTIVE OPTION

A new advance directive option was introduced recently with the intention of improving the situation. *Five Wishes* was developed by Aging with Dignity (2002), a nonprofit organization that can be contacted at (850) 681-2010; www.agingwithdignity.org. Why still another approach since we already have the LW, the PSDA, and natural death legislation in most states? There is a persuasive reason: Many patients still hesitate to exercise their rights to limit curative treatment and many physicians still hesitate to restrict themselves to palliative care. It is estimated that, at most, one person in five has completed an advance directive (I think the actual

number is even less). Often, medical students are given only approximately 3 hours of class time on working with terminally ill patients. This is not much preparation for interacting with dying patients and their families. Physicians seldom speak plainly to patients about the prognosis (probable outcome) of their illness when it is poor, preferring instead to talk about details of the treatment (Miyaji, 1993). Communication problems arise on all sides. For example, only approximately one of four hospital patients discuss advance directives (Silverman, 1995). For their part, hospitals often wait until the very morning of a major surgery before giving patients the opportunity to consider and sign an advance directive. There is considerable support for the use of other health care personnel to serve as patient advocates in the decision-making process, but this possibility remains largely undeveloped.

Communicating about end-of-life issues has not improved as much as hoped, although substantially more attention has been given to this topic in recent years. *Five Wishes* is a new version of the LW that is intended to help patients, families, and health care providers to communicate more effectively. It has been supported by a grant from the Robert Wood Johnson Foundation and refined with the assistance of the American Bar Association. More than 1.5 million families have already made use of the document, which is applicable for use by adults of any age, although the emphasis was originally on helping elderly people make end-of-life decisions. The Five Wishes directive has become legally valid in most states.[1] Physicians in states in which it is not legal may choose whether or not to honor a Five Wishes document, but this could nevertheless be used as part of the patient–doctor communication process. The following are basic facts about *Five Wishes*:

- It is a document that enables people to state clearly their preferences for end-of-life care.
- Identifying one or more people who will serve as health care agents is part of the decision package.
- The document is to be signed in the presence of two witnesses. (Some states also require notarization).

- Special witnessing requirements may be necessary for people who live in long-term care facilities, homes for the mentally retarded or developmentally disabled, or mental health institutions.
- The lists of possible actions are significant features of *Five Wishes*. Each list includes many of the key decision points that might otherwise not come to mind and therefore provides the kind of specific guidance that would be needed by physicians and other care providers who are willing to comply with the patient's wishes.

The Five Wishes

Following are abridged versions of the information and instructions that can be found in the official *Five Wishes* document. It is wise to review the complete document if this advance directive is of personal interest. The complete document is available from Aging with Dignity (P.O. Box 1661, Tallahassee, FL 32302-1661 or the Web site given previously).

Wish 1: The Person I Want to Make Care Decisions for Me When I Can't

If I am no longer able to make my own health care decision, this form names the persons I choose to make these choices for me. This person will be my Health Care Agent (or other term that may be used in my state, such as proxy, representative, or surrogate).

This person will make my health care choices if both of these things happen:

1. My attending doctor finds that I am no longer able to make health care choices, AND
2. Another health care professional agrees that this is true.
   - Your Health Care Agent should be at least 18 years of age or older (in Colorado, 21 years or older) and should not be
   - Your health care provider, including owner or operator of a health or residential or community care facility serving you;
   - An employee of your health care provider.

Identify the person you choose as your health care agent, providing name, phone number, and address. Identify two other people who you would choose if the first person is not available or willing to make the choices for you when the time comes. One can cancel or change the health care agent(s) identified in the form at any time.

I understand that my Health Care Agent can make health care decisions for me. I want my Agent to be able to do the following. Please cross out anything you **do not** want your Agent to do:

- Make choices for me about my medical care or services, such as tests, medicine, or surgery. It can also include care to keep me alive. If the treatment or care has already started, my Health Care Agent can keep it going or have it stopped.
- Interpret any instructions I have given in this form or given in other discussions, according to my Health Care Agent's understanding of my wishes and values.
- Arrange for admission to a hospital, hospice, or nursing home for me.
- Make the decision to request, take away, or not give medical treatments, including artificially provided food and water, and any other treatments to keep me alive.
- See and approve release of my medical records and personal files.
- Move me to another state to carry out my wishes.
- Take any legal action needed to carry out my wishes.
- Apply for Medicare, Medicaid, or other programs or insurance benefits for me. My Health Care Agent can see my personal files, such as bank records, to find out what is needed to fill out these forms.

Wish 2: The Kind of Medical Treatment I Want or Don't Want

I believe that my life is precious and I deserve to be treated with dignity. When the time comes that I am very sick and am not able to speak for myself, I want the following wishes, and any other instructions I have given to my Health Care Agent, to be respected and followed.

A. **General instructions**
   - I do not want to be in pain. I want my doctor to give me enough medicine to relieve my pain even if that means that I will be drowsy or sleep more than I would otherwise.
   - I do not want anything done or omitted by my doctors or nurses *with the intention of taking my life.*
   - I want to be offered food and fluids by mouth and kept clean and warm.

B. **Meaning of "life-support treatment"**
   Life-support treatment includes medical devices put in me to help me breathe, food and water supplied artificially by medical device (tube feeding), cardiopulmonary resuscitation, major surgery, blood transfusions, dialysis, and antibiotics.

   If I wish to limit the meaning of life-support treatment, I write this limitation in the space below....

C. **If I am close to death:**
   If my doctor and another health care professional both decide that I am likely to die within a short period of time, and life-support treatment would only postpone the moment of my death (**choose *one* of the following**):

   ___ I want to have life-support treatment.

   ___ I want to have life-support treatment if my doctor believes it could help, but I want my doctor to stop giving me life-support treatment if it is not helping my health condition or symptoms.

   ___ I do not want life-support treatment. If it has been started, I want it stopped.

D. **If I am in a coma and I am not expected to wake up or recover: (choose *one* of the following):**

   ___ I want to have life-support treatment.

   ___ I want to have life-support treatment if my doctor believes it could be help-

ful, but I want my doctor to stop giving me life-support treatment if it is not helping my health condition or symptoms.

   ___ I do not want life-support treatment. If it has been started, I want it stopped.

E. **If I have permanent and severe brain damage and I am not expected to recover:**
   If my doctor and another health care professional both decide that I have permanent and severe brain damage (e.g., I cannot open my eyes, or I cannot speak or understand) and I am not expected to recover, and life-support treatment would only postpone the moment of my death (**choose *one* of the following**):

   ___ I want to have life-support treatment.

   ___ I want to have life-support treatment if my doctor believes it could help, but I want my doctor to stop giving me life-support treatment if it is not helping my health condition or symptoms.

   ___ I do not want life-support treatment. If it has been started, I want it stopped.

F. **If I am in another condition under which I do not wish to be kept alive:**
   If there is another condition under which I do not wish to have life-support treatment, I describe it below. In this condition, I believe that the costs and burdens of life-support treatment are too much and not worth the benefits to me. Therefore, in this condition, I do not want life-support treatment. (Please write the condition or conditions in the space below, or leave the space blank if you have none.)

Wish 3: How Comfortable I Want To Be

I do not expect my wishes to place new or added legal duties on my doctors or other health care providers. I also do not expect these wishes to excuse my doctor or other health care providers from giving me the proper care asked for by law.

Please cross out anything that you **don't** agree with:

- I do not want to be in pain. I want my doctor to give me enough medicine to relieve my pain, even if that means that I will be drowsy or sleep more than I would otherwise.
- If I show signs of depression, nausea, shortness of breath, or hallucinations, I want my caregivers to do whatever they can to help me.
- I wish to have a cool, moist cloth put on my head if I have a fever.
- I want my lips and mouth kept moist to stop dryness.
- I wish to have warm baths often. I wish to be kept fresh and clean at all times.
- I wish to be massaged with warm oils as often as I can be.
- I wish to have my favorite music played when possible until my time of death.
- I wish to have personal care such as shaving, nail clipping, hair brushing, and teeth brushing, as long as they do not cause me pain or discomfort.
- I wish to have religious readings and well-loved poems read aloud when I am near death.

Wish 4: How I Want People to Treat Me

Please cross out anything that you **don't** agree with:

- I wish to have people with me when possible. I want someone to be with me when it seems that death may come at any time.
- I wish to have my hand held and to be talked to when possible, even if I don't seem to respond to the voice or touch of others.
- I wish to have others by my side praying for me when possible.
- I wish to have the members of my church or synagogue told that I am sick and asked to pray for me and visit me.
- I wish to be cared for with kindness and cheerfulness, and not sadness.
- I wish to have pictures of my loved ones in my room, near my bed.
- If I am not able to control my bowel or bladder functions, I wish for my clothes and bed linens to be kept clean, and for them to be changed as soon as they can be if they have been soiled.
- I want to die in my home, if that can be done.

Wish 5: What I Want My Loved Ones to Know

Please cross out anything that you **don't** agree with.

- I wish to have my family members and loved ones know that I love them.
- I wish to be forgiven for the times I have hurt my family, friends, and others.
- I wish to have my family members and friends know that I forgive them for what they may have done to me in my life.
- I wish for my family members and loved ones to know that because of the faith I have, I do not fear death itself. I think it is not the end, but a new beginning for me.
- I wish for all of my family members to make peace with each other before my death, if they can.
- I wish for my family and friends to think about what I was like before I had a terminal illness. I want them to remember me in this way after my death.
- I wish for my family and friends to look at my dying as a time of personal growth for everyone, including me. This will help me live a meaningful life in my final days.
- I wish for my family and friends to get counseling if they have trouble with my death. I want memories of my life to give them joy and not sorrow.

People are also given the opportunity to add other wishes that are not on any of the lists. There is also a place to tell others "how I want to be remembered, please say the following about me…" Additionally, people can specify the type of funeral and memorial service they prefer.

Next Steps for *Five Wishes*

Five Wishes offers far more detail than previous advance directives such as the LW. This same attention to detail might encourage more useful discussions but might also seem overwhelming to some people. There may also prove to be a problem in the shift of focus that occurs with the last two wishes. The first three wishes focus on the decisions we might want to make about our own medical care. This is a straightforward proposition. The last two wishes, however, attempt to influence the way *other* people feel and behave. Experience suggests that it is difficult even for willing people to alter their feelings and behaviors simply because they have been asked or commanded to do so.

There is little difficulty in complying with the wish "to have pictures of my loved ones in my room, near by bed." Nor is there any fundamental problem in asking to have "people with me when possible" and have "my hand held and to be talked to when possible, even if I don't seem to respond to the voice or touch of others." We encounter difficulties, however, when others are asked to provide care with "cheerfulness, and not sadness." Some people are very sad indeed as they see a friend or family member in failing health: Asking them to feel otherwise could increase stress. The wife who sits by her husband's side, holding his hand and trying to be "cheerful," may be so tense that she breaks down in tears the moment she leaves the room. Similarly, it may be difficult for family and friends "to look at my dying as a time of personal growth for everyone, including me." Some people do look at dying in this way, and others are capable of doing so. However, such a positive view can be difficult to sustain as a terminal illness progresses. Anxiety and conflict might well intensify if people believe they *must* experience the terminal illness of a friend or family member "as a time of personal growth."

Much will depend on the sensitivity with which the Five Wishes are communicated and interpreted. Clearly, the intention is to support and enhance the relationships between dying people and those who have been most important to them. This good intention will have to survive a tendency we have seen in many other spheres—to turn a useful suggestion or guideline into a task, a command, a requirement for conformity. In other words, the Five Wishes will probably be as helpful as our ability to use them well.

Recently, the sponsoring organization, Aging with Dignity, has taken what it calls the "next steps" in making Five Wishes both more available and more effective. The innovations include a workplace program. Employers can now choose to make Five Wishes available to their employees as part of the overall benefits package. The organization has also made available a video presentation and brochures that offer suggestions for carrying out various aspects of the Five Wishes procedure. Topics include how to discuss Five Wishes with loved ones and physicians, "how to be by the bedside," and how to answer questions. Examples of the sensible advice include

- Go over the pain and symptom control wishes very carefully with your doctor. "This is one you don't want to leave to chance."
- Tell your doctor how much you want to know about your illness and chance of recovery—all the details, or just a general outline.
- Let your doctor know if you want information about your condition shared with, or kept from, people close to you.

There are families and physicians who can communicate openly and effectively without the assistance of a procedure and document such as Five Wishes, but it is likely that many of us would discover something in the process that might otherwise have been neglected.

A RIGHT *NOT* TO DIE? THE CRYONICS ALTERNATIVE

Do we perhaps have a right *not* to die? Even if we are dead? To be more specific, did Walt Disney make this choice? Should the "Splendid Splinter" be given the opportunity to stand again in the late-inning shadows of Fenway Park and glare at a nervous pitcher? The answer to the first question is clear: Disney was not placed in cryostasis, despite lingering rumors to the contrary. The second question remains a matter of opinion—a dispute within Ted Williams' family, a prevailingly negative response from other baseball players and the sports community, and a challenge to the general public about who, if anybody, might deserve a second chance at life.

The cryonics alternative has been available since 1967, when the first person chose to have his certified dead body placed in a hypothermic (frozen) condition for the possibility of resuscitation at a later time. However, relatively few

"Neural preparations" (heads) as well as whole bodies are preserved in liquid nitrogen in Scottsdale, Arizona's Alcor facility, the largest cryonic foundation in the world, directed by Dr. Jerry Lemler.

people were aware of the cryonics movement until the controversy following Ted Williams' death in 2002. There were conflicting reports about Williams' final intentions and dissension among his surviving family members. The sports community was appalled by the unseemly family dispute but even more by the image of the near-legendary baseball player's body being "kept on ice," as some erroneously characterized the process. The cryonics alternative is worth considering here as a counterbalance to the current emphasis on right to die. It is also instructive not only for the alternative but for what the public's response might tell us about our attitudes toward life and death.

Historical Background

One of the most enduring themes in human history has been the desire to endure—that is, to extend our lives. This desire has taken many forms. In pretechnological times, it was attempted through a combination of physical ordeals, magical spells, secret rituals, and experiments with a seemingly endless variety of substances and concoctions. The impulse for life extension has often been associated with the quest for eternal or restored youth. An ancient Egyptian papyrus offers instructions on how to transform a person of 80 into a youth of 20 (reportedly, some of the suggestions have become incorporated into the modern cosmetic industry). Alchemists whose work eventually prepared the way for the physical sciences hoped to convert base metals such as lead into gold but hoped even more fervently that they could find the elixir to keep people alive and healthy for many more years.

We have seen in previous chapters that both life expectancy and healthy life expectancy have increased markedly in developed nations since public health and biomedical advances took hold in the early 19th century. Nevertheless, life still comes to an end, and for some people this ending seems to come much too soon.

Cryonics does not represent a completely new phenomenon. It is one more attempt in a long line of endeavors to extend life in a radical manner. The fact that having a large portion of one's intestines removed or receiving "monkey gland"

transplants did not accomplish this trick does not mean that cryonics or some other procedure based on scientific advances is necessarily doomed to failure. What is the mission and specific technique that is being offered for those who are interested in making an end-of-life decision that would somehow avoid having to die and stay dead?

Rationale and Method

Advocates of the cryonic approach believe it may be possible to maintain "deceased" people at very low temperatures for long periods of time. Eventually, medical breakthroughs will make it possible to cure the conditions that led to their "death" (Drexler, 1991). Some believe that resuscitation should wait even longer—until science has turned the key that will enable us to halt or even reverse the aging process. There are two levels of vision: (a) restoring a dead person to continue his or her life where it left off and (b) not only raising the dead but also equipping them with bodies that will be resistant to aging and other forces of mortality.

This scenario does sound like science fantasy and, in fact, has often been introduced in movies and works of fiction. Nevertheless, cryonics has roots in demonstrable reality. Surgeons routinely lower the patient's body temperature, especially for lengthy operations. Both human sperm and embryos have been maintained in a frozen condition until use—perhaps some readers of this book were given their lives in this manner by parents who could not conceive or safely deliver a baby in the usual way. Experiments have had some success in preserving body parts and even whole animals in a hypothermic state. More simply: Do you have a freezer unit in your kitchen?

The basic rationale is that we have a right to live or at least to seek a longer life. People make use of medications and other medical advances to maintain or restore their health. When diagnosed with a life-threatening condition, it is not unusual for people to seek an experimental or even a far-out treatment to give themselves another chance. Some of us watch our diet and include physical workouts in our routines of life.

The cryonics alternative may seem a lot different than the more commonly used methods for trying to survive, but it can serve the same purposes, perhaps even more effectively. In offering propositions along this line, cryonicists are sensitive about the criticism that it is selfish to desire a second chance at life. It is up to every person involved with end-of-life issues to decide whether the cryonic alternative is a legitimate exercise of individual rights or a demonstration of excessive ego.

I did not meet Dr. James H. Bedford personally, but I paused for a moment by the aluminum chamber that holds his physical remains. Bedford, a psychologist, was the first person to test the possibilities of cryonic preservation and restoration with his own body. He is now housed at the Alcor Life Extension Foundation in Scottsdale, Arizona. Stephen Bridge, former Alcor director, helped to transfer Bedford from his original cylinder to a newer model in 1984. He observes that Bedford looked to be as intact and "healthy" as when first placed into cryostasis. Bedford is one of 50 at that facility whose future depends on substantial new advances in knowledge and technology. One of the others is the mother of R. C. W. Ettinger, whose best selling book, *The Prospect of Immortality* (1966), brought keen but fleeting attention to the subject. Most other people in cryostasis with Alcor or other facilities have requested that their identities be kept confidential.

The cryonics procedure cannot begin until a physician has certified the patient as dead. To begin the procedure earlier would break the law and could be considered an act of homicide. A team of cryonicists immediately lower the body temperature and give injections to protect vital organs while a heart–lung machine circulates the cryoprotectant medications that are intended to protect against the hypothermic process. The body is brought to the nearest cryonics facility, where further preparations are made and the cooled and wrapped body is placed into a cylinder filled with liquid nitrogen. The cryonic organization maintains the level of liquid nitrogen (which is subject to evaporation over time) and ensures the integrity of the protective chamber. Sooner or later, or perhaps never, biomedical advances will make it possible to thaw, resuscitate, and cure the person from his or her "temporary death."

No such attempts have yet been made at Alcor, the largest of the life extension foundations, or any other facility.

Heads of Stone: A Radical New Development

The methods described previously were in use from the beginning of cryonics until very recently. There were improvements along the way, notably in the effectiveness of the cryoprotectants to prevent the formation of crystals as a result of freezing. Now, however, there have been two major changes: (a) neural (head-only) preservation has replaced whole-body preservation, and (b) the cooled tissues are vitrified (transformed into a stone-like substance) (Kastenbaum, 2002). These developments require a little explaining and more than a little reconsideration.

Why preserve only the head? Less cost, takes less space. It is the brain, not the head, that is the focus.

What is vitrification? It is a process that replaces most of the water inside cells with antifreeze compounds (that is what "cryoprotection" is all about). The temperature is then dropped to –130°C. The result is a rigid stone-like structure that is actually a form of glass. The vitrified tissues are no longer subject to biochemical processes and are expected to remain stable indefinitely. Vitrification has had other uses in medical research and education, so here it is a new application rather than a new procedure. Like earlier forms of cryostatis, though, no attempts have been made to reverse the process; scientists are awaiting further biomedical advances.

The neural vitrification process is considered by Alcor to be such an improvement that it is now its standard operating procedure. However, it requires an extra leap of faith on the part of potential participants. Two leaps, actually. First, that an entire body can be regenerated from neural DNA and, second, that glass can again become flesh. Cryonicists believe that whole-body regeneration will become feasible as cloning experiments continue. In the past, people who considered the cryonic alternative could at least envision a whole body (with its head) keeping cool until the time came for resuscitation. It is asking much more of people to imagine a glass–stone head that will somehow become a new or renewed person.

Questions, Concerns, and Current Status

Some of the most frequent questions have reasonably clear answers:

1. The cost for a neurosuspension is estimated at approximately $50,000; if full-body suspension is desired, the cost is approximately $120,000. Life insurance policies are among the arrangements that can be made in advance for covering the costs.
2. As already noted, there are legal sanctions against proceeding with cryostasis in advance of certified death, even if the individual wishes to have it done that way.
3. Time is of the essence. The cryostasis process must begin as soon as possible before nonreversible cell damage occurs. This requires careful prearrangements and the cooperation of hospitals, physicians, and other persons involved.
4. There are no guarantees. Cryonic experts are not in a position to promise that resuscitation efforts can be made at any particular time, or that these attempts would be successful. It is all an experiment in progress.

Here are some other questions and concerns that are far from settled. What do you think? Should we regard cryostasis

1. As body preservation, like mummification?
2. As body disposal (cryo-remains)?
3. As an affront to God and Nature, or just one more life-prolongation effort among others? As *denial* of or *resistance* to death?
4. As the potential realization of a long-cherished human desire, or just a fantasy that affluent people can afford?
5. As a new chapter in the ancient mythology of the journeys of the dead, or the related stories of a Sleeping Beauty waiting to be warmed by a lover's kiss?
6. As an occasional idea that is becoming a new social reality: a category of "sleepers" who are neither living nor dead in the traditional senses of the term?

Having left so many questions for your consideration, I venture an observation on one more issue. Counting all of Alcor's guests, there are fewer than 100 cryomains in the entire world. Although several hundred people have reportedly signed up for possible cryostasis, this is an astoundingly small number of people who have attempted to get past death in our high-technology era. Social and behavioral scientists have given little attention to this phenomenon. I must rely on a study that students and I conducted back in the 1960s in which we found that most respondents firmly rejected cryonic suspension even though they were open to many other end-of-life possibilities. "Freeze–wait–reanimate!", the slogan of the time, was a bad idea and also a scary one. Often mentioned was the fear of overstepping the human domain: It is not for us to challenge the mortality to which God has consigned us. There was also much concern about loss and distortion of relationships ("If I come back young, and my wife is old…"; "I wouldn't want to come back alone, without my people"). Others were distressed by the idea of losing so much control, along with distrust of how their fate would be managed by others. Although few said so explicitly, I had the feeling that there was also a fear akin to being buried alive.

The very idea of a procedure such as cryostasis presents us with many emotional, cognitive, and ethical challenges. What would we do if one of these days it actually works?

ORGAN DONATION

A much more frequently considered end-of-life decision is to make one's organs available to others rather than keeping them for future reference. Organ donation has saved many lives, although supply lags behind demand. The organs most sought for transplantation are kidneys and livers. Hearts, heart–lung sets, intestines, and pancreas are also on the waiting list.

Five factors clearly have restraining influences on the number of successful transplantations: (a) willingness of people to donate, (b) condition of the donated organs, (c) biological match between donor and recipient to avoid rejection, (d) whether the recipient is strong enough to survive with the new organ even if it is not rejected, and (e) expense and timely delivery. Furthermore, health care professionals may be caught in a stressful situation: required by federal regulations to ask families for permission but hesitant to impose on the grieving survivors, especially when the death occurred in a sudden and unexpected manner.

Organs are sometimes donated by living people who are likely to survive their anatomical gift (often a kidney). In these circumstances, it is possible to plan carefully for the future. The opportunity for cadaver donations, though, can occur with little or no advance notice and require prompt identification and action. Victims of fatal motor vehicle accidents are one of the most available sources. Organ donations by the living have increased over time, but the dead still contribute slightly more than half of the organs transplanted each year (United Network for Organ Sharing, 2002).

There is continuing concern about the gap between organs needed and organs available. Approximately 75,000 people are on the waiting list in the United States at any point in time, many in critical need. Competition has spurred conflict. For example, should an available organ go to the person who is in the most need and has the highest probability of surviving with it or to a person who resides in the local area from which the donation was received? There is also concern that some potential recipients face discrimination. Charges of discrimination against recipients on the basis of ethnicity or race have been made occasionally, but such a practice would violate accepted standards of care.

There are fears that disadvantaged people may be selling their organs for use by affluent patients. Reports from India continue to indicate that the sale of organs from living human donors is still brisk even though illegal (Devraj, 2002).

This practice is condemned by authorities both on ethical and on biomedical grounds: The donors, already suffering hardships and deprivations, increase their own risks of death. How common and widespread this practice may be has not been determined. It does stand as a compelling example of how a society's death system can virtually cannibalize itself.

In the medical community, one of the greatest concerns is the relationship between organ donation and the diagnosis of brain death (Chapter 3). Many people felt that brain death might be certified prematurely in order to advance the removal and transplantation of organs. This is a situation that deserves continued monitoring.

Anthropologist Margaret Lock offers a penetrating analysis of organ transplantation from a sociocultural standpoint in *Twice Dead* (2002). Readers interested in the way in which other cultures deal with this issue will find much of interest in Lock's book.

In our everyday lives, we might take the opportunity to consider the possibility of making one end-of-life decision rather early—organ donation. In some states, this can be done when obtaining or renewing a driver's license. Your physician or health care provider system can also provide information.

FUNERAL-RELATED DECISIONS

The funeral and memorialization process is discussed in Chapter 13. Individual decision making, though, can benefit from acquiring specific information, exploring alternatives, and discussing the situation with the important people in our lives. We focus on the practical matters of funeral and burial costs and arrangements.

It sounds rather cold to think of ourselves as "consumers" of funeral and burial services, but this is part of the reality. Here are several useful suggestions from the American Association for Retired People as well as other public interest groups:

- Funeral homes are required to provide price lists at their place of business, and some will mail the information. Although prices can also be disclosed by telephone, it is a good idea to have a written list that includes all options.

- Do thorough comparison shopping. The differences can be significant. Look at separate price lists for general services, caskets, and outer burial containers rather than only an overall cost estimate.
- Be aware of additional charges for additional services and products. For example, many funeral homes will prepare obituary notices or provide music, but for an additional charge.
- Do not hesitate to inquire about simple and immediate burials or about cremation. Again, check to learn what services are included in the basic fee.
- The most expensive item in a traditional funeral is the casket. Be aware that you can choose to purchase a casket from the Internet or other outside source and that a funeral home cannot charge you extra for this.
- Use your good judgment to resist agreeing to add-on services or products unless these are what you and your family really want.

There has been increasing pressure on the public in recent years to plan funerals well in advance and often to commit their money in advance as well. This development is part of a major change in the funeral industry. The family-owned community funeral home is rapidly being taken over or displaced by corporate expansion. Even though a familiar family name might still be seen, it could be that your local funeral home has become a franchise operation with national or international headquarters elsewhere. Funeral director Thomas Lynch (1997) is among the critics of this trend:

The firm in the next town was bought out last year by Service Corporation International (SCI)—The Big Mac of the mortuary trade. They own most of Paris and Australia, a lot of London and Manhattan. They buy guys like me. They want the brick and mortar, the 50 years of trading on the family name. They want to be like one of the family, mine and yours. At the moment these multinational firms own a fifth of the mortuary dollar volume in the United States. They are in a hurry to own more and more. (pp. 174–175)

Many others are concerned about the mega-corporation influence on funeral services. Funeral directors were once among the most respected citizens in small-town America (Holloway, 2002). Their families knew the families who came to them in time of need. Prepaid funeral and burial arrangements can be useful to some people, but the warning signs are evident: Let's build a database, discuss the options with family and friends, and make a decision that we are not likely to regret later.

A PERSPECTIVE ON END-OF-LIFE DECISIONS

Society is actively engaged in rethinking and restructuring the ways in which we treat each other near the end of life. Both the general public and health care professionals may at times feel uncomfortable because the rules have changed and are still changing. People are now being asked to make decisions that formerly seemed to make themselves. The physician generally was in the position of unquestioned decision maker. These decisions often flowed from the belief that one should do everything that might be done to extend life, even if there is little or no hope of success. Occasionally, the decision could be made (quietly and unobtrusively) to withhold or withdraw cure-oriented treatment to spare the patient further suffering. Now the physician is expected to share decision making with patient and family and to be responsive to other health care professionals and legislative measures as well.

The new social and medical climate for end-of-life decisions favors strengthened participation, communication, and patient's rights. We might therefore expect a widespread transformation and, consequently, find ourselves surprised and disappointed when these principles are neglected, as, for example, demonstrated by the SUPPORT study (Chapter 5) and in the stressful experiences of nursing home resident Millie Morrisey as described in a chapter-opening quotation. The old ways are difficult to change (but hasn't somebody said that before?). Nevertheless, discouraging results have stimulated renewed and more sophisticated efforts to improve physicians' responsiveness to patient and family needs at the

end of life. More physicians have become active in this cause. Millie Morrisey's distress was soon alleviated. The nursing home staff did become aware of her wishes and quickly removed the ventilator and offered her comfort care that resulted in a peaceful death a few days later (Field & Cassel, 1997). Furthermore, shaken by this experience, the nursing home made changes in its policies and practices to prevent such a situation from happening again.

We are in a difficult but promising situation: More people are concerned about making end-of-life decisions that respect patient and family wishes, but how to do this in an effective and timely way is a challenge that must be addressed. There may also be crucial personal situations to resolve. Should the terminally ill person try to overcome years of grudges and negative feelings toward a family member or friend? Is it better to hold on to the anger or seek resolution? Is it the terminally ill person's relationship with God that needs to find resolution one way or another? Still again, there may be a strong need to complete a project or mission. Near the end of his life, J. S. Bach (1685–1750) was so weakened by illness that his family tried to persuade him to remain in bed. He would not. Instead, he devoted practically every waking hour to *Art of Fugue,* one of the most remarkable compositions from one of the world's most remarkable composers. His mental and emotional powers remained at their peak despite his rapidly failing health. There are not many J. S. Bachs with such a monumental project to complete near the end of their lives, but there are others among us who have endeavors they are deeply committed to seeing through as long as possible. End-of-life decisions can take many forms, so we are well advised to be sensitive to the special needs of every individual.

SUMMARY

The responsibility for end-of-life decisions was once largely in the hands of physicians and the health care system. Today, there is more opportunity for patients and their families to participate in decision making. We observed at the outset, however, that not everybody feels prepared to take on the responsibility for exercising control

Johann Sebastian Bach continued to compose his monumental *Art of Fugue* until very nearly his last breath.

over the type of medical interventions that should be attempted near the end of their lives. The "ideal" patient from the standpoint of current thinking is somebody who values having control over the future, stands ready to make significant decisions, and has a cultural heritage in which individual choice is salient. One should be careful about imposing mainstream concepts of individual choice and control on people whose personalities or ethnic backgrounds are inclined to a different direction.

The first advance directive to gain wide attention was the LW. This document stimulated discussion of end-of-life issues within families as well as within the health care, legislative, and judicial spheres. Within a few years, most states had enacted legislation based on the LW concept that people should have the right to limit the kind of treatment they receive near the end of their lives. Courts established the *principle of informed consent,* which supports individual choice. Nevertheless, neither the LW nor the measures enacted by legislatures could overcome the many obstacles to fulfilling the promise of advance directives. The federal government then enacted *the Patients' Self-Determination Act* with the intention of increasing patient participation and hospital compliance. This measure has also proven to be only a limited success. A new and more detailed advance directive, *the Five Wishes,* has shown promise in generating patient instructions that could be used effectively by health care personnel. Cryostasis was discussed as a biotechnological attempt to provide another end-of-life decision option, though this approach currently provides more questions than answers.

In trying to develop a perspective on end-of-life decisions, we noted that we are in a difficult transition period from the previous physician-oriented approach to one in which the wishes and needs of patient and family are fully considered. We also noted that end-of-life decision making is not limited to health concerns but also may include important relationship, spiritual, economic, and personal challenges.

REFERENCES

Aging with Dignity. (1999). *Five wishes.* Tallahassee, FL: Author.

Devraj, R. (2002). *HEALTH-INDIA: Legal ban fails to check kidney "exports."* www.oneworld.org/ips2/dec00/11.

Drexler, K. E. (1991). *Unbounding the future.* New York: Morrow.

Ettinger, R. C. W. (1966). *The prospect of immortality.* New York: Mcfadden–Bartell.

Field, M. J., & Cassel, C. K. (Eds.). (1997). *Approaching death. Improving care at the end of life.* Washington, DC: National Academy Press.

Holloway, K. F. C. (2002) *Passed on. African American mourning stories.* Durham, NC: Duke University Press.

Kastenbaum, R. (2002). Cryonic suspension. In R. Kastenbaum (Ed.), *Macmillan encyclopedia of death and dying* (Vol. 1, pp. 192–195). New York: Macmillan.

Koenig, B. A. (1997). Cultural diversity in decision making about care at the end of life. In M. J. Field & C. K. Cassel (Eds.), *Approaching death. Improving care at the end of life* (pp. 363–382). Washington, DC: National Academic Press.

Lock, M. (2002) *Twice dead. Organ transplants and the reinvention of death.* Berkeley: University of California Press.

Lynch, T. (1997). *The undertaking. Life studies from the dismal trade.* New York: Penguin.

Miles, S. H., Koepp, R., & Weber, E. P. (1996). Advance end-of-life treatment planning: A research review. *Archives of Internal Medicine, 156,* 1062–1067.

Miyaji, N. T. (1993). The power of compassion: Truth-telling among American doctors in the care of dying patients. *Social Science and Medicine, 36,* 249–264.

Silverman, H. J. (1995). Implementation of the patient self-determination act in a hospital setting. An initial evaluation. *Archives of Internal Medicine, 5,* 502–510.

Taylor, J. (1977). *The rules and exercises of holy dying.* New York: Arno. (Original work published 1665)

United Network for Organ Sharing (2002). www.unos.org.

GLOSSARY

Advance Directive: A document that specifies the type of health care an individual wishes to receive should that individual not be in a position to express his or her wishes in a critical situation.

Assisted Death: An action taken by one person to end the life of another person at that other person's request.

Cryonics: An approach that attempts to preserve a body at low temperatures until medical advances have made it possible to cure the fatal condition.

Durable Power of Attorney for Health Care: The transfer of legal authority to a person who would make health care decisions for a person who at that time is unable to make or communicate his or her own decision.

Five Wishes: A new advance directive form (supported by law in some but not all states) that provides an expanded set of specific choices.

Informed Consent: The principle that patients should be provided with sufficient information to make decisions for or against accepting a treatment.

Living Will: The first type of advance directive to be introduced, requesting that no aggressive treatments be attempted if the individual is in the end phase of life.

Mercy Killing: The once more common term for what is now referred to as assisted death.

Patients' Self-Determination Act: A federal law that requires health care organizations to provide patients with the informed opportunity to establish an advance directive to limit medical treatment in specified situations.

Note:

1. The Five Wishes document is legally valid in the following states: Arizona, Arkansas, California, Connecticut, Delaware, District of Columbia, Florida, Georgia, Hawaii, Idaho, Illinois, Iowa, Louisiana, Maine, Maryland, Massachusetts, Michigan, Minnesota, Mississippi, Missouri, Montana, Nebraska, New Jersey, New Mexico, New York, North Carolina, North Dakota, Pennsylvania, Rhode Island, South Dakota, Tennessee, Virginia, Washington, West Virginia, and Wyoming. In the other states, Five Wishes is not illegal but does not have official status.

The Aokigahara Forest at the base of Mount Fuji is a favorite destination for day-trippers from Tokyo, but also for desperate people seeking to end their lives. An average of more than one suicide body per week has been reported. The students in this photo are reading a sign that reminds them: "Your life is a precious gift."

133 B.C. The inhabitants of the Spanish city Numance, after being besieged for 8 years by the Romans, rather than surrender, chose to slit the throats of their women and children. Afterward they set fire to the city and challenged each other to death; the last survivor threw himself off the ramparts.
—Mancinelli, Comparelli, Girardi, and Tatarelli (2002)

The younger you are, the worse things have gotten over the last decades of the 20th century in terms of headaches, indigestion, sleeplessness, as well as general satisfaction with life and even likelihood of taking your own life.
—Robert D. Putnam (2000)

Emmy, Susie, Tammy—My Dear Ones
Don't think badly of me. I am finally doing the right thing. I did so many things that were wrong or just plain stupid. Please remember one thing. That I love you and always have and always will. None of this was your fault. It was just time for me to get out of everybody's life so you can all have a life. Love you, love you, love you.
Mom
The bills are all paid.
—Suicide note of a 37-year-old woman

I remember sitting at this adding machine in this insurance office. These ladies were bossing me around and I'm adding numbers.… I decided right then: I already felt dead. Everything I did, I felt more dead. Nothing felt alive and nothing would help. I just felt it would be more congruent to be dead. Just not to have this body to keep being in.
—Karen, quoted by Richard Heckler (1994, p. 67)

His third try was to move out of the apartment that reminded him too much of Sadie and the life they had once shared. Max relocated to a sunbelt state,

but he hated it. Surrounded by strangers and an alien environment, he felt more isolated and lonely than ever. He finally went out and bought a handgun and spent an evening staring at it.
—Kastenbaum (1994)

Police have concluded that a west Valley man was trying to kill himself and his pregnant wife when he drove across a dirt median on the Loop 101 freeway and crashed head-on into a semi-tractor trailer earlier this month, sources have told The Tribune.
—Yantis and Burgard (1999, June 26)

A person sits alone, brooding and drinking. Another rejection, another relationship broken. Well, that's the way it always seems to go. What's the point of it all? Time to do something to stop this bleeding that's called life.

This is a mind-set from which many suicide attempts develop. Suicide can be the outcome of an individual's stressful and disappointing experiences, often lubricated by the use of alcohol or other drugs. However, throughout history, suicide has sometimes been a group response to a situation experienced as unbearable. For example, mass suicide has occurred repeatedly in Jewish history, with the Masada episode (73 A.D.) the most often remembered; however, it was followed by others throughout Europe from the 11th to the 13th centuries. In recent times, cult suicides such as Jonestown and Heaven's Gate have again demonstrated that a group of people can self-destruct for reasons that may or may not seem rational to others. Mass suicide can also include acts of homicide, as demonstrated by the besieged people of Numance and members of the Jonestown community who were forced to drink poison.

These mass deaths are dramatic examples of the connection between suicide and society, but there are many other connections as well. For example, political scientist Robert N. Putnam (2000) finds extensive research support for the proposition that American youth of today are more depressed and suicidal than those of past generations. For whatever reasons, our society seems to have become less supportive of the young. Putnam is also on solid ground in pointing out that other signs of distress, such as headaches, sleeplessness, and general dissatisfaction, often accompany suicidal ideas.

Can a dead woman kill herself? Yes, and dead men, too; it happens many times every year. Karen became emotionally numb to protect herself from her sorrows and stresses. Few people, if any, noticed. Feeling as though one were already dead may be protection from both life and death in the short term, but it can also be another step closer to a suicide attempt (Heckler, 1994).

The media paid no attention to Max during his more than 60 years of meeting his occupational, social, and family obligations. Little notice would have been taken had Max ended his life with his new handgun. He would have become just one more statistic: Anyone who cared about this topic would have already discovered that older white males have the highest suicide rate in the United States.

The woman who wrote a farewell note to her children had made two previous suicide attempts before taking a fatal overdose. She had been quiet and uncomplaining as she went about her responsibilities, so the family also went about its business and thought she would be all right. On the first anniversary of her death, the oldest daughter (age 13) made a serious but nonfatal suicide attempt. Individuals attempt and com-

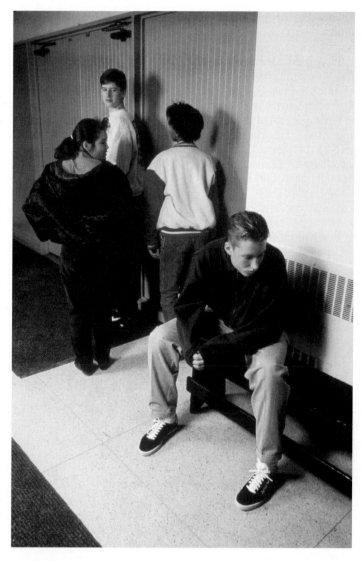

Depression can be deepened and suicidal thoughts aroused when a teenager or youth feels rejected by peers.

plete suicides, but self-destruction is frequently also a family matter.

Many deaths not recorded as suicides nevertheless were motivated by the intention to die. Unfortunately, some people also decide to take others with them. Motor vehicle accidents that are not entirely accidents and deliberate encoun-

ters with law enforcement officers ("suicide by cop") are among the ways in which a suicidal purpose is sometimes carried out. The September 11, 2001 terrorist attacks on the United States and a campaign of suicidal attacks in the Middle East have made self-destruction a part of political/religious agendas.

Suicide occurs at every age from childhood onward. The victims are males and females, the affluent and the impoverished, the seeming failures and the apparently successful. People take their own lives in rural Vermont and urban San Francisco, in crowded Tokyo and sparsely populated Lapland. The scope of the problem is worldwide and not limited to any particular class of person, although some groups are more at risk than others. Furthermore, the casualties of suicide include parents, children, spouses, lovers, and friends, all of whom are at risk for traumatic grief (Chapter 12).

We begin with a statistical profile of suicide attempts (also known as parasuicide) and completed suicides. More detailed attention is then given to gender differences; suicide among youth, elders, Native Americans, and Vietnam war veterans; and special circumstances in which there is a higher risk of self-destruction. Next, we examine both cultural and individual meanings of suicide, with special attention to the descent into suicide and the attempt itself. This background will prepare us to consider the challenge of suicide prevention.

WHAT DO THE STATISTICS TELL US?

Suicide has been among the leading causes of death in the United States ever since fairly reliable statistics have been available. The most recent national data (2000) reveal suicide to be the 11th most common cause. It would have been ranked higher, but several other causes of death (Alzheimer's, kidney disease, and septicemia) have become increasingly frequent and have overtaken suicide. Throughout the nation, there were 29,350 deaths certified as suicide (more than 80 per day). Experts believe that the actual toll is even greater. It is not unusual for a death to be classified in some other way (e.g., accidental) if the suicidal component has not been established beyond a doubt. Furthermore, many people still find it difficult to believe that a child might be capable of committing suicide, so the reported statistics among the very young may not be reliable. The suicides of ailing and socially isolated old men sometimes are recorded as arteriosclerosis or heart disease. Sympathetic medical examiners have also been known to shade the facts when there is any ambiguity as to cause of death at any age. The statistical profile, then, tends to underrepresent the actual incidence of suicide.

Interpreting the suicide rate has been made more difficult by changes in the procedure used by the International Classification of Diseases, Injuries, and Causes of Death (ICD). For example, in 1968 it was decided that death associated with self-inflicted injury would not be classified as suicide unless *the intentionality* of the act was specified. Intentionality is notoriously difficult to establish, especially when information is limited. This classification revision resulted in a misleading 6% decline in suicides. Changes in classification procedure have nothing to do with the actual number of suicides and make it difficult to compare rates over time. Another problem becomes evident when we examine the technique used to calculate suicide rate. It is based on the following formula:

$$Suicide\ rate\ = \frac{Number\ of\ suicides}{Population} \times 100,000$$

It is easy to make a mistake here. We are more accustomed to thinking of percentages than rates. The most recent data (Minino, Arias, Kochanek, Murphy, & Smith, 2002) show a suicide rate of 10.7. This is high enough, but it would seem catastrophic if we treat the number as a percentage. There would be approximately 30 million suicides in the United States each year if the 10.7 rate were a percentage of 10. Fortunately, the rate signifies that 10 or 11 people out of every 100,000 commit suicide during a year. The rate is also different from the *number* of total death by suicide. If, in fact, there were only 100,000 people in the United States, then only 10 or 11 would have committed suicide. The larger the population, the higher the number of deaths if the rate is held constant. It is possible, for example, to have more suicides per year as a population expands even if the rate remains constant or even declines slightly. Next, we consider the data and what they tell us about suicide in the United States and elsewhere. We first consider suicide in the United States as compared with other nations, and then examine more closely what is happening in our own nation.

World Suicide Rates

How suicidal is the U.S. population compared with other nations? Table 8-1 presents the most recent information reported by the World Health Organization (1999) and the U.S. Center for Health

TABLE 8-1

Suicide Throughout the World per 100,000 population

Nation	Men	Women	Total
Argentina	12.4	3.3	7.5
Australia	19.7	5.2	12.3
Austria	30.1	18.6	9.0
Belarus	66.8	10.2	36.0
Bulgaria	24.5	9.4	16.4
Canada	20.0	5.1	12.4
Costa Rica	11.8	2.3	7.0
Cuba	28.2	12.9	20.3
Estonia	68.9	13.0	38.4
Finland	44.0	11.8	27.4
France	29.0	9.8	18.8
Germany	21.7	6.8	13.7
Greece	5.9	0.1	3.4
Hungary	53.6	15.0	32.5
Hong Kong	16.7	4.1	12.9
Ireland	20.4	3.7	11.9
Israel	9.9	3.0	6.3
Italy	11.6	3.3	7.2
Kazakhstan	62.8	10.7	35. 0
Kirgyzstan	18.0	3.7	10.8
Mexico	7.3	1.0	4.0
The Netherlands	13.2	6.4	9.7
New Zealand	24.2	6.0	14.8
Norway	19.2	16.4	12.7
Poland	26.1	4.7	14.9
Portugal	10.2	2.5	5.9
Romania	23.2	4.2	13.4
Russian Federation	69.9	11.7	38.4
Singapore	17.1	8.6	12.6
Spain	12.4	3.3	7.5
Sweden	19.5	7.9	13.6
Ukraine	54.6	9.4	29.7
United Kingdom	11.2	3.1	7.1
United States	17.5	4.1	10.7

Statistics (Minino et al., 2002). Some countries are missing from this list because they did not provide such information on an official basis.

You have probably noticed at least two things about Table 8-1. Looking at the Total column, you can see how much the suicide rate varies from nation to nation as, for example, from the Russian Federation to Greece or from Estonia to Mexico. That suicide could be as much as 10 times more frequent in one country than another raises many questions. For example, are Russians so at risk for suicide because of long, difficult winters? Devastated economy and lack of opportunity? Governmental ineptitude? Vodka? A cultural history often characterized as "Slavic melancholy"? The decline in its position as a world power? Or prolonged grief reaction after the deaths of so many family members in Stalinist purges, two world wars, and various smaller military operations? There is reason to believe that all these factors contribute to high suicide rates in the Russian Federation, but there is no definitive way of determining how all these factors operate together.

You have noticed something else in Table 8-1. The suicide rate for men is substantially higher in all countries. Again, many questions are raised by this pattern. In the following section on gender and suicide, we discuss a major exception to this pattern. China is not included in Table 8-1 because data for the entire population have not been compiled, although the Chinese Bureau of Statistics is working to obtain more adequate data. Several research teams have estimated the rate in the People's Republic of China at 30+, making it one of the most suicide-prone nations in the world. The *number* of suicides is even more daunting than the rate: approximately 350,000 deaths in 1990 (most recent data available) and an estimated 534,000 suicides per year by 2020. Also in China, women have a higher suicide rate than men, especially in rural areas (Jianlin, 2000; Phillips, Liu, & Zhang, 1999).

The United States started the 21st century with a suicide rate of 10.7, which has remained constant for 2 years after gradually declining from a high of 12.4 in 1990. North Americans are not among the most suicidal of people, but there are important differences within our population.

Suicide Patterns
in the United States

Several basic facts have been well established through statistical information. We first consider completed suicides:

1. *Completed suicides occur most often among white males. At every age, white males are at greater risk for suicide* than females or black/nonwhite males. The difference is substantial: four of five suicides are by males, predominately whites.
2. *The white male suicide rate increases with age, but females and nonwhite males reach their peak vulnerability earlier in adult life.* Although the rate is highest among older white men, the *actual number* of suicidal deaths is higher for middle-aged men because there are more of them. Even a lower rate represents more fatalities.
3. *Suicide is the third leading cause of death among youth (ages 15–24).* There are approximately 4,000 certified suicidal deaths among youth each year.
4. *Bad economic times are usually associated with an increase in suicide rates.* The suicide peak in the United States occurred during the Great Depression of the 1930s, and a later period of recession resulted in another increase in suicide.

The "soup kitchen" became a fact of American life during The Great Depression that started in 1929. Unemployed men, unable to support their families and stressed by loss of occupation and self-esteem, were vulnerable to thoughts of suicide, as were those who had made and lost fortunes.

5. *The suicide rate is higher among people who (a) suffer from depression or other psychiatric problems; (b) use alcohol while depressed; (c) suffer from physical, especially irreversible, illness; (d) deal with challenges and frustrations in an impulsive way; (d) are divorced; (e) have lost an important relationship through death or breakup; and (f) live in certain areas of the country.*

It is not surprising that such factors as depression, drinking, impulsivity, and illness are linked to suicide. The geography of suicide may be less familiar, though. What patterns do you pick up in Table 8-2?

Is this what you expected? Such low suicide rates in competitive, crowded, fast-moving places, such as Massachusetts, New York, and the District of Columbia? Such high rates in scenic and spacious places such as Alaska, New Mexico, and Arizona? Lack of social support and connectedness seem be a key factor in differential suicide rates within the same nation. The highest suicide rates in the United States are in western states such as Nevada, New Mexico, and Arizona, especially in rural areas that offer relatively little opportunities for social interaction and support. The lowest rates are in high-density states in which it is very difficult not to bump into people all the time. However, who chooses to live in Nevada and who chooses to live in New Jersey? Are stresses greater in the "most suicidal" states, or are social support

TABLE 8-2

Suicide by State per 100,000 population

Rank	State	Rate	Number	Rank	State	Rate	Number
1	Alaska	22.0	137	27	Indiana	11.4	683
2	Nevada	21.3	400	28	Pennsylvania	11.3	1,356
3	New Mexico	18.7	327	29	South Carolina	11.3	443
4	Montana	17.8	158	30	Wisconsin	11.1	590
5	Wyoming	17.3	83	31	Virginia	11.0	768
6	Arizona	16.1	784	32	Delaware	10.8	82
7	Colorado	14.8	613	33	New Hampshire	10.8	131
8	Oregon	14.8	493	34	North Dakota	10.8	68
9	Oklahoma	14.7	497	35	Georgia	10.7	847
10	Utah	13.8	298	36	Louisiana	10.7	468
11	Florida	13.6	2,086	37	Mississippi	10.5	294
12	West Virginia	13.6	245	38	Texas	10.1	2,053
13	Arkansas	13.5	349	39	Iowa	10.0	289
14	Alabama	13.3	583	40	Michigan	9.8	974
15	Tennessee	13.2	730	41	Ohio	9.7	1,088
16	Idaho	13.1	167	42	Connecticut	9.2	304
17	Kentucky	13.1	521	43	Maryland	9.1	474
18	South Dakota	12.9	95	44	Minnesota	9.1	440
19	Vermont	12.9	77	45	California	8.8	2,969
20	Missouri	12.7	699	46	Illinois	8.2	1,003
21	North Carolina	12.5	971	47	Rhode Island	7.5	75
22	Washington	12.5	727	48	New Jersey	6.8	560
23	Kansas	12.2	325	49	Massachusetts	6.2	387
24	Maine	12.2	154	49	New York	6.2	1,132
25	Hawaii	11.6	137	51	Washington, DC	4.4	23
26	Nebraska	11.6	193	Total		10.7	29,350

Source: National Center for Health Statistics (2002).

systems less available? Clearly, detailed studies are necessary.

What about Suicide Attempts?

Up to this point, we have focused on completed suicides. It has been much more difficult to estimate the frequency of suicide attempts, many of which never appear in official documents. Now we finally have a useful estimate of suicidality that does not result in death. A large-scale telephone survey (Crosby, Cheltenham, & Sacks, 1999) found that suicidal ideas and thoughts are not uncommon in the general population. The authors estimated that more than 10 million people think of suicide. Of this number, approximately 2.7 million go so far as to plan how they would end their lives, and more than 1 million make some kind of actual attempt. We can see why mental health experts urge us to take suicidal thoughts seriously: Ideas can become plans, plans can lead to attempts, and attempts can lead to the loss of life. Parasuicide is considered further as we explore self-destructive actions in various populations and contexts.

The Human Side

The impact of suicide cannot be gauged by numbers alone. Even attempts that do not result in death can have significant consequences. For example, family and friends are put on alert and may respond either by renewed efforts to help the individual or by further emotional isolation of the attempter because of their own heightened anxiety. The suicide attempt is sometimes viewed as a manipulative action and thereby arouses resentment and hostility, or it might win some temporary gains and concessions.

I have observed a tremendous range of responses to suicide attempts. In one instance, colleagues became more sensitive to the individual's sense of despair and were able to provide valuable help with both emotional support and practical actions to change a frustrating situation. In another instance, however, the parents refused to be "impressed" by their adolescent daughter's near-fatal attempt and in effect challenged her to "finish the job." She did. A suicide attempt (or threat) is likely to alter interpersonal relationships as well as the individual's own feelings. Completed suicide often leaves the survivors shaken. The guilt can be disabling. Furthermore, the survivors may believe that they cannot speak openly about the death to others and therefore become socially isolated.

The social cost of suicide is high, although it is impossible to calculate precisely. Occasionally, one suicide seems to encourage another as some vulnerable people identify with the deceased and view self-destruction as an acceptable means of solving their problems. When the suicide of a young celebrity is reported vividly by the media, there may be a short-term increase in suicide attempts and completions by some people who have identified with the star and who have been having problems of their own. "Copycat suicide" has been shown to occur in many nations following the suicide of a person with whom some people closely identify, but these effects are usually limited and discontinue after a short time (Stack, 2000a).

The human side of suicide also includes children left without parents and therefore made more vulnerable to stress and self-doubts that can haunt them throughout their lives. Children with family members who attempted or completed suicide are more likely to make suicide attempts themselves at some point in their lives. Suicide has a ripple effect of stress and distress that starts with the immediate family and friends and may continue to widen. Behind each number in the suicide statistics there are families, friends, and colleagues who will never be quite the same again.

FOUR PROBLEM AREAS

A more detailed look at suicide among youth, elderly persons, Native Americans, and Vietnam war veterans will illustrate some of the many relationships between individual self destruction and society.

Youth Suicide

The suicide rate among adolescents and young adults (ages 15–24) nearly tripled between the mid-1960s and mid-1980s before decreasing and becoming more stable in recent years. The youth suicide rate is now 10.4, similar to that of the general population. Nevertheless, an estimated 500,000 serious attempts are made by American youths each year. In a society that is often characterized as youth oriented, it is enigmatic as well as alarming that completed and attempted suicide has become so prevalent among young people. Consider some additional facts:

1. *The increase in completed suicides is greater for males, although more suicide attempts are made by young women.*

2. *Both sexes use firearms and explosives as the most common method of self-destruction (even more frequent among males).* Poisoning or overdosing is the second most common method used by young women. Hanging and strangulation are also more frequent among young women.

3. *Academic pressure seems to be related to suicide among college students but not in a simple way.* Many undergraduates who commit suicide had a higher grade point average than their peers. Objectively, they were doing well. Subjectively, however, they had performed below their expectations—or what they considered to be their parents' expectations. "I couldn't face Dad and that big scene there would be after all the money he had spent on my education and how he had wanted to be proud of me and blah, blah, blah!" This is how one student explained his near-fatal suicide attempt to a counselor, and many others have had similar experiences.

4. *Most of those who have gone on to commit suicide expressed their despondency to others and made explicit comments about their intentions.* Unfortunately, most youths who were at risk for suicide did not receive mental health treatment or counseling (National Household Survey on Drug Abuse [NHSDA], 2002). Clinicians have long held that many suicidal people do issue a cry for help. This seems to be true of many of the youths who view suicide as a possible solution to their problems. Every expression of suicidal intent provides an opportunity for a helpful intervention.

5. *The immoderate use of alcohol and other drugs occurs more often with suicidal people than with the general population at all ages.* A sudden change in drinking habits may be a particularly important factor because the risk of suicide increases when a person goes on a "jag." Alcohol and drug abuse

have been identified as especially important factors in youth suicide. This was clearly illustrated in the pattern of substance abuse that preceded Kurt Cobain's suicide and was also found in the deaths of several other young rock-oriented singers. A major national study (NHSDA, 2002) confirmed that alcohol and drug use are associated with heightened suicide risk in youth. A particularly lethal combination is the loss of a valued relationship through rejection, separation, or death when it is followed by increased alcohol use (Hendin, 1995).

6. *The loss of a valued relationship is one of the most common triggering events for youth suicide.* This can involve the death of a parent, breaking up with a lover, having a quarrel with a close friend, being disappointed in a role model, or learning that one's favorite dog or cat has died. Many people experience these kinds of losses and stresses without becoming suicidal. However, some have become more intensely sensitized to loss and stress and lack other coping resources. Past experiences of loss, rejection, and unworthiness make some youths more vulnerable to suicide when new interpersonal problems occur. The college experience often does not generate a suicidal impulse for the first time but may have provided an occasion for its expression (Hendin, 1995).

7. *Heavy metal music attracts depressed and suicidal youth—it does not cause suicide* (Stack, 2000b). Many heavy metal fans come from dysfunctional families, experience difficulties in coping with the world, and have low self-esteem. The angry pounding rhythms resonate with their feelings, reducing their sense of aloneness, but they have not been shown to contribute directly to suicide. Depression creates an elevated risk for suicide among both youth and adults.

8. *Teens and adolescents who frequently change their place of residence are at a higher risk for suicide.* This connection is also found with youth who expect to move soon. Geographical mobility weakens interpersonal support as well as the comfort of a familiar environment. A research team notes that "frequency of moving, distance moved, recency of move, and difficulty in staying in touch were all factors that appear to be associated with increasing odds of nearly lethal suicide attempts" (Potter et al. 2001, p. 47).

The role of the family in youth suicide should not be ignored. Leenaars and Wenckstern (1991) identified the following family characteristics that tend to be seen in families of suicidal adolescents and young adults:

1. The families often impose rigid rules.
2. Communication patterns within the family are poor: People do not really listen to each other.
3. One parent may establish too strong an emotional bond with the youth (e.g., "smother love") while at the same time not encouraging the youth's progressive growth toward responsibility and independence.
4. Long-term patterns of dysfunction exist within the family (e.g., father or mother absence, divorce, alcoholism, and mental illness). For adolescent females with suicidal tendencies, there is also a much higher rate of incest than that for the population in general.

Leenaars and Wenckstern (1991) emphasize that "there are no evil, weak parents, only perturbed parents or, more accurately, perturbed and suicide-enhancing families" (p. 101). The suicidal youth may represent a distress call on the part of his or her entire family.

All of us may have the opportunity to help an adolescent or young adult find an alternative to suicide. This process begins with our willingness to take this measure of concern and responsibility. The next step is to become familiar with some of the most typical signs of suicide risk in this age group (Table 8-3). We must keep in mind that all young men and women have their own unique biographies and their own distinctive coping styles. We also want to avoid a mechanical approach to detecting possible suicidality, considering instead a particular person in his or her particular situation.

I add two other observations. First, many suicidal youths are misguided by vague and wishful thoughts about death. There is often the assumption that the person will be able to witness the response of survivors. "Look how upset they will be!" "They'll be sorry they treated me so bad." "They'll know I really meant it." I have also

TABLE 8-3
Youth Suicide: Factors Associated with Higher Risk

- There have been suicidal attempts by other members of the family.
- This person himself or herself has made a previous suicide attempt.
- There have been recent changes in this person's behavior, including level of social activity, sleeping, eating, choice of clothes, and use of alcohol or drugs. The behavior change can take either the direction of withdrawal from previous interests and activities or a sudden burst of pleasure-seeking and risk-taking activities. The clue is that in either case this person is acting very much differently than usual.
- A sense of hopelessness, apathy, and/or dread is expressed. "What's the point of trying again?" "There's nothing I can do about nothing." "So, who cares anyway? I don't!"
- Explicit or implicit statements are made about ending his or her life. "I've had enough of this crap!" "You're going to see me on the ten o'clock news!" "I want to get it all over with, and I will!"
- The thought process has narrowed to the point that everything seems open or closed; there is little or no ability to acknowledge shades of meaning and only extreme courses of action are envisioned. "I'll kill her, or I'll kill myself." "I can never get anything right." "He was the only person who understood me and I can't live without him." "There's only one way out of this mess."
- Abrupt flashes of anger interfere with activities and interactions. He or she becomes touchy and unpredictable and seems to overreact to small frustrations or provocations. There may also be an increase in glowering resentment and uncooperativeness even if this does not explode into overt displays of anger. Aggressive and antisocial behavior occurs more often among males than females as a forerunner of a suicide attempt.

heard many expressions of the assumption that death is "just a trip," perhaps similar to a pleasant alcohol or drug high. They have not read Greyson's (1992–1993) study in which he found that people who reported near-death experiences also reported very strong antisuicide attitudes. Another common presuicidal belief is that death is better than life (compared with the alternative view that death refers to the *absence* of life). A tendency to envision death as more rewarding than life may contribute to the decision to take one's life.

Second, it is important to remember that suicidal impulses do not have free reign. People of all ages also have strong reasons *not* to take their lives despite moods of discouragement and frustration. Thoughts of suicide are common in Hong Kong as well as in other nations where this tendency has been investigated. Although as many as two in five adolescents report having considered suicide, most have not and most likely will not make an attempt (Chan, 1995). One of the keys to suicide resistance among these youth is the fact that they have powerful reasons for wanting to live, such as the desire to experience more of life, discovering their own special purpose in life, wanting to grow together with friends, and not wanting to hurt family. Perhaps surprisingly, the adolescent respondents did not consider religious prohibitions against suicide, fear of hell, and the injunction that only God has the right to take life as significant barriers against suicide.

It may be tempting to try to prevent suicide by emphasizing religious and moral beliefs, but it is more effective to direct attention to all the life experiences that lie ahead and the other reasons frequently cited by the Hong Kong teenagers as well as by suicidal college students in the United States whose curiosity about and hopes for the future were their main reasons for not making a lethal attempt (Jobes & Mann, 1999). Inquiries into suicidal thought among young people should be balanced by inquiries into the hopes and values they hold that can only be fulfilled by overcoming challenges and growing into a rewarding adult life.

Do Children Commit Suicide?

Despite all the attention given in recent years to youth suicide, very little has been directed to those who are even younger. It has often been assumed that few if any children commit suicide. This assumption has been coming under increasing critical scrutiny. Children do think about death (Chapter 11) as well as the uncertainties and frustrations of life. It has been found that third graders have a clear understanding of suicide, and that even younger children realize that people can and do take their own lives (Mishara, 1999). Mishara (2002) adds that although almost all children at the second-grade level and higher have seen some form of suicide on television, these images are

> different from the vast majority of suicides in the real world. Those who commit suicide on television almost never suffer from severe depression or mental health problems, they are almost never ambivalent about whether or not they should kill themselves, and it is rare that children see suicidal persons receiving help or any form of prevention. (p. 836)

It could be useful for parents to monitor what their children see on television and help to correct misleading impressions that could affect their understanding of suicide and death. We should not be entirely surprised that suicide occasionally occurs during the grade school years and, more rarely, during the preschool years. Others do continue to be surprised, however, and some categorically deny that any person younger than age 13 or 14 could possibly intend to kill himself or herself (Orbach, 1988):

> Adults prefer to believe that children do not commit suicide. It seems inconceivable that children could become so desperate and suffer so much at their young age that they would choose death over life. Guilt and anxiety make us blind to the truth, even when it cries out to us. We are also blinded by false perceptions about childhood. (p. 23)

Israel Orbach and colleagues conducted a series of studies on "children who don't want to live." Orbach (1988) identified a typical progression toward a potentially lethal suicide attempt:

> The process starts with a harmless attempt, by which children can assess the effect it has on their

Children who are bullied at school are more likely to become depressed and suicidal.

surroundings. At the same time, this attempt represents a test of their ability to cope with their fear of death. A second attempt often follows the first—especially if there is only a minimal response from the social environment. This second attempt is a little more bold and dangerous, and has more serious consequences. (p. 27)

Orbach (1988) reports that angry parents have sometimes challenged children to try harder to kill themselves the next time. This is just what some children proceed to do. The observations made by Orbach and colleagues indicate that children often give a number of verbal and nonverbal messages about their desperation and their intent prior to a lethal suicide attempt. Often, adults simply do not believe the children mean what they say. Orbach's findings are consistent with those of Mishara, who noted that few young children report having discussed suicide with adults.

Detection of and response to suicidal thoughts and actions in childhood become even more important when we realize that this is also the foundation from which many suicides in adult life originate. For example, a young child who considers himself or herself unwanted and unloved may have thought of suicide repeatedly and even made one or more attempts that escaped notice. In adolescence or young adulthood, this person may encounter new experiences of rejection and disappointment that resonate with the earlier anxiety and self-destructive tendencies. This child, whose suicidal orientation was ignored years before, may become part of the suicide statistics in adolescence or the early adult years.

Furthermore, recent research (Yang & Clum, 2000) reveals that early stressful experiences in childhood can increase the risk of suicide in adult life by distorting the way the child thinks about self and world. The development of suicidal behavior in children and adults follows the same general pattern. This should not be surprising because all suicidal adults were once children. The earlier phases of this pattern include a sense of intolerable pressure from the family, a depressed attitude, and various coping attempts that do not work very well and that result in accumulated frustrations and a loss of self-confidence. If this stressful situation is not altered, the idea of suicide appears and the child or adult now attempts to cope through one or more types of self-destructive behavior. If others do not respond in a helpful and effective manner, the individual feels increasing pressure and a sense of failure that confirms the feeling that suicide is the only solution. Self-destructive behavior is often set into motion as early as childhood, but it may claim its casualty at any later developmental level as well.

Do children commit suicide? In returning to this question, we must reply, "Yes, sometimes. However, it is just as important to recognize that suicidal orientations may develop early in childhood and have their fatal outcomes later in life." Having faced this harsh reality, we are in a better position to be helpful both to the children who are at particular risk for development of a suicidal orientation and to the troubled families whose own anxieties are represented in the children's distress. Furthermore, there is much to work with in attempting to prevent the establishment of a self-destructive process. As Orbach and others have observed, even those children who are experiencing high levels of stress still have a desire to grow, to flourish, and to live. Given understanding, protection, and caring relationships, many of those at risk for self-destruction can embrace the alternative of life.

Suicide among Elderly Persons

We left Max staring at his newly purchased handgun, wondering if that was the way to solve his problems. The elderly white man remains the person most vulnerable to suicide. Since 1990, the largest increase in the suicide rate has been among people 85 years of age or older; furthermore, there is a worldwide tendency of increasing suicide rates among elders. Combine the increasing suicide rate with age and the fact that more people are living into the later adult years and we can see that there is a powerful trend toward self-termination as the world population ages. The suicide rates among white men increase from middle age onward. By

age 85 or older, the suicide rate increases to 19.4, which is much higher than the general rate of 10.7. However, despite this vulnerability, suicide among the elderly often fails to receive sufficient attention. The victim may have been socially isolated for some time before death, or the community may be less disturbed by the act than when a young person is involved (Kastenbaum, 1995). Nevertheless, suicide in later life represents not only the premature death of a fellow citizen but also an implicit commentary on the place of the elderly person in society. What is to be said about the current status of "the American dream" if, after a long life of responsible contributions, an elder finds himself or herself in a nightmare that suggests suicide as the only solution?

Physical illness and other sources of distress do not necessarily make self-destruction the plan of choice. My colleagues and I have worked with many older people who had reason to despair over the harsh realities of life. Often, these people were able to draw on their own personal resources and find the strength and will to live within a relatively short time. The key in some cases was a short reprieve from a stressful situation or objective changes to improve their quality of life; in other cases, it was a therapeutic alliance and counseling. Stress and despair can be experienced at any age, and the same is true of recovery. Several other findings about suicide in later life follow:

1. *The major demographic risk factors include being white, male, older than age 65, living alone, and residing either in a rural area or in a transient inner-city zone* (Osgood, 1992).
2. *Social isolation is a theme that runs through most of the risk factors.* Living alone is associated with a higher risk of suicide. Elderly suicide rates tend to be higher in areas where divorce rates and interstate migration are also higher (Conwell, 2001).
3. *Depression increases the risk of suicide.* In fact, recent research found that mood disorders are the strongest predictors of suicide attempts in elderly people (Beautrais, 2002). This is not the same as concluding that depression causes suicide. People cope with

depression in many ways, and not all suicidal elders show an obvious picture of clinical depression.

4. *Physical illness is a major risk factor for suicide
among elderly adults.* Again, it should be kept
in mind that (a) many elders cope with physical problems without becoming depressed
and (b) depression may occur without a basis
in significant physical problems.

5. *Alcohol use increases the risk of suicide among
elderly adults.* Alcohol abuse is approximately
twice as frequent among suicidal adults than
the population in general. Increased use of
alcohol is often intended to ward off depression and suicidal thoughts, but eventually
alcohol and/or drug abuse tends to increase
the probability of suicide because of the impact on social isolation, health, and clarity of
thought.

6. *Failure to cope with stress increases the risk of
suicide among elderly adults.* Persistent stress
syndromes (see Chapter 12) can develop
when individuals' coping responses are overwhelmed by life changes and crises encountered in the later adult years. Lack of
adequate social support systems can further
expose an individual's limitations. Once it
has started, the psychophysiological stress
reaction is difficult to terminate and can become a major stressor, sapping an individual's strength and producing anxiety.

7. Loss of relationships increases the risk of
suicide among elderly adults. Bereavement
and divorce are the most common types of
relationship loss for elderly adults. Some
older adults also experience a particularly
harrowing kind of loss of relationship when
the spouse is afflicted with Alzheimer's disease or a similar dementing condition. The
spouse is still there, but the familiar and
mutually supportive relationship has altered
radically.

The Lethality of Suicide Attempts in the Later Adult Years

In general, older adults are at even greater risk
for death when they make a suicide attempt. The
ratio of suicide attempts to deaths is much smaller
for elders, especially males. Overall, elders have a
4:1 ratio of attempts to completions, compared
with the young adults' ratio of 20:1. Several factors contribute to this difference:

- Both elderly males and females most often
choose firearms as their mode of suicide
(McIntosh, 1992). This is true for adults in
general in the United States. However, the
proportion of firearms use is even higher
among elders: Approximately three of every
four elderly male suicides involve the use of
firearms.

- Elders are less likely than younger adults to
give clear warnings of their suicidal intent.
This is particularly true of males, who seem
less inclined to share their personal feelings
and have a more limited social support network, especially if they live alone and have little participation in community activities.

- Elders are more likely to plan their suicides
and try to avoid discovery or interference.

- Elders are less likely to recover from suicide attempts that produce serious trauma but from
which a younger person might survive.

Preventing Suicide in the Later Adult Years

Some people are so anxious about the prospect
of their own aging that they feel that depression,
helplessness, and suicide are only to be expected.
For example, the middle-aged person who says
"I'll kill myself before I get that old!" is not likely
to be very helpful in understanding and preventing self-destructive behaviors of the elders in
their lives. Our first priority is to come to terms
with our own futures—those older people we
ourselves will be one of these days, if we are fortunate enough.

If the motivation is there, we can do much to
detect high suicide risk in elders and to help provide alternatives. Physicians and other human
service providers often have interactions with elders who are one step away from suicide. Studies
have found that up to half of the people who commit suicide had seen a physician within 1 month
of their death (Murphy, 1995). It is probable that
elders are overrepresented in this group because
relatively few physicians are trained in detecting
depression and suicidality. Increased awareness

of this risk on the part of service providers can result in timely interventions.

Older adults who are at elevated risk for suicide often show several of the characteristics identified in Table 8-4. Again, we do not want to use this information in a mechanical manner but, rather, to guide our further observations and interactions.

There is reason for optimism in the prevention of elder suicide. By and large, people do not reach their later adult years unless they have both resilience and skill. Max, for example, demonstrated competence in school, work, and interpersonal relationships throughout his life. He had overcome many challenges, savored some successes, and adjusted to some disappointments.

The death of his wife was a severe loss to him. Along with the sorrow, there was the question of how—and why—he should go on with his life. After several coping attempts had failed, Max decided to try a solution that is deeply engrained in the tradition of this nation: When all else fails, kill somebody (see Chapter 9). However, after staring at that gun, Max realized that this was not his solution. Just as he was not a person who was made for sitting around in the sun, so too he was not a person who dealt with problems in an explosive and violent manner. Max went on to find another solution. He returned to his old neighborhood and drifted naturally to the library that had been his home away from home in child-

TABLE 8-4

Elderly Adults: Ten Indicators of Possible Suicide Risk

1. Sad, dejected, or emotionally flat mood
2. Stooped, withdrawn, fatigued, lack of eye contact
3. Careless in grooming and dress
4. Restlessness, handwringing, constant motor activity
5. Inattention, lack of concentration, losing the thread of the conversation
6. Loss of appetite/weight
7. Sleep disturbance (insomnia or oversleeping)
8. Loss of interest in activities that previously were pleasurable
9. Loss of interest in other people
10. Preoccupied with vague and shifting physical complaints

hood. Max soon became first an unofficial assistant to the librarian and, eventually, a person who the children and youth of the neighborhood sought out for advice and companionship. Max not only *felt* useful and connected again—he *was* useful and connected. He took the money he received from selling the gun and plunked it into the library's fund to help low-income children purchase their own books.

We have been focusing on elder male suicide because this is the subpopulation that is most at risk. As we have seen, though, elderly women also tend to use lethal means when they attempt suicide. It is also probable that a large but undocumented number of elderly women hasten their deaths by not looking after their health and gradually withdrawing from social contact. Deaths of this type are known as subintentional. They are not certified as suicides, but those who are familiar with the situation often believe that the person contributed to the death in a significant although indirect manner.

Suicide among Native Americans

Throughout much of the world, the people native to a region have given way to forces from other lands who were equipped with more advanced military and technological techniques. *Indigenous populations* have often been deprived of their previous means of existence, victimized by discrimination, and subject to efforts to destroy their cultural heritage (Hunter & Harvey, 2002). Elevated suicide rates are often among the consequences. The indigenous people of Australia and Canada as well as the United States are prime examples. The white man's conquest and development of the New World was catastrophic to the ancestors of many of those who are now known as Native Americans. Although the infamous quotation, "The only good Indian is a dead Indian," was in fact a misquote, there is no denying that American history expressed a genocidal component in some of its dealings with the nation's original inhabitants. It is equally troubling to think that the current high suicide rate among Native Americans is a continuing part of that heritage. Whatever the actual connection might be, it is a matter of record that genocide has in fact been followed by high rates of suicide.

The following are the basic facts about suicide among Native Americans:

1. The rate is exceptionally high. Native Americans as a total group have the highest suicide rate of any ethnic or racial subpopulation.
2. Tribal differences in suicide rates are large and also vary over time.
3. Alcohol is a major factor in Native American suicide. Although there is a strong association between alcohol and suicide for the general population, it is even more so with Native Americans. Heavy alcohol consumption was associated with approximately two thirds of the suicides among American Indians in New Mexico during a 10-year period (May et al., 2002). Alcohol abuse has been related to high unemployment, prejudice, cultural conflict, and the loss of heritage, among other factors. Suicide is clearly a symptom of social stress and disorganization as well as a tragic outcome for the individual and his or her survivors.
4. *Unlike the general population, Native Americans are more at risk for suicide in youth than in old age.* Rates for elderly suicide are low; the peak occurs in the late teens and 20s.

Suicide is more common among Native Americans than the general population. The average life expectancy is relatively low for Native Americans. This unfortunate fact contributes to a youth-oriented structure in the population, and it is the young Native American who is most susceptible to overt self-destruction. (If a life foreshortened by alcoholism is to be regarded as a form of indirect suicide, then many older Native Americans must also be counted as victims.)

It is alarming that suicide is not only among the leading causes of death but also becomes salient very early in life. Suicide is the second leading cause of death for 10- to 14-year-olds and for those ages 15–34. The lives of many American Indians and Alaskan Natives end in self-destruction just when life should be opening up with all its opportunities and discoveries. Suicide is the sixth leading cause of death in the 35–44 age range but becomes uncommon for those older than age 44.

Those who survive into their later adult years seem to be highly resistant to suicide—quite the opposite of the life-span risk for suicide among whites.

It should be emphasized that suicide, motor vehicle accidents, and other forms of violent death did not become a salient part of Native American societies until they were exposed to prolonged and overwhelming stress and deprivation (Kozak, 1991). Programs that provide realistic opportunities for youth to pursue their goals and dreams and that strengthen tribal val-

Celebrating one's own cultural heritage and personal skills provides a strong counterforce against suicidality.

ues are likely to result in a sharp decrease in suicide.

Vietnam War Veterans

Television brought home some of the brutality and moral ambiguity of war. When the Americans who were called on to fight the Vietnam War came home, it was not to praise, parades, and warm-hearted welcome. The nation had been divided regarding both the mission and the conduct of the war. The disorienting experience of engaging in a confusing war in a remote land was often followed by a sense of being shunned back home. Posttraumatic stress disorders were also common. Many of the combatants could not help but take the war home with them. Although some medical and social services were offered to the veterans, many encountered significant problems in getting on with their lives. Years later, the Vietnam Memorial Wall would remind the nation of the sacrifices made by fellow Americans during the war and arouse more compassion (Chapter 12). In the meantime, there was often a sense of estrangement, depression, and, for some, suicide.

The actual number of suicides associated with the Vietnam War will probably never be determined, nor the number of attempts. The emergence of suicide as an option is described by Alexander Paul, himself a Vietnam veteran, in *Suicide Wall* (1996). Based on facts and first-hand experience, this book illustrates how readily a suicidal crisis could develop in the circumstances. Fortunately, support from friends and mental health professionals could often help the person make it through the crisis. Chuck Dean, also a veteran, attempts to estimate how many did commit suicide in his factual account, *Nam Vet* (1990). From various sources, he derived estimates ranging from 20,000 to 200,000. The highest figures include indirect suicide through single-car accidents and other deaths that were not officially classified as suicide. Even the most conservative estimate suggests that many veterans had to struggle with suicidal thoughts at some point during their reintegration into society. Perhaps many lives were saved by good friends, loving family, and, the returning veteran's own personality strengths. There is little

doubt, however, that society's discomfort with the Vietnam War increased the stress on men and women returning from the horrors of war.

High-Risk Situations for Suicide

The risk of suicide is increased in some situations. The following are several important examples. Again, keep in mind that these are useful generalizations but should not be substituted for knowledge of how particular people deal with particular circumstances.

1. *People with HIV/AIDS are at a higher risk for suicide.* The American Foundation for Suicide Prevention estimates that the risk of suicide is up to 20 times higher for people with HIV/AIDS than for the general population. Some people become suicidal when they first learn of their HIV infection, others when HIV converts into AIDS symptoms. The suicide decision is sometimes made in a mental state that is compromised by the illness and/or by the use of drugs and alcohol. Nevertheless, much of the suicidality in people with HIV/AIDS has been based on a rational assessment of the situation—the feared loss of function and increase in suffering (Werth, 1995). We should not overlook the grief experienced by many people with HIV/AIDS who have lost friends from the disease. Although suicide is a salient thought for many people with HIV/AIDS (Beckerman, 1995), many also respond positively to counseling and social support. The feeling of being isolated and rejected can contribute more to suicidality than the disease. As with other life crises, people with HIV/AIDS often come to terms with their situation and continue to live meaningful and useful lives. Furthermore, the improved survival outlook for people with HIV/AIDS in recent years is another protection against suicide.

2. *Gambling is associated with a higher risk of suicide.* The connection between gambling and suicide has often been observed. There are solid data to confirm this relationship (Phillips, Welty, & Smith, 1997):

> Las Vegas, the premier U.S. gambling setting, displays the highest levels of suicide in the nation, both for residents of Las Vegas and for visitors to that setting. In general, visitors to and residents of

major gambling communities experience elevated suicide rates. In Atlantic City, abnormally high suicide levels for visitors and residents appeared only after gambling casinos were opened. The findings do not seem to result merely because gaming settings attract suicidal individuals. (p. 373)

3. *Schoolyard bullies and peer harassment increase suicidality.* Children and teens who have been pushed around, insulted, threatened, and mocked by classmates not only feel miserable as a result but also are at a higher risk for depression and suicide (Rigby & Slee, 1999). This situation becomes even more dangerous when victims feel they have no social support from family, teachers, or friends. Bully and harassment victims report more suicide ideation. Homicidal thoughts may also occur. For example, the Columbine High School killers felt that they had been rejected and mocked by classmates and/or teachers. There is every reason to take notice of bullying and peer harassment and take action to prevent this kind of behavior and to offer social support to the victims.

4. *"Suicide by cop" has become an established term because so many incidents have occurred throughout the nation.* The term was introduced in 1983 by Dr. Karl B. Harris, chief medical examiner for the County of Los Angeles. He identified many instances in which an armed suicidal person confronted a police officer in such a way as to force the officer to shoot in self-defense. In these cases, it was later discovered that the suicidal person's gun was unloaded or nonfunctioning: The idea all along had been to force the officer to engage in the police version of assisted suicide. This type of confrontation is very stressful for the officers, both at the time and afterward. A creative and effective alternative has been developed by some law enforcement units (Blankenstein, 1998):

When deputies in the Antelope Valley were confronted earlier this month by an armed man who continued resisting after being shot with "bean-bag" rounds, they did an unusual thing for law enforcement officers—they just went away. The man eventually returned home, without harming himself or anyone else.

The phenomenon of cop suicide is a powerful reminder that we cannot deftly separate individual

"Suicide by cop" is a situation well known to law enforcement officers.

and societal responses, nor can we keep suicide and homicide in separate categories.

Gender and Suicide

We have already seen that women are less likely to commit suicide in the United States and most other nations. How should this fact be interpreted? First, we might remind ourselves that the death rate for males is generally higher at all age levels for all causes except those specific to females (e.g., pregnancy and birth). Sex differences in life expectancy have favored females since records have been kept (Stillion & McDowell, 2001/2002). Females born in 1850 had an average life expectancy of approximately 40 years—2 years more than males. A century later, this gap had expanded: Females born in 1950 had a life expectancy of 72 years, more than 5 years longer than their male peers. Today, females have an average life expectancy of nearly 80 years, 7 years more than males. Lower male life expectancies also occur in most other nations, including those in which fewer people survive into the middle and later adult years. Although voluntary self-destruction is much different from causes of death that have a clearer biological basis, it is difficult to avoid the inference that males are relatively more vulnerable to the stresses and hazards of life and, therefore, that suicide might be part of this overall picture.

Next, we consider a major exception to the rule. As mentioned previously, China has been undergoing a national suicide crisis. It has been estimated that China has 21% of the world's population but 44% of the suicides—and 56% of the world's female suicides (Canetto, 2002). Evidence suggests that most of these suicides are motivated by a sense of hopelessness. Painful and frustrating experiences have led many women to feel that they have little or no chance of a good life. The situation is especially desperate in rural areas where government policies, including limiting married couples to one child, have disrupted traditional family patterns and increased the stress of life (Jianlin, 2000). Abortion and infanticide (Chapter 10) have also increased under the intolerable pressure. Again, a high suicide rate is not only alarming but also represents an even more widespread sense of anxiety and desperation because some sufferers stop short of suicide.

Most of the female suicides in China seem to be of the type that sociologist Emile Durkheim classified as *fatalistic:* a death that is considered the only way out of an oppressed and hopeless life. (We consider Durkheim's influential theory later in this chapter.) Another approach has been articulated recently by psychologist Silvia Sara Canetto (2002). She notes that each society has its own models and rules for suicidal behavior. It is as though there were scripts to follow in the performance of self-destructive behavior. There is evidence that suicide is one of the more culturally acceptable scripts for desperate Chinese women who have few other choices available. Canetto applies the same concept to the gender–suicide link in the United States:

> Nonfatal suicidal behavior is considered less masculine than fatal suicidal behavior.... Males are particularly critical of other males who survive a suicidal act. Studies also show that killing oneself is seen as a masculine and relatively strong act.... Men who kill themselves are viewed as better adjusted than women who kill themselves, independent of the reasons for the suicide. (p. 817)

If the cultural script depicts completed suicide as masculine, then females may have less inclination to perform this role. A suicidal threat or nonfatal attempt would be more in accord with cultural expectations. The gender–suicide connection is still far from being understood, however, and we would not want to apply any general theory to all individual situations.

Balancing Individual and Cultural Influences on Suicide

It would be useful to find a balance between individual and sociocultural factors. The realities of everyday life and prospects for the future may differ appreciably for a white, Anglo-Saxon, Protestant undergraduate; an elderly African American widow; and a youth living on a poverty-stricken reservation. The same act of desperation can flow from many sources. Preventive and interventive efforts will be more effective in some circumstances if they are focused on the individual; in other circumstances, a broader social policy approach may be necessary. Next, we examine some major cultural and individual influences on suicide.

SOME CULTURAL MEANINGS OF SUICIDE

The act of suicide has been interpreted in many different ways throughout human history and tells us much about worldviews and values of societies that have come before us (Minois, 1999; Murray, 1998, 2000). Most of these earlier conceptions are still with us and still competing with each other. We are also faced with relatively new situations, such as persistent vegetative states and the intensified advocacy for "death on demand" and physician-assisted death (see Chapter 10). New interpretations of suicide may emerge from such new challenges.

Suicide as Sinful

The doctrine that suicide is sinful has been held for centuries by defenders of the Judeo-Christian faiths. Catholics, Protestants, and Jews generally have been taught that suicide is morally wrong. Condemnation of suicide has been emphasized by the Catholic Church since at least the 5th century. Why? What about suicide is so appalling that it must be condemned by all the authority that an organized religion can command? St. Augustine helped to establish the Catholic position by crystallizing two fundamental objections to suicide. The first depends on articles of faith that are not shared by all followers of the Judeo-Christian tradition—namely, that suicide precludes the opportunity to repent of other sins. However, the second objection is based on the Sixth Commandment, "Thou shalt not kill." Suicide is not exempt from this commandment in St. Augustine's judgment of 426. St. Augustine (426/1971) did have to volunteer some exceptions to his own rule:

> Abraham indeed was not merely deemed guiltless of cruelty, but was even applauded for his piety, because he was ready to slay his son in obedience to God, not to his own passion....

Samson, too, who drew down the house on himself and his foes together, is justified only on this ground, that the Spirit who wrought wonders by him had given him secret instructions to do this. (Book I, Chapter XXI)

Perhaps the most uncomfortable exception granted by St. Augustine concerns Jepththah's execution of his daughter because he had promised God he would sacrifice "whatever first met him as he returned victorious from the battle." Although very influential, this church father's pronouncement has troubled some believers through the centuries by ruling against suicide yet justifying a father's killing of his daughter in order to keep his own reckless promise.

In the 13th century, St. Thomas Aquinas (1279/1971) reaffirmed St. Augustine's conclusion and added another objection. God and only God has the power to grant life and death. Suicide is sinful because it represents a revolt against the ordained order of the universe. The self-murderer is engaging in a sin of pride, of self-assertion. This point was later advocated by a man whose ideas of human nature and society exerted great influence over the founding fathers of the United States. John Locke (1690/1971) refused to include self-destruction as one of the inherent liberties: "Every one...is bound to preserve himself, and not to quit his station willfully" (p. 26). A person who abandons his station thereby transgresses the law of nature. According to Locke, we are possessions and therefore not at liberty to dispose of ourselves. Great suffering does not entitle a person to suspend the "law of nature" and take life into his or her own hands.

Individuals who accept this cultural tradition are likely to believe that there is more to lose by suicide. The survivors have more to lose as well. The suicide of a family member could bring a strong sense of shame as well as the feelings of loss and grief that accompany bereavement from death produced by other causes. Some regimes seized on this idea to rule that the property of families in which a suicide had occurred must be turned over to the state.

Condemnation of suicide as a violation of the Sixth Commandment, however, is difficult to square with the tradition of warfare and violent death that has been not only condoned but also, occasionally, actively pursued by defenders of the faith. Religious wars and the persecution of heretics have repeatedly violated the edict, "Thou shalt not kill." As Jacques Choron (1972) observes, "during the Middle Ages, mass suicide was frequent among persecuted sects of Christian heretics and non-Christian minorities....The category of non-Christians included Moslems and Jews, who refused to be converted to Christianity and preferred to commit suicide" (pp. 25–26). The persecuted victims were sinners for committing suicide, but the persecutors, acting in the name of their religion, were not sinners, even if they had used threats and torture.

The image of the crucifixion, so powerful in the Christian tradition, is a sacrifice of suffering unto death with strong suicidal connotations. Some of the early Christian thinkers, in fact, regarded the death of Jesus as suicide (Brown, 1998), as did deeply reflecting Christians of later times, such as John Donne (1646/1977). Choron (1972) suggests that suicide through martyrdom became all too tempting to those who tried to follow Christ's pathway. It was glorious to die as a martyr. The Church found it advisable to protect some true believers from themselves, to reduce the attractiveness of death now that immortality had been proclaimed, and to discourage widespread emulation of the early martyrs. Admiration of martyrdom has persisted, however, and so has the moral condemnation of suicide (Smith, 1997). The Old and New Testaments do not directly prohibit suicide, nor do they even seem to find this action particularly remarkable.

Other influential voices within the Christian tradition have offered alternative interpretations. For example, philosopher David Hume (as quoted in Colt, 1991) reasoned along these lines:

I am not obliged to do a small good to society at the expense of a great harm to myself; why then should I prolong a miserable existence? If upon account of age and infirmities, I may lawfully resign any office, and employ my time altogether in fencing against these calamities, and alleviating as much as possible the miseries of my future life; why may I not cut short these miseries at once by an action which is no more prejudicial to society? (p. 43)

Suicide as Criminal

Is suicide a sin or a *crime?* The intertwining of church and state once made it easy to regard suicide as both criminal and sinful. Certainly, the sinful and the criminal interpretations of suicide have something in common. Both regard self-destruction as a willful violation of the basic ties that relate the individual to the universe.

Through the years, however, the civil and divine realms of authority have become more independent of each other. This has strengthened the view that suicide is crime, not sin. The word suicide seems first to have entered use in approximately the middle of the 17th century. The earliest citation given by *The Oxford English Dictionary* attributes the following statement to Walter Charleton in 1651: "To vindicate ones self from... inevitable Calamity, by Suicide is not...a Crime."

Suicide is more apt to be punished by human authority when it is interpreted as a crime as well as a sin. Suicide attempts have often brought severe punishment in addition to moral condemnation. This has included torture, defamation, and impoverishment. Surviving family members have sometimes also been punished by having their possessions confiscated by the state.

The interpretation of suicide as crime is waning. Criminal laws have been erased from the books. It was once common for insurance companies to treat suicide as a crime intended to defraud the underwriters. It is now possible to have death benefits associated with suicide, although with limitations and restrictions built into the contract. Decriminalization of suicide is based on the realization that penalties have not served as effective deterrents, and that few people were willing to enforce the laws. Law enforcement agencies have become effective frontline resources for suicide prevention in some communities, liberated from the obligation of treating the attempter as a criminal.

Suicide as Weakness or Madness

Some people who commit suicide can be classified as psychotic or severely disturbed, but some cannot. Individuals with diagnosed psychiatric conditions have a higher suicide rate than the population at large. People diagnosed as depressive psychotics tend to have the highest rates of completed suicides. Prevention of suicide does require diagnostic and therapeutic attention to people suffering from depression or other psychiatric disorders. However, psychiatric disorder is not entirely adequate as an explanation or predictor of suicide. Many people go through disturbed periods without attempting suicide. It would be tempting to believe that a person has to be crazy to commit suicide, but this is simply not true.

What about the related explanation that suicide is the outcome of weakness? This view gained additional support as a result of the survival of the fittest doctrine (Darwin, 1859/1971). Those who favor a rough-and-tumble, highly competitive struggle for power tried to rationalize these tactics with a speculative extension of the so-called survival of the fittest principle. Suicide is one of nature's ways to preserve the species by weeding out the less fit. This interpretation is not necessarily one that would have been endorsed by Darwin, who had no control over how society chose to use or abuse his ideas.

This position is not taken quite as openly today as in the heyday of rugged individualism and naive social applications of evolutionary theory. Nevertheless, we can still see it in operation. "If you can't stand the heat, get out of the kitchen!" was one type of comment heard after a spectacular suicide in New York City. A ranking executive of a major international corporation leaped to his death from an office high above Manhattan. Media coverage emphasized the length of time that his fallen body tied up traffic and other circumstantial aspects of the death. Little attention was given then or later to his state of mind, the meaning of his suicide, or the impact on survivors. Other executives throughout the nation commented off the record that some people just cannot take the gaff. There was a note of pride in such comments: "I am strong enough to cope with adversity; that other fellow wasn't." Is this a justified interpretation or simply a way of covering our own fears and asserting our own superiority?

Suicide as "The Great Death"

The Buddhist tradition in China and Japan includes the image of *daishi*, which translates roughly as "The Great Death." Through their own example, Zen masters have shown how a person might pass admirably from this life. The discipline and devotion of the master appealed to the warrior. The samurai would seek *daishi* on the battlefield. This influence remained strong enough through the centuries to enlist the self-sacrifices of *kamikaze* pilots in World War II (although some of these young men still had their doubts about carrying out missions that meant almost certain death).

Suicide has been honored as a form of *daishi*. *Seppuku* is a traditional form of suicide in Japan, better known in the West as *hara-kiri*. The act consists of disembowelment, usually with a sword. In some situations, this form of death has served as an honorable alternative to execution. A person condemned to death would be given the privilege of becoming his or her own executioner. Voluntary *seppuku*, in contrast, might flow from a number of different motives on the part of the individual (e.g., to follow a master into the great beyond or to protest an injustice). Placing your entire life at the disposal of an honorable or noble motive was a much admired action. In our own time, the self-immolation of Buddhist monks in Southeast Asia to emphasize their religious and political protests has also made a deep impression on observers.

Ritualized, honorable suicide of this Great Death type seems to integrate various levels of existence. By opening his abdomen, the individual is showing the world that his center of being (thought to be located there) is pure and undefiled. Specifically, the individual puts the sword to the *hara*, regarded as the locus of breath control, and breath is regarded as a link to both life and divinity. The terminal act therefore involves a network of physiological, individual, social, and religious referents.

The association of suicide with desirable death has not been limited to the Orient. It was one of the characteristic themes of the ancient Greeks and Romans (Colt, 1991):

> In Alexandria in the third century B.C. the philosopher Hegesias taught that life was so fleeting and full of cares that death was man's happiest lot. He lectured so eloquently that...many of his

listeners committed suicide. Two centuries later, during the reign of Cleopatra, herself a suicide, there seems to have existed...a school that taught the best ways of committing suicide. Some "students" were rumored to have killed themselves during sumptuous banquets. Such excess anticipated the Roman Empire. For if the Greeks rationalized suicide, the Romans made it a fashion, even a sport. (p. 148)

Thus the same action that later was considered a sin by some people and a crime by others was regarded by Romans of the classical period as perhaps the most noble and glorious thing a man (sic) could do.

Suicide as a Rational Alternative

The belief that suicide can bring a glorious death has a more subdued echo in another cultural tradition that dates from ancient times. This is the attitude that suicide is an acceptable, rational alternative to continued existence. It is a view often conditioned by adverse circumstances. "Life is not always preferable to death" is the thought here. Individuals do not destroy themselves in hope of thereby achieving a noble postmortem reputation or a place among the eternally blessed. Instead, they wish to subtract themselves from a life whose quality seems a worse evil than death.

Renaissance thinkers often praised death as the place of refuge from the cruelties and disappointments of life. Erasmus (1509) is but one of the eminent humanists who observed what a distance there is between our aspirations for the human race and the failings discovered on every side in daily life. The newly awakened spirit of hope and progress soon became shadowed by a sense of disappointment and resignation that, it sometimes seemed, only death could possibly swallow.

Much earlier in history there is also evidence that the harshness of life made suicide an appealing option to many. Stoicism, a philosophical position that was enunciated in ancient Athens and Rome and has since become virtually a synonym for rational control, was in actuality (Alvarez, 1970)

a last defense against the murderous squalor of Rome itself. When those calm heroes looked around them they saw a life so unspeakable, cruel, wanton, corrupt, and apparently unvalued that they clung to their ideas of reason much as the Christian poor used to cling to their belief in Paradise and the goodness of God despite, or because of, this misery of their lives on this earth. Stoicism, in short, was a philosophy of despair; it was not a coincidence that Seneca, who was its most powerful and influential spokesman, was also the teacher of the most vicious of all Roman emperors, Nero. (p. 66)

There have been many times in human history when misery was so general and the outlook so grim that it seemed natural to think seriously of suicide. The horrors of the plague years, for example, intensified by warfare and general social disorganization, led many to question the value of continued life. Nevertheless, careful attention should be given to the question of what it is that might make a suicide "rational." Brandt (1990) observes that what might seem rational from the standpoint of the individual contemplating suicide might not seem rational from another person's perspective. Furthermore, it can be difficult to determine whether a person is thinking in a rational manner when contemplating suicide, and it is impossible to do so after the fact.

The Judeo-Christian tradition has generally held that we should not dispose of life, no matter what the provocation or temptation. This message has been imperfectly delivered. At times, it has been contradicted by actions of the true believers. Nevertheless, enough of this spirit has come across to establish a challenging issue for all of us: Is life to be valued and fostered under *all* conditions because it has primary and intrinsic value? Or is the value of life relative to the circumstances? We encounter this issue repeatedly today, as in the prospect of health care rationing and the spectrum of right-to-die decisions.

A POWERFUL SOCIOLOGICAL THEORY OF SUICIDE

Emile Durkheim proposed a comprehensive sociological theory of self-destruction in 1897. *Le*

Suicide (1897/1951) became a cornerstone for the emerging science of sociology and remains one of the most influential theories of suicide. His ideas continue to command the attention of those who study and seek to prevent suicide. Durkheim's approach was audacious for its time. Suicide was not a matter of the individual's relationship to God, nor were moral values the primary focus. Instead, suicide could be viewed most accurately at a distance and by a cool observer who was more interested in the overall pattern of self-destruction than in any particular life and death.

The Importance of Social Integration

Why do people kill themselves? All individuals are more or less integrated into their societies. Suicide risk depends much on the extent of social integration between individual and society. Society may be stable, consistent, and supportive, or it may be falling apart under stress. The individual may be weakly or strongly integrated into a high- or low-solidarity culture, as shown in Table 8-5.

The crucial index for suicide can be found in the interaction between integration and solidarity. How much does the culture control the individual? Both the weakly integrated person in a cohesive society (low-high in Table 8-5) and the person trapped in a disorganized culture (high-low) are endangered because there is not enough group control. With lessened group control, there is a heightened possibility of suicide. However, suicide can also result from too much control by

TABLE 8-5

Types of Connection between Individual and Society

Individual's integration into society	Society's solidarity
High	High
High	Low
Low	High
Low	Low

society. Durkheim's theory invites attention to both the cohesiveness of society and the social integration of any particular individual.

Collective representations is another important Durkheimian concept. All cultures have collective representations that convey the spirit or personality of the culture as a whole, the guiding themes, moods, or emotional climate. Unfortunately, this group spirit can turn morose and self-destructive. Individuals who are well integrated into the culture may be especially vulnerable. They are more likely to absorb the pessimistic mood of the larger society and may act it out with fatal results. This aspect of Durkheim's theory suggests that the very forces that should hold a society together can take on the opposite character and lead to what we might call *sociocide*. The mass suicide and homicide in Jonestown, Guyana, that resulted in the eradication of a unique community and more than 900 lives is one such example.

Four Types of Suicide

Most of the attention to Durkheim today focuses on the four types of suicide he identified. Each represents a distinctive relationship between individual and society. The *egoistic suicide* is committed by people who do not have enough involvement with society. They are not under sufficient cultural control. The executive who literally fell from on high is one probable example. Individuals whose talents, inclinations, or stations in life place them in a special category, relatively immune from ordinary social restrictions, are especially vulnerable to egoistic suicide. The celebrity in the entertainment field, the creative artist who follows his or her own star, and the person in a relatively distinct or unique role all may go their own personal ways until they can no longer be reached effectively by cultural constraints. Intellectuals are also common in the category of egoistic suicide. They are more likely than others to pick up those collective representations described as sociocidic. Sensitive to underlying currents of melancholy and despair in the culture and, in a sense, lost in their own thoughts, they have little outside themselves to grasp when the suicide impulse arises.

French scholar Emile Durkheim was a pioneer in the study of suicide and one of the founders of the field of sociology.

Very different indeed is the *altruistic suicide.* Already mentioned were such examples as the *seppuku* tradition and the *kamikaze* combat death. *Suttee* (Sati), the now illegal Indian practice of a widow giving her life at her husband's funeral, is another dramatic example. According to Durkheim, altruistic suicide occurs when the individual has an exaggerated or excessive concern for the community. This is usually the strongly integrated person in a high solidarity culture (High–High, Table 8-5). Altruistic suicides tend to be less common in Western societies but often are admired when ᵗhey do occur. The soldier who volunteers for a "suicide mission" (one in which death is almost certain) in order to protect comrades or achieve a military

objective can be considered both a hero and an altruistic suicide.

The third type is called *anomic suicide.* Social breakdown is reflected most directly in the anomic suicide. Here it is less a question of the individual's integration with society and more a question of society's ability to function as it should. People are let down, cast adrift by the failure of social institutions. Unemployment is an important example. The person thrown out of work has lost a significant tie to society and through society's doing, not his or her own. Bad times, unemployment, suicide—a predictable sequence. Similarly, a person who is forced to leave his or her occupation because of age may enter an anomic condition that leads to suicide. When the rupture between individual and society is sudden and unexpected, the probability of suicide is thought to be especially high. This situation arises, for example, when the death of an important person drastically reduces the survivor's place in society.

For many years, it was this set of three suicide types that dominated the picture. Recently, however, more attention has been given to a fourth type that Durkheim introduced but treated more as a curiosity in a footnote: *fatalistic suicide.* A person may experience too much control by society, he suggested. A culture that stifles and oppresses some of its members may thereby encourage fatalistic suicide. The individual sees all opportunities and prospects blocked. Durkheim spoke of slavery as a condition that engenders fatalistic suicide but thought that civilization had put this kind of oppression well into the past. Oppression and subjugation have not disappeared from the human condition, however, because totalitarian regimes continue to manifest themselves into the 21st century.

Both the altruistic and the fatalistic suicide involve excessive control of the individual by society. In altruistic suicide the individuals appear to share wholeheartedly in the collective representations. They die for their people. In fatalistic suicide they die in despair of ever being able to actualize themselves in a culture that affords little opportunity for self-esteem and satisfaction.

Next, move from a sociological approach to the individual's own thoughts, motives, and lifestyle as factors in suicide.

SOME INDIVIDUAL MEANINGS OF SUICIDE

Just as the preceding discussion did not exhaust all the cultural and sociological meanings of suicide, so this section can only sample some of the individual meanings. The intent is to convey something of the various states of mind with which people approach a suicidal action.

Suicide for Reunion

The loss of a loved one can be experienced as so unbearable that the survivor is tempted to "join" the deceased. Recently bereaved people often experience the "presence" of the dead. This may be regarded as part of the normal response to the death of a loved person and may help to reduce the sense of abandonment. However, desperate longing may impel a person to follow the dead all the way to the other side if the relationship has been marked by extreme dependency. "I can't go on without him." "I am not complete without her." "What's to become of me? I can't manage by myself." Many people have feelings of this kind. Sometimes these feelings are accompanied by suicidal thoughts. Reunion fantasies may have some temporary value while bereaved individuals reconstruct their lives, but they can also lead to suicidal actions.

Some sociocultural themes can encourage suicidal reunion fantasies and actions. Heaven is such a delightful place, and it is so miserable here. Death is not real; it is only a portal to eternal life. Insurance advertisements have depicted a deceased husband gazing down with approval from the clouds. Messages of this type encourage a blurring of the distinction between the living and the dead.

Children are particularly vulnerable to reunion fantasies. The child is still in the process of attempting to establish identity as an individual. The parent or older sibling who has "gone off to heaven" has left the survivor with painful feelings of incompleteness and yearning. Some adults remain relatively childlike in their dependency on others and feel very much the same way when separated by death. Suicide to achieve reunion seems most likely when the person lacks a fully developed sense of selfhood, whether because of developmental level or personality constellation; when death has removed a significant source of support; and when there are salient cultural messages that make death appear unreal and the afterlife inviting.

Suicide for Rest and Refuge

Worn down by tribulations, a person may long for a "good rest" or a "secure harbor." This motivation can have many outcomes other than suicide. A vacation far away from the grinding routine may restore energy and confidence. Somebody else may appear on the scene to share the load. The vexed and fatigued person may simply drop his or her responsibilities for a while. Alternatives such as these may not work, however. Life may be experienced as too unrelenting and burdensome. The miracle of an ordinary good night's sleep may seem out of reach as depression deepens. In such circumstances, the fantasy of a prolonged, uninterrupted sleep may take on a heightened allure. The sleep–death analogy is readily available in America as in most other cultures (Chapter 3). It is tempting to take a few more pills than usual and just drift away.

This attitude toward suicide is also encouraged by individual and cultural tendencies to blur the distinctions between life and death. It falls well within the established cultural style of solving problems by taking something into our mouths (puff on a cigarette; suck on a pipe; or swallow pills for headaches, indigestion, and any form of distress). People with oral or escapist tendencies dominant in their personalities might be expected to be especially vulnerable to these lures of suicide.

Suicide for Revenge

The lover is rejected. The employee is passed over for promotion. Another child is preferred and pampered. The particular situation is not as important as the feeling of burning resentment and hurt left inside. It may not have been the first time. Some people repeatedly feel that they are treated unfairly. Their achievements never seem to be recognized. No matter how hard they try, love and appreciation are withheld. Others may not recognize the state of mind with which such a person approaches a situation and how intensely hope and doubt, anger and longing are intermingled.

> I felt crushed. Absolutely crushed. It was my first really good semester. No incompletes. No withdrawals. All A's and B's. And no "episodes." I kept myself going all semester. I really felt strong and independent. I knew I shouldn't expect too much when I went home, but I guess…I mean I know I expected a little appreciation. You know, like maybe Mother just smiling and saying, "Had a good semester, didn't you? I'm happy for you" or "I'm proud of you," though she would never say that.

This young woman believed that her achievement passed without notice—that, in fact, the family hardly noticed that she had come back home. Hurt and angry, she decided to get back by making a suicide attempt. If her family would not pay attention when she did something right, maybe they would when she did something wrong. "I wanted to hurt them—and hurt me—just enough." She slashed away at her wrist and arm. The self-wounding seemed to release some of her despair. She had not injured herself seriously, so she wrapped the wounded area in a bulky bandage. Nobody seemed to notice. A few days later she removed the bandage, exposing the patchwork of fresh scars. There still was no obvious response from the family. Instead, they were enthusiastically anticipating the graduation and upcoming marriage of one of her cousins.

She felt even more crushed and low when she was passed over in the wedding arrangements as well: "I couldn't even be part of somebody else's happiness…. I knew that revenge was stupid. But I felt like doing something stupid. Listen everybody: You're 100% right! I am a stupid person. And here is something really stupid to prove it!" She hurled herself from a rooftop.

> I wanted to kill myself then. I think I did. But I also wanted to see the look on their faces when they saw that bloody mess on the sidewalk. I could see myself standing alongside the rest of them, looking at that bloody mess of myself on the sidewalk, and looking at their shocked looks…. I didn't think what it would be like if I

half-killed myself and had to live with a crushed body. Maybe that was the really stupid part of it.

She survived a suicide attempt that might have been fatal. She was also fortunate in that her injuries did not prove permanently crippling, although she was disabled for months. The physical pain and trauma relieved some of her emotional tension for a while. However, she felt that she might "have to" do it again, perhaps "next time for keeps." She did not need a psychologist to suggest that her suicide attempts were efforts to punish others by punishing herself. She was also perfectly capable of pointing out that both attempts had been aimed at forcing either love or remorse from the people who had been letting her down for so long. (At last report, this woman was alive, well, and somehow a stronger person for the ordeals she had undergone.)

The example given here illustrates several other characteristics often shown by the person who is on a self-destructive footing. This woman's fantasy included witnessing the impact of her suicide. *She had divided herself into murderer and victim.* The revenge fantasy would have lost much of its appeal had she recognized that she would never be able to confirm or appreciate the hoped-for impact. People who attempt suicide for reasons other than revenge may also act on the assumption that, in a sense, they will survive the death to benefit by its effect.

She also experienced some tension release through the self-destructive action. It is not unusual for the sight of one's own blood to relieve built-up emotional pressures, if only for a while. Another woman who had slashed her wrists on several occasions told me, "I felt as if I had done something finally. I wasn't paralyzed anymore. I wasn't suffering helplessly. I took action into my own hands, and that felt good." Perhaps the experience of surviving this type of suicide attempt encourages the fantasy that one would still be around to feel better after a fatal attempt as well.

The low self-esteem of many suicide attempters is also evident in the instance given here. Having a very unfavorable opinion of yourself may be linked with a variety of other motivations in addition to the fantasy of revenge. The combination of the revenge fantasy and low self-esteem appears to be a particularly dangerous one, however.

Suicide as the Penalty for Failure

The victim of suicide may also be the victim of self-expectations that have not been fulfilled. The judgment "I have failed" is followed by the decision to enact a most severe penalty, one that will make further failures impossible. It is as though the person has been tried and found guilty of a capital offense in his or her own personal court. A completely unacceptable gap is felt between expectations and accomplishment. Some take the alternative of lowering expectations to close the gap. Others give themselves the benefit of the doubt in evaluating their accomplishments ("I really didn't do so badly, everything considered"). Still others keep trying to bring performance up to self-expectations. However, for some people a critical moment arrives when the discrepancy is experienced as too glaring and painful to be tolerated. If something has to be sacrificed, it may be themselves, not the perhaps excessively high standards by which the judgment has been made.

A sense of failure is prominent among many people who take their own lives. The psychological autopsy technique (a special kind of case review) often finds that adult male suicides have occurred after the person was fired, demoted, or passed over for promotion. Female suicides are more often related to real or perceived failures in relationships. Young female suicides often had a history of persistent troubles with men. Those who married and had children had further difficulties in meeting the responsibilities of the maternal role. Older women who take their lives often seem to have lost or given up most of their social roles and obligations. For women younger than 50 years old, work failure does not seem to be nearly as salient a factor in suicide as it is for men. However, often the suicidal person has experienced repeated failure in both personal relationships and occupational success.

Fortunately, not every person who experiences failure commits suicide. This has led to Warren Breed's (1972) influential concept of a basic suicidal syndrome. Failure plays a critical role but takes on more lethal potential because of its association with the other factors. The syndrome includes rigidity, commitment, shame, and isolation, as well as failure. The individual tends to be rigid in that he or she cannot shift from one role or goal to another or shift the level of aspiration. There is only one goal, one level of expectation, and only one way to achieve it. There is also a strong sense of commitment—that is, an intense desire to succeed. The sense of failure involves more than performing below self-expectations. It also includes a sense of culpability, of self-blame. The feeling is likely to go beyond guilt. A person who has failed or erred still might have a chance for redemption. The suicidal syndrome is characterized by a generalized sense of shame. It is not just that the individual has failed at something—he or she feels totally worthless. "I am no good. Never will be. I am nothing." From all these interacting factors, the individual may develop a sense of isolation. This syndrome has been found by Breed and his colleagues most conspicuously in white, middle-class adults, both men and women. It does not seem to hold for lower-class black men who kill themselves.

It is going too far to speak of this as *the* basic suicidal syndrome. Breed (1972) readily acknowledges that there are also other patterns associated with suicide. Several have already been sketched here. However, the high-aspiration, shame of failure dynamics revealed by his research do come close to the meaning of suicide for many in American society today. It does not tell us, however, why one person with a basic suicidal syndrome commits suicide while another finds a different solution to his or her problems.

Suicide as a Mistake

Death may be the intended outcome of an overdose or other self-destructive action, but the person might not die. A serious attempt may fall short of its objective for a number of reasons. An unexpected rescuer may appear on the scene, a determined self-mutilation may miss a vital spot, the overdose may induce vomiting instead of coma, and even a loaded gun may fail to fire.

The victim may "betray" himself or herself, as in the case of the bridge jumper who survives the often deadly fall and then swims desperately for life.

However, there can be a discrepancy between intention and outcome in the other direction as well. Some people kill themselves even though there is good reason to believe that they had not meant to do so. The victim had counted on being rescued. The overdose was not supposed to be lethal. Some kind of control or precaution had been exercised to limit the effect, and yet the outcome was death. We cannot automatically conclude that death was the intention any more than we can insist that a person did not intend to commit suicide because the attempt happened to abort. In suicide, as in most other actions, we do not always achieve the outcome we had in mind. The person may have wanted much to live, but a mood, a desperate maneuver, and a misjudgment brought life to a sudden close.

People who often work with the suicidal recognize that the individual contemplating a self-destructive act frequently is of two minds. This is the impression, for example, of volunteers who pick up the phone when a call is made to a suicide prevention hot line. The very fact that a person would reach out for human contact in this way suggests some continuing advocacy for life. We have no way of knowing if all people in a suicidal state of mind experience strong ambivalence. However, many people with suicide on their minds do go back and forth about it, experiencing conflicting life and death tugs simultaneously. A life-threatening act that emerges from a wavering or conflicting intention may show some apparent contradictions. Why would she have taken the overdose just a few minutes before her husband was due home if she was entirely of a mind to take her life? Yet she did take the pills, and if her husband happens to be delayed coming home this day, will this gesture have become indeed her final gesture?

Helping people to survive their own mistakes is an important part not only of suicide prevention but also of public health safety in general. Access to lethal means of self-destruction could be made more difficult, for example, thereby placing some time and distance between a momentary intention and a permanent error. Suicide rates decreased significantly in England after coke gas was no longer widely available as a mode of suicide in the home or when its toxicity was reduced.

Mental health specialists have persistently advocated the construction of a lower-span sidewalk for the Golden Gate Bridge, a place that has become known widely as a "suicide shrine." Seiden (1977) followed up on more than 700 people who had approached either the Golden Gate or Bay Bridge with suicidal intentions and who were intercepted by alert citizens or police before completing the action. Ninety-six percent of these people did not make subsequent fatal attempts, and all the survivors favored construction of a barrier. "If there had been a barrier every one of them reports they would have reconsidered" (p. 274). The suicidal intention had been strong but ambivalent. The attempters had given society a chance to catch them before making a fatal mistake. Seiden adds that "considering the transitory nature of suicidal crises, the presence of a highly lethal and easily available means such as the bridge must be regarded as equivalent to a loaded gun around the house ready to be used in an impulsive outburst" (p. 274). Society could take a more active role in protecting people from those critical moments when the possibility of making a fatal mistake is on the horizon.

A Psychoanalytical Approach to Suicide

Since life seeks to preserve itself, how could a being actively pursue its own destruction? Freud (1917/1959) first suggested that suicidal individuals turn a murderous wish against themselves. By destroying themselves, they symbolically destroy the other person. Suicide victims behave as though they are rooting out the inner representation of another person, a representation that might derive from early childhood when the distinction between self and other is incomplete. What looks to the world like a suicide may be the symbolic murder of a person whose compelling image has remained lodged in the mind.

Freud did not remain satisfied with this theory. Later, he (1923/1961) offered a more philosophical concept. We do not have just one basic instinctual drive. Each of us possesses a pair of drives that have different goals. These are a life instinct, *Eros*, and a death instinct, *Thanatos*. These drives constantly interact in our lives. When Thanatos gains the upper hand, we may engage in a self-destructive action. Vulnerability to suicide exists for all humans because there are many obstacles in our pathway to gratification and much of our aggression is forced inward.

This twin-instinct theory still has something to offer (Kastenbaum, 2000) but has not found much application in day-by-day interactions with people at suicidal risk, and researchers have yet to derive convincing ways of testing the theory. However, the psychoanalytical approach does alert us to the long developmental career that precedes a self-destructive action. The young child, for example, may internalize the negative attitudes conveyed by cruel or thoughtless parents. This burdens the child with a superego that is excessively oriented toward criticism and self-destructive action. Chaotic and inadequate parenting may also jeopardize the child by leaving him or her with a brittle ego that fragments and shatters under pressures that most other people are able to withstand.

Many present-day clinicians and researchers have modified the early psychoanalytical approach to take sociocultural factors more into account. For example, some Native Americans are at exceptionally high risk for suicide and other self-destructive actions. Their sense of low self-esteem comes from the deprivation and discrimination experienced in their contacts with mainstream U.S. society. The child is in danger of growing up with a severe lack of confidence in his or her identity and worth as well as with a tendency to keep aggressive impulses locked up under high pressure until efforts at control fail. This is in contrast with the pride and satisfaction a child would have taken in being, for example, a Cheyenne in preceding generations when the people were independent and possessed a favorable group self-image. These dynamics of low self-esteem and self-directed aggression can lead to fatal outcomes other than

suicide, as demonstrated by the high alcohol-related death rates on the same reservation. The psychoanalytical approach remains useful today, but its interpretation must be tested against experience, and other relevant factors should also be considered.

The Descent Toward Suicide

How do people move toward suicide? Are there enough common features to help us identify and understand the states of mind that culminate in a suicide attempt?

Richard Heckler (1994) offers a useful description of the events and states of mind that often precede a suicide attempt. The most basic and common experiences along the way to a possible suicide attempt, and possible death, are the following:

- An experience of loss and/or trauma that deprives the person of emotional support and sensitizes the person to the possibility of further losses. These hurtful experiences often occur early in life when the person is most vulnerable and most in need of support and guidance. For example, the father may have abandoned the family, followed by the mother's depression and drug addiction and then her death.
- The experience of losing hope for a satisfying life and losing the belief that the world is a coherent and rational place where good intentions and good actions have good consequences.
- The sense of descending, sinking, and falling slowly into a subhuman kind of existence. This is accompanied by low self-esteem and a feeling of helplessness, like trying to run through quicksand.
- Withdrawal and communication breakdown increasingly isolate the individual from others. There is often a mutual withdrawal from significant emotional interactions as family members and friends also find themselves unable to cope with the situation of loss and trauma.
- The presuicidal person now constructs a facade as protection against further emotional pain. Karen, quoted in the beginning of the chapter,

built a robot-like facade around her doubts, fears, and vulnerabilities. She was just there, doing her work, trying to be socially invisible to avoid interactions. In a sense, though, she was not there at all. Within the facade of a competent but distant and uninviting person, she experienced the deadening effect of this protective strategy and "just felt it would be more congruent to be dead. Just not to have this body to keep being in." Other people may construct other types of facades that offer protection but also exact a high price in restricting the quality of life.

- If the descent continues, the person enters a state of mind that Heckler believes can be described accurately as the suicidal trance. There is a greatly restricted range of thoughts and feelings. One is aware of one's suffering but of little else. There is a deepening conviction that the only options available are to continue suffering or to free themselves from suffering through death.

- The person now thinks and feels as though trapped in a tunnel. Death increasingly seems to be the only logical and possible exit.

- The movement toward suicide is likely to be accelerated by the impression that death is somehow beckoning to the individual, offering release, even commanding the act of self-destruction (for some people this takes the form of hallucinatory voices, but others are aware that it is their own mind that is making the decision).

- A precipitating event is likely to trigger the actual suicide attempt when the person is already primed toward death-as-release. Often, this precipitating event is some form of rejection from another person.

The descent toward suicide can be halted at any of these points by understanding and helpful interactions as well as by the individual's own resourceful efforts. The deeper the person has descended into the presuicidal sequence, however, the more difficult the challenge. Nevertheless, it is an encouraging fact that Heckler's (1994) case sample is drawn from people who did "wake up, alive." I was impressed by the courage and resourcefulness of many of the peo-

ple described by Heckler who fought uphill battles against despair before making suicide attempts. I have known some people like this myself, and perhaps you have, too. The private hells they have had to survive often were not at all of their own making.

FACTS, MYTHS, AND GUIDELINES

Some of the major social and individual meanings of suicide have been considered. Now we consider myths that have grown around the subject over the years. This will serve as a partial review and will also prepare us for a set of guidelines.

Popular Myths about Suicide

- *A person who talks about suicide will not actually take his or her own life. There is abundant evidence to show that this statement is not true.* Approximately three of every four people who eventually kill themselves give some detectable hint ahead of time, whether by less serious attempts or by verbal statements (the latter are sometimes as direct as can be, e.g., "I'm going to blow my head off" and "If things don't get better in a hurry, you'll be reading about me in the papers"). This is one of the most dangerous myths because it encourages us to ignore cries for help. As noted previously, the rejection of the communication can become the last straw for a person contemplating suicide.

- *Only a specific class of people commit suicide.* It is sometimes held that suicide is a particular risk of either the poor or the rich. The poor are supposed to feel helpless and deprived and the rich to be bored and aimless. These simplifications fail to consider the complexity of the individual's relationship to society. People in all income brackets and social echelons commit suicide. An explanation limited to economic or class distinctions alone is not adequate and contributes to our blind spots in the identification of individuals at risk.

- *Suicide has simple causes that are easily established.* It would be closer to the truth to say that many of us are easily satisfied with hasty and superficial explanations. This chapter has emphasized meanings and situations rather than causes of suicide, which are often far from simple.

- *Asking people about suicide will put that thought in their minds and encourage suicide attempts.* This is one of the most common of the mistaken assumptions. Many lives have been saved by opening communication on this topic.

- *Only depressed people commit suicide.* This misconception is held by some professionals as well as by the public. People with a psychiatric diagnosis of depression do have a higher suicide rate than those with other psychiatric syndromes or those without known syndromes. However, suicide may occur in any type of psychiatric disorder. The person may not even seem to be especially unhappy immediately before the fatal action. It is dangerous to overlook suicidal potential on the basis of the assumption that only depressed people take their lives.

- *Only crazy or insane people commit suicide.* This mistaken proposition is related to the one just described. Psychiatrists disagree on how many suicides are associated with obvious mental disorder, but some of the most qualified researchers and clinicians find that suicide is not invariably related to psychosis. Rational people can feel overwhelmed by circumstances.

- *Suicidal tendencies are inherited.* It is true that more than one person in the same family may commit suicide. Some families do have a suicidal tradition that seems to perpetuate itself. However, there is little evidence for a hereditary basis, even in studies of identical twins. The explanation for suicide must be sought elsewhere, with particular attention to family patterns of communication.

- *When a suicidal person shows improvement, the danger is over.* The period following an apparent improvement in overall condition is actually one of special danger. Sometimes this is because the client has improved enough to be discharged from a mental hospital and therefore has more opportunity to commit suicide. It may also be related to a recovery of enough energy and volition to take action. Sensitivity and

interpersonal support are especially needed when the person seems to be pulling out of a suicidal crisis.

- *People who are under a physician's care or who are hospitalized are not suicidal risks.* This is wishful thinking. Many people who commit suicide have received some form of medical or psychiatric attention within 6 months preceding the act. Suicides can and do occur in hospitals. Furthermore, the institutional situation can contribute to anxiety, low self-esteem, and other conditions conducive to suicide (Kastenbaum, 1995).

- *Suicide can be prevented only by a psychiatrist or mental hospital.* Some of the most successful suicide prevention efforts are being made by a variety of people in the community who bring concern, stamina, and sensitivity to the task. The human resources of the entire community may hold more hope than the limited cadres of professionals or the institution. It is neither necessary nor realistic to pass all the responsibility to a few.

SUICIDE PREVENTION

We have already touched on suicide prevention in several ways. Improving our ability to observe signs of possible heightened suicidal risk in children, youth, and adults is a useful first step. Recognizing that a number of common assumptions about suicide are not supported by fact is another useful step. Now we consider other contributions that we can make to suicide prevention as individuals and as a society.

Individual Guidelines to Suicide Prevention

Many suicides can be prevented. Perhaps you have already played a role in preventing suicide without realizing it. The companionship you offered a person during a crucial period or the confidence you displayed in a friend after he or she suffered a failure experience might have provided just enough support to dissolve a self-destructive pattern in the making. Whenever we bring sensitivity and a genuinely caring attitude to our relationships with other people, we may be decisively strengthening their life-affirming spirit.

How we should best proceed depends on who the suicidal person is, who we are, and what kind of relationship we have to go on together. A few general guidelines can be offered, however:

• *Take the suicidal concern seriously.* This does not mean panic or an exaggerated, unnatural response. It does mean time, attention, and active listening.

• *Do not issue a provocation to suicide.* Strange though it may seem, people sometimes react to the suicidal person in such a way as to provoke or intensify the attempt. Do not be one of those "friends" who dares this person to make good his or her threat or who intimates that he or she is too "chicken" to do so. Do not belittle or joke away the suicidal state of mind—this might intensify the need to do something desperate so that others will appreciate how bad he or she really feels.

• *Go easy on value judgments.* "You can't do that—it's wrong!" This is sometimes the exclamation that would come most readily to our lips, but it is seldom a useful one. It is not very helpful to inject value judgments when a troubled person is starting to confide self-destructive thoughts.

• *Do not get carried away by the "good reasons" a person has for suicide.* The interpersonal response to a suicidal individual sometimes involves much reading of our own thoughts and feelings into the other person's head. We may think, "If all of that were going wrong with my life, I'd want to kill myself too!" This conclusion might be attributed to the other person all too hastily. For every person who commits suicide when faced with realistically difficult problems, there are many others who find alternative solutions. It is possible to respect the reality factors in the suicidal individual's situation without lining up on the side of self-murder. This respectful, nonevaluative approach is taken by many of the people who pick up the phone when a crisis hot line call is put through.

• *Know what resources are available in the community.* Who else can help this person? What kind of help might this person find most acceptable? What services are available through local schools, religious groups, or mental health cen-

ters? Does your community have a crisis intervention service? How does it operate? Learn about and, if possible, participate in your community's efforts to help those who are in periods of special vulnerability.

• *Listen.* This is the advice you will hear repeatedly from people who have devoted themselves to suicide prevention. It is good advice. Listening is not the passive activity it might seem to be. It is an intent, self-giving action that shows the troubled person that you are there. Also, it is an opportunity for the person to discharge at least some of the tensions that have brought him or her to a certain point of self-destructive intent and to sort out other possibilities.

Systematic Approaches to Suicide Prevention

Many communities have crisis hot lines and other services that can be useful both to a suicidal person and to his or her worried family, friends, and colleagues. Large metropolitan areas also have centers specifically dedicated to suicide prevention. Mental health specialists in clinics or private practice are also available in many areas.

Suicide prevention centers usually offer 24-hour telephone counseling services. Some also provide walk-in clinics in which people may receive crisis counseling. Many of those who use these services are able to work through their crises without resorting to suicide. However, there are also many people with high suicidality who do not contact a center. Younger adults and women are more likely to seek help through a suicide prevention center than older adults and men. Suicide prevention centers often try various types of public information and outreach programs to encourage contacts from older adults and men. It is not easy to bring some of the people at greatest risk into the orbit of the suicide prevention center, so alternative ways of reducing suicide must also be pursued.

The community may decide to take other actions to reduce suicide risk. These programs range from making access to "jumping off places" more difficult to promoting both recreational and employment programs for youth.

Reducing access to guns could be a particularly effective component of a community's suicide prevention efforts for elders because they are less likely to shift to other modes of self-destruction.

One of the most promising systematic approaches to suicide prevention is through educational programs. School-based programs have been developed in the United States (Shaffer & Gould, 2000) and Europe (Mishara & Ystgaard, 2000). Educators and parents must first work through their own anxieties and become more familiar with the facts of suicide. Education directed at schoolchildren could be the most efficient way to increase the general public's ability to prevent suicide in the long-term. Gatekeeper training is another approach that shows promise. Clergy, teachers and staff members, police officers, bartenders, and physicians are among the people who often have contact with people who are in a suicidal crisis. Improving their ability to recognize and respond to the crisis can save many lives.

Please Note: Physician-assisted death, also known as physician-assisted suicide, is examined in Chapter 10.

SUMMARY

We have seen that suicide takes many forms, and that both thoughts and attempts are more common than we might have supposed. Suicide is the 11th most common cause of death in the general population of the United States, but it is even more common for adolescents and young adults. The United States, with its suicide rate of 10.7 per 100,000, is in the middle of those nations that report data to the World Health Organization. Male suicide rates are higher than female rates almost everywhere. The pattern is reversed in China, where many women, especially in rural areas, suffer from oppression and hopelessness and where female suicide is more in accord with cultural values than in most other nations. In the United States completed suicide tends to be regarded as "masculine" and nonfatal suicide attempts as "feminine." Special attention was given to youth suicide, particularly to males and college students who are at a

higher risk. Children can also be suicidal to the point of taking their lives if their concerns are ignored by adults. Suicide rates are highest among elderly people, especially white males. The risk factors were identified and discussed. Suicide rates are alarmingly high among young Native Americans and Alaskan Natives. Several situations were identified as holding increased risk of suicidality: having HIV/AIDS, gambling, victimization of bullies and other peers, and suicide by cop.

Several alternative meanings of suicide have been promulgated in society: suicide as sinful, as criminal, as weakness or madness, as The Great Death, and as a rational alternative. Sociobehavioral scientists and clinicians have offered their own explanations. Durkheim's pioneering sociological theory was reviewed, featuring his concepts of social integration, collective representations, and the altruistic, anomic, egoistic, and fatalistic types of suicide. Several individual meanings of suicide were then discussed: suicide as reunion, as rest and refuge, as revenge, as penalty for failure, and as mistake. Freud's first theory explained suicide as anger toward others that has been turned inward; his second theory proposed warring life *(Eros)* and death *(Thanatos)* instincts in which self-destructive tendencies may dominate because of problems experienced in early development.

Richard Heckler's description of the descent toward suicide added to our understanding of the sequence of problems, losses, and failed attempts at coping that can lead first to suicidal thoughts, and then to attempts and, finally, death.

We reviewed several popular myths about suicide (e.g., A person who talks about suicide will not actually take his or her own life) for the express purpose of noting that these statements are not supported by the facts. We concluded with a brief consideration of what we can do to prevent suicide as individuals and as citizens.

REFERENCES

Alvarez, A. (1970). *The savage god.* New York: Random House.

Beautrais, A. L. (2002). A case control study of suicide and attempted suicide in older adults. *Suicide and Life-Threatening Behavior, 32,* 1–9.

Beckerman, N. L. (1995). Suicide in relation to AIDS. *Death Studies, 19,* 223–234.

Blankenstein, A. (1998, August 24). Handling suspects who seek "suicide by cop." *Los Angeles Times,* p. A-1.

Brandt, R. B. (1990). The morality and rationality of suicide. In J. Donnelly (Ed.), *Suicide. Right or wrong?* (pp. 185–200) Buffalo, NY: Prometheus.

Breed, W. (1972). Five components of a basic suicide syndrome. *Life-Threatening Behavior, 3,* 3–18.

Brown, R. E. (1998). *The death of the messiah.* (2 vols). New York: Doubleday.

Canetto, S. S. (2002). Suicide influence and factors: Gender. In R. Kastenbaum (Ed.), *Macmillan encyclopedia of death and dying* (Vol 2, pp. 815–818). New York: Macmillan.

Chan, D. W. (1995). Reasons for living among Chinese adolescents in Hong Kong. *Suicide and Life-Threatening Behavior, 25,* 347–357.

Choron, J. (1972). *Suicide.* New York: Scribner.

Colt, G. H. (1991). *The enigma of suicide.* New York: Simon & Schuster.

Conwell, Y. (2001). Suicide in later life: A review and recommendation for prevention. *Suicide and Life-Threatening Behavior, 31* (Suppl.), 32–47.

Crosby, A. E., Cheltenham, M. P., & Sacks, J. J. (1999). Incidence of suicide ideation and behavior in the United States, 1994. *Suicide and Life-Threatening Behavior, 29,* 131–140.

Darwin, C. (1971). *Origin of the species.* Cambridge, MA: Harvard University Press. (Original work published 1859)

Dean, C. (1990). *Nam vet.* Portland, OR: Multnomah.

Donne, J. (1977). *Biathanatos.* New York: Arno. (Original work published 1646)

Durkheim, E. (1951). *Suicide* (J. A. Spaulding & G. Simpson, Trans.). New York: Free Press. (Original work published 1897)

Erasmus. *The praise of folly.* (Original work published 1509)

Freud, S. (1959). Mourning and melancholia. In *Collected papers* (Vol. 4, pp. 152–172). New York: Basic Books. (Original work published 1917)

Freud, S. (1961). *The ego and the id.* New York: Norton. (Original work published 1923)

Greyson, B. (1992–1993). Near-death experiences and antisuicidal attitudes. *Omega, Journal of Death and Dying, 26,* 81–90.

Heckler, R. A. (1994). *Waking up, alive.* New York: Ballantine.

Hendin, H. (1995). *Suicide in America* (Rev. ed.). New York: Norton.

Hunter, E., & Harvey, D. (2002). Suicide influences and practices: Indigenous populations. In R. Kastenbaum (Ed.), *Macmillan encyclopedia of death and dying* (Vol. 2, pp. 818–821). New York: Macmillan.

Jianlin, J. (2000). Suicide rates and mental health services in modern China. *Crisis, 21,* 118–121.

Jobes, D. A., & Mann, R. E. (1999). Reasons for living versus reasons for dying: Examining the internal debate of suicide. *Suicide & Life-Threatening Behavior, 29,* 97–104.

Kastenbaum, R. (1994). Alternatives to suicide. In L. Tallmer & D. Lester (Eds.), *Now I lay me down. Suicide in the elderly* (pp. 196–213). Philadelphia: Charles Press.

Kastenbaum, R. (1995). The impact of suicide on society. In B. L. Mishara (Ed.), *The impact of suicide,* (pp. 169–186). New York: Springer.

Kastenbaum, R. (2000). *The psychology of death* (3rd ed.). New York: Springer.

Kozak, D. L. (1991). Dying badly: Violent death and religious change among the Tohono O'Odham. *Omega, Journal of Death and Dying, 23,* 207-216.

Leenaars, A. A., & Wenckstern, S. (1991). *Suicide prevention in schools.* New York: Hemisphere.

Locke, J. (1971). Concerning the true original extent and end of civil government. In R. M. Hutchins (Ed.), *Great books of the Western world* (Vol. 35). Chicago: Encyclopedia Britannica. (Original work published 1690)

Mancinelli, I., Comparelli, A., Girardi, P., & Tatarelli, R. (2002). Mass suicide: Historical and psychodynamic considerations. *Suicide and Life-Threatening Behavior, 32,* 91–100.

May, P. A., Van Winkle, N. W., Williams, M. B., McFeeley, P. R., DeBruyn, L. M., & Serna, P. (2002). Alcohol and suicide death among American Indians of New Mexico: 1980–1998. *Suicide and Life-Threatening Behavior, 32:* 240–255.

McIntosh, J. L. (1992). Suicide: Native-American. In R. Kastenbaum & B. K. Kastenbaum (Eds.), *The encyclopedia of death* (pp. 238–239). Phoenix, AZ: Oryx Press.

Minino, A. M., Arias, E., Kochanek, K. D., Murphy, S. L., & Smith, B. L. (2000). Deaths: Final data for 2000. In *National vital statistics report,* Hyattsville, MD: National Center for Health Statistics.

Minois, G. (1999). *History of suicide. Voluntary death in Western culture.* Baltimore: Johns Hopkins University Press.

Mishara, B. L. (1999). Conceptions of death and suicide in children ages 6–12 and their implications for suicide prevention. *Suicide & Life-Threatening Behavior, 29,* 105–118.

Mishara, B. L. (2002). Suicide over the life span: Adolescents and youths. In R. Kastenbaum (Ed.), *Macmillan encyclopedia of death and dying* (Vol. 2, pp. 832–835) New York: Macmillan.

Mishara, B. L., & Ystgaard, M. (2000). Exploring the potential of primary prevention: Evaluation of the Befrienders International Reaching Young Europe Pilot Programme in Denmark. *Crisis, 21,* 4–7.

Murphy, G. E. (1995). 39 years of suicide research. *Suicide & Life-Threatening Behavior, 25,* 450–457.

Murray, A. (1998). *Suicide in the Middle Ages: Volume 1. The violent against themselves.* New York: Oxford University Press.

Murray, A. (2000). *Suicide in the Middle Ages: Volume 2. The curse on self-murder.* New York: Oxford University Press.

National Center for Health Statistics. (2002). *Suicide by state.* www.cdc.gov/nchs/faststats/suicide.htm.

National Household Survey on Drug Abuse. (2002). *Substance use and the risk of suicide among youths.* www.samhsa.gov/oas/2k2/suicide/suicide.htm.

Orbach, I. (1988). *Children who don't want to live.* San Francisco: Jossey-Bass.

Osgood, N. J. (1992). *Suicide in later life.* New York: Lexington.

Phillips, D. P., Welty, W. R., & Smith, M. M. (1997). Elevated suicide levels associated with legalized gambling. *Suicide & Life-Threatening Behavior, 27,* 373–378.

Phillips, M. R., Liu, H., & Zhang, Y. (1999). Suicide and social change in China. *Medicine and Psychiatry, 23,* 25–50.

Potter, L. B., Kesnow, M., Powell, K., Simon, T. R., Mercy, J. A., Lee, R. K., Frankowski, R. F., Swann, A. C., Bayer, T., & O'Carroll, P. W. (2001). The influence of geographic mobility on nearly lethal suicide attempts. *Suicide & Life-Threatening Behavior, 32* (Suppl.), 42–48.

Putnam, R. D. (2000). *Bowling alone.* New York: Simon & Schuster.

Rigby, K., & Slee, P. (1999). Suicidal ideation among adolescent school children, involvement in bully–victim problems, and perceived social support. *Suicide & Life-Threatening Behavior, 29,* 119–130.

St. Augustine. (1971). The city of God. In R. M. Hutchins (Ed.), *Great books of the Western world* (Vol. 18). Chicago: Encyclopedia Brittanica. (Original work published 426)

St. Thomas Aquinas. (1971). Summa theologica. In R. M. Hutchins (Ed.), *Great books of the Western world* (Vol. 19). Chicago: Encyclopedia Brittanica, Inc., (Original work published 1279).

Seiden, R. H. (1977). A tale of two bridges: Comparative suicide incidences on the Golden Gate and San Francisco–Oakland Bay bridges. *Crisis, 3,* 32–40.

Seiden, R. H. (1977). Suicide prevention: A public health/public policy approach. *Omega, Journal of Death and Dying, 8,* 267–276.

Shaffer, D., & Gould, M. (2000). Suicide prevention in schools. In K. Hawton & K. V. Heeringe (Eds.), *Suicide and attempted suicide* (pp. 76–91). New York: Wiley.

Smith, L. (1997). *Fools, martyrs, traitors: The story of martyrdom in the Western world.* New York: Knopf.

Stack, S. (2000a). Suicide: A 15-year review of the sociological literature: Part I. Cultural and economic factors. *Suicide & Life-Threatening Behavior, 30,* 145–162.

Stack, S. (2000b). Suicide: A 15-year review of the sociological literature: Part II. Modernization and social integration perspectives. *Suicide & Life-Threatening Behavior, 30,* 163–176.

Stillion, J. M., & McDowell, E. E. (2001–2002). The early demise of the "stronger" sex: Gender-related causes of sex differences in longevity. *Omega, Journal of Death and Dying, 44,* 301–318.

Werth, J. L., Jr., (1995). Rational suicide reconsidered: AIDS as an impetus for change. *Death Studies, 19,* 65–80.

Yang, B., & Clum, G. A. (2000). Childhood stress leads to suicidality via its effects on cognitive functioning. *Suicide & Life-Threatening Behavior, 30,* 183–198.

Yantis, J., & Burgard, M. (1999, June 26). Crash on 101 murder, suicide. *The Tribune* (Tempe, AZ).

GLOSSARY

Altruistic Suicide: Committed by people who have extremely high or excessive concern for society (Durkheim).

Anomic Suicide: Committed by people who fail to receive support and meaning from society (Durkheim).

Collective Representations: The symbols and themes that convey the spirit and mood of a culture.

Daishi: An ideal or "great death" in Buddhist tradition.

Egoistic Suicide: Committed by people who are not under sufficient control by societal norms and obligations (Durkheim).

Fatalistic Suicide: Committed by people who are stifled and oppressed by society (Durkheim).

Genocidal: A systematic plan and/or action that targets an entire population for death.

Intentionality: An action that places one's life at risk is classified as suicidal only when it has been established that the act was planned as self-destructive, as distinguished from accidental.

Parasuicide: Attempted suicide.

Samurai: Warrior who follows a strong code of honor (in Japanese tradition).

Seppuku: Suicide by ritualistic disembowelment (in Japanese tradition) Also known in the West as *hara-kiri.*

Social Integration Solidarity: The extent to which individuals are connected to a society that is more or less cohesive (Durkheim).

Stoicism: A philosophical tradition that emphasizes a rationality and the ability to withstand despair and emotional provocations and temptations.

Suicidal Trance: A state of mind in which a person sees death as the only way to relieve suffering and gives little attention to anything else.

Suicide: Self-murder.

Suicide Rate: A measure that is computed by multiplying the number of suicides by 100,000 and dividing by the population number. The suicide rate is not to be mistaken for a percentage.

A Cambodian man prays for Khmer Rouge victims in front of a map made from their skulls.

chapter 9

VIOLENT DEATH: MURDER, WAR, TERRORISM, DISASTER, AND ACCIDENT

For you Mr. Police. Call me God.... Your children are not safe at any time.
—John Allen Muhammad (as quoted in Smalley & Miller, 2002, p. A14)

My jobs from my agency have slowed down. I cannot make my rent this month. I am behind on my phone utilities, auto insurance, and child support. I don't drink, carouse, or have vacations. I have friends, but between work and school I never had time to socialize. I am tired, tired and weary.... I am going to end it now.
—Robert Stewart Flores Jr. (as quoted in the *Arizona Daily Star,* 2002, p. A1)

MOSCOW—The hostages had feared their lives would end in gunfire or the explosion of suicide bombs. Instead, Russian health officials acknowledged Sunday, 116 of the 118 captives who died after the theater was freed from Chechen rebel control were killed by a powerful gas that rescuers pumped into the auditorium through air ducts.
—John Daniszewski and David Holley (2002, p. A16)

Kendra Nowak, whose newborn baby was discovered in a garbage bag in her Michigan home, was a physically and emotionally abused teenager. She was 19 and single when she gave birth in the home she shared with her mother. No one had even known she was pregnant.... Authorities said the baby had lived for 2 days but had been dead for a week when it was found.
—Charles Patrick Ewing (1997, p. 85)

Anthony Robles, 3, wouldn't get dressed one morning, so his grandmother's boyfriend threw him down, slamming the toddler's head against a concrete

floor, police said. The boyfriend, 41, was baby-sitting the boy in the grandmother's Phoenix apartment, and the child's mother was in jail.
—Karina Bland (1996, p. A6)

KLM eight seven zero you are cleared to the Papa Beacon, climb to and maintain flight level nine zero, right turn after takeoff.
—Control tower to pilot (as quoted in Cushing, 1994, p. 19)

In this chapter, we consider deaths that stun and enrage, deaths that challenge our ability to comprehend the way that the world works and the way that our own minds work. We have already considered one difficult question: Why do people kill themselves? Now we must consider a larger spectrum of sudden and violent deaths. These deaths not only are experienced as painful losses by the survivors but also often lead to heightened fears and doubts: Fears that still other sudden and violent deaths might occur, and doubts that the world is as rational and safe a place as we would like to believe. Every society's death system is stressed by sudden and violent deaths. We have classified these events by the traditional categories of murder, suicide, accident, war, terrorism, and disaster. The distinctions are not always clear-cut, however, and the definitions may be subject to challenge. One person's "terrorism," for example, may be another person's legitimate "war." It is unpleasant to read or write about the human tragedies encompassed by this chapter, but to avoid doing so would be to avoid part of the reality of our relationship to death. Consider for a moment the events already noted—three of which occurred within the same month in 2002.

• Ten people were shot to death and three others wounded in the Washington, DC, area as they were going about their everyday affairs. The series of apparently random murders created an atmosphere of alarm and led to some school closings and other cautionary measures. Intensive police investigation and tips provided by the community led to the capture of John Allen Muhammad and 17-year-old John Lee Malvo. The arrests

put an end to the killings, but the lives of family and friends of the victims had been changed forever and the public's sense of security damaged. Meanwhile, law enforcement experts had a new development to reflect on: All previous serial murders had been committed by white men.
• A professor of nursing was working in her University of Arizona office when a student entered and shot her dead. Flores then walked into a classroom in which a test was in progress. He approached a professor who taught ethics and studied the relationship between health and spirituality in seriously ill patients. "I'm going to give you a lesson in spirituality," he said, and shot her in the chest. He shot her again in the chest and the head after she had fallen to the floor. Another professor had taken refuge behind a desk. Flores asked her if she was ready to meet her maker. She said "Yes," and he shot once and then twice more. Flores then killed himself. In his backpack were enough weapons and ammunition to have killed many more people. Depressed, flunking out of the nursing program, and having difficulties with every aspect of his life, Flores chose suicide—but not until he had murdered three faculty members who were admired by the students for their caring and helpful attitude. Why do some people decide that the only way to solve their problems is through both murder and suicide? What can be done to identify and prevent?
• Terrorism, seldom absent from human history, has become a worldwide threat. Unfortunately, counterterrorism can also claim casualties. People who were simply enjoying an evening in a theater became victims first of militants from the

People comfort each other outside the University of Arizona School of Nursing (Tucson), where a disturbed student had killed three faculty members.

ravaged republic of Chechnya and then from the rescue efforts of their own authorities. One of the more obvious lessons to be drawn from this and many other episodes is that terrorism, once in operation, cannot be restricted to any definitive boundaries or circumstances.

• The love of a mother for her baby is often intense and persevering even when the circumstances are difficult. How is it possible, then, for a woman to destroy her baby, and why does this kind of murder seem to be occurring more often today?

• One of the most unthinkable types of death has also been occurring with increasing frequency in American homes. Incidents of child abuse, including those with severe and lethal outcomes, have increased sharply in recent years.

What are we to make of the fact that adults are abusing, battering, and killing young children?

• Accidents are a different matter. By definition, accidents just happen. However, more often than might be supposed there is human error—especially lack of adequate foresight and communication—behind fatal accidents. The brief exchange between the control tower and a commercial jet pilot was followed a few seconds later by a catastrophe that resulted in the loss of 583 lives, the worst accident in aviation history. With better communication, these people would still be alive.

We now consider death by violence in a more systematic way, beginning with murder and continuing with war, terrorism, disaster, and accident. We will learn not only about violent death but also about some characteristics of the society in which we live.

MURDER

A person who takes the life of another has committed homicide. If a court rules that this killing was intentional and unlawful, then the act is judged to be murder. All murders are homicides; some homicides are murders. You may have committed "justifiable homicide" if you used lethal force to protect your own life, or you may be guilty of "negligent homicide" if your carelessness resulted in the death of another person. Distinctions of this kind can be very important in the judicial process. For the purposes of this chapter, however, we use the simplest and most direct word, murder.

The Statistical Picture

The United States has the highest murder rate (7.4 per 100,000) of all nations providing information to Interpol (Crissman & Parkin, 2002). It is difficult to escape the implication that there is something particularly "American" about this high rate. Neighboring Canada shares the North American continent and is comparable in many respects but has a murder rate (2.7) approximately two thirds lower. Western European nations, with whom we might also compare ourselves, generally have even lower murder rates than Canada. There is room for more than one explanation of the relatively high murder rate in the United States, but all theories must take into account the basic facts: *Who are the killers? Who are the victims? What are the trends?*

• Murder rates in the United States increased from a low of 4.0 in 1957 to a peak of 10.7 in 1980 and then gradually declined (Adler, Mueller, & Laufer, 2001). This decline has been variously attributed to a healthy economy, more efficient police work, and a slightly smaller percentage of young males in the population. The most recent FBI data, however, indicate that violent crime and other felonies increased in 2001. After a decade of steady decline, murder, armed robbery, rape, and burglary occurred more often. This increase in murder and other major crimes

might be related to the economic recession that led to unemployment and cutbacks in human services.

• The murderer is male in 8 of 10 cases. Approximately three of every four murder victims are male. The portrait of male as killer and male as victim has existed since reliable statistics have been compiled.

• A person in the United States is most at risk for becoming a homicide victim on the day he or she is born (Paulozzi & Sells, 2002). By far the greatest risk (95%) is for infants not born in a hospital. The risk starts to decrease significantly after the day of birth. Do statistics have something important to tell us? Paulozzi and Sells suggest that

> Preventing out-of-hospital births among high-risk women might help reduce the number of homicides on the day of birth. Home visitation and parenting programs, especially those that begin during infancy by focusing on the weeks of greatest risk early in infancy. (p. 2208)

• Other than the day of birth, youth (ages 15–24) are most at risk to become murder victims (rate, 12.5). The risk diminishes considerably but is still high (8.4) between ages 25 and 44. Murder is the second leading cause of all deaths for youth in the United States and is the sixth leading cause for 25- to 44-year-old adults. Adults from their mid-60s onward are not often victims of homicide, and their risk has continued to decline.

• Most murders (approximately 90%) are committed by killers who are of the same race as the victims. This fact is worth emphasizing because interracial murders often arouse more fear and anger. Newspapers and other media tend to give more attention to interracial murders and thereby "push the panic button" for many people.

• Murder rates are higher among African Americans, who are also more frequently the victims of murder. African Americans are six times more likely to become homicide victims and seven times more likely to commit homicide (Bureau of Justice Studies, 2002a). Arguments and illegal drug transactions are the situations that most often trigger homicide among African Americans. However, workplace and sex-related homicides are less common among African Americans.

• At least three of five murders are committed by people who are relatives, lovers, friends, neighbors, or colleagues of the victims. Again, the media tends to spotlight killings by strangers (e.g., in the course of a robbery or a freeway sniping). However, the fact remains that among both blacks and whites the killer and the victim usually are acquaintances if not relatives or intimate companions. Furthermore, family violence that results in serious injuries as well as death continues to be rampant. The most common type involves violence between spouses or ex-spouses. Women are at higher risk for murder by a killer who had an intimate or family relationship (Bureau of Justice Studies, 2002b).

• Murders are most common in large cities—approximately three times more frequent than the national average. Nevertheless, there has been a general decrease in homicide in large cities in recent years.

• Handguns are the most often used weapons of murder in the United States. Firearms in general are involved in approximately 7 of every 10 killings. Knives and other cutting or stabbing instruments are the next most common lethal weapons. Knives, however, are the weapons most frequently used in murders committed by those of Asian or Native American heritage. Gang-related murders are responsible for the largest number of gun-related killings (Bureau of Justice Studies, 2002c).

• Arguments are the most frequent provocations for murder, occurring approximately twice as often as in all other types of felonies combined. However, the provocations or reasons for murder remain unknown in many instances (Holmes & Holmes, 1994).

• Murder has become the leading cause of death for women in the workplace. Men are usually the killers. Some observers believe that male insecurity and rage may be intensified by increasing competition from women, especially during a time of high unemployment. Another possibility is that the workplace has become more dangerous for everybody because of the overall social climate of violence and ready access to firearms. Both men and women can become frustrated and angry in a variety of workplace situations, but men are more likely to respond with a lethal outburst.

• Both homicide rates and the use of guns in murder continue to be highest in the southern states, a long-established pattern. The lowest rates are found in the New England, mountain, and west north central regions (Bureau of Justice Studies, 2002d).

• Drug and alcohol use continue to have a strong association with murder. More than half of the state and federal prisoners serving time for murder were under the influence of drugs or alcohol when they took another person's life (Crissman & Parkin, 2002a).

Patterns of Murder in the United States

A man with a long criminal record ambushes and executes another criminal; this was his day's work. Another man nervously attempts his first hold up. Something goes wrong and he fires his gun at the clerk, then flees in panic. After a bout of drinking, a rejected lover breaks in on the woman, her children, and her new friend. Cursing them all, he sprays the room with bullets from a semiautomatic rifle. An emotionally fragile woman hears voices that tell her what to do in her predicament. Obeying the voices, she strangles her child and then attempts to take her own life. It is obvious that there cannot be any one, all-encompassing explanation for murder. It is important to examine some of the specific patterns that murder takes in the United States. We examine violence and abuse in the home, with spouse, children, or parents as victims; young men with guns, including school shootings; mass and serial killers; and political murders (assassination).

Domestic Violence

Law enforcement officers throughout the nation are well aware that they might encounter extreme violence when they respond to calls for a family situation. They are also aware that they could become homicide victims (though, fortunately, the number of law enforcement officers killed in the line of duty has declined since the early 1970s). As already noted, most killings involve people who knew each other, often in very close relationships. The killer is usually a man, whether the murder occurs from a domestic or criminal situation. Wives are the most common victims of intrafamilial killings, followed by husbands, sons, daughters, fathers, brothers, mothers, and sisters.

Men Who Kill Their Partners

Many women are subjected to repeated abuse and violence from their male partners. More than 1,000 a month are killed, even though they had previously sought help from the police or the courts. In four out of five spousal homicides, the police had been called to the home at least once. Ewing (1997) asks and answers the questions that come directly to mind: Why are so many battered women killed by their abusers, and why does the law fail to prevent these deaths?

> The overall likelihood that a battered woman will be killed by her batterer is directly proportional to the degree she resists being abused. Battered women who resist abuse or fight back are much more likely to be killed than battered women who suffer in silence. Battered women who leave or even try to leave their batterers are the most likely of all to be killed. (p. 22)

Many communities have responded to the desperate situation of battered women by providing shelters and counseling programs. This increase in community resources for battered women, however, has been accompanied by an increase in murders by their abusive partners. Ewing (1997) explains:

> Ironically, giving a battered woman a place to go makes it more likely that she will leave—or at least try to leave—her batterer, but that also increases the likelihood that she will be killed by him. The explanation lies in the dynamics of the battering relationship. Control is the ultimate issue in most of these relationships. Batterers have an obsessive if not a pathological need to control the lives of the women with whom they share intimate relationships. (p. 22)

Is it a mistake to offer haven and assistance to women who are trapped in an abusive and life-threatening relationship? Not really. Such assistance has helped some women to free themselves (and their children) from abusive relationships, literally saving their lives. It is probable, however, that the prevention of abuse and murder will re-

quire much more attention to the person who is committing these offenses, the male partner. Generally, these men have been victims of abuse in their youth. They treat women and children as personal possessions to compensate for their own low self-esteem. It is not unusual for the abusive male to feel he is being "the big man," who now has the dominant role that reverses the victim role he knew as a child.

Cultural tradition has given men enormous latitude for controlling the lives of their wives and children. Wife beating was seldom treated as a criminal offense in a society in which women were required to abide by their husband's decisions and denied the right to vote for more than a century. It was not long ago that an employed woman could not have a credit card unless it was registered in the name of her husband or father. The abusive and potentially murderous male partner is still supported to some extent by the unwritten law that women are here only to serve men. Programs that provide assistance to families threatened by a pattern of male abuse are part of the solution, but the men need to be fully involved in preventive programs—an approach that requires real commitment to the idea of equal rights and responsibilities.

Women Who Kill Their Partners

Women may also kill, especially when they have suffered humiliation, abuse, and injury at the hands of a man (Browne, 1987):

> "I'm going to kill you, you bitch. I'm going to kill you this night!" Bella ran from side to side in the room, but couldn't get to the door because Isaac had blocked it off. Isaac forced her into a corner, holding her up with a hand in her hair, and began hitting her repeatedly with his fist. Bella could hear the children screaming and kept crying to them to get help. She was sure Isaac would kill her if no one intervened. Then he began to bang her head against the wall. Bella was too dizzy to resist anymore, and just hung on. The attack ended a few minutes later when a relative stopped by and restrained him. (pp. 61–62)

This violent episode is typical of many others experienced by the battered women in Angela Browne's (1987) study. The rages were often sudden and unprovoked. The insults and accusations had little if any basis in anything the wife had done, and the attacks were savage. Many battered women described their husbands as having become entirely different people during the assaults: "He'd get a look in his eyes and start to breathe differently." "It was like dealing with a stranger." Repeatedly the victim of a man who might become crazed with fury at almost any time, these women lived in fear for themselves and their children. In Bella's case, she endured 20 years of severe abuse until one night Isaac went too far. He threatened to kill their oldest daughter when she came home. Isaac fell asleep first, however, and Bella and another daughter shot him and then set the house on fire. This removed one major threat from Bella's life but did not set her free. She was found guilty of murder in the first degree and sentenced to life imprisonment. Permanently disabled and in very poor health as a result of the repeated attacks from Isaac, she is considered to have a shortened life expectancy.

Each year there are approximately 1.5 million physical assaults on women by their male partners. Many of these men are in a drugged or intoxicated state at the time. It is the woman who usually suffers the injuries. Severely battered women, in contrast, seldom have behaved violently toward their mates, until a few such as Bella try to end their ordeals through murder. Most often, the battered women tried to placate their husbands and did what they could to avoid such episodes. Legal protection and social support for battered women are still quite inadequate in most places. This means that more women (and children) will continue to suffer, and more will be provoked to take extreme measures.

Unfortunately, "many states do not have self-defense laws, and in those states even the belief that one is in dire or fatal danger is not considered an adequate defense for the commission of homicide" (Holmes & Holmes, 1994, p. 33). Even where a self-defense provision exists, a woman may be found guilty of homicide if she is judged to have defended herself too effectively against partner assault.

It is ironic that the United States, with its commitment to preventing and treating life-threatening diseases and its support of hospice care, has been so slow to protect women from lethal attacks by their male partners. In a recent Arizona example, typical of many throughout the nation, a woman was repeatedly assaulted by her husband and the life of their infant daughter was placed in jeopardy. The health care system looked after her injuries, but the judicial system turned the husband loose after each incident, until he did kill her. What our society will do to save a life varies greatly depending on the person at risk, the situation, and the attitudinal context.

People Who Kill Children

Physicians, nurses, teachers, and other human service providers have something else to worry about these days. They see children who bear the physical and emotional marks of abuse. These injuries have been inflicted by their parents or by other adults in the home. A grade school teacher may have been speaking for many others when she told me,

> We don't want to notice. We don't want to suspect. We don't want to believe. But we have to notice, we have to suspect, and, more and more we have to believe…that this child is being very badly mistreated and is at risk for…everything. Including death. Including death.

It is no longer unusual to find police officers on the pediatric unit of a hospital. They have been called by a physician or nurse who recognizes a young child's injuries as being the result of abuse—beating, shaking, burning, throwing against a wall or down a flight of stairs, or neglect (starvation, dehydration, lack of physical care). A nurse on a unit devoted to the care of infants noted,

> The worst thing is that it happens at all. The next worst thing is that it is becoming almost routine. You see this incredibly beautiful baby. And you see what has happened to it. And you know that even though the baby makes it through this time, you know there very likely will be a next time. Some cases, as soon as we have our first look, we're on the phone to the police. Let me tell you, they hate it, too, maybe as much as we do.

In my home state of Arizona, Child Protective Services is overwhelmed by the magnitude of its responsibilities. The agency does not have the resources to respond promptly and adequately to all instances of child endangerment. Furthermore, the situations of many children at risk never reach the attention of this agency or any other until there has been serious injury or death. Similar problems are being experienced throughout much of the nation. The United States has the highest child murder rate of any industrialized nation in the world (Crissman & Beach, 2002). These deaths occur at the hands of parents, siblings, friends, acquaintances, and strangers. Abused children are at a greater risk to eventually become homicide victims, whether by direct violence or abandonment and neglect.

What is happening? Most observers attribute the increasing abuse and murder of children to dysfunctional families. The inability of families to care for their children is in turn attributed to such factors as unemployment, alcohol and drug use, and the abandonment of mothers and children by the father. There are at least three additional factors:

1. *Lack of parenting skills.* Many people who become threats to their own children have themselves had little opportunity to learn how to be caring and effective parents. Fortunately, these same people are often motivated to improve their parenting skills when given the opportunity through education and counseling.
2. *Mental disorder.* Postpartum psychosis is often involved in the murder of infants by their mothers. Anxiety and mood and impulse control disorders on the part of male as well as female adults are often involved in the deaths of children beyond infancy (Ewing, 1997).
3. *The replacement father syndrome.* This is my term for a situation that is responsible for many instances of severe and repeated child abuse, often with a fatal outcome. A woman is left to cope, along with one or more children. She takes a new lover. For this man, the children are just in the way—unwanted distractions and responsibilities. However, there is something else here as well: There is an impulse to destroy the children of the pre-

vious husband or lover. During an episode of stress or alcohol- or drug-clouded thinking, the new lover attacks the child. These attacks may also be premeditated and carried out in a deliberate way, sometimes with the passive acceptance or even the cooperation of the woman who does not want to lose her new man. When you come across reports of serious child abuse and murder, observe how often the perpetrator is the replacement father. Awareness of potential dangers to children in the replacement father situations might help to prevent such tragedies.

Neonaticide (the killing of a newborn baby) requires special attention. Most women who do so are young, white, unmarried, uneducated, and poor. They have very little social support and are suffering from depression and a sense of hopelessness. Sometimes they succeed in denying their pregnancy to themselves as well as concealing it from others until the last moment. Usually, they have made no plans for either the birth or the care of the child: They are simply overwhelmed and trying to make the problem go away. They are not likely to seek help because they do not expect anyone to help them. Abortion is not a strong option for a person who is denying and concealing pregnancy, and it becomes less of an option as time passes. Adoption is another possible option, but most of these young women do not feel sufficiently connected to and knowledgeable about society to explore this alternative (and, again, there is the denial/deception factor). How about leaving the baby someplace where there would be a good chance that it would be quickly discovered and cared for? Some young women in this predicament do leave the baby at a clinic or child care center. Nevertheless, many of these unwanted infants are placed in a plastic bag and tossed in a trash or garbage bin. Why? Because it is convenient, because it lessens the chance of a connection being made with the mother, and because the symbolism of trash and garbage resonates with the young woman's own feelings of worthlessness and horror. The mother is the person who would be held responsible for this death if the connection is ever discovered, but this killing must also be acknowledged as part of a larger

1. A pattern of family violence
2. Failed efforts by the adolescents to get help
3. Failed efforts by the adolescents to escape from the family situation
4. Isolation and few social outlets
5. A family situation that became increasingly intolerable
6. Increasing feelings of helplessness
7. Inability to cope with increasing stress, leading to a loss of self-control
8. Little or no previous involvement with the criminal justice system
9. Ready availability of a gun
10. Alcohol abuse and/or alcoholism in the home
11. Evidence that the adolescent may have been in a dissociative state at or near the time of the killing
12. Evidence that the adolescent offender and other family members felt relieved by the victim's death

Source: Heide (1992).

pattern of deprivation, abuse, and failure to develop positive bonds with the community.

Children Who Kill Parents

Each year, approximately 300 parents are killed by their children in the United States. Katherine Heide (1992) analyzed the pattern of parricide and found the following:

- Most of the murdered parents and stepparents are white and non-Hispanic.
- The victims are usually in their late 40s or 50s.
- Most of the killers are white, non-Hispanic males.
- A juvenile (younger than 18) is more likely to kill a parent than to kill anybody else.
- Most of the juveniles who kill their parents were victims of severe abuse by those parents.

Heide (1992) identifies 12 characteristics associated with adolescents who kill their parents (Box 9-1). These characteristics pretty much speak for themselves.

Young Men with Guns

The guns that kill are almost always in the hands of men, and most of the men are young.

Nine out of 10 law enforcement officers who are killed in the line of duty are victims of guns in the hands of young men. Many killings occur during drug-related transactions; others occur as part of gang rivalries. The general public tends to pay less attention to these deaths than to murders that seem to be casual, random, and unpredictable. The belief that such killings are becoming more common has led to the present state of anxiety in which schools, public offices, merchants, and private individuals feel the need for increased security—a need that has resulted in more purchases of guns for self-protection. Actually, the overall murder rate as well as rates of other violent crimes have decreased in the late 1990s and the early 21st century. It is difficult to feel reassured by recent statistics, though, when yellow police tape cordons off homes, shops, and streets where innocent people have been shot to death.

One of the most alarming developments is the apparent increase in drive-by shootings. We must use the term "apparent" increase because law enforcement agencies have not always tracked drive-by shootings as a special class of crime. Nevertheless, there are more reports than ever of gunfire from passing cars, sometimes resulting in death, and always resulting in fear and anger. Here is an excerpt from an incident reported by a local newspaper (DeBruin, 1994):

> Two teens charged with shooting bicyclists…last month exchanged high-fives after one shooting and joked about getting "20 points" for another, according to police reports. Michael James Sheehan and Damon Eli Richardson, both 18, were indicted Thursday on two counts each of aggravated assault and eight counts of endangerment.... Greg Whipperman, 35, and Robert Valdez, 33, were shot in the back while riding their bicycles in the early morning hours…Sheehan and Richardson also are accused of participating in eight drive-by shootings earlier that morning as part of a drunken spree.... "I just looked at him in my mirror and saw him fall. And I was like, "Yeah, you hit him. Good shot!" (pp. A1, A4)

In this incident and many others, the assailants had been using alcohol or drugs. Substance-impaired judgment, however, is not enough to account for such potentially lethal attacks on people unknown to them. How can we understand these incidents?

The approach I consider most useful investigates the following hypotheses:

1. The young males who engage in drive-by and other forms of gun violence have not developed a sense of identification with the human race at large. There is little awareness of how others think and feel, little empathy. Other people are objects. This arrested development of feelings for humanity is in all probability the outcome of earlier failures in socialization: They themselves were probably treated without understanding and compassion.

2. Peer acceptance, important for most young adults, is a dominating motivation for these men, who envision no other reward structure in their future.

3. Guns—and automobiles—provide remote devices for dealing death. One does not have to confront another human being, a confrontation in which mental and physical skills could determine the outcome. One can be a "man" by killing another human being as easily as one operates a remote control for the television set.

Every generation known to history has faced the challenge of socializing its young males and directing their spirit and energies into constructive uses. Our generation certainly has its work cut out for it.

School Shootings

Pranks and acts of vandalism have occurred in high schools for as long as anybody remembers. A successful businessman confessed to me that when he was in school, he and several other students had placed "For sale" signs on the high school and then gone to the trouble of filling the swimming pool with jello (orange flavor, mostly). Students with deeper grievances simply skipped or withdrew from school. Personal animosities were settled—or at least expressed—through a scuffle after school. Nobody would be seriously hurt, and the antagonists might even become friends afterward, as I discovered a time or two.

The ready availability of guns and recipes for bomb making have provided a much more dangerous avenue of expression for youth grievances. Furthermore, the victims are no longer limited to a particular person who is perceived as having rejected or harmed the killers. A pair of angry adolescents might choose an entire set of fellow students (e.g., athletes and people of a different race) or just let loose on anybody unfortunate enough to be on the scene. One "quiet kid, pretty much like the others" might bring a rifle and a backup pistol to school one day and fire at his classmates. Why?

- *Killing has gained more acceptance as a way of solving problems.* A nasty relationship can be ended this way, so can an unsatisfactory drug transaction. Suicide is another way in which problems can be made to go away (although not for the survivors). The higher rate of male suicide is related to the most frequently chosen method, guns, as a "manly" response to stress. The 14-year-olds who were charged with plotting to massacre students and teachers also planned to commit suicide afterward: This seems to be a common theme in school shootings. The 15-year-old shooter at Heritage High School (Conyers, Georgia) had already stuck a revolver in his mouth before the principal arrived in time to talk him out of killing himself. Guns have become readily available, making it easier to kill on impulse.
- *There is no other way to deal with rejection, frustration, and loss.* This belief is mistaken. Nevertheless, some teenagers become killers because they cannot think of any other way to deal with a threat to their relationships with their girlfriends. Young people usually have not had much experience in coping with disappointment and frustration. The thought process is therefore likely to be truncated, even reduced to the fatal "either/or": "Either she comes back to me or I have to kill—somebody, maybe everybody." A 15-year-old arrested for killing his parents and two classmates and wounding 20 others explained, "I had no other choice." Take frustration, inexperience, and oversimplified thought processes and add the availability of weapons and the potential for a lethal outcome is there.
- *The world is divided between Us and Them (or just Me and All of You).* Anybody who has survived

adolescence is likely to remember the "in groups," the students who seemed to get all the attention and all the breaks. Even people who were among the most popular students later report that they often suffered from feelings of uncertainty, anxiety, and being left out. Furthermore, all the prejudices that have been nurtured in society have the opportunity to play themselves out in the high school years. Many adolescents take advantage of this opportunity to become friends with people who differ in racial, religious, or ethnic background. Others, however, bring deeply ingrained prejudices with them that can easily be triggered. The Columbine High School shootings, for example, had a racist component that has been associated with the influence of skinhead organizations. There are always others to blame and attack when things go wrong in one's own life.

There are frequent calls for greater understanding between people of different races and backgrounds, more effective adult guidance, and decreased access to firearms. We should be listening, shouldn't we?

Mass and Serial Killers: Who Are They and Why Do They Do It?

Many killings appear to be understandable. A burglar picks the wrong home to burglarize and is shot dead. One drug dealer is ambushed by another in a turf dispute. A drunken brawl ends in death when one combatant goes for a knife. These killings disturb but do not puzzle us. Mass and serial killing, however, seem more remote from ordinary human experience. Who are these people and why do they kill so many? The mass killer is alarming to society both because of the many lives he destroys in one time and place and because his very existence appears to contradict our expectations of human feeling and conduct. There are similarities and differences between mass and serial killers, and both types of murder are indeed quite out of the ordinary.

A mass killing is one in which several people die in a single episode. The following are examples of mass killing in recent years:

- Twenty-one shot to death at a McDonald's restaurant in California (1984)

- Sixteen family members shot to death in Arkansas (1986)
- Eighty-seven die of smoke inhalation and burns in a deliberately set night club fire in New York City (1990)
- Twenty-two shot to death in a restaurant in Texas (1991)
- Three family members killed at home and nine shot to death in Atlanta brokerage offices (1999)
- Three professors of nursing shot to death at the University of Arizona (2002)

These examples of mass murder in the United States are typical in that all were the work of a lone killer (a male) and most involved firearms. Furthermore, in most of these instances the killer knew few if any of his victims. He may have wanted to get back at a particular person he thought had treated him badly (as in the night club arson) but had no compunction about slaying many others as well. The Atlanta killings had a disturbing new element that is discussed later. We also revisit the sniper killings in Virginia, Maryland, and Washington, DC, that broke from the typical multiple-murder pattern.

The public perception of the mass murderer has proven to be accurate—a person who feels rejected by society, angry at real or imagined mistreatment, and motivated to "get back" at all that has oppressed him, even though he has suffered no harm from the particular individuals he has killed. James Oliver Huberty personifies this description. He had lost his long-time job as a skilled worker when the plant had to downsize because of economic conditions. He moved to another state, found another job, but lost it. Over the years, he had often practiced shooting his rifles into the basement wall and occasionally frightening his neighbors by brandishing a weapon. One afternoon, he told his wife he was going to "hunt humans." She assumed that James was just trying to get her upset again. He kissed her good-bye and walked back to the McDonald's where he and his family had lunched a few hours earlier. He opened fire, killing 21 and wounding 19 before being felled by a police sharpshooter.

The available explanations remain inadequate, however, because many people have come from dysfunctional families and have later experienced rejection and hard times, but only a few become mass murderers. Holmes and Holmes (1994) find that mass murderers also have a strong suicidal streak: They are willing or even motivated to die at the scene of their crimes. This is in contrast to most serial killers, who intend to keep on killing as long as they can.

Some mass murderers are psychotic, but again, not all psychotic people become mass murderers. In general, mass murderers (and serial killers) do not attract much attention until they are apprehended or shot. Others have little sense of their own identity and are willing to become disciples of a charismatic person. Such was the situation with Charles Manson and several of his followers. Their mass killing episodes may also be compared with the hate group dynamics expressed by Nazis and emulated by skinheads. There have been many violent confrontations by skinheads toward people they have targeted as objects of their hatred both in the United States and in Germany, although not all these have resulted in fatalities.

The mass murderer is typically a white male in his late 20s or 30s (Lane, 1997). Rarely is the mass murderer a hardened criminal, although a spotty history of property crime is common (Fox & Levin, 2001). The killings sometime follow a spell of frustration when a particular event triggers sudden rage; however, in other cases, the killer is coolly pursuing some goal he cannot otherwise attain.

A few special aspects about mass killers are worth keeping in mind:

1. Mass killers do not draw their violence from the Southern tradition of homicide. Although murder is most common in the South—and often appears to be a lethal response to a challenge—relatively few mass murders occur in the South, nor do they take the form of a direct confrontation. There is reason to believe that Southerners have continued to provide more support for each other through neighborhoods, churches, and other community organizations, thereby reducing the sense of alienation that can lead to violence against others. "Even an unemployed or divorced man in the rural South was far less likely to be alone. His kin, congregation, or lodge were there to help" (Humphrey & Palmer, 1986/1987).

2. Boom cities attract many people whose high hopes fail to be fulfilled. They become bitter, disillusioned, and ready to try something different to get rid of their frustrations and anger (as was the case with Huberty).

3. The age and race correlates of murder in general do not apply to the mass or serial killer. Most murders are committed by young adults, with a higher rate among blacks. In contrast, most mass killers are white and in their 30s or 40s.

4. Most mass murders are not psychotic but have an antisocial personality (also known as "sociopath" or "psychopath"). This type of killer is not out of touch with reality and does not hear voices that order him to kill. Basically, the antisocial personality does not feel affection, empathy, or concern for other people. This is the person who uses other people without remorse. The antisocial personality is likely to have a low tolerance for frustration and to explode in rage when things go wrong.

Mark Barton, the Atlanta mass murderer, had some of the typical characteristics of the mass murderer, notably low tolerance for frustration and explosive rage when things go wrong. His interpersonal relationships were also deeply flawed. He was a father who neglected his children, kept to himself, and made few if any friends. He had little affection or empathy for others. However, Barton had worked as a chemist, had a middle-class lifestyle, and was not conspicuously on the outs with society. In fact, neighbors described him as a quiet, churchgoing man who worked all day on his computer.

There are two ominous characteristics of Barton and his rampage that could cause concern that more such mass killings will occur in the future. First, is it possible that people with limited social skills or empathy will further distance themselves from others by the availability of an all-consuming computer connection to the world—a virtual rather than an actual life? This computer-mediated lifestyle might have just enough of a further deadening effect on the user's sense of human bonds that it becomes as easy to squeeze a trigger as to click on an icon.

Second, day-trading is already becoming an addictive form of gambling, but one in which the stakes can get completely out of control. The high of making a "quick killing" on the stock market can be followed by loss of all one's savings and assets. Desperation becomes rage, and rage becomes murder. There is much more to Barton's story: He not only sprayed two brokerage offices with bullets but also had murdered his own family with a blunt instrument 1 or 2 days previously. Furthermore, he was the main suspect in the deaths of his first wife and her mother, soon after taking out a large insurance policy on her. Barton was not simply a man who became unhinged by losses in the stock market; he was already a manipulative and self-centered person with the habit of using and discarding other people for his own aims. This should come as something of a relief: Most day-traders will not become killers after a bad spell on the computer, but we also may not have seen the last of this kind of tragedy.

Serial killing occurs in other nations as well. Nineteenth-century London's "Jack the Ripper" is the prototypical serial killer. Like many other serial killers, "Jack" was a male who chose women for his victims. Prostitutes have long been at increased risk for serial killing. Some serial killers, however, have attacked children or hospital patients, and others have selected almost any available target.

David Lester (1995) notes,

> The motives of serial killers seem to have changed over the years. In preindustrial times, serial murderers tended to be depraved aristocrats preying on peasants; in the industrial era, seemingly respectable middle-class men killed prostitutes, homeless boys, and housemaids. Today serial murderers are often people who exist on the margins of society, those who have failed to achieve their personal expectations, who are mainly of working- and lower-middle-class origins, and who attack middle-class victims such as college students. (p. 187)

Holmes and Holmes (1994, p. 103) offer the chilling estimate that "from our contacts with law enforcement officials all over the United States, we believe that a more accurate estimate may be as high as 200." It is thought that many serial killers "limit" themselves to two or three murders a year and therefore draw less attention to themselves and are able to continue.

The sniper killings of 2002 did not follow the established pattern in that there were two gunmen working together and both were African American (John Allen Muhammad, 41, and John Lee Malvo, 17). There was nothing conspicuously racist or political about their violent actions. They gunned down blacks as well as whites and targeted men, women, and children who were not celebrities or power figures—just everyday people going about their lives. The victims did not know their killers and had done no harm to them. The motivation remains unclear, other than the attempt to extort money to stop the killings.

Serial killers draw a great deal of attention from the media. Sniper Muhammad, for example, left the Tarot card of death near the scene of one of the killings with his cryptic message, "For You, Mr. Police. Call me God." Other mass and serial killers have often acted in such a way as to attract widespread attention. Robert Stewart Flores Jr., who took his own life after shooting three professors of nursing, left much more than a suicide note (Tobin, 2002). In a 22-page letter, he disclosed his sense that everything in his life was falling apart. He accused his teachers of not respecting him because he was a male in a primarily female professional school. In fact, the teachers had extended themselves to help him make it through the program. Flores, like other multiple killers, used his violent actions as a way of calling attention to his grievances. In this, he was successful. A series of bloody murders becomes a Monday night movie. Some killers report that they wanted to be famous, just like the people they have seen on television. Protests and criticisms have been voiced repeatedly about the tendency of the media to capitalize on serial killing and other forms of violent death. The media's usual response is to note that the public has a right to be informed and also, incidentally, that it sells newspapers and raises the viewership ratings. So the death system keeps right on being the death system: The mass or serial killer becomes a commodity, and perhaps an inspiration to other potential killers.

A mother comforts her daughter after one of the D.C.-area sniper killings that seemed to target innocent people at random.

It would be a mistake to assume that mass murder in the United States is only a recent phenomenon. There have been such episodes since at least the middle of the 19th century, when a worker in Philadelphia hammered seven members of his employer's family to death. At least 49 members of black families were murdered by an unknown home invader in Texas and Louisiana in 1911 and 1912. In 1927, a Michigan farmer, enraged by a hike in his property tax, bombed a local school, killing himself and 39 others. Michael Newton (1999) provides a grim profile of the mass killer, one that fits most, if not all, the examples we have mentioned here:

He is depressed or moody, prone to blaming scapegoats for his private failures, cultivating fantasies of retribution and revenge. Unfortunately, in the high-stress modern world, such individuals are not rare. Most simmer quietly throughout their lives; a few explode. (p. 334)

Political Murder: Assassination in the United States

Abraham Lincoln, John F. Kennedy, Robert F. Kennedy, and Martin Luther King Jr.: The assassination of these four leaders has become a disturbing part of American history. The murder of a political leader has both its private and its public side. A child loses a father, a wife loses her husband. Some of the most prominent political assassinations in the United States are listed in Table 9-1.

TABLE 9-1

Political Assassination Attempts, United States

Year	Intended Victim	Assassin	Outcome
1835	Andrew Jackson	Richard Lawrence	Unharmed
1865	Abraham Lincoln	John Wilkes Booth	Killed
1881	James Garfield	Charles Guiteau	Killed
1901	William McKinley	Leon Czolgosz	Killed
1912	Theodore Roosevelt	John Schrank	Unharmed
1933	Franklin Roosevelt	Giuseppe Zangara	Unharmed[a]
1935	Huey Long	Carl Weiss	Killed
1950	Harry S. Truman	Oscar Collazo and Griselio Torresola	Unharmed[b]
1963	John F. Kennedy	Lee Harvey Oswald	Killed
1968	Martin Luther King Jr.	James Earl Ray	Killed
1968	Robert Kennedy	Sirhan Sirhan	Killed
1972	George Wallace	Arthur Bremer	Wounded
1974	Richard Nixon	Samuel Byck	Unharmed[c]
1975	Gerald Ford	Lynette Fromm	Unharmed
1975	Gerald Ford	Sara Moore	Unharmed
1981	Ronald Reagan	John W. Hinckley Jr.	Wounded

Sources: Clarke (1982) and Crissman and Beach (2002).

[a]Chicago Mayor Anton Cermak was killed and four others were wounded in the volley of shots fired at President Roosevelt.

[b]Security guards Leslie Coffelt and Joesph Downs were wounded; Coffelt died as he returned fire and killed Torresola.

[c]Byck killed two Delta pilots and wounded a cabin attendant in an aborted attempt to force the plane to crash into the White House.

Clarke (1982) found four types of assassins: Type I, political extremists; Type II, rejected and misguided people; Type III, antisocial personalities; and Type IV, psychotics. Three of these types were clearly in contact with reality and did not suffer from delusions, hallucinations, or other cognitive distortions. This is not to say that the assassins were without personal problems. Social isolation or disturbances of interpersonal relationships were characteristic of several types. They differed markedly in the primary motive for the assassination attempt. This can be most clearly seen when comparing the Type I and the Type IV assassin.

The public stereotype of the crazed assassin is represented by the men who threatened the lives of Andrew Jackson, James Garfield, and Theodore Roosevelt. These people were delusional and, at times, incoherent. Almost anybody would have easily recognized their distortions of reality and need for treatment. In keeping with their de-

fects in reality test testing, Lawrence, Guiteau, and Schrank were confused and idiosyncratic in their motivation. Guiteau, for example, had a friendly attitude toward Garfield but convinced himself that the president must be killed to "save the Republic." He would later say that God had made him do it. It was clear that in this and in most other matters Guiteau had a grossly distorted view of himself and the world.

In contrast, the Type I assassins were motivated by political objectives: as Clarke (1982) called them "rational extremists" (p. 262). Booth, Collazo, Torresola, and Sirhan were motivated by their identification with nationalistic aims. Czolgosz thought that by killing McKinley he would be striking a blow for "the good working people," a class-oriented political motivation. None of these men were insane (legal framework) or psychotic (psychiatric).

The people Clarke (1982) classifies as Type III assassins remind us of the antisocial personalities who committed mass murders. These men, such as Bremer, Byck, and Zangara, hated the society they believed had rejected and frustrated them. Unable to express feelings other than helplessness or rage, they cast about for a target that would symbolically represent those aspects of society they most disliked. They did not have personal animosity toward the leaders they attacked. Like the mass murderers, the Type III assassins showed no remorse. Although neither the typical mass murderer nor the Type III assassin is "crazy," each has a fundamental character flaw in the ability to feel and express ordinary human feeling.

This leaves still another kind of assassin. Oswald, Byck, Fromm, and Moore were very anxious people who felt rejected and unable to cope with the demands of life. They wanted to be taken seriously by somebody and to prove themselves in some way. Although a Type II assassin might attach himself or herself to a political cause, the basic objective is personal: to redeem one's own miserable life by a bold deed. As Clarke (1982) observes, the Type II assassins were misguided people but not insane.

This attention to the makeup of the individual assassin should not distract us from more systematic factors. For example, the emergence of television has generated an unprecedented type and degree of coverage for spectacular events. How often do we want to see the stricken man crumple from the bullet? Would we prefer to see it in slow-motion? Split-screen? Reverse angle? Whether the potential assassin's motivation is primarily political or personal, during the past several decades there has been an added incentive of flashing this event before the eyes of many millions of people. Another point to consider is that some potential assassins have political grievances that are not in themselves irrational. We will encounter this problem again when we examine terrorism. To recognize that reality-based political grievances can stimulate assassination attempts is not to condone such acts of violence. Instead, we may be better prepared as a society to prevent or respond to assassination attempts if we do not insist on believing that they are all the work of people who are mentally ill. A more general issue recurs here as it did when we considered mass murderers: Can we continue to be an open and trusting society and still improve our ability to protect ourselves, our children, and our leaders from the killers? The creation of a Homeland Security Department is responsive to growing fears of assassination and terrorism; how much intensified security measures will restrict individual exercise of freedom is almost certain to be a continuing issue.

TERRORISM

The September 11, 2001 terrorist attack on America has had a profound effect on the nation's sense of security. The world at large has seemed less secure as terrorist threats and actions continue to occur in many places. Actions in other parts of the world have also seemed to hit closer to home. Previously, the public had been grieved and shaken by the bomb that killed 168 people and demolished the Alfred P. Murrah Federal Building in Oklahoma City on April 19, 1995. Here, we will size up terrorism at large and then discuss events and concerns in the United States.

Who Is the Terrorist?

Terrorism is "violence or threat of violence, in which civilians or locations habituated by civilians are targets or are frequently involved in the conflict" (Picard, 1993, p. 11). This is a useful working definition of terrorism. It makes clear the facts that (a) terrorism operates as a threat as well as an actuality and (b) it usually claims civilians as victims. But who is the terrorist?

Is the terrorist a believer in a fundamentalist form of Islam who is prepared for his own death as he plans the massacre of others? Yes, sometimes. This was true on September 11, 2001, but also in previous suicidal attacks, such as on April 18, 1983, when a truck loaded with explosives killed 63 people in Beirut. What was new about these attacks was the willingness of the terrorist to ensure the success of the mission by sacrificing his own life. In such instances, terrorism combines murder with suicide and also resembles assassination since it is motivated by a political or religious cause.

Terrorism is by no means either a recent development or a tactic used only by some Shi'ite

Terrorism has taken lives and created tensions throughout much of the world.

extremists. Terrorism has had a long and diverse history. Some examples are listed in Table 9-2. Terrorism was a force as early as the 11th century. The killers whose name is still invoked today—the Assassins—were members of a small but highly disciplined Middle Eastern religious sect that believed in the imminent beginning of a new millennium. Mistreated by those in control at the time (the Seljuks), the Assassins carried out lethal terrorist operations for approximately 200 years. Disguising themselves in various ways and choosing the dagger as their weapon, the Assassins killed a number of powerful leaders and succeeded in creating a climate of terror. The Assassins expected to die as they completed their missions.

During this same period, Christian Crusaders fought for possession of the Holy Sepulchre (which actually no longer existed). The Crusaders were not a terrorist organization, but they did abandon themselves to episodes of massacre and atrocity. The major example occurred when they broke through the defenses in Jerusalem and slaughtered many of the inhabitants, including women and children. The Jews of this city, who had played no particular role in the hostilities, were herded into a mosque and burned alive. Institutionalized terroristic killing as part of the Christian establishment awaited the formation of the Inquisition in 1231. The persecu-

tion of suspected heretics and dissidents spread through much of Western Europe. Thousands were burned alive, and many others died while being questioned and tortured. The later Protestant version of religious persecution was no less cruel and deadly. Many conquerors have utilized terror tactics not only to destroy enemies but also to undermine the will to resist. Tamerlane, for example, buried thousands of his victims alive. Terrorism has accompanied many other military campaigns throughout history.

For the word *terrorism* itself, we must turn to the French Revolution. The new government rounded up suspected "enemies of the people" and sent approximately 30,000 to the newly invented guillotine. Robespierre seemed to believe that by making so many public examples of people guilty of unacceptable thoughts or conduct, he would create a new type of society in which everybody lived in love and harmony. Like most other terrorist actions, the "reign of terror" failed to achieve its objectives, and Robespierre himself went to the guillotine.

Terrorism occurred in many places and circumstances throughout the 19th century. The Thugs (or Thuggees) of India robbed travelers and strangled them with silk ties. The Thugs regarded the killing as an honorable and sacred act of religious devotion. Like many other murdering terrorists, Thugs professed to hold death in

TABLE 9-2

Some Terrorist Killers before the 20th Century

Terrorist Organization	Time	Place	Usual Methods
The Assassins	11th–13th centuries	Persia, Syria	Dagger
The Crusaders	11th century	Jerusalem	Burning alive
The Inquisition	13th–17th centuries	Europe	Burning alive
Tamerlane	14th century	Middle East	Burial alive
French Republic	1790s	Paris	Guillotine
The Thugs	19th century	India	Strangulation
Ku Klux Klan	1867–	United States	Lynching, guns, fire
Molly Maguires	1870s	United States	Explosives, guns
Narodnaya Volya	1869–1885	Russia	Guns, explosives, bomb-throwing
Anarchists (individuals)	1890s	Europe	Bomb-throwing

Sources: Dobson and Payne (1987), Hofstadter and Wallace (1971), Lacqueur (1987), Lea (1906/1907), O'Brien (1973), Raynor (1987), Wakin (1984).

contempt. The terrorist tradition includes a pattern of belief and behavior in which there is no compunction about killing others or about meeting one's own death through violence.

The Ku Klux Klan (KKK) and the Molly Maguires exemplify terrorist groups that formed in the United States shortly before and after the Civil War. Started in 1867, at first the KKK attempted to protect Southern whites from some of the threats and abuses that followed their defeat. Before long, however, the KKK had become a terrorist organization intended to keep the freed African Americans "in their place." The KKK did not specialize in mass killing; instead, threats, beatings, and property destruction were augmented by the occasional lynching. Perhaps the fact that the KKK often had the support of the local establishment (or actually was the local establishment under its robes) meant that the executions did not have to be numerous but simply had to remind potential victims that "uppityness" would not be tolerated. Historians of violence in the United States believe that much of this tradition was generated by the KKK and similar organizations after the Civil War to keep African Americans in a powerless position. We may also think here of the long-standing excess of murder in the southern region of the United States that continues to this day.

The Molly Maguires first made themselves known in the 1860s as some Irish Americans reacted to oppressive and dangerous circumstances. As one historian (Wakin, 1984) tells it,

> In Pennsylvania, the oppressors were mine owners who brutalized the miners and their families. The miners went down into the dangerous hell of the mines, often with their children along, digging up wealth for the owners and a marginal living for themselves. New waves of immigrants enabled the owners to keep wages low; workers were forced to live in company houses and buy at company stores in between periods of idleness when they earned nothing. Even while working, many a miner received, instead of his monthly pay, a "bobtail check" showing that he owed the company money. When workers tried to organize, the owners intimidated them, and when fledgling labor organizations protested or struck, they were crushed. (p. 147)

The Molly Maguires threatened and beat mine owners, then used bombs to create an atmosphere of terror, killing several people they considered to be oppressors. This underground movement did arouse fear and direct attention to the miners' predicaments; however, like so many other organizations that resorted to terror, it failed to achieve its basic objectives. Improved conditions for miners would still be a long time in coming, and clever detective work resulted in the conviction and hanging of 19 Molly Maguires—probably more men than the group killed during its decade or so of activity.

Terrorism can also be instructive: Did the Molly Maguires perhaps learn something from the ruthless methods of their bosses, and did both management and labor in the forthcoming years teach each other new lessons in brutal force? Did the prolonged exposure to threat and violence suggest something to the 19th century African American that is expressed in contemporary murder rates?

Twentieth-Century Terrorism

What will historians say about the recently elapsed 20th century? One fact will be impossible to overlook: the infliction of deprivation, cruelty, and death on millions of people. Throughout all of human history, there have never been so many casualties of man-made violence.

Numbers can be numbing. We can grasp and respond to the death of one person, to the death of a family, and perhaps to the death of all occupants of a jetliner. It is much more difficult to grasp both the individual and the mass tragedy when the victims are numbered in thousands or in millions. Table 9-3 looks much like any other table: some identifying information and a lot of numbers. However, for any thinking, feeling human being, there can be nothing "so what" about the horrors represented here.

There are survivors of all these campaigns of terror still among us who can recall their experiences with vivid immediacy. For example, there is an aged woman in Arizona who will never

TABLE 9-3

Examples of Large-Scale Terrorism in the 20th Century

Killers	Victims	Date	No. of Deaths
Turks	Armenians	1915	800,000
Soviet Communist Party	Russian peasants	1929–1932	11,000,000
Soviet Communist Party	Russian "dissidents"	1937–1938	500,000
Nazis	Jews	1933–1945	6,000,000
Japanese[a]	Chinese, Nanjing	Dec. 1937–Jan. 1938	360,000
Muslims[b]	Hindus, Sikhs	1946	1,000,000
Hindus, Sikhs[b]	Muslims	1946	
Sudanese Muslims	Sudanese, Africans	1955–1972	1,000,000
Indonesians	Communists	1965	600,000
Nigerians	Ibo	1966–1967	800,000
Khmer Rouge	Cambodians	1975–1977	2,000,000
Tutsi/Hutu[c]	Hutu/Tutsi	1972–1975	100,000
Hutu/Tutsi	Hutu/Tutsi	1994	500,000
Hutu/Tutsi (Burundi)	Tutsi/Hutu	1996	50,000+
Serbs	Ethnic Albanians	1999	10,000

Sources: Amnesty International (1984), Associated Press (1994), Becker (1986), Brook (2000), Chang (1998), Conquest (1986), "Descent into Mayhem" (1994), Grosscup (1987), Gutteridge (1986), Kuper (1981), Laqueur (1987), Morgan (1989), Payne (1973), and Sterling (1981). www.cnd.org/njmassacre. All data are best available estimates.

[a]Japanese soldiers burned, buried alive, bayoneted, and tortured at least this number of Chinese civilians in Nanjing during a six-week period. It has been estimated that more than 200,000 Chinese were killed by Japanese biological warfare experiments and that at least 30 million other Chinese died as a result of the Japanese invasion and occupation between 1931 and 1945. It is not clear how many of these deaths should be considered genocide and how many were the indirect result of oppression and crop failure due to the chaos of war.

[b]During the partition of India following World War II, Hindus and Sikhs moving east were slaughtered by Muslims, and Muslims moving west were slaughtered by Hindus and Sikhs.

[c]Terrorism, including massacre, was carried out by both the minority Tutsi and the majority Hutu peoples of Rwanda and Burundi. A new wave of ethnic/political violence erupted in April 1994, with reports of massacres and total social disorganization.

forget how her childhood and very nearly her life were destroyed when the Turks started their operation to eliminate the Armenian population. In her neighborhood, the men were rounded up for "routine questioning" that turned out to be excruciating torture followed by killing. As it became clear that this was only the beginning of the terror, she and her family barely managed to escape. If this had proved to be the only example of large-scale terrorism in the 20th century, then its memory might have been more firmly impressed on society in general. Approximately 800,000 people slaughtered—not killed in combat, but slaughtered!

There is nothing in the ordinary experience of most people that can serve as comparison. We know that thousands are killed in automobile

accidents. We are aware of AIDS as a newly emerged life-threatening disease. We may have read the names on the Vietnam Memorial Wall. However, years of highway fatalities, AIDS-related deaths, and Vietnam casualties are surpassed by what the armed forces of one nation did to the civilians of a differing ethnic group within a period of months.

This, in the eyes of some observers, was only a "sideshow" to World War I, and, as events would subsequently show, only one of numerous reigns of terror that have marked the 20th century. The total number of estimated deaths from the various persecutions and massacres listed in Table 9-3 exceeds 22 million men, women, and children. This number is larger, for example, than the populations of Finland and Holland combined and larger than the cities of Chicago, Los Angeles, Montreal, New York, Ottawa, and San Francisco combined. Without doubt, this total is also an underestimate. There is really no reliable estimate for the deaths suffered by Cambodians at the hands of the Khmer Rouge—hundreds of thousands, surely, and perhaps more than 1 million. For the other totals, relatively conservative estimates have been selected. It could be argued that more than 30 million perished as the direct result of the various reigns of terror listed in Table 9-3, and this list is not intended to be complete.

Many people with fresh memories of terror are still trying to recover their lives, such as families who fled war-torn Kosovo and then returned to devastated homes and communities. More than 10,000 others were killed during an operation that was peculiarly described as "ethnic cleansing." Is a person's ethnicity "dirty"? Are robbery, torture, eviction, and massacre "cleansing"? The assault on ethnic Albanians in Kosovo is one more devastating chapter in the attempt to acquire or keep political power through the use of terrorism and lethal force.

It is not within the scope of this book to examine these events in detail. However, we can offer a few observations that are based securely on the available evidence.

1. Terror has often been unleashed against people who share the same land and many of the same experiences and tribulations but who are *perceived as being different in some significant way.* Most German Jews, for example, were law-abiding and patriotic Germans, but when Hitler pushed the anti-Semitism button, Germans who also happened to be Jewish were ostracized and then slaughtered. Hindus, Sikhs, and Muslims alike had shared the hardships of drought, famine, and colonial subjugation, but the mutual perception that their religious differences were all-important led to widespread atrocities and killings during the partition of India and creation of Pakistan, and hostilities have recently resumed.

2. Killing is often preceded by ostracism, by *denying the other person's fundamental reality as a human being.* Our people are truly human. Those others are less than human. It would not really be killing a person to eradicate those vermin, waste those pigs. In this sense, *the murder takes place first in the mind.*

3. *Fear kills.* Reigns of terror have often been triggered or intensified because those in power have feared overthrow. The Stalinist purge of 1937 and 1938, for example, was directed almost exclusively at Soviet citizens who were suspected of harboring politically unreliable thoughts. An alleged plot against the government of Indonesia aroused fear-driven hysteria of such magnitude that 600,000 fellow citizens were slaughtered in a short period of time, most of whom were innocent of any crime or criminal intention.

4. *Cold-blooded "rationalism" kills.* There have been many episodes of terrorism in which the attackers have shown themselves as frenzied and brutal people, caught up and distorted by high passions. However, some of the most destructive terrorist operations have been systematically planned as "rational" ways to achieve political objectives. Did 11 million Russians actually die at the hands of fellow Russians in 1929–1932? Yes, that is no misprint. Stalin (who would later kill another half million people in a devastating purge) saw to it that millions of peasants died so that he could achieve his economic and political aims. Most died from planned starvation, but others were killed outright. (This incredible destruction of his own countrymen did not achieve its rational objectives either: Terrorism seldom, if ever, does.)

5. *Religious intolerance instigates and justifies terrorism.* Many people secure in their own religious beliefs have lived harmoniously with people of other faiths. Nevertheless, some of the bloodiest reigns of terror have been launched by people who were convinced both that they have the true religion and that they are therefore entitled to convert or destroy all others. The true believer becomes one of the most dangerous people when he or she turns killer. There is no hesitation, no reflection, and no compassion. True believers often appear on both sides of religious/ethnic issues.

I have known several mental patients who heard voices or felt strong impulses that brought them to the edge of killing another person. They suffered terribly because they did not want to kill and yet they could not stand the pressure, so they

The Holocaust took more than 6 million lives during World War II and left many others widowed and orphaned. Here are a few children who survived imprisonment in the Auschwitz (Poland) camp.

sought help. I have yet to learn of a religious cult that asked for help to rid itself of murderous impulses.

6. *Terrorism fails.* Seldom has a terrorist organization or movement achieved its objectives by

persecution and killing. The Nazi's "final solution," for example, was not only brutal and inhumane to the extreme but also it contributed significantly to Germany's defeat. Many of that nation's leading scientists, physicians, and other professionals were Jewish. *Germany without Jews* (Engelmann, 1984) was a weakened nation. Furthermore, Germany was left with a heritage of guilt and shame over the participation of many people not in the Nazi movement or hierarchy who became *Hitler's Willing Executioners* (Goldhagen, 1996). In an earlier epoch, an arrogant and intolerant Spanish monarch banished the Moors from what had been their homeland for centuries. The conditions of this banishment were so harsh that more men, women, and children died than survived to move on elsewhere. This "purification" or ethnic cleansing plan dealt Spain a blow from which it has never recovered. Repeatedly, terrorism has failed to achieve lasting success; often, it has brought about violent discord among the terrorists, retaliation from others, and the loss of opportunities for improving one's conditions by positive efforts.

The New Target: Innocent Bystanders

The primary target of terrorist attacks has changed over the years. Terrorism usually was targeted against selected adversaries (e.g., bombing a police station and ambushing a military patrol). In their analysis of worldwide data, Weimann and Winn (1994) found that police and military are no longer the chief targets of terrorist attacks. Furthermore, important installations, such as hydroelectric plants and other utilities, are seldom attacked. With a few exceptions, the top governmental leaders are also less frequently targeted. Who is the target then? Diplomats and ordinary citizens! Weimann and Winn note,

> As victims, diplomats embody a different symbolic meaning from that of policemen. In those autocratic countries that historically faced domestic terrorism, police forces represented violent repression, the flouting of law by authorities, and the abusive application of raw power. Contemporary diplomats do not conjure up the same imagery. They are by contrast the embodiment of conciliation, codes of conduct, and constraints on the use of power. (p. 34)

The targeting of diplomats is a profound violation of international law that has been for the most part respected even during periods of total war. It is also a way to slow the process of finding peaceful solutions to problems for those who want to retain the power of violence.

Attacks on ordinary citizens provide a way to mock powerful nations whose economic and military power does not necessarily protect individuals in the course of their everyday lives. As most brutally demonstrated by the events of September 11, 2001, ordinary citizens and business people have become the most common targets of terrorist attacks in recent years. There are no more innocent bystanders.

The Psychological Side of Terrorism

What about the psychological side of terrorism?

1. The terrorist has often been portrayed or perceived as an alluring and powerful figure, a new kind of romantic. Robin Morgan (1989) even suggested that the terrorist has become a contemporary version of the *Demon Lover:*

> He evokes pity because he lives in death. He emanates sexual power because he represents obliteration. He excites with the thrill of fear. He is the essential challenge to tenderness. He is at once a hero of risk and an antihero of mortality. (p. 24)

2. One person's terrorist is another person's hero. The popular figure of William Tell represented a terrorist to the authorities of the time. You and I might find ourselves in sympathy with some people who have carried out terrorist activities against brutal regimes. In fact, the rebellious spirit has often been considered to be an American specialty, and the film industry has been supplying us for decades with heroes who saddle up against the forces of unjust authority. There is some danger that the "terrorist" will be whoever those in control of the media choose to portray in those terms.

3. Some people clearly identify themselves with life and some with death. Death was a characteristic of the Nazi self-image (Friedlander, 1984); it can also be observed in the dress, speech, and behavior of some "skinheads" today. The terrorist, lacking a positive self-image and

filled with a generalized rage toward society, may be using the coping strategy of "identifying with the aggressor." Who is the aggressor of aggressors? Perhaps Death qualifies for that role. Some terrorists may be attempting to disguise and transform their personal fear of annihilation by entering Death's service.

4. "Sacred terror" is based on a different orientation to death. Former members of the National Security Council, Daniel Benjamin and Steven Simon (2002), believe that *jihad* (holy war) will be the most dangerous form of terrorism for years to come. It is a movement deeply rooted in the past that has risen again as Islamic fundamentalists attempt to assert themselves against what they view as a world dominated by the agents of Satan. To die as a hero on behalf of one's faith is to be assured Paradise for ever more. The psychology of the true believer can inspire individuals to violent and self-destructive actions in the name of God.

5. Freud's death instinct is a failed theory according to many critics, including the majority of psychoanalysts (Freud, 1923/1961; Kastenbaum, 2000). Nevertheless, it is difficult to escape the feeling that there is a propensity for destructiveness rooted in human nature. The terrorist, whether member of a furtive cult or a high-ranking government official, is a constant reminder that our death system does not include only the caring, compassionate, and life-protecting passions of society. The killer has always been with us and, on some horrifying occasions, has been us.

Recognizing, preventing, and ameliorating the terrorist mind-set might prove even more useful than constructing concrete barriers and introducing increasingly invasive security measures. However, we will have to learn more about our own minds as well to understand how inflicting death can seem to be the best way to improve life.

ACCIDENT AND DISASTER

Accidents and disasters have in common the fact that the deaths were not intentioned. Unfortunately, *intentionality* can be very difficult or even impossible to establish, as can be observed in many legal proceedings. Often, we cannot be sure of another person's state of mind, and some-times we may not be clear about our own intentions. Furthermore, a person may have conflicting and shifting intentions.

Intentionality is not the whole story. People may have a degree of *responsibility* for accident or disaster deaths even if they had no intention of doing so. Here is one of many examples in which a sequence of behaviors leads to an "accidental" death:

An 8 year-old girl became trapped by fire in her second-floor bedroom on October 28, 2002. Firefighters rushed to the scene but (Farmer, 2002)

> could not make the turn onto the girl's narrow street because of illegally parked cars. So they knocked down fences and plowed cars out of the way in a frantic effort to reach the dwelling. Officials say the delay in reaching the girl almost certainly contributed to her death. "When we say seconds count, it sounds cornball, but it's true," Fire Lt. William Dewan said yesterday at the station. (p. B1)

People who are familiar with the Boston area can easily visualize the situation. Illegally parked vehicles are commonplace, a chronic source of traffic congestion and driver stress. Although angry motorists frequently complain, this practice has been tacitly condoned as "just the way we do things here in Boston." It is probable that many other people's lives have been put at heightened risk over the years. Those who had made Bowen Street nearly impassable did not foresee or intend the death of Katie Orr, but it might be said that they had some responsibility for this outcome.

There was more than one aspect to this situation: The fire was started by her father in the early morning hours. He was in bed, using an oxygen tank and smoking a cigarette. It is almost certain that he had been repeatedly warned against smoking while using oxygen. It is probable that his serious respiratory illness had been caused by smoking. We can speculate about but we cannot be sure why he would not only further endanger his condition by smoking but also risk a fatal fire. Chances are that the agonized death of his daughter was not intentional, but the "accident" certainly was set up by his nonresponsible behavior as well as that of the drivers who illegally congested the street. Many other accidents result from a sequence of decisions and behaviors that have a share of the responsibility even if not intentioned to result in injury or death.

Despite these difficulties, the concept of unintentioned death provides a useful pathway through the kinds of death that are customarily called accidents or disasters.

Accidents

We begin with a statistical overview of accidents. We then examine more closely the contexts and dynamics that are often associated with accidental deaths.

The Statistical Picture

Accidents have always been a major cause of death. Today, we are especially aware of the death toll from motor vehicle accidents. What might be surprising is the fact that the rate of accidental deaths has declined appreciably throughout the 20th century. For example, industrial accidents (such as coal mine explosions or collapses) and fires are among the types of accident that take fewer lives today.

The number of accidental deaths has remained nearly constant in recent years. The most recent available data indicate that 97,3000 Americans died from all accidents, including motor vehicle crashes, poisonings, falls, and fires. The National Safety Council (2001) estimates that a disabling injury accident occurs every 1.5 seconds around the clock, and a death occurs every 5 minutes. Motor vehicle accidents, the most common type, were the leading cause of death for people ages 1–33 and the leading cause of accidental death in all age groups. There are significant age differences in the risk of fatal accidents. For example, fires and burns are more often the cause of death for very young children and people 75 years of age or older. Falls are another high risk for elderly adults. The vulnerability of elderly men and women is increased by preexisting health factors. Elders are more likely to have conditions that require medical treatment. They may also have more limited powers of recuperation from trauma and stress. Therefore, an accident from which a younger person might recover is more likely to prove fatal to an elderly person.

Alcohol intoxication remains a major factor, being involved in two out of every five motor vehicle deaths.

The general decline in the rate of accidental deaths in the United States over a recent 20-year period is shown in Table 9-4. Remember that the population has continued to increase during this time, so the *number* of deaths could remain about the same or increase even though the *rate* per 100,000 has declined. The rate is given first, with the number of deaths in parentheses.

The Human Side of Accident Fatalities

The statistical picture reminds us that all fatal accidents are not the same. The automobile passenger who is killed when broadsided by another vehicle was in a much different situation than the elderly pedestrian who slipped on an icy sidewalk or the young child who drowned in the family pool when, for one tragic moment, nobody was standing watch. There can be important differences within the same general type of fatal accident. For example, reckless driving is often responsible for fatal motor vehicle accidents in which a young person is behind the wheel; poor vehicle maintenance is often a contributing cause as well. In contrast, failure to take sufficient note of traffic conditions and slow reaction times are more often associated with fatal accidents for which elderly drivers are responsible. Additionally, the single car accident is often associated with use of alcohol or drugs and

TABLE 9-4

Leading Causes of Accidental Deaths in the United States, 1970–2000

Type of Accident	1970	2000
Motor vehicle	26.8 (54,633)	15.6 (43,000)
Falls	8.3 (16,926)	5.9 (16,200)
Poisoning	1.8 (3,679)	4.2 (11,700)
Drowning	3.9 (7,860)	1.4 (3,900)
Fires and burns	3.3 (6,718)	1.3 (3,600)
Ingestion of food, object	1.4 (2,753)	1.2 (3,400)
Firearms	1.2 (2,406)	0.2 (600)
Gas poisoning	0.8 (1,620)	0.1 (400)

Source: National Safety Council (2001).

sometimes with a self-destructive intention as well (in which case, the accident is not entirely an accident).

Some accidents truly are accidents. People behaving in a responsible manner may become victims of unforeseen equipment failures or unpredictable events. "Being in the wrong place at the right time" is sometimes a realistic explanation. On the other hand, some of the most devastating accidents have been primed by human error, indifference, or greed. In these instances, it is more accurate to speak of the lethal episode not as an accident but as a probable outcome.

Consider the following example. On April 27, 1865, the steamship *Sultana* started its voyage north from Vicksburg. Almost all the passengers were Union soldiers, including hundreds who had been incarcerated in prison camps under conditions of extreme stress and deprivation. They were all exhausted survivors of a long and bitter conflict, finally on their way home. Early the next morning, the steam boilers exploded, the ship splintered, and passengers and crew were hurled into the cold waters of the Mississippi River. Of the 2,200 people aboard, 1,700 died almost immediately, and another 200 later died of exposure and injuries. This represents the largest loss of life on an American ship, with the casualties exceeding even those of the Titanic.

An accident? The *Sultana* was built to accommodate 376 people. Approximately six times as many people were crowded aboard. Furthermore, there had been clear indications that the boilers were failing (Salecker, 1996). Greed and indifference to the safety of human lives created a situation that markedly increased the probability of catastrophe. The tragic outcome is classified officially as an accident, but this was far from an unpredictable event. The death toll was also increased by the fact that few of the passengers knew how to swim, largely because relatively few people in the United States at that time were proficient swimmers. There are numerous other examples throughout the world in which ships have gone down with a heavy loss of life because of overcrowding and neglect of safety measures. It is a dangerous misrepresentation to classify as accidents fatal events that were shaped by human error, indigence, and greed "Accident" implies that nothing could have been done to

prevent the loss of life, thereby contributing to lack of prevention in the future.

Airline catastrophes provide many examples in which human error has contributed significantly. Communication problems are often at the core, and these problems often occur because of ambiguity or other flaws in the entire system of communication that governs air travel. For example (Associated Press, 1996),

> The captain of an American Airlines jet that crashed in Colombia last December entered an incorrect one-letter computer command that sent the plane into a mountain, the airline said Friday. The crash killed all but four of the 163 people aboard.

The pilot had not made a careless error. He thought he was entering the coordinates for Cali, the intended destination:

> But, on most South American aeronautical charts, the one-letter code for Cali is the same as the one for Bogata, 132 miles in the opposite direction. The coordinates for Bogata directed the plane toward the mountain.

The ambiguity and confusion in the communication system included the fact that most computer databases used different codes for Bogata and Cali. The lack of standardization among computer databases led the captain to make one fatal keystroke. For all the efficiency and potential of computerized processes, there is also the risk of fatal error.

The following quote from control tower–pilot conversation was given at the beginning of the chapter: "KLM eight seven zero you are cleared to the Papa Beacon, climb to and maintain flight level nine zero, right turn after takeoff" (Cushing, 1994, p. 19). The runway was crowded and visibility was obscured by fog on March 27, 1977, in a Canary Islands airport. The pilot informed the tower that "We are at takeoff." What the pilot meant by this message was that the plane was actually lifting off. However, the air traffic controller interpreted the message as indicating that the plane was still on the runway and waiting for clearance. The controller thought he was giving instructions on what course to take when the plane did become airborne, and the pilot thought he had been given clearance to fly:

> The KLM pilot interprets the clearance as permission to fly to the Papa Beacon, but the Tower appears to have intended it as permission to fly to that beacon only after having received further clearance to leave the ground. The subsequent collision with another aircraft that was still on the runway resulted in the loss of 583 lives, the worst accident in aviation history. The use of alternative unambiguous phrases for the clearance would have enabled the controller to advise some action that might have averted the collision. (p. 10)

Cushing (1994) found dozens of instances in which inadequate communication resulted in either fatal accidents or near misses. Improved awareness of the communication process and its hazards could sharply reduce the possibility of accidents in aviation and other transportation situations. The automatic assumption that we have understood what the other person meant and that the other person has understood what we meant can produce what Cushing has aptly titled *Fatal Words* (1994).

We reduce the probabilities of a fatal accident happening to others or ourselves every time we check our assumptions, monitor our communications, and resist the temptation to rush full speed ahead without charting the waters. We also reduce the probabilities of a fatal accident with effective educational programs and well-designed laws. An important example is the substantial reduction in alcohol-related motor vehicle accidents by youthful drivers. A variety of educational programs and zero-tolerance laws are credited with persuading young drivers not to drink and drive (U.S. Department of Transportation, 2002). Although drinking is still prevalent among American youth, there is a strong trend toward abstaining from alcohol before taking the wheel. There has also been more acceptance of the designated driver option. Unfortunately, there has been little such change among older drivers.

Natural Disasters

"Natural" disasters includes earthquakes, volcano eruptions, storms, and floods. Catastrophic drought and crop failure have also been classified as natural disasters. Some of these disasters seem beyond human control. However, the choices we make in our lives and the changes we make in our physical environment can either increase or decrease the probability of a disaster. For example, the decision to live in an area with known environmental hazards is likely to increase the number of casualties should such events occur. Oceanfront living has attracted many people to coastal regions that are vulnerable to punishing storms. The beauty and privacy of a home in the woods places some people at risk for forest fires. Some of the areas in California that are considered at greatest risk for earthquakes are also some of the most highly populated areas. Many people are well aware of these risks and have made conscious choices to remain in hazardous areas because of their positive features. Others do not seem to realize the danger until they experience a near-disaster.

The term natural disaster customarily refers to an episode that occurs within a limited period of time. However, there are also slow, massive disasters. A fertile agricultural region becomes an arid desert because of poor farming practices. A forest that supports a diversified ecology is destroyed, resulting in long-term deprivation for the human as well as the animal population. A river dies. Fish disappear. A new blight or pest destroys crops. These events may occur over a period of years—sometimes centuries—and their impact on human lives may also occur gradually and in complex ways. It requires a perspective on long-term developments to understand slow, massive disasters and devise effective preventive or remedial measures.

Through the centuries, earthquakes have been responsible for the most devastating episodic disasters. The following are the earthquakes with the most fatalities as can be gleaned from historical as well as recent sources:

- 830,000 in Shaanxi, China: January 24, 1556
- 300,000 in Calcutta, India: October 11, 1737
- 250,000 in Antioch, Syria: May 20, 526
- 242,000 in Tangshan, China: July 28, 1976
- 200,000 in Yokohama, Japan: September 1, 1923
- 200,000 in Nan-Shan, China: May 22, 1927

A helping hand is usually offered when disaster strikes. Continued assistance in recovering from the disaster over the long-term is not as predictable.

As can be seen, the most destructive earthquakes known have been distributed throughout human history. It can also be seen that the scale of casualties can far exceed what has happened in the United States up to now. Consider earthquake-prone California. The earthquake that occurred during the 1989 baseball World Series in the San Francisco area resulted in 62 deaths. One person died in a southern California earthquake in 1992. The Northridge earthquake of 1994 resulted in 61 deaths. These episodes were important not only for their actual casualties and devastation but also for their forewarning of earthquakes to come. In the United States, we have little or no grasp of the extent of fatalities, injuries, and destruction that can result

when a powerful earthquake strikes a heavily populated area. Along with the great loss of life, a massive earthquake would also create a very large number of bereaved people who will have both short- and long-term needs for material and emotional support.

Researchers have found that persons and communities struck by disaster often experience four distinct phases of response (Weaver, 2002). First, there is a *heroic phase,* in which people demonstrate outstanding courage, stamina, and concern for others in trying to prevent loss of lives and property. Next is the *honeymoon phase,* in which a unified community works together toward recovery. Unfortunately, this optimistic period tends to be followed by the *disillusionment phase*, which is likely to endure for months or even longer.

> Social scientists sometimes call it the second disaster, as it is the time when the realities of bureaucratic paperwork and recovery delays set in. Outside help has often come and gone and people realize that they must do more themselves. Eventually, the *reconstruction phase* begins. This phase may take several years as normal functioning is gradually reestablished. (p. 237)

It is not difficult to see parallels between these phases and the responses to the terrorist attacks on America. The major difference, of course, is that earthquakes happen when they happen, but violence unleashed by a distant enemy arouses many other feelings and responses.

SUMMARY

Sudden and violent death takes the forms of murder, war, terrorism, disaster, and accident. The boundaries between these forms of violent death are not firm and stable, however. When is armed attack war and when is it terrorism? When is an accident actually homicide? We have also seen that there are many connections between individual actions that result in death and societal beliefs and practices. The fact that the United States continues to have the world's highest murder rate necessarily calls attention to characteristics of the society as well as individuals.

We first acquainted ourselves with overall murder rates and characteristics of the people who are most likely to be killers and victims. For example, most murders are committed by people who are of the same race as the victims, and in most cases the victims and the killers had previously been known to each other.

We then explored several types of murder. Domestic violence includes abusive men who kill their partners and women who kill the men who have been abusing them. The tragedy of adults who kill children, even newborn babies, was also examined, including the increasing incidence of child abuse and neglect, the lack of parenting skills, and the replacement father syndrome. Domestic violence includes parricide as well (children who kill their parents); often, these murders are preceded by years of abuse at the hands of the parents. Young men with guns account for the largest number of murders. The recent wave of lethal school shootings was discussed as a new dimension to youth violence.

Mass and serial killing are related patterns that differ from usual murders. We identified the typical characteristics of mass and serial killers and noted the possible emergence of a new type in the recent Atlanta massacre by an enraged daytrader who lost his money on a downturn in the stock market. Political assassination is another type of killing that should be distinguished from the others.

Terrorism was rampant throughout the 20th century, with perhaps 30 million people dead and many others tortured and abused. Early in the 21st century, terrorism appears to have taken additional forms.

Finally, we learned about disasters and accidents as causes of violent death. The accident rate in the United States has decreased over the years but could be sharply reduced if fewer intoxicated drivers were at the wheel.

REFERENCES

Adler, F., Mueller, G. O. W., & Laufer, W. S. (2001). *Criminology* (4th ed.). New York: McGraw-Hill.

Amnesty International. (1984). *Torture in the eighties.* London: Author.

Associated Press. (1994, April 16). *Rwanda massacre reports.* New York: Author

Associated Press (1996, August 24). *Colombia crash linked to pilot error.* New York: Author.

Becker, E. (1986). *When the war was over.* New York: Simon & Schuster.

Benjamin, D., & Simon, S. (2002). *The age of sacred terror.* New York: Random House

Bland, K. (1996, June 27). Child Protective Services opens files on 27 deaths. *The Arizona Republic,* p. A6.

Brook, T. (Ed.). (2000) *Documents on the rape of Nanking.* Ann Arbor: University of Michigan Press.

Browne, A. (1987). *When battered women kill.* New York: Free Press.

Bureau of Justice Studies. (2002a). *Homicide trends in the U.S. Trends by race.* http://www.ojp.usdoj.gov/bjs/homicide.race.htm.

Bureau of Justice Studies. (2002b). *Homicide trends in the U.S. Trends by gender.* http://www.ojp.usdoj.gov/bjs/homicide/hmrt.htm.

Bureau of Justice Studies. (2002c). *Homicide trends in the U.S. Long term trends and patterns.* http://www.ojp.usdoj.gov/bjs/homicide/hmrt.htm.

Bureau of Justice Studies. (2002d). *Homicide trends in the U.S. Regional trends.* http://www.ojp.usdoj.gov/bjs/homicide/hmrt.htm.

Chang, I. (1998). *The rape of Nanking: The forgotten holocaust of World War II.* New York: Penguin USA

China News Digest. Japanese Army's Atrocities: Nanjing Massacre. www.cnd.org/njmassacre.

Clarke, J. W. (1982). *American assassins.* Princeton, NJ: Princeton University Press.

Conquest, R. (1986). *The harvest of sorrow.* New York: Oxford University Press.

Crissman, J. K., & Beach, K. A. (2002). Assassination. In R. Kastenbaum (Ed.), *Macmillan encyclopedia of death and dying* (Vol. 1, pp. 41–44). New York: Macmillan.

Crissman, J. K., & Parkin, J. (2002). Homicide. In R. Kastenbaum (Ed.), *Macmillan encyclopedia of death and dying* (Vol. 1, pp. 423–426). New York: Macmillan.

Cushing, S. (1994). *Fatal words.* Chicago: University of Chicago Press.

Daniszewski, J., & Holley, D. (2002, October 28). Hostages killed by rescuers. *Los Angeles Times/East Valley Tribune* (Mesa, AZ), p. A16.

DeBruin, L. (1994, April 6). Suspects joked about shootings, police say. *Mesa Tribune,* pp. A1, A4.

Descent into mayhem. Tribal slaughter erupts in Rwanda. (1994, April 18). *Time,* 44.

Dobson, C., & Payne, R. (1987). *The never-ending war: Terrorism in the 80s.* New York: Facts on File.

Engelmann, B. (1984). *Germany without Jews.* New York: Bantam.

Ewing, C. P. (1997). *Fatal families. The dynamics of intrafamilial homicide.* Thousand Oaks, CA: Sage.

Farmer, T. (2002, November 12). Clear out: Menino launches parking crackdown after fatal fire. *Boston Herald,* p. B1.

Fox, J. A., & Levin, J. (2001). *The will to kill.* Boston: Allyn & Bacon.

Freud, S. (1961). *The ego and the id.* New York: Norton. (Original work published 1923)

Friedlander, S. (1984). *Reflections of Nazism.* New York: Harper & Row.

Goldhagen, D. J. (1996). *Hitler's willing executioners.* New York: Knopf.

Grosscup, B. (1987). *The explosion of terrorism.* Far Hills, NJ: New Horizon.

Gutteridge, W. (1986). *Contemporary terrorism.* New York: Facts on File.

Heide, K. M. (1992). *Why kids kill parents: Child abuse and adolescent homicide.* Columbus: The Ohio State University Press.

Hofstadter, R., & Wallace, M. (Eds.). (1971). *American violence: A documentary history.* New York: Random House.

Holmes, R. M., & Holmes, S. T. (1994). *Murder in America.* Thousand Oaks, CA: Sage.

Humphrey, J. A., & Palmer, S. (1986/1987). Stressful life events and criminal homicide. *Omega, Journal of Death and Dying, 17,* 299–308.

Kastenbaum, R. (2000). *The psychology of death.* 3rd ed. New York: Springer.

Kuper, L. (1981). *Genocide.* New Haven, CT: Yale University Press.

Laqueur, W. (1987). *The age of terrorism.* Boston: Little, Brown.

Lea, H. C. (1906/1907). *A history of the Inquisition of Spain* (4 vols.). New York: Macmillan.

Lester, D. (1995). *Serial killers.* Philadelphia: Charles Press.

Morgan, R. (1989). *The demon lover. On the sexuality of terrorism.* New York: Norton.

National Safety Council (2001). *Report on injuries in America, 2001.* www.nsc.org/library/rept2002.htm.

Newton, M. (1999). Mass murder: Individual perpetuators. In R. Gottesman (Ed.), *Violence in America: An encyclopedia* (Vol. 2, pp. 329–334). New York: Scribner.

O'Brien, J. (1973). *The Inquisition.* New York: Macmillan.

Paulozzi, L., & Sells, M. (2002). Variation in homicide risk during infancy—United States, 1989–1998. *Journal of the American Medical Association, 287,* 2208.

Picard, R. G. (1993). *Media portrayals of terrorism.* Ames: Iowa State University Press.

Raynor, T. P. (1987). *Terrorism: Past, present, future* (Rev. ed.). New York: Franklin Wats.

Salecker, G. E. (1996). *Disaster on the Mississippi.* Annapolis, MD: Naval Institute Press.

Smalley, S., & Miller, M. (2002, October 21). Dear Policeman, I am God. *Newsweek,* 25–32.

Sterling, C. (1981). *The terror network.* New York: Reader's Digest Press.

Tobin, Mitch. (2002, October 30). Killer sends 22-page letter to publisher. Arizona Daily Star, p. A1.

U.S. Department of Transportation. (2002). *Why there are fewer young alcohol-impaired drivers.* http://nhtsa.dot.gov/people/injury/FewerYoungDrivers.

Wakin, E. (1984). *Enter the Irish-American.* New York: Crowell.

Weaver, J. D. (2002) Disasters. In R. Kastenbaum (Ed.), *Macmillan Encyclopedia of Death and Dying* (Vol. 1, pp. 231–240). New York: Macmillan.

Weimann, G., & Winn, C. (1994). *The theater of terror.* New York: Longman.

GLOSSARY

Assassination: The murder of a public official or other political figure.

Branch Davidians: A Christian sect, some of whose members died in their compound near Waco, Texas, during an attack by federal agents.

Day Trader: A person who makes a continuing series of quick financial transactions through the internet.

Death instinct: A biological impulse present in all individuals that is aimed at reduction of stimulation and activity to the point of death; also known as Thanatos. It is countered by Eros, the impulse for growth, love, and new experiences (Freud).

Homicide: The act of killing a human being.

Interpol: International Police Organization, primarily an information-sharing agency.

Mass Killer: A person who murders a large (but not fixed) number of people in a single episode.

Mosque: An Islamic place of worship, a temple.

Murder: The criminal act of killing a human being.

Parricide: Murder of a parent.

Rational Extremists: A type of assassin who is motivated by political objectives; often mistakenly believed to be psychotic.

Replacement Father Syndrome: The new husband or lover engaged in abusive and life-threatening actions against the children of the wife's previous mate.

Serial killer: A person who commits murders on repeated occasions.

Terrorism: Violence or threat of violence in which civilians or places used by civilians are the targets.

Unabomber: The name given to himself by a person who sent explosive packages through the mail to kill or injure the recipients.

Hippocrates is often considered the father of medicine and the Hippocratic oath has long been regarded as a fundamental statement of the physician's mission. An unknown artist in the Middle East offered this depiction in the 3rd century B.C.

chapter 10

EUTHANASIA, ASSISTED DEATH, ABORTION, AND THE RIGHT TO DIE

We heard screaming coming from another crater a bit away.... He kept begging us to shoot him. But we couldn't shoot him. Who could shoot him? We stayed with him, watching him go down in the mud. And he died. He wasn't the only one. There must have been thousands up there who died in the mud. Or almost worse, suffered in it, wounded.
—Quoted by Winston Groom (2002, p. 215)

I swear by Apollo the physician, and Aesculapius, Hygeia and Panacea and all the gods and goddesses, that, according to my ability and judgment, I will keep this oath and this covenant. I will give no deadly medicine to anyone if asked, nor suggest any such counsel, and in like manner I will not give to a woman an abortive remedy. With purity and with holiness I will pass my life and practice my Art.
—The Hippocratic Oath (fifth-century B.C.)

Death Counseling
IS SOMEONE IN YOUR FAMILY TERMINALLY ILL?
Does he or she wish to die—and with dignity?
Call Physician Consultant [Telephone No.]
—Classified newspaper advertisement (June 1987)

The woman said the baby's naked body, spotted alongside a road in a small town in Hunan province, was still warm—she had been dumped and had just died. Many passers-by on their way to work ignored the child...while some stopped to look, then walked on, until an elderly man eventually put the tiny body into a box and carried it away.
—"China Uses Abortion" (2001)

You could find Nature in the South Bronx if you had legs enough to walk to a park where they kept grass and trees, even squirrels. You could also find Nature on the very sidewalks of New York as a single blade of grass succeeded in reaching for the sun between cracks in the pavement. Nature is famously insistent about filling earth, water, and sky with life-forms, and these life-forms are famously insistent about staying alive. Human nature, though, is replete with exceptions, such as suicide, homicide, and war. In this chapter, we examine other types of individual and societal practices that have the effect of terminating lives that could have continued. Euthanasia, assisted suicide, and abortion differ in significant ways, but all involve decision making under stressful conditions. We also examine the right-to-die movement (actually a cluster of advocates with a variety of concerns) that has generated ideas and programs while receiving both praise and criticism.

• "Mercy death" is probably the earliest and purest form of euthanasia. A dying person or animal is spared further suffering by a blow or shot that ends its life quickly. This kind of action has been known and respected on battlefields and accident sites for longer than anybody can remember. War memoirs are filled with instances in which a soldier provided mercy death for either a fallen comrade or enemy. In the example given previously, the British infantryman was not dying, but he would soon be dead. He was one of many soldiers on both sides of the war who would be slowly pulled into the depths of a bomb crater whose mud acted like quicksand. His comrades had tried to save him, but there was no way. As horrifiying as it was to watch him slowly sink into the mud, none of the young men could bring themselves to shoot him. That same day—and the next day for years to come—British, French, German, and other soldiers would be slowly dying in the zone accurately known as "no-man's land." The fatally wounded called out for relief while they still had breath. A comrade who responded to these pleas would most likely be cut to pieces by machine gun fire or blasted apart by a mortar round. Mercy death was almost a luxury in the trench warfare that relentlessly claimed the lives of the young men of Europe and, near the end, Ameri-

can reinforcements. Euthanasia, however, is not always such a straightforward proposition.

• What has become known as the Hippocratic Oath is thought to have been drawn from the writings of a physician who practiced on the Greek island of Cos 2,500 years ago (Edelstein, 1943). This ancient document is still very much at issue today: Should a physician violate the injunction to give no deadly medicine and still be a physician? Dr. Jack Kevorkian is not the only physician who has intentionally contributed to the death of his patients, but both his actions and his words have had a powerful influence on the right-to-die controversy. Furthermore, the shadow of involuntary euthanasia has been cast over the movement to provide assisted death. People who know their 20th-century history have concerns about any movement that would encourage and legalize the taking of a life. Are these concerns valid or misplaced?

• The dead and discarded baby alongside a road must have been profoundly painful even to the passersby who could not bring themselves to deal with it. Babies and children are considered precious in Chinese culture. Nevertheless, the people of China have been confronted with a combination of forced abortion and infanticide ever since the regime decided on a drastic policy of population control. Abortion issues, like euthanasia, take many forms. Seeing the more familiar form of the abortion controversy within a larger perspective could be helpful.

In this chapter, we consider the related topics of euthanasia, physician-assisted suicide, abortion, and the right to die. We also examine the Black Stork (Pernick, 1996) phenomenon to become aware of the connection between eugenics, euthanasia, and assisted death. We have prepared ourselves for this challenge by studying end-of-life decisions (Chapter 7), suicide (Chapter 8), and killing (Chapter 9). We begin with the Hippocratic Oath and then acquaint ourselves with key terms and concepts. This is followed by attention to public attitudes toward the set of right-to-die issues and a review of some of the major cases that have influenced the right-to-die controversy. We then examine the assisted-death issue in detail, with particular attention to Oregon, the only state in which there is a legal process for assisted termination. The emotionally and politically divisive issue of abortion concludes our exploration. Can we keep an open mind through it all?

"I SWEAR BY APOLLO THE PHYSICIAN": WHAT HAPPENED TO THE HIPPOCRATIC OATH?

Kevorkian's classified advertisement was a clear signal that "death with dignity" was becoming more than a rallying cry. Here was a physician who was offering to perform a service that most of his colleagues did not even want to talk about. It was a service, in fact, that seems to be specifically banned by the Hippocratic Oath.

We often assume that (a) all physicians have sworn allegiance to this oath and that (b) this covenant does in fact represent the core belief system for physicians from antiquity forward. Neither assumption is correct. Many physicians graduate from medical school without being asked to take the Hippocratic Oath. Kevorkian (1991) characterizes the oath as irrelevant. Furthermore, the Hippocratic Oath has encountered opposition since its inception. Many in the ancient world considered it reasonable and even honorable to seek release from the rigors, pains, and disappointments of life. The prohibition against giving "deadly medicine" was probably specified because taking deadly medicine had become a widespread practice. The concurrent prohibition against abortion was also contested, with Aristotle as one of the leading dissenters.

History suggests that opinion has often been divided on the physician's role in life and death decisions. Today, some physicians continue to rely on the Hippocratic Oath, but many have never entered into this covenant, and all are confronted with new and complex problems that Hippocrates never had to deal with. Even physicians who accept the Hippocratic Oath must find a way to reconcile these precepts with the decisions they must make day by day. Physicians in the United States generally work within the system. They must find ways to help their terminally ill patients without violating either their own moral code or the law of the land. Abandoning the patient or offering to provide assisted death are extremes that most physicians would not choose. Whatever one's position on physician-assisted death, though, one cannot simply invoke the Hippocratic Oath as the unquestionable authority. We must work things out for ourselves.

KEY TERMS AND CONCEPTS

We improve our ability to deal with these life-and-death issues by becoming more familiar with key terms and concepts.

A literal translation of the term *euthanasia* would be happy (*eu*) death (*thanasia*). However, it would be more accurate to understand this original usage as "dying without pain and suffering." It has seldom been assumed that dying is a great pleasure. At first, the euthanasia concept referred to the individual's state of being (e.g., "She died peacefully"). Later, euthanasia came to signify actions performed to hasten death. Today, the term euthanasia retains something of its original meaning: a peaceful, painless exit from life. However, it has taken on another meaning as well: the intentional foreshortening of a person's life to spare that person from further suffering.

Many people have emphasized the distinction between a life that is foreshortened by doing something and a life that is foreshortened by deciding not to do something. The term *active euthanasia* applies to actions that are intended to end the life of a person (or animal) that is suffering greatly and has no chance of recovery. A lethal injection or the administration of carbon monoxide are clear examples of active euthanasia. *Passive euthanasia* refers to the intentional withholding of treatment that might prolong life. Deciding not to place a person with massive brain trauma on a life-support system is an example of passive euthanasia, as is the decision not to treat pneumonia or an opportunistic infection in an immobilized and cognitively impaired long-term patient.

The health care provider or family member who feels that it is acceptable to "let him/her go" (passive euthanasia) might be deeply troubled by the prospect of giving direct assistance to death (active euthanasia). The legal system and society in general have been more tolerant of the "letting go" approach. Few are inclined to make trouble when health care providers and family members

An influential movement in the United States urged death for babies with birth defects and others who were considered to be burdens on society. The Black Stork was a symbol often used by critics of this movement.

agree that it would be pointless to introduce further procedures that would only prolong suffering or a vegetative state. The living will, the Patients Self-Determination Act, and Five Wishes (Chapter 7) provide further support for the passive euthanasia approach.

There is still substantial opposition to active euthanasia. Many physicians strenuously object to placing their services at the disposal of death. "Doctors are supposed to keep people alive. If doctors also kill people, then who can trust them?!" Some physicians and other health care providers are also strongly opposed on personal religious/moral grounds. Furthermore, there is no sheltered legal status for the person who engages in active euthanasia: It is likely to be classified as homicide. Such a person, whether physician or family member, may be charged with a crime.

We still hear about active and passive euthanasia because these were the original terms of the controversy. Today, however, most physicians and bioethicists speak instead of withdrawing or withholding life supports. This makes discussion simpler and more direct. Instead of dealing with the somewhat abstract and unwieldy concept of euthanasia, we can focus on whether or not certain practical actions should be done or undone.

The constant attention given to the passive/active distinction has its own critics. We can ask ourselves the same question they raise: How much does it really matter whether the life is terminated by passive or active means? The outcome is the same. What do you think?

For anybody with a knowledge of 20th-century history there is another difficult question to consider: *Can we detach ourselves from the memory of horrors that have been perpetrated in the name of euthanasia?* There are still many people among us who remember how the political, medical, economic, and military forces of a modern nation all collaborated in the murder of millions of people. The holocaust that eventually claimed millions of lives was preceded by Hitler's policy of *Vernichtun lebensunwerten Lebens.* Nazi doctors participated in the "extermination of valueless life" (Lifton, 1986). The victims were fellow German citizens, non-Jewish, who were invalids, infirm, unable to care for themselves—a large proportion of the institutionalized population. Killing these helpless people required the cooperation of physicians and other people who had been entrusted with their care.

This brutal program might have been rejected by German society had it been exposed for what it was. However, the murders were disguised as euthanasia. The Nazi leadership declared that these people were being put out of their misery *for their own good.* And, yes, it would also save the cost of feeding and housing them. Enough physicians believed (or pretended to believe) this explanation in order to make the program a success.

What the Nazis did to their helpless citizens had nothing at all to do with euthanasia. These people were not terminally ill. They were not suffering intractable pain. They did not ask to be killed. They were simply murdered, one by one, through a process that had a bureaucrat at one end and a physician at the other. Discovering that he could induce physicians, lawyers, and other responsible people to engage in "mercy killing," Hitler moved on to his genocidal assaults against Jews and Gypsies (Friedlander, 1995).

The Black Stork

An almost forgotten episode in United States history brings this issue even closer to us. A keen interest in both eugenics and euthanasia developed early in the 20th century. Preventive medicine was starting to reduce mortality rates and increase life expectancies. Why not go all the way? Why not keep "defective" people out of the population in the first place? Eugenicists proposed sterilization of people thought to have defective genes. Why not let defective newborn infants die? While we are at it, why not end the lives of patients as soon as it is clear that they are incurable? A crusade was born! Euthanasia was favored by those who did not think eugenics went far enough. A prominent Chicago surgeon, Harry J. Haiselden, combined eugenics with euthanasia. He boasted of having allowed the deaths of at least six "defective" infants. He urged other physicians to help him weed out those unfit for the new and improved version of society.

Physicians who saved defective infants came under attack by eugenicists (Pernick, 1996). At first, the public was divided in its response to the eugenics and euthanasia movements. By the 1920s, the public had pretty much rejected the euthanasia facet of the movement, but not before it had attracted the enthusiasm of some German physicians and political thinkers:

> By the 1930s racial hygiene, eugenics, and euthanasia played a complex but central role in the evolution of Nazi ideology and in the legitimization of Nazi genocide. Depicting their intended victims as carriers of racial "diseases" constituted a key feature of Nazi propaganda.... Programs for killing incurably ill institutional patients, such as the operation code named "T-4" that secretly gassed over 100,000 disabled Germans, pioneered the machinery and trained the medical personnel who were then transferred to run the death camps for the "racially diseased." (p. 164)

Can there be any wonder that the terms euthanasia and mercy killing now lead to fear, suspicion, and anger on the part of those who know how they have been so cruelly misused? The Native American woman who told me of the forced sterilization of many women in her tribe was not being paranoid: She was simply reporting facts.

The Ventilator as Example of Life-and-Death Decisions

"Withholding or withdrawing" treatment provides a more useful frame of reference for dealing with most life-and-death decisions in the health care system today. Even so, thoughtful people might disagree on what course of action should be taken. It is also possible to disagree on just how much significance should be given to the withholding/withdrawing distinction.

Consider, for example, the ventilator (Iserson, 2002). This is one of the most familiar pieces of equipment in the intensive care unit. It is frequently used in life-support situations. Suppose that a patient has been attached to a ventilator for weeks or even months. Families and hospital staff now agree that this person has no chance for recovery and is receiving no quality-of-life benefit from the life-support system. Somebody pulls the plug. In a little while, the patient is dead. This is an example of withdrawing treatment. However, suppose instead that a person has just been brought to the hospital after a massive stroke or with severe brain trauma from an accident. It is obvious to the medical team that the higher brain centers have been destroyed. Death will soon oc-

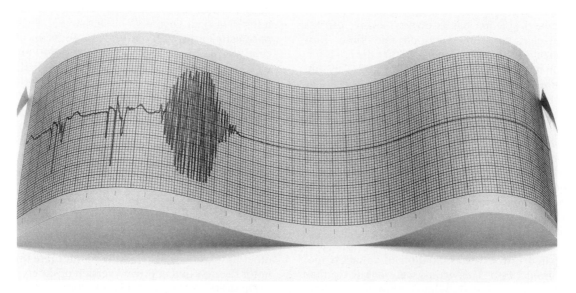

One criterion for determining death is the appearance of a flat line on an EEG read-out.

cur unless the unresponsive body is hooked up to a life-support system. The decision is made against using a ventilator. The patient is soon certified as dead.

The patient dies in both of these scenarios. The "instrument" of death in both scenarios is the ventilator. How much importance should we attach to the difference between withdrawing and withholding treatment? Are both methods equally moral and acceptable (or equally immoral and unacceptable?). What if it was up to you? Would pulling the plug be no more difficult than deciding not to connect the plug in the first place? Whatever your judgment and your decision, you are sure to find some experts in agreement and others in disagreement. We return to this problem later.

Euthanasia, assisted suicide, physician-assisted death, medicide, and other such terms all differ from suicide by involving the actions of another person. The suicidal person carries out his or her own intention. All forms of assisted death, by definition, require another person to contribute actively to the outcome. How much importance do you attach to this distinction? If a person really wants to have his or her life ended, do the details matter? "Yes," you might argue, "because it places a heavy responsibility on another person." "No," you might argue, "because it is the intention and the outcome that count, not the particular method." Attempts to legalize assisted deaths in the United States may hinge on the outcome of these counterarguments.

We use the *slippery slope* argument when we oppose a particular instance of assisted death because it could contribute to widespread abuse in other instances. "I can understand and sympathize with this person's request to be put out of her suffering," we might say, "But if society consents to 'mercy killing' in this instance, then tomorrow we will be asked to consent in a case where the right to die is not quite so clear. And so it will go, until we slide all the way down the slope."

Perhaps many people would give up too soon when confronted not only with a terminal illness but also with other challenges and crises. Death would become too easy an out. We might even expect people to kill themselves or seek assistance in ending their lives. Perhaps the physician will be increasingly expected to participate in as-

sisted death—and would that perhaps help to control the costs of health care in a graying society? Who can be sure that Nazi-style "euthanasia" might not come into fashion in the United States or elsewhere, again under the cover of deceptive terminology? There are sharp disagreements today regarding the applicability of the slippery slope argument to a particular life-and-death decision, and these disagreements are likely to continue for some time.

It is important to keep in mind that the living will and other advance directives do not include provisions for assisted death. Many people who support the living will as an expression of the individual's preferences do not support assisted death. However, one sentence in the standard living will does walk the boundary: "I do, however, ask that medication be mercifully administered to me to alleviate suffering even though this may shorten my remaining life."

Suppose that you are a physician. The patient you are attending at this moment has previously entrusted you with a signed and witnessed copy of her living will. She is dying. She is also in physical and emotional distress. "I want to die," she tells you. It had been your intention to control her pain with morphine. A heavier dose would not only relieve her pain but also hasten an easy death. Would you feel justified in prescribing a lethal dose because it is consistent with the advance directive ("even though this may shorten my remaining life")? Would you feel that you were dishonoring your profession or even committing murder? The living will, valuable instrument that it is, does not answer all the questions for us and, indeed, continues to raise new questions.

OUR CHANGING ATTITUDES TOWARD A RIGHT TO DIE

In recent years, the public has had more opportunity to learn about and reflect on right-to-die issues. As we have already seen (Chapter 7), the doctrine of informed consent has made a difference, and the public soon proved supportive of natural death acts that support advance directives such as the living will. A national survey was conducted while open discussion of right-to-die issues was still in its early phases (Times Mirror, 1983). Most Americans already believed that there were circumstances in which a person should be allowed to die and that terminally ill people do have the right to accept or reject treatment options. More personally, most people said they would ask their doctors to stop treatment if they were in great physical pain and unable to function in daily activities because of an incurable disease. However, there was also a consensus that medical personnel were not paying much attention to the patient's wishes (i.e., trying to resuscitate patients who had asked that this procedure not be done). Most respondents had heard about the living will and thought it a good idea, but few had actually completed such a document for themselves.

What about the possible next step—euthanasia or assisted death? Perhaps surprisingly, 7 of 10 people believed it was justified to terminate a life if a person was suffering terrible pain from a terminal disease. The survey question was specific to married couples: If the pain was severe and could not be relieved, it would be an act of mercy to end the life of one's dying spouse (with the consent of the spouse, of course). At this point, the role of the physician as terminator was not yet salient.

The attitudinal picture was not as clear-cut as it might seem from the findings already mentioned. Do people have the moral right to end their own lives if afflicted with an incurable disease? The public was divided on this question. There was a slight edge for those who agreed that there is a moral right to suicide in this circumstance, but there was firm disapproval for ending one's life simply because it has become burdensome to either one's self or family. Americans were also equally divided about whether they would want to have everything done to save their lives or choose comfort management instead. Note that there is a major difference between believing that it is morally acceptable to reject treatment and one's personal choice in the matter. The same distinction is true with the more controversial issue of terminating the life of a dying person: One might consider this to be a morally acceptable action in some circumstances but reject the idea of participating in such an action personally.

Much has happened since the 1980s. The establishment of hospice care programs to provide comfort, pain relief, and family support has alleviated the prospect of suffering for many people and, therefore, the desperate impulse to hasten the end of life. However, the opposite extreme has also become offered as an option: physician-assisted death (discussed later). How has public opinion responded to these and other recent developments?

The results of several national polls have been summarized by the Death with Dignity National Center (2002). In general, the public finds physician-assisted death to be an acceptable course of action in appropriate circumstances. The following is a typical question and response:

> Do you think that the law should allow doctors to comply with the wishes of a dying person in severe distress who asks to have his or her life ended, or not?
>
> "Yes, should allow"—65%
> "No, should not allow"—29%
> "Not sure"—6%

The same survey also asked specifically about the Oregon legislation that provides a legal basis for physician-assisted death. United States Attorney General Ashcroft had moved to overrule this majority vote: 35% agreed with Ashcroft and 58% disagreed. Obviously, there are still significant differences in American public opinion. Some polls indicate strong approval of the right for assisted death, but responses are fairly balanced between approval and disapproval in other polls. (None of the polls show clear disapproval of assisted death.)

One study tried to determine what factors are linked to approval or disapproval of assisted death (Worthen & Yeatts, 2000/2001). Interestingly, there was no relationship to age, gender, and previous experience in giving care to terminally ill friends or family members. Religious belief was influential, though, particularly the conviction that life belongs to God, physical suffering can be a blessing, and physician-assisted death is murder. For most respondents, the most important consideration was the actual situation. People wanted to focus on the particular person in that person's distinctive situation. Abstract ideas about right and wrong were less influential than the challenge of dealing with immediate re-

Karen Ann Quinlan never regained consciousness after her 1975 accident. The question of whether she should be disconnected from the life support apparatus became the subject of intense legal, medical, moral, and religious debate.

ality. Another finding from this study perhaps tells us something important about the American belief system: The typical response was that people should have the freedom to make choices about the ending of their own lives, but most of the respondents would not make the choice of assisted death.

THE RIGHT-TO-DIE DILEMMA: CASE EXAMPLES

We have examined some of the key concepts and learned how they are viewed by the public. Now it is time to look at some of the specific human experiences that have influenced the present status of the right-to-die issue in the United States and that will also play a role in future developments. We begin with the case that made the question of assisted death one that the nation could not easily ignore.

The Ethics of Withdrawing Treatment: The Landmark Quinlan Case

A young woman became the center of national attention when she lapsed into a coma after a party on the night of April 14, 1975. One friend applied mouth-to-mouth resuscitation while another called the police, who also attempted resuscitation and took her to a hospital. She started to breathe again, but Karen Ann Quinlan did not return to consciousness. Traces of valium and quinine were found in her blood. Drug-induced coma was the preliminary diagnosis. Later, this diagnosis was disputed and has never been fully clarified. Whatever the precipitating cause, Quinlan had suffered severe and irreversible brain damage as a result of oxygen deprivation.

Weeks and then months passed. Quinlan remained in the hospital. Her vegetative functions were maintained on a ventilator, with intravenous tubes providing fluids and nutrition. Her body gradually wasted away. After a few months, the once vital and attractive young woman had become a 60-pound shriveled form, curled into a fetal position. Talk of recovery and a miraculous return to life became less frequent as time went by. The hospital expenses continued to mount day by day.

Karen Ann was the adopted child of deeply religious parents. Joseph Quinlan maintained hope for nearly 6 months. Finally, his priest persuaded him that morality does not require that extraordinary means be used to prolong life. This communication did not resolve the moral issue, however; it simply exported it into other spheres. The Quinlans asked two physicians to turn off the ventilator. They declined to do so. The physicians were not sure of the moral implications of such an action. They were also naturally concerned about the possibility of facing malpractice or even felony charges. As we have seen, physicians may still be troubled by these concerns today after two decades of discussion and legal

rulings. For those physicians at that time, the request to "pull the plug" was almost equivalent to the first astronauts' walk in space.

What were the Quinlans to do? They pursued their request through the courts. The time-consuming legal process provided the opportunity for many opinions to be aired in the media and in professional circles as well as in the courts. Some confusion was also generated. For example, there was a tendency to speak of Karen Ann as though she were already dead. The fact was that electroencephalogram (EEG) tracings still showed weak electrical activity in the brain. A neurologist described her condition as a "persistent vegetative state." This phrase would be repeated many times about many other nonresponsive persons in the years to come. An attorney for New Jersey described a brief visit to her room (Kron, 1975):

> Her face is all distorted and she is sweating. Her eyes are open and blinking about twice a minute. She's sort of gasping. I've never seen anything like that.... I was there for 7 minutes and it seemed like 7 hours (p. 22)

Medical testimony was given that Karen Ann would die within a short time if removed from the ventilator.

The court ruled against the Quinlans' request. In this ruling, the court specifically rejected the argument that religious freedom should be the basis for approving the removal of the life-support system. This decision was appealed to the New Jersey Supreme Court. Here, for the first time, a court ruled that a ventilator could be turned off (in the popular mind this was soon translated into pulling the plug). However, the court imposed a condition: Physicians must first agree that Karen Ann had no reasonable chance of regaining consciousness. The New Jersey Attorney General decided not to challenge this decision. This meant that the U.S. Supreme Court was not asked at that time to make a precedent-setting decision for the entire nation. The U.S. Supreme Court's turn would come later in the Nancy Cruzan case.

Finally, 14 months after she had lapsed into a nonresponsive state, Karen Ann was disconnected from the ventilator. She was expected to die quickly. However, her persistent vegetative state proved persistent indeed. Karen Ann remained alive (in some sense of the word) for more than 10 years until she succumbed to pneumonia in 1985. Many a thoughtful observer drew the inference that expert opinion is not always respected by the forces that govern life and death.

Karen Ann's predicament was not the first example of its kind, but it became the starting place not only for discussion but also for efforts to develop due process in right-to-die issues. It was recognized that medical technology now made it possible for many people to be maintained in a persistent vegetative state, and that human judgment would often suggest that medical technology not be applied beyond a point of no return. Guidelines were needed, and a system of checks and balances should be established.

There has been a long and winding road from the Karen Ann Quinlan dilemma to the present day. It is now estimated that 10,000–25,000 Americans exist in persistent vegetative states (Iserson, 2002). Some will remain unresponsive but alive for years. Families and caregivers must deal with this difficult situation day after day. Since Karen Ann Quinlan's dilemma first captured public concern, there have been a number of proposed guidelines and systems of checks and balances. Court decisions have sometimes clouded and sometimes clarified our understanding. Meanwhile, physicians and other health care providers responded in various ways to their new challenges. One of these responses became the subject of a continuing controversy. The principals in this drama were a young physician and a young woman who became known as Debbie.

"It's over, Debbie": Compassion or Murder?

The Quinlan case was characterized by a long period of consultations, discussions, and legal proceedings. Many people participated in the decision making, and many facts were brought forward for public as well as family and professional scrutiny. A very different case was reported in a leading medical journal. No author's name was attributed to "It's over, Debbie" when this brief report was published in the *Journal of the American Medical Association* (Anonymous, 1988). The article was offered as a personal experience and

consisted of only three paragraphs. The following is the story.

A presumably young physician, a resident in gynecology, was on duty when called in the middle of the night. The request came from a nurse on the gynecologic–oncology (cancer) unit. This was not the physician's usual duty station. The doctor "trudged along, bumping sleepily against walls and corners and not believing I was up again." Upon reaching the unit, he picked up the patient's chart and was given some "hurried details" by the nurse. A 20-year-old patient was dying of ovarian cancer. An attempt had been made to sedate her by using an alcohol drip, but this had led her to vomit "unrelentingly."

Entering the patient's room, the resident saw that she was emaciated and appeared much older than her actual age. "She was receiving nasal oxygen, had an IV, and was sitting in bed suffering from what was obviously severe air hunger." There was another woman in the room who stood by the bed, holding the patient's hand. The physician had the impression that "the room seemed filled with the patient's desperate effort to survive." The physician also observed that the patient was breathing with great difficulty. The article states that she had not eaten or slept in 2 days, nor had she responded to chemotherapy. Presumably, this information had been gleaned from the doctor's quick glance at the patient's chart.

Trying to take in the whole situation, the resident felt that it was a "gallows scene, a cruel mockery of her youth and unfulfilled potential. Her only words to me were, 'Let's get this over with.'"

At this point, the physician returned to the nurses' station to think things over. There, the physician decided that he would "give her rest." The nurse was asked to draw morphine sulfate into a syringe. "'Enough,' I thought, 'to do the job.'" The physician returned to the patient's room and told the two women that he was going to give Debbie "something that would let her rest and to say good-bye." Within seconds of the intravenous injection, the patient's breathing slowed, her eyes closed, and her distress seemed to be at an end. The other woman stroked Debbie's hair as she slept.

The doctor "waited for the inevitable next effect of depressing the respiratory drive." Four minutes later, the breathing slowed further, sputtered, and came to an end. The dark-haired woman stood erect and seemed relieved. "It's all over, Debbie."

This brief report raised a furor among the readers of this widely read and respected medical journal. The media picked it up and the public was immediately drawn into the controversy as well. The response was divided, but critical reactions dominated.

Here are what I see as the most salient questions raised by this incident:

1. The physician had no prior acquaintance with the patient or her companion. This means that the life-and-death decision was made and carried out by a stranger. *Should a physician assist the death of a patient with whom he or she has no previous relationship and no background of knowledge?*

2. The decision was also made very quickly and without consultation. Did the decision have to be made that quickly? *Does a physician have the responsibility to get a second opinion before taking a life?*

3. The physician was fatigued. *Should physicians be able to take their own state of mind and body into account when on the verge of making important decisions?*

4. The physician's anxiety was heightened by the fact that the patient was also young. It became more difficult, then, to establish a sense of emotional distance: This terrible thing could also happen to the physician. The physician seems to have projected his or her own thoughts and feelings on the patient. The "gallows" and "cruel mockery" images emerged from the physician's own mind and may have had little resonance with Debbie's own thoughts. *Should physicians be required to demonstrate competency in dealing with their own emotions before being entrusted with other people's lives?*

5. At first the physician felt that "the room seemed filled with the patient's desperate effort to survive." A few minutes later, the physician ended Debbie's life. There was no indication in the published report that the physician ever tried to reconcile the impression with the action. *Should physicians be required to demonstrate the ability to monitor their own thoughts in an alert and critical manner before being entrusted with other people's lives?*

6. The nurse was ordered to prepare a lethal injection. *Is it morally defensible to order another person to participate in an assisted death? Should the nurse have been given the opportunity to express her feelings and philosophy? Did the nurse have the responsibility to refuse this order and inform the physician that she is reporting this incident immediately?*

7. The physician ordered a lethal dose of medication instead of a dose that might have provided relief without ending her life. This alternative does not seem to have been considered. *Does a physician have the right to end a life before attempting to relieve pain and other symptoms by nonlethal means?*

8. The patient's distress had been intensified by a procedure (the alcohol drip) that had produced new symptoms without alleviating the existing symptoms. *Did this hospital routinely fail to provide adequate pain relief because of ignorance, indifference, or the fear of making an addict out of a terminally ill patient? Was it the failure of the hospital's overall symptom relief program that placed both the young resident and the young woman in this extremely stressful situation?*

9. Debbie spoke only one sentence to the doctor. *Did the doctor try to converse with her or her companion? Did he/she or the companion hold her hand, establish eye contact, and attempt to have at least a little more guidance from her before making the decision to end her life? Should doctors be required to demonstrate communication competence in critical care situations before being entrusted with other people's lives?*

10. The doctor told the two women that he was giving Debbie something that (a) "would let her rest" and (b) and would "let her say good-bye." What actually happened, according to the report, was that Debbie closed her eyes and died shortly thereafter without having the chance to say good-bye or anything else. *Was the physician actually concerned with enabling leave-taking communication between Debbie and her companion? Did the physician really believe that death and "rest" are identical outcomes? Did the physician misrepresent what he was actually doing in order to reduce*

his own anxiety level? What responsibility to truth and open communication should be expected of the physician in critical care situations?

An Arrow through the Physician's Armor

One of the painful lessons in this particular episode involves the role of the physician's own physical, mental, and spiritual state and the nature of the health care system. A tired and probably overworked physician found himself in a stressful situation that neither medical training nor personal experience had equipped him to master. His own insulation from dying and death was pierced momentarily by seeing another young person in such a painful and vulnerable condition. The physician felt an urgent need to relieve Debbie's anguish as well as his own sense of personal vulnerability and inability to restore her health.

The physician had several options, including taking other measures to relieve the patient's distress and discontinuing those that were adding to her distress. The physician could have consulted with others, such as the nurses who had been caring for Debbie as well as more experienced physicians. Certainly, the physician could have made more effort to learn who Debbie was and what she wanted. It is not unusual for people to wish themselves dead when experiencing acute distress but to be grateful later that another alternative had been found.

All these options required time and patience, and time was not what this tired, poorly prepared, overmatched, and anxious physician could afford. The decision to end Debbie's life was influenced by the physician's urgent need to terminate a situation in which he felt powerless, vulnerable, and depressed. The needs and feelings of other people were barely considered, nor did the physician feel obliged to think of the philosophical, religious, sociopsychological, and legal factors that might lead one to hesitate before taking another person's life.

Much of the critical response called attention to the physician's disregard of standards and due procedure. Other doctors were aware that their images and reputations were endangered by such episodes. The ease with which one young physi-

cian disposed of Debbie's problems by disposing of Debbie in the middle of the night seems to be a prime example of how slippery the slope can be.

We should keep in mind, however, that the anxieties of doctors (or hospital administrators) can lead to the opposite outcome as well—bodies being maintained on life-support systems despite the obvious futility of this procedure and despite the family's and even the patient's expressed wishes. The legal justice system in our society, for all its flaws, does at least allow time and does require evidence. Decisions hastily made in the middle of the night by doctors who are poorly trained in self-monitoring and interpersonal communication afford few if any safeguards.

Does a Person Have to Be Dying to Have the Right to Die?

This odd phrase brings us to one of the issues that is becoming increasingly important. Much of the right-to-die controversy at first centered around people who were either locked into a persistent vegetative state (e.g., Karen Ann Quinlan) or alert and responsive but with little time to live (e.g., Debbie). As we have seen, there is increasing public support for the right to terminate life-sustaining procedures when a person is in either of these conditions. However, what are we to think about a case such as the following? As you read about this case, consider what decision you would have recommended at each point and why. Test your own decision-making skills and life-and-death philosophy.

Elizabeth Bouvia

A 26-year-old woman has earned a degree in social work and is seeking employment. Her husband leaves her. She becomes depressed and anxious. If she also becomes suicidal, would you recommend:

_____ Everything possible should be done to prevent her from committing suicide.

_____ Somebody should listen to her, offer advice and support, but not otherwise intervene.

_____ Some other course of action should be taken, namely _____

Why did you make this particular recommendation? _____

_____

_____

Now we add some additional information. This woman is also afflicted with cerebral palsy. She retains just enough muscular control to operate an electrically powered wheelchair, to speak, and to chew and swallow food when someone feeds her. Suppose that she expresses a strong wish to end her life. What course of action would you recommend?

_____ Everything possible should be done to prevent her from committing suicide.

_____ Somebody should listen to her, offer advice and support, but not otherwise intervene.

_____ Some other course of action should be taken, namely _____

_____

_____

Why did you make this particular recommendation? _____

_____

_____

There is a new development. The state will no longer provide assistance in transportation. This makes it almost certain that she will not be able to find and keep a job. She is now deprived of the opportunity to pursue the career for which she prepared herself and the chance to support herself. As a result of this discouraging development, she expresses a strong wish to end her life. What course of action do you recommend?

_____ Everything possible should be done to prevent her from committing suicide.

_____ Somebody should listen to her, offer advice and support, but not otherwise intervene.

_____ Some other course of action should be taken, namely _____

_____

_____

Nobody has agreed to help her commit suicide (remember that she does not have the physical ability to do so herself). She is desperate. What can she do? She arranges to have herself admitted to a hospital so she can be left alone and gradually starve herself to death. When she is admitted to the hospital, attempts are made to change her mind, but her purpose holds firm. At this point, what course of action would you recommend?

_____ Force her to take nourishment against her wishes.

_____ Allow her to carry out her plan while also providing her with companionship and the opportunity to discuss and reconsider her options if she so chooses.

_____ Some other course of action should be taken, namely _____

_____

_____

Why did you make this particular recommendation? _____

_____

_____

Now let's see what actually happened. Riverside (California) General Hospital refused to accept Elizabeth Bouvia's plan and brought the issue to court. The judge declared that Ms. Bouvia was fully competent and had made a decision that was both competent and sincere. However, he decided in favor of the hospital's position (Annas, 1984):

> The decisive point was that Ms. Bouvia was "not terminal" but "had a life expectancy of 15 to 20 years." He concluded, "The established ethics of the medical profession clearly outweigh…her own rights of self-determination." Therefore, "forced feeding, however invasive, would be administered for the purpose of saving the life of an otherwise nonterminal patient and should be permitted. There is no reasonable option." (p. 20)

George Annas, a professor of health law, argues that this was a poor decision that gave legal force to "brutal behavior." His key point is that medical care requires consent and is really no care at all when it is imposed against the patient's wishes. He reports that "four or more attendants wrestle her from her bed in the morning and restrain her while a nasogastric tube is rudely forced through her nose and into her stomach" (1984, p. 24). Hospital officials insisted that its staff should not be asked to become accessories to a suicide. (Apparently, there was no concern about asking the staff to participate in a group assault on a helpless person.)

The impasse was resolved when Ms. Bouvia checked herself out of the hospital and was admitted to a nursing home that promised not to force food on her. Once settled into the (unidentified) nursing home, Ms. Bouvia outlived the media's interest in her. She decided not to starve herself to death after all because this had proven to be too stressful a process.

Ms. Bouvia's predicament, and the predicament of all who became involved in the situation, illustrates what can happen when various rights come into conflicts. Here are some of the rights that were asserted or implied:

1. The right to end one's own life—for any reason that seems significant to that person.
2. The right to end one's own life when not terminally ill but facing years of infirmity and isolation.
3. The right to ask or require other people to help end one's life.
4. The right of society to oppose the wish of a person to end his or her life.
5. The right of "experts" (e.g., physicians, lawyers, and judges) to do what they think is best for a person even if this directly contradicts what that person seeks for himself or herself.

No judicial decision can resolve all the issues raised by competing claims of rights. Some of these issues are linked with our deepest personal values and beliefs and may therefore be highly resistant to change as per court order. In this instance, many people were outraged by the court's support of physical intervention to force Ms. Bouvia to take nourishment. The basic sense of fair play and compassion seemed to be violated when a disabled individual, innocent of any crime, could be so abused by the system and with a judge's consent. In situations such as these, judicial rulings might be "proper" on their own terms but are more likely to create than solve problems because they run counter to society's view of how people should treat each other.

Reflect for a moment on the recommendations you made at various points in the development of Ms. Bouvia's predicament. What perspective did you take? Were you placing yourself in Ms. Bouvia's situation, trying to see the situation from her standpoint? Did you see yourself instead as a hospital administrator or as the nurse responsible for her care? The priorities and pressures of the situation take on a different pattern as we shift perspective. It is a constant challenge to put ourselves in the position of all the people who may be involved in a life-and-death predicament. Even the question of "which right is the rightist?" may be answered in a different way, depending on our particular involvement and stake in the situation.

Ms. Bouvia's experience leaves us with three fundamental problems that neither society at large nor medical and legal experts have fully resolved: (a) If we have a "right to die," must this be limited to terminal illness and, if so, why?; (b) are there limits to the power that the state can legitimately exercise over an individual who wishes to die?; and (c) is it acceptable to ask others to help us die? Responsible people continue to disagree.

Competent to Decide?

The issue of consent to treatment has already come to the fore. Consent would have no meaning, however, if the individual were unable to comprehend the situation, the options, and the consequences. Due process requires a determination of competence before the issue of consent can be addressed. What should be done when it is ruled that the individual is not competent?

Joseph Saikewicz was a 67-year-old resident of the Belchertown State School (Massachusetts). He was considered to be profoundly retarded, with a mental age of less than 3 years. Because of this intellectual deficit, he was not considered competent to enter into legal contracts or make other significant decisions regarding his own welfare. A representative of the state would make decisions on his behalf. Saikewicz was robust, ambulatory, and usually enjoyed good health. He was able to make his wishes known only through gestures and grunts. He had adjusted fairly well to the sheltered institutional environment but was vulnerable and disoriented in other settings.

The need for decision making arose when Saikewicz was diagnosed as suffering from acute myeloblastic monocytic leukemia, a form of the disease that was considered to be incurable. Chemotherapy produces a remission in some patients, but this usually lasts only for several months. Unfortunately, the course of treatment can produce serious side effects. According to the medical testimony (Robbins, 1983),

> A patient in Saikewicz's condition would live for a matter of weeks, or perhaps, several months. A decision to allow the disease to run its natural course would not result in pain for the patient, and death would probably come without discomfort. (p. 38)

If Joseph Saikewicz had been capable of comprehending his condition, he would have been able to decide whether or not he wanted chemotherapy, with its prospect of extending survival for several months but also making him feel sicker. Because he was not capable of making this decision, it fell to the medical and administrative officials and eventually the courts. In this instance, a Massachusetts probate judge ordered that all reasonable and necessary supportive measures should be provided to Saikewicz, but that he was not to be subjected to chemotherapy. This decision was based on the consideration that the state had no applicable interests or claims that outweighed Saikewicz's right to be spared the discomfort of a treatment that could not save his life. The patient remained in his familiar institutional home until he died of pneumonia, a complication of the leukemia. Reportedly, he died without pain or discomfort.

Unlike the judicial decision that gave precedence to social institutions over the individual's (Bouvia's) own wishes, this ruling supports the position that the state does not necessarily have either the right or the obligation to subject a person to treatment simply because the treatment is available. Each new case that comes up for judicial review will have its own distinctive features. This means that even when competency or incompetency has been clearly established, the ruling may be affected by other factors. Furthermore, a judge may find cause to make a ruling that departs markedly from the decisions made in previous cases of a similar nature.

Joseph Saikewicz was known to have been incompetent to give or withhold consent because of his lifelong intellectual deficit. Nobody challenged the classification of mentally incompetent. This determination is not always so easy and free of dissent. For example, I have observed shifting levels of competence in aged residents of long-term care facilities. There are times when the person appears disoriented, out of touch with both the institutional environment and the larger world. On other occasions, the same person is alert, aware, and able to express preferences and intentions. Furthermore, this variable competency may be influenced much by how the person is being treated and what is going on around him or her. A change in medication (even in the dosage of the same medication) can result in either a spell of disorientation or a recovery from the fog. A person who has withdrawn from social interaction and has little to say may be assumed to be mentally incompetent when in fact he or she is suffering from a depressive reaction or can no longer hear conversations but is hesitant to ask for a hearing aid. If we assume that "old and institutionalized" means "incompetent," then we might slide into the habit of making decisions without the participation of that person. When such a pattern has developed, it is only a small step to assume that the person is mentally incompetent and unable to participate in a life-or-death situation.

At the other end of the age spectrum, we have already noted (Chapter 6) that children tend to be excluded from participation in decision making about their own care. The child is not considered competent to give or withhold informed consent for medical procedures in general. Does this mean that every possible treatment must be given (imposed) on a child? Who should decide?

A Supreme Court Ruling: The Nancy Cruzan Case

The U.S. Supreme Court issued its first direct ruling on the subject 15 years after the Quinlan case brought the right-to-die issue to public at-

Nancy Cruzan, another accident victim who suffered a permanent loss of consciousness, had her case brought before the United States Supreme Court.

tention. Nancy Cruzan, 26, had been critically injured in an automobile accident on January 11, 1983. When discovered by paramedics, Cruzan was lying face down in a ditch—no respiration, no heartbeat. The paramedics were able to revive her respiration and cardiac functions, but the young woman remained unresponsive. Physicians judged that she had suffered trauma to the brain and oxygen deprivation.

Three weeks later, she could grimace, display motor reflexes, and take a little nourishment by mouth. There may have been slight responsivity to pain and sound. Nevertheless, Nancy Cruzan did not respond to conversation, express thoughts and needs, or engage in either verbal or nonverbal communication. Surgeons implanted a feeding tube with the permission of her husband. It was not necessary to use a ventilator because she continued to breathe on her own. Rehabilitation efforts were attempted, but they failed. No improvement was noted or expected, but the young woman remained alive and the state of Missouri continued to pay for her care.

Two options were considered at this point: continue to support her life by tube feeding and nursing care or withdraw these services, thereby leading to her death. Nancy Cruzan's parents

asked hospital personnel to discontinue the tube feeding and hydration. It was understood by everybody involved that this action would result in the young woman's death. The hospital declined to do so without court authorization. This request would go all the way to the U.S. Supreme Court (1989). The following is a summary of what happened:

1. The trial court ruled that Nancy Cruzan had a fundamental right to refuse or accept the withdrawal of what it termed "death-prolonging procedures."

2. It was also ruled that she had expressed her general intent in a conversation with a close friend a year previously. Nancy had told her friend that if very ill or seriously injured, she would not want to continue her life unless she could live "at least halfway normally."

3. The Missouri Attorney General appealed this ruling to his state's supreme court. By a four to three margin, the lower court's ruling was overturned. The life-support procedures would have to be continued. A key point in this decision was the fact that Nancy had not prepared a living will or any other document that established her intent beyond a reasonable doubt.

4. The U.S. Supreme Court recognized the principle that "a competent person has a constitutionally protected...interest in refusing unwanted medical treatment" (p. 183). Nevertheless, by a five to four margin, the nation's highest court refused to overturn the decision. Nancy Cruzan had the right to refuse death-prolongation procedures, but the state of Missouri had the right to require what it considered to be clear and convincing evidence that this would really have been Ms. Cruzan's intentions if she could now express herself.

5. The Supreme Court, however, had created a way out of the dilemma. The state itself could reconsider the evidence and approve withdrawal of life-support activities. This is just what happened. Nancy Cruzan's physician had opposed withdrawal of life support. However, after 6 years, he had seen enough. A court-appointed guardian asked the physician if he still thought it was within the patient's interest to continue the tube feeding and hydration: "No, sir. I think it would be personally a living hell!" A Jasper County judge ruled that the parents' request could be honored. There were no further legal challenges this time, although a throng of protesters (not people who had known Nancy Cruzan personally) voiced their disapproval. The young woman died quietly 12 days after the tubes were removed.

What has been established by and learned from this ordeal? The U.S. Supreme Court did affirm, though indirectly, the principle that a competent person has the right to refuse treatment that would only prolong suffering, and that local jurisdictions could require due process. The Curzon vs. Missouri decision, however, did not address all the issues that can arise in right-to-die cases; it did not even address all the salient issues in the Curzon case. This laborious process of legislative action and judicial review is still with us.

What lessons can we draw? We can see that it would be useful to establish our wishes in some form of advance directive. Nancy Curzan's situation would have been resolved sooner and with less stress for everybody concerned had she executed a living will, but how many 23-year-olds (or 46-year-olds, for that matter) do you know

who have actually done this? We can also see that the decision to withdraw life support is a difficult one when respiratory, cardiac function, and motor reflexes persist without external aids. The Missouri State Supreme Court emphasized that "Nancy is diagnosed as in a persistent vegetative state. She is not dead. She is not terminally ill. Medical experts testified that she could live another 30 years" (U.S. Supreme Court, 1989, p. 180). We need to be well informed and secure in our understanding about what it means to be alive and a person.

Finally, we are left with the question of perceived social value. Both Karen Ann Quinlan and Nancy Cruzan were young people who seemed to have full lives ahead of them. What about elderly people who find themselves in similar predicaments? Hemlock Society author Donald W. Cox (1993) notes,

> On November 30, 2 weeks prior to Judge Teel's order to remove Nancy's feeding tube from her stomach, the Court of Common Pleas in Lackawanna County (Scranton), Pennyslvania held that a 64-year-old incompetent woman in a persistent vegetative state was entitled to have a nasogastric feeding tube withdrawn. The hospital removed the tube and the woman died peacefully and quietly, in sharp contrast to the front-page publicity that enveloped Cruzan's death a few weeks later. (p. 86)

Many elderly men and women have died in this manner. Others have died when health care personnel have decided against starting life-support procedures. As a nation, we seem to place less value on the lives of older adults. We assume that old people are supposed to be depressed and therefore seldom intervene therapeutically (Hinrichsen, 1993). When older people seem ready to die—well, that is what they are supposed to do, right?

DR. KEVORKIAN AND THE ASSISTED SUICIDE MOVEMENT

Society at large and the health care system in particular continue to struggle with the idea and practice of assisted death. Kevorkian's activities remained in the media spotlight until they reached a crescendo when the television program "60 Minutes" featured a video that showed him giving a lethal injection to Thomas Youk. He challenged prosecutors to try him for murder. They did so—successfully—and Kevorkian was subsequently convicted of second-degree murder and imprisoned. He decided against going on the hunger strike he had threatened and, at last report, was serving time in a Michigan penal facility. Kevorkian's words, actions, and personality have dominated the subject of assisted death in the United States for more than a decade. Nevertheless, we must also examine the broader picture here, starting again with terminology.

Kevorkian has often described his services as assisted suicide. This term locks in a particular interpretation (suicide) with which not all proponents of assisted death agree, and with which most suicidologists disagree. We use the more neutral term assisted death, which provides maneuvering room for a variety of interpretations. It should be noted that the most common term now in use is physician-assisted death. Despite its popularity, this term is unnecessarily limiting: People other than physicians can assist death.

Assisted death is examined briefly within several contexts: (1) the medicolegal situation in The Netherlands (Holland) and Australia; (2) Kevorkian's philosophy and practice; and (3) recent alternatives and developments, including Compassion in Dying and the Oregon Death with Dignity Act.

The Netherlands: A Social Experiment Watched Closely by the World

In recent years, The Netherlands' medicolegal system has been the focus of interest for both advocates and opponents of assisted death. It is this enterprising and often surprising nation that has provided the most tolerant social climate for assisted death. Dutch courts established a tradition of sanctioning cases of medically assisted death brought before them during the 1980s (Gomez, 1991). These were individual court decisions—interpretations of the existing laws—in individual situations. These decisions did not meet with total approval on the part of all legal experts, health care professionals, and the general public.

There was, and continues to be, critical and passionate dialogue between advocates and opponents within The Netherlands.

The Netherlands later enacted a law that made it legal for a physician to assist in ending a patient's life (Cox, 1993). The physician has to behave in compliance with a set of rules that include the requirements that (a) the patient is terminally ill, (b) the patient has made an explicit request for life termination, and (c) the physician informs the coroner of this action and provides a detailed check list regarding the patient's situation and the physician's own actions. Currently, The Netherlands is the only nation with a law that clearly sanctions (medically) assisted death. With the passage of this legislation, physicians have no concern about facing criminal charges, including murder, as long as they stay within the guidelines.

The issue is not so easily resolved, however. Some physicians and other health care providers in The Netherlands, as elsewhere, are opposed to assisted death for personal and/or moral reasons. Others are worried about the adequacy of the decision-making process: Do the people involved always communicate adequately with each other and have full knowledge of the available options? Still others accept the legalization of assisted death in its present form but harbor concerns about the possible extension of this practice into other spheres, fearing that their nation may have already taken a dangerous step down that slippery slope. This fear was intensified on April 29, 1995, when an infant born in terrible pain with a spinal column defect was injected with a muscular relaxant that stopped her breathing. The baby girl's parents had authorized the procedure, and it was carried out by her physician. The Dutch Ministry of Justice prosecuted the physician on the charge of premeditated murder. The physician was found guilty but not convicted. The trial was intended not to punish this physician but to establish new guidelines for assisted death (or, as some still prefer, euthanasia) for newborns with severe disabilities.

This case was important not only because it involved a newborn person but also because (a) the decision was in the form of substituted judgment and (b) despite its serious physical defect and pain, the infant was not terminally ill. The little girl could not speak for herself. Is it reasonable and moral for anybody to make the decision to end her life, even her parents? Is the acceptance of this act of assisted death a dangerous slide further down the slippery slope that could result in widespread killing of newborns and perhaps others who do not meet somebody's criteria for being an acceptable person? Opponents were concerned that the slope had now become much too slippery—one person could make the decision to end the life of another person. Euthanasia had become involuntary and therefore verged on homicide. However, proponents noted that the parents had loved their baby and accepted its disabilities. What they could not bear was the fact that the baby was suffering pain and the pain could not be relieved. From this perspective, the parents and the sanctioning government were approving a compassionate end to a life that would have been dominated by suffering.

In considering The Netherlands experiences with assisted death, we perhaps find more problems than answers. The answers, when forthcoming, sometimes are unexpected. For example, an institutionalized Dutch woman requested assisted death. The request was denied, but she was told that the institution could not force her to eat. She took no food and only a little water for several days and continued to express her wish to die. The institution then respected her decision and stopped offering her food. Well, they did give her some apple juice (Meijburg, 1995/1996):

> To the surprise of those who attended to her needs, her physical situation had not really deteriorated after 3 weeks. It was discovered that the contents of apple juice can keep people alive well over 100 days and that, if she kept drinking apple juice, she would probably not die from starvation at all. A week later the nurses happened to serve the residents a hot meal with french fried chicken. At the smell of this dish the woman all of a sudden asked whether she could have some, too. Ever since she has been eating her meals again and for many months afterward she happily participated in all different kinds of activities the nursing home had to offer. (p. 192)

Gradually, the woman's physical condition deteriorated and "she died a natural death." This is one of many vignettes suggesting that there may be many unknowns and a good deal of ambiguity in the interaction between a person requesting assisted death and those who must respond to this request in some way. Perhaps it is not surprising that physician-assisted death remains a deeply divisive issue in the nation that has been most receptive to the idea.

Australia: Yes, and Then No

The assisted death/right-to-die controversy is raging in many nations today. Australia provides another instructive example. The first law that specifically legalized euthanasia and assisted suicide was enacted by the Northern Territory Parliament, taking effect July 1, 1996. Less than 1 year later, the Australian Senate overturned this law and forbid any of its territories from passing any measures that would make assisted suicide legal. Clearly, the nation was in turmoil over this issue. As in other nations, the case for assisted death was made on the behalf of terminally ill people whose suffering had not been relieved. Again, as in other nations, the controversy served to alarm and educate the public about the situation experienced by terminally ill people. Should this person be granted her wish to avoid further suffering by assisted death, or should physicians be more conscientious and effective in providing relief for pain and other symptoms?

An additional pair of questions soon came into focus: What physician would agree to terminate a life, and what physician would be qualified to do so? Only one Australian physician, Dr. Philip Nitschke, agreed to take on this responsibility, and only after discovering that none of his colleagues would step forth. Obviously, passage of assisted death legislation does not ensure a readiness in the medical community to participate. The several terminally ill people seeking assisted death under the new (and later revoked) law and the one physician willing to respond to their wishes became the center of heated controversy that has not yet abated (Nitschke, 2000; Street & Kissane, 2000). There is also increasing concern in the United States regarding the qualifications that should be required of a physician who executes a patient's request for assisted death. Are all physicians qualified? What kind of skills and ex-

Jack Kevorkian with his suicide machine. Kevorkian was "present" at the death of more than a hundred people before being found guilty and imprisoned.

perience are needed? This issue is a long way from being resolved.

Assisted Death in the Kevorkian Manner

Assisted death in the Kevorkian manner should be seen within its sociomedical context. Consider first the principle objections of medical practitioners to any form of assisted death:

- *Taking a life is inconsistent with the responsibilities and values of a physician.* Nothing could more contradict and undermine the mission of the healer.
- *Religious convictions forbid taking a person's life in any circumstances with the possible exception of self-defense.* Some physicians could not even

begin to consider the possibility of assisting death because of their deeply held religious convictions.
- *The life might be mis-taken.* Nature does not always behave as the physician expects. The impulse to relieve suffering might result in ending a life that had potential for recovery.
- *Serious legal consequences might be expected to befall any physician who engaged in assisted death.* Malpractice suits and criminal charges would destroy the life of a physician reckless enough to take such action.
- *The dying person accuses the physician of being a failure.* Rather, it is the physician's self-accusation when the limits of medical art and science are exposed by incurable illness. Physicians were avoiding their dying persons in general. They certainly did not want to see

their patients' unrelieved suffering and perhaps hear their cries for help.

When Kevorkian started his one-person campaign in 1990, he had practically no support from either medical organizations or court rulings. He hoped to arouse the sympathetic interest of the public and thereby force the medical profession to change its position. This plan required Kevorkian to reveal rather than conceal his actions. Kevorkian was eminently successful in arousing public opinion on this subject through media attention and controversy.

People who have known Kevorkian over the years characterize him as a very intelligent man with a keen grasp of medical history. Families who have sought his services speak of him as a compassionate and understanding person. Critics remark on Kevorkian's verbal attacks on those who do not agree with him, his apparent delight in publicity, and his "lone wolf" approach. Although principles are more important than personality in the long run, what are perceived as positive and negative features of Jack Kevorkian, M.D., have influenced the reception to his words and actions.

Kevorkian's Agenda

Kevorkian would add planned death to the list of shattered taboos, now that legal sanctions against abortion and suicide have weakened. The agenda he presents also includes the establishment of centers in communities across the nation in which people could have assisted deaths on their request and also in which biomedical research could be done on dying and death. These *orbitoria* would go much further than previously has been possible to understand the nature of death. Perhaps you recall Kevorkian's long-term interest in the changes that occur near the time of death (Chapter 3). He is also a strong advocate for organ donations and attempted to establish a program through which condemned prisoners could donate their body parts.

Beyond assisted death, Kevorkia's objective is to complete what he sees as the long process of breaking away from concepts and values that once were dominant in Western society. This stance puts him into conflict with much (though not all) of the religious and legal as well as the medical establishment. Furthermore, he would extend biomedical science into a zone that makes many people very uncomfortable. His advocacy for research into the central nervous system of dying and dead people is reminiscent of the violent disputes that erupted when postmortem examinations were prohibited by church and state. Physicians had to obtain cadavers through shady practices and conduct their examinations under risk of discovery and punishment. There is no question but that major advances in medical knowledge derived from studying the dead, especially as this practice gradually won approval. This history does not mean that much of value would also be learned from the types of biomedical studies that Kevorkian has in mind, nor does it mean that these studies should be approved and supported. It is useful to be aware of this historical parallel, however, if only to recognize that Kevorkian has more on his mind than pain relief for suffering individuals.

Kevorkian's Method

People turned to Kevorkian when there did not seem to be hope for improvement in their condition or relief from suffering. He would discuss the situation with the patient and family members. Some of these sessions were recorded on videotape. Kevorkian has repeatedly emphasized that he puts no pressure on the patient to make the final decision quickly or to make that decision in the direction of assisted death. Carol Loving (1998) describes the final scene in which her son, Nick, was to be terminated by Kevorkian:

> Dr. Kevorkian kept telling him, "If you don't want to go through with this, you don't have to. You don't have to worry about hurting our feelings. If you want to postpone for a week, a month, a year, don't even hesitate." My son kept saying, "No, no, let's do it. I want to go. I want to go." So I helped him with his mask to get it all adjusted.... Dr. Kevorkian told him, "Now anytime you feel comfortable and ready you just go ahead and pull it. The gas will start." (p. 175)

The death of Nick Loving was accomplished through an apparatus constructed by Kevorkian that he sometimes referred to as the "Merciton" but that is better known in the media as the "suicide machine." Whether Kevorkian used this or some other procedure for a particular patient, it was intended to be the patient who took the decisive action. It is for this reason that Kevorkian could speak of having "assisted" at a death. The fact that Kevorkian did not himself take the final action also served as protection against charges of murder. He forfeited this protection and crossed the line he himself had specified when he gave Thomas Youk a lethal injection.

Evaluating Kevorkian's Approach

Physician-assisted death as advocated and practiced by Kevorkian has been subjected to many criticisms. There is the religious/moral objection that here is a physician playing God. Only God can give, and only God should take life. This objection is potent for those who hold a religious belief of this type and also influential for others who think that, for whatever reason, Kevorkian has stepped across a line that should be respected. There is also the objection, already noted, that the physician must always be on the side of life.

Additional problems demand attention when we examine the data for the deaths that Kevorkian has acknowledged facilitating. The most detailed presentation and analysis of these data has been provided in two articles written by Kalman J. Kaplan, director of a suicide research center in Chicago, and his research team (Kaplan, Lachenmeier, et al., 2000; Kaplan, O'Dell, et al., 2000). The most important data come from the medical examiners who have investigated the cases in detail. Information of this kind was available for 93 cases.

1. *Most of the people whose deaths have been assisted by Kevorkian were not terminally ill.* Only 28.3% were terminally ill. Since the majority (69.9%) were not terminally ill, significant questions must be raised: How adequate was Kevorkian's medical assessment of the patients? How valid is his claim for relieving the suffering of dying people if most were not dying? Do these data confirm the fears of a very slippery slope? In other words, did the availability of "death on demand" lead to premature death?

2. *The gender bias in Kevorkian's clientele suggests that his practice encouraged and increased suicidality among women.* We turn again to Kalman's data. Before the Michigan law against assisted suicide was signed by the governor, all of the deaths had been women. During the period in which Kevorkian was dealing with legal proceedings against him, he participated in the deaths of 11 men and 9 women. As soon as he was acquitted on charges of assisted suicide, Kevorkian returned to the original pattern in which by far the greater number were women. In the general population, women are much less likely than men to commit suicide. The reverse is true among Kevorkian's assisted death patients.

3. *The people assisted to death by Kevorkian fit the general profile of suicide attempters rather than terminally ill people.* For example, they had a high incidence of depression and dependency and a low incidence of the conditions that are the most common causes of death in the United States. The implication is that Kevorkian either stimulated or was the receptive target for unhappy people who might otherwise have either attempted nonfatal suicide attempts or found other ways to deal with their situation. Another disturbing implication was Kevorkian's failure to diagnose or treat their depression. Many people with depressive episodes or tendencies are effectively treated every day. Some of these people do express the desire to end their lives in order to end their miseries. Competent medical help has often contributed to a restoration of their spirits, but competent medical help with their lives is not what they received from Kevorkian.

4. *Kevorkian functioned without adequate medical information and consultation.* He seldom asked for a second opinion—and did so increasingly less as he continued his practice. This was especially unfortunate because Kevorkian did not have expertise in many of the specific medical conditions that affected his patients, nor in psychiatric evaluation or palliative care. Part of the problem was due to the unwillingness of other physicians to cooperate with him. He could have done much more, however, to make sure his patients had the advantage of medical and psychiatric expertise before assisting them to death.

5. *Death is much too extreme a solution to the relief of suffering.* For those people who are in severe pain

(most of his patients were not), there were alternatives. It is interesting to consider an international example. There was a sharp negative response after an eminent Japanese physician administered a lethal drug to his patient. The director of a hospice (Kato, 1996) wrote,

> Even if there is so much pain that it cannot be eliminated through the use of painkilling drugs like morphine, it is possible to enable the patient to sleep without feeling the pain by using large doses of tranquilizers or anesthetics. Physical pain is not a reason for permitting euthanasia.

Japanese Philosopher Histake Kato (1996) reported an incident in which a friend of his was in excruciating pain during an attack of pancreatitis. The first doctor he saw did not take painkilling measures. His friend switched to another hospital, where the pain was removed: "In other words, both doctors who have the best know-how about eliminating pain and doctors who have no know-how at all exist side by side in the Japanese medical system."

Kevorkian did not established his credentials for the up-to-date and effective relief of pain, and he has shown little familiarity or interest in the hospice movement. He did not offer an alternative other than death.

6. *Despite his disclaimers, it appears that Kevorkian has rushed people into assisted death without adequate safeguards and consideration.* His very first case, Janet Adkins, was in good health, suffering no pain, and, in fact, had been playing tennis with her teenage son. Kevorkian seemed to become her instrument of destruction on the promptings of her husband. There are other cases as well in which Kevorkian seems to have strayed from his own criteria (Box 10-1). Data show that as time went on, Kevorkian moved more rapidly from first meeting with the patient to the death. He increasingly violated the criteria he had himself insisted on in his public statements. One of these cases is reported by Kaplan (1998):

> Gale, a 72-year-old former merchant marine, was suffering from emphysema. There is no question that he asked to die, but there is clear evidence that Gale had a great deal of ambivalence after the gas mask was put on his face, asking twice that it be removed. Kevorkian's original record of the incident…found in a garbage bag outside his assistant's house, indicated that Kevorkian removed the mask in response to Gale's first request, but did not remove it in response to the second. (p. 173)

7. *Kevorkian uses "silencing" techniques to defend his actions.* This pattern is clear in his book and in many of his presentations through the media. It is only the physician who should assist deaths. It is only the physician who understands. This attitude dismisses the experiences, values, knowledge, and feelings of a great many other people, including clergy, nurses, social workers, attorneys, sociologists, anthropologists, and philo-

---

BOX 10-1
KEVORKIAN'S STANDARDS AND KEVORKIAN'S ACTIONS

Kevorkian's standards	*Kevorkian's actions*
• Call for psychiatric consultation	• Rarely called for consultation
• Call for pain specialist consultation	• Rarely called for pain specialist
• 24-hour waiting period after final request	• Most deaths in less than 1 day
• Extensive patient counseling	• Brief conversations; no professional counseling
• Stop the process if any sign that patient is ambivalent	• Some patients were clearly ambivalent, but assisted death carried out

sphers. Kevorkian is open to the charge of excessively medicalizing dying and death.

Oakland County (Michigan) Judge Jessica Cooper offered her own evaluation of Kevorkian's activities when she sentenced him to a term of 10–25 years when he was found guilty of second-degree murder (www.catholic.org/euthanasia/kevsen.html):

> This trial was not about the political or moral correctness of euthanasia. It was all about you, sir. It was about lawlessness. It was about disrespect for a society that exists and flourishes because of the strength of the legal system. No one, sir, is above the law. No one. You were on bond to another judge when you committed this offense; you were not licensed to practice medicine when you committed this offense, and you hadn't been licensed for 8 years. And you had the audacity to go on national television, show the world what you did and dare the legal system to stop you. Well, sir, consider yourself stopped.

Kevorkian was convicted on charges of second-degree murder after he invited CBS's "60 Minutes" program to show a videotape in which he administered a lethal injection (a departure from only "assisting" in a death). He started serving a 10- to 25-year sentence in 1999, lost an appeal to overturn the verdict, and the U.S. Supreme Court declined to consider another appeal in October, 2002.

Compassion in Dying: An Alternative Model

A different approach to assisted death was introduced by Compassion in Dying, a nonprofit organization based in Seattle (P.O. Box 16483, Seattle, WA 98116; telephone, 1-206-624-2775). It has become a model for other organizations that attempt to meet the needs of terminally ill people who express a desire for death without violating legal or ethical principles. The guidelines and safeguards established by Compassion in Dying are summarized in Table 10-1.

Compassion in Dying emphasizes time, communication, and counseling. Representatives of the organization help patients and families to consider their alternatives. Founder and director Ralph Mero reports that hospice care is one of the

TABLE 10-1

Compassion in Dying: Guidelines and Safeguards

Guidelines

Eligibility
- Limited to adult, mentally competent patients who are terminally ill.
- Patient's condition must cause severe, intolerable suffering.
- Patient must understand condition, prognosis, and alternatives.
- Independent physician must examine patient, review records, and consult with primary care physician to verify eligibility.

Quality of care
- Request for hastened death must not result from inadequate comfort care.
- Request must not be motivated by economic concerns or lack of health insurance.

Process of requesting assistance
- Request must originate with the patient.
- All requests will be kept confidential.
- Any indication of uncertainty cancels the process.
- Requests cannot be made through advance directives.

Mental health considerations
- Professional evaluation may be required to rule out emotional distress.
- Patient must understand and take responsibility for the decision.

Family and religious considerations
- Family must give its approval.
- Spiritual or emotional counseling may be arranged.

Safeguards (partial list)
- Patient must provide three signed written requests.
- There must be a 48-hour waiting period between second and third requests.
- Compassion in Dying representatives meet in person with patient and family.
- Any sign of indecision on the part of the patient, or opposition by the immediate family, cancels the process.
- Review team meets regularly to confirm eligibility and if assistance is warranted.
- The patient may request that Compassion in Dying be present at the time of the death.
- Actual means of hastening death is prescribed by patient's physician and varies according to underlying condition.

alternatives that is explored (Kastenbaum, 1994/1995):

> The development of the hospice movement is one we strongly support. Many patients are able to endure the process of dying because of the

generous provision of morphine and other pain medications which hospice offers. We have an experienced hospice nurse on our board of directors, and we value the advice we receive from hospice personnel. Most of our patients have been certified by their physicians as eligible for hospice care, and some were enrolled in hospice programs when they contacted us. (p. 9)

How does Compassion in Dying respond to the slippery slope question?

COMPASSION can hardly be accused of providing "death on demand." We usually spend at least a month with patients between initial contact and time of death. Our somewhat complicated protocol slows down the process toward suicide to the degree that some patients feel it is not happening fast enough.... COMPASSION seeks to demonstrate that assistance with suicide can be provided carefully and thoughtfully, under the guidance of sensible constraints, and in a manner which will not jeopardize the well-being of vulnerable persons. If anything, our work enables some persons to postpone suicide or avoid it all together. Just the knowledge that control has been regained may be enough to permit some patients to endure their illness until natural death. (p. 9)

We can see that people who favor the sanctioning of assisted death may take markedly different approaches. Please see Table 10-2 for a summary of some of the major differences between the Kevorkian and the Compassion in Dying approaches.

The Oregon Death with Dignity Act

The voters of Oregon took one step further by supporting a measure legalizing assisted death in 1994 and reaffirming it in 1997. The act applies only to terminally ill adults in Oregon. This obviously would have excluded most of the people at whose deaths Dr. Kevorkian assisted because they were not terminally ill. The issue of assisted death for children is seldom discussed. Eligibility for assisted death in Oregon requires that the person be older than 18 years of age and have an incurable and irreversible disease that will proba-

bly produce death within 6 months. This rules out people who have progressively deteriorating conditions but who are not at a high risk for death at the present time.

Numerous procedures and safeguards are built into the law to prevent its abuse, including a 15-day waiting period after the request has been made and a repeat of this request before the physician can write a prescription for a lethal dose of medication. The Oregon Death with Dignity Act has faced repeated challenges from federal courts and the U.S. Justice Department under Attorney General John Ashcroft. There have also been efforts to prohibit federal funding for medical assistance, which would mostly impact low-income people. Oregon's program will continue to receive intense scrutiny by both advocates and opponents of assisted suicide.

What has happened so far? In 2001, 33 physicians wrote 44 prescriptions for lethal doses of medication (Oregon Public Health Services, 2002). Not all these patients actually used the medication, and not all have died. Nineteen ingested the medication, 14 died from their underlying diseases, and 11 were still alive at the end of the

TABLE 10-2

Two Approaches to Assisted Death in the United States

	Kevorkian		Compassion in Dying	
	Yes	*No*	*Yes*	*No*
Patient must be terminally ill.		√	√	
Emotional distress is evaluated by mental health professional.		√	√	
Consultation by a second physician is required.		√	√	
Patient confidentiality is maintained.		√	√	
Close contact is maintained with hospice organizations.		√	√	
Provides the means of death.	√			√

year. The following are the available numbers since inception of the program

Year	Number of Deaths
1998	16
1999	27
2000	27
2001	19

Approximately 30,000 people die in Oregon each year. As can be seen, those choosing the assisted death option comprise a very small fraction of the total. The practicing physicians who participated had an average of 20 years experience and were mostly in the specialties of internal medicine, oncology, and family medicine. The prescribing physician or other health care providers were present at the time of all the deaths. Most of the patients were in their late 60s, and cancer was by far the most common primary illness.

There has been an interesting side effect of the Oregon program: Physicians report that they have been improving their knowledge of pain medications for the terminally ill as well as their skill in recognizing depression and are also referring patients to hospice more frequently (Gazini et al., 2001).

ABORTION

For the past three decades, there has been increasing public and legal support for making one's own life-and-death decisions. The question remains: How far can or should this go? A key concern has been the individual's right to decide. The abortion debate has intensified during the same period. Again, there has been an increase in public and legal support and, again, the nation wrestles with the issue of what conditions or limits should be placed on abortion. However, there is also an obvious difference. A competent adult can decline medical treatment and a limited precedent has been set for requesting assisted death. Courts, legislators, and ethics committees have tried to ensure that the decision represents the individual's own intentions and not the guesses, beliefs, or wishes of others.

The fetus, however, cannot participate in the decision-making process. Who, then, has the right to decide? The woman? Her partner? A doctor? A judge? A religious establishment? Society at large? Everybody? Nobody? The debate about whose decision should stand often brings the rights of the individual and the rights of societal institutions into sharp conflict. The tension crackles among institutions as well. For example, which interpretation of which set of religious teachings should be taken as the will of God? The abortion controversy has its rational arguments pro and con, but powerful emotions often dominate and can lead to actions as extreme as the murder of physicians. It makes sense to begin with some basic facts about abortion.

Basic Facts about Abortion

Some pregnancies do not result in the birth of a live and viable infant. These spontaneous abortions are usually classified as miscarriages, although statisticians sometimes use the term fetal loss. "Strictly defined, abortion is the expulsion or removal of an embryo or fetus from the uterus before it has developed sufficiently to survive outside the mother (before viability)" (DeFrain, 2002, p. 1). This definition implies that we are dealing with infanticide, not abortion, if a healthy fetus, mature enough to be viable, is destroyed or allowed to die from neglect. We focus here on abortion as a choice, an intentioned action.

Most abortions are performed in the first 12 weeks of pregnancy. The earlier the abortion, the simpler the procedure. In recent years, a combination of two drugs (mifepristone and misoprostol) has become frequently used to halt development and expel the embryo. Few serious medical complications have been reported with this procedure. This pharmaceutical innovation is having implications for the abortion debate, as DeFrain (2002) notes:

> Clinics that perform abortions are regularly picketed by antiabortion protesters in the United States, making the experience of obtaining a legal abortion difficult for many women. If use of this method spreads in spite of opposition from antiabortion groups, abortion will become an almost invisible, personal, and relatively private act. (p. 2)

Three other abortion techniques are commonly used during the first trimester. Vacuum aspiration uses a tube to extract fetal tissue. Dilation and curettage and dilation and evacuation are more complex procedures that are performed under general anesthesia in a hospital and also involve the extraction of fetal tissue. These related procedures are mostly used early in the second trimester. Induced labor is sometimes used between the fourth and sixth months. Medications result in the delivery of a lifeless fetus. Most radical and controversial are late-term abortions, conducted 4 or 5 months into the pregnancy. Now also known as partial-birth abortions, this procedure destroys the brain of the infant and delivers the body. This type of abortion has been banned by laws in 23 states, and others might follow.[1] Approximately 9 out of 10 abortions in the United States occur in the first trimester and therefore require the less invasive procedures. Abortion is not rare. An estimated 46 million abortions occur throughout the world each year, of which nearly 4 out of 5 are in developing countries in which family size exceeds available resources.

Abortion was neither a crime nor a major issue in the United States until it came to public attention when newspapers started to advertise abortion-inducing preparations. Moralists quickly rallied against abortion as a way of concealing extramarital affairs and thereby corrupting the nation's values. Antiabortion measures were signed into law throughout most of the nation by the early 1900s. Women had no enfranchised voice in this development because almost all politicians were males and women had not yet been given the constitutional right to vote. It is unknown how many potential abortions were prevented by the criminalization of abortion. However, it soon became clear that abortions were still taking place but under more unsanitary and dangerous conditions, too often at the hands of careless or unskilled practitioners.

The rules changed again in 1973 in the historic Roe vs. Wade case when the U.S. Supreme Court concluded that states did not have the right to regulate early term abortions: This decision must be left to the woman and her physician. However, some power was placed in the hands of local jurisdictions: States could regulate facilities and personnel who performed second-trimester abortions and could not only regulate but also ban third-trimester abortions except when necessary to preserve the mother's health or life. Legal abortion in the United States has proven to have a low risk to the mother's health, although the risk increases with advancing stage of pregnancy. For example, the risk of a mother's death as a result of an abortion performed in the first 9 weeks is approximately 1 in 500,000, but increases to 1 in 67,000 between 9 and 12 weeks and 1 in 8,700 after 16 weeks (Gee, 2002). By comparison, the risk for death during pregnancy and childbirth is 1 in 14,300.

The continuing opposition to abortion has been expressed in campaigns to overturn the Roe vs. Wade decision. Meanwhile, public opinion has taken a "permit but discourage" attitude, favoring the continued legality and availability of abortion but suggesting that more efforts be made to reduce the number of abortions (Alan Guttmacher Institute, 1999).

Difficult Issues and Questions

It is not an exaggeration to say that many thoughtful people are tormented by abortion-related issues. I have not come across anybody who believes it is a good thing to destroy a fetus that would otherwise be viable. People on both sides of the issue would prefer that the situation never arises in which a woman feels unable or unwilling to see a pregnancy through. The same person can feel compassion for a woman in a stressful, even overwhelming situation, but also pain for the child who never will be. Unfortunately, mutual respect and effective communication have sometimes been blocked by the strong feelings that are understandably associated with the abortion controversy.

Here are three of the issues that remain as challenges to our hearts and minds:

1. *State policy vs. individual and family needs.* The Chinese government has been severely criticized by international human rights organizations for its policy of limiting married couples to one child and one child only. The policy started with the good intentions of controlling population growth and therefore extricating China from its long-standing cycle of poverty and becoming a more

technologically advanced nation. China has indeed made significant strides toward both goals. The government claims it has prevented 250 million births. However, the stress and pain suffered by the Chinese people, especially in the vast rural regions, has been enormous. The pleasures and supports of family life have been denied to many people—children have been growing up without brothers and sisters. More to the point, the systematic abortion and infanticide of girls has become a national horror and disgrace. An estimated 500,000–750,000 female fetuses are aborted every year after (illegal) ultrasound screening ("China Uses Abortion," 2001). That number does not include the many other babies who are delivered live but then killed or abandoned out of parental desperation. In Chinese tradition, boys have been crucial for supporting the parents in their later years and keeping the family going. The punishment for disobeying the law is harsh, and many abortions are forced on women who want desperately to have the child (Lifesite.net, 2001). The government has been trying to make its policy more humane, but there are still reports of oppression, reprisal, and forced abortion. *How far can or should a government go to regulate birth and pressure for the death of the unborn? What rule or guide would you establish?*

2. *General principle or particular situation?* The Catholic Church's rejection of abortion is the most prominent example of applying a general rule to individual situations. The opposite extreme would be the position that a woman has the right to do whatever she chooses with her body, including its contents. Other positions could also be identified or imagined. However, are any two circumstances identical? Should the realities of a particular situation be considered with an open mind, or is it best to deal with all cases on the basis of a firm and simple rule? (This is not a new dilemma for the Catholic Church: For centuries, "case books" have been prepared to help priests bridge the gap between general rules and the many unique situations they were likely to encounter.) *How would you have it? Establish a general rule and abide by it, encourage flexibility in understanding and responding to particular situations, or somehow find a way to accept rule-oriented guidance but also rely on good judgment in the individual situation?*

3. *When does life and when does personhood begin?* The question of when or in what circumstances life ends (Chapter 3) has its counterpart here. A moment's reflection teaches us that the beginning of a life and the beginning of a human life are not necessarily the same. Sperm and ova are life-forms even if they never meet. The embryo is a different proposition from either sperm or ova. The developing fetus has signficant new attributes. It would be difficult to deny the existence of life before birth. However, when does this become a human life, a person? We can choose to approach this question by reading theological discourses on when in the course of development the soul is created, implanted, or transformed. Instead, we might prefer to rely on developmental psychobiology and judge on the basis of the functions available to a fetus or infant. Then again, we might feel that the anthropologists hold the key to this question as they describe the ways in which a society either bestows or denies personhood even to adults. It has not been unusual for one group of people to consider other groups less than human and, therefore, not equal, not deserving, and not exempt from enslavement and killing. *What is the most realistic, sensible, and humane way to regard the life and personhood of the unborn?*

SUMMARY

There was a time when a few people discussed the right to die from a theoretical perspective. Today, many people are intensely involved in this issue on a personal and practical level. Should terminally ill people have the right to ask a physician to end their suffering by ending their lives? This question has become complicated by factors such as memories of the abuse of eugenics and so-called euthanasia through the past century; differing interpretations of the power of the Hippocratic Oath; concerns about the adequacy of care offered to terminally ill people by physicians; concerns about the failure to take advantage of the palliative care (hospice) options that are now available; the attempt to broaden physician-assisted suicide to include any person who wants to die, terminally ill or not; and the gap between theory and practice in carrying out physician-assisted death. Moral and religious considerations play a significant role in all these issues. While defining our key terms, we explored the unsavory side of some past euthanasia programs and then examined current attitudes toward a right-to-die. We next acquainted ourselves with some of the most important individual cases that brought the right to die issue to national attention and led to the first round of rulings and decision making. Although each case was unique, all revealed the complexities and ambiguities that often confront us in life-and-death situations.

We then devoted sustained attention to physician-assisted suicide, starting with brief looks at developments in The Netherlands and Australia and then focusing on the approach taken by Jack Kevorkian. We learned that there are many troubling questions about the practice of physician-assisted death as carried out by Kevorkian. Next, we examined alternative approaches, such as Compassion in Dying and the Oregon Death with Dignity Act. Finally, we explored the key issues surrounding the abortion issue.

NOTE

1. The following states have banned partial-birth abortion: Alabama, Alaska, Arizona, Arkansas, Florida, Georgia, Illinois, Indiana, Kansas, Louisiana, Michigan, Mississippi, Montana, Nebraska, New Jersey, Ohio, Oklahoma, Rhode Island, South Carolina, South Dakota, Tennessee, Utah, and Virginia. It is possible that other states will be added to this list (www.abortionfacts.com).

REFERENCES

Aging with Dignity. www.agingwithdignity.org.

Alan Guttmacher Institute. (1999). *Induced abortion worldwide.* New York: Author. www.agi-usa-org/pubs/fb-induced-abortion.html.

Annas, G. J. (1984). When suicide prevention becomes brutality: The case of Elizabeth Bouvia. *Hastings Center Report, 13,* 20–21.

Anonymous. (1988). It's over, Debbie. *Journal of the American Medical Association, 259,* 272.

China uses abortion as female genocide. (2001, February 15). CNSNews.com. www.newsmax.com/cgi-bin

Cox, D. W. (1993). *Hemlock's cup.* Buffalo, NY: Prometheus.

DeFrain, J. (2002). Abortion. In R. Kastenbaum (Ed.), *Macmillan encyclopedia of death and dying* (Vol. 1, pp. 1–5). New York: Macmillan.

Edelstein, L. (1943). *The Hippocratic Oath: Text, translation, and interpretation.* Baltimore: Johns Hopkins University Press.

Friedlander, H. (1995). *The origins of Nazi genocide.* Chapel Hill: University of North Carolina Press.

Gazini, L., Nelson, H. D., Schmidt, T. A., Kraemer, D. F., Delorit, M. A., & Lee, M. A. (2001). Physicians' experiences with the Oregon Death with Dignity Act. *New England Journal of Medicine, 342,* 557–563.

Gee, E. (2002) Mortality, childbirth. In R. Kastenbaum (Ed.), *Macmillan encyclopedia of death and dying* (Vol. 2, pp. 585–588). New York: Macmillan.

Gomez, C. R. (1991). *Regulating death.* New York: Free Press.

Groom, W. (2002). *A Storm in Flanders. Tragedy and triumph on the western front.* New York: Atlantic Monthly Press.

Hinrichsen, G. A. (1993). Depression. In R. Kastenbaum (Ed.), *The encyclopedia of adult development* (pp. 106–111). Phoenix, AZ: Oryx Press.

Iserson, K. V. (2002). Persistent vegetative state. In R. Kastenbaum (Ed.), *Macmillan encyclopedia of death and dying* (Vol. 2, pp. 668–669). New York: Macmillan.

Kaplan, K. J. (1998). The case of Dr. Kevorkian and Mr. Gale: A brief historical note. *Omega, Journal of Death and Dying, 36,* 169–176.

Kaplan, K. J., Lachenmeier, F., Harrow, M., O'Dell, J. C., Uziel, O., Schneiderhan, M., & Cheyfitz, K. (2000). Psychosocial versus biomedical risk factors in Kevorkian's first 47 physician-assisted deaths. *Omega, Journal of Death and Dying, 40,* 109–164.

Kaplan, K. J., O'Dell, J., Dragovic, L. J., McKeon, C., Bentley, E., & Telmet, K. J. (2000). An update on Devorkian–Reding 93 physician-assisted deaths in Michigan: Is Kevorkian a savior, serial-killer or suicidal martyr? *Omega, Journal of Death and Dying, 40,* 209–230.

Kastenbaum, R. (1994/1995). Ralph Mero: An Omega interview. *Omega, Journal of Death and Dying, 29,* 1–16.

Kato, H. (1996, June 25). Doctors need re-educating. *Sankei Shimbun (Kyoto).*

Kevorkian, J. (1991). *Prescription: Medicide.* Buffalo, NY: Prometheus.

Kron, J. (1975, October 6). The girl in the coma. *New York Magazine,* 17–24.

Lifton, R. J. (1986). *The Nazi doctors.* New York: Basic Books.

Loving, C. (1995/1996). Nick Loving and Dr. Jack Kevorkian: An Omega interview with Carol Loving. *Omega, Journal of Death and Dying, 32,* 165–178.

Meijburg, H. H. V. D. K. (1995/1996). How health care institutions in The Netherlands approach physician assisted death. *Omega, Journal of Death and Dying, 32,* 179–196.

Nitschke, P. (2000). "Desiring death, dispensing death" by Annette Street and David Kissane: A commentary. *Omega, Journal of Death and Dying, 40,* 249–254.

Oregon's Death with Dignity Annual Report 2002. www.ohd.hr.state.or.us/chs/pas/ar-index.cfm.

Pernick, M. S. (1996). *The black stork.* New York: Oxford University Press.

Quill, T. E. (1993). *Death and dignity.* New York: Free Press.

Robbins, B. (1983). *Last wish.* New York: Linden Press/ Simon & Schuster.

Street, A., & Kissane, D. (2000). Desiring death, dispensing death. *Omega, Journal of Death and Dying, 40,* 231–248.

Times Mirror Center for the People and the Press. (1983). *Reflections of the times: The right to die.* Washington, DC: Author.

U.S. Supreme Court. (1989). Missouri vs. Cruzan. In R. M. Baird & S. E. Rosenbaum (Eds.), *Euthanasia. The moral issues* (pp. 179–212). Buffalo, New York: Prometheus.

GLOSSARY

Advance Directive: A document that specifies the type of health care an individual wishes to receive should that individual not be in a position to express his or her wishes in a critical situation.

Assisted Death: An action taken by one person to end the life of another person, at that other person's request.

Competence: The mental ability to make a rational decision about important matters in one's life (a law concept).

Durable Power of Attorney for Health Care: The transfer of legal authority to a person who would make health care decisions for a person who at that time is unable to make or communicate his or her own decisions.

EEG Tracings: Electrical activity of the brain as displayed on a moving scroll or computer monitor using an electroencephalogram.

Euthanasia: Originally, a pleasant death, one without suffering. Later applied also to actions taken to end a life. "Active" euthanasia involves an action that ends the life; "passive" euthanasia refers to withdrawal or withholding of actions that might prolong life.

Hippocratic Oath: A code presenting ethical principles for the practice of medicine, attributed to a Greek physician of the fifth-century B.C.

Informed Consent: The principle that patients should be provided with sufficient information to make decisions for or against accepting a treatment.

Living Will: The first type of advance directive to be introduced, requesting that no aggressive treatments be attempted if the individual is in the end phase of life.

Mercy Killing: The once again common term for what is now referred to as assisted death.

Orbitoria: Clinics or centers at which assisted death would be provided at patients' request and in which biomedical studies would be conducted.

Patients' Self-Determination Act: A federal law that requires health care organizations to provide patients with the informed opportunity to establish an advance directive to limit medical treatment in specified situations.

Slippery Slope Argument: Holds that accepting assisted death for any person will lead to a moral "slide" that will increase the demand and approval of death for many other people.

Ventilator: A machine that provides respiration for people who are unable to breathe adequately on their own.

For Better or For Worse®   by Lynn Johnston

Do rabbits have spirits, Mom?

I would say that they do.

All living things are filled with energy, and when they die— that energy goes somewhere!

To Heaven?

Maybe

Then... there are pets in Heaven?

I hope so!

'Cause if there's no pets allowed, ...I don't want to go there either!

Is he ok?

Your dad gave him some medication... so he's not in pain.

But, Mom... is he ok?

You know he's not ok, honey. We have a very sick bunny

Do you think he knows what's happening?

I think all animals know when their time has come, April. And they accept it quietly and patiently.

Then, why can't I?

What's April doing?

Holding her bunny. She doesn't want to let him go.

Dear me. When he was healthy, she ignored him most of the time, and now that he's not going to be here much longer, she wants to be with him

But, I guess we're all like that to some extent. We take life for granted, and then when it's too late, we wish we'd spent more time.

That reminds me... I've been meaning to call my folks.

chapter 11

DEATH IN THE WORLD OF CHILDHOOD

The mother died in the hospital, where the children were not allowed to see her. I came to the funeral with the children, where they saw their mother's body in the open casket. The two older children seemed satisfied with just touching their mother and giving her a kiss, but the youngest one wanted to do more. He was about 3 years old, and he wanted to see if he could wake her up.
—Margarita M. Saurez and Susan J. McFeaters (2000, p. 58)

One night, after visiting the cemetery, Coleen asked her father how deep her mother was buried. She seemed relieved when Joseph explained that it was very deep—six feet. Coleen was consoled because she had stepped on the mound and was worried that she had stepped on her mother.
—Grace Hyslop Christ (2000, p. 103)

How was the frog? The frog was dead, dead, dead. What else could it be? We buried it a whole summer ago!
—A 3-year-old girl's report after she and her older brothers checked out the place where they had held the funeral and burial for a frog briefly known the previous summer.

I love the juice, but the sun goes up; I see the stars
and the moonstar goes up,
And there always goes today. And the sun
Love people. But one always dies.
Dogs will die very sooner
Than mummies and daddies and sisters and
brothers because
They'll not die till a hundred an
Because I love them dearly
—Hilary-Anne Farley, age 5, as quoted in Lewis (1966, p. 143)

Children are much more observant of death-related phenomena than many adults have supposed. The ability to enter the child's world of life and death can be immensely valuable in responding to the needs of children as illness, death, and grief enter their lives in one form or another.

RESPECTING THE CHILD'S CONCERN AND CURIOSITY

Mental health professionals as well as the general public often underestimate the child's concern and curiosity about death. It is assumed that children are too young to comprehend the realities of death. We begin by calling this assumption into question.

A publication of the Philadelphia Child Guidance Center (1993) asserts that

> Lacking the ability to appreciate the permanence and gravity of death, very young children are not likely to respond to a specific death with strong emotions.... A child this young does not appear to experience the type of immediate, prolonged, and demonstrative grieving period for a dead loved one that an older child or adult typically does, nor should she or he be influenced to do so. (p. 74)

This dismissal of young children's sensitivity to death and loss is just plain wrong. The youngest of the three children at the funeral wanted to see if he could wake his mother up. (Saurez & McFeaters, 2000):

> I let him try, and he did it as little ones do. First he tried to open her eyelids, and then he touched her face. Finally he called her name. After several attempts he turned to me and said, "I cannot wake her up." He wanted to try again, and I let him try one more time, because through my own Latina cultural filters, there was nothing wrong or disrespectful in touching a dead body. (p. 58)

Did this 3-year-old recognize that death was something of great importance? Did he feel the need to try to bring his mother back to life? Did he have the courage to put his hands on this strangely unresponsive form? Was he lost in a child' fairy-tale world or involved in, literally, a hands-on effort to discover more about death and test the possibilities of resuscitation? How, and why, would we want to dismiss this young child's response as shallow or unrealistic? What about the courage and perspective shown by the adult companion who permitted him to try, even though she knew this would be painful to watch? Observations such as these have been made so often that society has to work very hard at minimizing the importance of death in the world of childhood.

And yet it is true that the young child's conception of death and the dead is the same as the adult's. Coleen had not arrived at the conclusion that the dead feel nothing, not even when you walk on a grave. This attribution of life qualities to the dead probably comes from three factors: her level of mental development, limited experience with death situations, and the cultural milieu from which she was drawing her language, concepts, and attitudes. We will examine these factors in more detail later.

The 3-year-old girl and her brothers who were checking out the frog's grave were indulging their curiosity about the same issue: What is the difference between being alive and dead? Almost all children share this curiosity, and many conduct their own little experiments, often without their parents' knowledge. Burying the frog in the first place (note that it was dead at the time!) was a way of acquiring a sense of partial control over the mysterious phenomena of coming into being and disappearing into nonbeing. The funeral service was not simply an imitation of adult rituals but also a way for them to experience the birth–death–rebirth cycle. None had expected but all had hoped that perhaps the frog would be alive and kicking again. Already sensitive to the fragility of life, these healthy children were vicariously burying and attempting to restore a little of themselves through the fate of the bog dweller.

Hilary-Anne Farley, a Canadian girl only 5 years of age at the time, created a poem that confronted the universal tension between love and death, the very themes that have stimulated so much adult poetry and philosophy through the centuries. She is bursting with love but is acutely aware that time and loss are inevitable: "And there always goes today"; "But one always die." Does this sound like a child who has no clue

Children often learn of death through the loss of a pet. Here a father helps his daughter with the funeral for her goldfish.

about the reality and universality of death? She even recognizes differential longevity and the ambiguity of time. Here is time as the enemy that takes people away, but here also is time as insulation between now and death ("They'll not die till a hundred"). Young Ms. Farley calls on the force of her love and need to protect her family from death. They will live until a hundred "Because I love them dearly." Wish fulfillment? Of course. However, the poem as a whole resolutely faces the reality of death and loss.

It is understandable that adults would want to protect children from the anxiety and sorrow associated with the death of a loved person and from intimations of their own mortality. This impulse to shield children from threatening realities

is almost certainly bound to fail, however. No child is spared the possibility of losing loved ones. No child is exempt from life-threatening risks. No child grows up without noticing that sometimes what is here today is gone tomorrow. Whether we are ready to accept it or not, death is a part of the child's world.

Our exploration begins with the adult's conception of the child's conception of death. Next, we explore the child's understanding of death as observed in both research and natural settings. This is followed by learning how children cope with the death of others and how we can be helpful to them in their grief experiences. Some children also must cope with the possibility of their own death. We will learn much from listening to what these children have said. We then examine our society's tradition of excluding children from participating in life and death decisions that are of personal concern to them. The chapter concludes with guidelines for sharing and responding to children's death concerns.

ADULT ASSUMPTIONS ABOUT CHILDREN AND DEATH

How was the subject of death treated in your home when you were a child? This is the first of several questions that are raised in Box 11-1. Please turn to these questions now. These questions will help you to bring your childhood experiences forward into the present. The activity of writing down your memories will also help you to compare your experiences with those of other people and to think about how these experiences may have influenced your life.

Here are some of the most frequent responses to the first question:

- They sat in dark rooms and became quiet.
- Very hushed and away from us as children. There were 2 deaths and 3 near deaths, from when I was 7 to when I was 10. I felt like I was left out of all of them. No one ever explained anything to me.
- I don't remember any conversations about death with my parents. My Mom went back East for my uncle's funeral and my grandparents' funerals, but I did not go.
- Death was not something that was discussed with children. When my grandfather died, though, it was chaotic. The adults talked to each other about how the death took place. Everyone offered opinions of how the wake and funeral should be carried out. There were arguments and disagreements. All of us kids were completely left out.
- Since I am and come from a Christian home, death was addressed often as a concept and limited to an afterlife. When someone actually did die it was put in perspective with God at the center. For example, "He or she is in a better place…" At times I found this very comforting; at other moments I felt put off by their rehearsed responses.
- After the cat died, we were told about death in that the life is gone. No more movement, no more breath, etc. It seemed to make sense.

BOX 11-1
EXPLORING YOUR EXPERIENCES WITH DEATH IN CHILDHOOD

Write your answers on a separate sheet of paper.

1. How was the subject of death treated in your home when you were a child? What questions did you ask of your parents? What answers did you receive?

2. What most interested or puzzled you about death when you were a young child?

3. Do you remember the death of a pet or other animal at some time in your childhood? What were the circumstances? How did you feel about it? How did other people respond to your feelings?

4. Do you remember the death of a person at some time in your childhood? What were the circumstances? How did you feel about it? How did other people respond to your feelings?

5. Can you identify any ways in which childhood experiences with death may have influenced you to this day?

6. What do you now think is the best thing a parent could say to or do with a child in a death situation and why?

7. What do you now think is the worst thing a person could say to or do with a child in a death situation and why?

Some people remember being given straightforward, naturalistic information, such as that given after the death of the cat. Often, however, families seemed to be following a rule of silence so far as communicating about death with children is concerned. Families develop both explicit and implicit rules to govern their conversations. Book (1996) found that a primary family rule was often: "Do the right thing." This was a "coded" rule in that it really meant "Don't say what you think about death; don't say what you feel about death." Studies of family communication tend to support the impression that children are seldom given the opportunity to participate in open discussion on death-related topics (Corr & Corr, 2002).

Studies also indicate that many adults do not understand how children of a particular age or developmental stage think about death. Blano (1988), for example, not only found that adults misread their children's understanding of death but also, as a consequence, tend to respond inappropriately when interacting with children in death-related situations. Children therefore may be deprived of effective parental comfort and guidance because the two world of experience—the child's and the adult's—have not been bridged.

Why do adults often have such difficulty in communicating with children about death? The answer has much to do with the adults' own fears, doubts, and conflicts. Even in this era of hospice care, grief support groups, and university seminars, many people continue to avoid thinking and speaking of death whenever they can. Perhaps Sigmund Freud (1914) was on the mark when he suggested that, having lost their own childhood innocence, adults want very much to believe that their children live in a fairy-tale world, safe from the stings of reality.

Next, we learn how children themselves think and feel about death. This information can help us to develop more effective ways of responding to children's needs and our own.

CHILDREN DO THINK ABOUT DEATH

The most basic fact has been well established: Children, even young children, do think about death. Evidence comes from many sources.

Early Experiences with Death in Childhood

One of America's first distinguished psychologists, G. Stanley Hall (1922), was also among the first to study aging and death. Hall and his student, Colin Scott, asked adults to recall their earliest experiences with death. These childhood experiences evidently had made a lasting impression because they were recalled in vivid detail:

> The child's exquisite temperature sense feels a chill where it formerly felt heat. Then comes the immobility of face and body where it used to find prompt movements of response. There is no answering kiss, pat, or smile.... Often the half-opened eyes are noticed with awe. The silence and tearfulness of friends are also impressive to the child, who often weeps reflexly or sympathetically. (p. 440)

Hall (1922) adds that funeral and burial scenes sometimes were the very earliest of all memories for the adults he studied. Recent studies also find death experiences to be common among adults' earliest memories, as I have found in some of my own research. For example, an Italian American butcher shared his earliest memory with me:

> I was still in the old country. We all lived in a big old house, me, my family and all kinds of relatives. I remember it was just a few days after my fourth birthday, and there was grandmother laid out on a table in the front room. The room was full of women crying their eyes out. Hey, I didn't want any part of it, but somebody said grandmother was just sleeping. I doubted that very much. Grandmother never slept on a table in the front room with everybody crying their eyes out before. But what I really remember most is what I want to forget most. "Kiss your grandmother!" Yeah, that's right. They made me walk right up and kiss grandmother. I can still see her face. And I can still feel her face. Is that crazy? I mean, after all these years, I can still feel her cold dead face and my lips against it.

Although this man was the owner of a specialty meat shop and its chief butcher, he reported feeling panic on those few occasions when he has been in the presence of a human corpse. The early childhood experience with death had somehow become part of his adult personality. Another compelling example was reported by a college student to another researcher who was inquiring into earliest memories (Dickinson, 1986):

> As a young child, I would receive ducks and chickens as an Easter present. One of these chicks was able to survive the playing and was able to grow into a nice white hen. She was my pride and joy, following me and coming when I called. The hen stayed at my grandmother's. One Sunday dinner the main course was "fried chicken." It took me several minutes to realize just what had happened. To say the least, I was devastated and do not eat chicken to this day. (p. 83)

In a follow-up study, Dickinson (1992) found that college students still had intense memories of their early childhood experiences with death. It was startling to learn how anger, "outright hatred at times," continued to be felt toward "a parent who had killed the (pet) animal, whether it was a parent who had accidentally run over the animal or the vet who 'put the animal to sleep'" (p. 172). The explanations given to them by their parents in childhood were often felt to be unsatisfactory. Often, the children had been told that a deceased person had gone to heaven. Some had been reassured because heaven was said to be a happy place. One 4-year-old girl, however, became upset when her father told her that her kitten "went to heaven to be with God." She responded, "Why does God want a dead kitten?" A 3-year-old also became angry when told her grandmother had gone to heaven: "I don't want her in heaven. I want her here!" Not only are young children affected by death-related events but also they may recall these experiences with intense emotions many years later.

The childhood loss and death theme was again evident in research interviews several students and I conducted with residents of Sun City and Sun City West, Arizona. These people were asked not for their earliest experiences with death but for their earliest memories of any kind. The respondents went back at least 60 years and sometimes more than 80 for their memories. Many incidents were pleasant to recall; others were odd and difficult to explain. However, more than one

person in three reported an earliest memory that conveyed some encounter with death, loss, or separation:

- "The green chair nobody sat in anymore. I remember going into the room and out of the room and back into the room time after time. Maybe grandfather would be sitting in his chair the next time I entered the room. I know I was 4 because I just had a birthday with four candles on the cake."
- "There were lots of people in the street, and there had been some kind of accident. I wanted to see what. A horse was on the ground and there was a twisted up, tipped over cart behind it. Somebody, a man, was saying they ought to shoot it. I got one look and then somebody pushed me away or led me away. I don't know what I thought about it at the time, but I can still see that horse."

Studies such as these indicate that the young child's experiences of death and loss may become lifelong memories for the adult. Perhaps you also found some death or loss/separation memories coming to mind when you answered the questions about your own childhood experiences. Some readers of this book have taken their early memories as the starting point for their personal research. One young woman, for example, recalled having felt very much alone and frightened, "and there was something about the ocean and the beach in it." No other details came to mind from this memory that seemed to have taken place just before her kindergarten days. She decided to ask her parents what had actually happened. They were reluctant, but,

> then we had one of our best talks ever! Mom had had a miscarriage and the doctor had said she couldn't have any more babies or she might die herself. It never occurred to them to say any of this to a little kid like me. But while we were talking I suddenly remembered them getting rid of baby things, a crib and all, giving them away, and my mother looking real strange and distant. And that was when they sent me to live with a family I didn't like much so they could also get away a few days, together, and try to feel normal again. I can understand that perfectly now. But then, it

was like they were going to get rid of me, too! And in my little kid's mind, the beach and the ocean were part of it all. Maybe they were going to leave me all by myself on the beach, or maybe a big wave was going to come and get me!

This student had developed a pattern of avoiding beaches and large bodies of water, although she was also attracted to these places. The frank conversation with her family not only helped her understand the unpleasant and unaccountable early memory but also dissipated her anxieties about going to the beach. Many other students have found that it was possible to gain a better understanding of some of their ways of thinking simply by bringing early memories to mind. A graduate student of social work reported that "I think I know now why I'm so crazy about stuffed animals! I had my favorite kitten squashed by a truck, and then the mother cat, too, by some kind of vehicle. And then, all in the same short period of time, a coyote killed our old family dog. Stuffed animals have a much better life expectancy!"

Your childhood memories of death-related experiences may be quite different from these. It would be going much too far to say that a particular childhood experience "causes" us to behave or feel in a particular way in adult life. Nevertheless, it is clear that childhood experiences tinged with death, loss, or separation can become significant influences on the way we view life and cope with death. Most of us carry in our memories our own personal historical evidence for childhood encounters with death.

Death in the Songs and Games of Childhood

Cultural history provides examples of a broader scale. The "innocent" songs and games of childhood through the centuries have often centered on death themes. The familiar ring-around-the rosie song and game achieved popularity during the peak years of the plague in 14th-century Europe. The "rosies" referred to one of the symptoms of the disease; the "all fall down" is self-explanatory. The children who enacted this little drama were acutely aware that people all around

them were falling victim to the plague. We can imagine the security they sought by joining hands. The ritual impersonated the trauma and separation of death. Helpless passivity and fear were transformed into a group effort to actively master the threat. Today, this game may seem quaint and innocuous. In its heyday, though, ring-around-the-rosie represented both an acknowledgment of the prevalence of uncontrolled death in the environment and the impulse to share and master death-related anxiety. The children who had fallen to the earth would leap to their feet with joyful shouts after completing the ring-around-the-rosie dance. For the moment, at least, they were still very much alive.

The death theme is explicit in many hide-and-seek and tag games, such as "Dead Man Arise!" This type of game has many names and local variations. In Sicily, for example, children played "A Morsi Sanzuni" (Opie & Opie, 1969):

One child lay down pretending to be dead while his companions sang a dirge, occasionally going up to the body and lifting an arm or a leg to make sure the player was dead, and nearly stifling the child with parting kisses. Suddenly he would jump up, chase his mourners, and try to mount the back of one of them…. In Czechoslovakia… the recumbent player was covered with leaves, or had her frock held over her face. The players then made a circle and counted the chimes of the clock, but each time "Death" replied, "I must still sleep." This continued until the clock struck 12 when, as in some other European games, the sleeping player sprung to life and tried to catch someone. (p. 107)

In tag games the person who is "It" must not peek or move while the other players conceal themselves. The touch of "It" is both scary and thrilling—almost a training ground for future Count Draculas. Even the slightest touch has grave significance: The victim instantly is transformed from lively participant to death personified ("It"). Further resemblances to death are suggested in those variations in which the victim must freeze (enter suspended animation?) until rescued by one who is still free (alive?).

Historical observations strongly suggest that concern with death has been a common theme in children's play through the centuries. This tradition continues today with computer-mediated destruction games that compete with each other for violent special effects. As a child in the streets of New York, my friends and I played variations of cops-and-robbers, mostly sporting wooden guns (some armed with rubber bands). In other streets many centuries before, medieval children brandished their "swords" as they replayed the Crusader–Saracen battles. Our technologically advanced society provides children and adolescents with ready-made games in which there is no personal relationship between killer and slain and in which the object often is to inflict death in violent and humiliating ways. There is well-founded concern that aggressive video games (and television violence) increase similar behavior on the part of children (Wass, 2002). It is also possible that the child's attitude toward death can be distorted by emphasis on the act rather than the consequences of killing. A coalition of parents persuaded major retail stores to remove the most extreme of these games from their shelves. Nevertheless, it remains a paradox that death games should be such a popular item in a society that finds it so difficult to think of death and to communicate about death with its children.

Research and Clinical Evidence

It is the rule rather than the exception for children to include death among their interests and concerns. The following are examples from my collection of verified observations:

• A boy, aged 16 months, was taken to a public garden by his father, an eminent biomedical scientist. This was a regular visit, one of their favorite expeditions together. The boy's attention was captured by a fuzzy caterpillar creeping along the sidewalk. Suddenly, large adult feet came into view, and the caterpillar was crushed (unwittingly) by another visitor to the garden. Immediately the boy showed an alarmed expression. He then bent over the remains, studying them intently. After a long moment, he stood up and informed his father, in a sad and resigned voice, "No more!" "No more!" Can there be a more direct and concise comment? From that moment the boy expressed an aversion to being in the public garden, looking with distress at fallen blossoms that he had not previously seemed to notice. It took several comforting attempts from his father before he would again visit this place of beauty and of death.

• An 18-month-old discovered a dead bird on the ground as he and his father walked through the woods. The boy crouched over by the bird, his face taking on an expression of the classic Greek mask of tragedy. "Bird!" he said. "Yes," his father replied, "A bird; a dead bird." For the next several days the boy would make sure to visit the dead bird, looking at it very carefully but not saying anything. One day there was a crisp autumn breeze, and leaves floated down from the trees. The boy picked up a leaf and handed it to his father, insisting with great determination that his father place the leaf back on the tree. The father said this could not be done, but, with the boy's insistence, he tried. The leaf would not stay put. The father tried again and again. The boy then looked sad and turned away. He never asked again to have a leaf restored to its tree, nor did he look again at the dead bird.

There was no doubt in the minds of these very young children that death was something special that required special thoughts and actions. Older children explored ways of expressing and overcoming the sorrow of loss:

• An 8-year-old boy was improvising—loudly—at the piano. His father approached him with the intention of asking him to cease and desist but noticed that the pianist was in a mood of deep contemplation, not just idly banging away. "What are you playing?" the father asked. The boy replied, "A funeral song for Lovey" (the family cat, which was recently killed on the highway). As the boy continued his improvisations, he explained the meaning of each passage, "This is Lovey sharpening her claws on a tree.... This is Lovey when she has just heard the can opener.... This is Lovey curled up and purring."

Again, there can be no doubt that this child understood something of death's significance and felt the need and obligation to perform some ritual in honor of the deceased. From direct observation, clinical experience, and systematic research there is ample evidence that children do think of death. We examine this development in more detail next, drawing first on research case histories and then on larger scale studies.

Research Case Histories

Research findings are usually conveyed through statistics, and appropriately so. This custom, however, often fails to convey the reality of individual differences as well as the patterning of thoughts and actions within the individual. Three brief case histories drawn from my research will enable you to glimpse individual and family patterns. A general review of research findings will follow. For the present purposes, this section concentrates on data obtained in structured interviews with the mothers of school children.

Teresa

Teresa is a 7-year-old described by her mother as a quiet girl who enjoys her own company: "She's just a very nice girl, not afraid to express any emotions at all." Teresa is especially inter-

ested in plants and how they grow and is much involved in her family as a unit. The following is an interview with Teresa's mother.

INTERVIEWER: Has death come into Teresa's life?

MOTHER: My mother died, her grandmother, in January of this year…we all knew she was dying. I told Teresa and I told June [her sister] that she was dying. They wanted to know, "What is dying, where is she going to go, why is she going, why is she leaving me? She's my Grandma! I don't want her to die!"…And she was just very curious about the whole business of the wake and the funeral and "Why do we have to do this, why do we have to do that." The big thing was, "I don't want to see other people sad, because it makes me sad."

INTERVIEWER: How did Teresa respond to the death when it actually came?

MOTHER: She comforted me. She came to me. She would cry when I cried. She would put her arms around me and she would say, "Please don't cry; everything will be all right. Grandma

Children who have been touched by death, especially sudden and violent, may find expression for their feelings in games of destruction.

isn't suffering anymore. Grandma is happy now."

The death was experienced as a major loss by everybody in the family. Grandma was 54 at the time of her death and had been very close to the whole family although not living with them. "My mother was my best friend and she was also my children's best friend," Teresa's mother said.

INTERVIEWER: What did Teresa understand about Grandma's death?

MOTHER: She understands that she [Grandma] was put in the ground in that cold outer casket, but Teresa realizes that she is not there. She's in spirit, beside her, watching and loving her always. And Teresa sees a bird—my mother was a bird freak—and she said, "I wonder if Grandma can see that bird?" You know, she's very much into, very aware that Grandma is around her, spiritually, not physically.

INTERVIEWER: What did Teresa not understand about this death?

MOTHER: She still doesn't understand why. You know, why take her from us now, she wasn't old; she was a young woman. Why was she so sick, you know. What did she do? Did she do something bad?

INTERVIEWER: Does Teresa have any death concerns or fears?

MOTHER: I think she'd be very much afraid of losing me at this point because since my mother has died she's becoming extremely touchy with me; she gets a little bit upset when I have to go out, you know. "Please come back soon!" I think she relates it to losing me, to maybe her fears of losing her own mother.

INTERVIEWER: How have you answered her questions about death?

MOTHER: Well, as far as the religious, we don't get into it at my house, you know. I don't want to get into hell and heaven and that, because I don't want them to get hung up on it.... I really don't think we discussed it, you know, before it actually hit us;

we never really discussed it with the children.

INTERVIEWER: Has it been difficult to discuss death with Teresa?

MOTHER: Not with Teresa, not at all. With June, yes, but not with Teresa.

INTERVIEWER: How do you feel in general about the way Teresa thinks about death?

MOTHER: I think she's got her head pretty well together. She's really probably done better than I have.... Two or 3 months after my mother died, I was sitting by myself, having my crying jag and getting it all out, and Teresa got up out of bed. You know, I was sitting in the dark. I just knew it was coming. I had put them to bed. So she got up, and she came beside me and she said, "Mama, I know why you're crying." And I said, "Why, Teresa?" And she said, "Because you miss your mother." And I said, "You're right." And Teresa said, "But you always have to remember, how good she was to us, remember she used to take us uptown and buy us ice cream and she used to sing us songs and remember when she bought me this bracelet." And within a matter of, say 3 minutes, I felt so relieved, like, you know, tons had been lifted off me; from this 7-year-old child, you know, really laying it on me and telling me, come on, you know, you got to go on living.... And the oldest one (June) will not discuss it at all. You know, it's too bad.

INTERVIEWER: Do you have any questions of your own about what to do with a child in things related to death?

MOTHER: There are things I don't know, and so I wouldn't know how to explain it to them. I don't know how to make it easier for them.... This is a society where everybody dies—why do you grieve then? Why is there a wake, why is there a funeral? There are things I don't understand so I'm sure they don't understand, you know, why the pain?

INTERVIEWER: Should parents and children discuss death together?

MOTHER: It's very important, so very important! I can remember my own first experience with death and how frightened I was of it. I think it's something that should be talked about in a family and…I'm having a hard time expressing myself, but I really think that when people die, that we love, we shouldn't have to grieve…why do they put us through the wakes, the funeral? This is what we saw when we were children; we saw grieving after death—and my children will grieve over death.

INTERVIEWER: What is the worst thing a parent could say or do with a child in a death situation?

MOTHER: I would hate to stifle emotions. I would hate to say, "Stop all that crying!" Or, the other thing is, "He's gone away for a vacation. He's left us, but he'll come back." That's a bunch of lies and children see through these things.

INTERVIEWER: What is the best thing a parent could say or do with a child in a death situation?

MOTHER: Let the children see what goes on. Let them be totally involved with the family, to be able to express with the family their own emotions and to be totally included in what goes on instead of shifted off to a friend's house.

INTERVIEWER: How curious about death were you when you were Teresa's age?

MOTHER: I wasn't at all…until I was about 10 years old.… I lost my cat and I remember, I cried all day upstairs in my room because I thought: This is death. I'm going to lose my mother. And I cried and cried and I was so scared and I had nightmares.

INTERVIEWER: How was death handled in your home when you were growing up?

MOTHER: It wasn't. I said to my mother once, "I'm so afraid that you were going to die." And she just said, "I'm not going to die." And…she died. [These words were spoken very softly and sadly.]

INTERVIEWER: Was that the way she should have handled it, or what do you think she should have done instead?

MOTHER: I think that she should have drawn more out of me and really given me time that I needed, and maybe have said—well, I don't know what you can say to a child to make it any easier when there is a threat, a scare of losing a parent, but just be able to sit down and discuss it.

INTERVIEWER: What are your thoughts and feelings about death now?

MOTHER: Since my first death was my mother, I think it was very hard.… I just accept the fact that she is dead and I will no longer see her, but I just hang on to the thought that she's not suffering and that she knew she was dying even though nobody told her.… She said more with her eyes, more than anything else in the world. I feel very…I feel peace within myself.

INTERVIEWER: Did she tell you her thoughts or feelings at all?

MOTHER: No, she was aphasic…and paralyzed. She couldn't talk. The only thing she could do was move one arm and one hand and the night before she died, we went in there and they took her out of the special care unit and just took off the respirator and let her die and she just kept pointing up to heaven. She knew she was dying and she just…made us feel at ease. Because I was glad she knew, and she knew that I knew so we wouldn't have to play the game: "Okay, Ma, we'll get you out of here in a couple of weeks." It was kind of peace, you know, that we shared.

INTERVIEWER: Is there anything you would like to add?

MOTHER: I think we should teach children about death in schools. I don't mean we shouldn't teach them at home, but in school, too. Let people know what often happens in grief, so they won't be so surprised.... Should start early because it's like sex education, you know, you almost don't talk about it until it happens, until there is a problem.

Stanley

Stanley is another 7-year-old who is described by his mother as "just the nicest boy a mother could ever want. Does what you tell him to—most of the time.... His life is pretty much centered around the family and his dog."

INTERVIEWER: What does Stanley understand about death?

MOTHER: That whoever would die they're not going to see again and that's about all. As far as feeling for the person, he hasn't come to that stage yet.... We have a dog and if he died I wouldn't know what he would feel. I really don't. I would say he would be too little to think much about it.

INTERVIEWER: What does Stanley not understand about death?

MOTHER: What the purpose of death is. Why we were put on the earth for a reason and why we're going to die. Stanley is definitely too little to understand why somebody's laying in a casket. Especially if it is somebody young. Why is that person dead? You try to explain to him that God put him on this earth but He called him back. He wanted him back. I don't think he can comprehend that at all.... When a little boy dies, I tell him the little boy was very sick and God wanted him back.

INTERVIEWER: How have you answered Stanley's questions about death?

MOTHER: Sometimes I tell him that the person was very old and very sick. If it was a little boy, that the little boy was very sick and God wanted him back.... God put us here but He isn't going to let us stay here. We're all here temporarily and even though you boys are little doesn't mean you couldn't die tomorrow. Even Stanley, I told

him, you could die tomorrow. I could die tomorrow. We don't know when. God doesn't tell us. It doesn't mean that just sick people die. Anybody can die—people get hit by cars.

INTERVIEWER: What is the worst thing a parent could say or do with a child in a death situation?

MOTHER: To hide it from them. If you want to cry, cry. That's the best thing. Make him experience it with you. Why not? They've got to be exposed to it the way it is.

INTERVIEWER: How was death handled in your home when you were growing up?

MOTHER: My parents shielded us from all of that.... We never got the answers we really wanted, so as a result we stopped asking. That was about anything, even about death.... But death can bring people together, it's just that in our family it didn't. Would have been nice if our parents had let us join in, instead of getting our relatives to babysit us while they went and did it all...going to the funerals and all of that.... I would have liked to have been at their side.

INTERVIEWER: What are your thoughts and feelings about death now?

MOTHER: I'm very conscious about death now. It panics me, truthfully, it really panics me. I know we can't live forever. If I knew I was dying, I just wouldn't want to wake up in the morning, that's all. That's how I would want it to be for me and yet it's probably the easy way out. I'm not too happy about other people dying either.... Dead people are supposed to be with God. We're supposed to be happy but we still can't. Part of us says we are—part of us says we're not!

Brian

Brian is 8 years old and "a bright boy with lots of curiosity. He's especially interested in rocks and minerals, gems, animals, underwater stories. He reads about them all the time, and talks about anything. But not death."

INTERVIEWER: What does Brian understand about death?

MOTHER: Oh, he understands it…I think. But he doesn't really like to talk about it. He doesn't like the idea that any of us will die. Like he said to me, "You'll never, never die, Mom." I tried to explain to him, well, that's not true, that I will die and so will Daddy, and when that time comes he must accept it because that's part of living. He understands what I'm saying. You can see that from the look in his eyes. But it makes him very, very sad, and he'll go, "I don't want to talk about that, I'd rather not—please, Mom!"

INTERVIEWER: What does Brian not understand about death?

MOTHER: Only one thing I can think of. His Daddy likes to hunt. He goes deer hunting and he killed, you know, a young deer. Brian couldn't quite understand that. He thought the deer was so beautiful and to kill him…. Well, we had to tell him why he killed the deer, and the deer hurt, and if he wasn't killed, if so many deer weren't killed a year, the balance of nature would be off.

INTERVIEWER: Does Brian have any death concerns or fears?

MOTHER: Losing one of us that he loves. He's very, very close to Cris [his sister] so, of course, he doesn't want her to leave the house. He's often said this. If she doesn't come home when she said she's supposed to come home he'll call me and say, "I'm awfully worried because she's out in the car, if she has an accident and gets killed, Mom, I don't know what I'll do." And I mean upset. I've seen him cry and tears going down his face and he'll say, "I would just die if my Crissy dies."

INTERVIEWER: What is the worst thing a parent could say or do with a child in a death situation?

MOTHER: Well, I'm going to say this from experience. I think the worst thing to do is not let the child grieve. To tell them they can't cry…bottling up these emotions does something to that person and carries on into their adult life. It does irreparable damage if you ask me, and I guess you did.

INTERVIEWER: How was death handled in your home when you were growing up?

MOTHER: Nobody prepared me for it, nobody answered my questions, nobody told me one thing or the other. "I don't want to talk about it," would be the answer, or, "I don't know why you ask me such foolish questions."

INTERVIEWER: What are your thoughts and feelings about death now?

MOTHER: Now, it's much different. I feel the more I think of it, the more at peace I feel with the fact that death is going to come. When I was younger I was hoping, oh, I'd never die, and now I know that I am, and the time comes I don't think I'll be afraid to die…. I have more acceptance of the fact of death now than I did when I was—even 10 years ago or even 5 years ago…. I think it comes with time, you're more at peace with yourself. Even so, having children makes death more important in a way, too, your responsibility to them.

Reflections and Questions

Young as they are, Teresa, Stanley, and Brian already differ in their experiences and concerns. A thorough analysis of their orientations toward death would need to take into account both their individual personalities and what they have in common as children growing up at a particular time in history. The following are a few reflections and questions on these research case history excerpts:

1. It is not so much death in general, but the death of particular people or animals that arouses the children's concern: Grandma for Teresa and Crissy and the deer for Brian. The possibility (Crissy) as well as the actuality (Grandma) of death can stimulate thought and feeling. Stanley is confronted with specific death concerns by his

mother ("you could die tomorrow. I could die tomorrow"). Many studies have focused on the ability of the child to formulate abstract conceptions of death. Although this is a significant question, it should not lead us to forget that thoughts of death most often arise around specific incidents and contexts. Children do not have to comprehend death in its most abstract aspects to recognize that it threatens their relationships with the people who are important to them.

2. Could we understand the differing death orientations of Teresa, Stanley, and Brian if we focused only on the children? It is doubtful. Experiences, attitudes, and ways of coping with death are part of the intimate flow of life between children and their parents. The influence can go in both directions. Brian's questions about the slain deer, for example, and his apparently exaggerated fear for Crissy's well-being present challenges for the parents' own attitudes toward death.

3. There may be differing orientations toward death within the same household. Teresa and June, for example, differ in their openness to discussion of death. A specific death may have varying effects on the children, depending on their developmental phase, personality, and position in the family. It is important to become well acquainted with the entire family constellation if we want to understand the implications of one particular child's view of death. From other data it was clear that Brian, as the only boy in the family, wanted very much to be like his father—but does this mean he, too, will have to go deer hunting? If he were not first in the "line of succession," perhaps the slain deer would have taken on a different meaning.

4. Teresa's mother is a sensitive person who favors an open communication process and who reflects thoughtfully on her own behavior as well as her children's. However, she has not been able to cope with death-related problems to her own complete satisfaction. She has unresolved questions in some areas, such as the value of funerals and the grief process in particular. Despite these unresolved concerns, Teresa's mother shows flexibility and the ability to learn from experience. In contrast, Stanley's mother does not seem to have sorted out her own assumptions about life and death. When Stanley notices a death-related incident, his mother is not likely to use this as an occasion to reflect on her own thoughts and values or really share the experience with her son. Instead, she relies on passing along a received dogma that has been familiar to her since her own childhood but never much thought about. The abstraction level and tone of her explanation were of doubtful help to Stanley. Parents who are not able to cope with a child's death-related curiosity on a simple, naturalistic level because of their own discomfort may be perpetuating the anxieties for still another generation. Imagine Stanley's thoughts after his mother's explanation: "God does not want healthy people? Is it wrong to want people to live? Is God the enemy who takes my friends away? Do I have to get very sick and die to be loved by God?" I have, in fact, heard reflections of this type from children whose curiosity about death was answered by verbose patter that seemed to place the blame on God. On the topic of death, as on any other topic, it is useful to understand something of the child's frame of reference before unloading one of our "standard explanations."

5. Although Teresa's mother had a warm and loving childhood, the topic of death had been glossed over by her parents. This has made it more difficult to cope with both the death of her mother—who had promised she was not going to die—and the feelings of her own daughters. Brian's and Stanley's mothers likewise grew up in homes in which death was not to be discussed with the children. This background of death avoidance in the childhood home is typical for the mothers in our study. Today's young mothers in general seem to be more aware of the value of discussing death with their children as part of their general preparation for life. However, most often they have not benefited from such good examples in their own homes while growing up. *We now have a transitional generation of parents who are trying to relate to their children in an area that was off limits when they themselves were young. This leads to second guessing of their own responses:* "Did I say the right thing?" Eventually, however, the new openness should make death a less divisive topic between parent and child in generations to come.

It is not by accident that the research case histories sampled here are based on the mothers' reports (Box 11-2). Children have fathers, too, but they have been less willing to discuss this subject. Family death education seems to be viewed as something for mothers to handle.

CONCEPTS OF DEATH: DEVELOPING THROUGH EXPERIENCE

It is clear that death has a place in the thoughts of children. But just what do children make of death? How do their ideas develop from early childhood onward? Early studies emphasized the importance of maturation. Children's understanding of death improved along with the general development of their mental abilities. Later studies indicate that life experiences also play a significant role. A 13-year-old, for example, generally will show an understanding of death that is more accurate and complete than that of a 4-year-old. However, is this because the older child has developed more advanced cognitive structures, or is it simply because the older child has had an additional 9 years of life experience from which to learn?

Recent studies indicate that the child's understanding of death is influenced by both maturation level and life experience, although much remains to be learned about the interaction of these factors. The specific interplay between maturation and experience is difficult to establish, no matter whether we are concerned with concepts of death or any other facet of the child's overall comprehension of reality.

"Auntie Death's" Pioneering Study

Our understanding of the way children think about death has been greatly influenced by a pioneering study that is worth reviewing in detail. Hungarian psychologist Maria Nagy (1948/ 1969) invited 378 children, ranging in age from 3 to 10 years, to express their death-related thoughts and feelings. The children came from a variety of social and religious backgrounds. The older children were asked to draw pictures and to "write down everything that comes to your mind about death." Children of all ages were engaged in conversation on the subject. As she reviewed the children's words and pictures, Nagy found that three age-related stages could be established (Table 11-1).

Stage 1

Stage 1 includes the youngest children, from the third until approximately the fifth year. These very young children regarded death as a continuation of life but in a diminished form. The dead are simply less alive. They cannot see and hear—well, maybe they can, but not very well. They are not as hungry as the living. They do not do much. Being dead and being asleep are

---

BOX 11-2
LESSONS FROM THE RESEARCH CASE HISTORIES

- It is the death of particular people or animals that enlists the child's concern.

- Death-related experiences, attitudes, and behaviors are part of the intimate flow of life between children and their parents.

- There may be several different orientations toward death within the same household.

- Parents whose own discomfort interferes with their response to their children's death-related

curiosity are likely to perpetuate these anxieties for another generation.

- There is now a transitional generation of parents who are trying to communicate in an open manner with their children, although their own experience was of family silence about death.

TABLE 11-1

Stages of Death Comprehension in Childhood (Nagy)

Stage	Age Range	Interpretation of Death
1	3–5	Death is separation. The dead are less alive. Very curious about death.
2	5–9	Death is final, but one might escape it! Death is seen as a person.
3	9–adult	Death is personal, universal, final, and inevitable.

seen as similar conditions. The youngest children also thought of death as temporary. The dead might return, just as the sleeping might wake up (remember the 3-year-old boy at his mother's funeral?). Uppermost in the minds of many children was the theme of death as departure and separation.

We might call this a functional conception based on the survivor's own situation: The dead person is gone, not with us, and not able to provide comfort, companionship, and protection. What has actually become of the dead person may be a matter of guesswork, imagination, and wishful thinking, sleep is a familiar activity that offers a promising comparison. However, it is the *absence* of that person that is most obvious and most compelling.

Nagy noticed that the preschoolers were very curious about death. They were full of questions about the details of the funeral, the coffin, the cemetery, and so on. The child's active engagement with the challenge of comprehending death was also noted repeatedly by Sylvia Anthony (1940/1972). These very young children did not seem to understand death adequately by adult standards, but what they did think about it was powerful enough to arouse negative feelings (Brian's anxiety comes to mind, as do the childhood experiences of all three mothers in the case history excerpts). For Nagy's respondents, death at the very least did not seem to be much fun— lying around in a coffin all day, and all night, too. The dead might be sleeping, which is acceptable

but boring, or they might be scared and lonely, away from all their friends. It would seem that young children were attributing some of their own thoughts and feelings to the dead.

The combination of what the young child knows and does not know about death can arouse anxiety. "He would like to come out, but the coffin is nailed down," one 5-year-old told "Auntie Death," the name bestowed on the psychologist by the children. This comment suggests the fear of being buried alive that in some times and places has also been prevalent among adults. It also suggests that people are being cruel to the deceased by nailing down the coffin. The possibilities for further misinterpretations and ill feelings based on this limited conception of death are considerable, especially if the adults on the scene fail to understand how the child is likely to interpret death-related phenomena.

Stage 2

Stage 2 begins at age 5 or 6 and persists until about the ninth year. The child now recognizes that *death is final*. The older the child within this age range, the more firm the conclusion. The dead do not return. Another new theme also emerged during this stage in Nagy's (1948/1969) sample. Many of the children represented death as a person. Interestingly, personification is one of humankind's most ancient modes of expressing the relationship with death. One 9-year-old confided,

> Death is very dangerous. You never know what minute he is going to carry you off with him. Death is invisible, something nobody has ever seen in all the world. But at night he comes to everybody and carries them off with him. Death is like a skeleton. All the parts are made of bone. But then when it begins to be light, when it's morning, there's not a trace of him. It's that dangerous, death. (p. 11)

The association of death with darkness is an ancient habit of mind, expressed by people in the earliest civilizations that have left us record. The other side of this idea is the equation of light with life. It is not unusual for the child's conception of death to include elements that once were the common property of adults.

The personification of death as a skeleton was fairly common in Nagy's sample of 5- to 9-year-olds. For Nagy's respondents, death personifications were often fearful, representing enormous if mysterious power. Some Stage 2 children added threats or lethal wishes to their personifications. As Nagy (1948/1969) reports, "Kill the death-man so we will not die" was a frequent comment. Some children also depicted death as a circus clown—supposedly the embodiment of mirth and good times. Other children saw dead people as representing death, whereas still others personified death in the form of angels. Even angelic death, however, did not remove the sting of fear. "The death angels are great enemies of people," declared a 7-year-old. "Death is the king of the angels. The angels work for death."

There is at least one more significant characteristic of Stage 2, according to Nagy (1948/1969). *The realization of death's finality is accompanied by the belief that this fate might still be eluded.* The clever or fortunate person might not be caught by the "death-man." This idea also shows up in specific modes of death. A child might be killed crossing the street, for example. However, if children are very careful in crossing the street, they will not be run over, and therefore they will not die. In other words, children in this age range tend to see death as an outside force or personified agent. "It's that dangerous, death." However, the saving grace is that you do not absolutely have to die. Death is not recognized as universal and personal. Perhaps, just perhaps, you can be lucky or clever enough to elude it.

Stage 3

The final stage identified by Nagy (1948/1969) begins at approximately age 9 or 10 and is assumed to continue thereafter. By Stage 3, the child understands that death is *personal, universal, and inevitable* as well as final. All that lives must die, including oneself.

Discussion of death at this age has an adult quality: "Death is the termination of life. Death is destiny. We finish our earthly life. Death is the end of life on earth," declared one 9-year-old boy. A 10-year-old girl added a moral and poetic dimension: "It means the passing of the body. Death is a great squaring of accounts in our lives.

It is a thing from which our bodies cannot be resurrected. It is like the withering of flowers."

This new awareness is compatible with belief in some form of afterlife, as with the 9-year-old boy who said, "Everyone has to die once, but the soul lives on." In fact, it might be argued that the child does not really have a grasp of afterlife concepts until death is appreciated as final and inevitable.

Evaluating Nagy's Contributions

Nagy's findings remain useful today, although the tendency to personify death between ages of 5 and 9 seems to have diminished greatly, according to most follow-up studies. Perhaps this is a change wrought by the new childhood with its exposure to mass media, high technology, and postmodern changes. "Death is like the computer's down and you can't get it started again," one 7-year-old told his mother recently. There also seems to be a tendency for children in America today to move through the stages at an earlier age than did the children studied by Nagy. This may be part of a larger trend in which some aspects of children's cognitive development has been accelerated through exposure to the diverse experiences they encounter in the "information age."

Five-year-old Michael provides an example of the way some young children today are integrating technological developments into their dawning conceptions of dying and death. Researcher E. J. Deveau (1995) comments on his drawing (Fig. 11-1). The researcher notes that

> Michael…is concerned with burial, fantasy, and the world beyond. He integrates modern technology into his account of how god converts the dead into angels after hauling them up to heaven. His description of how people die is very concrete and practical, in keeping with what might be expected at this age. (p. 86)

In the picture, according to Michael, "God uses a machine that turns them into an angel." People die "when they eat bad food, the bad food sticks to their heart and the blood can't get in the heart and then you have a heart attack…or something like that."

FIGURE 11-1
Michael's God Machine. Reprinted with permission from D. W. Adams & E. J. Deveau (eds.), *Beyond the Innocence of Childhood.* Vol. 1; "Perceptions of Death Through the Eyes of Children and Adolescents," Amityville, NY: Baywood, 1995.

It is also probable, as Deveau (1995) suggested, that the stages are not absolute and fixed but, rather, represent temporary "resting places" in the child's continuing attempt to come to terms with death both cognitively and emotionally.

Nagy's portrait of the child's development of death concepts has served as a useful guide for many years. We now examine some of the major additions to her findings.

Are Concepts of Death Related to Cognitive Level, Gender, and Social Class?

Nagy organized her findings around the chronological age of her young respondents. This approach worked well, but later researchers have introduced a useful refinement. All children are not alike at a particular age. Some are further along in their physical, mental, social, and emotional development. A review of the literature (Kenyon, 2001) concludes that children with superior intellectual and verbal skills demonstrate more advanced concepts of death than other children of the same age. Kenyon cautions, however, that children with limited verbal ability may also comprehend death concepts well but have difficulty in communicating their understanding. Kenyon discovered few effects of gender or social economic status, with the exception that boys are more likely than girls to depict violent causes of death.

Does Anxiety Influence Children's Thoughts about Death?

Death is an emotionally laden subject for both children and adults, as we have glimpsed in the research case histories. Anxiety in general serves as an alarm signal for us—there is something potentially dangerous in this situation. A quick surge of anxiety can be helpful in directing our attention to the source of possible danger. Persistent or intense anxiety, however, tends to have dysfunctional effects on our perceptions and cognitions (Freeman & DiTomasso, 1994). If anxiety can influence adult thought processes, then what effects might anxiety have on the child's incomplete and rapidly changing view of the world?

Considerations such as these have led a number of researchers to examine the influence of anxiety and related emotions on children's conceptions of death. Separation anxiety has been the central theme here. Even brief separations can lead to fears of abandonment and loss. Because children are naturally dependent on adults, it is a reasonable hypothesis that they are highly susceptible to separation anxiety. Perhaps all separations are tinged with death anxiety. Reports of childhood experiences suggest that bedtime rituals can have the function of reducing separation anxiety and preparing people for coping with death-related situations in their adult lives (Kastenbaum, in press).

A young child's seeming immature concept of death may represent defensive strategies for avoiding emotional pain. We might be underestimating the child's ability to understand the finality, universality, and inevitability of death if we neglected the anxiety–defense dynamics. The force of logic and intellect gradually liberates itself from separation/death anxiety. This does not mean that older children are free of separation or death anxiety. It does mean, however, that the children can now think at their most mature level when confronting the fear of losing a loved one. Do we ever completely free our thought processes of death anxiety? This is an unanswered question.

This inquiry into the emotional side of children's death conceptions may help to illuminate the challenges and conflicts that adults experience as well. For example, Lonetto (1980) asked children to draw pictures about death and then talk about them. The younger children expressed more separation anxiety. However, Lonetto also observed that the older children were more disturbed by other aspects of death: "The happy smiles of the dead depicted by the younger children have all but faded away in the representations given by 10-year-olds, who show the dead with closed mouths and eyes" (p. 146). The older children were more likely to depict death as scary and horrible, and they also focused more on their own possible death compared with others.

By age 11, there was more use of abstract symbols in the drawings, indicating a new way of coping with death. They could hint at death and

Bombs and artillery shells ravaged Sarajevo and took many lives. Children find the opportunity for their own snowball war.

represent its meanings (e.g., a valentine with tears pouring down its face) without having to draw all the unpleasant details. Interestingly, the use of black as the only color became dominant among the older children. This also showed up in their verbal comments. Jenny, aged 11 years, 10 months, said (Lonetto, 1980)

> Death is blackness…Like when you close your eyes. It's cold and when you die your body is cold. Frightening, I don't want to die…. I wonder then, how I'm going to die…. I feel scared and I try to forget it. When I feel like this, I try to forget it and just put something else into my mind. (p. 154)

An 8-year-old boy in Lonetto's (1980) study offered this solemn meditation:

> When my pet died I felt sorry for him. Because he was only a kitten. When my mom buried him he

might be turned into bones. When people die they just turned into bones too. When you die you cannot talk, see, write, or anything like that. When you die they bury you in a little yard. I think everybody will die. (p. 119)

We seem to pay a price for developing more mature and realistic conceptions of death. It is more difficult to fall back on the idea that dead people are happy. Jenny has already put a new defensive strategy into operation, one that characterizes many adults as well: "I try to forget it and just put something else in my mind."

Developmental studies and observations made in natural settings all indicate that children are aware of death from an early age. The child does not begin with the realization that death is inevitable, universal, and final but does quickly grasp the implications of separation and loss. It is likely that the questions posed to the child's mind by death stimulate the desire to learn more about the ways of the world and contribute to overall mental development. Chronological age is a rough indicator of the cognitive level of a child's view of death; independent measures of the child's verbal conceptual development provide a more refined indicator.

How did the September 11, 2001, terrorist attacks affect children's thoughts and feelings about death? It may be a while before enough information is compiled to draw firm conclusions. We know already, though, that a great many children learned about the attack and its effects on people's lives through the repeated images on television. Did their parents explore the children's responses and help them to interpret the events? Did the younger children add more intensive "knock down the tower" games to their play? Did some children become more anxious that their own parents would not come home from work, and especially concerned when a family member had to take a plane trip? The heaviest burden is on the children who were bereaved by the terrorist attacks, but many others have had to deal with the alarming possibility of the sudden and traumatic loss of a family member.

Cultural Influences on Children's Concepts of Death

What children emphasize most in their thoughts about death may depend on cultural influences. For example, children in Sweden and the United States had similar concepts of death at the same age. However, U.S. children more often depicted violent causes of death, and Swedish children more often depicted chapels in cemeteries, tombstones, crosses on church steeples, caskets, and other cultural symbols. It is possible that the much greater frequency of violence and death on U.S. television compared with Swedish television may have a strong bearing on these differences in children's representations of death (Wass, 2002; Wenestam & Wass, 1987).

The role of religious beliefs and expectations is suggested by a study of Muslim girls, ages 6–10, in South Africa (Anthony & Bhana, 1988/1989). The realization that death is universal and inevita-

ble seemed to be grasped at an earlier age by Muslim children, but this did not mean that they also *accepted* the irreversibility of death. "They believe that the dead come alive again under certain circumstances, such as when angels question them in the grave. It can, thus, be seen that the responses of the children are characteristic of their cultural and religious environments" (p. 225). The Muslim children were also more likely to believe in the importance of praying for the dead. No doubt there are many other variations in children's thinking about death as they respond to the ideas, actions, and symbols of their cultural backgrounds. The type and frequency of exposure to death seem to influence how rapidly children develop their concepts. This includes not only direct exposure to death but also the effects of religious teachings and media.

Children in some other areas of the world have been facing personal threats from warfare, terrorism, and the diseases and malnutrition that are bred in these circumstances. The world spotlight has moved away from the violence in Bosnia as other "hot spots" have become prominent. Nevertheless, the children of Kosovo are still being affected by unforgettable experiences of life-threatening episodes or loss of loved ones. To a child in Buranda, Guatemala, the Sudan, and many other places, the death of others and the possibility of one's own sudden death have become a deeply rooted part of their lives.

Those who have grown up in a hazardous and unpredictable environment may take sudden death as the norm. Among refugees of the Lebanese war, it was observed that children made lethal weapons their playthings and often gunned each other down (Cutting, 1988). Observations of this type have also been made in other war-torn settings. The idea of killing might be part of any child's development of the overall concept of death (Anthony, 1948/1972). For children to emphasize and enact the role of killer, however, suggests that situational factors can have a very strong impact.

Over a longer arch of time, children born before and after the conquest of fatal childhood diseases and the introduction of television might differ in their experiences and concepts of death. My father would occasionally speak of his brothers who died of diphtheria in childhood. Many other long-lived adults have memories of family members dying from contagions and infections that are seldom encountered today. Every new generation of children brings distinctive experiences to its understanding of death-related issues.

HOW DO CHILDREN COPE WITH BEREAVEMENT?

For some children, death has already become a reality. They have lost a person who had been very important in their lives. We now examine the effects of bereavement on children and the ways in which they attempt to cope. We will see that an increasing number of American children may be at risk for prolonged and disturbing grief reactions as a result of a traumatic bereavement.

A Death in the Family: Effects on the Child

A death in the family often draws attention and energy away from the needs of the children. When a parent dies, for example, the surviving parent's grief can interfere temporarily with the ability to care for the emotional or even the physical needs of the children. It can be very difficult for lone parents to manage both their own sorrow and the needs of their children.

Sometimes it is a sibling who dies. In this situation, the parents may be so involved in the plight of the dying child that other children are neglected. The surviving children may face two sources of stress. First, as already mentioned, the grieving parent may not be able to provide as much emotional support as well as guidance through the problems of everyday life. Second, the children have their own anxieties and sorrows to suffer through. The surviving children may feel isolated if the adults fail to recognize their distress signals. Sensitive adults will take into account both the child's developmental level and the role that the deceased person had played in the child's life. What did this child understand about separation and death? Does the child understand that death is final and universal? Was the deceased person an older sibling whom the child had looked up to? Was the deceased a younger sibling whom the child had resented as a competitor for parental competition? Does the surviving child believe that she could join the lost sibling if she managed to get herself killed?

Furthermore, attention should be given to the quality of the child's personal and family situation prior to the bereavement. Had this been a tightly knit family in which the child enjoyed a strong sense of love and security? Was it a broken or bent family characterized by anxiety and insecurity? The impact of bereavement is influenced by the child's developmental level, the specific loss that has been experienced, and the previous pattern of family security and affection.

Bereaved children may express their distress in ways that do not seem closely associated with the loss. Serious problems in school may appear for the first time. Children may turn on playmates with sudden anger. Fear of the dark or of being alone may reappear. There are many ways in which the child's life pattern can show the effect of bereavement without an obvious show of sorrow. The child may be further inhibited from direct expression if commanded by the surviving parent to be "brave." Tears are then stigmatized as signs of weakness and disobedience.

Young children tend to express their memories of a lost parent through specific activities that had linked them together. An adult can preserve a valued relationship by replaying memories in private or sharing them with others. However, a 2-year-old boy who loses his father is more likely to express his longing and sadness through actions (Furman, 1974):

> For weeks he spent much of his time repeating the daily play activities that had constituted the essence of his relationship with his father. He also insisted, over and over, on taking the walks he had taken with his father, stopping at the stores where his father had shopped and recalled specific items. (p. 55)

The toddler's need added to the mother's emotional pain, but she recognized that it was the best way he had to adjust to the loss.

In remembering the deceased person, young children are likely to focus on a few strong images, in contrast to the bereaved spouse, who has many recollections from all the years of marriage. The young child carries much of the remembrance of the lost parent in the form of scenes and activities in which intense feelings have been invested. Years after the death the child may suddenly be overwhelmed with sadness when he or she encounters a situation that touches off a precious memory.

The mental image of the lost parent often remains with children long after the death. Adults sometimes make it easier on themselves by assuming that a child forgets quickly. The child may contribute to this assumption by an apparent lack of grief and mourning—what adults perceive as a lack of response. For example, the child goes back to watching television, a behavior that suggests to the adult that he or she probably does not understand what has happened. This assumption is contradicted by most clinicians and researchers who have observed childhood bereavement in detail. Although "some children could bear an astonishing amount of pain alone...most needed a loved person who could either share their grief or empathize with them and support their tolerance and expression of affect" (Furman, 1974, p. 57). The silent sadness of the bereaved child can be painful for the adult to acknowledge. But how are we to support and comfort unless we can accept the reality of the child's suffering?

It can be even more difficult to accept the child's response when it includes anger. The surviving parent may be horrified to hear criticisms of the deceased parent coming from the children. This may happen precisely at the time that the widowed spouse is at the peak of idealizing the lost husband or wife. Yet the expression of anger may be a necessary part of the child's adaptation to the loss. Such expressions do not mean that the child does not love and miss the lost parent— quite the opposite. One of the reasons some adults find it very painful to accept the child's expression of mixed feelings toward the deceased is that these feelings are within them as well. Whoever helps a bereaved spouse express grief openly and begin the long process of recovery is also helping the children by returning the strength and sensitivity of their remaining parent.

Most studies of children's parental bereavement have concentrated on the loss of the father. Several consistent differences have been found in the behavior of children who have suffered parental bereavement compared with children who have both parents living.

Children whose father died

- Tend to be more submissive, dependent, and introverted
- Show a higher frequency of maladjustment and emotional disturbance, including suicidality (suicide in children is considered in Chapter 9)
- Show a higher frequency of delinquent and criminal behavior
- Perform less adequately in school and on tests of cognitive functioning
- Experience more physical symptoms
- Become more concerned that the family will fall apart

Coleen, the girl who was afraid she had hurt her mother by stepping on her grave, experienced several of these difficulties. Within a month of the death, she reported headaches and stomachaches and became extremely worried about her father's increased drinking and grouchiness. To make it even worse, her father and her sister were giving each other a hard time. "Mother used to make it better and stop them, but she isn't here anymore" (Christ, 2000, p. 103). It is useful to note that many of Coleen's concerns were linked with specific situations, and she was already exploring ways of dealing with these problems. For example, she would soon be a junior bridesmaid for her cousin, but Mom would not be there with her—"but I'll pretend she is watching me from heaven." *Pretend!* She had the mental flexibility to find comfort in the idea of her mother watching her from heaven while not necessarily taking this to be an objective fact. Coleen was also anxious about the way her friends would treat her when she returned to school: Would they be asking a lot of uncomfortable questions, or what?

As it turned out, the friends were supportive and understanding, sending her many condolence and encouragement cards even before she returned to school. It was that much better when she was chosen to dance in a show at school. Coleen was fortunate in having a supportive family and the opportunity to meet with a school counselor, but she also demonstrated her own resourcefulness in coping with her situation. We see bereaved children's realistic concerns and strenuous efforts to deal with them repeatedly in case histories such as those described by Christ (2000). Although children may have incomplete conceptions of death, their ability to recognize and deal with the realities should not be underestimated. The more fully we can enter into the child's private world of hurt and fear, the better position we are in to provide understanding and comfort.

Posttraumatic Stress Disorder Following a Violent Death

Sudden, unexpected death has a more severe impact on the survivors, whether children or adults (see Chapter 13). This impact can be further intensified by especially threatening features of the death (e.g., a drive-by shooting, a suicide, or mutilation of the corpse in an accident). Some teachers and school systems have already developed programs and techniques for reaching out to children who have been exposed to traumatic death. It would be useful to bring awareness of this problem to all school systems as well as parents and the general public.

Central to this awareness is the syndrome known as posttraumatic stress disorder (PTSD). This condition was officially recognized as a diagnostic entity in 1980. The phenomenon has been known for many years: A person survives extremely stressful situations and then, at a later time, suffers "flashbacks" in which the traumatic events are reexperienced. During these episodes the individual behaves in seemingly irrational, bizarre, and perhaps dangerous ways—not at all in keeping with his or her previous personality. These episodes are often frightening to family, friends, and the individual experiencing them. The definitive description of PTSD is given in Table 11-2.

Awareness of PTSD in adults was heightened by the experiences of some people who served in the Vietnam War. Recognition of PTSD in children who have experienced traumatic bereavements or other encounters with death is now starting to receive some of the attention it deserves (Corr & Corr, 1996; Doka, 2000). Children

whose PTSD is not recognized may have difficulty paying attention, concentrating, and making and keeping friends. Such a dysfunctional pattern is especially harmful in childhood when so many basic personal and interpersonal skills are being developed. No less important, the child with PTSD is likely to be frightened, as shown by the following brief excerpt from a psychotherapy session with Webb (1993) in which Susan, age 9, shares her reaction to the automobile death of a schoolmate:

SUSAN:	I'm having bad dreams that wake me up every night. Then in the morning I don't want to get up. I'm tired all the time, even when I go to bed at 8 o'clock.
WEBB:	That sounds pretty bad! Can you tell me what the dreams are like?
SUSAN:	I dream that there is a gorilla in my closet and that he is going to sneak up to my bed and grab me and then take me away and roast me on a barbecue.
WEBB:	That must be pretty scary! Does the dream wake you up?
SUSAN:	Yes, and then I run into my mom's bed. (p. 196)

Children can be helped to overcome PTSD, but first we must be observant enough to recognize their distress and its possible connection to a disturbing death-related experience.

Long-Term Effects of Childhood Bereavement

The effects of childhood bereavement are not limited to childhood. Loss of a significant person in childhood can have an important effect on subsequent development. Major physical and mental illnesses occur more often in the adult lives of those who were bereaved as children. Other children develop in ways that perhaps can best be described as unusual. For example, some children take on the identity of their dead sibling or, more rarely, a dead parent. This is most likely to happen when the family had given preference to the child who is now deceased and then responds with approval to the impersonation. This borrowed iden-

TABLE 11-2

Diagnostic Criteria for Posttraumatic Stress Disorder

A. The person has experienced an event that is outside the range of usual human experience and that would be markedly distressing to almost anyone (e.g., serious threat to one's life or physical integrity; serious threat or harm to one's children, spouse, or other close relatives and friends; sudden destruction of one's home or community; or seeing another person who has recently been, or is being, seriously injured or killed as the result of an accident or physical violence).

B. The traumatic event is persistently reexperienced in at least one of the following ways:
   1. Recurrent intrusive distressing recollections of the event (in young children, repetitive play in which themes or aspects of the trauma are expressed)
   2. Recurrent distressing dreams of the events
   3. Sudden acting or feeling as if the traumatic events were recurring (includes a sense of reliving the experience, illusions, hallucinations, and dissociative [flashback] episodes, even those that occur upon awakening or when intoxicated).
   4. Intense psychological distress at exposure to events that symbolize or resemble any aspect of the traumatic event, including anniversaries of the trauma

C. Persistent avoidance of stimuli associated with the trauma or numbing of general responsiveness (not present before the trauma), as indicated by at least three of the following:
   1. Efforts to avoid thoughts or feelings associated with the trauma
   2. Efforts to avoid activities or situations that arouse recollections of the trauma
   3. Inability to recall an important aspect of the trauma (psycho-genic amnesia)
   4. Markedly diminished interest in significant activities (in young children, loss of recently acquired developmental skills, such as toilet training or language skills)
   5. Feelings of detachment or estrangement from others
   6. Restricted range of affect (e.g., unable to have loving feelings)
   7. Sense of a foreshortened future (e.g., does not expect to have a career, marriage, children, or a long life).

D. Persistent symptoms of increased arousal (not present before the trauma), as indicated by at least two of the following:
   1. Difficulty falling or staying asleep
   2. Irritability or outbursts of anger
   3. Difficulty concentrating
   4. Hypervigilance
   5. Exaggerated startle response
   6. Physiological reactivity upon exposure to events that symbolize or resemble an aspect of the traumatic event (e.g., a woman who was raped in an elevator breaks out in a sweat when entering any elevator)

E. Duration of the disturbance (symptoms in B–D) of at least 1 month.

tity may seem to serve its purpose well for a period of time, but it is likely to generate significant problems at some point in adult life.

Zall (1994) found that mothers whose own mothers had died in childhood showed symptoms of depression, worried about their own death, were overprotective, and were perfectionist. Despite these problems, however, many proved to be effective mothers. They seemed to respond to the challenge of the parental role by completing their unfinished grieving over the deaths of their mothers. One of the women who exemplified this positive outcome offered the following comments:

For many years I didn't want children. I decided to take the risk, with my husband's encourage-ment, and the experience of motherhood has been the most challenging and even more delightful than I ever dreamed. Because of my early loss and fear of dying and leaving my children, I have been extremely conscientious about teaching the children to separate from me very early in their lives. I tend to spend a great deal of time with them.

Parental bereavement can be found in the childhood of many people who made exceptional achievements in adulthood. Consider, for example, the great naturalist Charles Darwin. Throughout his life, Darwin retained the memory of his mother's deathbed, her black velvet gown, and the worktable. Curiously, though, he remembered hardly anything of her appearance and his conversations with her. Darwin's memory of his mother's death when he was 8 years old was vivid but fragmentary. He remembered being sent for, going into her room, being greeted by his father, and crying afterward. Even stranger, Darwin had much more detailed recollections of the funeral of a soldier that he attended a few weeks later.

Biographer Ralph Colp (1975) was struck by Darwin's apparent repression of many of his memories of his mother and her death while details of the soldier's death remained fresh in his mind. Colp found that death-related themes were closely interwoven with Darwin's work throughout his life. These themes showed up even in the notes he made in the margins of books as well as in his dreams. One of the major themes disclosed was a "keen instinct against death." Colp and others believe there is a connection between Darwin's ardent advocacy of life and his fascination with the evolution of new life-forms.

Darwin's own observations confronted him with a challenge on both the personal and the scientific level. His growing awareness of a process of natural selection in which entire species die off resonated with the feelings he still carried from the time of his mother's death. In his middle adult years, Darwin expressed fear of sudden death and regarded his theory as an indirect form of continued personal survival. Darwin had more bereavements to suffer in his adult life, notably the death of his much-loved daughter, Annie.

Above all, Darwin's personal experiences with death and his scientific perspective on the destruction of entire species contributed to his ardent love of life. Unable to believe in any doctrine of survival of death, Darwin had to bear with his own "intolerable vision of slow and cold death—death irrevocably, and, finally, ascendant over all life" (Colp, 1975, p. 200). However, he also had the example of his father to inspire him. The elder Darwin lived to age 83 with a lively mind right up to the end. Vivid memories of a father who was strong and admirable throughout a long life helped to sustain him during the course of his own life's work that was so burdened with death-related experiences and observation.

Near the end of his life, Darwin felt too ill to pursue major research, but he returned to the first creatures that interested him as a young boy—worms. He had enjoyed fishing and had mixed feelings about sacrificing worms to this cause. As an elderly man, Darwin did little studies of worms. In Colp's (1975) words, "Thus, the old man, who as a boy had killed worms, now, night after night, observed how he would soon be eaten by worms" (p. 200). This line of thinking was not altogether as morbid as it might sound. It was, after all, a continuation of Darwin's incessant fascination with life and death. Scientist Darwin respected worms as coinhabitants of planet Earth that have a key role in maintaining the living ecology by literally passing the earth through themselves. That he, too, Charles Darwin, would become part of the worm and part of the earth again was not a cliché or a horror story but an acceptable aspect of our natural history.

Ten thousand examples would provide 10,000 different stories of the direct and indirect ways in which childhood bereavement influences the entire life course. How each story turns out years later is likely to depend much on the kind of attention and support the child receives. We next examine some approaches that have proven useful.

Helping Children Cope with Bereavement

1. *Develop and maintain an open communication pattern with children.* It is unrealistic to wait until a crisis situation has developed before including children in the discussion of significant issues. The child who is shunted aside whenever there are "important things" to talk about will have had little opportunity to learn the communication skills that are required to deal with difficult situations. Although limited by their levels of maturation and experience, children observe, think, and make choices. The family in which children feel that they can communicate about anything and everything with their parents and receive a careful and sympathetic hearing is the family that will be able to cope more resourcefully together when faced with bereavement or other stressful life

events. Phyllis Silverman (2000) offers further guidance for parents and other adults who are interested in improving their ability to communicate with bereaved children.

2. *Give children the opportunity to decide about attending the funeral.* Adults often assume that children would either not understand funerals or be harmed by the experience (Silverman & Worden, 1992). Parents give only the illusion of choice: "You don't want to go, do you? No, I know that you don't." As research has found, children appreciate the opportunity to make their own decisions (Silverman & Worden, 1992). In some cases, families encouraged children to make specific recommendations about the funeral (e.g., "outside, with lots of flowers, and with bright colors so we can remember all the good things"). Furthermore, those who attended the funeral were better able to cope with the loss of the parent. The researchers conclude that

> funerals meet similar needs in children and in adults. By being included in the family drama, children felt acknowledged and thereby supported by their families, thus setting the stage for legitimating their roles as mourners.... The funeral becomes an opportunity to say good-bye, to feel close to their parent for one last time, and for the community to join them in doing this. (p. 329)

Nevertheless, the child who has decided against attending the funeral should not be forced to do so against his or her wishes.

Many children occasionally seek comfort from a parent at bed time. This need is stronger in children who have lost a parent or other loved one and fear further abandonment.

3. *Find out what the child is thinking and feeling—do not assume that we know what the death means to him or her.* For example, Hersh (1995) noted,

> With children never interpret a head nod when you are explaining something to them as you would with an adult. They have learned the gesture from adults, but frequently it is for the child simply the easiest way to get the "helping" adult to leave them alone.... Always gently ask the child to tell you what they have just heard and to explain it to you in their own words. (p. 91)

4. *Encourage the expression of feelings.* This point was made by many of the mothers in our own study. Mental health professionals agree. The grieving child's thoughts and feelings are a part of reality that cannot be wished away or kept under wraps without adding to the already existing emotional burden. Young children are likely to find valuable means of expression through play and drawings, often accompanied by storytelling. Feelings can also be expressed through a variety of physical activities, including vigorous games through which tension and anger can be discharged. Children of all ages can benefit from open communication with their surviving parent and other empathic adults. An especially valuable way for children to express their feelings is to help comfort others. Even very young children can do this. For example, one child attending a funeral later reported that "At the end while I was crying, my little cousin came up to me and gave me a hug and said it was okay. She was only three" (Silverman & Worden, 1992, p. 329). Comforting and altruistic behavior can begin very early in life.

5. *Provide convincing assurance that there will always be somebody to love and look after the child.* The death of a parent arouses or intensifies fears that the surviving parent and other important people may also abandon the child. Verbal assurances are useful but not likely to be sufficient. Children may become anxious when the surviving parent is out of sight or has not come home at the expected time. Sending the children away for a while is a practice that often intensifies the anxiety of abandonment. Adult relatives and friends who spend time with the children after their bereavement are helping the surviving parent to provide reassurance that there will always be somebody there for them.

6. *Professional counseling should be considered if the bereaved children are at special risk.* The death of both parents, for example, constitutes a special risk, as does a death for which the children might feel that they are somehow to blame. There is one special risk that each year arises for thousands of children (Carolyn and Kristin as quoted in Dahlke, 1994):

> Mom told us to sit down and she said, "Girls, your Dad died." We both cried right away. We went down to the garage where everybody was. People began holding us and trying to make us feel better. No one knew what to say. We felt like everyone was just staring at us. It was like a big, bad dream. And to make matters worse, we found out from our Mom that Dad had killed himself.... It still is hard for us to understand. We were only 5 and 9 years old. (pp. 116–117)

The two girls had to contend, suddenly, with both the death of their father and the puzzle and possible stigma of his suicide. Their consuming question was, "If Daddy loved me, why did he leave me?" This became the title of a book that the girls wrote together over a period of time. In addition to their supportive mother, Carolyn and Kristen had the skilled services of a professional counselor, David Dahlke. Every page of the girls' book reflects their personal growth experience as they explored their thoughts, feelings, values, and choices with the counselor's assistance.

Dahlke (1994) offers a detailed account of the counseling process along with the girls' own thoughts and comments by the mother. We learn, for example, that the children became afraid that if mother married again her new husband would also commit suicide. We also learn that the possibility of the father's suicide had already affected them before the act took place. As Carolyn reported, "I felt Dad threatened suicide a lot. I asked him, 'What if you kill yourself?' and he said, 'I won't do that!'...But he did. He lied to us...Dad was mixed up."

Carolyn and Kristin showed both insight and resilience as they dealt with their loss and all the questions it raised. Other children who suffer parental bereavement under especially traumatic and stressful conditions can also receive valuable assistance from qualified counselors. Additional information on counseling is provided by Stevenson (2002) and Doka (2000). Fristad, Cerel, Goldman, Weller, and Weller (2000–2001) discuss the role of ritual in comforting bereaved children.

THE DYING CHILD

Children sometimes think about death, loss, and separation even when there has been no obvious event to arouse their curiosity or concern. Writing about his own childhood, Spalding Gray (1986) recalls

> the time when I woke up in the middle of the night and saw my brother Rocky standing on his bed, blue in the face and gasping for air, crying out that he was dying. My mother and father were standing beside the bed trying to quiet him, and Mom said, "Calm down, dear, it's all in your mind." And after he calmed down, my father went back to bed, and my mother turned out the light and sat on the edge of Rocky's bed in the dark.... We were all there, very quiet, in the dark, and then Rocky would start in, "Mom, when I die, is it forever?" And she said, "Yes, dear." And then Rocky said, "Mom, when I die, is it forever, and ever, and ever?" and she said, "Uh-huh, dear." And he said, "Mom, when I die, is it forever and ever and ever…?" I just went right off to this. (p. 14)

Many other healthy children also may have moments when they imagine themselves dying and worry about what it means to be dead. It should not be surprising, then, to learn that children who actually are afflicted with life-threatening illnesses are keenly aware of their predicaments.

Sometimes the failure to communicate adequately with dying children arises from a death taboo. This was documented in a study that compared children suffering from uncontrolled leukemia with other children who were hospitalized with orthopedic conditions that posed no threats to their lives. All the children were Chinese. Those with leukemia were more tense, detached, and guarded. Given projective tests, the life-threatened leukemic children also expressed stronger feelings of being isolated and abandoned while at the same time tending to deny the seriousness of their illness.

The authors, themselves Chinese, observed that in their ethnic group parents are especially reluctant to discuss death with their children (Lee, Lieh-Mak, Hung, & Luk, 1983/1984). Death is a taboo subject in general and even more so when children are involved. The child, whether healthy or fatally ill, is left to develop and test death concepts with little or no adult guidance. Inadvertently, the parents convey the impression that they are rejecting their dying children—why else, wonder the children, would their parents spend so little time with them and seem to take so little interest in their illness? Wherever such a taboo prevails, both the dying child and the parents are likely to suffer additional anguish because of the communication barrier.

Fortunately, there are also many examples of sensitive communication within families that face the impending death of a child. Shira Putter, who died at the age of 9 from a rare form of diabetes, left a diary that offers the opportunity to learn how a child may interpret his or her own situation (Grollman, 1988). Problems in communication did arise along the way. At one point, Shira was feeling that "Daddy doesn't care about me. I know he comes to visit me practically every day, but once he comes he always seems so far away. It's like he can't wait to leave again." She was reluctant to share this concern with her mother because "I didn't want her to get upset." However, she did tell her mother, who then explained "that Daddy does love me and that was part of the problem. He loves me so much that it hurts him to see me sick and in pain. She asked me to please try to understand" (p. 12). This episode put everybody more at ease, including Daddy, and restored the usual family pattern of warm and caring interactions.

Dying children may hesitate to share their concerns because of the fear that this will only make their parents feel even worse. On other occasions, Shira did remain silent when she could see that her parents were upset by new complications in her condition. So, far from being unaware of the perils they face, children may take a kind of parental role themselves and try to protect adults from anxiety and sorrow.

First-hand accounts of the child's experience of terminal illness are also valuable in reminding us that each day can bring some new threat or challenge. Shira, for example, had to cope with the fact that her favorite doctor took himself off her case because he was so upset by her continued physical decline. The fear of abandonment by the most important people in the child's life is often a major concern of the dying child—and too often based on the way that some adults do distance themselves from the child.

Shira and her family were able to maintain their closeness and mutual support until the very end. In one of her last diary entries, Shira writes of their Passover celebration (Grollman, 1988),

> In a way, it seemed like any other Passover. We said all the prayers. We sang all the songs. But when we were reciting the blessing, thanking God for letting us celebrate this special occasion, everyone started crying. Then, for about a minute, we all stood together quietly, holding hands. It was as if, without saying anything, I was telling everyone what was in my heart. That I loved them and wanted to be with them, but I couldn't make it much longer. That I wasn't afraid of dying anymore, so they had to let me go. They just had to. (p. 70)

Anthropologist Myra Bluebond-Langner (1977, 1988) spent many hours with hospitalized children, listening to them and observing their interactions with parents and staff. There was no question about the children's keen awareness of their total situation. One morning, for example, Jeffrey made a point of asking Bluebond-Langner to read to him from the classic children's book, *Charlotte's Web* (White, 1952). He wanted to hear again "the part where Charlotte dies." This chapter, "Last Day," offers a combination of humor, drama, and consolation. "Nothing can harm you now" is one of its thoughts. Another is "No one was with her when she died." When Bluebond-Langner completed her reading of the chapter, Jeffrey dozed off. He died that afternoon.

Many of the terminally ill children observed by Bluebond-Langner passed through five stages in the acquisition of information:

1. I have a serious illness.
2. I know what drugs I am receiving and what they are supposed to do.
3. I know the relationship between my symptoms and the kind of treatment I am getting.
4. I realize now that I am going through a cycle of feeling worse, getting better, then getting worse again. The medicines don't work all the time.
5. I know that this will not go on forever. There is an end to the remissions and the relapses and to the kind of medicine they have for me. When the drugs stop working, I will die pretty soon.

The children soon became sophisticated about hospital routines. They learned the names of all their drugs and how to tell one kind of staff member from another. Little escaped them. Staff members would have been astonished had they realized how much the children picked up on hospital processes and purposes. Most of all, perhaps, the children learned from each other. They would notice that they were now on the last drug that another child had received before his or her death or that people were now starting to treat them differently, meaning that something important had changed in their condition.

Seriously ill children work hard to understand what is happening to them. They are aware of the possibility of death but must also give attention to the specific changes that are taking place in their bodies, the kind of treatment they are receiving, and how their family and friends are responding to them. The adult who assumes that a sick child is too young to understand anything is probably making a serious mistake. Consider the sequence reported by Sourkes (1996):

A 3-year-old boy played the same game with a stuffed duck and a toy ambulance each time he was hospitalized. The duck would be sick and need to go to the hospital by ambulance. The boy would move the ambulance, making siren noises.

THERAPIST: How is the duck?
CHILD: Sick.

THERAPIST: Where is he going?
CHILD: To the hospital.
THERAPIST: What are they going to do?
CHILD: Make him better.

During what turned out to be the boy's terminal admission, he played the same game with the duck. However, the outcome of the ritual changed dramatically:

THERAPIST: How is the duck?
CHILD: Sick
THERAPIST: Is he going to get better?
CHILD: (Shaking his head slowly): Ducky not get better. Ducky die. (pp. 157–158)

Two days later, the boy drew a picture of "a vibrant firefly, smiling broadly as it emerges from the blackness into the…light." He explained: "Fireflies glow in the dark and show others the way." He died that evening.

Further insight into the world of the dying child is offered by Judi Bertoia (1993), an expressive therapist who worked with 7-year-old Rachel, who was losing her battle with leukemia. Rachel expressed her thoughts and feelings through her drawings as well as her conversations with Bertoia. There could be little doubt that Rachel understood much of what was happening to her—one had only to view the crumbling houses and distorted bodies that were among her drawings. All was not fear and dread, however. Rachel showed a continued growth in knowledge and emotional material as time went on. Bertoia noted that Rachel's increasing understanding progressed in the stages that had been reported by Bluebond-Langner in her studies of dying children. Rachel also expressed her distinctive individuality through the drawings. She could not be reduced to a "type" or "stage": She was always Rachel, trying to understand and cope with her life-threatening illness in the best ways she knew how. Who can do any better than that?

Care of the Dying Child

Along with emotional support and sensitive communication, dying children are also likely to need a variety of medical, nursing, and other support services. In recent years, the hospice approach to terminal care has been extended to include children. The basic philosophy is the same as with hospice care in general: to help the dying person enjoy the highest quality of life possible in the circumstances. This is accomplished by skillfully controlling pain and other symptoms and by working with the family to support their own caregiving efforts.

Although circumstances may arise in which a hospital stay seems to be necessary, the focus is usually on home care. Children as well as adults often feel most secure within their own homes. Because there can be situations in which neither the hospital nor the home seem to be the best place to care for the dying child, some hospice organizations have also established respite care facilities. These are usually small, home-like centers in which the child can receive care for a few days or weeks while the family copes with other problems.

Levetown (2002) points out that the children's own view of their situation is more likely to be understood and respected if the care team includes a child psychologist or child life therapist. The American Academy of Pediatrics has endorsed the inclusion of a child therapist, but this has not yet become a standard practice.

Whether the child is at home, in a respite care center, or in a hospital-based hospice service, the overall philosophy remains the same: Give comfort, relieve distress, and help the patient and family preserve their most basic values of life during this difficult time. Currently, there are relatively few children's hospice programs, but a growing number of pediatric caregivers are applying hospice principles and techniques. Up-to-date information can be obtained from Children's Hospice International (800-24CHILD or chiorg@aol.com).

Whether or not a hospice approach is used, the care of the dying child is likely to be enhanced by attention to the following needs, which have much in common with the situation of the bereaved child:

1. The opportunity to express his or her concerns through conversation, play, drawing, writing—whatever modality is most effective

and natural for the particular child. Such creative activities as modeling clay figures or drawing pictures of the family may help to transform inner feelings into a tangible communication that can be shared with others. The very process of creative transformation—feelings into art—can itself have a therapeutic value. Resentment and anger may be expressed on occasion in the child's play or art; this is usually part of one's natural response to overwhelming circumstances, and the opportunity to "get it out" often proves valuable.

2. Confirmation that he or she is still a normal and valuable person, despite the impairments and limitations imposed by illness. Sensitive parents and other caregivers will find ways to affirm and strengthen the child's basic sense of self. They will not allow "dyingness" to overshadow every interaction, every plan, and every project. Instead, opportunities will be found for the child to do things that are still within his or her sphere of competence and to stay involved with roles and activities that have brought pleasure. One 10-year-old boy, for example, taught his younger siblings how to play chess while he was dying of leukemia; a girl, also 10, kept the statistics and figured the batting averages for her softball team after she could no longer play. With the availability of home computers, it is now also possible for children to enjoy computer-assisted learning programs, drawing, writing, and games with relatively little expenditure of energy.

3. Assurance that family members and other important people will not abandon the dying child, no matter what happens. Nonverbal behavior is a vital component of interaction that can either affirm or undermine the family's words of reassurance. As illustrated by Shira's diary, children are quite aware of discomfort, tension, and conflict on the part of the adults in their lives. By their everyday actions as well as their words, parents and other caregivers must continue to convey their dedication to being with—to staying with—the dying child, come what may.

4. Reassurance that he or she will not be forgotten. Often, dying children fear they will not be a part of what will happen in the family when they are no longer there. They may also fear that they will be replaced in the family constellation by another child instead of remembered and valued for their uniqueness. In some situations, it may be useful to use mental imagery exercises to help the child prepare for impending separation and to participate in the future through imagination. Children may also come up with their own ways of feeling a part of the future, requiring of the adults only their sympathetic attention and cooperation. For example, a child may wish to give some favorite toys to a sibling or friend or to make a cassette that can be listened to on birthdays or other special occasions.

In addition to these common needs and themes, each child with a life-threatening illness is almost certain to have distinctive ideas, hopes, and apprehensions. What special wish or secret fear is on the mind of this particular child? There is no substitute for careful listening and observation and for respecting the individuality of each child.

Siblings of the Dying Child

He's been sick a lot this year…But I kind of get used to him being sick…I really want to know what it's like to stay home and watch and take care of my brother for a whole day when he's sick. And I know what to do. Every night you [a person with cystic fibrosis] have to get on this machine. And it's because you get all this mucus in your lungs and it's hard to breathe. And when you get sick, you really get sick…And sometimes you die at an early age. But I don't think that will happen to Jason, because he's in pretty good shape. That's about it. (Bluebond-Langner, 1996, pp. 78–79)

Eleven-year-old Regan and her family lived every day with 9-year-old Jason's illness and with the prospect of his early death. She adjusted to this situation as did everybody else in the family: Life has to go on and people have to do what they have to do. She was well informed about her brother's condition and had personal knowledge of somebody who had died young of the same medical condition, cystic fibrosis. Nobody had died—yet. Nobody was dying—yet.

Nevertheless, Regan's own childhood experiences were shadowed by the possibility of her brother's death and by the family's daily efforts to carry on "normally" despite their burden of anxiety.

Anxiety and sorrow about the dying child can lead to neglect of other family needs. Parents may not give adequate attention to their own health, for example. The continuing stress can lead to a narrowing of attention, a concentration on "just what most needs to be done," and increased irritability and distraction even on the part of the most devoted parents. Also, as recent findings suggest, the brothers and sisters of dying children may be at particular risk during this difficult period.

Bluebond-Langner (1988) observes,

"The well siblings of terminally ill children live in houses of chronic sorrow. The signs of sorrow, illness, and death are everywhere, whether or not they are spoken of. The signs are written on parents' faces: "My mother always looks tired now," and "Even my Dad's crying a lot." The signs are there in hushed conversations: "You learn everything by listening in on the [phone] extension." (p. 9)

The following problems are among those observed in well siblings in the course of Bluebond-Langner's research (1988):

1. Confusion about what role they are supposed to play in the family. Should they try to be like the sick child? Should they try to become "assistant parents"? Should they become invisible, "just blend into the woodwork and get out of the way"?
2. A feeling of being deceived or rejected by their parents: "They don't tell me the truth.... Nobody really cares about me anymore."
3. Uncertainty about the future: "What's to become of all of us?...Does it do any good to have plans anymore?"
4. Changes in the relationships among the siblings: For example, the illness and hospitalization of the sick child deprive the others of a companion:

Siblings often find that they cannot give reciprocally to one another.... For example, while Jake lay dying, complaining of his back hurting him and not being able to breathe, his brothers offered to rub his back. He pushed them away saying, "no, no, not you. Only Mommy now." The ill child's alliances shift from a closeness to both the parent and the sibling to a closeness with the parent divorced from that of the sibling. (p. 13)

5. Feelings of guilt and ambivalence: The well siblings are distressed by the suffering of the sick child but may also feel relieved—and feel guilty about feeling relieved—that they are not the ones who are dying.
6. Frustrated in not being able to express their feelings and fears to their parents, who are so preoccupied with the dying child and with their own feelings.

Not all well siblings had all these reactions, nor did these feelings occur all the time. In some families, few obvious problems developed until the sick child had become extremely frail and disabled. Until that time, the parents had managed to find some time and energy for the other children and keep a semblance of normal family life going. However, the well siblings often took account of changes in the sick child's condition and needs. They recognized that the sick child now required a great deal of attention from the parents, and they were less likely to feel rejected or in competition.

Compassionate relatives, friends, neighbors, and teachers can lighten the burden by giving attention to the well siblings during and after the terminal process and by unobtrusively helping the parents in coping with the responsibilities of everyday life. The family with a dying child certainly needs and deserves sensitive, understanding, and mature companionship from all the community.

The Stress of Working with Dying Children

All who are called on to provide care for dying children are vulnerable to anxiety and sorrow—sometimes a sense of guilt as well because they are unable to save the child. Unfortunately, not much has been done to prepare health care professionals for this challenging kind of work. Papadatou (1997) believes that the medical profession's traditional emphasis on diagnosis and treatment of the disease has contributed to neglect of the dying child as a person—and neglect of the feelings of those who work closely with the dying child. Papadatou describes an innovative educational program for pediatric nurses at Children's Hospital, Athens, Greece. Pediatric nurses are provided with close and supportive supervision as they work with dying children and their families. They are given the opportunity to discuss their cases with a psychologist and work with a supportive professional team. A sensitivity group experience is also included and their personal reflection is enhanced by keeping a journal of their experiences. These and other techniques now being evaluated in Athens might well provide a new model that will help to prepare nurses throughout the world to provide care for dying children while also reducing their own stress. A follow-up study (Papadatou, Papazoglou, Petraki, & Bellali, 1999) revealed that friends and relatives are seldom prepared to support nurses who are experiencing stress related to their work with dying children. Mutual support—nurse to nurse—seems to be a more effective approach.

SHARING THE CHILD'S DEATH CONCERNS: A FEW GUIDELINES

Adults may hope to shield children from death concerns, but it is in the child's interest to identify and understand threats to his or her well-being. This has been all too true in situations in which children have been left to survive as they can with little assistance from the adult world. However, it remains true even within the harbor of a loving family. Our children will encounter death in many forms—close and distant, imaginary and realistic. Many parents today received little guidance in death-related matters when they were young. It is not unusual for adults to face inner struggles when called on to respond to a child's questions.

This is not a "how-to" book, but it might be useful to present a few guidelines that have been helpful in relating to children on the subject of death:

1. *Be a good observer.* Notice how the child is behaving. Listen to what he or she is really saying. Do not rush in with explanations, reassurances, or diversions unless there is some overriding necessity to do so. You will be more helpful to the child if you are relaxed, patient, and attentive enough to learn what questions or needs the child actually is expressing rather than those you might assume to be there. For example, the child who suddenly asks a parent, "Are you going to be dead?" might have been thinking about something grandmother said last week or any number of other happenings that aroused this concern. Taking a moment to learn how this question arose in the child's mind could also help to provide an appropriate response.

2. *Do not wait or plan for "one big tell-all."* Maintain a continuing dialogue with the children in your life as occasions present themselves. The death of pets, scenes in movies, newspaper articles, or television presentations—whatever brushes with mortality the children have—all can offer the opportunity for discussion. This does not mean, of course, that parents should remain poised to jump on a death dialogue opportunity. However, it is more natural and effective to include death as one of the many topics that adults and children can discuss together. We are more likely to be helpful when we are not ourselves caught up in the midst of a death situation. Combine a child who has been kept ignorant about death with an adult who is grief stricken or uptight and you have something less than the most desirable situation.

3. *Do not expect all of the child's responses to be obvious and immediate.* When a death has occurred or is impending, the child's total response is likely to unfold over time and to express itself in many ways. Changes in sleeping habits, mood, relationships with other children, and demands on adults may reflect part of the child's reaction to the death, even though the connection may not be obvious. Be patient; be available.

4. *Help the child remain secure as part of the family.* Sometimes, adults have the panicked impulse to remove children from the scene when death has

come too close (e.g., sending them off to a relative or neighbor). Examine such impulses before acting on them. Whatever practical decisions you reach, consider what the children might learn from the opportunity to participate in the family's response and what lingering questions, misinterpretations, and fears might remain if they are excluded.

5. *Use simple and direct language.* Too often, what adults say to children becomes a sermon, peppered with words and concepts that mean little to them. Try to provide children with accurate information. See if they understand what you have said (e.g., by having them explain it back to you) and make sure that you have responded to what they really wanted to know in the first place.

6. *Be accessible.* The child's sense of comfort will be strengthened by the very fact that you are available to talk about death when the need arises. Your expression of feelings that are natural to the situation (worry, sorrow, and perhaps even anger) are not likely to harm the child but rather will provide a basis for sorting out and expressing his or her own feelings.

7. *Be aware of all the children in the family.* It is natural to concentrate the family's resources and attentions on the seriously ill child. Other children in the family continue to need love and reassurance, however, and need to participate somehow in the total process.

8. *Keep the relationship going.* How a life-threatened child responds at a particular moment might be disturbing to parents and other adults. We do not want to see or hear certain responses. Losing the closeness and support of important adults is a great danger to the child. This, in fact, is one of the reasons why children may not share their thoughts and feelings with us. We do not have to approve or agree with everything the child tells us about death, but we do have to maintain a supportive relationship.

THE "RIGHT" TO DECIDE: SHOULD THE CHILD'S VOICE BE HEARD?

The controversial "right-to-die" issue (Chapter 10) usually focuses on adults. This issue also

can arise with children. Consider Marie, for example (Meagher & Leff, 1989/1990). Marie was a patient for most of her young life; Marie had little opportunity to experience a normal childhood because of severe kidney disease and the effects of treatment:

> During Marie's short life, she experienced numerous hospitalizations and separations from her family, who eventually abandoned her. Massive nosebleeds…terrified her mother and lead to seven emergency hospitalizations and transfusions. Marie's lonely, monotonous hospital days were interrupted only by traumatic episodes which affected her both physically and emotionally. (p. 178)

Marie was especially fearful of and stressed by the kidney dialysis sessions. She would be put in restraints for this procedure, producing long periods of unrelenting discomfort. "Marie's mother would not be waiting for her after the ordeal had ended. Sedatives would not be used to ease the passage of time." In fact, Marie did not receive medication for her pain whether in or out of dialysis. A dialysis nurse stated that giving her sedatives would only "spoil" Marie—she must learn to cope with pain.

When Marie cried out for relief from pain, her pediatricians went through an elaborate placebo procedure, attempting to deceive the girl rather than offering actual medications. The placebo stunt did not relieve Marie's pain, and no other relief was offered. Marie's agony, anger, and fear all intensified until she became comatose and died.

How could this little girl have been allowed to suffer so long and so greatly? Did this pattern of "care" represent a violation of her rights? We might feel very strongly that the medical regime had been abusive and unsympathetic, but do children have rights? Specifically, do children have the right to participate in decisions regarding the quality of their own lives and the prospect of their own deaths? These questions have been avoided by many of the philosophers, policymakers, and physicians who analyze treatment decisions from ethical and legal standpoints.

Meagher and Leff (1989/1990) are firm in their own opinion: "Marie has the absolute right to expect that any procedure or course of treatment be in her best interest" (p. 283). She has the right to be spared the pain and stress of undergoing procedures that offer no reasonable probability of extending her life for a sustained period. She would seem to have the right "at least to participate in the decision to refuse treatment or to withhold further interventions." However, as Meagher and Leff point out, the law does not agree with this conclusion. A person must be competent in the eyes of the law in order to make decisions, and "competent" is invariably part of the phrase, "competent adult. "

The idea of a "competent child" has long remained outside the judicial and legislative systems. I find it unsettling that the basis for determining competency differs for children and adults. The competency of adults is determined on a case-by-case basis: Some adults are competent, others are not, and this status may change with time and circumstance. In contrast, children are considered not competent as a class. This two-track system of legalistic logic has a powerful effect on the policies enacted in our society's death system. It should be challenged, don't you think?

Historian Viviana A. Zelizer (1994) compiled evidence for an interesting transition in society's image of the child. She finds that until fairly recent times children were valued mainly for their contribution to the economy: cheap labor at home, in the fields, and in factories. The modern image of the child started to emerge around the turn of the 20th century as children became less of an economic asset and became valued instead as "emotionally priceless." Our heritage features the child as a cheap and expendable source of labor who had the responsibility of obeying adult authority and had few if any intrinsic rights. Several generations later, it appears that society has yet to adjust its moral and legal perspective.

Fortunately, there is a growing movement toward giving children more of a say in the management of their conditions. The American Academy of Pediatrics has recommended that children be included in medical decision making, and the National Commission for Protection of Human Subjects of Biomedical and Behavioral Research has proposed that by age 7, a child should be given the opportunity to accept or reject participation in a research project (Hinds, Bradshaw, Oakes, & Pritchard, 2002).

SUMMARY

Adults often believe, or want to believe, that children do not understand death and should be protected from all death-related situations. The facts are quite different. Children are naturally curious about loss, disappearance, and death. Furthermore, no child is too young to experience the anxiety associated with separation experiences. Most studies indicate that children do not have a firm grasp of death's finality, irreversibility, and universality until approximately age 10. Nevertheless, even very young children have moments of sudden discovery (e.g., the frog was "dead, dead, dead. What else could it be?"), and the mystery of death is very much in their minds throughout their developmental process. Many of today's parents grew up in homes in which death was never to be discussed, especially in the presence of children. This increases their difficulties in communicating about death with their own children. We learned something about the interaction between parents and children on the subject of death through a sampling of research case histories. It is clear that experiences, attitudes, and ways of coping with death are part of the intimate flow of life between children and their parents, and it is also clear that it is the death of particular people or animals that evokes the child's concern.

Studies indicate that the young child's experiences of death and loss often become lifelong memories for the adult. Psychologist Maria Nagy ("Auntie Death") found three stages of progressive understanding of death in her pioneering research. The youngest children thought of death as a continuation of life in a diminished form. The realization that death is final occurs in the next stage, at approximately age 5, but there is still hope that one can be smart or lucky enough to elude death. By age 10 (Stage 3), most children understand that death is personal, universal, and inevitable as well as final.

Recent studies emphasize the relationship between separation anxiety and children's thoughts of death. For children as well as adults, our thoughts about death are often if not always tinged with anxiety. There are basic similarities in death conceptions among children in various cultures but also some culture-specific characteristics.

The death of a parent or other family member is highly stressful to children. We have seen that the child's response to this stress may be deeper and more intense than what appears on the surface. PTSD is a particularly disturbing response to a particularly disturbing death—one that has occurred in a sudden and violent manner. PTSD has become increasingly recognized as a major problem for some adults, but it is not often recognized in children. Suggestions were made for helping children cope with bereavement.

Dying children often understand more about their condition than adults realize but also often have little voice in how their condition is managed, as we discovered in Marie's situation. Nurses and others who work closely with dying children also experience high levels of stress. Fortunately, attention is now being given to helping nurses prepare themselves for serving the needs of dying children while reducing their own stress.

The family with open and supportive communication patterns can offer much to children as they discover death and loss in its many forms. Many of us, though, must first overcome our own reluctance to accept the fact that death does touch children and that children are very much attuned to loss and separation experiences.

REFERENCES

Anthony, S. (1972). *The discovery of death in childhood and after.* New York: Basic Books. (Revision of *The child's discovery of death.* New York: Harcourt Brace and World, 1940)

Anthony, Z., & Bhana, K. (1988/1989). An exploratory study of Muslim girls' understanding of death. *Omega, Journal of Death and Dying, 19,* 215–228.

Bertoia, J. (1993). *Drawings from a dying child: Insights into death from a Jungian perspective.* London: Routledge.

Blano, M. K. (1988). *A study of the level on which adults understand and respond to children in death-related situations.* Doctoral dissertation, Georgia State University.

Bluebond-Langner, M. (1977). Meanings of death to children. In H. Feifel (Ed.), *New meanings of death.* New York: McGraw-Hill.

Bluebond-Langner, M. (1988). Worlds of dying children and their well siblings. *Death Studies, 13,* 1–16.

Bluebond-Langner, M. (1996). *In the shadow of illness.* Princeton, NJ: Princeton University Press.

Book, P. (1996). How does the family narrative influence the individual's ability to communicate about death? *Omega, Journal of Death and Dying, 33,* 323–342.

Christ, G. H. (2000). *Healing children's grief.* New York: Oxford University Press.

Colp, R. J. (1975). The evolution of Charles Darwin's thoughts about death. *Journal of Thanatology 3,* 191–206.

Corr, C. A., & Corr, D. M. (Eds.). (1996). *Handbook of childhood death and bereavement.* New York: Springer.

Corr, C. A., & Corr, D. M. (2002). Children. In R. Kastenbaum (ed.), *Macmillan encyclopedia of death and dying* (Vol. 1, pp. 123–130). New York: Macmillan.

Cutting, P. (1988). *Children of the siege.* New York: St. Martin's.

Dahlke, D. (1994). Therapy-assisted growth after parental suicide: From a personal and professional perspective. *Omega, Journal of Death and Dying, 23,* 113–152.

Deveau, E. J. (1995). Perceptions of death through the eyes of children and adolescents. In D. W. Adams & E. J. Deveau (Eds.), *Beyond the innocence of childhood* (Vol. 1, pp. 55–92). New York: Baywood.

Dickinson, G. (1992). First childhood death experiences. *Omega, Journal of Death and Dying, 25,* 169–182.

Doka, K. J. (2000). Using ritual with children and adolescents. In K. J. Doka (Ed.), *Living with grief. Children, adolescents, and loss* (pp. 153–160). New York: Brunner/Mazel.

Freeman, A., & DiTomasso, R. A. (1994). The cognitive theory of anxiety. In B. J. Wolman & G. Stricker (Eds.), *Anxiety and related disorders* (pp. 74–90). New York: Wiley–Interscience.

Freud, S. (1914). On narcissism: An introduction. In *Collective works* (Vol. 4, pp. 30–59). London: Hogart.

Fristad, M. A., Cerel, J., Goldman, M., Weller, E. B., & Weller, R. A. (2000–2002). The role of ritual in children's bereavement. *Omega, Journal of Death and Dying, 42,* 321–340.

Furman, E. F. (1974). *A child's parent dies: Studies in childhood bereavement.* New Haven, CT: Yale University Press.

Gray, S. (1986). *Sex and death to the age 14.* New York: Vintage.

Grollman, S. (1988). *A legacy of courage.* New York: Doubleday.

Hall, G. S. (1992). *Senescense: The last half of life.* New York: Appleton.

Hersh, S. P. (1995). How can we help? In K. J. Doka (Ed.), *Children mourning; Mourning children.* (pp. 93–96). Washington, DC: Hospice Foundation of America.

Hinds, P. S., Bradshaw, G., Oakes, L. L., & Pritchard, M. (2002). Children and their rights in life and death situations. In R. Kastenbaum (Ed.), *Macmillan encyclopedia of death and dying* (Vol. 1, pp. 139–147). New York: Macmillan.

Kastenbaum, R. (in press). *On our way: The final passage through life and death.* Berkeley: University of California Press.

Kenyon, B. L. (2001). Current research in children's conceptions of death: A critical review. *Omega, Journal of Death and Dying, 43,* 63–91.

Lee, P. W. H., Lieh-Mak, F., Hung, B. K. M., & Luk, S. L. (1983/1984). Death anxiety in leukemic Chinese children. *International Journal of Psychiatry in Medicine, 13,* 281–290.

Levetown, M. (2002). Children, caring for when life-threatened or dying. In R. Kastenbaum (Ed.), *Macmillan encyclopedia of death and dying* (Vol. 1, pp. 147–154.) New York: Macmillan.

Lonetto, R. (1980). *Children's conceptions of death.* New York: Springer.

Meagher, D. K., & Leff, P. T. (1989/1990). In Marie's memory: The rights of the child with life-threatening or terminal illness. *Omega, Journal of Death and Dying, 20,* 177–191.

Nagy, M. H. (1969). The child's theories concerning death. In H. Feifel (Ed.), *The meaning of death.* New York: McGraw-Hill. (Reprinted from *Journal of Genetic Psychology, 73,* 3–27, 1948).

Opie, I., & Opie, R. (1969). *Children's games in street and playground.* London: Oxford University Press.

Papadatou, D. (1997). Training health professionals in caring for dying children and grieving families. *Death Studies, 6,* 575–600.

Papadatou, D., Papazoglou, I., Petraki, D., & Bellali, T. (1999). Mutual support among nurses who provide care to dying children. *Illness, Crisis, and Loss, 7,* 37–48.

Philadelphia Child Guidance Center. (1993). *Your child's emotional health.* New York: Macmillan.

Saurez, M. M., & McFeaters, S. J. (2000). Culture and class: The different worlds of children and adolescents. In K. J. Doka (Ed.), *Living with grief. Children, adolescents, and loss* (pp. 55–70). New York: Brunner/Mazel.

Silverman, P. R. (2000). When parents die. In K. J. Doka (Ed.), *Living with grief. Children, adolescents, and loss* (pp. 215–228). New York: Brunner/Mazel.

Silverman, P. R., & Worden, J. W. (1992). Children's understanding of funeral ritual. *Omega, Journal of Death and Dying, 25,* 319–332.

Sourkes, B. M. (1996). *Armfuls of time. The psychological experience of the child with a life-threatening disease.* Pittsburgh, PA: University of Pittsburgh Press.

Stevenson, K. G. (2000). The role of death education in helping students to cope with loss (pp. 195–206). In K. J. Doka (Ed.), *Living with grief. Children, adolescents, and loss.* New York: Brunner/Mazel.

Wass, H. (2002). Children and media violence. In R. Kastenbaum (Ed.), *Macmillan encyclopedia of death and dying* (Vol. 1, pp. 133–139). New York: Macmillan.

Webb, N. B. (1993). Traumatic death of friend/peers: Case of Susan, age 9. In N. B. Webb (Ed.), *Helping bereaved children* (pp. 189–211). New York: Guilford.

Wenestam, C-G., & Wass, H. (1987). Swedish and U.S. children's thinking about death: A qualitative study and cross-cultural comparison. *Death Studies, 11,* 99–122.

White, E. B. (1952). *Charlotte's web.* New York: Harper & Row.

Zall, D. S. (1994). The long term effects of childhood bereavement: Impact on roles as mothers. *Omega, Journal of Death and Dying, 29,* 219–230.

Zelizer, V. A. (1994). *Pricing the priceless child.* Princeton, NJ: Princeton University Press.

GLOSSARY

Affect: Emotion.

Aphasic: Unable to speak, most often a consequence of a cerebrovascular accident (also known as a stroke).

Bereavement: The loss of a loved one through death.

Cystic Fibrosis: A hereditary disorder in which lungs and other organ systems are blocked by abnormal mucus secretions. A life-threatening condition.

Death Anxiety: Emotional distress and insecurity aroused by encounters with dead bodies, grieving people, or other reminders of mortality, including one's own thoughts.

Dissociative Episodes: Experiences that are not well integrated into the individual's basic personality and that therefore may be interpreted as coming from some other source.

Heuristic: A stimulus to further achievements, events, or knowledge.

Introversion: The personality characteristic of turning one's attention and energies inward, as contrasted with extroversion, the direction of one's interests toward other people.

Leukemia: A progressive disease that produces distorted and dysfunctional white blood cells, increasing susceptibility to infection, bleeding, and anemia. Sometimes a life-threatening condition.

Personification: Representing an idea or feeling as a human or human-like form.

Plague: The plague that resulted in the deaths of at least one-fourth of the population of Europe in the late 14th century is generally considered to have been bubonic disease, carried by rats and fleas as well as stricken humans. Also known as "The Black Death."

Posttraumatic Stress Disorder: A (sometimes delayed) response to a death that has occurred under highly stressful conditions. The traumatic event is reexperienced repeatedly, and other disturbances of feeling, thought, and behavior are also likely to occur.

Separation Anxiety: Emotional distress and insecurity aroused by loss of contact with a valued and protective person (also observed in animal behavior)

Sibling: A brother or sister.

Trauma: A wound, injury, or emotional shock that produces injury.

Local people affected by the crash of a hijacked airliner in a Shanksville, Pennsylvania, field established their own simple memorials to honor the victims.

chapter 12

BEREAVEMENT, GRIEF, AND MOURNING

I've seen my father, literally seen him standing in the lane with his hand out to me. I talk to him all the time. I talk to my mother. I saw my son standing by the road waiting to be picked up a couple of times. And then it wouldn't be anybody there, or it would be a post, or it would be somebody who looked like him.
—Terkel (2001, p. 273)

A fleet of unlicensed vehicles would close off a street, heavily armed men in plainclothes would storm an apartment or house, terrify the family, break in and pillage possessions, then assault and kidnap one or more family members, usually a young adult. The victims were taken to centers hidden around Buenos Aires and the rest of the country where they would be brutally tortured for hours to days to months before being killed.
—Thornton (2000, p. 281)

I'm an island. And I'm not happy with it.... I stay at home with my dog. I insulate myself. I'm waiting on the sidelines. I'm waiting for a sign that things will be all-clear.
—Chethik (2001, p. 53)

My father died at age 86 following a lengthy bout with lung cancer and heart problems.... His request to me the night before he died was, "I want you to care for Mother. I know it won't be easy, but all I'm asking is that you do this the best you can." Those words are as clear today as they were 16 years ago. They haunted me when Mother died. I had failed to take care of her.
—Bozeman (1999, p. 94)

I used to wish that she would die. I remember before I brought her home from the hospital thinking, God, I wish she would just die and then I

wouldn't have to bring her home and go through this and put the kids through this. And I just couldn't have been more wrong.
—Milo (1997, p. 457)

There's always this great hole inside that hurts…it didn't matter what you did, it was there. So I felt all these things I was doing, as if I was building a pattern, a life around it. I couldn't—you can't ever fill it, but you build a life around.
—Bennett and Bennett (2000/2001, p. 244)

Many of us can remember the moment that we learned a treasured life was taken away from us. Perhaps it was a telephone call or a knock on the door. Perhaps we had been there to witness the passing for ourselves. Whether the death was sudden or long expected, usually there was a moment in time in which the event fractured our lives. Some of us continue to live with or within that moment even many years later. Almost all of us discover that the loss has remained an ongoing part of our lives even when the moment of separation has long passed. We are the bereaved. We are the grieving. We are the mourning. And, as will be seen, we are also the vulnerable.

The related experiences of bereavement, grief, and mourning are powerful aspects of both our individual lives and the mood and functioning of our society. This chapter examines one of the most profound links with the whole procession of the human race: the capacity to suffer deeply and yet to renew our commitment to life when separated by death from a beloved person.

SOME RESPONSES TO LOSS

We have stepped briefly into the lives of several people who responded to a death in several ways. Folk singer Rosalie Sorrels had known many deaths during her long life, starting with her childhood on a farm. "You know, I never thought of death as unfriendly" (Terkel, 2001, p. 266). Furthermore, she did not think it strange

or alarming that she still seems to come across some of her favorite dead people from time to time. In her interview with Studs Terkel, the distinguished oral historian, Sorrels was comfortable in describing a continuing bond with the dead. Is this unusual? Is it "pathological" or "healthy"? We explore what becomes and what should become of a relationship after it has been interrupted by death.

Death squads terrorized the citizens of Argentina during the oppressive 8-year (1976–1983) military regime. This was terrorism of perhaps the most brutal kind—carried out not by outsiders or a few dissidents but as a core feature of government policy. People were afraid to protest or even ask questions because of the constant threat that one might be the next to disappear without notice. *Los Madres de la Plaza de Mayo* was an improbable response to this intolerable situation. One by one, women whose children had been kidnapped by the regime reached out to each other for support. Many had already tried to contact the authorities to learn what had happened but were rudely dismissed. There seemed to be nothing left for them to do but to continue with their anxiety and sorrow. The slow process of healing could not really begin while the fate of their children remained unknown.

That the women should band together to protest against the terrorist regime was almost unbelievable. Women were supposed to restrict themselves to their duties at home and not meddle in public affairs, even when these affairs affected them deeply (Thornton, 2000):

When ordered to move on by the police, they... started *la ronda,* the walk around and around the Plaza, which was to become a trademark of their peaceful protest.... The women were threatened with weapons and dogs, sometimes had cocked guns put to their heads, and sprayed with water cannons or tear gas. (p. 282)

Despite intimidation, ridicule, and some "disappearances" within their ranks, the mothers persevered. Hebe de Bonafini, mother of two missing sons, explains why (de Bonafini, 1991):

If they cannot be here, then I have had to take their place, to shout for them...I feel them present in my banners, in my unending fatigue, in my mind and body, in everything I do I think that their absence has left me pregnant forever. (p. 287)

The Mothers of the Plaza experienced an inner transformation through which they realized that they were rebelling not only against the constricted role of women in their society but also against a militaristic regime in which force and violence were systematically employed against the public at large. The public eventually responded to their example, contributing to the downfall of the militaristic government: "They were discovering a new self—one of courage, dignity, and worth. Their grief was being transformed into action for the good of all (Thornton, 2000, p. 283). Grief can be a powerful motivating force for individuals and for society.

John Donne, one of the greatest poets of the 18th or any other century, had written in one of his devotions that "No man is an island." Nevertheless, Seth (Chethik, 2001) felt that he was an island after the death of his father. How adult men experience the death of their fathers was, until recently, one of the most neglected topics in bereavement research. Neil Chethik's *FatherLoss* (2001) describes the varied ways in which the relationship between a father and son affects the grief and recovery process. One quickly learns how much difference a breakthrough in a distant or conflicted relationship can make in both the father–son ongoing relationship and the quality of the son's life after bereavement. Seth did give himself his own all-clear sign 4 years after the death and moved on to a more satisfying and productive life.

Grief is painful, but we usually get over it in a year or so—right? Wrong! Jeanine Cannon Bozeman, a professor of social work at New Orleans Baptist Theological Seminary, describes the lasting impact of her mother's death on her. After 16 years, she reported still having difficulty in accepting this loss and in forgiving the driver of the car in which her mother had been a passenger. Is 16 years a long time to grieve? I have known people who were still caught up in deaths that occurred more than half a century ago, feeling that there just might have been something else they could have done or should have done. Time does not always heal, and what has become known as unresolved grief accompanies many people throughout their lives.

In this chapter, we carefully examine the grief and recovery process for parents who have lost children and children who have lost parents. We also consider husbands who have lost wives and wives who have lost husbands and siblings who have lost siblings. Sometimes, though, we do not seem to have the right to grieve—we were not family, but the pain is there. Accordingly, we also examine hidden or disenfranchised grief.

There are also circumstances in which none of us are "supposed" to grieve because the person who died was not considered to be really a person in the full sense of the word. This was the subject of research by Elisabeth Moulton Milo (1997), who studied mothers who received little social support or understanding upon the death of their developmentally disabled children.

We must be attentive to the way society and the individual regard the person who has died and to the questions of value and meaning that can become insistent after a death.

A sound general understanding of bereavement, grief, and mourning would be helpful before we examine specific issues. We begin by clarifying basic concepts and becoming acquainted with major theories of grief. How people actually cope with loss is then examined in detail, drawing on the most useful of both classic and current research. This includes attention to the impact of grief on the survival of the survivors: Is grief hazardous to our health? Although we will discover common patterns and themes, we will also become aware of great individual differences and of the role played by sociocultural expectations. Finally, we build on these observations to improve our ability to recognize and respond helpfully to the grief experience, whether in ourselves or in others.

DEFINING OUR TERMS: BEREAVEMENT, GRIEF, MOURNING

Bereavement, grief, and mourning—these words cannot convey the impact that a death can have on the survivors. However, let us at least begin with these words and see how they can best be understood.

Bereavement: An Objective Fact

Bereavement is an objective fact. We are bereaved when a person close to us dies. The term is usually applied when the person who has died is part of our family or a close friend. There is no hard and fast rule about how far this term should be extended. The death of a coworker, for example, might or might not be considered a bereavement, depending on the relationship that had existed. Bereavement conveys the idea of a tearing-apart, forcible separation that results in the loss of something we once had. That "something" is a vital and perhaps sustaining relationship.

Bereavement is also a change in status. A child becomes an orphan, a wife a widow, a husband a widower. Bereavement status can only suggest what the survivors might be experiencing and how they have adapted to the loss. It is an objective fact that serves as a clue to possible psychological, social, and physical distress.

Bereavement is also an outcome of large-scale social phenomena. Widowhood and orphanhood are major consequences of natural disaster, terrorism, and war. Thousands of families had their lives shattered by deaths in the terrorist attacks of September 11, 2001. The lethal events were swift; the consequences will be enduring. Perhaps we can spare a thought for the millions who were bereaved by the killing fields and trenches of World

War I (the "War to End All Wars"). Thousands of men died each day. Approximately 100,000 of the brightest and most educated German youth were sent quickly to their deaths in the first battle of Ypres (Groom, 2002), with many more deaths yet to come. British, French, and Belgian losses were also horrendous. All the adversary nations were deprived of fathers, husbands, sons, and brothers and left with a population of survivors who could not be expected to pick up their lives as usual when the war ended. World War I slaughter and bereavement had a profound and continuing effect on society and, to a greater or lesser extent, the same can be said of other catastrophes in which the large-scale loss of life led to substantial changes in societal patterns as well as individual experience.

Bereavement can also occur on a large scale in a much less conspicuous way. Although more people now live longer, there are also more widows than ever. Social isolation and loneliness have become recognized as a major source of stress and vulnerability. Although bereavement by itself is only a bare objective fact, it is also a fact that tends to generate increased vulnerability and stress.

Grief: A Painful Response

Grief is a response to bereavement; it is how the survivor feels. It is also how the survivor thinks, eats, sleeps, and makes it through the day. The term does not explain anything. Grief requires careful understanding on a person-by-person basis; it is not a word that can be taken as a simple explanation of what is being experienced and why.

Furthermore, grief is not the only possible response to bereavement. There may be anger or indifference, for example. Some individuals show what psychiatrists term a *dissociative flight* from the impact of death—a pattern of denial that can become so extreme that it forms the core of a psychotic reaction. Some people clearly recognize their loss but appear unable or unwilling to grieve at a particular time. Nevertheless, the grief response is so frequent and so painful that it is of primary importance for those who wish to understand and comfort the bereaved.

A useful distinction is often made between the grief experienced at the first recognition of the loss and the grief that continues long afterward.

Thousands of soldiers on both sides of "No Man's Land" lived and died in trenches during World War I.

The following is a classic description of the observable physical symptoms of acute grief (Lindemann, 1944):

> The picture shown by people in acute grief is remarkably uniform. Common to all is the following syndrome: sensations of somatic distress occurring in waves lasting from 20 minutes to an hour at a time, a feeling of tightness in the throat, choking with shortness of breath, need for sighing, an empty feeling in the abdomen, lack of muscular power, and an intensive subjective distress described as tension or pain. (p. 145)

Other symptoms also commonly seen were insomnia, failures of memory, absent-mindedness, problems in concentrating, and the tendency to do the same things repeatedly.

This classic description by psychiatrist Eric Lindemann (1994) should be considered in context. He was working with people who had been stunned by the sudden death of loved ones in the Cocoanut Grove fire (Boston, 1942), in which 400 people perished in less than 15 minutes and others died later of severe burns and smoke inhalation. It has since been learned that the total symptom picture seen by Lindemann may not be expressed by every person who has an acute grief reaction. Nevertheless, Lindmann's description conveys a vivid sense of what it is like to be overwhelmed by grief.

Grief affects all spheres of life. The grieving person's body does not work very well. George Engel (1963) was among the first to suggest that an intensive or sustained grief reaction can precipitate serious illness, even death, in bereaved individu- als who have underlying physical problems. Cur- rent theory and research continue to provide support for considering grief to be a physical dis- order as well as a personal crisis. It is the whole person who grieves, and this person is part of a network of interpersonal relationships. Grieving takes place both within and between people and shows its effects in all spheres. Consider, for ex- ample, a few of the major changes in the way our bodies function, and the way in which grief can influence our thoughts and relationships.

Neuroendocrine Changes in Grief

The grief experience operates as a stressor. The biochemical and physiological concomitants of grief place additional strain on the weak links in the bereaved person's physical systems, with the particular type of somatic reaction that develops depending on the particular weak link or defect that preexisted in the bereaved (Hall & Irwin, 2001) Individual differences in cognitive, behav- ioral, and relational responses influence the neu- roendocrine system's response to the stress of grief.

Each response to the loss can also contribute to further distress. For example, if we become with- drawn and inactive, we might become more vul- nerable to opportunistic infections because of lowered body tone. Furthermore, new problems continue to arise as the survivor attempts to ad- just to an altered life situation. The homeostatic mechanisms of the body try to moderate the stress as the first shock of the loss is followed by a period of active grieving. This protective response can result in *adaptation to chronic stress.* It is possible for the protective response of the neuroendocrine system to contribute to a new form of homeosta- sis, one that assumes the continued existence of stress. Some grief responses become increasingly difficult to "get over" because our central nervous system has dedicated itself so effectively to mod- erating the effect of the stress. In other words, we may have to deal with our physiological response to stress as well as the stress itself.

Studies indicate that the stress of grief pro- duces much wear and tear on the body, along with increased risk of cardiovascular, infectious, and inflammatory disorders. Furthermore, there is evidence that stress-related hormones become

more active. Hall and Irwin (2001) report that the higher levels of cortisol, epinephrine, and norephrine are signs that grieving people are un- dergoing a destabilization of their physiological systems. These changes can be regarded as warn- ings of possible risk to health and survival.

The immune system, our primary defense against pathogens, appears to be especially vul- nerable to the stress of grief. The "killer cells" that destroy threatening invaders have been shown to become fewer and less active in women who have either experienced a death or are living with the anxious expectation of a death. Unfor- tunately, there are also some indications that this heightened vulnerability may persist over an ex- tended period of time.

The link between physiological response and in- terpersonal relationships will become more fully understood with continuing research, but there are already some provocative findings. For exam- ple, infant monkeys show significant immunolog- ical and other physiological changes when they are separated from their mothers for even a short time (Laudenslager, Boccia, & Reite, 1993). The infant monkeys who were most agitated, slouch- ing, and withdrawn were also those whose im- mune systems were most affected by the stress of separation. However, when the mother and in- fant are reunited, the young monkey's immune system returns to normal. (It would be interesting to know what is happening to the mother's im- mune system during this time as well.)

Furthermore, the young monkeys show less be- havioral and physiological stress during maternal separation if they are kept in a familiar environ- ment and can see their peers. Familiar surround- ings seem to have some value in buffering the effects of the loss experience. Monkeys as well as humans experience both behavioral and physio- logical stress when separated from their "signifi- cant others," and monkeys as well as humans can cope with this stress more successfully when pro- vided with social support before and during the grief process.

Physical aspects of distress can be intensified by how the person responds to the loss. Going with- out proper nutrition and rest and neglecting self- care are a dysfunctional pattern—add alcohol and indiscriminate use of medications and it becomes worse. Both behavioral and physiological responses to the stress of loss can place the bereaved person at heightened risk. Just how high is this risk? Are grieving people at special risk for death? We will consider this question later.

Personal and Interpersonal Responses to the Stress of Grief

The mind of the grieving person may not work as well as usual. Problems with attention, concentration, and memory increase the person's risk to self and others. A person who is usually alert and responsible becomes an inattentive driver, a parent who fails to notice household hazards, or a worker who becomes careless on the job. It is the emotional side of grief that often besets the survivor with the greatest distress, however. The person may be tossed between opposite extremes of reaction (Glick, Weiss, & Parkes, 1974):

> When I got home from the morgue, I was just out for the rest of the day. I just couldn't help myself. I thought I would have a nervous breakdown, and my heart was going so fast. The man at the morgue said, "Well, if you don't stop crying, you're going to have a nervous breakdown." But all I could do was cry. That's all I could do. And I told him, "If I don't cry, God, my heart will burst." I had to cry, because he wasn't going to be back no more. (p. 17)

This woman had just found herself transformed from wife to widow. She first experienced shock and could not feel or think at all. Then she could not stop herself from feeling and crying. She feared for her self-control, even for her sanity. People in acute grief sometimes feel that they are "going crazy," that they will keep "getting worse and worse and then just fall all apart." Those who have previously experienced such intense grief and have since found their way back can be very helpful to those who are in the midst of such experiences.

Distress does not end with the first wave of shock and grief. It is not enough to realize that a loved one is dead. One now faces the further realization that life is supposed to go on. Depending on the individual and the situation at the time of the death, there may be further waves of confusion, anxiety, rage, and other painful inner states. The sense of numbness can also return,

sometimes to linger as though it would never go away.

That grief can return in wave after wave of distress was discovered in an important study of 19th-century American diaries. Paul Rosenblatt (1983) found that recurring experiences of grief were common to the bereaved. A period of time would go by in which thoughts and feelings turned to other matters. Suddenly, the memories would come flooding back, sometimes as painful as ever. People who felt they had recovered completely from the pangs of grief might be engulfed in a wave of distress months or years later. Some of the diary entries expressed a more profound sense of grief years after the loss than they had at the time of the loss: "I think of Ma so much, and the horror of her taking never leaves me. Why should that condition come to her. Why should she keep it secret so long. What would have prevented it" (p. 23). This entry was written two and one-half years after the death of this man's wife. He had expressed no sense of grief for her in some time.

Many occasions could renew the sense of grief: "I think of Henry every time I sit at the table and see his place is vacant." "[Sitting again] in our old pew, I could not help thinking of my dear parents and before I could stop myself was crying bitterly" (Rosenblatt, 1983, p. 27).

Anniversaries, places that rekindle a memory, and people who remind us of the lost person all have the power to start a new wave of grief long after the death. Grief may return again and again, long after the bereavement. Most people seem to recover well from their first intense grief episode. The vulnerability often remains, although subsequent episodes are likely to be much briefer—an image, a sudden pang, a catch of the breath, a readiness to weep…and then, after a pause, a going on with life.

Mourning: A Signal of Distress

Mourning is the culturally patterned expression of the bereaved person's thoughts and feelings. Bereavement is a universal experience. No society, ancient or contemporary, has been spared the loss of people it valued, loved, and depended on. How people express their loss is not universal, however. These expressions vary from culture to culture and also change over time. Dennis Klass (2002) observes that even the basic concepts of grief and mourning differ appreciably across cultures:

> Grief as a real subjective state grows from a culture that prizes and cultivates individual experience. There is no equivalent to the term *grief* in some other languages; indeed, in some cultures, as in Japan, the concept of emotions that are only in the individual seems foreign. (p. 383)

Perhaps the connection between inner state (grief) and outer expression (mourning) is so close in some societies that we should not try to separate them. However, since most of us do live within a society that emphasizes individual experience, the distinction between mourning and grief can remain helpful.

Recent studies have shown that there is often a real-life distinction between grief and mourning. Terry Martin and Kenneth Doka (2000) identified a *dissonant pattern* among some bereaved people: "Here there is dissonance between the way a person experiences grief and the manner in which that person expresses and adapts to grief. This usually occurs with an individual who…finds it difficult to express that emotion" (p. 160). The dissonant pattern was found more often with men, although there are marked differences in grief and mourning within each gender.

From World War I to September 11, 2001

Geoffrey Gorer (1977) observed striking changes in mourning behavior within the same culture during his own lifetime. When his father died aboard the *Lusitania,* capsized by a torpedo in 1915, his mother became "a tragic, almost a frightening figure in the full panoply of widow's weeds and unrelieved black, a crepe veil shrouding her…so that she was visibly withdrawn from the world." However, within a few months the death toll from World War I had become visibly represented throughout all of England: "Widows in mourning became increasingly frequent in the streets, so that Mother no longer stood out in the crowd." Eventually, signs of mourning were modified, reduced. Too many people were being touched too closely by death. The functioning of society as a whole would have been impaired had every bereaved person pursued every step of the

traditional mourning ritual, which included a long period of withdrawal from everyday life. The previous tradition of mourning maintained its place so long as death was occasional; a new pattern had to be developed when death was rampant in everybody's neighborhood almost all the time.

There have been times when individual bereavement and grief come across clearly even in a complex and diversified society such as the United States. The gold star in the window of many a home in the United States during World War II indicated that a very particular life had been lost. That particular death however, represented part of a national, shared cause. Each gold star mother had her special bereavement, but collectively they signified a loss felt by the entire nation. Where are the "gold star mothers" for Americans who died in Vietnam? Acknowledgment, sympathy, and support for families grieving for loved ones killed in Vietnam were much less in evidence than in most previous military engagements (but consider the delayed response in the form of the Vietnam Memorial Wall later in this chapter). By the time American armed forces had withdrawn from Vietnam, the war had become a divisive rather than a unified national cause.

The Gulf War produced another different type of mourning response. Death was notably absent from the messages about the Gulf War that reached viewers and readers in the United States (Umberson & Henderson, 1992). Smart bombs "serviced" their targets, and not-so-smart bombs resulted in "collateral damage." The attempt to eliminate images of death from Gulf War reports may have contributed to the public's difficulty in mourning those who died on all sides of the conflict. It was a little different with Kosovo and Afghanistan. The remarkable absence of U.S. combat casualties during the military operation in Kosovo and the few in Afghanistan spared families grief and mourning, although not the anxiety of separation.

The Oklahoma City bombing aroused sorrow and anger throughout the general public. The community and its leadership worked together in a sense of sustained purpose that not only resulted in an innovative memorial (see Chapter 13) for the victims but also made it evident that healing was everybody's endeavor.

Mourning for the September 11, 2001, victims has had even larger dimensions. There have been numerous memorial services, some informal and limited to the people most closely concerned and some replete with prominent officials, celebrities, and national television coverage. As previously observed (Chapter 1), strenuous efforts were made to identify and recover remains so that family mourning could begin. Two other facets of the mourning for terrorist attack victims also stand out: The individuality of each victim was recognized at every opportunity (e.g., reading of the names and displaying their photographs), and New York City was treated as victim (e.g., sorrow for loss of the World Trade Center towers and, indirectly, for the blow to the image and stature of a city that had been the first destination of many immigrants and the long-time symbol of American power). Some catastrophes strike so severely at the core of a people that intensive mourning seems to be essential for recovery even to begin.

Culturally Varied Patterns of Mourning

Mourning occurs on a smaller and more personal scale for most of us in private life. Still, the

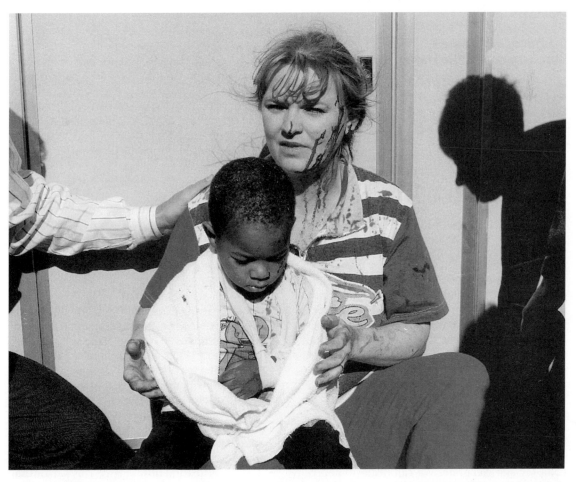

Comfort is offered to a child who survived the bombing of the Alfred E. Murrah Federal Building in Oklahoma City. Acts of violence not only take lives, but also place survivors at risk for post-traumatic stress disorder and other complicated grief reactions.

ways in which we express the recognition of death reflect the attitudes and customs of society. Nations as varied as the United States offer many patterns of mourning—compare those of Americans who are of African, Chinese, Korean, Japanese, Italian, or Central European–Jewish heritage, for example. Furthermore, traditions of mourning are subject to change. Many people have been uprooted from their native lands or have chosen to move elsewhere in search of opportunities for an improved quality of life. Because of their beliefs and practices, though, they may encounter difficulties in the process of acculturation. Traditional expressions of mourning can be affected, as with the Hmong when relocated to the United States.

Hmong Mourning Practices in Laos and in the United States

The Hmong people have been known to history for almost 5,000 years. Those who selected Laos as their home became involved in that nation's violent political upheavals during the 1960s. Many fled in fear for their lives in the mid-1970s, and of these refugees approximately 120,000 relocated to the United States.

Mourning in Hmong Homelands

Hmong mourning practices are closely related to their religious beliefs. There is thought to be a spiritual world that coexists with the physical world. The newborn infant is under the care of spirit-parents before its birth and must therefore be inducted into the world of the living through an appropriate ritual. Ancestor-spirits are among the many types of spirits that interact with the world of living people. These spirits can either help or harm the living. It is important, therefore, to show all possible respect to the dead. Failure to treat the dead with respect could lead to adverse effects on the health and prosperity of the surviving family members.

In Laos and other Hmong homelands, the process of showing respect for a deceased person through funeral and mourning practices is complex and elaborate. We can begin to appreciate the significance attached to appropriate mourning by focusing on the large number of helpers who are required. Bliatout (1993) iden-

tified the following types of helpers who must be available:

- *Guide to the spirit world:* This person will recite the *Qhuab Ke* verses from memory. Included in this recitation must be a mention of every place in which the deceased lived. Unless this recitation is offered, the deceased will not know that he or she has died and also will not be able to find his or her way back to the place of birth. It is crucial to return to one's birth place because the placenta has been buried there and is needed if the soul is to make it safely back to the spirit world.
- *Reed pipe player and drummer:* Usually two musicians are required. Their music verifies the fact that a death has occurred and provides safe passage to the soul of the deceased from one world to the other. The performance makes great demands on the stamina of the musicians, and the instruments themselves are sacred. Mourning has not properly started without this music.
- *Counselor to the family:* An elder is selected to sing comforting traditional songs to the family on the evening before the funeral.
- *Counselor to the dead:* Only deceased elders receive this special attention in which texts are recited that are helpful to the soul on its journey between the world of the living and the world of ancestral spirits. Funeral, safe passage, and mourning rituals are more elaborate in general for elders than for younger members of the society.
- *Funeral director and an assistant:* They serve mainly as coordinators to make sure that all tasks are being carried out properly by others.
- *Shoe maker:* This person constructs special shoes from woven hemp. "These special shoes turn up at the toe; without them, the souls will be unable to cross the big river, walk the treacherous paths, step over valleys of snakes …and arrive at the spirit world" (p. 87).
- *Stretcher-maker:* This person creates a symbolic horse from bamboo thatch and two long wooden poles. The deceased will lie on this pallet for several days until the burial.
- *Geomancer* (a kind of shaman): This person discovers the best time for the burial to take place.
- *Food server:* This person is specially trained to communicate with the souls of the deceased.

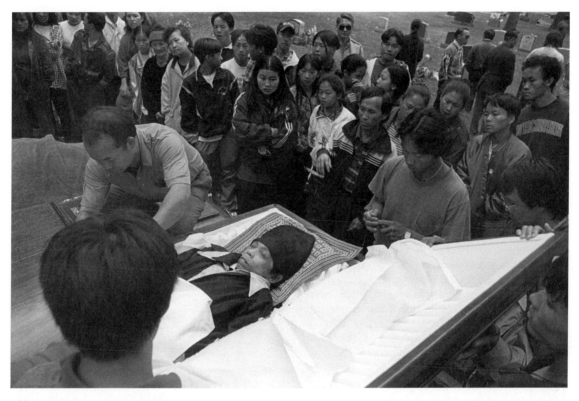

Hmong funerals include complex rituals for the passage of the deceased person to the next life and the safety of the family. Here a body is being checked for metal or other foreign objects that might leave a curse on the family.

- *Warrior:* The warrior shoots arrows or fires his gun in the air and engages in other rituals to help protect the deceased on his or her journey.
- *Coffin makers:* They must locate the right tree to cut down and use. There must be no metal in the coffin or any material other than the specific wood that is required.
- *Sacrificial ox slayers:* They must choose the right ox or oxen for this purpose. A whole day may be devoted to rituals associated with the sacrifices.

This list of helpers is incomplete, but the point has surely been made. For Hmong living in their homelands, the death of a family member cannot be mourned appropriately unless the funeral process involves many people carrying out specified roles with specified materials in specified ways. The funeral and mourning processes blend into

each other all along the way. The process is an extensive one: for example, the 13th Day End ritual must be performed after that amount of time has passed since the burial. It is on this occasion that the soul is finally released from its body and is free to journey to the spirit world. In the meantime, nobody works at their normal tasks other than preparation of food and other basic life-support activities.

Hmong Mourning in the United States

What happens when Hmong relocate to the United States? As you can easily imagine, a great many problems arise. Here is a sampling of the problems that Bliatout (1993) has identified:

- *The American medical system urges or require autopsies in some cases.* "This is considered one of the most horrible things that can happen to a Hmong person, as it is believed that the person will be born mutilated in the next life" (p. 96).

- *Often, there is no opportunity for the Hmong to wash, dress, lay out the body themselves, or provide the symbolic (stretcher) horse.* This can lead to fears that one is not serving the deceased properly and therefore interfere significantly with the grieving and mourning process.
- *The reed pipes and funeral drum may not be allowed because they might disturb the neighbors.* Again, mourners may fear that they are jeopardizing the safety of the deceased soul as well as their own lives because of this failure to honor and protect their dead. The sacrifice of oxen, the firing of guns, and other traditional rituals are also likely to be banned or to become impractical in their new environment.
- *Some Hmongs convert to Christianity and adopt lifestyles associated with our industrial–technical, mass media culture.* This can lead to a rift within and between Hmong families that, in turn, is likely to interfere with their established patterns of communal mourning.

The Hmong story—still in the process of transition—has many other parallels in our pluralistic society. Few if any ethnic/racial traditions of mourning are immune from influence and challenge.

Appreciating Universality and Diversity in the Response to Bereavement: An African American Example

People living within one culture have been known to misinterpret the bereavement responses of people within another culture. The mistaken assumption that life is cheap in Asia, for example, has been fostered by outsider ignorance of culturally expressed modes of mourning. Our difficulties in comprehending what another person is experiencing when bereaved are often compounded by cultural differences, but even within the "same" culture there can be a lack of understanding about what the bereaved person goes through.

Pulitzer Prize-winning poet and novelist Alice Walker has described some of her own personal experiences that help to illuminate both what is universal and what is distinctive about a particular culture's response to grief. In a book written

primarily for children, *To Hell with Dying* (1988), Walker tells of her love for an old man by the name of Mr. Sweet. He was not the usual type of elderly person who would be invited to be the main character in a children's story: "Mr. Sweet was a diabetic and an alcoholic and a guitar player and lived down the road from us on a neglected cotton farm" (p. 1). Nevertheless, he was a continual source of delight and instruction for Walker and her older brothers and sisters. One of Mr. Sweet's specialties was dying. He seemed very close to death on several occasions but was rescued by the Walker children who, on a signal from their father, would

> come crowding around the bed and throw themselves on the covers, and whoever was the smallest at the time would kiss him all over his wrinkled brown face and begin to tickle him so that he would laugh all down in his stomach, and his mustache, which was long and sort of straggly, would shake like Spanish moss and was also that color. (p. 3).

As told by the adult Alice Walker (1988), Mr. Sweet had long ago learned that the careers he wanted for himself—doctor, lawyer, or sailor—were at that time out of reach for a poor black boy. In this sense, he might have been living in grief all his life, having lost his childhood vision of an exciting and rewarding career. However, he excelled in bringing joy to the children in his rural neighborhood. Alice Walker, belonging to a new generation, moved away for the college education that eventually contributed to her notable career as a writer. Using these writing skills, she has given us a portrait of love and grief during a period of time in American history when many people of African heritage were denied equal access to opportunity.

The smiles and tears of *To Hell with Dying* (1988) have universal resonance, but the *particulars* of the experiences shared by Mr. Sweet and the Walker family reflect the unique patterns of life in a rural black community during a recent period of our society. An outsider, for example, would have no way of knowing that the old guitar in a young black woman's hands was a tangible expression of both loss and continuity, grief and love.

How do Africans cope with grief and mourning when they are in their homelands? There are as many answers as there are varied heritages, but an instructive example comes from the Yoruba of Western Nigeria (Adamolekun, 1999). There is a strong tradition of support for people in mourning. Even the salutations or greetings that one person gives to another play a role in this support system. Every person in mourning is greeted by other members of the community with expressions of concern, support, and encouragement. These expressions are specific to the kind of bereavement that was experienced (e.g., a spouse, parent, or child), how the death occurred (e.g., long illness or sudden accident), and to the age, gender, and situation of the mourning person. This careful differentiation of message makes it clear that the society is aware of the distinctive loss that has been experienced. All of the salutations acknowledge the pain of the loss and many congratulate the mourner for having the courage to bear up to this sorrow. An example of the salutation being made relevant to the mourner's specific situation is the reminder to take good care of oneself in order to meet obligations for the family:

> This is more pertinent when a young widow is so overwhelmed with her grief that she feels she were dead or even tries to harm herself physically. Other survivors, like brothers, sisters, cousins, and nephews are sometimes prevented, through some phrases, from hurting themselves. This is more so when death is sudden and the deceased is in the prime of life. (p. 282)

The Yoruba response clearly shows that the community is aware of the grieving person's loss, recognizes the sorrow and stress, and encourages the person to go on with life. This community-wide support is seldom evident in the United States and other urbanized, technologically driven nations in which there is little patience with the mourning process.

Perhaps you have a cherished possession that reminds you of a person who is no longer with you. Perhaps, like Alice Walker, the memories represented by this object or picture help to nourish your sense of personal identity across all the years of your life. Getting rid of Mr. Sweet's old guitar might seem like a good idea—we would not have to look at it and have our sorrows rekindled. However, this might also deprive us of a precious link to the past and those who have meant much to us. Perhaps you agree that it is both more natural and more helpful to directly acknowledge the mourner's grief rather than avoid the subject or, worse, avoid the person.

THEORETICAL PERSPECTIVES ON GRIEF

We are mainly concerned with grief throughout the remainder of this chapter. Bereavement is a significant event in the life of the survivors, and mourning is a significant process of interaction between survivors and their society. Grief, however, is the major source of emotional distress for the individual and can lead both to long-term dysfunction and increased risk of death for the survivor. Theoretical perspectives on grief can help us to make sense of the sometimes puzzling responses and outcomes that can be observed in the wake of a death. Theory might also guide us in making more precise and sensitive observations. Most important, a sound understanding of grief can help survivors cope with their losses.

TYPES OF GRIEF

It is clear that the grieving process is not identical for all people in all circumstances. There is an ongoing effort by clinicians and researchers to make the most useful distinctions among types of grief. We examine several terms that have been applied to forms of grief: normal, pathological, complicated, traumatic, resolved, unresolved, and anticipatory.

Normal as Distinguished from Pathological, Complicated, or Traumatic Grief

Mental health experts have learned over the years that grief is basically a human and not a pathological or abnormal response to loss. This is an important point of agreement because it discredits the assumption that people should just take the loss of a loved one in stride and get on with their lives without making a fuss. It also implies that before we judge that a person is "crazy with grief" we should check to see if perhaps it is our own discomfort with emotional expression that is at work. As Klass and others have cautioned, we might consider that people are grieving "too much" as well as "too little" because of our differing cultural orientations. Nevertheless, there are situations in which grief is so extreme, so debilitating, and so enduring that the individual seems headed for catastrophe. There is general agreement that a grief response can become more than painful: It can jeopardize the person's ability to cope with life and meet crucial responsibilities such as parenting or the ability to perform critical tasks such as providing health care or operating a vehicle.

I do not much care for the term normal grief because one is likely to feel anything but normal. However, there is an element of accuracy in the term. Distinguished researcher Margaret Stroebe suggests that grief is normal when it stays within the bounds of a particular cultural tradition (i.e., follows the norm) (Stroebe, 2001). What about pathological grief? Here, Stroebe affirms a position that has become increasingly prevalent in recent years. Pathological grief smacks too much of a biomedical approach. Although there are certainly physical changes involved in the stress of grief, the total experience includes much more, both of the person and of the society. Stroebe therefore would replace "pathological" with "complicated." The grief response can be complicated in several ways. The common feature is that the bereaved person does not move from the shock and pain of loss toward a substantial return to an active and fulfilling life.

Traumatic grief is a more recent concept that is starting to receive general acceptance (Jacobs, 1999; Range, 2002). It refers to a severe and disabling response to sudden, unexpected, and often violent death. Family and friends of terrorist attack victims, in the United States and elsewhere, are especially vulnerable to traumatic grief. The survivor's whole world seems to have collapsed, and it is extremely difficult to restore a sense of meaning and purpose. We might consider traumatic grief to be an especially severe type of complicated grief. Helping people who are experiencing the traumatic form of grief often seems to require professional counseling or therapy and special attention to the circumstances surrounding the death.

Anticipatory Grief

That people sometimes begin grieving before a death occurs has been recognized since the phenomenon was described by Lindemann in 1944. It is believed that anticipatory grief has become increasingly common in recent years as people live longer with life-threatening conditions (Beder, 2002). There is more time to worry, more time to plan, more time to experience stress, and more time to make decisions, clarify values, and strengthen relationships. Anticipatory grief can have both positive and negative consequences. It is how people cope with this expectation of loss that seems to make the difference. Experts are beginning to draw the conclusion that anticipatory grief cushions the impact of the loss to some extent when it does occur, but that the pain and sorrow still come through.

Resolved and Unresolved Grief

There are competing points of view on recovery from grief. Some experts believe that grief can and should be "resolved" within a reasonable (but not standard and fixed) period of time. Others believe that the loss of a crucial relationship is never completely resolved: We can recover much of our function and go on with our lives, but we will never again be the same. This controversy is significant because it can influence the way we respond to grieving people. What should we expect of them (or ourselves, when the loss is personal)? For what it is worth, I doubt that it is useful to push people toward resolution on any external time schedule, and I also doubt that a profound bereavement can disappear simply with the passage of time and change of circumstance. From the practical standpoint, though, we can be helpful by attending to signs of movement or lack of movement toward recovery from the most debilitating effects of grief. Resolved and unresolved grief can be useful concepts when linked to careful observations, as we will see later.

THEORIES OF GRIEF

Theories of grief try to explain not only the general or normal process but also why this experience sometimes overwhelms the bereaved person and what might be done to help.

The Griefwork Theory

The first influential theory was introduced by Sigmund Freud (1919/1959) following the mass death and bereavement of World War I. Freud was shaken to discover that nations so priding themselves on their highly cultivated civilization could behave so brutally toward each other. From his personal sorrows as well as his observation of widespread grief and mourning, Freud offered the following propositions that, taken together, lay down the foundation for griefwork theory:

1. *Grief is an adaptive response to loss.* It is not just an expression of emotional pain. Grief is also a kind of work that must be performed. Our "pay" for this work is the restoration of our own peace of mind and social competence.

2. *The work of grief is difficult and time-consuming.* We cannot take a few days off and pick up normal life as though the loss had not occurred. Both the bereaved person and society should appreciate this fact. Demanding that one's self or others should quickly snap back to the preloss pattern of life can only be stressful and increase the difficulties in carrying out griefwork.

3. *The basic goal of griefwork is to accept the reality of the death and thereby liberate ones self from the strong attachment one had to the "lost object."* Some people make strong emotional investments in each other (e.g., parent and child, husband and wife). Freud used the term *cathexis* in discussing these vital interpersonal bonds. We must somehow recover the emotional investment we made in the deceased person so that we can reinvest it in other relationships and values. How do we go about the detachment (*decathexis*) process? We must accept the fact that the loved one is really and truly lost to us. We cannot keep clinging to memory, hope, or fantasy. This acceptance must be accomplished on a deep emotional level; it is not enough to have only an intellectual acknowledgment of the loss.

4. *Griefwork is carried out through a long series of confrontations with the reality of the loss.* Survivors must deal with all the feelings, all the memories, and all the daily life encounters that bring to mind their attachment to the deceased person. Often, one must confront the same point of attachment repeatedly. For example, the survivor might have to listen repeatedly to a particular song that was a favorite of the deceased person before this song loses its power to overwhelm him or her with anxiety and sorrow.

5. *The process is complicated by the survivor's resistance to letting go of the attachment.* We want to stay in touch with the "lost object" in any way we can. The need to hold on to the attachment tends to sabotage our efforts to accept the loss and return to normal life.

6. *The failure of griefwork results in continued misery and dysfunction.* Time itself does not heal. In fact, we do not reenter the mainstream of time until we have liberated ourselves from attachment to the deceased person. Survivors who remain intensely attached to the deceased person over a prolonged period of time are considered to be suffering from *pathological grief.* (We would now call it complicated grief and not expect resolution neatly within the first year of bereavement.)

Freud's griefwork theory filled a major gap at the time. Through the centuries, poets, dramatists, novelists, artists, and composers had recognized grief as a devastating experience that was part of the human condition. It was not until the griefwork theory, however, that sociobehavioral sciences had a conceptualization that took grief seriously, described some of its main characteristics, and offered guidance for interventions. Despite its limitations, griefwork theory deserves much credit for encouraging sensitive attention to the experiences of the bereaved person.

Interpersonal Applications of Griefwork Theory

Freud's original theory emphasized the intrapsychic response to loss—how we attempt to deal with our own thoughts and feelings. Later contributors have called more attention to the interpersonal context of griefwork: how a loss affects our relationships. British psychiatrist John Bowlby (1969, 1973, 1980) expanded on Freud's observations and developed a broad framework for understanding attachment as well as loss.

The current interest in attachment behavior and bonding owes much to Bowlby's investigations. Bowlby sees a strong connection between the biological need for survival and the phenomena of grief and mourning. Animal as well as human behavior provides him with examples. The vulnerable young of many species exhibit distress and attempt to draw their absent mother to their side by whatever sounds and other communication signals they may have in their repertoire. The mother also seeks her missing young by calling or signaling to them. Neither the young nor the mother can relax until they have rejoined each other.

Adults also show the need for attachment when there is danger afoot. For example, citing a study of baboons, Bowlby (1969) notes,

> Not only infants but adults also when under stress are strongly disposed to cling to a companion. Thus an adult female, when alarmed, clings to the back of her husband or is embraced by him. Conversely, when he is under stress during a fight, a male is likely to embrace one of his wives.... The persistence into adult life of patterns of behaviour seen first and at greatest intensity during infancy is found, then, to be a regular species of the behavioral repertoire of other primate species. (p. 130)

Adult grief resonates with our early experiences of separation. Every dog has been a frightened puppy, every cat a stressed kitten, and every adult human an anxious baby. We have all had the anxiety of separation experiences in our life histories, even if these were but fleeting episodes. The depressive state of a bereaved spouse has its precedent in the infant who felt himself or herself to be abandoned and vulnerable. The feeling that "I can't live without you" may have its roots in the sense of vulnerability and anxiety that also accompanies separation between parent–young and mate–mate in many other species.

Why is griefwork so difficult? Bowlby (1980) answers this question through his general theory of *attachment behavior.* The goal of attachment behavior is to maintain the security provided by a significant interpersonal relationship. Any situation that threatens this bond will call forth

> action designed to preserve it; and the greater the danger of loss appears to be, the more intense and varied are the actions elicited to prevent it. In such circumstances all the most powerful forms of attachment behaviour become activated—clinging, crying, and perhaps angry coercion. This is the phase of protest and one of acute physiological

stress and emotional distress. *When these actions are successful the bond is restored, the activities cease, and the states of stress and distress are alleviated.* (p. 42)

I have added italics to the last sentence because here Bowlby provides a valuable insight for understanding the intensity and persistence of grief responses. In some situations, we can respond effectively to a threatened loss of relationship. We communicate our concern and put ourselves on full alert. When, however, it is death that separates us from a loved person, none of our efforts prevail. We do everything within our power, and yet the other person does not return. This persistent absence may be accompanied by persistent stress. What is the survivor to do when efforts to restore the relationship by yearning, remembering, crying, praying, and raging have failed? The survivor may keep trying and trying (Bowlby, 1980):

> Evidence shows that, at perhaps increasingly long intervals, the effort to restore the bond is renewed: The pangs of grief and perhaps an urge to search are then experienced afresh. This means that the person's attachment behaviour is remaining constantly primed.... The condition of the organism is then one of chronic stress and is experienced as one of chronic distress. At intervals, moreover, both stress and distress are likely again to become acute. (p. 42)

Bowly's description is consistent with ongoing research into the physiological stress of bereavement. Our response to the stress of loss may become the source of continuing stress: *We cannot get what we want and we cannot stop trying and, in the meantime, not much else gets done.* Griefwork is so difficult because it must overcome our strong tendency to try to restore the lost love object through fantasies and emotions. We need patience and we need persistence—and some help from our understanding friends.

Another British researcher, Colin Parkes, has also made significant contributions that focus on the interpersonal dimensions of bereavement, grief, and mourning. He has conducted some of the most important studies of the *psychosocial transitions* involved in coping with the loss of a loved person. How do people attempt to get on with their lives among other people after bereavement? Under what conditions does griefwork fail, leaving the survivor in a state of prolonged social and personal dysfunction? These are examples of the questions that Parkes has been trying to answer. Parkes (2001) has identified three basic components of griefwork:

- *Preoccupation with thoughts of the deceased person:* This represents a continuing search process (reminding us of the attachment-seeking signals and behaviors described by Bowlby in many species).
- *Repeatedly going over the loss experience in one's mind:* This is a painful process in which the survivor seems to be testing the reality of the loss (Did this terrible thing really happen?).
- *Attempts to explain the loss:* It is easier to accept the reality of a death and get on with one's own life if the loss somehow makes sense and had a reason behind it. During this part of the griefwork process, the survivor is asking self and others "Why, why, *why?*"

Evaluation of the Griefwork Theory

The griefwork theory has offered valuable insights and stimulated useful research. There is little doubt that our understanding of grief has been enriched by the contributions of Freud, Bowlby, Parkes, and others who have cultivated this approach. Nevertheless, the griefwork theory has limits.

Margaret Stroebe (1992/1993) suggested that griefwork theory was accepted too quickly and without adequate examination. There was much basic research yet to be done. Stroebe and colleagues are among those who have been doing some of this additional research, and their findings have not entirely supported griefwork theory. Some bereaved persons had not devoted themselves to griefwork but were functioning well and free of depression, and some who were hard at griefwork had shown only limited signs of recovery. These outcomes do not support the proposition that it is absolutely essential to detach oneself from emotional bonding to the deceased person through a long, difficult, and painful process. Nevertheless, the absence of griefwork was related to adjustment problems for some individuals, mostly on the part of widowers who attempted to distract themselves from the loss. In light of these findings, it is useful to give more at-

tention to individual differences in personality and coping styles. A review of the literature affirmed that "apparently, not all bereaved persons need to express themselves in the same way or share the same experiences in order to manage the difficulties of this highly stressful process" (Lund & Caserta, 1997/1998, p. 288). Camille Wortman and Roxanne Cohen Silver (2001, p. 423) are even more emphatic: "The studies reviewed provide no evidence to suggest that people who attempt to confront and process the loss do better than those who do not." The lesson, they believe, is that we must look more closely at the relationship that has been lost (e.g., mother–child or husband–wife) and all the circumstances involved.

Cultural differences are also emphasized again. As Stroebe points out, bereaved persons in Bali are expected to distract themselves and participate in cheerful interactions, whereas those in Egypt are encouraged to share their pain and sorrow with others. Quite possibly there is more than one way to cope effectively with the loss and stress of bereavement, with both personality style and sociocultural expectations having their influence.

Other Theoretical Approaches to Understanding Grief

There are now alternatives to griefwork theory. Most of these approaches have been suggested by counselors and therapists as a result of their clinical observations, but some have also come from a biological perspective. None of these theoretical positions have been adequately tested, but each offers something useful to think about.

Task Theories

There are certain tasks a person must accomplish in order to move through the grief experience and return to a meaningful, satisfying, and effectively functioning life. This is the basic premise in task theories offered by distinguished clinician–researchers such as William Worden (2001) and Teresa Rando (1992/1993). For Rando, the grieving person does not have to set aside attachments to the deceased to the extent that Freud has been thought to have suggested (whether he actually insisted on rigorous detachment is not entirely clear). Rando's basic message might be stated: "We can still keep a

TABLE 12-1

Two Task Theories of Grief

Worden	Rando
1. Accept the loss.	1. Accept the loss.
2. Work through the pain.	2. React to the separation.
3. Adjust to life without the person who has died.	3. Remember and reexperience the lost person and relationship.
4. Place the lost person in the past.	4. Give up the attachment to the person and the life that used to be.
	5. Move into the new life but remember the old.
	6. Reinvest emotions and energies in other relationships and activities.

cherished memory of our relationship with the lost person while we remake our lives and cultivate other relationships and activities." Rando and Worden offer similar but not identical sets of tasks for the bereaved person (Table 12-1).

There is still a good bit of griefwork theory here—emotional investments are to be withdrawn from the lost person and reinvested in other people and activities. There are other things to notice about all the task theories:

- They import the attitudes of middle-class, achievement-oriented society into the grief process. What is life? A series of tasks to be completed. What is grieving? The same. This is a culturally shaped viewpoint, and so it may feel plausible and appropriate when applied to those who share this belief system. However, we really do not have to think of either living or grieving as tasks, no matter how familiar this idea might be. This can be a useful perspective, but it is not the only one.
- The theories are prescriptive. They emphasize what we *should* do. The theorists are all expert observers whose writings promote understanding of the grief process; nevertheless, the descriptive and the prescriptive are mixed together and can be difficult to disentangle.

Stage Theories

The Kübler-Ross (1969) stage theory of dying has also been frequently applied to grieving. Stage theorists specify that the first response to bereavement is shock, numbness, and disbelief. The final phase is the reestablishment of physical and mental balance. Descriptions of the middle phases of the grief process and the total number of phases differ from one stage theorist to another.

It is clear that many grieving people experience some of the feelings and attempt some of the coping strategies that are included in the various stage theories. It is not clear, however, that everybody in fact does go through all these stages or under what conditions reintegration is either established or fails to be established. Stage theorists provide useful observations and guidelines, but there is little independent evidence to verify this model of the grief process. If anything, there is now more evidence for individual and cultural differences in response to grief.

An Integrated Individual–Family Model

A promising new approach was introduced by Nancy Moos (1995) and taken up effectively by other researchers. The grieving person is often part of a family. The interaction patterns within the family could be as important as the "tasks" or "stages" that occupy individuals.

Moos (1995) identified many symptoms of family grief, including the following:

- Changes in who talks to whom and in what way
- Reconnection or cutoff of certain family members
- Confusion in family roles (who is in charge, and who has what responsibilities)
- Overprotecting each other
- Family becoming isolated from friends and support network

Changes such as these within family dynamics obviously differ from symptoms of grief that affect individuals (e.g., tightness in throat, shortness of breath, and disturbed sleep patterns). The individual symptoms are familiar in grief research and are taken into account in all theories. However, less attention has been given to interaction processes within the family. The emotional bond among family members can be threatened as individuals retreat into their own distress or form relationships with others outside the family.

Children who have lost a mother or father through death often have a need to revisit the places they had seen with their deceased parent.

These changes often begin before the family member has died, sometimes as soon as a life-threatening diagnosis has been made. Elliot Rosen (1998) observed that the family's early response to a threatened loss frequently sets the pattern for how they will function later when the person has died. There is much opportunity to strengthen family responses that are likely to prove helpful and avoid or overcome responses that might intensify stress and conflict.

Families are not all alike, so we would not expect that responses to death will be the same. Dorothy Becvar (2001) and Reiko Schwab (2002) provided useful analyses of the ways in which family characteristics affect their grieving process. It is not surprising that an ongoing pattern of open and flexible communication within the family proves beneficial when the members must deal with the stress of impending or actual loss. However, research suggests that a family can be too "tight," the members too strongly bonded with each other. Schwab concludes that the crisis of loss is most effectively handled by families whose members are connected to each other and yet can also function independently. In contrast, "in disengaged families, members are emotionally distant and unable to rely on one another for support or problem solving while in enmeshed families members are excessively close, demanding loyalty and lacking personal separateness" (p. 353).

It has also become evident that a death in the family tends to open old emotional wounds and intensify conflicts and insecurities. Families can become stronger as they unite to cope with the stress of grief or can be fractured and even destroyed by the experience. Mutual respect and affection and communication patterns that are in good working order will prove invaluable in coping with the threat or reality of loss.

An Evolutionary Biology Model of Grief

Much different from the approaches to grief that we have been considering is the evolutionary perspective offered by John Archer (2001). He raises a question that has seldom been considered by social and behavioral scientists: Is grief *adaptive*? In other words, does this devastating experience have a positive function in natural selection and survival of the species?

Archer's (2001) first conclusion is that grief is not just a human universal; a grief-like reaction also occurs in social birds and mammals when they lose a significant other through either death or separation. This conclusion had already been reached by John Bowlby and by Charles Darwin (1972). Archer has a more refined version of this principle, though: The grief expressed by birds and mammals is similar to that of young children rather than adult humans. The distress is acute but less complicated.

Archer's (2001) second conclusion is that grief is maladaptive: It has detrimental effects on the survival of the bereaved animal or person. This is a puzzle from the evolutionary perspective: Why would humans and other animals have such a strong response pattern that jeopardizes survival?

> Why were individuals who grieved not replaced by those who greeted the death of a mate or offspring with emotional indifference? Such individuals would, it seems, be better able to carry on with essential maintenance activities and be more motivated and able to find a mate and raise offspring. (pp. 268–269)

Archer answers this question in a fascinating way. The grief itself is not adaptive, but social bonds are very much advantageous for survival. Grief is an unavoidable by-product of a bird, mammal, or human determination to build and maintain strong emotional bonds with others. A journey to the evolutionary biology realm offers a renewed appreciation for the significance of intimate relationships. The pain of separation is a risk that comes with attachment to another person (or dog, cat, horse, or macaw). By implication, when we decide against having any close relationships, we may be reducing the sorrow and anxiety of bereavement but also the benefits of social support.

HOW DO PEOPLE RECOVER FROM GRIEF?

We have already seen that there are more ways than one to cope with the stress and loss of bereavement. In this section, we explore these patterns in more detail. First, we consider what has been learned about the death of a spouse. This includes a harrowing visit with Third World widows. Next, we consider responses to the death of children, the grief and death of elderly adults, and survivors of traumatic or stigmatized death. We complete our examination of the impact of grief by examining the most extreme outcome—death of the bereaved person.

When a Spouse Dies

"Until death us do part." This traditional phrase in marriage vows continues to be meaningful. Death as the event that ends a marriage occurs ever more frequently in the later adult years. Consider the situation at age 65 and older: the U.S. Census Bureau estimates that in 2001 approximately 45% of women and 14% of men who had been married were now widows or widowers. At age 85 and older, spousal bereavement increases to 80% for women and 43% for men. These numbers would be even higher were it not for the increase in divorce. Coping with the loss of a marital partner and somehow going on with life are challenges that many people will face at some point. Fortunately, spousal bereavement has been the subject of many careful studies that have included interviews as well as background information. We first draw on findings from major studies conducted in the United States and England by Colin Murray Parkes and colleagues (Glick et al., 1974; Parkes, 2001; Parkes & Weiss, 1983).

The Immediate Impact of Spousal Bereavement

Most women had been experiencing anticipatory grief. Often, a woman expressed relief that her husband's long period of suffering had ended. However, the impact of the actual death was still felt deeply. Those who found themselves suddenly transformed into widows suffered more intensively, however. They felt overwhelmed, anguished, and as though there were no limits to the catastrophe that had befallen them. The newly and suddenly bereaved woman might feel so numb that she feared she would never again move, act, or think, or she might cry as though she would never be able to stop.

The husband who became a widower usually responded to the impact of the death very much as the widow did. The men differed, however, in how they interpreted their feelings. Although the women often emphasized a sense of abandonment, the men reported feeling a sort of *dismemberment*. The women would speak of being left alone, deprived of a comforting and protecting person. The men were more likely to feel "like both my arms were being cut off." These differences seemed related to what marriage had meant for widow and widower. Marriage had sustained the man's capacity to work. For the woman, marriage had provided a sphere of interpersonal engagement.

Emotional and Physical Reactions Soon after Bereavement

Bewilderment and despair often continued beyond the first impact of loss. There were still periods of weeping, especially for women. Physical symptoms appeared and sometimes lingered for weeks or months. Aches and pains, poor appetite, loss of stamina, headaches, dizziness, and menstrual irregularities were reported by many. Sleep disturbances were common. Often, a widow would wake up in the middle of the night and remain tormented by grief and the reality of her partner's absence. Instead of offering temporary relief from sorrow, the night often held anxieties of its own. Some women tried to tire themselves out by working hard and staying up late. Others turned to sleeping medications. The dread and emptiness of facing the night alone were relieved for some of the bereaved by having close friends or relatives who could listen to them and keep them company until sleep finally took over.

Most of the widows tried hard to maintain emotional control. Often, the newly bereaved woman would long for somebody else to take over and organize life for her. Each woman had to find her own balance between the desire to receive help and the fear of becoming dependent on others. The widowers were more often uncomfortable with direct emotional expression of their distress. The typical widower attempted to maintain control over his feelings because he considered it unmanly to let go. Such statements as "It's not fair!" were seldom made by men, although they were fairly often made by women. Although less troubled by anger than the widow, the widower did have difficulty with guilt. He was more likely to blame himself: "I wasn't sensitive enough to her" "I should have made things easier." The widower's guilt reaction, however, tended to subside fairly soon, although the need for rational control over all responses to the death persisted.

Leave-Taking Ceremonies

The realities of daily life continue during the process of grief and recuperation. One of the major demands of the period soon after bereavement is the necessity to bid farewell to the lost spouse through some type of funeral process. The leave-taking ceremonies went well for most of the bereaved in this study. They often found it helpful to hear from others that they had done their part to ensure a proper farewell. This bolstered their sense of confidence in managing difficult affairs despite their shock and suffering. The widow was seen by all as the final authority on what should be done, regardless of different wishes that, for example, the husband's family might have. In this way, the widow began to gain public acceptance as the new head of the family. The widows often felt that in arranging the ceremonies, they were able to continue the expression of their love, devotion, and attachment.

The funeral directors usually were seen as supportive and caring persons. Nevertheless, there were painful moments despite all the support available. Some widows suddenly felt the full pangs of their late husband's death at a particular point during the funeral process, such as the last viewing of the body. The funeral emphasized the reality of the death, cutting through the haze of unreality in which many of the newly bereaved functioned despite their outward control and competence. The complete realization of the death, however, did not seem to dawn on the bereaved at any one moment in time, although some of the moments were critical steps toward this realization.

Most widows seemed to be operating on very limited emotional energy. They neither sought out nor took in what the clergy might have had to say. Understandably, the widows tended to be absorbed in their own feelings. Many of the widows were religious, however, and seemed to find some comfort in clergymen's repetitions of traditional beliefs about the continuation of soul or spirit after death.

The leave-taking ceremonies did not seem to be quite as important to most of the widowers in this study. They gave less attention to the details and did not express as much gratitude toward the funeral directors. They were also more likely to feel that the cost of the funeral was too high. The emotional significance of the funeral may have been relatively less important for the men because they were primarily concerned with how they would manage in the months to come. The funeral and all that it involved was something that they had to "get through" rather than the milestone it represented for many widows.

Grief and Recovery: The First Year

The long months after the funeral were often the most difficult for both widow and widower. For a short time, there was concentrated attention on the needs of the bereaved. However, the deceased spouse remains dead and the bereaved person's emotional and pragmatic problems continue day after day.

The Widows' Response

The widows in this study were left with the realization that they had to reorganize their lives, but now they lacked the clustering of help that had been available to them in the first days after bereavement. The widows seemed to feel that they should not burden others with their sorrow. They felt that a "decent" amount of time had to pass before they could reenter ordinary life and yet did not feel comfortable with a full-blown expression of mourning such as is customary in some societies.

Feelings of sorrow and anxiety remained intense even though the widows no longer spoke of their grief. Many engaged in *obsessional reviews*. Events surrounding the husband's death were relived over and over. The "worry work" of obsessional review might have been helpful by integrating the realities of the loss into ongoing life. Mulling over the death is a component of griefwork that, as Stroebe found, seems to be helpful to some but not all survivors.

The obsessional reviews often were concerned with what *might* have happened instead of what actually did happen. How could the accident have been avoided? How might it all have turned out differently? The widows frequently searched for meaning through these reviews. *Why* had their husbands been taken away? It was not the name of the disease or the technical reason for the accident that concerned the widow so much as the need to make sense of the death. If "Why *me?*" is the question some people ask when they learn of their own terminal illness, then "Why *him?*" seems to be the survivor's parallel question. These questions often lost some of their intensity over time, but the search for meaning continued to linger. Convincing answers proved difficult to find.

Although it remained painful to review the events leading up to the death, memories of the husband and of shared experiences generally were positive. This was especially true in the early weeks and months. A tendency to *idealize* the lost spouse was observed. The deceased husband was the best man who ever lived, a wonderful husband, a marvelous father—he had no faults whatsoever. Later, a more balanced view usually emerged. The widow would still think about him frequently and positively, but now some of his quirks and imperfections gained recognition as well. Surges of anger—sometimes very intense—occasionally broke in between the early tendency to idealize and the later, more balanced view. For example, the widow might find herself suddenly angry at the husband for leaving her with the children to raise by herself. These episodes of negative feelings seemed to be part of the long process of developing a realistic attitude that the widow could live with through the years.

Often, the widow's feelings about her husband went beyond vivid memories. *She might have a strong sense that he was still there with her.* This impression made itself felt soon after the death or a few weeks later. Once the widow developed the experience of her husband's presence, it was likely to remain with her off and on for a long time. The sense of presence was especially persistent for women who had experienced the sudden loss of their spouses. More extensive haunting experiences were reported by women who had had no opportunity to prepare themselves for the loss. For most of the widows, it was comforting to feel that the husband was still there somehow. However, the widow knew the difference even when the sense of presence was vivid. She knew that her husband was really dead, even though her sense of his presence was also real in its own way. It was neither unusual nor crazy for a widow to feel this sense of presence.

During the first year of the widow's bereavement, there was a gradual movement away from absorption in the loss and toward reconstruction of her life. This was not a smooth process and there was seldom a decisive severing of thoughts and feelings about the past. Instead, the widow continued to feel a sense of attachment to her deceased spouse but had called back enough emotional energy to cope more adequately with her current life situation.

Widows with children at home usually recognized their responsibilities clearly and believed that the need to provide parental care helped to keep them from becoming lost in their own grief. They attempted to help the children feel that the world was still a good place—that life could and would go on. Often, there was a new resolve to be a good mother. The widows felt the need to be straightforward and realistic with the children but also to shelter and protect them and keep their spirits up. The widows were in a difficult position in trying to provide answers to their children while still searching for answers themselves.

The Widowers' Response

Although the bereaved man was almost as likely to feel the presence of his wife soon after the bereavement, as time went by this phenomenon became much less common than it was for the widows. The man's need for control and realism expressed itself also in the tendency to cut off obsessional review after just a few weeks. The widower did not seem as tolerant of his impulse to dwell on the past; he pushed himself right back to immediate realities, although, like the widow, he too felt a desire to replay the circumstances of the death. The widowers were also less likely to speak openly about their feelings. They did not usually seek out the opportunity to share either the events or their personal reactions.

When widows and widowers were compared at the same points in their bereavement, it usually *seemed* that the men were making a more rapid adjustment. However, the researchers had reason to doubt. It was true that the men returned more quickly to their previous roles and functions; they were also even less likely than the widows to go through a period of conspicuous mourning. The typical widower gave no outward sign of his grief. However, a close look at the quality of the widower's personal life, including the occupational sphere, indicated a decrease in energy, competence, and satisfaction.

The widower usually made a more rapid *social* recovery but a slower *emotional* recovery than the widow. A year after his wife's death, the widower was much more likely than the widow to feel lonely and depressed.

Types of Recovery from the Impact of Marital Bereavement

Several important points for identifying those at risk for complicated or unresolved grief emerged from these studies. *People who did not have the opportunity to prepare for the spouse's death suffered more distress, not only immediately but also for some time afterward.* More than 1 year later, the spouse who had experienced sudden, unexpected bereavement was more socially withdrawn, remained more preoccupied with the details of the death, had more difficulty in accepting the reality of the loss, and in general was experiencing more disorganization in daily life.

We cannot rely on the passage of time by itself to facilitate recuperation from the trauma. Social support is needed both in the early period of acute bereavement and over the many months and even years required to adjust to the devastating loss.

The response to early bereavement provides useful clues as to how the individual will respond as the months go by. *Those who were most disturbed*

Although emotionally painful as reminder of the loss, a cemetery visit can also be a consoling way of affirming one's love.

a few weeks after the death usually were the ones who continued to be disturbed 1 year later. The person who had strong feelings that the death was unreal and who tried to behave as though the spouse were still alive was also likely to have more difficulty than others over an extended time.

The quality of the marital relationship influences the grief and recovery process. When the partners had very mixed feelings toward each other, the experiences associated with bereavement were often more disturbing. Similarly, it was more difficult for the survivor to adjust if the relationship had been based on a clinging dependence. If soon after bereavement the surviving spouse felt cast

adrift, empty, and helpless because the mate was no longer around to make life run properly, then difficulties in adjustment were likely to be more prolonged.

Unresolved Grief

All of the newly bereaved people studied had to face the question of who they were now, having lost part of their identities with the loss of their spouses. Two years later, some had made substantial recoveries from grief. Those still in despair had not formed a conception of the death that they found coherent and acceptable, nor were they able to modify their self-images in preparation for a new life without the husband or wife. Furthermore, they were more likely to use tranquilizers, drink and/or smoke heavily, and to wonder whether anything in life was worthwhile. Why did some people experience such complications in the grief and recovery process? Why do some people fall into one pattern and some into the other?

Careful study of individual case histories distinguished among three concepts of *unresolved grief:*

• The *unexpected grief syndrome* occurs in some people when the spouse dies without warning; therefore, they do not have the opportunity to prepare themselves for the overwhelming loss. Disbelief and intense anxiety often become not only the first but also the continued response.

• The *conflicted grief syndrome* can occur when death ends a troubled relationship, often one in which separation or divorce had been contemplated. Some of the marriages in the study had been to alcoholic men whose behavior had created a climate of fear and disorder. Other marriages leading to the conflicted grief syndrome had been marked by depression and the withdrawal of the survivor. The unresolved grief experienced by survivors of a troubled marriage appears in a sense to be a continuation of the frustrations and disappointments that had characterized the relationship while the spouse was alive.

• The *chronic grief syndrome* is marked by the survivor's strong feelings of dependency. Although some distress may be experienced at the time of the death, the more compelling and lasting response is a deep sense of yearning for the lost one. Yearning for the deceased is often a part of any grief experience, but for people with this syndrome it becomes predominant. The survivor has unusually powerful dependence on the deceased spouse and does not feel personally capable of taking on the responsibilities of life with his or her partner gone.

Awareness of the nature of the marriage relationship that has been sundered by death and by the circumstances of the death (sudden or anticipated) could improve our ability to identify those who are at particular risk for intense and prolonged distress. Whatever the particular circumstances of the death, however, the grief process can be so disabling that the bereaved person is essentially out of commission for an extended time. Suicide attempts and severe depressive reactions requiring psychiatric treatment are among the risks. Parkes' studies and many others indicate that most bereaved men and women make their way through their distress without reaching extremes of despair or self-destructiveness. Nevertheless, we should not lose sight of the fact that some people do remain locked in their grief and mourning for an extended period of time to the extent that they cannot derive satisfaction from their own lives or meet the needs of others.

In another useful study (Lieberman, 1996), it was also discovered that not all "help" from other people was actually experienced as helpful by the widow or widower. There are usually expectations that certain people will come forth to provide support during this difficult period. If these people do not respond as expected or hoped for, the widowed person may feel hurt, rejected, and angry. A stranger or a human services professional might offer potentially valuable support, but this will not "count" as much to the widow who feels she has been let down by her own family, friends, or colleagues. Adult children are especially valued as sources of help by older widows and widowers. This help includes practical assistance, such as home maintenance, shopping, and coping with insurance and other financial transactions.

The Psychosocial Transition

After many years of bereavement research, Parkes (2001) reflects again on the *psychosocial transition*—in other words, the change from who we were to who we are now after a death has altered our lives. He reminds us that the death of a person we love is not the only situation that can transform our views of ourselves and the world. For example, people who lose vision, hearing, or the ability to walk must somehow come to new terms with life. People who have been diagnosed with a life-threatening illness often start to rethink what is most important to them and how best to make use of what could be a foreshortened life expectancy.

Parkes (2001) emphasizes the impact of bereavement not only on our emotions but also on our entire conception of who we are and what the world is really about:

> All of us, from the moment of our birth, have been building inside ourselves a model of the world, a set of assumptions on the basis of which we recognize the world that we meet and plan our behaviour accordingly.... Not only does a major psychosocial transition require us to revise a great number of assumptions about the world, but most of these assumptions have become habits of thought and behaviour that are now virtually automatic. A widow will come down for breakfast in the morning and find that she has laid the table for two when there is now only one person to eat it. (p. 91)

It is a difficult mental as well as emotional task to revise our assumptions and alter our habits. One must somehow keep the way it used to be in mind because that is such an important part of the self but also recognize the changed reality and find ways to cope with it.

I add two parallels with the situation of a person who is trying to make the psychosocial transition after bereavement. Anthropologists (Gennep, 1960; Turner, 1969, 1992) have made good use of the concept of *rites of passage.* Whether through physical or symbolic space, a person might need to move from "here" to "there" and in so doing shed an existing status for a new one. This happens, for example, when a youth is initiated into adulthood through traditional rituals or two single people go through a wedding ceremony. People are most vulnerable when they are *between* "here" and "there." This can be a lengthy period during which one is not quite who one used to be and not yet who he or she will become. That is clearly the situation for a person in the midst of psychosocial transition after bereavement, and it suggests that social rituals could be helpful in guiding and protecting the individual during this precarious time.

The other parallel is with one of the basic functions of a society's death system—the discovery or affirmation of meaning. The bereaved individual who is trying to reconstruct both personal identity and worldview might find either guidance or confusion in society's interpretation of why things happen as they do.

The Family That Has Lost a Child

Losing a child to death is one of the most painful of all human experiences. The immediate anguish may be followed by many years of sorrow. Acquaintances of grieving family members are almost certain to observe the powerful impact that follows soon after a child's death. What others might not realize, however, is that the distress continues long beyond this acute phase, and that the lives of the grieving family members may be altered in many ways, not all of which are obvious to outsiders.

Shadow Grief: Perinatal Death

The sorrow of a child's death often seems to follow a family like a shadow. After observing the reactions of mothers who had lost a baby before or soon after birth, Peppers and Knapp (1980) introduced the term *shadow grief.* Years after the death, many of the mothers were still feeling the anguish. In a later study, Knapp (1986) found the same phenomenon among parents who had lost older children to death. They were no longer completely dominated by grief, but the shadow or cloud had a way of making itself known as they moved through life:

> On the surface most observers would say that the "grief work" has been accomplished. But this is not the case. Shadow grief reveals itself more in the form of an emotional "dullness," where the person is unable to respond fully and completely to outer stimulation and where normal activity is moderately inhibited.... Under certain circumstances and on certain occasions, comes bubbling to the surface, sometimes in the form of tears, sometimes not, but always accompanied by a feeling of sadness and a mild sense of anxiety. (pp. 40–41)

Knapp's findings are consistent with the observations of many others. Parents who have lost a child often feel that their own lives also changed at that moment. Furthermore, they may not want to relinquish the grief. The pain is part of the memory—and the memory is precious.

It is significant that shadow grief was first recognized in a study of mothers who had lost newborn infants. The death of so young a child has often been given relatively little attention by society. The lack of communal recognition and support can isolate the parents in their grief. Some newspapers even prohibit publication of newborn death notices and it is difficult to find sympathy cards on the market for *perinatal death*. This term refers to infants who die at any point from the 20th week after conception through the first month after birth. Premature birth is still the most common cause of perinatal death, although advances in medical and nursing techniques have saved some neonates who otherwise would have died. Deaths also occur for a variety of other reasons (e.g., a genetic defect or a prenatal infection) and sometimes for reasons that are never clearly determined. We cannot exclude socioeconomic causes, either. Even in the United States, many pregnant women still do not have access to perinatal health services. Others do not seem to realize that such services are available and could improve the odds in favor of a healthy mother and a healthy baby. The bottom line is that society does not seem to realize the extent and intensity of shadow grief.

Complications of Perinatal Grief

Grief over a perinatal death is similar in many respects to grief over any loss. There are, however, some circumstances and consequences that are more likely to be present. For example, the mother may still be sedated or exhausted at the time she learns of her child's death. She is also likely to be ready to mother her baby, both physically and emotionally. This total readiness, including lactation to provide breast milk, now has no opportunity to express itself directly. Another significant problem can arise in families that have other children. Parents may have to listen to such unhelpful comments as "Well, you still have other children," and they may also find it difficult to explain the loss and provide comfort to the other children while they are troubled by their own grief.

Sensitive caregivers have learned that their first step is to recognize that a significant loss has occurred (or is about to occur, if the infant is still alive but not expected to survive). We can be more helpful to the parents and siblings when we ourselves comprehend the meaning of this loss. The family that has experienced perinatal death often feels misunderstood and abandoned by others (Cordell & Thomas, 1997):

> Most bereaved parents tell us that the support they received from others at the time of the baby's death did not continue very long. They think that others do not continue to "live" their grief as they do. Others expect them to recover within a few short weeks. (p. 299)

Even more devastating is the experience of having more than one baby die either during gestation or soon after. It is estimated that this happens more than twice as often among low-income blacks compared to whites in the United States (Guyer et al., 1997). Fortunately, mothers who believe that they were treated with competence and compassion at the time of the first perinatal death may be able to cope as well as possible with a subsequent loss.

There have been particularly effective responses by some nurses and physicians in situations in which the mother and her nonviable baby are still in the hospital. The family is encouraged to interact with the infant in a natural and loving way. Photographs may be taken of parents holding the baby and various memorabilia (such as the child's first footprints or a lock of hair) given to them. "Bereavement protocols" that help prepare hospital staff to provide emotional support for family members are becoming more common and group counseling has also proved helpful (Cordell & Thomas, 1997).

Effects of a Child's Death on the Parents' Worldview

The loss and sorrow that follow the death of the child may be intensified by a crisis of belief or faith. This response appears to be especially strong when the child's life was taken by murder (Wickie & Marwit, 2000/2001) and is thought to occur in other sudden and traumatic types of death as well. The parents may feel that the world no longer makes sense, that one can count on neither God nor community.

There is evidence that preserving an emotional connection with the deceased child helps to prevent the destruction of the parents' worldview. Klass (1992/1993) found that the "inner representation" of the dead child continues to be experienced by the parents for many years, if not throughout all their lives. He defines inner representations as "characterizations or thematic memories of the deceased, and the emotional states connected with these characterizations and memories." Parents can interact with their inner representations of the child through such means as

- *Memory:* bringing the child to mind often
- *A sense of presence:* the feeling that the child is still there with them in some way
- *Hallucinations:* the experience of seeing or hearing the child
- *Incorporation* of the characteristics or virtues of the child into their own personalities (e.g., rescuing lost animals as the child had often done)

Staying in contact with the inner representation of the dead child makes it easier for the survivors to keep their worldviews intact. The sorrow and sense of loss are still there, but the feeling that something of the child still lives with or within them seems to reduce doubts about their worldviews. These symbolic interactions with the deceased are not signs of pathology; for example, it is not "crazy" to sense the child's presence or even to catch fleeting glimpses of the child.

Some mothers have not only come through the grief of perinatal death but also become stronger persons as a result. Talbot (1998/1999) found that the hardiness of some mothers

> seems to have been forged in the fire of agonizing grief—grief which has been consciously confronted and transformed into the gift of compassion.... They have lit a pathway to survival and personal growth: By identifying and incorporating a loved one's best characteristics, it is possible to find ways to honor the past while building a future. By understanding what has been learned from loss and grief, it is possible to reach out and help make the world a better place for self and others. (p. 184)

The Future of the Marital Relationship after the Death of a Child

The loss of a child creates stress and strain for the family unit as a whole (Rubin & Malkinson,

2001). For example, sexual intimacy can diminish, even though many couples report an increased need for physical contact and comfort. The parents often report feeling more irritable and more likely to direct anger at each other. This can become particularly destructive when one parent blames the other either for the death or for past actions related to the lost child. Furthermore, communication tends to break down for bereaved couples. The parents may withdraw into their own grief and therefore away from each other. There may also be a reduction in self-disclosure and emotional exchange—an avoidance of the core issues. Despite these and other problems, most couples do not divorce or even seriously consider this possibility after the death of a child.

Overall, the available research indicates that the death of a child is catastrophic for some but not all marital relationships. Concluding their recent analysis of the research literature, Rubin and Malkinson (2001) observe that "the losses of children will require a continuing lifelong accommodation, at some level, to the shifting meanings of the loss and to the...memories and thoughts associated with the deceased" (p. 233).

The Grief of Grandparents

Grandparents and parents experience many of the same feelings of loss. In addition, grandparents are also likely to experience vicarious grief for the parents (Kastenbaum, 1987; Rando, 2002) as well as their own direct grief over the death of the child. It hurts them to realize how much their adult children are sorrowing for the death of the grandchild. Furthermore, it is even more unexpected for people to outlive their grandchildren. Such an unexpected and "untimely" death can generate a worldview crisis just as in the case of the parents.

White (1999) found that the death of a grandchild causes extreme anguish, regardless of the child's age. Most of the bereaved grandparents had a strong need to talk about their grandchildren. This need could be frustrated if the family has responded with withdrawal and silence or if communication patterns between the grandparents and their adult children had previously been inadequate. Some grandparents felt helpless because they could not protect their adult children from the pain of loss—similar, perhaps, to the frequent desire of parents to shield their young children from awareness of death and dying. Nevertheless, grandparents often did provide valuable support to the bereaved parents just by being there with them as well as by helping with chores and expenses. The overall message is clear: Grandparents often are much affected by the death of a child and have a significant role to play in the family's response.

BEREAVEMENT IN LATER LIFE

We are vulnerable to bereavement at any age. In the later adult years, there is an increased vulnerability but also a vitality and resilience that exceeds what one might have expected.

Sorrow upon Sorrow, Loss upon Loss

Life satisfaction does not necessarily decline with age. Gerontologists have discredited the assumption that usefulness and the enjoyment of life end at a certain age. Nevertheless, it is also true that the longer a person lives and forms loving attachments, the more there is to lose. Loss may follow upon loss, taxing the individual's ability to cope. This is the concept of *bereavement overload* (Kastenbaum, 1969). Long-lived people usually have survived many people with whom they were deeply attached. Furthermore, loss of physical abilities, employment, social respect, and familiar environments are all life changes that can trigger responses similar to what occurs when an interpersonal relationship is terminated by death. We accumulate these losses just by staying alive for an extended period of time.

What changes would be expected in people *of any age* who have been forced to cope with too many losses in too short a period of time? They might try to reconstitute their personal world by replacing the losses, or they might lose themselves in work or other engrossing activities. These alternatives, however, are often closed to elders. What now? One might become increasingly preoccupied with bodily functions and experience less free energy to invest in new activities or relationships. Furthermore, the experience of

multiple losses may lead to a sense of extreme caution. "I had better not care about anybody or anything else. Sooner or later I will lose these people and things as well. And I just cannot bear to lose and mourn again."

The whole constellation of "old behaviors" can develop from multiple, unbearable bereavement. Suicide attempts can also be generated from such a psychological state. The individual may give up when stricken by a relatively minor ailment and allow the condition to worsen or reduce his or her activities so drastically that both body and mind are in poor tone to respond to any kind of stress. Such considerations suggest that bereavement in old age is a condition deserving careful and systematic attention.

The older person is vulnerable to deaths of many kinds. Most common is the death of siblings (Moss, Moss, & Hansson, 2001). However, elderly adults also lose a spouse, adult children, grandchildren, and even parents. I have stood at the side of a 74-year-old man as tears ran down his cheeks because his 97-year-old father was dead. The outsider might rush to the conclusion that the death of a very old parent should not mean so much to a child also advanced in years. Consider, however, how long this relationship had to develop and flourish and what a blow it now was to go on without the father he had known for three-fourths of a century.

It is not just the death of a member of the family that can prove devastating. On several occasions, I discovered that an elderly patient with whom I was working first sank into a depressed, no-point-in-living state following the death of an animal companion. What might seem to be "the depression that comes with age" can turn out to be a grief reaction to the death of an animal companion as well as to the death of a human companion.

However, the overall picture is more positive than it has usually been assumed. Older widowed persons often have effective coping abilities that help them to get on with their lives even though they regard the death of their spouse as having been the most stressful event they have ever experienced. After months of high stress after the death of their spouse, many elderly persons are able to restore order and hope to their lives. Resiliency does not mean that words such as "recovery" or "renewal" describe their situation, however, nor does it mean that bereaved elders go through a standard set of stages. For example, the elderly widows studied by Bennett and Bennett (2000/2001) experienced the feelings described by stage theories but not in any particular order (no fixed sequence → no stages). They also explained that life goes on for them, but it is not really the same life. As one widow stated, "there's always this great hole inside that hurts, and…I was building a pattern, a life round it. I couldn't—you can't ever fill it, but you build a life round" (p. 244).

The elderly bereaved person often has a wealth of experience and skills that can be applied not only to reintegrating his or her own life but also to enrich the lives of others. Often, this person needs only positive human companionship and a little help with some of the details of everyday life in order to continue as a resourceful and well-integrated member of society.

ARE BEREAVED PEOPLE AT HIGHER RISK FOR DEATH?

In general, the risk of illness and death does increase following the loss of a person who has been very important to us. The more alert we are to this risk, the more we can do to protect ourselves and others through the most dangerous times and circumstances. Most grieving people experience some physical distress, and most make strong recoveries. "A broken heart," though, is not just a picturesque phrase. Research supports folk knowledge here, the message being that we would not want to underestimate the physical effects of sorrow and anxiety.

Differential Mortality Risk: The Statistical Pattern

The typical study compares the mortality (death) rates of bereaved and nonbereaved people. It is understood, of course, that all groups will have mortality rates. When one population has a higher mortality ratio it is said to have *excessive mortality*. What has been found? *Almost all studies have found excessive mortality rates for bereaved persons* (Goodkin et al., 2001; Stroebe & Stroebe, 1993). (The exceptions are a few studies with

small samples.) This pattern holds true in Europe and Japan as well as in North America, and it has been consistent throughout the 20th century.

Who Is Most at Risk?

Some people are more at risk than others. Widows and widowers are at higher risk than married men and women. This risk is even greater for widowers. The overall mortality rate is higher for males than females at every adult age level, and bereavement has the effect of further increasing the differential.

The relationship with age is not what one might have expected. Younger adults have a relatively higher excessive mortality rate after bereavement. The death of a spouse seems to produce a sudden increase in the mortality risk of young adults who otherwise are at relatively low risk of death. Most at risk is the young man whose wife has recently died. This risk is intensified if the death was sudden and unexpected. The bereavement-related deaths often occur within 6 months. These findings suggest that more attention should be given to the vulnerability of bereaved young men in the period of time immediately following the death. Lichtenberg (1990) offers his personal reflection on what a bereaved young man is likely to experience upon the sudden death of his wife. Lichtenberg survived and recovered—with the help of his friends—but remembers having felt "out of control: One moment I was torn apart, and the next moment I was calm. It was frightening to hurt, to be numb, to feel panic, and I worried that I would collapse" (p. 86). We never want to forget that there is always a human story behind the statistics.

What Are the Leading Causes of Death among the Bereaved?

The leading causes of death among bereaved people are the same as those for the population in general: heart disease and cancer. However, there is another type of death that increases greatly after bereavement—dying suddenly and violently.

The single greatest cause of excessive mortality among bereaved people is some form of heart disease, usually cardiovascular. These deaths often occur soon after the bereavement. There is evidence that liver cirrhosis, cancer, and infectious diseases also produce more deaths among bereaved people, but these patterns are more difficult to establish because of the lower incidence and other factors. For example, there are many types of cancer and these may vary in their progression after the stress of bereavement and are also likely to take more time before reaching a terminal phase.

The most striking changes, however, occur with violent deaths, especially suicide. Stroebe and Stroebe (1993) reported that within the *first week* after bereavement, the suicide rate for men was 66 times higher than would have been expected. The suicide rate for women was more than 9 times higher than expected. Suicide has the greatest increase among all causes of death, although heart disease accounts for most of the fatalities.

As noted earlier, the body's ability to resist infection through the immune system can also be impaired during the turmoil of grief, as it is in other types of stressful situations (Goodkin et al., 2001). We do not have to be medical experts to offer companionship and support to bereaved person—and by so doing, perhaps reduce stress levels, protect immune functioning, and perhaps even save a life.

Hidden and Disenfranchised Grief

Grief may be intensified and its resolution delayed when the bereaved are denied the opportunity to express their feelings. This is the basic concern that researchers and counselors have in mind when they discuss "hidden" or "disenfranchised" grief. We may speak of a person's grief as hidden when it is not recognized by others because the individual has attempted to keep either the loss or the feelings about the loss to himself or herself. For example, Gail, a school teacher, did not believe she had the right to express her grief in the presence of her students (Rowling, 1995):

> I knew I was heading towards a class in an hour's time. I knew that even within an hour I would not have myself pulled together enough to face the class. I mean, if you went and sat in front of a class and cried for 40 minutes they would riot, because they haven't got the rapport with what is happening with you at the moment. (p. 323)

Many other people also believe that it is inappropriate or forbidden to share their feelings of loss and sorrow with others. The grief may be hidden because the individual is not considered "entitled" to these feelings. In such a case, it can be said that the grief is disenfranchised.

I have observed many examples of hidden and disenfranchised grief among nurses and other caregivers. For example, staff members of a long-term care facility may become very much attached to the people in their care. An aged woman with no living relatives may be "adopted" by a nurse who has lost her own grandparents. The caregiver may experience grief when this resident dies. However, our society does not generally acknowledge the right of a caregiver to grieve and mourn. The health care system in particular has had a history of being intolerant of professionals who become "too involved" with their patients and "too upset" at their deaths. This tendency is still strong, although the emergence of the hospice movement and peer support groups is providing an alternative approach in some settings. The bereaved nurse who is not accorded the right to grieve and mourn has to find some other way to deal with the stress. My colleagues and I in a geriatric hospital noticed that staff members who had been emotionally close to recently deceased patients were more likely to be involved in single-car accidents and to experience a variety of illnesses requiring "sick days." These negative outcomes were sharply reduced after the staff organized peer support groups and gave each other permission to love and mourn their patients.

AIDS has brought many additional examples of disenfranchised grief. The lover-companion of a person with AIDS may not be considered "family" and therefore denied the right to mourn. In fact, lovers in general have often been excluded from supportive interactions because their relationship to the deceased person was not that of spouse, parent, child, or sibling. Social attitudes do change, however, and there is increasing recognition that lovers have both the need and the right to mourn. Unfortunately, though, there is still not adequate professional support for nurses and other caregivers who work with AIDS patients (Ingram, Jones, & Smith, 2001).

Hidden and disenfranchised grief take many other forms. We have already noted that parents of stillborn babies often have been forced to keep their grief to themselves. The sorrow of losing a companion animal has also been excluded from serious consideration by society in many instances. Fortunately, there is growing awareness that authentic grief can occur in both instances and deserves society's recognition and compassion.

Lavin (1989) brings one of the most neglected forms of hidden grief to our attention in discussing the situation of the bereaved person who is developmentally disabled:

> If they have been sheltered all their lives, they may face the death of a loved one unprepared. Often parents shield their normal children from death and are reluctant to include them in the rites of mourning, keeping them away from wakes and funerals. There is a greater tendency for the parents of the developmentally disabled to continue the shielding process longer. Thus the disabled...may be denied access to mourning rituals...and therefore are not exposed to role models who show them how to cope effectively with loss. (p. 231)

In both private homes and institutions, developmentally disabled people tend to be deprived of the opportunity to learn how to express and cope with their grief. Unfortunately, society may also persist in its assumption that the developmentally disabled are incapable of experiencing the loss, sorrow, and stress of bereavement. Adequate comfort and support may not be forthcoming because, in society's eyes, the grief does not exist. In an opening quotation we read the words of a mother whose developmentally disabled child had died (Milo, 1997). The mother's grief was real and intense, even though other people might have assumed that this death could not have been so important.

You are likely to encounter other types of hidden and disenfranchised grief as you go through life—in others or in yourself. Awareness that a person is attempting to cope with unexpressed sorrow and loss is the first step to sharing this burden and opening the way for recovery.

LIMITED SUPPORT FOR THE BEREAVED

The widower is reducing his colleagues' anxieties when he goes right back to work and gives no indication that he expects special concern. "I am OK," he is saying in effect, "I am not mourning." The widow releases others from the more obvious forms of obligation by refraining from displays of mourning. "She's a strong woman," her friends say with admiration. The bereaved person among us tends to be more socially acceptable if signs of mourning are set aside. However, the absence of mourning behaviors too easily gives the illusion that the person is "over" the grief action. This may be one of the reasons why some bereaved people have fears of going crazy. All of the anxiety and confusion, all the depths of feeling, seem to be on the inside. The rest of the world continues to move along in its usual way. With little social recognition or tolerance for grieving, the individual can be made to feel as though his or her responses were abnormal or pathological.

American Society's Discomfort with Grief and Mourning

How well a culture's death system is functioning can be determined by examining the support it provides for the bereaved. It is questionable if a mass, time- and efficiency-oriented society can pass this test. Mourning gets in the way. It may not seem to serve any real purpose. Pressures have been increasing against the expression of loss in many forms. There are still places in the United States where people will stop what they are doing when a funeral procession goes by. Pedestrians stand in respectful silence and motorists wait patiently, whether or not they know the identity of the deceased. However, the funeral procession has become a target of efficiency practitioners in many metropolitan areas. Abolition or restriction of this practice has been urged because it slows traffic. Similarly, there are pressures against the use of land for cemeteries. In some areas of the United States, it is now almost impossible to open new cemeteries, and existing cemeteries have been criticized as wasteful and out of step with the times. Nevertheless, the ability to join together in mourning and memorialization has not been lost, as the events of September 11, 2001, so clearly demonstrated.

Memorialization of the dead and support for the bereaved have fallen relatively low on the list of priorities of the mainstream American death system. People still gather around for the funeral—often with reluctance—and for a short period of ritual and visiting. After that, however, the bereaved is frequently left alone. How long do colleagues sympathize with somebody who has suffered a significant loss? How long are relatives and neighbors prepared to be sensitive and supportive? I have noticed an increasing impatience with grief. The mourner is supposed to shape up after a short time and let others get on with their lives. In this cultural context, it is not surprising to come across a doctoral dissertation featuring a "prescribed degriefing intervention method (DIM)" that requires but a single treatment session (DiMeo, 1978). DIM, indeed! Quicker is cheaper, better, and more cost-effective. But are we really prepared to line up for "degriefing" when overcome by profound sorrow and loss? There are still powerful local customs, though, in which the living offer their companionship unstintingly to the dead and the grieving. James Crissman (1994) describes such practices in *Living and Dying in Central Appalachia*.

Perhaps our impatience with grief is one of the reasons why so much attention is given to the question of how long grief is supposed to endure. It is one of the questions most frequently raised by the public and bruited about by professionals. The sense of chronic time urgency that characterizes the Type A personality also seems to characterize much of American society in general. We are reluctant to pause for death, and thinking about the dead is regarded as a waste of time.

American society's withdrawal of support from the bereaved represents a break from most historical traditions. In some religious and ethnic groups there remains a sense of closeness, of reconfirming bonds with each other. This may even include a legitimized relationship with the dead (as in the Hmong). The survivors may have prayers to say, offerings to make, and vigils to keep. Within such a context, there is time and opportunity for personal grief to find expression in a socially approved form. The newly dead can remain as an important person during a critical period of psychological adjustment to the loss. The bereaved need not pretend that the funeral marks the end of the relationship with the parent, spouse, sibling, child, or friend. It is possible to have thoughts and feelings about the deceased, even to sense the presence vividly, with-

out violating social norms. In this sense, societies that have functioned with less technological sophistication often have embodied more insights into the psychological needs of the bereaved. As a society, Americans may be uncomfortable with the seeming irrationality or inefficiency of grief. If so, this says more about dominant values in the United States than about the realities of core human experience.

MEANINGFUL HELP FOR BEREAVED PEOPLE

Society is coming to realize that we can help each other through our times of grief. One person who has contributed much to this encouraging development is Phyllis Silverman, founder of the Widow-to-Widow program. Silverman's *Omega* interview (Kastenbaum, 1993/1994) reveals many of the conceptual and practical issues that had to be resolved in establishing this pioneering peer-support program.

Widow-to-Widow: The Phyllis Silverman Interview

There were no peer support programs to deal with bereavement, grief, and mourning when Silverman was completing her doctoral studies at Harvard. It was thought that grief was a kind of illness that had to run its course. Did Silverman accept this medical model?

> When we talk of grief as illness, we make it sound like a foreign or alien object that has invaded our bodies and which we must in some way expunge, as, for example, a wound that heals after the scab falls off, or a cold that must run its course. With the "proper treatment" we can make it go away. With this model we maintain a sense of ourselves as machines.... We get no sense of context, of the complexity of an experience, and of its fullness.

Silverman observed grief to be a central fact of human existence, not simply an illness from which we hope to recover:

> Grief shapes our experiences and who we are.... We can't get through life without having such experiences all the time. We grow, mature, meet people, leave people. People, living or dead, are part of who and what we are.... We don't "get

over" people. We live in a web of relationships. We are still connected to the dead.... Because my father died, I haven't stopped being his daughter. When someone important dies we are changed by this loss. Our lives will never be the same.... The self we knew with that other person is gone. We need to reorganize, find a place for this relationship, and develop other selves.

Silverman does not believe that we must detach ourselves from the deceased in order to get on with our lives. She does agree, however, that grieving is work, and very hard work at that. In fact, one of her first research findings was that grief did not simply fade away after a brief period of crisis. Public health specialists at the time were endorsing a crisis theory of mental health and illness. With skillful professional intervention, the crisis should be resolved within approximately 2 weeks (well in keeping with our society's expectations for a "quick fix" to grief and anything else that ails us):

> When I first offered this view to the widowed women I was working with, they laughed at me! They said that if you had your act together in 2 years—so that your head felt screwed on, so you could look ahead—you were lucky! The more I talked with the widowed, the more I realized that our models of grief were not correct.

Silverman eventually came up with a different model and with a different approach to helping bereaved people. This model includes the following principles:

• *Grief does not have a final outcome.* Bereavement leads to a series of changes over many years. "People grow, gain new perspective on who they are, and learn how to deal more resourcefully with their own feelings and with other people."
• *Grief can most usefully be regarded as a life transition.* Although bereavement does produce a crisis and grief does have significant physiological aspects, it is basically a human experience that alters one's relationship to self and others. Life does go on, but it goes on somewhat differently.
• *People can help each other.* One does not necessarily have to turn to professional assistance, although this may be indicated in some circumstances. Peer support (e.g., widows comforting each other) can be highly effective. Furthermore,

when people with similar problems help each other they do not thereby become "patients" who are dependent on the medical system. Support should also come from family members.

> A network of social support is needed, and this support should include family members. There are usually several mourners in the death of a spouse, and they need each other to share their feelings about the deceased, to remember together, and to support each other as they acknowledge their pain and loss. They need friends to help with the concrete tasks of living and managing their family from the time before the funeral to the establishment of a lifestyle appropriate to their new situation.

Silverman introduced the Widow-to-Widow program at a time when neither professional grief counselors nor other peer support groups had appeared. The program was very successful and soon became replicated throughout much of the nation. A variety of other peer support groups have since emerged (e.g., the Compassionate Friends, which helps parents who have lost a child through death) (Klass, 1993). Silverman thinks of peer support as "the first line of defense. Most of us get through major crises in our lives with help from our friends." When people with similar problems help each other, all discover that they are not alone and all are in a position to learn valuable coping skills from each other.

Although many people seem to have found comfort in peer support groups of various types, there are hazards here as well. Julie Wambach (1983) also conducted a series of participant–observer contacts with self-help bereavement groups. She observed an inflexible philosophy that assumed widows should go through a sequence of stages of mourning in a prescribed time period. This rigid timetable and the concept of stages had no adequate basis in fact. Many widows felt pressured by the timetable and rigid expectations. Discrimination against the older widows was also observed. As Wambach also notes, there are probably many important differences in the nature and functioning of self-help bereavement groups, so a reasonable degree of caution is recommended. Even the best of ideas can go wrong.

Helpful and Unhelpful Responses to the Bereaved Person

Not everything that we communicate to bereaved people is helpful. Range, Walston, and Polles, (1992) obtained ratings (from "most helpful to "least helpful" on a 5-point scale) for a number of statements that are often made to bereaved people. The statements rated most and least helpful are shown in (Table 12-2).

As you can see from Table 12-2, the most appreciated statements are those that expressed the individual's commitment to being there for the bereaved. (The first two statements were by far the most favorably rated.) Asking specific questions or reminding them of specific sources of distress (e.g., "It was so sudden!") were comments that bereaved people felt they could do without. We should not generalize too much from one study, but it does suggest that we have our own thoughts and feelings in order before we volunteer such statements. There is one question in particular that it may be useful to ask of ourselves: "Is my message intended to comfort the bereaved person or control my own anxiety?"

Professional Help

Professional help has become more widely available in recent years. There are now counselors who have special training and experience with grieving people (Wolfe, 2002). When the

TABLE 12-2

Five Most and Least Helpful Statements to Bereaved People

Most Helpful	*Least Helpful*
"I'm here if you need somebody to talk to."	"Didn't the funeral home do a good job?"
"If there is anything I can do, please let me know."	"Did you know this was going to happen?"
"Put your faith in God."	"Was he/she in much pain?"
"Tell me how you are feeling."	"It's okay to be angry at God."
"He/she will always be alive in your memories."	"It was so sudden!"

Source: Range et al. (1992).

response to bereavement is especially traumatic, painful, debilitating, or prolonged, it is clear that sensitive professional interventions can be useful. One source of information is the Association for Death Education and Counseling, 638 Prospect Avenue, Hartford, CT 06105-4298; (203) 586-7503; fax: (203) 586-7550.

WIDOWS IN THIRD WORLD NATIONS

We have been considering bereavement, grief, and mourning with some attention to world cultures but mostly to our own experiences in the United States and other developed countries. There are cultures, though, in which both life and death are more difficult for most people. We are now being taught to understand and respect cultural traditions other than our own. There are certainly many ways to interpret the world and live our lives, and certainly the danger of criticizing somebody else's customs without really comprehending them. However, there are also practices that are very difficult if not impossible to condone. This bring us to the plight of widows in Third World nations. We begin with the universal fact of spousal bereavement: the permanent loss of a person who was of great importance in one's life. Recall the stresses and challenges that are encountered even when the widow has significant support from the community. Imagine what it would be like if she not only had to deal with what most widows have to deal with but also faced the absolute devastation of her life from that point forward. This is the fate even today of many widows in developing or Third World countries.

Widows in Third World countries are often deprived of the most basic human rights. Margaret Owen (1996, 2002) makes this situation unmistakably clear. She observes that spousal bereavement is a kind of death for the women as well, a social death. Widowhood deprives them almost completely of status (Owen, 2002), and

consigns them to the very margins of society where they suffer the most extreme forms of discrimination and stigma. Widows in these regions are generally the poorest of the poor and least protected by the law because their lives are likely to be determined by local, patriarchal interpretations of tradition, custom, and religion. Unmarried women are the property and under the control of their fathers; married women belong to their husbands. Widowed women are in limbo and no longer have any protector. (p. 947)

Here is an unfortunate example of the ways in which ingrained societal practices can generate misery and risk associated with death. Discrimination and oppression operate as forces throughout life and may become even more harsh when a person has been stricken by the death of a significant other. It may require extra reflection to realize that the excess misery inflicted on Third World widows is not a matter of chance or particular circumstance: It is rooted in cultural values and practices and is not restricted to just a few countries (Owen, 2002):

> Across cultures they become outcasts and are often vulnerable to physical, sexual, and mental abuse. It is as if they are in some way responsible for their husband's death and must be made to suffer for this calamity for the remainder of their lives. Indeed, it is not uncommon for a widow—especially in the context of the AIDS pandemic—to be accused of having murdered her husband, for example, by using witchcraft. (p. 947)

The AIDS pandemic mentioned by Owen is creating many more widows who themselves are at increased risk for this disease as they become sexually available to male relatives of the deceased husband and to other men as they become impoverished and unprotected. In Nigeria and other places, there is even the expectation that widows will submit to "ritual cleansing by sex" through taking on strangers or other men designated by their husband's family. Far from "cleansing," of course, this practice further increases the risk of contracting a sexually transmitted disease. Many other women have also been widowed and subject to rape as a consequence of violence and war in such nations as Afghanistan, Angola, Cambodia, Rwanda, Sierra Leone, and Uganda.

Fortunately, this large-scale abuse of widows has started to attract international attention. A nongovernmental organization, Empowering Widows in Development, has been established as an umbrella group for more than 50 grassroots organizations of widows in East Asia, South Asia, Africa, and Eastern Europe as well, where some of the same conditions have been observed. Operating with limited funds and not much cooperation from some world governments, advocates for Third World widows are hoping to educate the public about this mostly neglected tragedy and encourage corrective efforts.

SUMMARY

A person important to us dies. This loss is known as bereavement. We experience a mix of feelings, including anxiety, anger, and confusion. This condition is known as grief. We express our bereavement and loss to others in ways that are culturally patterned. This is known as mourning. In this chapter, we have seen that grief does not necessarily run its course in a year or any other fixed period of time. Instead, each individual and family has its own pattern of response and recovery that depends much on the nature of the death and the survivor's own general patterns of coping with stress and loss. Grief is more than an emotional state: It is also accompanied by the body's response to stress, especially in the neuroendocrine system. The health and even the survival of the survivors can be endangered by a severe or prolonged stress reaction. There are marked cultural differences in the way people have learned to respond to a death, and these differences are represented within the diverse U.S. population as well as in other societies, as we have seen through numerous examples. In attempting to understand how people cope with loss, many counselors have turned to Freud's griefwork theory, which emphasizes that it is a long and arduous process to accept the reality of the death and liberate oneself from the emotional pull of the deceased. Recently, counselors and researchers have suggested that it is not necessary to cast off the lost loved one; instead, one can reconstruct the relationship and keep it going in a revised and more adaptive way. We have also seen that people differ considerably in how they recover—or fail to recover—from bereavement. Gender differences and the way in which the person died (e.g., suddenly, or with time to prepare for the loss) are among the important influencing factors, but also is the nature of the relationship between the deceased person and the survivor. Particular attention was given to grief and recovery when the deceased person is a child or spouse, as well as bereavement among grandparents and other elderly people. The limited support given to bereaved people in the United States was a subject of concern, and suggestions were offered for providing support to the bereaved people in our own lives.

REFERENCES

Adamolekun, K. (1999). Bereavement salutations among the Yorubas of Western Nigeria. *Omega, Journal of Death and Dying, 39,* 277–286.

Archer, J. (2001). Grief from an evolutionary perspective. In M. S. Stroebe, R. O. Hansson, W. Stroebe, & H. Schut (Eds.), *Handbook of bereavement research* (pp. 263–284). Washington, DC: American Psychological Association.

Becvar, D. S. (2001). *In the presence of grief: Helping family members resolve death.* New York: Guilford Press.

Beder, J. (2002). Grief: Anticipatory. In R. Kastenbaum (Ed.), *Macmillan encyclopedia of death and dying* (Vol. 1, pp. 353–355). New York: Macmillan.

Bennett, K. M., & Bennett, G. (2000/2001). "And there's always this great hole inside that hurts": An empirical study of bereavement in later life. *Omega, Journal of Death and Dying, 42,* 237–252.

Bliatout, B. T. (1993). Hmong death customs: Traditional and acculturated. In D. P. Irish, K. F. Lundquist, & V. J. Nelsen (Eds.), *Ethnic variations in dying, death, and grief* (pp. 79–100). Washington, DC: Taylor & Francis.

Bowlby, J. (1969). *Attachment.* New York: Basic Books.

Bowlby, J. (1973). *Separation.* New York: Basic Books.

Bowlby, J. (1980). *Loss.* New York: Basic Books.

Bozeman, J. C. (1999). A journey through grief: An analysis of an adult child's grief in the loss of a mother. *Illness, Crisis, and Loss, 7,* 91–99.

Chethik, N. (2001). *FatherLoss. How sons of all ages come to terms with the deaths of their dads.* New York: Hyperion.

Cordell, A. S., & Thomas, N. (1997). Perinatal loss: Intensity and duration of emotional recovery. *Omega, Journal of Death and Dying, 35,* 297–308.

Crissman, J. K. (1994). *Death and dying in Central Appalachia.* Urbana, IL: University of Illinois Press.

De Bonafini (1991). Life stories. In S. Castro-Klaren, S. Malloy, & B. Sarlo (Eds.). *Womens' writing in Latin America: An anthology* (pp. 280–289). Boulder: Westview.

DiMeo, V. V. (1978). *Mourning and melancholia: A prescribed degriefing intervention method (DIM) for the reduction of depression and/or belated grief.* Unpublished doctoral dissertation, United States International University, San Diego.

Engel, G. L. (1963). A unified theory of health and disease. In D. Ingele (Ed.), *Life and disease* (pp. 7–24). New York: Basic Books.

Freud, S. (1959). Mourning and melancholia. In *Collected papers* (Vol. 4). New York: Basic Books. (Original work published 1919)

Gennep, A. V. (1960). *The rites of passage.* Chicago: University of Chicago Press. (Original work published 1909)

Glick, L. O., Weiss, R. S., & Parkes, C. M. (1974). *The first year of bereavement.* New York: Wiley.

Goodkin, K., Baldewitz, T. T., Blaney, N. T., Asthana, D., Kumar, M., & Zheng, W. L. (2001). Physiological effects of bereavement and bereavement support group interventions. In M. S. Stroebe, R. O. Hansson, W. Stroebe, & H. Schut (Eds.), *Handbook of bereavement research* (pp. 671–704). Washington, DC: American Psychological Association.

Gorer, G. D. (1977). *Grief and mourning.* New York: Arno.

Groom, W. (2002). *A storm in Flanders. Tragedy and triumph on the Western front.* New York: Atlantic Monthly.

Guyer, B., Martin, J. A., MacDorman, M. F., Anderson, R. N., & Strobino, D. M. (1997). Annual summary of vital statistics—1996. *Pediatrics, 100,* 905–918.

Hall, M., & Irwin, M. (2001). Physiological indices of functioning in bereavement. In M. S. Stroebe, R. O. Hansson, W. Stroebe, & H. Schut (Eds.), *Handbook of bereavement research* (pp. 473–492). Washington, DC: American Psychological Association.

Ingram, K. M., Jones, D. A., & Smith, N. G. (2001). Adjustment among people who have experienced AIDS-related multiple loss: The role of unsupportive social interactions, social support, and coping. *Omega, Journal of Death and Dying, 43,* 287–310.

Jacobs, S. (1999). *Traumatic grief.* New York: Brunner/Mazel.

Kastenbaum, R. (1969). Death and bereavement in later life. In A. H. Kutscher (Ed.), *Death and bereavement* (pp. 27–54). Springfield, IL: Charles C. Thomas.

Kastenbaum, R. (1987). Vicarious grief: An intergenerational phenomenon? *Death Studies, 11,* 447–454.

Kastenbaum, R. (1993/1994). Phyllis R. Silverman: An *Omega* interview. *Omega, Journal of Death and Dying, 28,* 251–260.

Klass, D. (1992/1993). The inner representation of the dead child and the worldviews of bereaved parents. *Omega, Journal of Death and Dying, 26,* 255–273.

Klass, D. (1993). Compassionate Friends. In R. Kastenbaum & B. K. Kastenbaum (Eds.), *Encyclopedia of death* (p. 56). Phoenix, AZ: Oryx Press.

Klass, D. (2002). Grief and mourning in cross-cultural perspective. In R. Kastenbaum (Ed.), *Macmillan encyclopedia of death and dying* (Vol. 1, pp. 382–389). New York: Macmillan.

Knapp, R. J. (1986). *Beyond endurance.* New York: Schocken.

Kübler-Ross, E. (1969). *On death and dying.* New York: Prentice-Hall.

Laudenslager, M. K. (1988). The psychology of loss: Lessons from humans and nonhuman primates. *Journal of Social Issues, 44,* 19–36.

Laudenslager, M. K., Boccia, M. L., & Reite, M. L. (1993). Consequences of loss in nonhuman primates: Individual differences. In M. S. Stroebe, W. Stroebe, & R. G. Hansson (Eds.), *Handbook of bereavement* (pp. 129–142). Cambridge, UK: Cambridge University Press.

Lavin, C. (1989). Disenfranchised grief and the developmentally disabled. In K. J. Doka (Ed.), *Disenfranchised grief* (pp. 229–238). Lexington, MA: Lexington Books.

Lichtenberg, P. A. (1990). Remembering Becky. *Omega, Journal of Death and Dying, 21,* 83–89.

Lieberman, M. (1996). *Doors close, doors open.* New York: Putnam.

Lindemann, E. (1944). The symptomatology and management of acute grief. *American Journal of Psychiatry, 101,* 141–148.

Lund, D. A., & Caserta, M. S. (1997/1998). Future directions in adult bereavement research. *Omega, Journal of Death and Dying, 36,* 287–304.

Martin, T. L., & Doka, K. J. (2000). *Men don't cry...women do.* New York: Brunner/Mazel.

Milo, E. M. (1997). Maternal responses to the life and death of a child with a developmental disability. *Death Studies, 21,* 443–476.

Moos, N. L. (1995). An integrative model of grief. *Death Studies, 19,* 337–364.

Moss, M. S., Moss, S. Z., & Hansson, R. O. (2001). Bereavement and old age. In M. S. Stroebe, R. O. Hansson, W. Stroebe, & H. Schut (Eds.), *Handbook of bereavement research* (pp. 241–260). Washington, DC: American Psychological Association.

Owen, M. (1996). *A world of widows.* London: ZED Books.

Owen, M. (2002). Widows in Third World nations. In R. Kastenbaum (Ed.), *Macmillan encyclopedia of death* (Vol. 2, pp. 947–952). New York: Macmillan.

Parkes, C. M. (2001). *Bereavement.* (3rd ed.). New York: International Universities Press.

Parkes, C. M., & Weiss, R. S. (1983). *Recovery from bereavement.* New York: Basic Books.

Peppers, L. G., & Knapp, R. J. (1980). *Motherhood and mourning. Perinatal death.* New York: Praeger.

Rando, T. A. (1992/1993). The increasing prevalence of complicated mourning: The onslaught is just beginning. *Omega, Journal of Death and Dying, 26,* 43–60.

Rando, T. A. (2002). Bereavement, vicarious. In R. Kastenbaum (Ed.), *Macmillan encyclopedia of death and dying* (Vol. 1, pp. 59–60). New York: Macmillan.

Range, L. (2002). Grief: Traumatic. In R. Kastenbaum (Ed.), *Macmillan encyclopedia of death and dying* (Vol. 1, pp. 379–382). New York: Macmillan.

Range, L. M., Walston, A., & Polles, P. M. (1992). Helpful and unhelpful comments after suicide, homicide, accident, or natural death. *Omega, Journal of Death and Dying, 25,* 25–32.

Rosen, E. J. (1998). *Families facing death.* San Francisco: Jossey-Bass.

Rosenblatt, P. C. (1983). *Bitter, bitter tears.* Minneapolis: University of Minnesota Press.

Rowling, L. (1995). The disenfranchising grief of teachers. *Omega, Journal of Death and Dying, 31,* 317–330.

Rubin, S. S., & Malkinson, R. (2001). Parental response to child loss across the life cycle: Clinical and research perspectives. In M. S. Stroebe, R. O. Hansson, W. Stroebe, & H. Schut (Eds.), *Handbook of bereavement research* (pp. 219–240). Washington, DC: American Psychological Association.

Schwab, R. (2002). Grief: Family. In R. Kastenbaum (Ed.), *Macmillan encyclopedia of death and dying* (Vol. 1, pp. 362–366). New York: Macmillan.

Stroebe, M. S. (1992/1993). Coping with bereavement: A review of the grief work hypothesis. *Omega, Journal of Death and Dying, 26,* 19–42.

Stroebe, M. S., & Stroebe, W. (1993). The mortality of bereavement: A review. In M. S. Stroebe, W. Stroebe, & R. O. Hansson (Eds.), *Handbook of bereavement* (pp. 175–195). Cambridge, UK: Cambridge University Press.

Stroebe, M. S. (2001). Introduction: Concepts and issues in contemporary research on bereavement (pp. 3–22). In M. S. Stroebe, R. O. Hansson, W. Stroebe, & H. Schut (Eds.), *Handbook of bereavement research.* Washington, DC: American Psychological Association.

Talbot, K. (1998/1999). Mothers now childless: Personal transformation after the death of an only child. *Omega, Journal of Death and Dying, 38,* 167–186.

Terkel, S. (2001). *Will the circle be unbroken? Reflections on death, rebirth, and human hunger for a faith.* New York: New Press.

Thornton, S. W. (2000). Grief transformed: The mothers of Plaza de Mayo. *Omega, Journal of Death and Dying, 41,* 279–290.

Turner, V. (1969). *The ritual process: Structure and anti-structure.* Chicago: Aldine.

Turner, V. (1992). Death and the dead in the pilgrimage process. In E. Turner (Ed.), *Blazing the trail. Way marks in the exploration of symbols.* Tucson: University of Arizona Press.

Umberson, D., & Henderson, K. (1992). The social construction of death in the Gulf War. *Omega, Journal of Death and Dying, 25,* 1–16.

Walker, A. (1988). *To hell with dying.* San Diego: Harcourt Brace Jovanovich.

Wambach, I. A. (1983). *Timetables for grief and mourning with and without support groups.* Unpublished doctoral dissertation, Arizona State University, Tempe.

White, D. L. (1999). Grandparent participation in times of family bereavement. In B. de Vries (Ed.), *End of life issues* (pp. 145–166). New York: Springer.

Wickie, S. K., & Marwit, S. J. (2000/2001). Assumptive world views and the grief reactions of parents of murdered children. *Omega, Journal of Death and Dying, 42,* 101–114.

Wolfe, B. (2002). Grief counseling and therapy. In R. Kastenbaum (Ed.), *Macmillan encyclopedia of death.* Vol. 1, pp. 389–393. New York: Macmillan Reference USA.

Worden, W. (2001). *Grief counseling and grief therapy: A handbook for the mental health practitioner.* (Rev. ed.). New York: Springer.

Wortman, C. B., & Silver, R. C. (2001). The myths of coping with loss revisited. In M. S. Stroebe, R. O. Hansson, W. Stroebe, & H. Schut (Eds.), *Handbook of bereavement research* (pp. 405–430). Washington, DC: American Psychological Association.

GLOSSARY

Anticipatory Grief: Anxiety and sorrow experienced prior to an expected death.

Attachment Behavior: Originally, the communications and actions by which a mother and her young seek to preserve their proximity and security. Now, the same in relation to any individuals.

Bereavement: The status of having lost a family member, friend, colleague, or other significant person through death.

Disenfranchised Grief: A response to a death in which the individual is not regarded as having the right to grieve and must keep the sorrow hidden.

Dissociative Flight: An extreme avoidant or denial response to a death.

Grief: The complex emotional, mental, social, and physical response to the death of a loved one.

Griefwork Theory: The process of gradually accepting the reality of the loss and liberating oneself from attachment to the deceased (Freud).

Intrapsychic: Within the mind.

Mourning: The expression of the sorrow of loss and grief in a manner understood and approved by the culture.

Spontaneous Memorialization: Voluntary public response to the death of a person by violence; characterized by expression of personal feelings, and bringing mementos to the site of the death.

Stigmatized Grief: The response to a death that has occurred in a manner that is considered immoral or shameful.

Traumatic Grief: The response to a death that has occurred in a sudden and violent manner.

This funeral procession is traditional among the Balinese, but the occasion bears the mark of contemporary worldwide violence. Nearly 200 people were killed in a terrorist attack on a nightclub in Bali, Indonesia on Oct. 22, 2002.

chapter 13

THE FUNERAL PROCESS

The wind blew the head down one night in 1685. A sentry secreted it beneath his cloak and took it home. Then began its long wandering, passing from hand to hand and indignity to indignity before obtaining a decent burial almost two centuries later.
—Edwin Murphy (1995) p. 20

The parent who brought her child to see a body followed a tradition grown out of an experienced ritual—a passed-on narrative for the African American community. "I came to bring my son," said one father. Another explained that he planned to bring his children back to the funeral home to let them understand "you're not too young to die."
—Karla Holloway (2002) p. 136

I have no weddings or baptisms in the funeral home and the folks that pay me have maybe lost sight of the obvious connections between the life and the death of us.
—Thomas Lynch (1997) p. 36

Pre-prepared funeral tributes. Solve funeral eulogy problems for ONLY $15. These funeral tributes come in sets of three all of which are about 1 minute long. They are especially written to enable you to mix and match them.... Send us your credit card details.
—A commercial Web site (2002)

There are powerful reasons for respecting the dead and their physical remains. The most powerful might be the most personal, as upon the death of a person we have loved and respected. However, there are also reasons that extend beyond our personal relationships.

I respect the dead because

- This also shows respect to the people who were close to them.
- It would violate social expectations if I did not show respect.

- We cannot go on with our individual and communal lives until feelings and issues aroused by the death have been settled amicably.
- I am troubled by death, so this is a way to do something positive.
- The dead have moved into a spirit realm whose god or gods I must respect.
- The spirits of the dead might take revenge on me if I did not show respect.
- I hope that my physical remains will be treated with respect when the time comes.

You might not agree with all of these statements, but you probably do not disagree with all of them, either. Furthermore, as a decent person, you probably do not have to think twice about treating the dead and their remains with respect.

It is all the more striking that there have been so many exceptions. Also, as usual, we can learn from the exceptions as well as the more common practices.

A SAMPLER OF RESPONSES TO THE DEAD

The toppled head in question had suffered six ax wounds on the neck because the executioner was having a bad day. Perhaps he was nervous about the assignment. Oliver Cromwell had been, until recently, the Lord Protector of England. He was perhaps the most formidable person in the kingdom until his adversaries gained the upper hand. The postmortem abuse of Cromwell (Murphy, 1995) was as intentional as can be. His head had been hung on a spike so that all could see what becomes of traitors. There was an additional twist of disrespect here, since it was usually common criminals who were treated in this manner. In this case, the abuse of the dead was a political action to intimidate Cromwell's supporters and anybody else who was of a mind to threaten the Crown.

Concealing the remains and preventing dignified burial is another way of disrespecting both the dead and their mourners. Tatanka Yotanka was such a victim. The leader of the Hunkpapa Teton Sioux (also known as Sitting Bull) was assassinated while in federal custody. The scene was chaotic and bloody. The government refused to release his body for traditional Sioux funeral rituals. Neither at that moment nor for many years later would the government turn his physical remains over to his people, despite family requests, religious protests, and court proceedings. This pattern of disrespect was taken to represent an entrenched discrimination against Native Americans and a persistent and misguided fear that returning Sitting Bull's remains would incite an uprising. (It was not until 1953 that a raiding party composed of his descendants and the town mortician succeeded in "kidnapping" the remains and providing a burial on Sioux land—much too late for the family and community that had lost him in 1890.)

Funerals have often been deeply significant events in African American life. Karla Holloway (2002) illuminates this tradition in *Passed On: African American Mourning Stories*. Racial discrimination and risk were conditions that many African Americans had to live with and sometimes die from. It was not realistic to raise children as though life would always be safe and sweet. Funerals were occasions to educate the young and to express the strong emotions of the adults within a positive and supportive framework. Cromwell and Tatanka Yotanka had exceptional lives but were flagrantly disrespected in death by mainstream society. Many African Americans have had to cope with disrespect from mainstream society during their lives but were honored and cherished by their own people in death.

The funeral director of Milford, Michigan, was reflecting on fundamental changes in the American way of life throughout the 20th century. In the past, most people were born and died at home (Lynch, 1997):

> There were households in which, just as babies were being birthed, grandparents were aging upstairs with chicken soup and doctors' home visits until, alas, they died and were taken downstairs to the same room the babies were christened in to get what was then called "laid out." Between the births and deaths were the courtships—sparkings and spoonings between boys and girls just barely out of their teens, overseen by a maiden aunt.... The smitten young people would sit on a "love seat"—large enough to look into each other's eyes and hold hands, small enough to prevent them getting horizontal. (p. 35)

As time went on, though, increasingly more of life's activities took place outside the home, although the professional establishment that prepares the dead for final disposition became known as the funeral home. Lynch's (1997) observations make it clear that we cannot understand how a society cares for its dead without also understanding how that society lives. Specifically, death in the United States has become increasingly removed from intimate family life, although there are signs of a reversal (e.g., hospice home care).

Lynch (1997) made his analysis prior to the terrorist attacks of September 11, 2001. We now should add another observation: The saturated television coverage of the disaster and the grieving survivors brought death into millions of homes. Many people experienced a form of *vicarious grief*: sorrowing for the losses suffered by others (Kastenbaum, 1987; Rando, 2002) (Chapter 12). The terrorist victims had not died in their homes nor were they members of their families. Television, the Internet, and other developments in communication have shown the potential for creating a much larger, if temporary, *virtual family* that can grieve and support the survivors of what Dan Leviton (1991) called "horrendous death."

It is one thing to witness funeral and memorial services and another thing to be a participant. Many people feel uncomfortable and unsure about what to do. For example, some people feel overwhelmed by the challenge of speaking at a funeral. "What should I say? What if I say the wrong thing?" This anxiety has created a potential consumer market that has not gone unnoticed by opportunistic salespeople. Purchase "pre-prepared funeral tributes" and we will not have to think for ourselves, not have to work through our own personal experiences, thoughts, and feelings. The real cost, though, is not the fee but the lost opportunity to say what is really in our hearts rather than take a generic tribute package off somebody's shelf (somebody who does not know either ourselves or the deceased).

Today, there are more options than ever about our own participation in funeral and memorial observances, and each decision either affirms or weakens our sense of meaningful involvement. It has therefore become increasingly important to enhance our understanding of the funeral process.

WHAT DO FUNERALS MEAN TO US?

The funeral is an event that occurs at a particular occasion at a particular place. We take final leave of one of our companions, "pay our respects," and then get on with our lives again. Why go to a funeral? What good does that do anybody? In fact, why have funerals at all? Some people view the funeral as an outdated practice. Perhaps we should replace the expensive and inconvenient funeral service with the click-click of the computer keyboard as we visit the departed at their cyberspace addresses. Perhaps not. Perhaps there is something so fundamental in the human response to death that we need the physicality of the funeral.

I believe the funeral is part of a deeper and more complex process in which we both separate ourselves from the dead and try to establish a new relationship with the dead and with each other. This chapter, therefore, examines not only the funeral but also the total process through which society responds to the death of one of its members. We examine both what is happening today and the cultural traditions from which our own needs, beliefs, and practices have emerged.

British sociologist Tony Walter (1992) asks us to confront the possibility that today we are long past the time when investing in the dead was a major value and source of satisfaction for society:

> It is one thing today to have a simple Georgian headstone or a well-constructed table tomb gently weathering in a country churchyard. It is something else to have a municipal cemetery stuffed with tottering Victorian sentimentality in which the once so affected heirs have long since lost interest. (p. 106)

Reaching much further back into history, we read of David's sense of responsibility both to his father and to his son *after their deaths:*

> David went and took the bones of Saul and the bones of his son Jonathan from the men of Jabesh-gilead, who had stolen them from the public square of Beth-shan. And they buried the bones of Saul and his son Jonathan in the land of Benjamin in Zela, in the tomb of Kish his father. (Old Testament, Sam. 21:12, 14)

King David's enemies valued these remains as negotiable symbols. Those who possessed these bones also possessed power. Politics aside, David was a son who would be in torment until he did the right thing by his father. A great many other people, before and after King David, have felt the same way: A proper funeral and secure disposition of the body are essential for the family's peace of mind.

The powerful need to possess and respect the physical remains of the dead was demonstrated immediately after the terrorist attacks of September 11, 2001. Emphasis at first was on rescue efforts and hope. Later, the emphasis shifted to recovery and identification of the remains. A proper funeral and burial would not heal the grief, but it would help to begin the process of healing. Nevertheless, there is also significant resistance to the funeral process as it has been commonly practiced in mainstream society. It has been variously criticized as too costly, too time-consuming, too depressing, and too artificial.

These are only a few examples, however, of the considerations that come to the surface when we inquire into the meaning of the funeral process. Let us make this inquiry more personal: What are *your* thoughts and feelings about the funeral process? Please answer the questions presented for your consideration in Box 13-1.

Respondents to these questions tend to be of two major types: *rationalist* and *romantic.* A thoroughgoing rationalist would agree that funerals are an expensive waste of time that make people too emotional. Cemeteries should be phased out so the land can be used more productively; cremation might therefore be the ticket. It is sensible to recycle one's better organs, but forget that morbid open-casket stuff. *Recognize yourself?* In contrast, a romanticist would observe that funerals are a comfort to the next of kin and suggest they are not all that expensive when one considers their meaning. Funerals are decisive and memorable events. Furthermore, people should show more, not less, emotion at funerals and not begrudge the dead a peaceful place to rest their bones. *Recognize yourself?*

Not all the questions bear on the rationalist/romantic attitude split, however. We return to these questions after we survey the funeral process.

An angel presides over a grave in Richmond, Virginia's Hollywood Cemetery. Rich and powerful families once demonstrated status by building impressive funerary structures.

BOX 13-1
THE FUNERAL PROCESS: A SELF-EXAMINATION OF ATTITUDES, FEELINGS, AND KNOWLEDGE

---

1. Funerals are a waste of time.

   Agree___   Tend to agree___
   Tend to disagree___   Disagree___

2. Bodies should be donated for scientific use.

   Agree___   Tend to agree___
   Tend to disagree___   Disagree___

3. Funerals are a comfort to the next of kin.

   Agree___   Tend to agree___
   Tend to disagree___   Disagree___

4. People often are too emotional at funerals.

   Agree___   Tend to agree___
   Tend to disagree___   Disagree___

5. The death of a family member should be published in the newspaper.

   Agree___   Tend to agree___
   Tend to disagree___   Disagree___

6. All things considered, most funerals are not excessively costly.

   Agree___   Tend to agree___
   Tend to disagree___   Disagree___

7. People often do not show enough emotion at funerals.

   Agree___   Tend to agree___
   Tend to disagree___   Disagree___

8. The size, length, and expense of a funeral should depend on the importance of the deceased person.

   Agree___   Tend to agree___
   Tend to disagree___   Disagree___

9. Allowing for some exceptions, cemeteries waste valuable space and should be diverted to other uses.

   Agree___   Tend to agree___
   Tend to disagree___   Disagree___

10. It would be preferable to be cremated.

    Agree___   Tend to agree___
    Tend to disagree___   Disagree___

11. It would be preferable to be buried in a cemetery.

    Agree___   Tend to agree___
    Tend to disagree___   Disagree___

12. A funeral director should be required to give a summary of laws stating what is and what is not required before the bereaved purchase a funeral.

    Agree___   Tend to agree___
    Tend to disagree___   Disagree___

13. The average cost of a funeral in the United States is between $_____ and $____.

14. Embalming the body is required:

    Always___
    In certain specified circumstances___
    Never___

15. An open casket funeral can be held after body organs are donated:

    Always___   Usually___
    Seldom___   Never___

16. My idea of the perfect funeral process is the following:

    _____

    _____

    _____

17. For me, the best or most useful aspects of a funeral are

    _____

    _____

    _____

18. For me, the worst or most distressing aspects of a funeral are

    _____

    _____

    _____

FROM DEAD BODY TO LIVING MEMORY: A PROCESS APPROACH

How do we transform our relationship to a living person into our acknowledgment of this person's death and a lasting memory that is integrated into our ongoing lives? This process has many dimensions, ranging from the legal, technical, and financial to the personal and the symbolic. Sometimes, the survivors succeed in converting what has become a dead body into a living memory. Sometimes, the process fails, and the survivors must shoulder a burden of unresolved feelings and unanswered questions.

Common Elements of the Funeral Process

We have already reflected on the passage from life to death (Chapters 3, 5, and 7). It is a biological process, a societal rite of passage, and, perhaps most of all, a mystery. The funeral process (or its absence) has a significant role in the symbolic transformation of a person into a corpse and the corpse into—what? Cultures differ in their beliefs about the new status taken on by the dead, and these differences are apparent in funeral and mourning practices. Although specific customs differ tremendously, certain basic elements can often be found.

Premortem Preparations

The law recognizes that actions taken in contemplation of death are unique. Gifts made under the shadow of death, for example, are often taxed more severely. The Internal Revenue Service is dead set against allowing dying people to give money away to their loved ones and thereby have them escape taxation. Economic issues are often important in all types of society (Clignet, 1992; Goody, 1962; Middleton, 1996). The premortem period is of economic concern to band-and-village societies as well as highly industrialized nations—the community wants to be reassured that debts will be paid and properly distributed according to the rules (Kastenbaum, in press).

The dying person sometimes takes the initiative, giving instructions for cremation or burial, disposal of personal property, and so on. It might be a family member who contacts family and friends so they can make plans to visit the dying person or at least attend the funeral. Colleagues may have a different type of preparation to make, such as replacing the coworker who will not be coming back to the job. The physician may be interested in removing an organ for transplant or in conducting an autopsy to determine the precise cause of death and therefore must decide how best to obtain permission. A funeral director may have already been consulted and carried out preliminary arrangements to see that the wishes of the family are respected. It may seem as though others are simply waiting and holding their breath, but often there is considerable activity in preparation for dealing with the event when it does occur.

Immediate Postdeath Activities

The death becomes official when it is certified by a physician. Certificates vary slightly from state to state but, as seen in Fig. 13-1, always require information on time, place, and cause of death. One immediate postdeath activity is to convert the person into a statistic or, more accurately, to complete the record keeping that started with the certificate of birth. Another immediate action is to contact next of kin should they not already be on the scene. It is common for the body to be cleaned and wrapped in a shroud (usually a plastic sheet). If the death occurred in a hospital, the body will either be kept in the same room or transferred to an available nearby room pending the arrival of the next of kin. If a hospital is pressed for space, the decision may be made to remove the body to the morgue after a short time.

Preparations for Burial or Cremation

The interval between death and the final disposal of the body is important in its own right. Often, there are both practical and symbolic reasons for placing a "space of time" between death and final disposition. One of the most common is to allow time for distant friends and relatives to gather for the funeral. Some deaths also raise questions that require action in the public interest. Was this death caused by negligence, suicide, or murder? Was the deceased the victim of a disease that poses a hazard to the general popula-

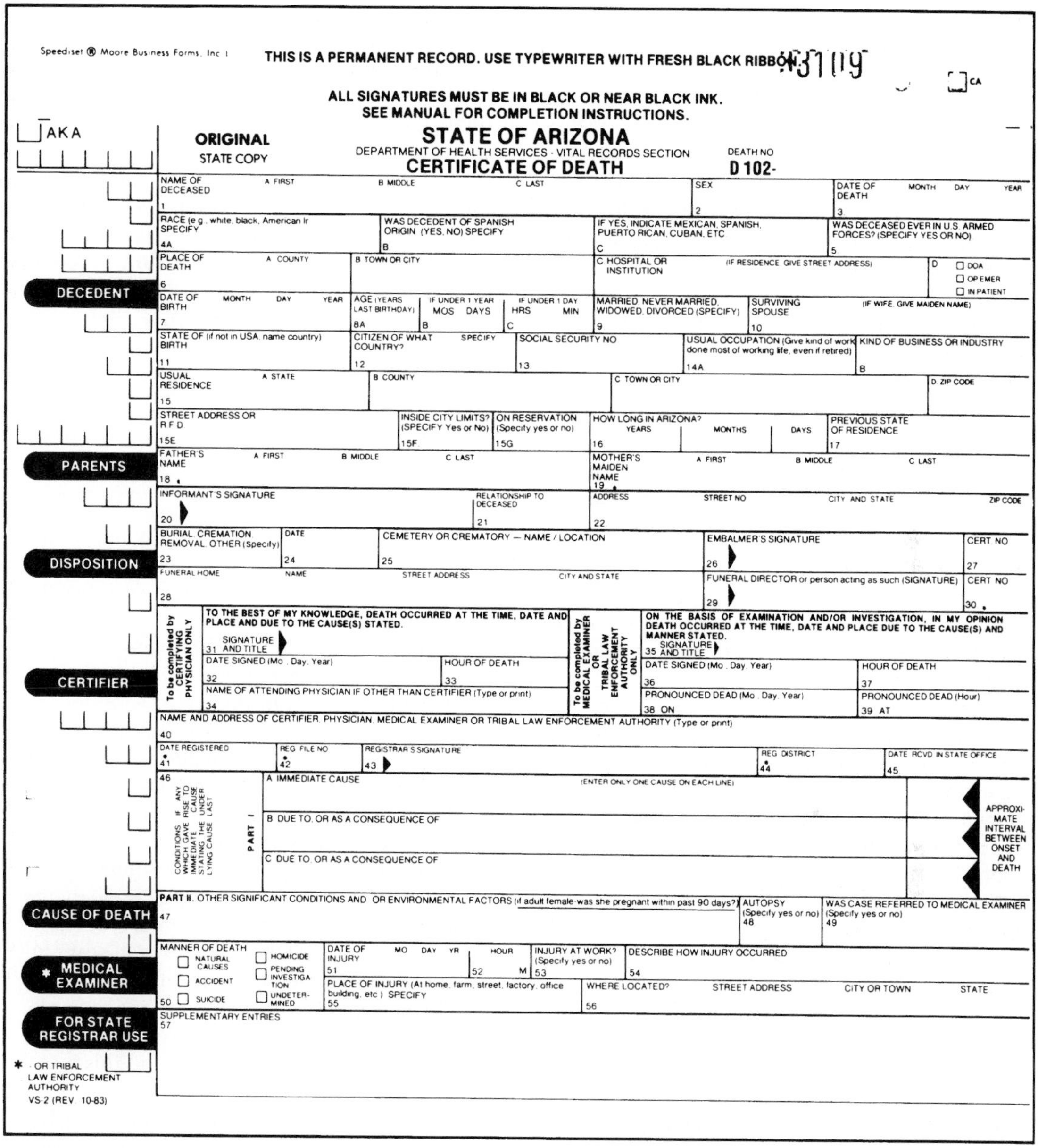
Speediset ® Moore Business Forms, Inc.

THIS IS A PERMANENT RECORD. USE TYPEWRITER WITH FRESH BLACK RIBBON. 31119

ALL SIGNATURES MUST BE IN BLACK OR NEAR BLACK INK.
SEE MANUAL FOR COMPLETION INSTRUCTIONS.

AKA

ORIGINAL
STATE COPY

STATE OF ARIZONA
DEPARTMENT OF HEALTH SERVICES - VITAL RECORDS SECTION
CERTIFICATE OF DEATH

DEATH NO
D 102-

DECEDENT
NAME OF DECEASED 1 — A FIRST — B MIDDLE — C LAST
SEX 2
DATE OF DEATH 3 — MONTH DAY YEAR
RACE (e.g., white, black, American Indian) SPECIFY 4A
WAS DECEDENT OF SPANISH ORIGIN (YES, NO) SPECIFY B
IF YES, INDICATE MEXICAN, SPANISH, PUERTO RICAN, CUBAN, ETC C
WAS DECEASED EVER IN U.S. ARMED FORCES? (SPECIFY YES OR NO) 5
PLACE OF DEATH 6 — A COUNTY — B TOWN OR CITY — C HOSPITAL OR INSTITUTION (IF RESIDENCE, GIVE STREET ADDRESS) — D ☐ DOA ☐ OP EMER ☐ IN PATIENT
DATE OF BIRTH 7 — MONTH DAY YEAR
AGE (YEARS LAST BIRTHDAY) 8A — IF UNDER 1 YEAR MOS DAYS B — IF UNDER 1 DAY HRS MIN C
MARRIED, NEVER MARRIED, WIDOWED, DIVORCED (SPECIFY) 9
SURVIVING SPOUSE 10 (IF WIFE, GIVE MAIDEN NAME)
STATE OF BIRTH (if not in USA, name country) 11
CITIZEN OF WHAT COUNTRY? SPECIFY 12
SOCIAL SECURITY NO 13
USUAL OCCUPATION (Give kind of work done most of working life, even if retired) 14A
KIND OF BUSINESS OR INDUSTRY B
USUAL RESIDENCE 15 — A STATE — B COUNTY — C TOWN OR CITY — D ZIP CODE
STREET ADDRESS OR RFD 15E
INSIDE CITY LIMITS? (SPECIFY Yes or No) 15F
ON RESERVATION (Specify yes or no) 15G
HOW LONG IN ARIZONA? YEARS MONTHS DAYS 16
PREVIOUS STATE OF RESIDENCE 17

PARENTS
FATHER'S NAME 18 — A FIRST — B MIDDLE — C LAST
MOTHER'S MAIDEN NAME 19 — A FIRST — B MIDDLE — C LAST
INFORMANT'S SIGNATURE 20
RELATIONSHIP TO DECEASED 21
ADDRESS 22 — STREET NO — CITY AND STATE — ZIP CODE

DISPOSITION
BURIAL, CREMATION, REMOVAL, OTHER (Specify) 23
DATE 24
CEMETERY OR CREMATORY — NAME / LOCATION 25
EMBALMER'S SIGNATURE 26
CERT NO 27
FUNERAL HOME 28 — NAME — STREET ADDRESS — CITY AND STATE
FUNERAL DIRECTOR or person acting as such (SIGNATURE) 29
CERT NO 30

CERTIFIER
To be completed by CERTIFYING PHYSICIAN ONLY
TO THE BEST OF MY KNOWLEDGE, DEATH OCCURRED AT THE TIME, DATE AND PLACE AND DUE TO THE CAUSE(S) STATED.
SIGNATURE AND TITLE 31
DATE SIGNED (Mo., Day, Year) 32
HOUR OF DEATH 33
NAME OF ATTENDING PHYSICIAN IF OTHER THAN CERTIFIER (Type or print) 34
To be completed by MEDICAL EXAMINER OR TRIBAL LAW ENFORCEMENT AUTHORITY ONLY
ON THE BASIS OF EXAMINATION AND/OR INVESTIGATION, IN MY OPINION DEATH OCCURRED AT THE TIME, DATE AND PLACE DUE TO THE CAUSE(S) AND MANNER STATED.
SIGNATURE AND TITLE 35
DATE SIGNED (Mo., Day, Year) 36
HOUR OF DEATH 37
PRONOUNCED DEAD (Mo., Day, Year) 38 ON
PRONOUNCED DEAD (Hour) 39 AT
NAME AND ADDRESS OF CERTIFIER, PHYSICIAN, MEDICAL EXAMINER OR TRIBAL LAW ENFORCEMENT AUTHORITY (Type or print) 40
DATE REGISTERED 41
REG. FILE NO 42
REGISTRAR'S SIGNATURE 43
REG. DISTRICT 44
DATE RCVD IN STATE OFFICE 45

CAUSE OF DEATH
46 PART I — CONDITIONS, IF ANY, WHICH GAVE RISE TO IMMEDIATE CAUSE, STATING THE UNDERLYING CAUSE LAST
A IMMEDIATE CAUSE (ENTER ONLY ONE CAUSE ON EACH LINE)
B DUE TO, OR AS A CONSEQUENCE OF
C DUE TO, OR AS A CONSEQUENCE OF
APPROXIMATE INTERVAL BETWEEN ONSET AND DEATH
PART II. OTHER SIGNIFICANT CONDITIONS AND OR ENVIRONMENTAL FACTORS (if adult female-was she pregnant within past 90 days?) 47
AUTOPSY (Specify yes or no) 48
WAS CASE REFERRED TO MEDICAL EXAMINER (Specify yes or no) 49

* MEDICAL EXAMINER
MANNER OF DEATH 50 — ☐ NATURAL CAUSES ☐ ACCIDENT ☐ SUICIDE ☐ HOMICIDE ☐ PENDING INVESTIGATION ☐ UNDETERMINED
DATE OF INJURY 51 — MO DAY YR
HOUR 52 M
INJURY AT WORK? (Specify yes or no) 53
DESCRIBE HOW INJURY OCCURRED 54
PLACE OF INJURY (At home, farm, street, factory, office building, etc.) SPECIFY 55
WHERE LOCATED? 56 — STREET ADDRESS — CITY OR TOWN — STATE

FOR STATE REGISTRAR USE
SUPPLEMENTARY ENTRIES 57

* OR TRIBAL LAW ENFORCEMENT AUTHORITY
VS-2 (REV. 10-83)

FIGURE 13-1
Death certificate in use in Arizona.

tion? When such questions exist, it is usually the medical examiner (or coroner) who must decide whether or not a full investigation is needed. A particular death can initiate a sequence of investigative and public health actions. If the case is particularly difficult or controversial, the services of a medical specialist known as a *death investigator* may be sought.

For an example of the challenges that may confront a death investigator, see Box 13-2.

An autopsy may be ordered by the medical examiner (in usual circumstances the autopsy is an optional procedure that requires consent of the next of kin). When special public health problems exist, a person whose death has certain characteristics may become the focus of investigation. This happened when swine flu and Legionnaire's disease became problems in the 1970s. Recently, attention has focused on deaths that might have been caused by the West Nile virus,

whose spread is being closely monitored. Post-mortem exams in such instances can provide important information for protecting others.

Disposition of the body may also have to await financial arrangements. Did the deceased have an insurance policy with funeral benefits? Precisely who is prepared to spend how much for the funeral? Has a clear choice been made between whole body burial and cremation? Sorting out all of this may require some time before final arrangements can be made. Problems arise in less bureaucratic societies as well. Was there sorcery

---

BOX 13-2
A DEATH INVESTIGATOR'S CHALLENGE: WAS THIS REALLY A SUICIDE?

The following is excerpted from the author's interview with Bruce Danto, M.D. (Kastenbaum, 1994/1995).

Would you give us an example of the kind of situation in which a death investigator's services might be called upon?

Perhaps most common is the case in which the cause or mode of death is equivocal. Relatives may want to prove that a suicide is a murder because at stake is a considerable inheritance from an insurance contract which prohibits suicide. Relatives may want a death studied because they don't like the members of the family who are survivors of the deceased. Insurance investigators may suspect fraud. A police department may feel that an intradepartmental investigation of a death is either insufficient or the bereaved family members may simply feel that they cannot get over the death until they are certain that the cause and circumstances have been firmly established.

Here is an example. A 20-year-old soldier was found dead in his vehicle in a federal park area. His rifle was between his legs. He was declared a suicide after an autopsy was conducted in the Army camp. It was 20 years later that the case came to my attention because a former military policeman had a guilty conscience. He had been called to the scene of that death and for years was bothered by the facts that photographs of the death scene had been taken after the dead

body had been removed to the hospital. He felt that those photographs were staged.... Now both he and the soldier's sister wanted to learn the truth, if possible.

All that was at hand was the autopsy report and the death photographs.... It became apparent that the wounds in the chest were not entrance wounds. There were two wounds, one of which was small and elliptical due to the forceful expulsion of the bullet's metal jacket from the body. This finding was suspicious to me because the autopsy described the entrance wound as being in the chest.... How could a person take a 30/30-caliber deer rifle and shoot himself in the back in a small automobile when the deceased himself was 6'5" tall? Photographs of the car's interior showed a bullet scar in the driver's door.... Finally, he kept his rifle on post as was required, but there was no sign-out slip. This means that the weapon somehow materialized in this man's hands without proper authority.

When the death investigator completed his work, it appeared that the soldier had been a homicide, not a suicide victim. This revised interpretation did not bring the man back to life, but it did confirm the sister's belief that he had not committed suicide. Many years of doubt and anxiety might have been spared and a killer might have been apprehended if more time had been given for a thorough investigation of this death before burial.

at work in this death? If so, was it a personal enemy within the tribe who must confess and make amends or was it caused by another tribe, therefore demanding lethal retribution?

The time interval also allows symbolic and psychological needs to be met. Among some ethnic and religious groups, the survivors have specific tasks to perform after death. These tasks help survivors express their affection for the deceased and support each other during the period of acute loss. Carrying out these responsibilities is also believed to be an act of piety. Society and its gods expect selected individuals to prepare special foods or create special objects to be placed in the grave. The symbolic meaning is often more important than the length of the interval. The Cheyenne, for example, buried their dead quickly so that the ghosts would swiftly take their departure. In contrast, societies as distant as Egypt and Greenland (Hansen, Meldgaard-Jorgen, & Nordqvis, 1991) mummified their dead as a way of keeping them part of the community, calling on their symbolic powers or enhancing their chances for a brilliant afterlife.

The process of preparing the body varies greatly from society to society. For example, embalming is far from universal, and it was seldom practiced in the United States until thousands of soldiers died far from home during the Civil War. Embalming is now a widespread practice in the United States, although it is not required by law unless the body is to be transported out of state or for some other clearly specified reason. Embalming can serve emotional and symbolic needs. For example, each year Arizona ships more than 3,000 bodies to the hometowns of those people who had left to spend their retirement in Arizona. "Postmortem emigration" also occurs in other Sun Belt states so that a body may be brought to a family plot in the hometown cemetery.

In some societies, attempts to embellish as well as preserve the body have taken considerable time, effort, and art. The ancient Egyptians' creation of mummies (Box 13-3) is the most famous but not the only example. Some rich and powerful people in Western nations have also demanded and received extensive postmortem treatment before burial. The wife of Louis XVI's minister "ordered her body to be preserved in al-

Many cultures have devoted skills and resources to the care of the dead and their progress into the afterworld. The dynastic Egyptians, however, brought the art of mummification to its highest level.

cohol, like an embryo" so that her widowed spouse could spend the rest of his life gazing at her beautiful face (Aries, 1981, p. 386). Less is known about the circumstances that led to mummifications (known as the Bog People) in northern Europe approximately 2,000 years ago, although ritualized killing is suspected for at least some of the cases. Societies throughout the world have found methods to achieve some form of preserving remains if they had a compelling reason for doing so. We consider an example from our own society after reviewing the Egyptian approach.

And now we have *plastination*. This is a process that converts organic material into durable objects. Dr. Roy Glover (2002) of the University of Michigan Medical School explains that

water and tissue are replaced with silicone in a process which, for most specimens, takes about 1 month. Preserved tissue is first dissected and then

---

BOX 13-3
THE SACRED ART OF MUMMIFICATION: HOW AND WHY?

How were mummies made in ancient Egypt?

- The family selects the grade and price level of mummification, choosing from several wooden models. Royal mummification is, of course, the highest quality whatever the expense. It is a first-class mummification that is described here.
- The internal organs are removed—the brain first, caught on an iron hook and fished out through the (slit) nostrils. The abdominal organs are then removed through an incision.
- In royal mummifications, the heart is replaced by the carved replica of a scarab (a dung beetle), symbolizing the perpetual cycle of life into death and death into life. The internal organs are transferred to canopic jars (stone vessels).
- The body cavity is thoroughly rinsed with palm wine.
- The face and body may be reshaped to restore blemishes and disfigurations that occurred during the final illness or the mummification procedure. This could include reshaping the breasts to provide a more natural appearance for a woman.
- Spices and many other aromatic substances are placed inside the body, which is then sewn up.
- The body is then covered by "divine salts" to foster drying and preservation. The standard period of time for the drying phase is 40 days, followed by another 30 days for final preparations.
- The salted and dried body is washed and wrapped in linen strips that are undercoated with gum. Features such as eyes and eyebrows are drawn in ink on the linen to recreate the face.

- The mummy of a powerful person is placed in a tapered coffin and the coffin itself is lodged within a sarcophagus (stone chamber), which itself is sealed into a tomb.
- It should be emphasized that this is mummification on the grand scale. The procedure was simplified and less expensive measures were used for people who lacked regal or other high-power status.

But why?

- The practical aim was to preserve the body by emptying the body of its fluids and the parts most subject to rapid decay, producing a dehydrated but otherwise faithful—almost lifelike—version of the deceased person. When conducted by skillful embalmers and not desecrated by tomb robbers, the results could be very impressive. There are pharaohs who look as though they are ready to reclaim their thrones more than 3,000 years after they drew their last breath. The high art of mummification was achieved only after many years of trial and error, with frequent failures.
- The more crucial aim was to guide a spirit that departed from the body at death—the *ba*—back to its former physical home where its companion spirit—the *ka*—awaited its nightly visits. The preserved body made it easier for the winged ba to locate its companion spirit, ka. Some archeologists believe that the great pyramids were constructed not only to honor the sacred dead and protect their bodies but also as a sort of astral communications center that provided a stronger signal for the communion of the spirits.

Principle sources: Ikram and Dodson (1998) and Harris (1973).

dehydrated with acetone. It is immersed in a silicone bath under vacuum until the replacement of acetone is completed.

Why?

The resulting tissue is safe to handle, the tissue has no odor and it is extremely durable. Thus, the anatomical specimens are safer to use, more pleasant to use, and are much more durable and have a much longer shelf life. (p. 1)

Plastination is currently used to prepare anatomical specimens for biomedical education. But how long will this efficient technological process be so restricted? Perhaps all it takes for plastination to become an option for human remains is a clever advertising campaign and public demand. (Or perhaps not!)

Settling into Earth

So familiar is the practice of embalming a deceased person, placing that person horizontally in a coffin, and placing that coffin horizontally in a cemetery gravesite that we might consider this to be a natural and universal tradition. Not so. For example, many tribal societies believe that one's afterlife is critically affected by the precise way in which that person's corpse is managed. One of the most common practices has been to place the body in a fetal position. The body is usually then wrapped or bound so that it will maintain this position, and then it is placed on its side. Is this position intended to resemble sleep and keep the spirit comfortable until it is ready to depart with the feeling of having been well served by the community? Some anthropologists think so; we really do not know. The fetal position might also be seen as an attempt to return the deceased to the womb of earth to be reborn. There have also been societies in which people were buried in a seated position or even upside down. Sometimes, members of a tribal society have clearly expressed their reasons, as when Solomon Islanders at the turn of the 20th century reported that they tightly bound their dead in seated positions so they would not come back to terrify or annoy them. Cynical observers in Western societies have claimed that grave stones are intended to accomplish the same purpose.

Up in Flames: The Cremation Alternative

Cremation is an ancient practice whose beginnings are lost in prehistory. Some of the earliest writings referred to cremation (e.g., the works attributed to Homer, Ovid, and Virgil, as well as Buddhist, Hindu, and Jewish scriptures). Historians believe that most ancient peoples (the Egyptians are one of the exceptions) chose cremation (Prothero, 2001). Some cultures have regarded assignment to the flames as a form of purification that helped to free the soul for its new form of existence. The Vikings, for example, would build a spectacular long boat to set afire with the corpse of their chief aboard. The flaming vessel would then cross to the spirit domain, taking along not only their chief but also his selected sacrificial companions. Practical considerations influenced a society's method: Cremation was not a realistic option for people who lived where trees were scarce. Some cultures had multiple ways of dealing with the dead. In former days, for example, Adaman Islanders would bury those who died very young or very old in a shallow hole, but those who perished in their prime received the prestigious treatment of having their bodies placed on a tree platform. Dead strangers were cut into pieces and consumed by fire without ceremony because their ghosts immediately left for their homeland and therefore posed no local danger.

Cremation was generally opposed by Christianity from the later Middle Ages until the establishment of Protestantism. Martin Luther rejected most of the Catholic rites for the dead and indirectly shifted attention away from the status of the body to the spiritual salvation of the individual. Cremation gradually became less of a threat to one's fate in the afterlife. Several events prepared Europe to at least consider the cremation alternative. One of the most influential was the death of English poet Percy Bysshe Shelley in 1822. He died in a shipwreck and his body was cremated on a pyre by his fellow poet and friend, Lord Byron, who then reached into the flames to rescue Shelley's heart. (Years later, Shelley's heart was buried with his widow, Mary Wollstonecraft Shelley, who, while in her teens, had written a novel called *Frankenstein*.) Cremation had started to take on images and resonances of its own. By the middle of the 19th century, an international movement composed of medical experts was criticizing burial as a breeding ground for disease and recommending its replacement with cremation. Not long after, Queen Victoria's personal physician wrote a procremation work that started a spark in the United States (Prothero, 2001).

There were *two* "first" cremations of Euro-Americans. The official first cremation occurred on December 6, 1876, in Washington, Pennsylvania. Baron Joseph Henry Louis Charles De Palm's cremation was hailed by some as a significant achievement in transforming society from sentimentality to science and denounced by others as satanic blasphemy. The debate was on, and it has continued to this day. The actual first cremation occurred much earlier. Henry Laurens, a former president of the Continental Congress, was given the open-air cremation he desired, although over the misgivings of practically everybody else. Why did he make so unusual and so unpopular a choice? Because he was afraid of being buried alive (see Chapter 3). Why was he afraid of that? Because his daughter, pronounced dead of smallpox, was close to being placed in the grave when she suddenly revived just in time. However, even Laurens' cremation was not the first to have taken place in North America. Cremation had been practiced by some Native American peoples (such as the Tolkotin of Oregon) before the first Europeans came ashore.

Today in the United States, cremation is selected by approximately one person in four. There are significant differences by state. Cremations are still uncommon (10% or less) in Alabama, Kentucky, Louisiana, Mississippi, Tennessee, and West Virginia. In contrast, approximately 60% of deaths are cremated in Alaska, Arizona, Colorado, Florida, Idaho, Kansas, Montana, Nevada, New Hampsire, New Jersey, New Mexico, Oregon, and Washington. Obviously, local circumstances and traditions have their influence. Estimates of cremation rates in other nations place Japan clearly at the top (95%). Cremation has also become the most common practice throughout Europe in general (63%), as well as in Australia/New Zealand, Britain, China, and India. Religious cus-

toms and other influences have made cremation rare, however, in sub-Saharan Africa, Islamic countries, and Israel.

The cremation option is being considered by many individuals today, but it also continues to be a large-scale economic, religious, and political issue in some lands. In India, for example, there is a shortage of kindling material and a danger that remaining forest land will be depleted. Governmental efforts either to promote or to discourage cremation for practical reasons often face determined resistance by people who prefer to care for their dead in their customary ways.

The Funeral Service

Both whole body burial and cremation offer the possibility of conducting a funeral service. This service is usually the centerpiece of the entire process. Two major purposes are achieved by the funeral service: final placement of the remains and society's public recognition that one of its members has made the transition from life to death. Perhaps the most familiar form is the church funeral service, in which respects are paid to the deceased in a church or funeral home and then mourners gather in the cemetery to hear eulogies and witness the casket being placed in the grave. Often, the arrangements for the service are carried out by the funeral director—ordering flowers, providing the hearse and possibly other vehicles, and so on. A member of the clergy usually presides over the commemorative services. In "small-town America," the clergyperson often knew the family well; this seems to be less common today.

Some rural areas still continue a more family- and neighbor-oriented process in which the funeral director has a less significant role. James Crissman (1994) provides a valuable description of a traditional approach that is being affected by changing times in *Death and Dying in Central Appalachia*. He speaks of "the code of the mountains" in which both independence and loyalty help people to survive hard times. Not much is expected—or wanted—from outsiders.

The funeral service can be influenced and distorted by intrusive events. Different factions of the family, for example, may collide because of long-standing grievances and hidden resentments. The tension can distract from the central purpose of the funeral services. An elaborate funeral can also attract so much attention that it is difficult to keep a focus on the deceased. A lack of consensus among the mourners can also be a distraction. One common example is the decision to have either an open or closed casket. These two choices are of almost equal popularity. This virtually guarantees that some participants will be displeased with whatever choice is made. Even those who prefer an open casket may disagree on the way it has been accomplished. Should Louise's visage be restored into a semblance of the robust person she was most of her life or with the lines of exhaustion that developed during her last illness? Should Harry be displayed in his favorite old sloppy clothes or an elegant dark suit that he would literally never have been caught dead in? The mourner can be distracted or disturbed by details of the funeral service. Nevertheless, the underlying purposes remain: to make a final disposition of the body and to use this occasion as a way of acknowledging that a life has passed from among us.

Memorializing the Deceased

Most societies attempt to fix the deceased in memory. In the United States, a death notice is often (but not always) published in a local newspaper. An obituary may also appear, especially if requested by the family. There is often a fee required by the newspaper to print an obituary unless the individual is considered especially "newsworthy." Furthermore, in recent years metropolitan newspapers have been reducing the number of obituaries published because of space and economical pressures. Is this trend weakening the ability of our death system to meet the need of survivors? Do people feel alienated because the deaths of their loved ones are not acknowledged in the state's major newspaper? We do not yet know the answers to these questions, but it is obvious that traditional acknowledgments and responses to death are vulnerable to general social trends.

Traditional burial is almost always accompanied by a grave marker, whether simple or elaborate. This identified site provides the opportunity for survivors to return and pay homage to the de-

ceased. Survivors often experience severe stress when war, terrorist attack, or natural catastrophe make it impossible to know precisely which grave is that of a relative or dear friend. Tens of thousands of unidentified soldiers lie buried in foreign lands, their graves usually marked by simple crosses. Many American families visited World War I burial grounds such as Flanders Field so they could at least be close to the place where their loved ones had fallen. In our own time, there are families who have experienced emotional pain for years because a member is still listed as "missing in action" in Vietnam. The increasing use of DNA testing may assist in the identification of people who have died in war or catastrophe and thereby ease some of the survivors' grief. There was some success in identifying the victims of the September 11, 2001, terrorist attacks. Whether it takes the form of lighting a candle on the deceased's birthday, saying prayers, or making sacrifices or gifts in the name of the deceased, memorialization appears to be one of humankind's deepest needs when separated from a loved one by death.

Getting on with Life

The funeral process is devoted to both completing society's obligations to the deceased and supporting the survivors in their grief. The "life must go on" motif has often taken the form of a festive occasion. Family, neighbors, and best friends gather to eat, drink, and share lively conversation. In former generations the food was usually prepared by family members, representing a gift in the service of life. It was a mark of pride to offer the fine ethnic delicacies in abundance, along with the beverages most favored by the guests. The prevailing mood would be much different from the previous phases of the funeral process. The guests were now expected to enjoy themselves, to be vital and frisky. There might be dancing and, as the feasting proceeds, even some romancing.

This type of festivity started to give way as society became more impersonal, mobile, and technologically oriented, and as efforts were made to banish death from public awareness. A cup of coffee with a few family members and friends has sometimes replaced the elaborate proceedings of earlier generations. Although the size and splendor of the postfuneral gathering may differ greatly, the underlying function is usually the same—to help people redirect their attention to the continuation and renewal of life. This is why conversation may seem unnaturally lively and why people may seem to eat, drink, and laugh too much considering the recent death of an intimate. If you happen to walk in while a risqué story is being told, it is easy to be offended and think that insensitivity and disrespect are afoot. However, lively and lusty behaviors after a funeral can represent a partial release from tension and the compelling need to show each other that life can and should go on—"Harry (or Louise) would have wanted it that way!"

MAKING DEATH "LEGAL"

Society's claim on the individual is demonstrated clearly at the points of entry and exit. Births and deaths have been recorded at the neighborhood church since medieval times. Demands of the faith required that each soul be entered into the books and therefore subject to the expectations of God and the state. A written notice was also required as the soul was released to join its maker—proof that the clergyman was carefully watching over his flock. These records would be consulted if questions arose about kinship rights and obligations. Now, centuries later, the surviving records continue to be of social value. Historians seeking to understand the effects of a harsh winter in rural England in the 17th century or migration patterns in northern Italy 100 years later are almost certain to consult entries preserved at the local parish.

Certificates of death (Figure 13-1) and birth today serve similar functions in a more secular society. The newborn and the deceased are affirmed as citizens beginning or ending their active roles in society. Church records now provide supplementary rather than official documentation. Despite all the changes that have occurred through the years, governing authorities still insist on "keeping the book" on the individual. This may seem a peculiar insistence—that we must not only be alive but also have proof of birth, that we must not only be deceased but also have proof of death! However, it represents the Western world's view of the social contract. I recently met a woman who had the task of persuading the Social Security Administration (SSA) that she was still alive, despite its "proof" of her death. (The SSA finally agreed with her opinion that she was still alive and proved it by giving her another stack of forms to complete.) Society presumes that none of us belong entirely to ourselves but are subject to "legalizations" both coming and going.

We now examine in more detail some of the major features of making death legal as part of the contemporary funeral process.

Establishing the Facts of Death

A death is real but not official until certified. Today, it is usually a physician who is called on to perform this task. It is the responsibility of the physician to establish the principal facts of the death and to initiate an investigation if serious questions arise. *Cause* of death often requires the physician to identify several contributing factors. The following are examples:

- Cardiovascular accident, secondary to hypertension
- Pneumonia, secondary to lung cancer
- Hemorrhage, secondary to cancer of the larynx
- Septicemia, secondary to extensive third-degree burns

The actual situation may be even more complicated than the death certificate can express. A woman in her 80s suffers from heart and urinary tract disorders in addition to a loss of bone mass and resiliency (osteoporosis). One day while she is simply ascending a staircase, the brittle bones give way. She falls. Both hips are broken. Her already impaired cardiovascular system is subjected to further stress. Internal bleeding proves difficult to control. Confined to bed and fitted with a catheter, she develops an infection that further saps her strength. Medical and nursing management becomes very difficult because treatments that might improve one condition can worsen another. Her lungs soon fill with fluid, and she dies. What is *the* cause? What is the precise relationship among the many interacting factors that lead to death? The physician may or may not be able to give a definite answer but often can specify the two or three major contributing causes.

The death certificate has its limits as a source of research data. Even so, it can provide useful information. For example, the information about this elderly woman adds to a growing body of data that emphasizes the need for better understanding and clinical and environmental management to prevent falls.

Occasionally, people dare to ask about the accuracy and reliability of the "cause of death" entries. The answers can be unsettling. Relatively few death certificates specify the underlying cause (Hanzlick, 1993; Kaplan & Hanzlick, 1993). Many death certificates also omit other information that would be needed to understand the circumstances of the individual's death. It is difficult to escape the inference that some physicians are not giving much priority to completing thorough and accurate death certificates.

The cause of death is often the most salient item of information required on the certificate, but the other entries are also of potential significance. Who is the next of kin? Was the death related to occupational hazard or stress? Has there been an unusually high rate of death from the same cause in this geographical area in the past few years? Questions such as these can have many implications for the well-being of surviving individuals.

The Medical Examiner and the Autopsy

The legalization of death occasionally requires the intervention of the coroner or medical examiner. Funeral arrangements will be suspended until the investigation is completed or the coroner decides that it is unnecessary. This procedure can distress the survivors, but it can also serve important purposes. It is possible, for example, that the death may have been caused by a condition that poses a continuing danger to the populace. Legionnaire's disease was not well understood when it was first encountered in 1976. Public health authorities had no way of knowing if this life-threatening affliction had resulted from some unusual combination of circumstances or if it represented a new threat of major proportions. A decade later, autopsies again became vital sources of information as another essentially unknown condition began to claim its victims:

AIDS. In both instances, public health authorities had to determine whether they were dealing with a limited or an extensive and uncontrolled threat to life. Physicians would have been remiss if they certified the deaths in a routine manner, as would public health authorities if they did not immediately examine both living and deceased victims. Certain diseases trigger automatic reports to the coroner's office when discovered by a physician in a living patient or during an autopsy. In the southwestern states, for example, physicians must report cases suggestive of plague. Such cases are very rare, almost always involving contact with disease-bearing fleas on dead or dying wild animals. Nevertheless, history has taught us to beware of any possible outbreak. The health care system's quick response to the emergence of a new type of life-threatening virus carried by rodents (hantavirus) was facilitated by the contributions of medical examiners. The spread of the West Nile virus, and SARS (severe acute respiratory syndrome) are among the public health threats that are being closely monitored at this time.

Inquests will also be ordered when there is reason to suspect that the death was the outcome of negligence or error. Was this patient given the wrong medication? Had this prisoner been held too long in an unheated jail cell? Did nursing home personnel fail to provide adequate nourishment to a "difficult" resident? It is obvious from all these examples that the interests of society can be served on occasion by requiring an investigation after death.

The examination can vary in scope and effort. In some instances, it may be sufficient to look for one or two telltale signs (e.g., the trace of certain substances in the lungs or intestines or the presence or absence of cerebral hemorrhage). Dissection and examination of the body may be considered necessary, along with a variety of laboratory tests, including bacteriological and toxicological. The popular television drama *Crime Scene Investigation* has acquainted many viewers with both standard and special forensic examination techniques.

Sometimes it is necessary to *exhume* a corpse for a further investigation of the cause of death. Removing a corpse from its burial site is a serious matter that requires careful thought and good judgment. Courts may order exhumation to obtain bullets, hair fragments, or other physical evidence that could bear on the cause of death in criminal cases, including malpractice. Corpses are also sometimes exhumed by accident, as when a graveyard is disturbed by flood or construction activities.

Autopsies require permission from the next of kin or a person who has been given power of attorney. In my experience, the decision whether or not to grant autopsy permission often depends on situational factors—the state of mind of the next of kin, for example, and that person's relationship to the deceased and to the physician. The request for autopsy permission can be difficult for all parties. The physician may hesitate to make this request so soon after the death, and the next of kin may have conflicting thoughts and fluctuating feelings. Effective communication and mutual trust are very important.

WHAT DOES THE FUNERAL PROCESS ACCOMPLISH?

The funeral process would not have become so important to so many societies unless it served significant needs and values. Some of the meanings have already been noted. This section considers a broader range of funeral observations and memorializations that will reveal even more about death system dynamics and the values that are at stake.

When Great People Die

Every life and therefore every death should perhaps be considered of equal importance. In practice, however, societies consider some people more important than others. The loss of a great person often triggers a massive response. The question, "Who does this society consider really important?" can be answered by observing the funeral process. However, it can be observed from another perspective as well: *Given that a great person has died, what is it that society feels it must accomplish through the funeral and memorialization process?* The following are examples that illustrate the dynamics and principles involved.

The Silent Army of Ch'in Shih-huang-ti

Ch'in Shih-huang-ti was one of the most powerful monarchs who ever appeared in either the East or the West. He unified the peoples of an enormous and diversified region into nationhood

and stimulated the development of a vigorous and distinctive culture. It was Ch'in, as the first Emperor of China, who built the Great Wall more than two centuries before the birth of Christ.

In 1974, Ch'in's tomb was discovered. It is one of the most incredible archaeological finds of all time. The tomb is encased within a large mound whose location was selected through the ancient Chinese practice of *feng-shui*, an occult art intended to deter evil spirits from disturbing either the deceased or the living. To call the site a tomb is an understatement—it answers better to the name of "palace." There are a variety of funerary buildings, each with a specific purpose; additionally, there had once been a set of double walls to protect the complex and provide housing for guards and attendants. Ch'in's tomb was built near the graves of earlier rulers and was clearly designed to surpass them all.

Several of the huge underground chambers have been excavated. Pit No. 1, for example, is a rectangle approximately 700 by 200 feet. It is divided into 11 parallel corridors, with the entire structure skillfully constructed by a combination of rammed earth, bricks, and timber crossbeams. In this pit excavators found an entire army! Arthur Cotterell (1981) describes the scene:

> The chambers are arranged in the battle order of an infantry regiment…3,210 terracotta foot soldiers. They do not wear helmets; only Ch'in officers have these. But most of the infantry soldiers wear armour. These armoured men are divided into 40 files; they stand four abreast in the nine wide corridors, and form two files in each of the narrow ones. The head of the regiment in the eastern gallery comprises a vanguard of nearly 200 sharpshooters, the ancient equivalent of artillery. They would have fired their arrows from a distance, once contact was made with the enemy. The majority between these sharpshooters and the armoured infantry are six chariots and three unarmoured infantry squads. Each chariot is pulled by four terracotta horses and manned by a charioteer and one or two soldiers. The guards would have wielded long flexible lances, measuring as much as 6 meters (20 feet), in order to stop enemy soldiers from cutting off the heads of the horses. (pp. 22–23)

The artistic craftsmanship devoted to the creation of this subterranean army and the enormous economic resources poured into the enterprise are truly staggering. What purpose was served by such a vast expenditure of labor and resources? Ch'in's motivation probably included the following components:

- To support his claims as the greatest of all monarchs.
- To impress the deities and ensure his place among the immortals.
- To confound his enemies and secure a continuation of his royal succession.

Ch'in made history, but he also made enemies. His military adventures placed enormous strains on the economy. He was also not the most tolerant of men. Scholars who displeased him were buried alive, and any person who displeased him was thereby in mortal danger. Revolution was prevented only by Ch'in's might and vigilance. The impressive tomb served to display his ability to defend his regime even from the grave, but it had another purpose as well.

Like many other rulers, the first Emperor of China craved immortality. The fantastic tomb at Mount Li culminated his self-aggrandizing lifestyle. Just as he literally required his subjects to sing his praises throughout his life, so he established a mute army to protect his afterlife from both earthly and spiritual foe. Didn't work, though. A fierce peasant revolution soon toppled the regime, and it is only in our own time that China has been able to recover detailed knowledge about its first Emperor.

Death Makes a Hero

Dynamics of a very different sort produced one of the most elaborate funeral processes of the 19th century. England's Prince Consort died unexpectedly after a short illness at the age of 42. Prince Albert of Saxe Coburg-Gotha had been married to the illustrious Queen Victoria. A proper and respectful tribute was in order, even though the public had disliked Albert because he was not an Englishman. What happened, though, went well beyond the proper and respectful: A national cult developed around the late Prince Consort.

Much of the evidence remains available for inspection today. Simply examine the monuments and portraits throughout the British Isles—Balmoral, Aberdeen, Edinburgh, Nottingham-

shire, South Kensington, Whippingham, Frogmore, Manchester, and so on. Among the physical tributes in London alone there is a memorial chapel in Windsor Castle and the Albert Memorial, which is only part of the impressive Victoria and Albert Museum. Existing parks and facilities were renamed in his memory. Many small statues and other items were manufactured and sold as memorabilia. One could purchase Prince Albert belt clasps, lamps, pencil cases, and stationery. Eventually, his handsome likeness would be put on packages and cans of tobacco. Alfred Lord Tennyson wrote one of his most famous poems to honor him (*Idylls of the King*). Upon his death, the late Prince Consort quickly became the most popular image and topic in the land and also something of an industry. Albert's widow, the Queen of England, demonstrated a worshipful attitude toward her late husband and would not allow people to speak of him in the past tense. His private rooms at three favorite residences were preserved just as they had been during his life. A nobleman who visited the Queen observed (Darby & Smith, 1983),

> She talked upon all sorts of subjects as usual and referred to the sayings and doings of the Prince as if he was in the next room. It was difficult to believe that he was not, but in his own room where she received me everything was set out on his table and the pen and his blotting-book, his handkerchief on the sofa, his watch going, fresh flowers in the glass, etc., etc., as I had always been accustomed to see them, and as if he might come in at any moment. (p. 4)

The observant Lord Clarendon noted a subtle contradiction in the arrangements. On the one hand, there were the fresh clothes, jug of hot water, and clean towels laid out for the use of the Prince, but a tinted photograph of his corpse hung by the side of his bed. Obviously, the Queen was having difficulty in reconciling her conflicting needs to acknowledge reality and to preserve the illusion that her beloved was still with her.

What purposes were achieved by the funeral and memorialization process for Prince Albert? I suggest the following:

1. *The elaborate memorialization process served the function of symbolically incorporating Albert into the British Empire.* In effect, he became an Englishman after his death. This was both a gesture of

Queen Victoria of England gave her name to an entire age. She remained in mourning long after the death of her beloved husband, Prince Albert, and maintained his rooms as though he were about to return any day. One of her most comforting companions also is seen here: Sharp, who had a natural gift for looking mournful.

support for their Queen and a way of grafting Albert's attributes onto the national self-image. His noble figure would always stand at alert attention or gracefully sit astride a beautiful horse. The memorialization also tried to make up for their cool attitude toward the foreigner Albert while he was alive. The need to incorporate and preserve what were now seen as his heroic at-

tributes, however, was probably more powerful than the gesture of reconciliation.

2. *Albert's death provided an excellent opportunity to express current sentiment and belief.* Victorian England had developed increasingly elaborate mourning practices. There was even competition to see who could express bereavement most impressively through dark clothing ("widow's

weeds"), withdrawal from customary social activities and responsibilities, and idealization of the deceased. Cemetery architecture prospered as affluent mourners commissioned impressive statuary art that aggrandized the departed and, therefore, the survivors as well. These customs affirmed the prevailing belief in the certainty and blessings of immortal life, although skeptics were abundant and wondered what other motives were being served or disguised by ostentatious mourning. It was the Victorian age, after all, that provided Sigmund Freud with the raw material for his exploration of hidden motives and thwarted impulses (Gay, 1984). Albert's death provided an opportunity to overcome personal fears and doubts with displays of public confidence in divine justice and mercy.

The postmortem cult of the Prince Consort would not have developed had not the spirit of the times been so conducive. Albert could easily be seen as an ideal representation of the virtues his generation would have liked to claim for its own. Furthermore, once the man was dead, his memory could be polished and fixed for posterity without the danger of competition from his ongoing life. It is often easier to admire dead heroes. They are less likely to turn around and do something that would force us to alter our judgment.

Many more examples could be given of elaborate memorialization processes for illustrious people. A common feature is the slow, stately tempo favored for the funeral procession and for the arrangements in general. This provides more time for the realization of the death and its meanings to sink in. In contrast, the final arrangements for a person without fame or influence are likely to be simple, routine, and brisk. At Vienna's Central Cemetery, for example, most funeral services are run by the clock, with every element determined by the status (i.e., the level of expense) of the deceased. The disassembly line is more efficient than many a factory assembly-line.

Throughout the world, some people who have been deprived and disadvantaged in life have yearned for a funeral that offers dignity if not splendor. Within the same society, then, we may find a few people who receive lavish attention in the funerary process and others who anxiously

hope and pray that their deaths will be given the basic respect due a human being.

The 20th century also provided examples of the lengths to which a society will go to memorialize one of its members—and of the political and emotional power that can remain associated with the corpse for many years. Consider, for example, the public afterlife of Vladimir Ilyich Ulyanov.

From Revolutionary to Relic

I'm standing beside Lenin. The man himself. Can it be true he died 10 years ago? I really feel like I'm looking at a man sleeping. You find yourself walking on tiptoe so as not to wake him. In preserving the body of its historic leader the USSR has achieved the seemingly impossible. The embalming of Lenin is the most perfect example I've ever seen of the art—better even than the mummies of ancient Egypt. Don't the Russian scientists say Vladimir Ilyich's body may be preserved for all eternity, without ever suffering the ravages of time? (An American visitor, quoted by Zbarsky & Hutchinson, 1997, p. 91)

The basic facts about Lenin's life and death are well known. He was the architect of a failed revolution in Czarist Russia in 1905 and fled the country. In 1917, Russia was in crisis as the government proved unable to conduct its war efforts successfully and meet the needs of the people at home. Nicholas II was overthrown, and the provisional government was beset with problems on all sides. It was at this moment in history that a mysterious sealed train entered Russia from neutral Switzerland. Lenin was its most important passenger. Within a short time his effective and ruthless leadership brought the Bolshevik Party to power, and the Soviet Union was thereby created. Germany, Russia's adversary in World War I, had financed this venture in order to knock Russia out of the war. Lenin had become the founding father of a new nation, and the Communist experiment had been given its first major opportunity.

Seven years later, Lenin was dead. Wounded and then partially debilitated by one or more strokes, Lenin became more of a symbol than an active leader during the last year of his life. Few, if any, shed tears. Lenin was consistently described as an ice-cold person who was obsessed by his plans and determined to see them through, no matter the consequences to other people. However, his death created a national crisis: The founding father had fallen, those hoping to take his place were engaged in savage infighting. (The genocidal Josef Stalin was the winner, and millions of Russian people were thereby doomed to suffering and death.)

The newly formed Soviet Union could not afford to lose its father figure. What if Lenin's corpse could be preserved indefinitely in a lifelike condition? What if this corpse could be placed within a grand mausoleum that would dominate Red Square, the spiritual heart of the nation? What if people could visit and see for themselves that their founding father, their peerless leader, was still with them?

The irony here was obvious to all who dared to take notice. Lenin's Soviet Union had no use for religion, no use for the ornate grandeur of the abolished czarist regime, and no use for "the cult of personality." Nevertheless, a shrine was created for Lenin so he could be revered as a de facto patron saint. However, the task of preserving Lenin's body for the ages had been bungled. Zbarsky and Hutchinson (1997) report that the first efforts were primitive, leading to serious deterioration of the body. The face and hands still looked presentable and were regularly touched up with an ointment to prevent drying and cracking. The body was in such bad condition that serious thought was given to burial, but this would have been a national scandal—the admission that Soviet science had failed. Zbarsky and Hutchinson describe the innovative techniques that they had to come up with in order to preserve the already deteriorated body. The restoration process included cosmetic repair of the face and substitu-

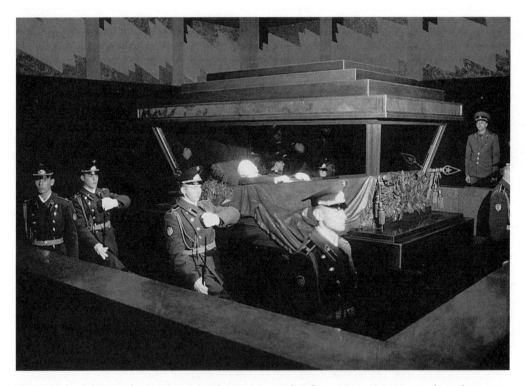

Russian physicians and scientists gained new respect for the ancient Egyptians when they were ordered to preserve the body of Lenin and did not completely succeed. Soldiers guard the tomb of Lenin whose postmortem political status has suffered a decline.

tion of false for real eyes to prevent the sockets from further shrinking.

How has Lenin fared as a relic? Very well, and not so well. Millions of people have visited his tomb, which became one of the most visible symbols both of Russia and of Communism. For several decades a visit to Lenin's tomb was emotionally significant to many Russians. However, statues of Lenin were pulled down in countries that had been subservient to Moscow soon after the Soviet Union ceased to exist. The Russian people have increasingly expressed their desire to bury Lenin's body. Rumors are regularly heard that Lenin's mummified corpse will be stolen some night and buried before the police can react (or perhaps even with police involvement).

Strange, strange, strange—but then, not so strange after all. Many societies have not only venerated but also used their powerful dead. For example, the skulls of past chiefs may be consulted for advice, and the shrines of saints have been thought to offer the promise of miraculous healing and other mercies. What we see in the memorial process for Lenin is an instructive reminder that a core of ancient belief and feeling has retained its potency into modern times. This emotional core was strong enough to entice a materialistic antireligious regime to devote itself to enshrining a corpse with so much determination that it might have earned grudging praise from the ancient Egyptians, but for intent more than craftmanship.

Balancing the Claims of the Living and the Dead

Another major function of the funeral process is to achieve a balance between the competing claims of the living and the dead. This may sound like a strange idea. We often hear it said that funerals are for the living. However, the need to honor the claims of the dead is also well entrenched in most death systems. It is expressed most clearly in funeral processes that are rooted in long-standing cultural traditions. Some of these traditions have been eroded by changing social conditions. Nevertheless, even today the need to balance the claims of the dead and the living can still be seen if we look beneath the surface. First consider how this process is expressed in three

traditional contexts: rural Greece, the Kotas of southern India, and orthodox Judaism.

In the Shadow of Mount Olympus

Potamia is a village in northern Greece not far from Mount Olympus. The 600 people who live there remain in close physical and symbolic contact with the dead. The small cemetery is crowded with 20 or more grave markers that memorialize villagers who have died in the past few years. Anthropologist Alexander Tsiaras (1982) entered a building in the corner of the cemetery:

> Although I knew what I would find inside, I was still not fully prepared for the sight that confronted me when I opened the door. Beyond a small floor-space a ladder led down to a dark, musty-smelling area filled with the bones of many generations of villagers. Near the top of the huge pile the remains of each person were bound up separately in a white cloth. Toward the bottom of the pile the bones—skulls, pelvises, ribs, the long bones of countless arms, and legs—lay in tangled disarray, having lost all trace of belonging to distinct individuals with the disintegration of the cloth wrappings. Stacked in one corner of the building were metal boxes and small suitcases with names, dates, and photographs identifying the people whose bones lay securely within. (pp. 10–11)

Bodies remain in the graveyard for 5 years and then are removed to the bone house. During this temporary burial the survivors have ample time to visit their lost loved ones. The survivors' feelings often become expressed with great intensity as the time nears to exhume and transfer the body. Tsiaras (1982) recorded a mother's lament:

> Eleni, Eleni, you died far from home with no one near you. I've shouted and cried for 5 years, Eleni, my unlucky one, but you haven't heard me. I don't have the courage to shout anymore. Eleni, Eleni, my lost soul. You were a young plant, but they didn't let you blossom. You've been here for 5 years. Soon you'll leave. Then where will I go? What will I do? Five years ago I put a beautiful bird into the ground, a beautiful partridge. But now what will I take out? What will I find? (p. 15)

The Ismall graveyard in Potamia is often filled with mourners, usually women. They come not only to express their sorrows through song, speech, and prayer but also to tend the graves. Candles are kept burning at the foot of each grave, and the grounds are tended with scrupulous care. Then they sit and talk to their dead and to each other. The conversation may center on death, and one mourner may seek to comfort another. However, the conversation may also include other events and concerns. The village's communal life is strengthened through their role as survivors of the dead. For the women especially, the graveyard provides an opportunity to express their *ponos* (the pain of grief). The men find a variety of outlets, but the women are usually expected to be at home and to keep their feelings to themselves. "A woman performs the necessary rites of passage and cares for the graves of the dead 'in order to get everything out of her system'" (Tsiaras, 1982, p. 144).

Through their graveside laments and rituals, the women try for a balance between the dead and the living. The custom of temporary burial is helpful in this process. The deceased is still treated as an individual and as a member of the community. In effect, the deceased suffers a second and final death when the physical remains are deposited among the bones of the anonymous dead. It is easier to cope with the symbolic claims of the dead when a definite time limit has been set—in this case, a rather generous 5-year period. Although the memory of the deceased will continue to be honored, removal of the remains to the bone house represents the reemergence of the life-oriented needs of the survivors.

The survivors are *obliged* to tend the graves and carry out other responsibilities to the deceased. As Tsiaras (1982) points out, this process involves a symbolic interaction and continuation between the living and the dead. *The dead have the right to expect it, just as those who are now among the living can expect their survivors to honor their postmortem rights when the time comes.* In Potamia and in some other communities in which traditional value systems remain in place, the obligations of the living to the dead are clear, specific, and well known.

Kotas and Orthodox Jews

Peoples as different as the Kotas of southern India and Orthodox Jews dispersed throughout the world continue to carry out extensive rituals to ensure that both the dead and the living re-

ceive their due. Their observations differ greatly in detail. The Kotas, who cremate their dead (Goldberg, 1981/1982),

> believe that death is contaminating and all who come into contact with death are defiled. Through the rituals of two funerals, the Green Funeral and the Dry Funeral, the spirit of the deceased is assisted in departing to the "Motherland" and the survivors are thereby cleansed so that they might resume their normal life within the society. Since the concept of an afterlife is not clear to most Kotas, the adherence to ritual is seen more as a cleansing process for the survivors, than for the attainment of existence in another world for the deceased. (p. 119)

Orthodox Jews obey strict laws that reject embalming and cremation and require that funeral arrangements be simple and standard no matter what the family's financial status. The interval between death and burial is regarded as quite apart from usual time and custom. This period is known as *Aninut,* a time in which time stands still (Schindler, 1996). During Aninut, the grieving survivors are exempted from all social and religious obligations, other than arranging for the funeral. One should be devoted to honoring the dead and reflecting on the loss. Aninut therefore helps the survivors to begin the long process of recovery from grief by providing time to focus on the death in their own private ways without other distractions. The *Kaddish* prayer affirms faith in God; *Shiva,* the 7 days of morning, unites the family in grief.

Interestingly, the ritual action of washing hands before sitting at *Shiva* has its parallel in the more elaborate purification rites of the Kotas. The Kota, the Orthodox Jew, the rural Greek villager, and many others with long ethnic traditions must fulfill obligations to the dead. When these obligations have at last been faithfully performed, however, it is time for the living to again turn their full attention to life.

MEMORIES OF OUR PEOPLE: CEMETERIES IN THE UNITED STATES

At first a nation of farmers who visited small towns with their artisans and shops, the United States quickly became a coast-to-coast industrial power with humming factories, crowded cities, opportunistic ventures in every direction, and a large and mobile population. The history of cemeteries has faithfully moved in concert with our changing ways of life. In Colonial times, most of the dead were buried in a church graveyard. This practice continued into the early years of the republic. As the population increased, however, these early burial grounds often proved inadequate. The dead as well as the living were becoming crowded. Furthermore, cemetery upkeep was too often neglected, resulted in conditions that were not only unpleasant for the visitor but also dangerous to public health.

The New Haven Burying Ground is a surviving example of the response to this emerging need. The city had established a cemetery in 1639 in what is now the center of New Haven, Connecticut (Plunkett, 1999). Graves were dug by friends and relatives who placed them wherever it seemed suitable or convenient to them, and they also marked and tended the graves as they saw fit. Just 20 years later, there was already concern that the burial ground had become too crowded, but nothing was done about it. The poorly tended and helter-skelter burial ground had the virtue of being adjacent to a church but was otherwise becoming an increasing eyesore in the growing community. The closely packed grave sites did not speak well for dignity and respect. Moreover, the seasonal death toll from diseases such as malaria and tuberculosis further strained the resources of the graveyard. People with some awareness of public health concerns could not help but worry about the possibility that the burial ground might be a source of infection.

The community finally responded in 1796 with the establishment of the New Haven Burying Ground (also known as the Grove Street Cemetery). Care was taken to select land that was accessible and yet would not block further community development. Furthermore, each grave lot became the property of a purchasing family—here was one of the first cemeteries in which "the family plot" became established. Future generations could return to view their family plot and to consider whether they would also end up there. The New Burial Ground was added under similar regulations a few years later. Unfortunately, though, even cemeteries planned with personal and social dignity and public health in mind are vul-

nerable to conflict and change. Some citizens advocated and some opposed new church constructions that would create problems for the again overcrowded burying ground. Many grave sites were neglected. Animals and vandals invaded at night—the former digging up graves, and the latter desecrating memorial stones and littering. The people of New Haven again rallied and protected their cemetery. This basic story has been repeated for many cemeteries as communities must cope with the challenges of urban change and the consequences of neglect.

Major changes in cemeteries occurred throughout the 19th century. One of the most important was the introduction of "memorial parks," also known as "garden parks" and "landscapes of memory" (Linden-Ward, 1989; Morris, 2002). The first of these was Mount Auburn Cemetery (Cambridge, Massachusetts), whose spacious and inviting grounds quickly became the inspiration for similar developments throughout the nation. The park lawn-type establishment had its origins in the sensitivity of community leaders who believed that a visit to the dead should bring us into comforting touch with nature. The other major development was the establishment of national cemeteries to honor those who had fallen in war. Lincoln's Gettysburg Address on November 11, 1963, was given to dedicate the first national cemetery. By the end of the Civil War, there were 14 national cemeteries for both Union and Confederate dead. The National Cemetery System today tends to the graves of more than 2 million veterans in more than 100 sites throughout the country. In history's odd way of doing things, the United States became that much more of a nation when the dead of the Blue and the dead of the Gray were placed to rest in the same meadows.

The Neighborhood Cemetery

There are still pockets of traditional symbolic interaction with the dead in American cities. While interviewing older people in small industrial cities, I often heard reference to the neighborhood cemetery. Although the cemetery may have been surrounded by deteriorating industrial buildings, it still remained the focal point of continuity. One octogenarian, for example, said

> I know I should get out of this neighborhood. Hell, it isn't even a neighborhood any more, not

like the old days. But how can I sell this house? It's where my mother and father lived and died. And who'd look after them?... Oh, sure, I'm out there every Sunday at least to keep things as nice as I can. It's not their fault what's happened to this neighborhood. Me and a few others still meet there, we keep up the graves. And it's not just my parents. Just about everybody else is there, too, I mean, 6 feet under. I keep them company. They keep me company.

This man, by the way, was not at all of morbid disposition. He had an active and well-integrated lifestyle but drew some of his strength and self-esteem from the knowledge that he was continuing to fulfill his obligations to the dead.

There are many other examples of continued bonding or symbolic transactions between the living and the dead that can be associated with the funeral and memorialization process. Even in bustling, urban America, survivors often se-lect images, materials, and objects connected with the deceased to somehow keep the beloved alive as part of themselves. Salient or treasured aspects of the deceased's personality become part of the survivor's lifestyle, and therefore the memorialization process continues well beyond the funeral.

Ethnic Cemeteries in the United States

The shores of the United States have attracted millions of people who sought to make new lives for themselves and their children. Others were brought here involuntarily, wrenched from their homelands and sold into slavery. Still other people lived freely in forests and plains until they encountered the aggressive newcomers who would eventually transform a wilderness into a powerful industry-driven nation. Memories of this in-

The village cemetery can be a place for comforting socialization as people gather to look after family graves.

credible variety of people remain with us in many forms. Poet Stephen Vincent Benet (1942) reflects on this heritage:

> I have fallen in love with American names,
> The sharp names that never get fat,
> The snakeskin-titles of mining-claims,
> The plumed war-bonnet of Medicine Hat,
> Tucson and Deadwood and Lost Mule Flat....
> I will remember Carquinez Straits,
> Little French Lick and Lundy's Lane,
> The Yankee ships and the Yankee dates
> And the bullet-towns of Calamity Jane.
> I will remember Skunktown Plain....
> I shall not rest quiet in Montparnasse.
> I shall not lie easy at Winchelsea.
> You may bury my body in Sussex grass,
> You may bury my tongue at Champmedy.
> I shall not be there. I shall rise and pass.
> Bury my heart at Wounded Knee.

The land also remembers. Ethnic cemeteries, often overlooked by society at large, still affirm that "our people" lived their own distinctive lives here and contributed to the nation's history. The following are examples of cemeteries whose responsibility is to preserve not physical remains but memories and symbols of those who have gone before us.

1. *Afro-American Section, the Common Burying Ground, Newport, Rhode Island:* This colonial cemetery dates from 1650. More than 8,000 people were buried here until it became a historical site. Only a few years ago, a visitor realized that this was probably the only remaining burial site of African Americans in colonial New England. Ann Tashjian and her husband, Dickran Tashjian (1989), photographed and transcribed the gravestones and researched the history. Many of the grave markers described the deceased as "servant," which is thought to have been a euphemism for "slave" (a term considered too harsh, even though accurate, in New England households of the time). Some of the gravestones are elaborate in design and execution, suggesting that the deceased had been held in high regard by the white families they served.

Do the gravestones or burial sites show any trace of the cultures and belief systems that the African Americans had left behind when they were brought to the American colonies? Not a trace. Whatever beliefs and practices these people may have continued to cherish from their own tradition, upon their deaths it was the dominant white American culture of the time that prevailed. If you visit this cemetery, make your way to the northern edge and you will see those African American grave markers that have survived the vicissitudes of time. You will see that they are similar to the other grave markers of the same time periods. Cherubs, for example, were popular adornments, and these appear alike on white and African American grave markers.

The cemetery tells us something about the subordinate place of African Americans in colonial New England; in death as in life, their own culture was denied expression. The Tashjians (1989) found that a Free African Union Society, active in the 18th century, had encouraged African Americans to "assume a dignified public appearance (at funerals) to protect the integrity of private grief" (p. 192). Along with other evidence, this suggests that the occasion of death was seen as having potential for racial tension, with the dominant white society seeking to maintain its control over the funeral services and burial. The longing to be free, so often expressed in gospel song, takes on added significance here. In death, an African American would become free of servitude, but the public memory of his or her existence would still be under the control of the dominant society.

2. *Navajo and Mormon companions, Ramah Cemetery, Ramah, New Mexico:* Members of The Church of the Latter-day Saints (often referred to as Mormons) started a community in Ramah, New Mexico, in 1876. The Ramah people of the Navajo Nation had previously taken up residence in this area. The same graveyard serves families of both cultures, although their beliefs and practices differ markedly. The cemetery was established by the Mormons on a knoll surrounded by farm and ranch land. There are no large memorial statues, and the ground is covered by native grasses and weeds.

The Navajo section includes 71 graves that could be positively identified. A few recent graves have commercially manufactured gravestones. A few others are decorated with artificial flowers, but most are undecorated. Cunningham (1989) noted

> There is no indication of any attempt to bury family members side by side or close together. All the graves are approximately the same distance apart and are laid out in what is basically a straight line. The headstone or other marker and the grave are placed so that the main side of the marker and the head of the deceased point toward the West, and the deceased would face East if sitting or standing. (p. 204)

This description tells only part of the story, however. Beneath the earth, the Navajo culture expresses itself through valued objects that are placed with the dead. Turquoise jewelry is thought to have special powers, attributed both to the gemstones and to the spirituality transmitted by the artists. In burying this jewelry with the deceased, the family both speeds its spirit on its journey to the afterlife and confuses and thwarts any *ch'iidii* (evil ghosts) that might covet these powerful objects.

The Mormon section (209 graves) has numerous markers, some of them homemade by family members. These markers display a large variety of styles and materials, in contrast with the simple metal markers that identify the Navajo graves. The Mormon markers include examples of folk art revival (e.g., in red sandstone carvings) and such others as "an actual picture of the deceased as a part of their design and contemporary sandblasted stones which allow very intricate and exact representations of floral motifs and even recognizable representations of Mormon temples at Mesa, Arizona, and Salt Lake City, Utah" (Cunningham, 1989, p. 204). The Mormon graves also differ from the Navajo in their spatial arrangement: They are usually grouped according to family relationships, including some joint stones for husband and wife. The memorial stones also provide more information about the deceased.

The Navajo and Mormon dead in New Mexico appear to be more companionable than the African Americans and colonial whites in Newport. The cemetery blends easily into its surroundings, with the "landscaping" for both Navajo and Mormon left to nature. The family-oriented Mormons preserved this orientation in the arrangement of graves and markers but did not impose their beliefs and practices on their Native American neighbors or object to the jewelry burials. For their part, some Navajos have chosen to become Mormon, or "semi-Mormon," and have expressed the thought that the worst of the evil spirits have departed from the burial grounds because of the Mormons' presence. Ironically, perhaps, the Mormons believe this cemetery meets their needs because it pays respect to the dead in an appropriate manner, while the traditional Navajos find it satisfactory as a place that keeps the dead (and the dangerous ghosts they attract) away from the living. Navajo and Mormon appear to have respected and learned from each other in life and to have shared the land in a manner acceptable to both. Now, in death, they can lie under the same ground without requiring one faith to bow to the wishes of the other.

3. *Mexican Americans in San Antonio's San Fernando Cemetery:* The standardization of American life extends to many urban cemeteries: This one does not look much different from that one. Lynn Gosnell and Suzanne Gott (1989) describe some of the activity at a cemetery that has retained its special character:

> Throughout the year, but especially during religious and secular holidays, including Halloween, All Souls' Day, Christmas, Valentine's Day, Easter, Mother's Day, and Father's Day, the visitor to San Fernando takes part in an energetic practice of grave decoration and visual display. During these days, cars and trucks jam the narrow traffic lanes which provide access to each block of this 93-acre cemetery. Relatives crowd the burial grounds, bringing with them gardening tools, flowers, and other decorative materials.... Some people busily tend to a gravesite, while others take time to chat and remark on a particularly well-decorated grave site. Still others stand quietly, singly or in groups, near the grave of a loved one. Grave decorating days within San Fernando Cemetery are therefore marked by a lively social interaction between the living and a heightened interaction between families and their deceased loved ones. (p. 218)

How important is this cemetery? Each family could remember and honor its own dead privately. However, having a cemetery to share with other people who hold similar beliefs and values enhances the memorial process. The dead have their special place that the living can visit (just like one living person might visit another). Furthermore, when one arrives at the gravesites, there are things to do for the loved ones (again, reminiscent of what one living family member might do for another). No less important is the vista: "We are not the only people to have lost a loved one. It is the human condition. We are, all of us, together in our respect for the dead and our celebration of life." Finally, after the trip, the decorating, and the interaction, the family returns home and is able to separate, for a while, from the dead. Some outsiders might be puzzled or even annoyed by all this activity at a cemetery: Have they never felt isolated by a loss and never carried a death around with them, unable to set it down even for a moment?

These are but three examples of the ethnic cemetery in the United States today. Are there examples in your area? What stories do they tell?

THE PLACE OF THE DEAD IN SOCIETY: YESTERDAY AND TODAY

Society today places a strong emphasis on curing illness and preventing death. In contrast, most death systems in the past emphasized relationships with the dead. Here is a brief comparison of the place of the dead in the past that will prepare us to consider the meaning and impact of the Vietnam Veterans Memorial—and the World Trade Center memorial that is yet to come.

When Are the Dead Important to the Living?

1. *The dead are more secure in past-oriented societies.* They maintain a role in the symbolic continuity of people with shared language and cultural values who have lived in the same place for many generations, perhaps for centuries. If the past is known, valued, and seen as relevant to daily life, then the dead are likely to be respected. For example, the Penang Gang people of central Borneo give new names or titles to their family members when they die. This practice conveys their continuing affection for deceased people

they loved and also provides them with powerful words (the death names) that can be called on in vows and curses (Brosius, 1995/1996). In contrast, in future-oriented societies the past is often seen as something to be set aside and improved on. Technological knowledge and devices are more valued than the achievements and wisdom of the dead past, and the dead themselves might almost not have existed, except when we are in a particularly sentimental or patriotic mood.

2. *Geographical detachment from the dead will cause distress to the living, especially in past-oriented societies.* Vietnamese families who were relocated by the American military during "pacification" efforts expressed great anguish in having to depart from the land where the spirits of their remote and recent ancestors held sway. Native Americans were subject to the same kind of stress and loss for many years, and there are still active cases in which tribes are being pressured to move from their sacred ancestral lands. The world today is filled with people from many traditional backgrounds who have been forced to leave their homelands and, therefore, their ancestors. Perhaps when we have all become ancestors there will be less concern for the dead because fewer people will have formed deep, long-term attachments to particular places (Scheidt, 1993).

3. *The dead will be remembered and "used" more often in societies in which children are highly valued as continuing the family soul over the gap created by death.* The only available study (Kastenbaum, 1974) suggests that young couples do not regard children as important for this purpose. Each individual (and each generation) is seen as having its own moment in the sun, free to pursue its own pleasures and values. It is not one generation's responsibility to project the "family soul" across the death line to the next generation. (We could certainly use more research on this topic.)

4. *Longer life expectancy and low vested power of the elderly make the dead less important.* In earlier times many people died at an age we would now consider premature. Such deaths are often especially painful and disruptive to the survivors. The incomplete lives are therefore more likely to be carried forth in memory, propelled by their unfinishedness. Today, more people live to an advanced age, and the survivors do not have a sense of incompleteness that needs to be compensated for by

memorialization. Furthermore, in today's youth-oriented world the older person does not as often control property and wealth and therefore is less likely to command respect and services. Now, there are so many long-lived people around that they have lost some of the status reserved for rarities. Older people also seem to be losing some of the special status once enjoyed when they were thought of as close to the gods and ancestral spirits.

5. *A society lacking unifying and transcending themes will assimilate the funeral and memorialization process into its utilitarian motives.* The funeral process loses its special status when a society does not share strong beliefs about who they are as a people. Without unifying beliefs, societies start to doubt and quibble about funerals. For example, the cost of the funeral may become the most salient concern. If the living no longer attach importance to the dead, then the funeral might as well be as inexpensive as possible. Similarly, not too much time should be "wasted" on funeral rituals. (Even in the slower paced, rural South, I have heard mourners complain that a funeral was "dragged on too long. One flower girl wasn't enough! They had to have three, and all of them took their own sweet time!") *For the dead to be useful, they will have to be functional, just like everybody else, and earn their place.* If public recognition of the dead continues to diminish, then donating organs may be one of the few ways in which the dead can remain a part of society.

6. *Societies that live close to nature need the assistance of the dead to promote fertility and regeneration.* The Merina of Madagascar, for example, make sure that the female element (the body) has thoroughly decomposed so that the male element (the bleached bones) can emerge purified and ensure that both the people and their harvests are fertile (Bloch, 1982). The decomposition process is thought to be dangerous, but it is also very important. A Merina cannot shrink from the reality of decay as people tend to do at Western funeral services because it is from decay that the miracle of regeneration is wrought. Bloch sees one of the major functions of the Merina funeral process as transforming death into life. The dead are very important because it is literally from their breath and bones that the species regenerates itself.

American Memory and the Vietnam Veterans Memorial

With the rise of technology and industrialization, the dead have been losing status. There are signs, however, that many people have been longing to reintegrate the dead into their lives. One of the most striking examples is the way in which the people of the United States have taken the Vietnam Veterans Memorial to their hearts. What would persuade a nation so often described as death denying to become so moved by a memorial to a war that we wanted to forget as quickly as possible? Why would so many people not only make a pilgrimage to the memorial but also bring objects of personal and symbolic meaning to leave by the wall?

Kristin Ann Hass (1998) recounts the fierce objections to Maya Lin's design for the memorial wall. It was too abstract, too intellectual. The black stone suggested mourning rather than heroism. The divided response to the design clearly revealed the nation's divided response to the war: Had we won a noble victory or had the war been a human disaster, a senseless killing field? One of the decisive factors in the decision to create the memorial was the support given by many veterans of the conflict who felt that making war should not be celebrated, but that the names of their buddies deserved to be honored and remembered.

The innovative design of the memorial wall proved to be ideally suited for its purpose. Everything about the wall invites reflection and personal involvement. The reflection is literal as well as symbolic: Visitors see themselves mirrored by the wall at the same time that they read the names. We all become part of the wall and its memories, if only for the moment. Furthermore, how the names are *not* arranged makes its own point. The conventional and arbitrary was set aside when it was decided not to present the names in alphabetical order. Rank, military unit, and home state were also ignored. Instead, with unassailable logic, the names are placed in the order of their deaths. It would be difficult to devise a more compelling way to make it clear that men and women died as individuals and should be remembered as such.

The Vietnam Memorial has had such a deep impression on so many people because the record

The Vietnam Memorial Wall initially faced a wall of criticism, but since has been recognized as a compelling remembrance of the men and women who did not return from the war.

of deaths reminds us of the personal lives of those who have become names on the wall. It has made such a deep impression because it makes public the private griefs of so many people. It has made such a deep impression because it encourages reflection and healing of the nation after a painful and divisive chapter in our history—one that bears some comparison with the Civil War in that regard. That so many people continue to bring something of their own to leave at the wall also suggests that this memorial still has much work to do (Hass, 1998):

> The things left at the Wall make a lot of noise. They constitute a remarkable conversation. It is a conversation about the shape of the nation, the status of the citizen, and the problem of patriotism. It is a conversation about the impossibility of loss, the deaths of sons, and the births of

granddaughters.... It is impassioned and unfinished, and it gives us a tremendous opportunity to witness the process of ordinary Americans struggling to make meanings of, to make sense of, the Vietnam War and all of its difficult and complicated legacies.

child's painting	*red panties*	*Zippo lighter*
eagle feather	*cornhusk*	*cookie*
stuffed dog	*poem*	*key chain*
tissue with lipstick (pp. 123–124)		

Remembering those who died during the Vietnam War has contributed much to the national consciousness about death in general. Hass (1998) observes that the AIDS quilt and a number of other large-scale remembrances of death have followed in the wake of the wall. In other words, as a nation we are once again finding a way to integrate those who we have lost in our ongoing lives. This can only make us stronger.

What Memorial for Victims of the Terrorist Attacks on the United States?

While the smoke was still rising from Ground Zero, there were already calls for creating a memorial to the World Trade Center victims. Attention has remained focused on this largest site of death and destruction, although the need to memorialize has also been under consideration for the Pentagon and the Pennsylvania field where the other hijacked jets crashed. Multiple plans have been developed and subjected to criticism. There seem to be easily as many critics as planners, partly because design and construction will be complicated and expensive, and partly because the nation has not yet decided just how it wants to fix the disaster in its collective memory. (The one suggestion I have not heard seriously made is "no memorial.")

There are daunting practical concerns; for example, how to restore a major international business center while also constructing—or growing—a suitable monument, and how to rebuild in a way that could provide more protection for people and property. The symbolic and emotional concerns are no less daunting. What should the memorial express and accomplish? Should it be designed primarily to honor the dead? To comfort the bereaved? To restore a sense of security in the general public? To tell the world that American business is still in business? To discourage other possible terrorists? To demonstrate the skill and creativity of the memorial planners? To become a prime tourist attraction? These and possibly other purposes might be served together, but not equally well served.

Another city, victimized by a domestic terrorist attack, has developed an innovative memorial that might serve as a model. The lives of 168 were lost when The Murrah Building, a federal building in Oklahoma City, Oklahoma, was destroyed on April 19, 1995. The people of Oklahoma City realized that clearing away the debris was not enough: A memorial should be erected on the site. They invited designs from around the world, but the decision was made by a committee that included family members, survivors, and rescuers as well as design professionals. The result was the Oklahoma City National Memorial and Memorial Center Museum. It includes an institute for the prevention of terrorism as well as an education and outreach service. The most compelling feature, though, is a room-to-room procession that illuminates the course of events from the chaos of the explosion, through the rescue and recovery efforts, and culminating in a tribute to hope in the form of a "water wall" that flows over a dark stone background. For many visitors the most moving experience occurs in the "Gallery of Honor." Here, there is a photograph or other image of each person who was killed in the bombing. The images are accompanied by a personal object that was selected by a family member. As a whole, this memorial demonstrates the individuality of the victims and the caring response of family and community. The human tragedy is not distanced by a monumental and impersonal structure. By practically all accounts, this memorial and the process that created it were ideal for the people of Oklahoma City. Would this approach be as successful in New York City and other places?

Suppose the World Trade Center rebuilding project were yours. What kind of memorial would you design, and why? Congratulations in advance if you come up with the perfect suggestion. Congratulations also if you just put in the effort to think through the issues involved—the issues here, and also the more universal issue: How should we remember the dead and how do we fathom that they would want to be remembered?

On the Treatment of Human Remains: The Vermillion Accord

Another important example of our renewed appreciation for the symbolic relationship between the dead and the living is illustrated by the Vermillion Accord and the actions that have since followed.

Strong protests by Native Americans over the desecration of gravesites and the appropriation of human remains and sacred artifacts provided much of the stimulus for the First Intercongress on the Disposition of the Dead (Davidson, 1990). Sponsored by the World Archaeological Congress, this unusual meeting brought representatives of native peoples around the world together with scientists and others who have a special interest in the topic. One of the outcomes of this conference was a statement that became known as the Vermillion Accord (the meetings were held in Vermillion, South Dakota).

The following are main points of the Accord:

- Universal respect shall be given to the mortal remains of the dead.
- Disposition of human remains will be made in accordance with the wishes of the dead themselves whenever this is known or can be reasonably inferred.
- The wishes of the local community will be respected "whenever possible, reasonable, and lawful."
- The scientific value of studying human remains will be respected whenever such value can be demonstrated to exist.
- Negotiations with an attitude of mutual respect shall be conducted to accommodate both the legitimate concerns of communities for the proper disposition of their ancestors and the legitimate concerns of science and education (Day, 1990).

Arizona's celebrated Heard Museum anticipated the Accord by several years when it voluntary returned some of the most valuable artifacts it had received from private collectors to Native American tribes. The museum directors explained that these sacred objects would have been used by the Native American community as a whole— for them to have been hidden away by collectors was equivalent to theft. Some other museums have since done the same. The Vermillion Accord did not immediately correct all grievances and ensure that mutual respect will prevail from now on. It did, however, establish both a goal and an affirmation of a principle that could help to heal society in general. Today, there is more understanding and cooperation than ever before between scientists who want to learn from human remains and cultural artifacts and native peoples who want to bring their ancestors home.

"You Were the Best Dog Ever": The Pet Cemetery

I have turned over the rocky ground of Massachusetts and the dry sands of Arizona to bury several very important cats. When the first dog of the family died quietly in his basket-bed, none of us could regard Toby's body as only the corpse of an animal. The same was true when Honey, the second dog, asked to go outside and moved with a purpose and stride we no longer expected in her enfeebled condition. A few minutes later she was still beautiful, but dead. Millions of other people have had close attachments to their pets or to animals with which they have worked: the horse who drew the milkman's wagon, the dog who guided its visually impaired owner, and the elephant who hauled lumber. Attachment does not end at the moment of death, whether the loss be that of another human or of an animal companion.

The pet cemetery is one instructive example of the way in which some people attempt to cope with the death of an animal companion. The modern version of the pet cemetery seems to have started in France around the turn of the 20th century. Not only dogs and cats but also horses, monkeys, rabbits, and birds (and a lioness) have been buried there. Perhaps the most famous "resident" is Rin-Tin-Tin, once the reigning animal star of Hollywood. However, the impulse to honor the memory of an animal companion through a funeral and burial process has been expressed throughout history. There are examples among the ancient Greeks and in the early years of our own nation. In the United States, there are currently 145 pet cemeteries that are affiliated with the organization that attempts to set professional standards and provide public information, the International Association of Pet Cemeteries. It is estimated that there are perhaps another 250 that have not affiliated themselves.

Pet cemeteries in the United States express some of the same mixed and changing attitudes toward death that characterize our society in general. For example, consider Pet Rest Memorial Mortuary and Cemetery. Once located just up the road from Arizona State University in Tempe, Pet Rest provided the opportunity for a study by Vivian Spiegelman and myself (1990). At the time of our visits, Pet Rest resembled many another small cemetery—a fenced-in, park-like space with a variety of grave markers. Some graves were decorated with plastic flowers; some markers included a photographic or sculptured representation of the deceased. Ceramic cats played inside a white picket fence at one gravesite. However, we also noticed that the burial ground was not well cared for. Some monuments had already fallen into the weedy grass, and there was a general impression of neglect. What has happened?

Pet Rest had already become a "dead cemetery"—that is, no more burials were allowed, nor had anybody accepted the responsibility for maintenance. If there is a villain to this piece, it was the pressure of urban development. The continuing influx of people into Arizona, the change from an agricultural to a residential community, and the transformation of a small college into one of the nation's largest universities are among the factors that contributed to the decline and eventual destruction of Pet Rest. The land had become too valuable and officials were uncomfortable with having death on display while attempting to upscale commercial properties. The "final resting place" had proven vulnerable to the economic pressure and social change that also affect many "people" cemeteries across the nation. Now, just a few years after our study, Pet Rest no longer exists; its "eternal memory" is on the way to being replaced by a nationally franchised restaurant.

Those who see the pet cemetery as a meaningful way of remembering animal companions may have to confront some painful economic and political realities. However, other people have found it consoling to conduct their own memorial services upon the death of a pet and to satisfy themselves with photographs in the family album and, perhaps, a trip to the local animal shelter to save a life that might otherwise be lost. (After a while, we made the trip again, and came home with Angel, The Incredible Leaping Dog and now dutiful servant to the three resident cats.)

Pet cemeteries have invited parody and mockery. Nevertheless, those who understand and value the bonds of affection that can form between one creature and another may judge that "too much" love is not the worst thing that might be said of a person.

CURRENT CHALLENGES AND DEVELOPMENTS: THE FUNERAL DIRECTOR'S PERSPECTIVE

As we have already seen, funeral and memorialization practices are very much a part of the world of the living and, therefore, subject to change. An interview with funeral director Tom

Carrick proved helpful in identifying some of the major challenges and developments:

• *The impact of AIDS?* "Everybody in the funeral industry overreacted at first. Now we realize that we can do our part in dealing with AIDS and cannot behave in a discriminatory manner. We do give more attention to personal safety. Precautions are used in handling all cases now because one can never be certain about AIDS. For example, we wear gloves every time we touch a cadaver. Instead of smocks, we now use rubber aprons and complete protective clothing, including eyewear. All 'sharps' go into specified and controlled waste containers. Essentially, funeral personnel are doing the same things that health care providers and other people who provide personal services are doing—being more careful."

• *Have there been changes in the way that funeral directors do business over the past few years?* "Enormous changes. Laws have changed and regulations have increased. For example, we are now mandated to provide full price disclosures to the public. Written consents are required for embalming. Employees must be given time off for continuing education sessions. Fair employment practices have increased access by women who are entering this field in larger numbers than ever before. These changes provide benefits to the public.

• *Have these regulations affected your cost of operations?* Yes, considerably so. Every funeral home has had to remodel to provide access for handicapped individuals and to meet other health and safety standards. For example, chemicals must be stored in sealed compartments with security locks so that people do not become exposed to any risk from them. Most of these changes are worthwhile, but they are costly. We feel a little oppressed not by legitimate requirements, but by the confusing and overlapping levels of regulatory authority that can take much of our time and energy away from direct service to the public."

• *You mentioned that more women have become funeral directors in recent years. How has this change been received and perceived?* "The public has had a favorable response. Many client families feel more comfortable in dealing with women. Frequently it is a widow who is making the arrangements. She may perceive a woman funeral director as more understanding and sympathetic. In the past there was a reluctance to hire women and only a few women were qualified. Part of this reluctance came from the enormous amount of lifting that is involved. But now women work in construction; women drive trucks; women work successfully in many occupations that were thought to be for men only. It's not that the conditions of work have changed so much—it's the *attitudes* that have changed about what women can and should do. Funeral directing is a very conservative business that tends to be slow in adapting to change. In metropolitan areas we see more rapid change than in rural areas."

• *What does a person have to know to become a funeral director?* "A person needs to become proficient in anatomy, chemistry, restorative art, pathology, business, accounting, and some law. These subjects are included in the licensure exams. Once a person is licensed it is important to keep up with new developments through continued education, for example, handling situations in which contagious diseases might be involved. Unfortunately, there has been a tendency for continued education sessions to be oriented toward marketing and sales, rather than consumer services. Our field could benefit by increasing the quantity and quality of continued education—and, fortunately, the trend is in this direction."

• *Can you take us through a typical funeral?* "The funeral itself will typically begin with a musical prelude, followed by an opening prayer. About half the people we deal with are 'churched.' This leaves the other half in need of a presiding clergyperson, so we frequently recommend one. Some families give a high priority to the choice of a particular clergyperson. Others say, 'I don't care who you get for my Mom's funeral. I want it brief!' This illustrates the larger differences in how families approach funeral planning. Some are concerned about every detail; some couldn't care less.

"After the opening prayer there are often introductory remarks by a person who represents the family. In recent years there has been more participation by family and friends. In particular, more teens are stepping up to contribute to the memorialization. Any number of family and friends may give scripture readings, recite poetry, eulogize the deceased, or play music, either live or recorded. Words of comfort are usually offered by the cler-

gyperson, but others may also express themselves in their own words."

• *What is the usual time length of a funeral these days?* "The typical funeral lasts between 20 and 40 minutes. The public seems to prefer brief services. I don't really know why this is the case.

• *And what about the question of open or closed casket?* "Most people still prefer the casket open for a portion of the time. Today it is most common for the deceased to wear their own clothing. It is usually a suit, shirt, and tie for man, a dress for a woman. There are regional differences, however. Yesterday we had a funeral in which the man wore a western shirt and jeans. This might seem unusual in New York City, but not here (Arizona) or in Aspen. If somebody never wore a suit or necktie, why should they be forced to change their habits now? If a lady was always seen in a pink dress, they're probably going to bury her in a pink dress, and get pink flowers."

• *How much is the typical funeral likely to cost?* "The national average is between $6,000 and $8,000 for a complete traditional funeral. This includes both mortuary and cemetery expenses, such as the burial plot, flowers, clergy, musicians, and limousine. The cost differs somewhat from one place to another. It tends to be higher in the eastern than in the western states. "

• *How common is cremation?* "It's now close to 50% in Arizona. Cremation is much more likely to be chosen in Sunbelt areas where people have relocated late in their lives and are away from their roots. We are a more mobile society these days, so more people find themselves in this situation. Solely from the standpoints of economy and simplicity, it is easier to cremate and have the ashes sent to Iowa.

"About half of those who choose cremation also choose earth burial. This may be a significant development because less space is needed for urn burial as compared with an adult grave. For those who are concerned about the availability or cost of cemetery space, cremation followed by earth burial could contribute to the solution. Churches are now starting to add *columbaria*. These are walls—either inside or outside—that contain niches for the placement of ashes [or, *cremains*, as these are often called]."

• *What is your experience with preplanning funerals?* "This has become a big issue. Preplanning is strongly encouraged both by industry and consumer groups. It can be very useful to the family in avoiding the need to make numerous major decisions at the time of death. Disagreements can arise within the family that add tension and conflict to the loss and sorrow. Preplanning can be done either with or without prepayment. The advantage of prepaying is that it locks in the price. If this is not a concern, then the family still can benefit by preplanning."

• *There are different opinions about the appropriateness of including children in the funeral process. How do you see this?* "I'm all for it. Death is part of life. Children should be exposed to it as often as it occurs. Parents may be poorly prepared to educate our kids about death and dying, but the best way to do that is to attend funerals when opportunity presents itself. We shouldn't be running and hiding from death. The ideal funeral should be an uplifting experience, reinforcing all the values this person stood for, and why we loved this person and are here today."

• *From the practical standpoint, in your role as a funeral director what is your worse case scenario about what might go wrong?* "I worry most about breakdown of equipment. What if the hearse breaks down, or the air conditioning fails in the summer months either in the building or the limousine?

"In some 30,000 funerals only one stands out as a total embarrassment to me personally. I call it 'The Funeral from Hell.' Every conceivable thing went wrong—from equipment failures right down to the cemetery digging the wrong grave! Mom's name was even on the headstone, but they dug 25 feet away on a 115-degree day. To make it even worse, the death was a sudden and tragic one. Oh, yes, and the sound system at the church picked that day to quit working; actually, it exploded! A key family member was late, one limo didn't show up, and another broke down. There was a mix-up with the flowers as well. Fortunately, this was the memorable exception and I don't feel the need to have another funeral memorable in this way, ever!

• *Looking back over 30 years as a funeral director, what stands out as most important to you personally?* "I've walked in the shoes they're walking in, and I think people appreciate that. I identify with their loss, so it is natural for me to offer all the time they need and all the understanding I can

bring to the situation. I remind myself each time that I am a total stranger who has been invited into a family's life at a time of loss and sorrow. My challenge is to put them at ease. This is not easy: 'How can I relax—my mother just died!' I derive my satisfaction from helping people through these stressful situations.

"I would like the readers of this book to know that we, as a society in general, need to understand how much death is part of life. As parents and teachers we don't do a particularly good job of it. We are still a death-denying society. We don't talk about funerals unless we just came from one!"

IMPROVING THE FUNERAL PROCESS

This chapter began with the question, "Why have funerals?" You were offered a set of questions to help you identify your personal attitudes and knowledge base. Now we have explored some major aspects of the funeral process together and, along the way, found answers to the questions of fact. You are now in a position to review your own attitudes toward the funeral process in general as well as your own personal involvement. Perhaps you will select for yourself one of the extreme positions: that funerals are either an expensive and morbid waste of time and money or that funerals should constitute the central juncture of private and public interactions. A position somewhere between these extremes would hold that the funeral process does serve important human needs, but that the process could be improved. Many of the purposes underlying funeral processes have already been noted. Perhaps the most basic need of all is to help the survivors achieve the emotional realization that one of their fellow mortals has in fact died and that they must find a way to go on in this person's absence. Nevertheless, many are convinced that the traditional commercial funeral process does not always meet these needs adequately and that alternatives should be explored.

Alternative Funerals

The usual suggested alternative is for a swift, simple, and inexpensive form of body disposal rather than a more elaborate, public process. Active participation in some aspect of the funeral process is likely to be of value to the survivors. An increasing number of funeral directors welcome greater participation by the families and are receptive to requests for special elements in the funeral process.

The death awareness movement has improved the ability of both the survivors and the funeral director to respond to the specific situation rather than to rely on a standardized ritual and service. The nature and the scope of the funeral arrangements can be designed through the collaboration of the survivors and the funeral director. At times, the dying person will also be willing and able to specify important details. In answering the open-ended questions at the beginning of this chapter, you may have come up with some valuable ideas for alternative funeral arrangements. An attitudinal climate is now developing in which it is becoming easier to consider alternatives. This requires more open communication among the survivors and between the survivors and the funeral director than what has often taken place.

Today, many observers believe that our society also needs ritual more than ever before. We are faced with so many changes in our lives and have such a difficult time in relating simultaneously to past, present, and future that rituals can serve the vital function of confirming our bonds with people and symbols beyond the moment. Ritual can be traditional, elaborate, and institutionalized or a simple ceremony devised by a particular family. It is also possible for several religious and ethnic traditions to contribute to the same memorial ritual.

Those who prefer a simple and inexpensive funeral are likely to find support and assistance through *memorial societies,* which are nonprofit organizations that help people to arrange funerals and memorial gatherings that are basic, dignified, and economical. The type of funeral process cultivated by memorial societies could be characterized as "down to earth" and has appealed to many people who have other priorities for their limited financial resources and/or disapprove of elaborate funeral observations. (For up-to-date information on local memorial societies, write to Continental Association of Funeral and Memorial Societies, Inc., 1828 L Street, N.W., Suite 1100, Washington, DC 20036; or Memorial Society Association of Canada, Box 96, Station A, Weston, Ontario M9N 3M6, Canada.)

Americans have long been known for individualism, so there continue to be more unusual types of farewell from life.

Virtual Memorials

Stone has long been a valued material for marking grave sites. It is very solid. It seems so enduring. It rises from a particular location and stands as a beacon to draw visitors near. Now, however, a nearly dimensionless form of memorialization is becoming increasingly popular. An Internet memorial occupies no fixed space. It is everywhere and nowhere. We cannot touch it or observe the changes that time and weather have wrought. Little is known about the relationship between "virtual memorials" and more traditional forms of postdeath care and remembrance. There is no evidence to indicate that virtual memorials are replacing cemetery sites and markers. It is just as likely that bereaved people are making use of the Internet as a supplement, another way to express their regards for the person who has died and call this death to the attention of a larger "virtual community."

Pamela Roberts (2002) notes that bereaved persons have their choice of creating a new memorial Web page or placing a memorial in one of the existing Web cemeteries. Virtual Memorial Gardens (http://catless.ncl.ac.uk/vmg) and Dearly Departed (www.dearlydeparted.net) seem to have been the first Web cemeteries to be established and both offer free services. Establishing a personal Web page requires computer expertise and upkeep effort that not all bereaved people can manage.

According to Roberts (2002), virtual memorials devoted to deceased children are the most common. Many of these Web sites offer the store of the child's life and death, photographs and other images, and a guestbook or e-mail link for visitors.

Roberts (2002) cautions that memorial Web site, like others, are not necessarily permanent (but, then, of course, stone is not either). Many physical cemeteries, both for humans and for their animal companions, have fallen into ruin or been taken over for other purposes. There is also some concern that virtual memorials might become too much relied on, substituting for more direct, interpersonal ways of sharing. Whatever the future may hold for virtual memorials, this avenue of expression is already adding a new dimension of sharing and remembrance.

Spontaneous Memorialization in Response to Violent Death

We turn now to an alternative type of response to a death that has become increasingly common in recent years. It is markedly different from both the traditional funeral and memorialization process in American society and the other alternatives that have emerged in recent years.

Spontaneous memorialization has been defined as a public response to deaths that are violent and unanticipated (Haney, Leimer, & Lowery, 1997). This response develops when people who are not supposed to be at risk for death are killed in vicious and senseless ways. Not all violent deaths elicit this response: The public must feel a sense of connection or identification with the victim. The spontaneous public response to the attacks of September 11, 2001, provided a dramatic example. Spontaneous memorialization seldom replaces traditional funeral rituals.

Spontaneous memorializaton usually takes place at the site of the death or some other place that is associated with the deceased. It differs in this respect from traditional services that take place at a funeral home, church, or cemetery. Each individual makes a personal decision about participating: No one is automatically included or excluded. People who did not know the deceased person may be touched by the death and decide to participate. As Haney et al. (1997) stated, "Spontaneous memorializtion extends the boundaries of who is allowed or expected to participate in the mourning process." There is no formal organization of the response to the death, at least at first. People respond out of their shock, sorrow, or anger, and together find a way of expressing their feelings. There are also no set time limits:

Spontaneous memorialization ebbs and flows as individual mourners make their pilgrimages and contribute their offerings either immediately af-

ter the death or during the weeks or months that follow.… Individual mourners may visit the site once or return again and again, either alone or accompanied by others. (p. 162)

Mementos are left at the site of the death. These may include a wide variety of objects—flowers, teddy bears, bibles, and even beer cans. A few of the objects that have been left at the Vietnam Memorial Wall have already been mentioned. These objects usually have meaning to the individual mourner and some connection to the victim's life. The mourners often raise funds to assist survivors of the victim and may also become advocates for improved public safety measures.

Spontaneous memorialization is focused on the feelings of many individuals toward the person who has been a victim of violence. It is also a response to the increasing tide of violence that threatens society's values and sense of security. Here we see individuals coming together of their own volition to create a memorialization process that demonstrates community solidarity and concern in the face of deaths that should not have happened. Violent deaths shatter our expectations that people should be able to enjoy a long life before succumbing to "natural causes." Society's death system has not proven capable of *preventing* violent deaths and often cannot even *explain* them very well. The emergence of spontaneous memorialization, however, reveals that in opening our hearts to victims of violent death and their survivors we are affirming values that are at the core of our existence as a society.

SUMMARY

The funeral is part of a deeper and more complex process in which we both separate ourselves from the dead and try to establish a new relationship with them that we can carry forward in our lives. We have examined the meaning of the funeral process in many places and times, including our own. It has become clear that how a society cares for its dead tells us much about the beliefs and lifestyles of that society in general. You were invited to reflect on your own attitudes, feelings, and knowledge about the funeral process, considering whether you are more the rationalist or more the romantic. Much attention was given to the process of transforming a dead body to a living memory. We identified basic elements of the funeral process, such as establishing the facts of death, the autopsy, the death investigator, legal issues, organ donation, premortem preparations, immediate postdeath activities, preparations for burial or cremation and the types of options that have been used, the funeral service, and the longer process of memorializing the deceased. Along the way we gave particular attention to the sacred art of mummification as brought to a high level by the ancient Egyptians. We gained further insight through the case histories of three influential people whose deaths were occasion for extraordinary memorialization: *Ch'in shih-huang-ti*, the first emperor of China; *Prince Albert*, husband of Queen Victoria; and *Lenin*, founder of the Soviet Union. Another major function of the funeral and memorialization process is to achieve a balance between the competing claims of the living and the dead. We learned how the dead have been regarded within three traditional contexts: rural Greece, the Kotas of southern India, and orthodox Judaism. Next, we discussed how cemeteries in the United States have been shaping memories from colonial times to the present and how the nature and upkeep of these cemeteries have been closely related to powerful events, such as the Civil War, and sociotechnological change, such as population pressures. We also visited several ethnic cemeteries to see how the challenges of diverse people living together are reflected in the way their deaths are memorialized. We wondered in what circumstances the dead are most important to the living and learned that the dead are more secure in past-oriented societies (and under several other conditions that were identified). The Vietnam Veterans Memorial was seen to be a compelling new development that has helped to heal a divided nation, long given to avoiding death but urgently needing a way of remembering those who died so soon and so far away. How the victims of the September 11, 2001, terrorist attack on the World Trade Center should be memorialized has raised questions about both the short- and long-term meanings of such a disaster, with lessons perhaps to be learned from the moving and effective memorial established for the victims of the 1995 Oklahoma City bombing.

We also learned of increased sensitivity and sense of responsibility for the disposition of human remains, as made salient through the Vermillion Accord. Memorialization of our animal companions was also considered through a visit to Pest Rest Memorial Mortuary and Cemetery (itself a recent casualty to urban development). Our curiosity about the current status of funeral practice led us to an interview with a funeral director who provided frank and engaging answers to many of our questions. We then reminded ourselves that there are a variety of alternative funeral and memorialization possibilities, including the ever more common phenomenon of public spontaneous response to a particularly disturbing death or deaths.

REFERENCES

Aries, P. (1981). *The hour of our death*. New York: Knopf.

Benet, S. V. (1942). American names. In *Poetry of Stephen Vincent Benet* (pp. 367–368). New York: Farrar & Rinehart.

Bloch, M. (1982). Death, women, and power. In M. Bloch & J. Parry (Eds.), *Death and the regeneration of life* (pp. 1–44). Cambridge, UK: Cambridge University Press.

Brosius, J. P. (1995/1996). Father dead, mother dead: Bereavement and fictive death in Penan Gang society. *Omega, Journal of Death and Dying, 32*, 197–226.

Clignet, R. (1992). *Death, deeds, and descendants*. Hawthorne, NY: Gruyter.

Cotterell, A. (1981). *The first emperor of China*. New York: Holt, Rinehart & Winston.

Crissman, J. K. (1994). *Death and dying in central Appalachia*. Urbana: University of Illinois Press.

Cunningham, K. (1989). Navajo, Mormon, Zuni graves: Navajo, Mormon, Zuni ways. In R. E. Meyer (Ed.), *Cemeteries and gravemarkers* (pp. 197–216). Ann Arbor: University of Michigan Research Press.

Darby, E., & Smith, N. (1983). *The cult of the prince consort*. New Haven, CT: Yale University Press.

Davidson, G. W. (1990). Human remains: Contemporary issues. *Death Studies, 14*, 491–502.

Day, M. H. (1990). The Vermillion Accord. *Death Studies, 14*, 641.

Gay, P. (1984). *Education of the senses*. New York: Oxford University Press.

Glover, R. (2001). *Plastination laboratory*. www.med.umich.edu/anatomy/plastinate.

Goldberg, H. S. (1981/1982). Funeral and bereavement rituals of Kota Indians and Orthodox Jews. *Omega, Journal of Death & Dying, 12*, 117–128.

Goody, J. (1962). *Death, property, and the ancestors: A study of the mortuary customs of the Lo Dagaa of West Africa*. Palo Alto, CA: Stanford University Press.

Gosnell, L., & Gott, S. (1989). San Fernando Cemetery: Decorations of loss in a Mexican-American community. In R. E. Meyer (Ed.), *Cemeteries and gravemarkers* (pp. 217–236). Ann Arbor: University of Michigan Research Press.

Haney, C. A., Leimer, C., & Lowery, J. (1997). Spontaneous memorialization: Violent death and emerging mourning ritual. *Omega, Journal of Death and Dying, 35,* 159–172.

Hansen, J. P., Meldgaard-Jorgen, J., & Nordqvis, J. (1991). *The Greenland mummies.* Washington, DC: Smithsonian Institution Press.

Hanzlick, R. (1993). Improving accuracy of death certificates. *Journal of the American Medical Association, 269,* 2850.

Harris, J. E. (1973). *X-raying the pharaohs.* New York: Scribner.

Hass, K. A. (1998). *Carried to the wall.* Berkeley: University of California Press.

Holloway, K. F. C. (2002). *Passed on: African American mourning stories.* Durham, NC: Duke University Press.

Ikram, S., & Dodson, A. (1998). *The mummy in ancient Egypt.* London: Thames & Hudson.

Kaplan, J., & Hanzlick, R. (1993). Improving the accuracy of death certificates. *Journal of the American Medical Association, 270,* 1426.

Kastenbaum, R. (1974). Fertility and the fear of death. *Journal of Social Issues, 30,* 63–78.

Kastenbaum, R. (1987). Vicarious grief: An intergenerational phenomenon? *Death Studies, 11,* 447–453.

Kastenbaum, R. (1994–1995). Bruce L. Danto, M.D.: An *Omega* interview. *Omega, Journal of Death and Dying, 30,* 79–104.

Kastenbaum, R. (in press). *On our way: The final passage through life and death.* Berkeley, CA: University of California Press.

Leviton, D. (1991). *Horrendous death, health, and well-being.* New York: Hemisphere.

Linden-Ward, B. (1989). *Silent city on a hill: Landscapes of memory and Boston's Mount Auburn Cemetery.* Columbus: Ohio State University Press.

Lynch, T. (1997). *The undertaking. Life studies from the dismal trade.* New York: Penguin.

Middleton, J. (1996). Lugbara death. In M. Block & J. Parry (Eds.), *Death and the regeneration of life* (pp. 134–154). Cambridge, UK: Cambridge University Press.

Morris, R. (2002). Lawn garden cemeteries. In R. Kastenbaum (Ed.), *Macmillan encyclopedia of death and dying* (Vol. 2, pp. 518–520). New York: Macmillan.

Murphy, E. (1995). *After the funeral. The posthumous adventures of famous corpses.* New York: Barnes & Noble.

Plunkett, T. (1999). *The New Haven burying ground. A brief history and discussion of the Grove Street Cemetery.* http://archnet.asu.edu/archnet/uconn%5Fextras/historic/grove%5Fstreet.html.

Prothero, S. (2001). *Purified by fire. A history of cremation in America.* Berkeley: University of California Press.

Rando, T. A. (2002). Bereavement, vicarious. In R. Kastenbaum (Ed.), *Macmillan encyclopedia of death and dying* (Vol. 1, pp. 59–60). New York: Macmillan.

Roberts, P. (2002). Memorial, virtual. In R. Kastenbaum (ed.), *Macmillan encyclopedia of death and dying.* Vol. 2 (pp. 570–574). New York: Macmillan Reference USA.

Scheidt, R. J. (1993). Place and personality in adult development. In R. Kastenbaum (Ed.), *The encyclopedia of adult development* (pp. 370–376). Phoenix, AZ: Oryx Press.

Schindler, R. (1996). Mourning and bereavement among Jewish religious families: A time for reflection and recovery. *Omega, Journal of Death and Dying, 33,* 121–130.

Spiegelman, V., & Kastenbaum, R. (1990). Pet Rest Cemetery: Is eternity running out of time? *Omega, Journal of Death and Dying, 21,* 1–13.

Tashjian, A., & Tashjian, D. (1989). The Afro-American section of Newport, Rhode Island's common burying ground. In R. E. Meyer (Ed.), *Cemeteries and gravemarkers* (pp. 163–196). Ann Arbor: University of Michigan Research Press.

Tsiarias, A. (1982). *The death rituals of rural Greece.* Princeton, NJ: Princeton University Press.

Walter, T. (1992). *Funerals and how to improve them.* North Pomfret, VT: Hodder & Stoughton.

Zbarsky, I., & Hutchinson, S. (1997). *Lenin's embalmers.* London: Harvill.

GLOSSARY

Aninut: The interval between death and burial in which "time stands still" and family members are given the opportunity to grieve in private (Jewish).

Autopsy: Medical examination performed on a corpse.

Cemetery: A place set aside for burial of the dead.

Ch'iidii: Evil ghosts who rob graves (Navajo).

Cremation: Reduction of a corpse to ashes in a burning chamber.

Cryonic Suspension: Preserving a (certified dead) person at a near-freezing temperature with the intention of subsequent revival, treatment, and restoration to healthy life.

Death Certificate: Required legal form that is completed or verified by a physician and includes basic information on the deceased person and cause(s) of death.

Death Investigator: Physician who examines autopsy findings and other evidence when there are questions about circumstances and cause of death.

Embalming: A procedure that retards physical deterioration of a corpse; includes introduction of a preservative fluid.

Eulogy: Words said or written to respect and praise a deceased person.

Exhumation: Also known as disinterment, this is the removal of a corpse from its place of burial.

Funeral: The rituals, observances, and procedures that accompany the burial or other disposition of the body of a deceased person.

Kaddish: Prayer on behalf of a deceased person (Jewish) (see Kaddish prayer in appendix).

Obituary: A (usually brief) published report that provides information on a person's life after his or her death.

Organ Donation: Providing a heart, kidney, cornea, or other tissues available for the benefit of another person. Some types of organ donations can be made by living donors; others are available only from people who have been certified as dead.

Ponos: The pain of grief (Greek).

Postmortem: After death.

Premortem: Before death.

Spontaneous Memorialization: Voluntary public response to the death of a person by violence; characterized by expression of personal feelings and bringing mementos to the site of the death.

Vermillion Accord: A position statement on the ethical principles that should govern our treatment of human remains (based on a conference in Vermillion, South Dakota).

The message of Christianity's victory over death was enhanced by reports that Jesus had brought a dead man back to life, as depicted in Rembrandt's (1630) *The Raising of Lazarus*.

chapter 14

DO WE SURVIVE DEATH?

The four men were sitting at a table outside a trailer park after their night on the town and entered into an argument about religion. The talk became heated when the subject turned to who would go to heaven and who would go to hell. Stoker said he would settle the argument and went into a house and returned with a shotgun, which he loaded and placed in his mouth.
—Reuters (2002)

The skeleton he will cause to be put together in such a manner that the whole figure may be seated in a chair usually occupied by me when living, in the attitude in which I am sitting when engaged in thought.... He will cause the skeleton to be clad in one of the suits of black occasionally worn by me.... If it should so happen that my personal friends and other disciples should be disposed to meet together...for the purpose of commemorating the founder of the greatest happiness system of morals and legislation my executor will from time to time cause to be conveyed to the room in which they meet the said box or case with the contents therein to be stationed in such part of the room as the assembled shall deem meet.
—Jeremy Bentham (1832)

That cadavers of the dead, borne by I know not what spirit, leave their tombs to wander among the living, terrorizing them and annihilating them, then return to their tombs which open by themselves before them, is a fact that would be difficult to accept if in our age numerous examples didn't prove it and if accounts did not abound.
—William of Newburgh, 12th century (as quoted in Schmitt, 1998, pp. 61–62).

I found myself looking down on myself, and the doctors and nurses around me. I could hear everything they were saying, and I wanted to tell them not to feel so bad. I was somewhere it was so beautiful and peaceful that I wanted to stay there forever. There was a bright, but soft light, and I felt the

most comforting sense of peace. Suddenly I thought, "B (my husband) can't possibly bring up M alone. I had better go back." And that is the last thing I remember. I am absolutely positive that I decided to come back. Since that time I have no fear of dying.
—From the near-death experiences report archives of
Ian Stevenson, M.D.

As Lord Krishna said to his disciple:
Who thinks that he can be a slayer,
Who thinks that he is slain,
Both these lack knowledge:
He slays not, is not slain.
Never is he born nor dies;
Unborn, eternal, everlasting be.
—K. Kramer (1988, p. 32)

Behold, I show you a mystery; We shall not all sleep, but we shall all be changed, in a moment, in the twinkling of an eye…for the trumpet shall sound, and the dead shall be raised incorruptible, and we shall be changed.… So when this corruptible shall have put on incorruption, and this mortal shall have put on immortality, then shall be brought to pass the saying that is written, Death is swallowed up in victory, O death, where is thy sting? O grave, where is thy victory?
—I Corinthians, 15

Life in paradise meant leisure and loving in a natural setting. Men and women were naked. Generally paired, they spent their time relaxing in the grass, bathing and swimming, or simply strolling about.… Troops of young men meet in sport with gentle maidens, and Love never lets his warfare cease. There are all on whom Death swooped because of love.
—C. McDaniel and B. Lang (1988, p. 125)

The prospect of the survival of death has stimulated faith, hope, and curiosity but also dread, violence, and skepticism through the centuries. Reports that the terrorists of September 11, 2001, expected to be rewarded for their deeds in a hero's afterlife were a sharp reminder that belief in survival can have powerful consequences.

However, I have also seen another sort of consequence: the person whose long life is about to end but who is well comforted by the belief that he or she is going to a better place. Before examining the present scene, we give ourselves the advantages of a selective historical review. We sample some of the ways in which other people have tried to come to terms with the certainty of death and the uncertainty of what happens next. We then consider the question of whether survival is something that needs to be proved. Several types of possible evidence for survival are explored, beginning with near-death experiences, which have been the focus of interest for the past three decades. Next, we examine how two phenomena from antiquity—ghosts and reincarnation—are faring today. *The Pearly Gates of Cyberspace* (Wertheim, 1999) is among the emerging options that we will consider as technology attempts to do its bit for survival of death. Finally, we return to the question of whether survival (and what kind of survival) would be a good thing and conclude with a consideration of the links between survival beliefs and death by suicide or other forms of killing.

CONCEPT OF SURVIVAL IN HISTORICAL PERSPECTIVE

The opening quotations remind us that survival of death has stimulated a wide diversity of responses. Let's revisit them:

1. There have been countless arguments about heaven and hell through the centuries, but on a July evening in Godley, Texas, two young men concluded their discussion by putting the matter to a test. Clayton Frank Stoker swallowed as much of the shotgun as he could with the apparent intention of discovering whether he would go to heaven or hell. Johnny Joslin snatched the gun out of his friends mouth, saying, "If you have to shoot somebody, shoot me." The shotgun fired (circumstances unclear), and it was Joslin who would be first to discover whether he was going to heaven or hell. (Yes, both had been drinking that night.) Along with everything else that might be said about this incident, we would not want to forget that the afterlife had become perhaps as urgent concern for two young men in 21st-century America as for many people 1,000 years ago when the fires and torments of hell were dominant images.

2. Jeremy Bentham was as cool, collected, and sober as always when he drew up his last will and testament in London on April 30. Although not an especially lighthearted fellow, Bentham was indeed the founder of a major social theory with

British philosopher Jeremy Bentham decided that his afterlife would include occasional appearances at faculty meetings, complete with a sturdy walking stick to maintain discipline.

the goal of making possible the greatest amount of happiness to the largest number of people. Bentham's writings have had a strong influence on the philosophy of government and the purpose of society. What mostly interests us here is Bentham's way of answering the question of what he should do after his death: He should continue to look like himself as much as possible, keep his trusty walking stick, and attend occasional faculty meetings. Presenting a caricature of survival—a well-dressed skeleton with a mummified head—was his alternative to a spiritual transformation. (There are unverified reports that Benthams have multiplied, attending faculty meetings in many universities with glazed eyes and mummified heads.)

3. An educated man of the 12th century was reluctant to believe that there were dangerous ghosts roaming the English countryside, but he judged that the evidence was too overwhelming to ignore or deny. Historians and anthropologists tell us that dangerous ghosts have been making people nervous throughout the world since ancient times. For example, the Romani (more commonly known as gypsies) have long feared that the *mulo* (the living dead) might take revenge against those who mistreated them in life (Crowe, 1996). There is also a special kind of evil spirit, the *marime,* that inhabits even the amiable dead, so corpses must not be touched. It is dangerous even to mention the name of the dead. The Brits and the Romani had plenty of company in these beliefs. There was a widespread conviction that the dead mingle with the living and often in ways that are not exactly comforting.

4. In contrast, the near-death experience (NDE) presents itself as immediate and vivid reality to the individual. The death that it suggests does not belong to somebody else's wandering spirit: It is one's own adventure, a private experience. One might try to describe this episode to others, but only the experiencing individual knows the NDE from the inside. Although near-death experience reports (NDERs) are not new, it is only in recent years that they have received widespread attention.

5. The Kramer (1988) quotation is from the Hindu tradition in which birth as well as death are seen as illusions. The spirit or soul is always in process. There is no death that one must survive. It is in our nature to be "everlasting," even though we may not have a conscious memory of who we have been in previous incarnations. The Buddhist tradition offers a different vision of reincarnation. The self is not a fixed entity that perishes at death and returns to life in another physical form. What in Western cultures we usually think of as the self is fluid, everchanging. The self cannot die because the self never exists as a fixed entity: On the other hand, we are always dying and undergoing rebirth through the course of our lives. This process continues after "death." What survives is the pattern of consciousness that has been shaped through many previous births, lives, and deaths.

6. The passage from I Corinthians—among the most influential words in the history of Western culture—presents still another view of human survival. This message has been subjected to several interpretations over the years. For example, does this transformation occur for all or only some people? Does it occur on a person-by-person basis or for all eligible humans in one ultimate "twinkling"? There is an obvious attitudinal difference between the New Testament vision and those associated with NDERs and the Hindu and Buddhist traditions. Death had been the enemy, the relentless adversary against which no human strength or strategy could prevail. Now it is death that has been defeated, its sting made harmless, consigned to its own grave ("swallowed up in victory"). This electrifying message from the early years of Christianity differs from the experience of "the most comforting sense of peace" in NDERs. There is no sense of a victory over a formidable enemy, no mocking of death. One might make a speculative case for the NDE as proof that death has indeed had its sting deactivated, but there is little or nothing of the Corinthian attitude in NDERs.

People have come to these differing interpretations of survival by different routes. NDEs often make a very strong impression on the individual: How can we *not* believe our own perceptions and feelings? In contrast, reincarnation has for centuries been a guiding vision of life to many Hindus and Buddhists. NDEs persuade on the basis of personal experience; reincarnation doctrine persuades on the basis of its intrinsic appeal and cultural heritage. Eternal life as victory over death also has intrinsic appeal, supported by the persuasive power of a strong religious and cultural heritage. A direct experience of triumph over death has not been salient in mainstream Christian belief. Those who are on the conservative side of the Christian spectrum sometimes judge that the NDE is a distraction and perhaps even an illusion that detracts from the core message of the faith.

The final quote given in the chapter opening takes us directly to heaven—or at least one version of heaven. If there is survival, then what? There was an appealing answer in the Roman air about a century before the birth and death of Jesus. The poet Tibullus pictured the afterlife as a paradise garden where lovers would enjoy each other's company forevermore. Tibullus asserted that in times gone by (the so-called Golden Age), people enjoyed free and uninhibited lovemaking. This pleasure was no longer available in the "modern" world but still awaited those who die young and in love. The paradise garden vision with its naked lovers strolling and rolling in the grass was revived in poetry and art many years later as humanism emerged from the middle ages. However, just around the corner of time from Tibullus was the life and death of Jesus and the church doctrines authored by Paul. The garden paradise as well as the much more melancholy afterlife scenarios held by the Jewish faith were soon to be overshadowed by the Christian vision. As we will see, questions still remain about not only the survival of death but also the form in which this survival occurs.

The Journey: Of the Dead and to the Dead

Many world cultures have persuaded themselves that the souls or spirits of the dead undertake a perilous journey after death. "Undertake" is the right word because dark passages under the earth as well as the crossing of dangerous waters often are involved. The journey of the dead is the final rite of passage. Every mortal embarks on this journey. A few exceptional people journey to the Land of the Dead in exceptional circumstances. Why would they do that? The answer is instructive.

Young lovers who died before they could experience the fulfillment of their union might find themselves in the Elysian Fields for an eternity of pleasure, or so a Roman poet suggested.

Consider first the king of Uruk, the mythical king who ruled that Mesopotamian city-state perhaps 5,000 years ago (Westwood, 2002). Gilgamesh is coveted by Ishtar. He rejects her advances, knowing that her ex-lovers tend to have had very short lives. The goddess of love tries to take her revenge, but her "hit man," the Bull of Heaven, is slain by Gilgamesh and his best friend, Enkidu. (Sorry if this sounds like a meld of *Xena* and *The Sopranos,* but that's mythology!) Offended, the gods unite and kill Enkidu. Here is where it gets interesting: Gilgamesh now begins to reflect on his own mortality. Even though he has a pair of gods for his own parents, the young king must come to terms with the same fate as other mortals. He has a dream or vision of the miserable underworld that is humanity's final destination. Gilgamesh dares to journey to the underworld in hope of persuading the one immortal man to grant him the same favor. (The gods had spared Utnapishtim from The Great Flood when they realized they needed some people around to offer them praise and sacrifices.) Many adventures and misadventures ensue. At the end, the brave and mighty Gilgamesh fails in his quest. He will not be an immortal. No human will ever escape death. This difficult lesson has been passed on for thousands of years: If the great Gilgamesh with his god connections could not escape death, who can? Immortality is only for the gods, if for anybody.

Orpheus lost not his best friend but his beloved wife, the nymph Eurydice. Like Enkidu, she died as a result of mischief from the gods, who had a serpent bite her. Orpheus was the son of a mixed marriage (the King of Thrace and Calliope, one of the nine divine muses). The grief-stricken husband ventured into the underworld where his music and song charmed even Cerberus, the three-headed vicious watchdog. Orpheus persuaded the gods of Hades to allow Eurydice to return with him on condition that he not look back at her until they reached the border. He could not resist, though, and Eurydice was gone forever. Cultural history has transformed the difficult lesson that the dead must remain so. Music is a sacred art that raises our life beyond an animal existence and places us in harmony with the gods. Orpheus has become the mythological embodiment of humanity's higher nature as expressed through music.

The journey of all mortals to the land of the dead has taken many forms. In Greek mythology, it was the boatman Charon who would ferry the dead across the river Styx to Hades. There were many discussions of the crossing fee demanded by Charon, who was generally regarded as a cranky and unpleasant fellow. The poet Virgil even suggested a specific location for Hades (a predecessor of the Christian Hell): The entrance can be found near the volcanic Mount Vesuvius, where pent-up vapors and mysterious sounds issue from the mysterious realm below.

In Islamic belief, the final journey begins after the Day of Judgment. Notice that the crossing of water is involved here as it is in many other journeys of the dead (Hanson, 2002):

> Humanity proceeds to a bridge known as the *sirat,* which crosses over hell. The Muslims who make it safely across are greeted by Muhammad, who will take them to a great pool and give them a drink that will quench their thirst forever.... Muslims see death as a transition to the other side. Islam is seen as the vehicle that will take one safely there. It is only in paradise that the believer finds ultimate peace and happiness. (p. 488)

Whether unlimited misery and despair or ultimate peace and happiness lie at the end, the journey of the dead is one of the most striking themes among world cultures in contemplation of the mysteries of death.

DOES SURVIVAL HAVE TO BE PROVED?

Most people in most societies took survival as a fact. Sometimes, the dead were buried with tools and other objects useful in the next life. Even more common was the assumption that the dead continued their interest in the living, either as guides and advisors or as malevolent, vengeful spirits. Ideas about the afterlife became elaborated and woven into theology, philosophy, poetry, song, and drama as civilizations arose.

The survival beliefs varied in their details. Often, the next life was seen to be perilous or otherwise undesirable, with such welcome exceptions as Tibullus' vision of a paradise garden. Although belief was dominant, the words of a

Lust was one of the seven deadly sins that lead to damnation and torment in hell. Each sin had its own punishment: being smothered in fire and brimstone was reserved for the lustful as illustrated by this 15th-century woodcut.

few dissenters have survived. Titus Lucretius Carus (54 B.C.) made the argument that "nothing can be produced from nothing" and that "a thing …never returns to nothing, but all things after disruption go back into the first bodies of matter." Nature continually shapes, destroys, and reshapes her basic materials. Although there is no complete annihilation, there is also no imperishable soul that is immune from the general principle of transformation.

Love, death, and the brevity of life have been the concern of poets since ancient times. A poet whose name has been lost to history was one of the many who took up his post as urgent counselor to the living:

> All who come into being as flesh
>   Pass on—and all men rest in the grave.
> So, seize the day! Hold holiday!
>   Be unwearied, unceasingly alive,
>   You and your own true love;
> Let not your heart be troubled during your
> sojourn on earth,
>   But seize the day as it passes!

This excerpt is from a poem written more than 3,000 years ago somewhere in Mesopotamia (Washburn & Majors, 1998, p. 22). The poet is not comforting us with a vision of paradise or any escape route from mortality: Here is life today—enjoy the moment with those we love, for all who have become before us have passed on, and the same will be true of us.

Poets aside, the ancient world generally assumed some type of survival. Major systems of religious thought and practice arose later in both the East and the West. Survival beliefs became important elements in Buddhist, Chinese, Hindu, Islamic, and Christian thought. Standing on the verge of the Christian message was the rather complex and contradictory set of beliefs held within Judaism. McDannel and Lang (1988) identified three currents within Jewish survival belief:

1. *Yahweh is the god of life—and this life is all that we have.* We should therefore live for this one life in this one world that God has given to us. This belief has been attributed to the Sadducee sect, most of whom were in the upper-class of society and therefore in a superior position to enjoy life and exercise power. It was the Sadducee's con-

tention that the holy scriptures offer no promise of an afterlife. One can experience the presence of God in everyday life, so there is no need to ask for more.

2. *The faithful among the dead will arise to participate in a new and improved society.* This concept, associated with the Pharisees, shared the Sadducee's primary interest in life on Earth. Bad things happen to good people, however, and there are many obstacles to worshipping and living as one would choose to do. This dilemma would be resolved when "the dry bones of a conquered Israel would rise up and claim their place on a renewed earth" (p. 21). Only the right kind of person would live again, however, and the main point of this return was to create a more perfect society on Earth.

3. *There is a spiritual rather than a physical afterlife in which the individual soul contemplates God.* This concept, associated with the Essenes, shifted the emphasis from materialistic life on Earth to a more liberated and purified existence on another plane. They were not political activists hoping to restore the independence of Israel but rather, people of a philosophical disposition who had their eyes turned toward the prospect of a spiritual immortality.

The Essene conception was the last of the three major belief systems to emerge within the Judaic tradition and had some features that were already pointing toward the Christian interpretation.

These new religious systems eventually gained dominance over the numerous local cults as well as such fading theocracies as the pantheon of gods on Mount Olympus. Survival beliefs started to change character within the new systems. There was now a stronger emphasis on the afterlife as a reward for goodness or punishment for sloth and evil. Believers were motivated to develop certain virtues and obey certain rules in order to enhance their chances of a favorable afterlife. There were bitter disputes about the specifics of the afterlife and its relationship to life on Earth. Nevertheless, relatively few people denied the existence of a divine purpose and power or the survival of death.

The rise of independent thought and the achievements of the scientific method started to "rock the boat" of faith in the 18th century, and the turbulence continues today. Many thoughtful people struggled to reconcile science and religion; others believed that they had to choose between progress and salvation. Nineteenth-century thinkers often felt impelled to write about immortality or survival, especially in the wake of Darwin's research. This trend continued into the early years of the 20th century. Some writers attacked religious beliefs in the name of science, whereas others performed the opposite service for religion. Strenuous efforts were made to defend belief in afterlife on the basis of scientific concepts and evidence.

Interest in the science versus religion controversy on survival eventually subsided among scholars and influential thinkers. Many people came to their own conclusions and had less interest in the debate. The questions have not gone away, however, and historical events have given the issue new momentum from time to time. The suffering and death generated by World War II had an impact on a new generation of thinkers, from whom the existentialism movement developed (Kastenbaum, 1993a). Death had once again become a philosophical problem, this time in association with the problem of evil. What kind of world is this and what kind of creature are we if we so often behave so brutally toward each other? Have we abandoned God, or has God abandoned us? Nineteenth-century philosopher Frederick Nietzsche (1885/1975) contended that the old gods have perished, failed to survive into modern times. This idea returned stronger than ever in the second half of the 20th century as "death of God" theology (Allitzer, 2002; Geering, 2002). Although taking several forms, this revisionistic theology urged people not to rely on their customary views of God but, rather, to achieve a more insightful faith and take more responsibility for their own lives. The meaning of death would also have to be reflected on anew by those who found merit in this challenging position.

Genocide, massacre, persistent vegetative states, the AIDS epidemic, the hospice movement, the living will, and physician-assisted suicide are among other developments that have altered the context within which the survival question is considered. We are confronting new kinds of life-and-death decisions, such as the response to people who are in a persistent vegetative state, the birth of a child with severe defects, and the demand for euthanasia or assisted suicide. These situations are stimulating some people to examine the survival question again. In fact, one of these emerging phenomena (NDE) has become a popular source of information suggestive of survival. A heightening of interest in "past lives" has done the same for evidence that might support reincarnation.

Basically, survival of death is a question for some people and an answer for others. These differences have persisted to the moment of death. Adam Smith, the famed economist, quipped to his friends, "I believe we must adjourn this meeting to some other place." Poet John Milton said farewell with the words, "Death is the great key that opens the palace of eternity." Others have died with their doubts and questions still intact. A tough-minded New England farmer, in his 90th year and within a day of his death, shared his thoughts with me: "Everybody I know's dead has stayed dead. Stubborn damn bunch, they get something in their mind!" [What are your plans?] "I'll rise at rosey-damn dawn with wings on my ass or I'll just (laughs, coughs)—I'll go on rotting like I been rotting. Ask me tomorrow!"

There are still other reasons to give careful consideration to this topic: If there is survival, what form does it take? How has the idea of survival been used and abused? What should the prospects of cessation or survival mean to us? Is survival the most or the least desirable possibility? Perhaps the most practical question is how do our attitudes and beliefs regarding survival influence the ways in which we live and die?

What do you think of all this? Please complete the self-quiz in Box 14-1. This will give you the opportunity to bring some of your own attitudes and beliefs to the surface and to compare them with what others have reported.

WHAT OTHER PEOPLE BELIEVE

Belief in life after death has been at least holding steady if not increasing in the United States since the 1980s (Gallup Poll, 1999; Greeley & Hout, 1999; Hayslip & Peverto, in press; Lester et al., 2000/2001; Morin, 2000). One survey finds that people who entered adulthood in different

---

BOX 14-1
SURVIVAL OF DEATH? A SELF-QUIZ

1. I believe in some form of life after death.

   ____Yes   ____No

2. I have the following degree of confidence that my answer is correct.

   ____Completely sure   ____Very sure
   ____Somewhat sure   ____Not sure at all

3. If you *believe* in some form of afterlife, describe on a separate sheet of paper precisely how you picture or understand the nature of life after death. If you *do not believe* in life after death, describe what you think it would be like if it were true.

4. Suppose that you really wanted to convince somebody that there is *not* life after death. What evidence, experiences, or line of reasoning would you use? Be as specific as possible and put your heart into it, as though you wanted very much to convince a person that there is no afterlife and had to call upon the strongest objections to this belief.

5. Suppose now that you wanted to convince somebody that there *is* life after death. What evidence, experiences, or line of reasoning would you use? Again, be specific and put your best efforts into it.

6. You have already stated your own ideas and beliefs. What kind of experience, evidence, or logic could persuade you to change your mind? It does not matter if you consider the contrary evidence or experience to be very unlikely. What might lead you to change your mind if it did happen or were true?

7. Suppose that you actually have changed your mind. You have discovered that your present belief is mistaken. What difference would it make in your life? In what ways and to what extent would your life be different if you had to accept the opposite of your present belief about life after death?

8. What influence has your actual belief or disbelief had on the way you live? What decisions has it influenced and in what way?

9. What do you think would be the best thing about life after death (whether or not you are a believer)?

10. What could be the worst thing about life after death?

11. How did you come to your present belief or disbelief about life after death?

12. What would you tell a child who asks what happens when a person dies?

---

generations have about the same degree of confidence in afterlife, while other studies find increases from one decade to the next. The findings of the various surveys cannot simply be combined because they ask somewhat different questions and draw on different samples. Nevertheless, at the very least there is no sound evidence for the proposition that Americans have forsaken their faith in a future life. There are more believers than non-believers in all the major studies, usually by a decisive margin. Morin notes that even

people who say they have no religious preference are more likely (63%) to believe in an afterlife compared to people in the 1970s (44%). Furthermore, the afterlife is overwhelmingly envisioned in positive terms. Most respondents expect it to be comforting, and many believe it includes reunion with family and friends. There was also consensus that any physical problems they have in this life would not be carried over to the next (e.g., the blind would see). Most (71%) respondents to the Fox News Survey (Morin, 1997) were sure that hell is a real place, but even more (88%) said the same of heaven.

Nevertheless, there was a sense of risk and foreboding as well. For example, most Gallup Poll (1999) respondents believed that there will be a day of judgment to determine who belongs among the blessed, but they were evenly divided on whether a good person can go to heaven without a belief in God.

Hayslip and Peverto (in press) repeated a detailed study reported by Richard Kalish and David Reynolds in 1976 (see Chapter 4). They found that a greater percentage of participants believed in an afterlife compared with the earlier study. This increase occurred in all four ethnic groups that were sampled: African American, Asian, Caucasian, and Hispanic. Although each of these groups had distinctive ways of thinking about dying and death, they were all part of the trend toward a more prevalent belief in an afterlife. One finding from the Kalish–Reynolds study did not appear in the follow-up: Older adults now were not more likely to believe in an afterlife. This finding could represent the way a new generation of aging adults thinks about life and death, or it could just be an artifact of sampling differences. Whatever the underlying reason, it is difficult to find research support for the proposition that the afterlife becomes more salient and convincing as people grow older.

The New Testament and accepted tradition are most often cited as sources that would be used to convince others of survival. The next most common answer is that we need faith in God and immortality to make it through the tribulations of life. Believers rarely specified any possible evidence, event, or experience that might lead them to change their opinion about survival, whereas almost all nonbelievers could think of something (e.g., a general "scientific breakthrough" or "a powerful personal experience, like really having a dead person I know very well come back to me in some kind of vision and say things that made me realize I wasn't making it up myself") Highly confident believers were even less likely to imagine anything that could lead them to change their minds.

Believers tended to say that they drew strength from the prospect of survival but did not often specify examples. Beliefs were formed early in childhood, according to almost all respondents, but the non-believers were more likely to have reconsidered this topic in recent years. What to tell a child proved to be most difficult for those who were not very sure of their position on survival, whether believers or non-believers. Non-believers more frequently expressed some conflict or uncertainty in what to say, but wavering believers also had their difficulties. Responding to a child's questions can test our own belief system (Chapter 11).

NEAR-DEATH EXPERIENCES: NEW EVIDENCE FOR SURVIVAL?

Renewed attention was given to the survival question with the publication of *Life After Life* in 1975. Physician and philosopher Raymond Moody, Jr., listened to the experiences of men and women who had recovered after coming close to death. Some of these people had suffered cardiac arrest; all had been in serious peril. Moody's report and discussion of these NDERs became a surprise best-seller. Almost immediately, additional NDERs appeared from many sources. Some people had had such experiences years before but were reluctant to speak about them until Moody's book brought the phenomenon into the open.

Moody selected 50 cases from his collection for analysis. Some of these people were said to have been pronounced dead by a physician; all appeared to have been close to the end. The following is an example from Moody's collection:

I was hospitalized for a severe kidney condition, and I was in a coma for approximately a week.... During this period when I was unconscious, I felt as though I were lifted right up, just as though I didn't have a physical body at all. A brilliant white light appeared to me. The light was so bright that I could not see through it, but going into its presence was so calming and so wonderful. There is just no experience on Earth like it. In the presence of the light, the thoughts or words came into my mind: "Do you want to die?" And I replied that I didn't know since I knew nothing about death. Then the white light said, "Come over this line and you will learn." I felt that I knew where the line was in front of me, although

I could not actually see it. As I went across the line, the most wonderful feelings came over me—feelings of peace, tranquillity, a vanishing of all worries." (p. 56)

This report illustrates some of the major features of the primary NDE. Instead of panic or despair, there is a sense of serenity and well-being. The sensation of being "lifted right up" is also one of the most striking characteristics. Known popularly as the "out-of-body experience," this state has a more technical name, the *autoscopic experience*. Rising and floating are also common experiences reported, as well as a sense of journey, a going toward something. A "brilliant white light" may be discovered as the journey continues. Furthermore, there is often a turning-point encounter (Moody, 1975):

The most common feelings reported in the first few moments following death are a desperate desire to get back into the body and an intense regret over one's demise. However, once the dying person reaches a certain depth in his experience, he does not want to come back, and he may even resist the return to the body. As one man put it most emphatically, "I never wanted to leave the presence of this being." (p. 11)

It later became clear that NDEs have been known for many centuries (Zaleski, 1987). Other researchers also found an abundance of NDEs

(Ring, 1989). Obviously, the type of experience confided to Moody was not limited to the survivors who had happened to come his way.

The question now arose: How is this remarkable experience to be explained? It is here that we enter the realm of continuing controversy. Does the NDER constitute proof for survival of death?

Evidence Favoring the NDE as Proof of Survival

Moody (as quoted in Kastenbaum, 1995a) has stated that the reports he collected do not provide evidence for survival:

"I am a complete skeptic regarding the possibility that science as we know it or any sort of conventionally established methodological procedures will be able to get evidence of life after death or to come to some sort of rational determination of this question." (p. 95)

Moody's own disavowal of NDEs as proof of survival, however, did not discourage many others from drawing this conclusion.

What has been learned from systematic research? Psychologist Kenneth Ring took the lead (1980; 1992). He developed and applied a scale to assess the depth of intensity of an NDE. The components of this scale are summarized in Box 14-2. A very intense NDE includes all these possible

---

BOX 14-2
COMPONENTS OF A NEAR DEATH EXPERIENCE

- I felt as though I were dead.
- I felt at peace; a pleasant experience; no suffering.
- I was separated from my body. I entered a dark region.
- I heard a voice…I encountered a kind of presence.
- I could see this spiritual being…I spoke with the spirit.

- I reviewed my whole life.
- I saw lights ahead of me….lights all around me.
- I actually entered into the light.
- I saw the most beautiful colors.

Source: Based on Greyson's (1999) revision of Ring's NDE scale.

components, some of which are also rated according to their vividness or depth.

Ring found that age, sex, economic status, and the type of NDE (e.g., automobile accident and surgery) did not seem to make a difference. NDEs occur in many types of situations and among many kinds of people. Ring (1989) also found that the NDE seems to have had a powerful effect on many survivors. Subsequent studies have confirmed this finding. After a brush with death, people often have a renewed sense of purpose in life. Daily life also becomes more precious to them. What about the fear of death? Many survivors report that they have become much less concerned about dying and death; there was something very comforting and reassuring about their close encounter. Those who recalled intense NDEs were much more likely to think of these as spiritual experiences that had changed their lives, whether or not religion had played an important role for them before these experiences.

Biomedical Attempts to Verify NDE Phenomena

What is the relationship of NDE reports to what actually was taking place in the body? This key question is difficult to investigate in clinical settings because medical care is the highest priority and there are so many things going on. Another major limitation is the retrospective nature of the usual NDE report: The experiencer is not identified until some time after the event. Until recently, there was one pioneering study that stood by itself. Cardiologist Michael Sabom (1982) and colleagues attempted to compare the survivor's subjective reports with the information available in hospital records and retrievable from staff members. Could a person in the midst of an NDE make accurate observations while trapped within a horizontal, impaired, and endangered body? Sabom knew that people who have not been adequately anesthetized occasionally show a memory for events that happened during their surgery. Could the NDE be the same sort of occurrence? He thought not. The NDER bears "no resemblance to the nightmarish experiences reported by inadequately anesthetized patients. Visual details of an operation are not later retrievable by hypnosis from the subconscious minds of patients who had been anesthetized, although spoken words can sometimes be recalled" (p. 80).

Sabom was able to establish a positive correspondence between what a few patients "saw" and what in fact took place during a life-and-death medical procedure. In a preliminary study he learned what kind of educated guesses people tend to make about cardiopulmonary resuscitation (CPR) so that he would not credit a survivor with a specific and accurate description unless it was justified by the evidence. The key information came from six survivors who recalled details of their near-death crisis. In each of these cases, the individual recalled having seen one or more specific events that could not have been obtained through guesswork or prior knowledge of CPR. This could be taken as independent evidence that some individuals had acquired information consistent with out-of-body status.

Sabom did not rush to the conclusion that his findings proved survival of death. Nevertheless, he believes that the autoscopic phenomenon may be authentic, that some type of split between mind and body can occur during times of crisis, and that during this altered state a person can make accurate observations of immediate reality as well as enter into the mystical state of being often reported for NDEs.

A few other researchers attempted follow-up studies but had difficulty finding with NDE cases in circumstances from which conclusions could be drawn. Recently, though, a team of cardiologists in The Netherlands identified 344 consecutive cardiac patients who had been resuscitated after cardiac arrest over a period of up to 4 years. Some had been resuscitated more than once. All these patients had been "clinically dead," according to electrocardiogram records. In other words, they had lost consciousness because of insufficient blood supply and/or circulation within the brain. The patients were interviewed soon after resuscitation, and those who were still alive and willing to participate were interviewed again 2 years and 8 years later. Pim von Lommel and colleagues (2001) found that NDERs were uncommon (18%):

Furthermore, seriousness of the crisis was not related to occurrence or depth of the experience. If purely physiological factors resulting from cerebral anoxia caused NDE, most of our patients

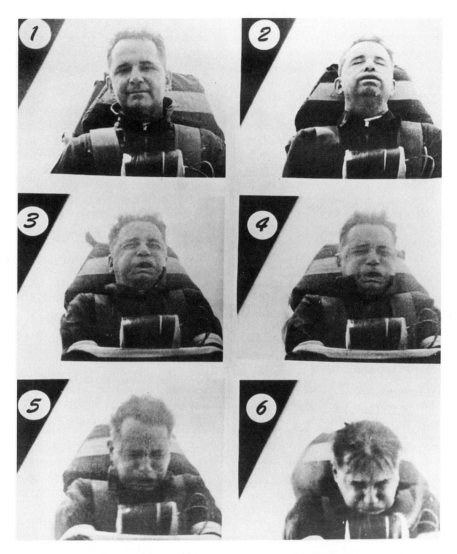

G-LOCK is a physical and mental phenomenon that occurs under the acceleration stress that is being experienced here by a pilot in a centrifugal chamber. It has been suggested that near-death reports have much in common with this experience.

should have had this experience. Patients' medication was also unrelated to frequency of NDE. Psychological factors are unlikely to be important as fear was not associated with NDE. (p. 2043)

The NDEs Lommel et al. (2001) did find were similar to those reported by Moody, Ring, and other researchers. They also found additional support for previous findings that people often believe their attitude toward life has been positively transformed by their NDE. There was also an interesting new finding that was made possible by the repeated interviews in their study: Positive changes, such as becoming more intuitive and having no fear of death, actually became more evident years after the event. The authors suggest that the profound impact of the NDE might take years to become fully integrated in the individual's personality. Nobody reported having had a frightening NDE.

However, what about the proposition that the mind or spirit is so free of the body during an NDE that one can see and hear things that should have been impossible to detect? Unfortunately, Lommel et al. (2001) could not provide evidence one way or the other. The authors, though, were struck by the realization that some very clear, vivid, and consistent memories had been reported despite the fact that the brain (supposedly) does not function during clinical death with a flat electroencephalogram. Other experienced researchers (Kelly, Greyson, & Stevenson, 1999/ 2000) have also made the point that a clear memory is remarkable under those conditions, even if it is difficult to prove that the patient had a paranormal or transcendent way of acquiring the information.

A similar study was performed by British researchers Sam Parnia and Peter Fenwick (2002). They also found that memories are rare after resuscitation from cardiac arrest. The relatively few memories (11% of the sample) did have some features of a NDE and were usually pleasant. There was a hint that NDEs were more common among patients who had more oxygenation and therefore better brain function during the resuscitation. These researchers tried to determine if the patients with NDEs had seen events from an out-of-body floating perspective, but there was insufficient data to draw a conclusion. The large number of NDERs that are in circulation may have led investigators to expect that they would find many cases in their prospective studies, but actually few have been found.

Eliminating Other Explanations

Other researchers favored explanations that do not require the assumption that a person had returned from the dead. Glen Gabbard and Stuart Twemlow (1984) were among the first to make a strong case against several of the competing theories.

1. NDEs are not caused by nor are they necessarily symptoms of mental illness. Very few people who reported NDEs showed signs of psychopathology.

2. NDEs are not related to level of education. Therefore, it cannot be said that the NDE is either something that is "imagined" by people with little formal education or "created" by people with perhaps too much education.

3. There is no evidence that NDEs occur mostly among people who previously had been fascinated by mystic or other unusual phenomena.

4. The NDE does not have much similarity to dreams. In comparing their NDERs with studies of normal dreams, Gabbard and Twemlow observed more differences than similarities. Therefore, it cannot be said that the survivors "dreamed" their experiences, if we use the term "dream" in its usual sense.

These findings suggest that NDEs cannot be easily explained as a dream state or as a function of easily known factors, such as education or mental illness. However, there are other alternative hypotheses to consider, as well as some problems with the data and logic of the survival interpretation.

The Case against the Near-Death Experience as Proof of Survival

There are a number of logical as well as empirical objections to interpreting NDEs as evidence for survival:

1. Many people who return from a close encounter with death do not report NDEs. They recall nothing at all or only vague and dreamlike fragments. Why are NDEs so uncommon among people who have been resuscitated after clinical death? (The answer might have a lot to do with such medical factors as the age of the patient, the level of oxygenation, and the length of time in a state of clinical death, as various studies have suggested.)

2. Some survivors return with nightmarish experiences. Atwater (1992) reports that these cases are more frequent than previously thought and can be compared with visions of Hell. I have collected both positive and negative reports myself (Box 14-3).

3. NDEs sometimes occurs in situations in which the individual is in no bodily peril of death. The out-of-body component of the NDE

has also been reported frequently in parapsychological experiments in which there is no life-threatening situation. Gabbard and Twemlow (1991) conclude that "the state of *mind* of the near-death subject is far more important than the state of the *body*" (p. 46). NDEs may be triggered by the belief that one is close to death or some other impending catastrophe.

4. Careful research of medical records shows that many people who report NDEs actually had not come close to death. The most thorough study found that only approximately half of the NDE reporters had survived a life-threatening illness or injury. Nevertheless, they believed that they had been dead or very near death even if they had not been in serious danger. Some patients had decided for themselves that they had been "dead" or "clinically dead." Others misinterpreted what they had been told by doctors or nurses. Stevenson, Cook, and McClean-Rice (1989/1990) comment that "having had the NDE itself may have led some people to believe retrospectively that their condition must have been worse than it otherwise seemed" (p. 52).

5. People who had been in severe pain were more likely than others to experience a sense of distance from their bodies. Gabbard and Twemlow (1984) note that in hypnotic pain experiments, it is a common suggestion to dissociate the painful part from the body so that it is treated as "not self." Furthermore, patients who had been under anesthesia were especially likely to see brilliant lights and hear unusual sounds. These effects occur with many people who have been anesthetized, whether or not their conditions were life threatening. Results such as these indicate that the overall picture is not that simple.

6. We hear NDEs only from the survivors. There is no evidence that what happens when a person really dies "and stays dead" has any relationship to the experiences reported by those who have recovered from a life-threatening episode. In fact, it is difficult to imagine how there could ever be such evidence; the very fact that a person has recovered disqualifies his or her report of "permanent death." There is always an observing self that categorizes the observed self as inert or dead. This split consciousness may result in the opinion that "I was dead," but there was always another "I" lively and perceptive enough to make that judgment.

BOX 14-3
SOME FRIGHTENING NEAR-DEATH EXPERIENCES[a]

- "There were so many pews on each side, and each pew was filled with people wearing black robes with hoods. I couldn't see their faces but if I turned my eyes I could see the inside of the hoods were lined with red.... I stood there wondering where I was and what I was doing there, when a door opened to the right of the altar and out came the devil.... I saw that what he was pouring from the jug was fire, and I screamed, dropped the goblet, and started to run" (Irwin & Bramwell, 1988, p. 42).

- "I was thrilled to meet this person or was it an angel and then all at once I saw that she or it was truly horrible. Where the eyes were supposed to be were slits and kind of blue-green flames flickered through them, through the eye-places. I can still see this demon, this whatever-it-was. With my eyes wide open, I can still see it."

- "She told me to go back. I didn't want to. I said I was so happy being where I was, not that I knew where I was. I thought she was being mean to make me go back into that bloody wrecked body. I could feel myself shaking and crying. I didn't feel good anymore."

[a]Told to the authors by survivors of motor vehicle accidents.

Mystical, Depersonalization, and Hyperalertness Responses to Crisis

Several explanations have been offered as alternatives to the conclusion that NDE survivors have actually returned from the dead. These explanations do not deny the experiences as such, nor the emotional significance and meanings that might be drawn from them. The alternative explanations, however, do attempt to provide interpretations that are plausible and that remain within the framework of basic clinical and research knowledge.

What are these alternative explanations? Psychiatrist Russell Noyes, Jr. (1979) and colleagues conducted a series of studies on people who survived a variety of life-threatening crises. They found three common dimensions in these reports: mystical, depersonalization, and hyperalertness.

The *mystical* dimension of experiences close to death includes the feeling of great understanding, sharp and vivid images, revival of memories, the sense of harmony, unity, joy, and revelation. There may also be visions and strange bodily sensations. The depersonalization dimension includes loss of emotion, the sense of the self being detached from both the body and the world, an altered sense of time objects appearing small and far away, strange sounds, and the body having been altered in some strange way. The *hyperalertness* dimension includes the feeling that vision and hearing have become sharper, thoughts either more vivid or more dull, and speeded up or blurred. One has an overall feeling of being mechanical in both thoughts and movements.

Hyperalertness and depersonalization are interpreted as part of a neural mechanism whose function is to help the human organism react to dangerous circumstances. Noyes (1979) suggests that this is an adaptive mechanism that combines opposing reaction tendencies: "the one serving to intensify alertness and the other to dampen potentially disorganizing emotion" (p. 78). When this mechanism is working properly, a person is able to cope exceptionally well (coolly, calmly, and objectively) in the midst of a crisis. Noyes suggests that

> depersonalization may be interpreted as a defense against the threat of death. Not only did people in the studies...find themselves calm in

otherwise frightening situations but they also felt detached from what was happening.... *The depersonalized state is one that mimics death* [italics added]. In it a person experiences himself as empty, lifeless, and unfamiliar. In a sense he escapes death, for what has already happened cannot happen again; he cannot die, because he is already dead. (p. 79)

Mystical consciousness occurs most often with people who are dying from physical disease. Noyes (1979) suggests that the physiological changes associated with terminal illness may induce altered states of consciousness in which experiences of a mystical type are more likely to occur.

When Do People *Not* Have NDEs? An Alternative Explanation

I have suggested a related possible explanation with two components (Kastenbaum, 1995b). First, you might expect that those who are closest to death—in the most perilous physical condition—should be the most likely to have intense NDEs. The available evidence, however, indicates just the opposite (Parnia, Waller, Yeates, & Fenwick, 2001). Survivors who had been very close to death reported fewer experiences of any kind than those who had been less jeopardized. This weakens the assumed connection between the NDE and death. It also highlights a question that has not been clearly answered: Precisely when does the NDE occur? Quite possibly, the NDE is a memory created on the way back. In other words, it is not necessarily what the person experiences at the peak of the crisis but rather an attempt to make sense of the profound yet confusing events. Some people may be able to integrate their extraordinary but chaotic experiences through a memory story whose content and texture are drawn from the psychobiological response as well as individual and cultural factors.

A second component of the NDE might arise from the type of the life-threatening condition. I suggest we consider the individual's role in the crisis. A driver faced with an impending collision is much more likely to make an emergency maneuver than to split off into an autoscopic experience. We engage in instrumental actions—we do something—when the circumstances permit.

This is a survival mechanism: action to avoid catastrophe. The NDE is more likely to occur when the jeopardized person has no instrumental action available. In such a situation, the NDE serves a quieting, energy-conserving function. The sense of serenity implies the activation of self-produced brain opiates (endorphins). This altered state enables body functions to continue at a basic level with minimum expenditure of energy and is represented at the psychic level by comforting imagery. The imagery becomes more coherent as the individual recovers, although in retrospect it is attributed to an earlier phase of the crisis.

Are NDEs Hallucinations?

Still another explanation has been offered by psychologist Ronald Siegel. He regards NDEs as having a hallucinatory character, based on his research on the neuropsychology of drug effects (Siegel, 1992). The specific content of hallucinations is influenced by the individual's expectations and the nature of the physical and psychological environment. When facing death, or believing that one is facing death, one may experience the activation of memories that have been stored in the brain for many years…going back even to prenatal existence (Siegel, 1980):

> The feelings of peace and quiet may be related to the original state of intrauterine existence when there is complete biological equilibrium with the environment. The experience of moving down a dark tunnel may be associated with the clinical stage of delivery in which the cervix is open and there is a gradual propulsion through the birth canal…the dying or near-death experience triggers a flashback or retrieval of an equally dramatic and emotional memory of the birth experience…. To the extent that this reasoning is correct, the experience of dying and rebirth in the afterlife may be a special case of state-dependent recall of birth itself.

Why the hallucinations in the first place? Siegel notes that the sensory world of the terminally ill person may be drastically reduced. This lack of external stimulation encourages the release or escape of stored memories. These memories reenter conscious awareness as though they were perceptions. The result is the experiential state known as the hallucination. This interesting idea has yet to be tested.

NDEs as Exercises in Religious Imagination?

Carol Zaleski, an expert in religious studies, examines what she calls *Otherworld Journeys* (1987) that have been reported from ancient times to the present. The following is one of her examples:

> Four days ago, I died and was taken by two angels to the height of heaven. And it was just as though I rose above not only this squalid earth, but even the sun and moon, the clouds and stars. Then I went through a gate that was brighter than normal daylight, into a place where the entire floor shone like gold and silver. The light was indescribable, and I can't tell you how vast it was. (p. 58)

This quotation is from a deeply religious man by the name of Salvius who had been left for dead one evening on a funeral bier. He was said to have revived and, inspired by his vision, became a bishop. Zaleski's perceptive review of "otherworldly journeys" offers some interesting comments along with the wealth of examples. She concludes that there is "a fundamental kinship" between these visions (or NDEs) and the imaginative powers that we use in everyday life:

> We are all, in a sense, otherworld travelers. Otherworld visions are products of the same imaginative power that is active in our ordinary ways of visualizing death; our tendency to portray ideas in concrete, embodied, and dramatic forms; the capacity of our inner states to transfigure our perception of outer landscapes; our need to internalize the cultural map of the physical universe; and our drive to experience that universe as a moral and spiritual cosmos in which we belong and have a purpose…. Near-death testimony is one way in which the religious imagination mediates the search for ultimate truth. (p. 205)

The NDER as a Healing and Illuminating Metaphor

Zaleski is among those who regard NDERs as productions of minds that find themselves in extraordinary situations. The NDER attempts to explain and make the best of the situation. The experience may include a sense of going some-place one has never been before, proceeding from the known to the marvelously unknown.

Allan Kellehear (1996) finds that the pattern of response expressed in NDERs has much in common with the way people respond to a variety of other crisis situations. What the NDE presents to us is a vivid example of the human mind attempting to cope with unusual and threatening events. These events might have either a direct or a symbolic relationship with death. For example, people who believe that all they have worked and hoped for in their lives is being destroyed may experience symbolic death imagery even though they are not in an actual life-or-death situation. The NDE might be one example of a larger class of experiences in which we try to re-organize ourselves in a threatening situation. These situations often hold promise for emerging with a stronger and wiser self, but there is also the possibility that one may come out of these episodes as a damaged or even shattered self. In this view, the NDE tells us something about the way we try to survive an episode that can be either disastrous or illuminating.

The NDER can also be viewed as a narrative text that contributes to healing and illuminating the individual who feels caught in a make-or-break situation. A profoundly unsettling and chaotic experience is transformed into a text through which the individual finds meaning and can therefore continue with his or her life as an integrated person (Kastenbaum, 1996). In studying unusual personal narratives, I noticed a feature that might be called the *enabling metaphor*. Discovery of the enabling metaphor in a personal narrative makes it possible to understand perceptions, images, and feelings that previously appeared obscure, incoherent, and inconsistent. It is a "Rosetta Stone" through which we can translate sequences of unusual, even bizarre, events such as those found in many NDERs. The images and impressions are difficult to catch in our usual categories of meaning—often people characterize their NDEs as basically "indescribable." If the individual can come up with a metaphor that encompasses the entire experience, however, it becomes possible to create a coherent and meaningful narrative out of the many vivid but unconnected impressions.

The metaphor of an out-of-body journey serves this purpose well in NDERs. Wilson (1996) examined the enabling metaphor in 50 NDERs. The guiding metaphor of an out-of-body journey played a significant role in the individual's ability to come out of the episode with the conviction that there is order and meaning in the universe that goes beyond the limits of one's own conscious existence. It is this sense of order, often characterized specifically as "peace and harmony," that may provide an enduring sense of comfort with life and death after a NDE.

What Are We Learning from Near-Death Experience Reports?

The NDE clearly is of interest as a remarkable human experience. However, were the survivors really dead? Do such reports provide evidence for survival of death? These questions remain controversial. The case studies reported by Kelley et al. (1999/2000) are encouraging to those who believe that NDERs could possibly provide evidence for survival:

> There are three features that we believe suggest the possibility of survival, especially when they all occur in the same experience. These features are enhanced mental processes at a time when physiological functioning is seriously impaired; the experience of being out of the body and viewing events going on around it as from a position above; and the awareness of remote events not accessible to the person's ordinary senses. (p. 513)

There is also a heightened interest among medical researchers who are fascinated by the interplay between mind and body as involved in NDEs. In their review of research on this topic, Parnia and Fenwick (2002) call for more attention to brain function near the end of life. They are open to the possibility that there might be major discoveries yet to be made about the way in which we cope with extreme stress, even when we seem to have little or no brain functioning to call upon. However, imagination can also create persuasive false memories.

Another interesting new approach has also focused on altered states of consciousness. Whinnery (1997) compares the loss of consciousness that occurs with acceleration during fighter air-craft operation (or ground-based centrifuge sim-ulation) with NDE reports. The G-LOC problem, as it is known, continues to present a challenge to fighter aviation medicine. Pilots who black out under acceleration stress are in danger for their lives. Whinnery concludes that

> the major characteristics of G-LOC experiences that are shared in common with NDEs include tunnel vision and bright lights, floating sensa-tions, automatic movement, autoscopy, out-of-body experiences, not wanting to be disturbed, paralysis, vivid dreamlets of beautiful places, pleasurable sensations, psychological alterations of euphoria and dissociation, inclusion of friends and family, inclusion of prior memories and thoughts, the experience being very memorable (when it can be remembered), confabulation, and a strong urge to understand the experience. (p. 245)

Clearly, there is much in common between typical NDE reports and the reports given by pilots who have experienced G-LOC. These simi-larities do not prove anything but certainly en-courage further exploration of both experiential states and the physiological conditions that influ-ence them so strongly.

From early childhood onward, we are strenu-ously influenced by society not only to behave but also to think and feel in conformity with ex-pectations. Mass media bombard us with an un-relenting profusion of images and messages that encourage us to fit into the mold. Near-death ex-periences, whatever else they might be, are asser-tions of our own individual inner lives—and perhaps also of something universal in human nature that is not entirely overridden by societal pressures (Kastenbaum, 1998a, 1998b).

THE DEAD AS EVIDENCE FOR SURVIVAL

People have searched for proof of survival for many centuries, long before the health sciences enabled people to survive close calls with death and thereby increased the frequency of the NDE. Often, what has been taken as proof are encounters with spirits of the dead. If the living and the dead can communicate with each other,

then there must be some form of afterlife. This is a big "If," but one that has enticed and con-vinced many people. We consider several types of reported encounters, starting with the death-bed escort.

Deathbed Escorts: Safe Conduct to the Other World

Mythology and folklore provide many exam-ples of a guide who escorts the living across the border to death. This guide often takes a form very similar to the "gentle comforter" personifi-cation of death discussed in a previous chapter.

One of the most famous in recent times fea-tures a "gray lady" who started to appear to dying patients in a London hospital many years ago. When a modern physician decided to examine this legend, he discovered that new instances were still being reported. Dying patients insisted that the gray lady visited them often and even filled their water jugs. The reports were always of a gray uniform, but the staff nurses actually wore blue. These patients had not known that gray was the color of the nurses' uniforms when the hospital had been new. For other examples, Sir William Barrett's (often criticized, but interesting to read) *Deathbed Visions* (1926/1986) might be consulted.

Karlis Osis and colleagues (Osis, 1961; Osis & Haraldsson, 1977) collected observations from more than 2,000 physicians and nurses in India and the United States. Wat did they find?

1. Patients at times were observed to be inter-acting with a visitor or apparition that others could not see. These patients were clear of mind and in possession of their mental faculties, not drugged, confused, or delusional.

2. The visitations usually come to people who were known to be dying, but there were also in-stances in which the deathbed escort appeared to a person who was not thought to be gravely ill—and that person did pass away soon afterward.

3. The visitations were not always welcome. It sometimes appeared as though the escort had to convince the patient that the time was near.

4. The escorts were varied. Some people saw the apparition of one of their parents; others be-lieved they were interacting with an angel or messenger of God.

FIGURE 14.1
A person's spirit floats over her body in an out-of-body experience.

5. Occasionally, something happened that the physicians or nurses could witness (Osis & Haraldsson, 1977):

> In the room where he was lying, there was a staircase leading to the second floor. Suddenly he exclaimed "See, the angels are coming down the stairs. The glass has fallen and broken." All of us in the room looked toward the staircase where a drinking glass had been placed on one of the steps. As we looked, we saw the glass break into a thousand pieces without any apparent cause. It did not fall; it simply exploded. The angels, of course, we did not see. A happy and peaceful expression came over the patient's face and the next moment he expired. Even after his death the serene, peaceful expression remained on his face. (p. 42)

The deathbed visions had similar features in the United States and India, despite the substantial cultural differences. The visions could be distinguished easily from ordinary hallucinations, and many had received no sedation.

Do these reports provide evidence for survival? The data were retrospective and therefore memory dependent, and they could not be independently verified. Furthermore, it is possible that many if not all of the deathbed visitors were wish-fulfilling fantasies and perhaps released by physiological changes such as decreased oxygen uptake in the brain. The escorts may have been created by the dying person's own unconscious and projected into the outer world, where it would then be experienced as "real." *One part of the dying person's self would therefore be able to communicate with another part through the hallucination.*

This trick of conversing with ourselves by attributing one of our "voices" to an external person or being has long been familiar to mental health experts

I have witnessed perhaps a dozen incidents in which a person near death seemed to be interacting with a companion that we could not see, and I have been told of others, but there is no basis for holding that all or even most people near death have such experiences. Perhaps deathbed escorts are highly selective in their visitations, but perhaps they exist in the mind of the dying person and nowhere else.

Angels have played the role of *psychopomps*, spiritual messengers dispatched by the gods to escort the soul of the dying person safely to the next life. Hermes/Mercury, the dashing Greek/Roman god, was, among other things, an elite psychopomp. The angel as deathbed escort has figured in religious traditions that preceded the Christian era and is still to be discovered in other traditions today. The "beings of light" that are encountered in some NDEs might qualify as guardian angels, as also indicated by the enduring sense of well-being that people have reported years after the experience.

Communicating with the Dead? The Medium and the Channeler

Today, there are "channelers" through whom the dead speak, or so believers believe. This is not new. In the past, practitioners went by a different name, however. The *medium* was a person who was considered to have an unusual sensitivity to communications from the deceased. Interest in "spiritism" ran high from the middle of the 19th century onward, faded away, then rebounded in recent years with a new vocabulary. These alleged communications with the dead were taken as proof of survival by many people.

When Spiritism Was in Flower

Bogus mediums have been exposed repeatedly. Unprincipled charlatans have often preyed on the sorrows and hopes of the bereaved and the uncritical innocence of the curious. There were repeated exposures of bogus mediums (e.g., by the celebrated illusionist, Harry Hou-

dini) and many eventually confessed to their deceptions. A core of ardent believers in spiritual contact with the dead remained undeterred by the numerous exposures and deceptions. Other investigators have written off the entire spiritism enterprise as an exercise in which some people, driven by their emotional needs, lined up and paid well to be deceived.

Interest in alleged communication with the dead was intensified after many families suffered bereavement during World War I. Meanwhile, science and technology seemed to have endangered belief in an afterlife. Some people fought against science, others decided to apply the scientific method to prove survival, if possible. People of both types joined in the establishment of the British Society of Psychical Research (SPR) in 1882. The scholars and scientists who founded this group included some of the most respected people of their time.

A Census of Hallucinations was taken (one of the first major public surveys). Personal observations suggestive of communications with the deceased were critically examined, and most were discarded. This left a core of incidents that the SPR believed deserved to be taken more seriously. Myers (1903/1975) presented many of these in his monumental two-volume work, *Human Personality and Its Survival of Bodily Death*. A "spirit photography" approach also became popular for a while: How could we not believe in spirits of the departed if we could see them with our own eyes? These productions were also quickly discredited by professional photographers and astute observers who discovered how easy it was to produce pictures of deceased people and disembodied forms. Seeing was not necessarily believing after all.

Of more promise were *automatic writing* and *trance reception*. Automatic writing was a *dissociative state*. A person would write rapidly—sometimes amazingly so—while seeming to be unaware of this activity. The thoughts seemed to write themselves down, as messages from some other person, whether living or deceased. Trance phenomena then appeared, which these days would be called an altered state of consciousness. In the trance state, individuals become receptive to thoughts and personalities that appeared alien to themselves.

Automatic writing provided a written text that could be examined at leisure and checked against external data. Trance states could be witnessed and monitored. Strategies were devised to detect fraud and self-deceit. The "sensitive" or "medium" became the focus of survival research. The life of more than one impressive medium was made miserable by the controls and invasions of privacy demanded by skeptical investigators. Many a medium was in fact exposed as fraudulent—sometimes merely by turning a light on at the wrong (or right) time. Few of these mediums passed through investigations unscathed, and even these cases have remained controversial.

Few *seances* have been conducted and reported under conditions exacting enough to be evidential, and fewer still have produced survivalistic communications. One can choose to hold fast to a few reports that have not been "debunked," or one can choose to emphasize the preponderance of fraudulent and inadequate reports. Spiritism (often called spiritualism) is still around. John Wallis (2001) notes that people who have become lonely in their bereavement often find comfort in sharing their interest in communicating with the dead. Furthermore, today there is also some effort on the part of spirit advisors to help bereaved people to accept the loss and move on with their lives.

Channeling and Past Life Regression

The change of terminology from *medium* to *channeler* has not altered the situation in any significant respect. Few channeling interactions have been conducted and reported in a manner that could be taken as evidential. Popular television exhibitions of reputed conversations with the dead would have been scoffed away by diligent researchers a century ago. Scientific evidence is rarely the primary goal of channeling sessions, and it is not easy to establish a situation that is favorable to both the (supposed) channeling process and to its scientific evaluation.

Perhaps the most famous case of channeling in recent times is the story of Bridey Murphy. Under hypnosis, Ruth Simmons, a 20th-century American, recounted her experiences as "Bridey Mur-

phy," who was said to have been born in Ireland in 1768 and to have died there in 1864. The book reporting this account (Bernstein, 1965) became a best-seller and stimulated interest in so-called past life regression. Unfortunately, this good story was later found to be a concoction from a variety of experiences Simmons had had in her own everyday life but that had emerged during the hypnotic sessions as hidden memories that were organized into coherent narratives. The most authentic-sounding memories of Ireland had slipped into her mind from her childhood visit to the World's Fair in St. Louis, where an Irish village had been recreated. There have been a great many reports of past lives since Bridey Murphy came and went, and the same doubts and limitations remain. "My past life" seems to function as an enabling metaphor that opens the door to memory fragments and fantasies that come together as though reports of an actual set of meaningful experiences.

Ghosts

It is not easy to take ghosts seriously today, even if we substitute the more respectable-sounding term *apparitions.* Ghosts have been for so long the stuff of campfire stories, parodies, and late-night movies that they might seem to be the least promising source of evidence for survival. However, ghosts deserve a little better than that. Ghosts have had a long and respectable place in culture, religion, and drama. Many societies have accepted ghosts as quasi-citizens. Everyday life without the possibility of interaction with departed spirits just would not be the same. For example, we could not hope to understand the beliefs and practices of villagers in the Delhi region of India if we did not also appreciate the power of ghosts and the need to take great care in dealing with them. The villagers also must be cautious in their dealing with each other because an aggrieved neighbor could become quite a troublesome ghost (Freed & Freed, 1993). Ghosts have a formidable social reality in many cultures.

At the beginning of a new millennium in an urban society, everyday people still report encountering everyday-type ghosts. These are not at all like the stereotypes associated with haunted houses. They are an entire family downstairs in the rented house, making breakfast for themselves, the aroma of freshly brewed coffee rising to the visitor's bedroom. The ghost is an old man who sits quietly reading a newspaper at the same hour in the early evening. The ghost is a cat who visits so often that it is considered a part of the family (even by the dog) and whose habits have become as familiar to them as their own. The quite down-to-earth and sensible woman who told me about the ghost cat had not at first thought it was even worth mentioning because "it was just part of our life; it was just there when it wanted to be." Myers (1903/1975) was more impressed with such innocuous ghosts than with the more elaborate reports he collected of formidable apparitions with their mysterious purposes and profound messages. Who would have invented such useless ghosts, and why have bothered? Apparitions that did not fit into cultural belief systems and did not seem to have any particular agenda or message seemed more credible to Myers than those who have been featured in ghost stories.

Nevertheless, it is the consequential spirit that has attracted the most attention and that has most often been taken as proof of survival. Perhaps most common is the ghost who visits to provide comfort during a time of crisis. For example (Green & McCreery, 1989),

> My mother died in June. One Sunday morning early, we had a terrible thunderstorm. My husband was working away at the time, and as I have always been very nervous of storms, I went downstairs, taking the baby with me, and my eldest daughter also came down with me. She could see how I was shaking with fright. Suddenly I felt a very slight pressure on my shoulders, and heard my Mother's voice say, "don't be afraid Winnie dear, nothing will harm you." I immediately stopped shaking, and felt quite calm, and my daughter noticed the change in me, and said, "What's happened, Mum, you don't look frightened anymore." (Green & McCreery, 1989, p. 201)

Another popular ghost figure is the one who warns us of danger: There is a problem with the electrical system in the new house, the bridge is unsafe to cross, and so on. How should a person respond to episodes in which one seems to have been comforted or warned by a ghost? Most of the people who have related such experiences to me were not quite sure just what had happened. Was that really a ghost? Are there really such things as ghosts? They had no way of knowing for certain. On the other hand, it was nice to be comforted, and there was no harm in taking the warning seriously enough to check it out.

Ghosts have not fared well in research—the tighter and more controlled the situation, the less inviting for spirit visitors. In the heyday of spiritism, some mediums regularly produced apparitions at their seances and were often discovered to have created these ectoplasmic beings from materials such as a quickly inflated goat's bladder. Still, there is something cheerful about thinking that there might be a form of survival that enables friendly spirits to visit now and again. In the ancient world, the living, the dead, and the inbetween were on closer terms, so perhaps we miss this entire realm of beings.

Unfortunately, as noted in the quotation that opened this chapter, ghosts sometimes do go bad—very bad! Fear of the dead is closely related to fear of angry or evil ghosts. This gives us a connection between two facets of the death system: how a society respects and cares for the dead and how it tries to go on with life after that living person has become a memory. Some of us might speak of "griefwork," but others might speak instead of trying to placate the discontented dead. Plainly, it is not always comforting to believe in an afterlife—not when it is stressful enough to motivate spirits to do mean and vicious things, and not when one is on the receiving end of such mischief.

The Ghost Dance: A Peaceful Vision Becomes a Tragedy

Beliefs have consequences, whether or not these beliefs are grounded in fact. Freed and Freed (1993), for example, have shown how ghost beliefs have interfered with the adoption of hygienic measures and health care interventions that could have saved lives. Sometimes, the ghosts become innocent bystanders in a tragedy for the living. Consider an example in which a belief in ghosts and survival contributed to one of the most shameful pages in U.S. history.

By the 1880s, life had changed radically for the Native American peoples who had once called this

The Lakota Sioux (shown here in 1892) and other Native American tribes performed exhausting dance rituals hoping to invoke their ancestors to rescue them from invaders, who had taken over their lands and driven them to the very edge of survival.

land their own. The whites were in control practically everywhere. Some of the tribes living in the Great Plains had continued to fight for their independence and just recently been defeated. Hard times indeed. Meanwhile, Jack Wilson, a Paiute orphan, was being raised by a white family on a Nevada ranch. It was thought that he was the son of Tavibo, a Paiute who had prophesied that the whites would be literally swallowed up by the earth and all the dead Native Americans would then return to life as part of the great celebration.

Jack Wilson was chopping wood one day when he heard a great noise, headed off to see where it came from, and then fainted. He had a spiritual vision while in this altered state of consciousness and awakened with a new mission—to persuade his people to live a righteous life in the eyes of God. Wovoka (the new name he had

taken) had been to heaven, met his mother and other deceased people, and conversed with God (Hittman, 1990). He now dedicated himself to teaching his people that they must not drink whiskey or fight. Instead, they must love one another and live in peace with the whites.

Wovoka encouraged his followers to continue their traditional circle dance while singing religious songs. This was a way of affirming their community bonds and also dedicating themselves to God and the right life. There was nothing warlike about this ceremony, but some nervous settlers became disturbed by a ritual they did not understand. Eventually, a militant spirit did arise around some campfires (Mooney, 1996). The earlier prophecy about the destruction of the whites and the raising of the dead became associated with the new movement. Another ominous development occurred: Some of the tribes recently defeated in combat with the U.S. Army came to believe that the dead could protect them. The ghost dance was created in the depths of their desperation.

Fasting and dancing to the point of trance and exhaustion brought the warriors into contact with the powerful spirits of the dead who were also longing for liberation. From these rituals came the idea of a sacred article of clothing that could protect them from the white man's bullets. They would be safe in their ghost shirts if attacked by soldiers. With rituals, courage, and perseverance, they would overcome. Accordingly, they did not give as much attention to defensive precautions as they would have without such special protection. They were in no position to defend themselves when attacked in their encampment at Wounded Knee, an attack that was more slaughter than military operation. Belief in ghosts and their powers had contributed to the massacre, though the savagery of the attack on women and children became the shame of the Army when the facts became known.

These are but a few of the examples that can be drawn from history. The belief that spirits of the dead can have crucial influence on our lives has led some people to misplace their trust and to neglect opportunities for protecting and enhancing their own lives.

Reincarnation

The ancient belief in reincarnation has come back to life in recent years in Europe, Australia, and North America, having remained influential in Asia and Africa through the centuries. Although Hindu and Buddhist versions of the reincarnation doctrine are the most widely known, other religions of more limited domain have also featured this idea. Judeo-Christian religious authorities generally have opposed reincarnation beliefs, but with only partial success. The idea of living more than one life seems to thrive even when it does not fit well into a particular religious dogma. Many in the United States today who believe in reincarnation were raised in the Christian tradition but became attracted to the concept of life as a continuing journey from one embodiment to another. The popularity of this belief was stimulated by so-called past life regressions (as with Bridey Murphy) and by heightened interest

in survival of death as NDERs made the rounds. Reincarnation beliefs have a long heritage and are cherished by many people in many lands.

Is there any evidence for reincarnation that would be persuasive to people who are not easy to persuade? One researcher stands out for his many years of careful investigation. Ian Stevenson's *Twenty Cases Suggestive of Reincarnation* (1974) did much to establish the credibility of reincarnation research. He has since produced many other books and articles on the subject. A hallmark of Stevenson's approach is intensive case-by-case analysis. Readers are left to draw their own conclusions. His work is lucid, systematic, and detailed, and his series of case histories is a model of its kind. A typical case "suggestive of reincarnation" starts early in childhood, usually between ages 2 and 4 years.

> The child often begins talking about this previous life as soon as he gains any ability to speak, and sometimes before his capacity for verbal expression matches his need to communicate. Some children make only 3 or 4 different statements about a previous life, but others may be credited with 60 or 70 separate items pertaining to different details in the life remembered. In most cases the volume and clarity of the child's statements increase until at the age of between 5 and 6 he usually starts to forget the memories; or, if he does not forget them, he begins to talk about them less. Spontaneous remarks about the previous life have usually ceased by the time the child has reached the age of 8 and often before. Unexpected behavior…nearly always accompanies the statements the child makes about the previous life he claims to remember, or occurs contemporary with them. This behavior is unusual for a child of the subject's family, but concordant with what he says concerning the previous life, and in most instances it is found to correspond with what other informants say concerning the behavior of the deceased person about whom the subject has been talking, if such a person is traced. (p. 324)

In an *Omega* I interview, I asked Stevenson about the difficulties involved in his research (Kastenbaum, 1993c).

> The effort to exclude the normal transmission of information exists even in cases in which the two families are completely unknown to each other and perhaps live many miles apart. I have often

had to content myself with saying that normal communication was improbable; only rarely can I say it was impossible. For example, in a case in Delhi the two families concerned did not live far apart, but an immense gulf of wealth, education, and religion made it unlikely that they could ever have met; and they said they had not. Yet we learned that both families had bought vegetables at the same market. Could the subject's family have overheard someone in the market talking about the murder of which he subject spoke? I cannot be sure that this did not happen, although it seems unlikely (p. 169).

Stevenson has investigated cases from Burma, India, Sri Lanka, Turkey, Lebanon, and Native Americans. Smaller sets of cases have come from Brazil, Nigeria, Finland, Thailand, the United Kingdom, and the United States. Cases seem to come to attention more readily in cultures that favor belief in reincarnation. Whether belief somehow generates the experiences or whether the experiences simply are easier to share within a sympathetic cultural milieu is difficult to determine. The specific elements in each case would have to be explained in any event.

Stevenson crowned his long research career by publishing a mammoth collection of case studies that are accompanied by medical records and photographs bearing on the validity of children's statements about a past life. He selected cases that had all the following characteristics:

1. The child has described the way he or she died in a past life.
2. The child has a birthmark or birth defect that is consistent with that form of death (e.g., two bullet wounds in the chest, or a knife wound on the neck).
3. An investigator identifies a deceased person whose life and death match the past life story given by the child.
4. Medical records documenting the specific cause of death and condition of the body are obtained.
5. There is a very close match between the fatal wounds suffered by the deceased person and the marks or defects found on the child at birth.

Stevenson offers these physical evidence match-ups as the best evidence available that is "suggestive of reincarnation." Readers who wish to examine these cases in-depth to draw their own conclusions will want to consult *Reincarnation and Biology* (1997a), a two-volume set of more than 2,000 pages with many photographs. A summary and discussion of these findings is presented in *Where Reincarnation and Biology Intersect* (1997b). Now that Stevenson's remarkable contributions are available for study, one might well hesitate to draw conclusions about reincarnation until reading this material with the care that the author took in collecting, analyzing, and presenting the cases.

Two of the many questions that might be asked about Stevenson's cases are worth mentioning. First, why were so many of the reported past lives ended by sudden and violent death? The number of murders and other violent deaths in Stevenson's sample goes well beyond general expectations. Second, how could anybody be reincarnated unless everybody is reincarnated? What do you think?

There is an even more radical possibility: Death may not be the same for everybody. Of all the possibilities considered in this chapter, the prospect of pluralistic death might well be the most extreme. This possibility may most challenge our basic assumptions about the nature of life and the universe. There is survival of death, or there is not survival—or so it is generally believed. The rational mind may find either of these alternatives more acceptable than the possibility that death might be different at different times to different people in different situations. Nevertheless, as I have suggested elsewhere, this seemingly bizarre idea appears consistent with some basic precepts of the philosophy of science (Kastenbaum, 1993c). The idea that death might be relative to life and context opens the possibility that there might be both survival and nonsurvival!

SHOULD WE SURVIVE DEATH?

Should we survive death? This is a question that perhaps should be asked more often. Let's begin with responses from college students to item 3 in the self-quiz given in this chapter:

• I really can't answer that question. That's funny, isn't it? Here I am, a good Christian and I believe in heaven and all that, but I can't get what it's all about clear in my mind. I think my problem is in the idea of a literal heaven, a Sunday school fairy tale. I can't really accept that anymore, but I don't have anything to replace it. • You tell me! I imagine eternity as a state of perfection. No more worries, no more problems. Best of all, no more deadlines and exams! But then what? All I can imagine is God and all the rest of us posing forever for our portrait with this transcendental smile on our faces. I'd go crazy! I need to worry and rush around or I'm not really myself. It will be beautiful and peaceful. More beautiful and peaceful than anything we can know on Earth. Maybe the closest would be a long and relaxed Sunday afternoon. What makes a Sunday afternoon so great, though, is that it comes after one hectic week and before another. I don't know how I would do if there was only Sunday afternoon. This is probably a dumb way to think about heaven, but it's the best I can do.

These respondents were hesitant about survival of death because the "what do we do after we get there?" image was unclear. Perhaps there is more appeal in the type of afterlife that has been envisioned by many tribal peoples: It was much like the familiar here-and-now life with such understandable activities as hunting, fishing, preparing and enjoying feasts, outsmarting adversaries, demonstrating valor, and so forth. Such conceptions of the afterlife involve not only continuing activity but also change, risk, and danger. The intellectual and the mystic may have ways of envisioning a Christian afterlife that is neither literal nor dull. Some believers, however, are uncomfortable with a heaven that seems just too heavenly and therefore remote from their own lives and thoughts.

A more radical orientation can also be taken toward the desirability of survival. There are two main components here: We do not deserve survival, and the prospect of survival encourages the worst side of human nature.

The first component is supported by all the cruelty, stupidity, greed, and pettiness that can be found in the lives of individuals and societies through the centuries. Make your own list. How many examples of genocide will you include? How many examples of fortunes being made by inflicting suffering on others? How many corpo-rate executives deceiving the public and destroying their own employees' retirement funds? How many examples of wanton destruction, of royal whim or bureaucratic arrogance? There are more examples than we can use. Whatever items we may choose for our list, the conclusion might be the same: *Homo sapiens* has not earned the right for survival beyond the grave. We might also count against ourselves the ways in which we often waste time and therefore life. Should eternal life be granted to those who have demonstrated so little ability to use the hours and days of earthly life? If much of our discretionary time is merely filled or killed, what claim dare we make on immortality?

The second component also places the human race in a harsh light. One of the arguments here is that the prospect of eternal life has been used repeatedly to manipulate believers in the service of power and greed and, at times, raging fanaticism. Again, we cannot help but think about the September 11, 2001, terrorists, who believed that they were earning admission to paradise. The guarantee of immortal blessing for those who die while slaughtering designated enemies has led to some of history's most ferocious battles. The moral case against survival is that we might be forced to become better people and learn to make more constructive use of our time on Earth if we did not have the prospect of an afterlife as either an all-dominating or fail-safe goal.

A thorough consideration of Eastern thought and practice would add still other dimensions. The way of the Buddha, for example, differs greatly from the Christian conception of life–death–afterlife (Bonney, 2002). "Death," in effect, disappears for those who can attain a heightened spiritual development in which birth and beginnings, cravings and ambitions, also dissolve. The character of the Buddhist survival doctrine is also distinctive in its implications for both individual and social action. Militant violence against others, for example, does not flow readily from this tradition.

Nevertheless, arguments can still be advanced against the desirability of this survival doctrine. Consider a single example: The Buddhist philosophy encourages inwardness, the cultivation of the inner self. The turning inward, however, with its cosmic agenda, can lead to neglect of pressing concerns on the worldly plane. Detachment from worldly affairs in pursuit of spiritual development could inadvertently contribute to the persistence of poverty, suffering, and inequality. Neither the Buddhists nor the Christians necessarily ignore the everyday human condition. There have always been activists who envision their own mission as both individual and social/humanitarian. Nevertheless, the question can be raised: Does a dominating vision of the afterlife divert and obstruct attention from flesh-and-blood realities here and now?

WHAT KIND OF SURVIVAL?

Suppose that there is survival after death. I can imagine a roomful of people who are in agreement with this statement, but each person might have a very different conception of the afterlife. The following is what they might tell us:

• "Survival? Yes, as a burst of pure energy. At the last moment of life there is a discharge of electromagnetic radiation (or something like that). Does this death flash continue in some form, and does it encode and preserve the individual's identity? Perhaps, perhaps not. But the burst of electromagnetic radiation can be documented. This is a long way from immortality, but a burst of glory—isn't that something?"

• "Have you seen a ghost? Most apparitions seem rather lost and slow-witted, not like the real people they once were, more like shadows or representations. What sometimes happens after death is that a temporary trace of the person remains in the locale. You might call this a force-field. This 'person-shaped force-field' exists in nature; but it does not exist for long and it is not the survived person, merely his or her energy traces, and these will soon fade. Like the death flash, the ghost is a kind of survival, but not much to write home about."

• "Fading, that is just what happens, but not in the way that you have proposed. When people die they move from the realm of light to the realm of darkness. There is survival here, in this underworld, but oh what a sad survival, a slow fading away to blank, characterless beings who lose all that made them passionate and knowing individuals. The Greeks called them shades. Poor lost souls, poor wandering creatures in a cosmic nightmare."

• "These quaint ideas miss the real point. There is true immortality—but not for everybody. Like much else in life, survival of death is *conditional*. What is it conditional on? This surpasses our understanding at present—but some wise people have believed that those who develop great spiritual strength will not perish along with their bodies. The soul does not possess immortality; rather, it may have the *potential* for immortality, depending on the person. The lives of some people may continue after death because they have become real in a different way."

• "Survival? How can you avoid it? We are born but to die, and die but to be reborn. Not only those of us who are at the moment human beings, but all living things (and perhaps 'inanimate' things as well) go through cycle after cycle of existence. There are so many beginnings and so many ends: but, for most of us, no Beginning and no End."

• "We live. We die. We are judged. We are damned or we are granted salvation through the mercy of the Lord. The righteous dwell forever with the Lord; those who live in ignorance or defiance will know the fires of hell."

• "Human life is—or should be—a progression toward enlightenment, toward spiritual development. This does not have much to do with the external forms of religion, but rather with each person's journey from ignorance to understanding, from concern with individuality and materiality to becoming part of a more universal consciousness. The passage from life to death is but one transition in this long journey, and what the person brings to death—and takes from death—depends upon his or her level of spiritual development at that point."

• "Leaving this life produces an altered state of consciousness. In this sense, somebody survives, but this is not quite the same somebody we have been all along. There are many examples of altered states as part of our life experiences, so death may be simply the most impressive and transfiguring of these changes."

• "What crazy people! The juice of the silly-berry has made you see things as they are not and fail to see things as they are. A person dies, of course. This always happens. And then that person just goes on with his life or with her life. This always happens, too. The next life is much like this one. There are pleasures. There are troubles. One can say the wrong thing or touch the wrong person and get oneself killed again, too. What else is a person to do in the next life but those things this person has always known and has always tried to do? These strange stories I hear from you—well, I do not like them very much, but maybe I will like them better if you have saved some of that powerful silly-berry juice for me!"

All the views paraphrased here have been expressed at various times. The concept of the next life being essentially a continuation of the present life has been held by many tribal peoples over the centuries. In contrast, the "death flash" theory is based on controversial experiments on electromagnetic radiation in living tissues (Slawinski, 1987), and the "trace-field" theory seems to have been first suggested by Myers (1903/1975). "Conditional immortality" was suggested by one of the few 20th-century philosophers who took the question of survival as a serious intellectual issue (Hocking, 1957). A specialist in the study of altered states suggests that death results in—what else?—an altered state (Tart, 1990).

It is not likely that a person in mainstream society today will find all these versions equally plausible or appealing. Nevertheless, we have reminded ourselves that more than one possibility has been envisioned in the ongoing scrimmage between the evident fact of death and the vast reaches of imagination and desire.

ASSISTED AND SYMBOLIC SURVIVAL

There are two other types of possible survival that are so different from those already identified that we need to give them separate attention here. *Symbolic immortality* is the more familiar and

better established of these concepts (Box 14-4). The other type is emerging strongly in our own society today—let's call it *assisted survival.*

Symbolic Immortality

Somebody—actually, several somebodies—had carved their initials into the old desk where I did a lot of my daydreaming in Public School 35, the Bronx. Third graders before me had made at least these marks in the world, if no others. I doubt they were thinking much about immortality just then. However, the impulse to leave some continuing mark on the world begins early in life and is not at all uncommon. Times of danger seem to intensify this need. "Kilroy was here!" became a famous phrase during World War II, found scrawled on practically every wall or object that could be scrawled upon, mostly by young men and women in the armed forces who were assigned to unfamiliar places in hazardous conditions. "Kilroy" represented each of the millions who were far from home and family and might never return—but they had been here, meaning they had been alive, had existed, and had done something.

The concept of symbolic immortality became salient through the writings of Robert Jay Lifton (1979) as he reflected on the psychological effects of World War II as death had become increasingly difficult to deny while fewer people were consoled by belief in a traditional afterlife. There was a subtle shift from talk of "soul" to "self." What was to become of the self when the body was finished? Perhaps it could live on in the memories of others. This was not a new idea; many world cultures had already worked out their ways of keeping their dead alive in memory and ritual. In our own society, fund-raisers had already practiced the art of persuading people to pay for buildings

---

BOX 14-4
WE'LL NEVER FORGET WHAT'S HIS NAME: PART 1

Fill in the blanks

_____'s great poem _____ describes a classic example of the way in which time can cancel the symbolic immortality of a once-mighty person.

that would bear their names forever. What was new was the upsurge of interest in symbolic immortality. Again, some of this passionate concern for living on in memory was aroused by the brutality of war. Holocaust survivors often saw themselves as witnesses with the responsibility to bear testimony: "We saw these things happen. We knew and loved these good people who were tormented and killed!" The horrendous deaths (Leviton; Chapter 16) of genocide were crimes against humanity that could not and should not be forgotten. Passing the memories of the victims on to the next generation was a priority, whether it took the form of conversation, writings, museums, or memorial sites.

There are many other motives and methods for symbolic immortality. We might be motivated by the desire to stay in control, or at least influential, after death. Even if there is a satisfactory afterlife ready for us, it might also be rewarding to know that we still have a significant vicarious role in earthly matters. We might also welcome symbolic immortality as confirmation of the good people we were and the good things we did. Late in my seemingly endless days as a graduate student, I happened to meet an elfin and spry old man with a flowing white beard and a merry demeanor. He could have come straight from the Black Forest and any number of folk tales. Rufus von Kleinschmidt lives in my memory as an extraordinary person, and I suppose I am mentioning this brief encounter because I would like to continue his symbolic immortality through you. However, the former chancellor of the University of Southern California is now officially immortal through a large building that carries his name. It is a beautiful building, but I miss the man. There are many people who achieve symbolic immortality without seeking or realizing it. Teachers, for

example, can become role models who influence their former students throughout their lives. There is now research confirming that a mentor can survive not only in memory but also as an inner representation that influences a person's life in many ways (Marwit & Lessor, 2000).

The desire for symbolic immortality can be just one part of a person's motivational repertoire, or it can become a driving and, therefore, distorting force. It is natural, for example, to hope that something of one's self might live on in our children and grandchildren, but it is a little out of control if we are obsessed with shaping their lives to fit this purpose. Passing on the family genes is perhaps the most ancient way of achieving a form of symbolic immortality. Other natural ways of achieving a kind of symbolic immortality include passing along some good (or fascinatingly bad) family stories that will then be retold to later generations, as well as giving family videos and cherished possessions. Desperation and poor judgment, however, can lead to destructive attempts at symbolic immortality (i.e., those who commit acts of violence so that they will be remembered and perhaps even admired) (Kearl, 2002).

The "immortality" in symbolic immortality is vulnerable to time and circumstance. The remembering people themselves die. Once-famous events and achievements become obscure. Buildings are destroyed and memorials are worn down or defaced (Box 14-5).

Assisted Immortality

Technology has been offering assistance to the quest for symbolic immortality. Recorded images and sounds, so familiar to us now, were an historic breakthrough: So much more of the past could now be part of the present. Even faces we

---

BOX 14-5
WE'LL NEVER FORGET WHAT'S HIS NAME: PART 2

Percy Bysshe Shelley's great poem, *Ozymandias,* describes a classic example of the way in which time can cancel the symbolic immortality of a once-mighty person. Is this, or any, poet still remembered, or have those who reflected on symbolic immortality lost theirs as well?

had never seen and voices we had never heard could survive to reach us. Furthermore, some of the most brilliant applied scientists labored to invent devices that would prove or ensure survival of death. Marconi made radio possible and Edison helped to bring forth the practical use of electricity, but both considered themselves failures because an immortality machine had eluded their efforts. The ever-increasing scope of technology still encourages some people to use this modality to overcome the finality of death. It is reasonable to suppose that technologically assisted survival is an especially attractive idea for people who do not have a strong faith in a religion that promises an afterlife. We do not have dependable information on this, however, and it would not be unusual if some believers also were interested in hedging their bets with technology.

The following are some modes of assisted survival that are current at this time. (*Cryonic resuscitation* is in a class by itself, and was considered in Chapter 7):

Clone thyself. Make a perfect copy of a document or a compact disk? We do things like that all the time now. Science could soon make it possible to duplicate ourselves, so won't that be the way to go? Or, actually, not to go! Cloning is also known as "twinning," in reference to the naturally occurring process that results in identical twins in humans and other mammals. The identical twins come from genetic contributions by both parents. Experimental cloning works differently to achieve the same result. The most famous sheep since Mary's Little Lamb was created through nuclear transfer: The nucleus of a cell was removed from an adult ewe, implanted in an egg, developed into an embryo, and then placed within a surrogate ewe that became Dolly's birth, though not biological, mother (Wilmut et al., 2001). This was neither the first nor the last laboratory production of a cloned animal. J. B. Gurdon (2001) and colleagues spawned swimming tadpoles by nuclear transfers, and soon there were also monkeys scrambling about who had no mother or father in the traditional sense. A newsrelease ("Wildlife Park," 2002) hinted that Japanese scientists are working to clone the extinct wooly mammoth from the DNA of a specimen found buried in an avalanche site. (An Indian elephant would be the mother.)

Most cloning research has been directed toward the production of improved food crops or the development of genetic fixes for life-threatening conditions. These goals can be achieved—with skill, patience, and good luck—by converting undifferentiated cells into specialist cells that can perform vital functions in plant or animal life-forms. There has already been success in producing rice and grain that flourish in difficult environments and resist insects and diseases. Many biomedical researchers believe that gene therapy, making use of cloning and other techniques, will introduce a quantum leap in improving the quality and length of life. These uses have been obscured by the controversy over the desirability of human cloning. There are powerful religious, economic, and political arguments on both sides of the controversy. These are fascinating issues that are being addressed by many writers (McGee, 2002; Maienschein, 2003; Ruse & Sheppard, 2001).

What mostly concerns us here is cloning as a possible form of assisted survival. The most encouraging element is the most obvious: A replicate of one's own body would be created. If all went well, there would be a new edition of one's very own self. Furthermore, this would not be an electronic/mechanical contraption but the familiar *H. sapien* form customized to replace a specific individual. There are significant negatives and questions as well. Note first that the successful cloning is the exception. There were many failures in the attempts to produce viable tadpoles and sheep (and pity for the elephants who may be required to carry hopeful little wooly mammoths that are not going to make it). Along with the absolutely failed clones are others that come forth with major problems, and so the issue of dealing with genetically defective infants will be expanded.

The most fundamental question, though, is whether the clone will actually be the original in significant respects. Yes, Clone looks like Original, and perhaps walks and talks like Original. Perhaps Clone even thinks pretty much like Original. But hold on! Does Clone have the same life history as Original? Did Clone grow up during the same sociohistorical period? Was Clone influenced by the same unique mix of personal experiences that have become so deeply ingrained into the texture of Original's personality? Genetic wizardry might have given Clone a strong inclination to develop as did Original, but the cumulative impact of lived experiences should not be underestimated. And hold on again—has Original's consciousness become installed in Clone? Can science replicate our inner sense of self and our immediate awareness of life? "Consciousness" is such a complex and tricky concept that philosophers and neuroscientists tried for awhile to banish it. Now, though, consciousness is one of the hottest topics in the neurosciences (Dennett, 1991; Pinkner, 1997). This topic deserves careful reevaluation rather than simplistic conclusion. Nevertheless, there is definitely much to be said for consciousness as something "real," even though it's difficult to say what kind of real. The most perfect Clone will not be the Original if it does not experience itself and the world through the consciousness of the Original. If a person's consciousness does not survive, that person will not even be aware of his or her "survival." How much good is that?

There is another issue with both practical and ethical resonances. Should individuals be created only to be sacrificed? A human cloning process would almost certainly result in the generation of many flawed embryos and infants. There would be an inclination to destroy these failures. Recently this scenario has been enacted with an endangered species of wild cattle. Two bantengs were birthed by a cow on an Iowa experimental farm (Elias, 2003). One is considered to be a candidate for breeding and therefore extending the species. The other was much larger than expected and was put to death. Fourteen other cloned pregnancies had previously failed. This issue is likely to become more intense as cloning experiments continue. Advocates urge cloning to give endangered species an opportunity for survival; opponents are disturbed by the large number of failures, each of which results in the death of an individual.

Become a smart chip. Perhaps bodies are overhyped. Perhaps we would be better off without them. There is already advocacy for preserving memory and cognitive skills after death. William Gibson's futuristic novel, *Neuromancer* (1986), dismisses bodies as "meat"—useless burdens that we should abandon to enjoy the infinite delights of "the matrix." Margaret Wertheim (1999) touches on several versions of technologically assisted sur-

vival that are now fiction but perhaps could morph into reality one of these days. She notes, for example, a story by Nicole Stengel (1991) in which people are able to download themselves into computers. Recently, this hypothetical process has been relabeled as "uploading." Joslyn, Turchin, and Heylighen (1997) suggest that

> we might imagine computer systems which interact so intimately…that they would "get to know" that user so well that they could anticipate every reaction or desire. Since user and computer system would continuously work together, they would in a sense "merge": It would become meaningless to separate the one from the other. If at a certain stage the biological individual of this symbiotic couple would die, the computational part might carry on as if nothing had happened. The individual's mind could then be said to have survived in the nonorganic part of the system. (pp. 1–2)

The technology invoked in this vision does not strain our credibility, but again we may have questions about precisely who or what it is that survives, and what is that elusive something that perhaps does not survive?

Mail ourselves to the future. Time capsules have been around for awhile. It is interesting to think about what we would like future generations to know about our own lives and times and then to place some associated items in a capsule to be opened at a later date. Could this be a form of assisted survival? A commercial organization known as Highway Products, Inc. assures us that an Infinity Time Capsule is not only "the best gift you can give to your future generation" but also "your chance at immortality." This is, of course, a variant on the more familiar symbolic immortality theme of staying alive in other people's memories. The technological assist in this case is through argon, which is a dry, inert gas intended to prevent deterioration of objects by acid, oxidation, or ultraviolet light. "Each Infinity Time Capsule is then punched with a serial number which we record and keep as a record. Your valuable contents are now safe and secured from the elements until your ancestors open your Infinity Time Capsule" (Joslyn et al., 1997, p. 2).

I would definitely be intrigued, perhaps thrilled, if such a time capsule came my way from ancestors of, for example, a century or two ago of whom I know so little. However, would this make them immortal in any meaningful sense of the term? We return once again to a question each person will probably have to decide: What would be a meaningful or essential form of survival, and would I make use of a technological assist, if available?

THE SUICIDE/SURVIVAL CONNECTION

Risking death and ensuring the bliss of eternal life have been closely linked at times. When Christianity was a new sect, many tried to emulate Jesus through martyrdom at the hands of the Roman authorities. A thousand years later, both Islamic and Christian warriors sought deaths that would earn them entry into their respective realms of eternal bliss. A thousand years after that, four hijacked jets headed toward a suicide mission. The idea that people who die a heroic death will find an eternal reward has been a motif in many cultures. See a production of Wagner's music drama, *Der Valkyrie*, and you will be treated to an imaginative reenactment of an ancient Norse legend in which fallen heroes are scooped up from the field of battle and escorted to Valhalla, a Viking warrior's version of heaven.

Today, we are experiencing an ever-shifting mixture of both ancient and contemporary themes. It may be useful to open our eyes to the new configurations of suicide/survival ideation and behavior. Greyson (1992/1993) finds that people who report NDEs subsequently have stronger antisuicide attitudes. One might have expected the opposite. The NDEs are often experienced as liberating and pleasant; shouldn't this make death more attractive? Well, yes, it does for many people. However, the NDE seems to inspire a greater appreciation for life. Most of the NDE survivors believe in an afterlife but are staunch in their rejection of the idea of foreshortening this life in order to reach the next life more rapidly.

What about those who believe that there simply is no death? This is by far the most common response we are finding in an ongoing study of people who identify themselves with the "New Age" movement. As one respondent stated, death "is just changing clothes." What remains to be learned is whether or not suicide will be seen as

an action that is unimportant and therefore not to be prevented or mourned. Some respondents have already expressed the view that what seems to be a premature and tragic death is nothing to be upset about because (a) death really is not anything and (b) if it happened that way, that is the way it was supposed to be. What do you think?

We have known for some time what Hamlet thinks. In that most famous of monologues (Act III, Scene 1), he begins with the question: "To be or not to be?" For a moment it looks as though death, not-being, will be his answer:

> And by a sleep to say we end
> The heart-ache and the thousand natural shocks
> That flesh is heir to, 'tis a consummation
> Devoutly to be wish'd. To die, to sleep.

He would not continue to suffer the "natural shocks that flesh is heir to." Understandable, of course. However, notice how that subtle mind proceeds to deceive himself or to attempt deception: "'tis a consummation Devoutly to be wish'd." Is death really a consummation? If he copes differently with his ordeal, Hamlet and Ophelia might yet have each other—now there would be a consummation! The imagery of sexual fulfillment is substituted for the reality of death, making it easier to edge his way toward the grave. He continues to blur the reality of death by again reassuring himself: "To die, to sleep." That is all that death is—sleep—and who's afraid of sleep? So, he is going to pack it in then, right? Not so fast!

> To sleep: perchance to dream: ay, there's the rub;
> For in that sleep of death what dreams may come
> When we have shuffled off this mortal coil,
> Must give us pause.

Hamlet pauses. In a moment he arrives at the image of bloody suicide "When he himself might his quietus make with a bare bodkin." However, there is that one troubling reason to stay his hand:

> the dread of something after death,
> the undiscover'd country from whose bourn
> No traveller returns, puzzles the will
> And makes us rather bear those ills we have
> Than fly to others that we know not of.

Every day there are people who confront their own "to be or not to be" dilemmas. Each person, each dilemma is unique. Nevertheless, all involve assumptions about life, death, and afterlife. Perhaps we can be wiser companions in these situations if we have explored our own undiscovered countries deeply enough to offer them a life-giving pause.

SUMMARY

Most people in most societies throughout the centuries have believed in some form of survival. Several of these belief systems were described. Only since the rise of science and technology have there been substantial widespread doubt and question. Much of this chapter, therefore, was concerned with evidence. You were asked to put your own ideas and beliefs on the line in a self-quiz. We then examined NDEs in detail because these reports have often been taken as proof of survival. The basic NDE was described (summarized in Box 14-2), and we noted that many who have had this kind of experience also reported that their lives had changed—for the better—as a result. The NDE material offered as proof of survival was reviewed and critiqued. We also considered several theories that attempt to explain the NDE. These included the spiritual/survival explanation and also alternatives that interpret the NDE as (a) a split-off psychological reaction to stress; (b) a quieting, energy-conserving function when we can do nothing to extricate ourselves from a life-threatening situation; (c) a hallucination produced by psychophysiological changes; (d) an exercise in religious imagination; (e) a healing and illuminating metaphor; and, recently, (f) a stress response that parallels the G-LOC experience of pilots subjected to extreme acceleration pressure. Next, we examined another source of possible evidence for survival: the dead themselves, or their spirit representatives. This discussion included deathbed escorts or visions, guardian angels, contacts made through mediums and channelers, and my personal favorite, ghosts. The tragic consequences of belief in the reality and power of ghosts were illustrated by the Ghost Dance through which some Native American peoples hoped to invoke the protection of their ancestors and raise them from the dead but instead exposed themselves to massacre. Reincarnation, although usually associated with Asian and African belief systems, has gained a large following in the United States and other Western nations in recent years. Ian Stevenson's careful and prolific research into "evidence suggestive of reincarnation" was the center of our attention. Before concluding, we considered the question, *should* we survive death? This was followed by perhaps an even more unsettling question: What kind of survival? After considering several traditional concepts of how we survive death, attention was given to symbolic immortality, cloning, and becoming a kind of "smart chip" that enters into the cosmic matrix. We then reviewed your thoughts on the survival question and took note of the subtle but significant links between survival beliefs and suicide.

REFERENCES

Alitzer, T. J. (1967). *Toward a new Christian reading of the death of God.* New York: Harcourt.

Atwater, P. M. H. (1992). Is there a Hell? Surprising observations about the near-death experience. *Journal of Near-Death Studies, 10,* 149–160.

Barret, W. (1986). *Death-bed visions.* Northampton: Aquarian. (Original work published 1926)

Bernstein, W. (1965). *The search for Bridey Murphy.* Garden City, NY: Doubleday.

Bonney, R. (2002). Buddhism. In R. Kastenbaum (Ed.), *Macmillan encyclopedia of death and dying* (Vol. 1, pp. 74–80). New York: Macmillan.

Crowe, D. M. (1996). *A history of the Gypsies of Eastern Europe and Russia.* New York: St. Martin's/Griffin.

Dennett, D. C. (1991). *Consciousness explained.* Boston: Little, Brown.

Elias, P. (April 8, 2003). Birth of cloned endangered cattle praised. Channels.netscape.com/ns/news/story.jsp?floc =FF-APO&idq=ff/story/0001%2F20030408.

Freed, R. S., & Freed, S. A. (1993). *Ghosts: Life and death in North India* (Anthropological Papers, No 72). New York: American Museum of Natural History.

Gabbard, G. O., & Twemlow, S. W. (1984). *With the eyes of the mind.* New York: Praeger.

Gabbard, G. O., & Twemlow, S. W. (1991). Do "near-death experiences" occur only near-death? *Journal of Near-Death Studies, 10,* 41–48.

Gallup Poll Survey No. GO 129321. (1999, December). CNN/*USA Today.*

Geering, L. G. (2002). *Christianity without God.* Santa Rosa, CA: Polebridge.

Gibson, W. (1986). *Neuromancer.* New York: Ace Books.

Greeley, A. M., & Hout, M. (1999). Belief in life after death increasing in the United States. *American Sociological Review, 64,* 813–836.

Green, C., & McCreery, C. (1989). *Apparitions.* Oxford, UK: Institute of Psychophysical Research.

Greyson, B. (1992/1993). Near-death experiences and anti-suicidal attitudes. *Omega, Journal of Death & Dying, 26,* 81–90.

Gurdon, J. B. (2001). The birth of cloning. In M. Ruse & A. Sheppard (Eds.), *Cloning* (pp. 39–48). Amherst, NY: Prometheus.

Hanson, H. Y. (2002). Islam. In R. Kastenbaum (ed.), *Macmillan encyclopedia of death and dying* (Vol. 1, pp. 484–489). New York: Macmillan.

Hayslip, B., & Peverto, C. (in press). *Historical shifts in attitudes toward death, dying, and bereavement.* Amityville, NY: Baywood.

Hittman, M. (1990). *Wovoka and the ghost dance.* Lincoln: University of Nebraska Press.

Hocking, W. E. (1957). *The meaning of immortality in human experience.* New York: Harper.

Irwin, H. J., & Bramwell, A. B. (1988). The devil in heaven: A near-death experience with both positive and negative facets. *Journal of Near-Death Experiences, 7,* 38–43.

Josyln, C., Turchin, V., & Heylighen, F. (1997). *Cyberbetic immortality.* Principia Cybernetica Web: www.pespmc1.vub.ac.be/CYBIMM.html.

Kalish, R. A., & Reynolds, D. K. (1976). *Death and ethnicity. A psychocultural study.* Los Angeles: University of Southern California Press.

Kastenbaum, R. (1993a). Psychopomp. In R. Kastenbaum & B. K. Kastenbaum (Eds.), *The encyclopedia of death* (p. 211). New York: Avon.

Kastenbaum, R. (1993b). Reconstructing death in postmodern society. *Omega, Journal of Death and Dying, 27,* 75–90.

Kastenbaum, R. (1993c). Ian Stevenson: An *Omega* interview. *Omega, Journal of Death and Dying, 28,* 165–182.

Kastenbaum, R. (1995a). Raymond A. Moody, Jr.: An *Omega* interview. *Omega, Journal of Death and Dying, 31,* 87–98.

Kastenbaum, R. (1995b). *Is there life after death?* London: Prion.

Kastenbaum, R. (1996). Near-death reports: Evidence for survival of death? In L. W. Bailey & J. Yates (Eds.), *The near-death experience reader* (pp. 245–264). New York: Routledge.

Kastenbaum, R. (1998a). Near death reports. Evidence for survival of death? In L. W. Bailey & J. Yates (Eds.), *The near-death experience reader* (pp. 245–264). New York: Routledge.

Kastenbaum, R. (1998b). Temporarily dead. *Readings, 13,* 16–21.

Kearl, M. C. (2002). Immortality, symbolic. In R. Kastenbaum (Ed.), *Macmillan encyclopedia of death and dying* (Vol. 2, pp. 461–464). New York: Macmillan.

Kellehear, A. (1996). *Experiences near death.* New York: Oxford University Press.

Kelly, E. W., Greyson, B., & Stevenson, I. (1999/2000). Can experiences near death furnish evidence of life after death? *Omega, Journal of Death and Dying.*

Kramer, K. (1988). *The sacred art of dying.* Mahwah, NY: Paulist Press.

Lester, D., Aldridge, M., Aspenberg, C., Boyle, K., Radsniak, P., & Waldron, C. (2001/2002). What is the afterlife like? Undergraduate beliefs about the afterlife. *Omega, Journal of Death and Dying, 44,* 113–126.

Leviton, D. (1991). *Horrendous death, health, and well-being.* New York: Hemisphere.

Lifton, R. J. (1979). *The broken connection. On death and the continuity of life.* New York: Simon & Schuster.

Lommel, P. V., Wees, R. V., Meyers, V., & Elfferich, I. (2001). Near-death experience in survivors of cardiac arrest: A prospective study in the Netherlands. *Lancet, 358,* 2039–2045.

Lucretius (Titus Lucretius Carus). *On the nature of things.* (Original work 54 B.C.)

McDannel, C., & Lang, B. (1988). *Heaven. A history.* New Haven, CT: Yale University Press.

McGee, G. (Ed.). (2002). *The human cloning debate.* Berkeley, CA: Berkeley Hills Books.

Marwit, S. J., & Lessor, C. (2000). Role of deceased mentors in the ongoing lives of proteges. *Omega, Journal of Death and Dying, 41,* 125–138.

Maienschein, J. (2003). *Whose view of life?* Cambridge: Harvard University Press.

Moody, R. A., Jr. (1975). *Life after life.* Atlanta: Mockingbird.

Mooney, J. (1996). *The ghost dance.* North Dighton, MA: JG Press.

Morin, R. (2000, April 24). Do Americans believe in God? www.washingtonpost.com/wp-srv/politics/polls/wat/archive.

Myers, F. W. H. (1975). *Human personality and its survival of bodily death.* New York: Arno. (Original work published 1903)

Nietzsche, F. W. (1975). *Also sprach Zarathustra.* New York: Modern Library. (Original work published 1885)

Noyes, R., Jr. (1979). Near-death experiences: Their interpretation. In R. Kastenbaum (Ed.), *Between life and death* (pp. 73–88). New York: Springer.

Osis, K. (1961). *Deathbed observations by physicians and nurses.* New York: Parapsychology Foundation.

Osis, K., & Haraldsson, E. (1977). *At the hour of death.* New York: Avon.

Parnia, S., & Fenwick, P. (2002). Near death experiences in cardiac arrest: Visions of a dying brain or visions of a new science of consciousness. *Resuscitation, 52,* 5–11.

Parnia, S., Waller, D. G., Yeates, R., & Fenwick, P. (2001). A qualitative and quantitative study of the incidence, features, and aetiology of near death experiences in cardiac arrest survivors. *Resuscitation, 48,* 149–156.

Pinkner, S. (1997). *How the mind works.* New York: Norton

Reuters. (2002). *Man shot dead over heaven and hell argument.* www.channels.Netscape.com/ns/news/ns/story.

Ring, K. (1980). *Life at death.* New York: Coward, McCann & Geoghegan.

Ring, K. (1989). Near-death experiences. In R. Kastenbaum & B. K. Kastenbaum (Eds.), *The encyclopedia of death* (pp. 193–196), Phoenix: Oryx Press.

Ring, K. (1992). *The Omega Project.* New York: Morrow.

Ruse, M., & Sheppard, A. (Eds.). (2001). *Cloning.* Amherst, NY: Prometheus.

Sabom, M. B. (1982). *Recollections of death.* New York: Simon & Schuster.

Schmitt, J.-C. (1998). *Ghosts in the Middle Ages.* Chicago: University of Chicago Press.

Siegel, R. K. (1980). The psychology of life after death. *American Psychologist, 35,* 911–931.

Siegel, R. K. (1992). *Fire in the brain.* New York: Dutton.

Slawinski, J. (1987). Electrometic radiation and the afterlife. *Journal of Near-Death Studies, 6,* 79–94.

Stengel, N. (1991). Mind is a leaking rainbow. In M. Benedict (Ed.), *Cyberspace: First steps* (pp. 55–68). Cambridge, MA: MIT Press

Stevenson, I. (1974). *Twenty cases suggestive of reincarnation* (Rev. ed.). Charlottesville: University Press of Virginia.

Stevenson, I. (1997a). *Reincarnation and biology. A contribution to the etiology of birthmarks and birth defects.* Westport, CT: Praeger.

Stevenson, I. (1997b). *Where reincarnation and biology intersect.* Westport, CT: Praeger.

Stevenson, I., Cook, C. W., & McClean-Rice, N. (1989/1990). Are persons reporting "near-death experiences" really near death? A study of medical records. *Omega, Journal of Death and Dying, 20,* 45–54.

Tart, C. (1990). Who survives? Implications of modern consciousness research. In G. Doore (Ed.), *What survives?* (pp. 138–152). Los Angeles: Tarchers.

Wallis, J. (2001). Continuing bonds: Relationships between the living and the dead within contemporary spiritualism. *Mortalty, 6,* 127–145.

Washburn, K., & Majors, J. S. (1998). *World poetry: An anthology of verses from antiquity to our time.* New York: W. W. Norton.

Wertheim, M. (1999). *The pearly gates of cyberspace.* New York: Norton.

Westwood, J. (2002). Gilgamesh. In R. Kastenbaum (Ed). *Macmillan encyclopedia of death and dying* (Vol. 1, pp. 331–334). New York: Macmillan.

Whinnery, J. E. (1997). Psychophysiologic correlates of unconsciousness and near-death experiences. *Journal of Near-Death Studies, 15,* 231–258.

Wildlife park to add mammoth attraction (2002, August 21). www.cnn.com/2002/TECH/08/21/clone.mammth/index.html.

Wilmut, I., Schnieke, A. E., McWhir, A., Kind, A. F., & Campbell, K. H. S. (2001). Viable offspring derived from fetal and adult mammalian cells. In M. Ruse & A. Sheppard (Eds), *Cloning* (pp. 31–38). New York: Prometheus Books.

Wilson, M. (1996). *A study of enabling metaphors in near-death experience reports.* Unpublished masters thesis, Arizona State University, Tempe.

Zaleski, C. (1987). *Otherworld journeys.* New York: Oxford University Press.

GLOSSARY

Autoscopic Experience: Perceiving one's own body as though from above, a facet of the out-of-the body experience.

Channeler: A person with the reputed power to communicate with the past lives of oneself or others.

Depersonalization: A sense of emotional distance from one's own body and self.

Endorphins: The most thoroughly studied of a class of substances produced by the brain with effects on mood and awareness.

G-LOC: An altered state of consciousness with many similarities to near-death experiences but produced by the stress of extreme acceleration in fighter planes or ground simulations.

Holographic memory: A vivid mental state in which one does not simply recall but actually seems to be experiencing past situations.

Hyperalertness: A state of heightened attention, usually to danger signals.

Immortality: The persistence of spirit, soul, or personality after death. Not all afterlife beliefs hold that people survive death on a permanent basis; therefore, not all survival has immortal status.

Medium: A person with the reputed power of receiving messages from the dead.

Metaphor: Something that represents something else. The *enabling metaphor* represents a large and complex set of events or experiences.

Near-Death Experience (NDE): Images, perceptions, and feelings that are recalled by some people after a life-threatening episode. The near-death experience report (NDER) is the account of such experiences as shared with others.

Psychometric-Type Measures: Questionnaires and tests whose responses can be quantified.

Reincarnation: The return of the spirit or soul in another physical form after death.

Rosetta Stone: An ancient tablet whose inscription, when decoded, made it possible to understand a forgotten language.

Seance: Literally, a sitting; the name given to sessions with a medium.

Yahweh: A name given to God in the Old Testament.

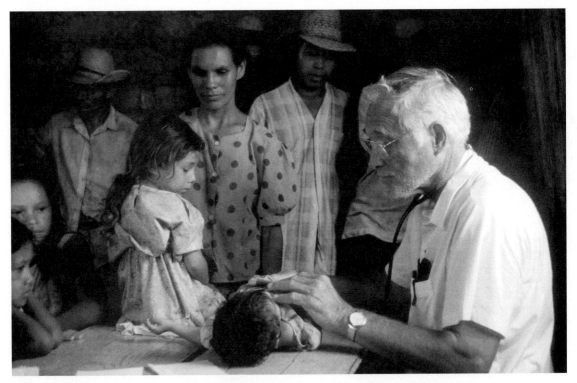

Doctors Without Borders provides life-enhancing and life-saving care in third world nations. The spirit and achievements of this nonprofit organization were honored with a Nobel Prize in 1992.

chapter *15*

HOW CAN WE HELP?

The Promise of Death Education and Counseling

I picked him up, ran out here, and laid him on the counter and called 911. And of course screamed hysterically into the phone. "Help me!" And they said they called the paramedics and they were on the way, and they want you to do CPR. And I had been trained in CPR [crying]. I probably didn't do it the way I should have. I'm sure I didn't. They did stay on the line with me. I think a woman answered first, and I think they put a man on the phone. He kind of talked me through the CPR.
—Gail (as quoted in Rosenblatt, 2000, p. 34)

In the weeks that followed Josh's [19-month old] sudden death, Toby [2½ years old] began to imitate all Joshua's mannerisms, including his baby talk. It was as though, in a desperate attempt to make everything better for the grown-ups, he had decided to "be" his dead brother, a notion I find particularly heart-wrenching.
—R. W. Weinbach (as quoted in Iserson, 1999, p. 136)

With little peeks over his shoulder as his mother was rolled out the door, Tristen told me when he becomes president, he's going to make a law that no one's mother will have to be carried out in a plastic bag. I told him it was a good law to make.
—Laura R. Smith (1996, p. 16)

Before he got sick, the most physical contact we would have was a warm handshake. A real blessing during that last month in the hospital was that we both felt more free to display affection…I would kiss him on the forehead. I massaged his feet with lotion. I could tell he liked it. So did I.
—A man reflecting on caring for his dying father (as quoted in Chethik, 2001, p. 113)

The fellow sitting across the dining room table thumbed casually through one of his company's forms, offered my wife a companionable little smile, then dropped his voice into a lower register. "You're such nice people and you have such a nice home," he volunteered. "But what if something should happen to Robert?" Robert, being me, dropped into his (my) lower register and whispered, "But what could possibly 'happen' to me?" Several changes of expression competed on the insurance agent's face, until he gave up his act and joined in the fun: "You're right, Robert, what the hell could happen to you—or any of us?" Something about that statement troubled the dog, though, so Angel moved to our side with that protective look on her face.
—The author's home, not so long ago.

On a medical floor, with perhaps two thirds of the patients suffering eventually fatal diseases, I say to a nurse, "What's happening?" and she replies, walking on down the hall, "Same ol' same ol.'" Nothing new, nothing exciting. On an Intensive Care Unit in the same hospital, "What's going on?" The resident replies, with a little shrug of her shoulders, "People are living, people are dying." Again, no surprises, nothing new. The routine goes on.
—Daniel F. Chambliss (1996, p. 119)

Prayer, I guess, is my way of "checking in" with God whenever I feel the need or desire to do so.
—A hospice volunteer (as quoted in Schneider & Kastenbaum, 1993, p. 477)

At a funeral, an older person who seems stoic and is not showing a lot of grief may be feeling grief much more deeply than younger persons.
—Donald Powell (as quoted in Goldberg, 2002, p. 18)

Loss and grief enter almost every person's life. The challenge of coping with life-threatening and terminal illness is also experienced by almost every person. We can benefit from honest, sensitive, and effective help when our turn comes. In the meantime, we can provide care and comfort to others who are trying to cope with death-related stress. Many people have demonstrated that it is possible to help each other through those difficult times. There are now certified grief counselors as well as teachers, nurses, social workers, and other service providers who have developed skills in comforting and guiding people who are attempting to cope with dying, death, and loss. However, many of us can be helpful even though we may not have a professional level of education and experience, as this chapter will show.

Life-or-death emergencies can occur any time, any place. In recent years, the nation has developed a system of quick response by emergency medical technicians, paramedics, and other specialists. Technology plays a significant role, but effective human communication is still a key factor ("They did stay on the line with me"). It is not unusual for students in a death education class to become professionals or volunteers in the emergency response system, but we can also be helpful by supporting community efforts to sustain and expand these services.

The parents of young Toby and even younger Josh recognized that the surviving child's reversion to baby talk was a meaningful and intentional action. Somebody else might have dismissed Toby's behavior as silly and not have connected it with Josh's death or may even have punished the boy for being so childish. Fortunately, Toby's parents took a different approach (Iserson, 1999):

> It was very important then to let Toby know that we loved him for being himself, and that he did not have to "become" Josh to gain our approval. So we never admonished him for taking the role of Josh, but we did remind him often that we loved him very much. (p. 136)

It was a certified death educator and counselor in Oregon who helped 10-year-old Tristen and his 8-year-old brother Clayton through the end phase of their young mother's terminal illness. During their sixth visit together in the hospital room, she started to discuss with the brothers the various times in people's lives when they have to say good-bye to places, things, and each other (Smith, 1996):

> Tristen crawled up right in front of me and looked me in the eyes. "In case you didn't notice. I don't want to talk about this." His look was steady. I was so proud of him for speaking up. "Thank you, Tristen. I'm really glad you told me and I respect your need not to talk about this right now." I patted his shoulder and we went on to play with something else. (pp. 13–14)

"I cried all the way home and into the night," Smith reports, but she also felt the sense of love that the dying woman, her fiancee, and her children had shared with each other. She knew the road ahead for the children, though very difficult, had been made that much easier by loving memories.

It was not a death educator but an adult son who spent many hours by his father's bedside as the older man died of kidney failure. The son experienced a sense of closeness and closure. Journalist Neil Chethik (2001) interviewed men to learn how they dealt with the deaths of their fathers. In general, he found that sons who spent time caring for the fathers before the death or talking with them directly about the death reported that such actions helped them in their grieving process afterward. Communication and sharing did much both to comfort the dying fathers and to help the sons go on with their lives.

Communication often sounds a false note, however, when the subject of death is touched during conversation, even if it is a conversation about life insurance. The insurance agent was hesitant to speak openly about that "something" that just possibly might "happen." An otherwise frank and open person, he fiddled with his words out of apprehension that clients might fall apart when reminded of their mortality. It is not only the insurance agent who is often in this fix. Many of us have difficulty in broaching or responding to the subject of death because we fear that other people will not be able to handle it. In my experience, the "other people" usually believe that they can handle it, but they have doubts about us!

The implicit rules that govern the communications and behaviors of health care personnel are intended to protect them from emotional wounds. The transition from life to death is transformed from the momentous and mysterious to the ordinary (Chambliss, 1996). Not just the individual nurse or physician but also the entire system of beliefs and procedures reduce the humanity of the dying person to the routine—unless there happens to be something special and exciting about the case. The doctors and nurses may suffer greatly when this protective system breaks down or when a staff member has not been sufficiently socialized into the system.

In contrast, doctors, nurses, and community volunteers who choose to work with hospice programs are usually able to focus more on the whole person rather than just the terminal illness. They also usually have less need to protect themselves

Hospice volunteers report that they draw personal strength from prayer, though they do not impose their own religious beliefs and practices on patients and families.

from the impact of dying and death. Their work does not become a "failure" when the person dies, nor do their own death anxieties explode. We (Kastenbaum & Schneider, 1991; Schneider & Kastenbaum, 1993) found that most hospice staff and volunteers call on personal prayer—a communication just between themselves and God—to give them the strength to go on. One volunteer was speaking for many others when she told us, "I feel it is a privilege to be with a person at this vulnerable and sacred time of their lives." No respondents described themselves as discovering prayer or becoming religious as a result of their experiences with dying persons: It was the other way around. People who had already found prayer to be a source of strength continued to call on this source as they encountered the challenges of hospice work. They did not ask for divine intervention or miracles in their prayers, nor did they impose these prayers on patients and families. Praying was a way of staying in touch with themselves and their deepest beliefs.

We have other alternatives. These include trivialization and avoidance of the dying person, crippling episodes of personal anxiety, or integrating dying, death, and grief into the fabric of our lives. Understanding and developing positive alternatives to avoidance and anxiety is one of the prime challenges faced by death educators and counselors.

We often rely on beliefs, habits, and that popular buzz term "gut reactions" when trying to cope with stressful situations. Facts are important, too, though. There are many streams of research that bear on dying, death, and grief. Responsible death educators continually educate themselves to take account of new findings. Powell's (2002) study is one example worth nothing. He measured the responses of young, middle-aged, and older adults to a series of slides with emotional content. He learned that the older respondents actually reported more intense emotional responses than the younger ones, even though they did not show as much obvious emotionality. As educators, counselors, friends, or family members, we might find it useful to question the common assumption that elderly people have less intense feelings.

DEATH EDUCATORS AND COUNSELORS: THE "BORDER PATROL"

Most people who serve as death educators and counselors draw on personal experiences as well as academic and professional education. Most realize that the boundary between the land of the living and the land of the dead is as subtle as the next breath we take.

Some people still have difficulty understanding how death can be studied or taught. Others are fearful that strangers under the guise of educators and counselors might invade the sanctity of their innermost beliefs. Questions may also be raised by researchers, educators, and counselors in other fields. Is there a solid basis for this field, or does death education purvey only untested assumptions and fancies? What do people derive from death education and counseling? What *should* people derive?

We begin our exploration with a brief historical introduction, then examine the current scene in death education and counseling, and conclude with some observations about future prospects and challenges.

DEATH EDUCATION IN HISTORICAL PERSPECTIVE

The term "death education" and the field to which it refers did not become a recognizable part of our society until the 1960s, as noted in Chapter 4. In the broader sense, however, we have never been without some form of instruction and guidance.

From Ancient Times

Ancient documents from Tibet and dynastic Egypt offer detailed accounts of what becomes of the soul after death and what preparations can be made ahead of time to improve chances for a safe passage. These documents have become known in the Western world as "books of the dead." Their emphasis is heavily weighted toward funeral and memorial practices and the fate of the soul after death. For example, it helps if one knows the names of the underworld demons and deities and the challenges they will put to the spirits of the deceased. It is crucial to be well prepared. In dynastic Egypt, 42 gods sit in judgment as the newly dead person confesses a lifetime's worth of faults and misdeeds. One's soul is then measured against a feather: Paradise is ahead if the scale balances perfectly. What happens if the soul fails to pass this test is something we really would not want to know. Ancient death education often focused on how one should prepare for the ordeal of judgment after taking that last breath.

In contrast, much of contemporary death education focuses on people attempting to cope with death in the midst of life (e.g., the hospice nurse, the grieving family member, and the individual who has just learned that he or she has a life-threatening disease). It might seem odd to us that some cultures would emphasize education for the dead and the mourners. The ancient Egyptian or Tibetan, however, might also have difficulty with our approach. For example, the layered mass of regulations for hospice care eligibility and reimbursement could appear as formidable as the priestly instruction for how to behave in the underworld.

Through the centuries, many religious leaders, philosophers, and creative artists have offered a variety of images and ideas about our relationship to death. One of the most basic and common themes has been the fleeting nature of life. Job (13:12) laments, "Man that is born of a woman is of few days, and full of trouble. He cometh forth like a flower, and is cut down: He fleeth also as a shadow, and continueth not." The *Old Testament* repeatedly compares human life with the grass that withers and is blown away by the whirlwind. The evanescence of life is linked with the limits of human knowledge and power. Do we suppose ourselves to be lordly beings? Proverbs (27:1) quickly deflates us: "Boast not thyself of tomorrow; for thou knowest not what a day may bring forth." If we cannot even be sure of having a tomorrow, how can we claim knowledge and power?

It is not only the Judeo-Christian tradition that has attempted to bring awareness of our mortality to the fore. The collection of stories known as *The Arabian Nights* is best known for its celebration of sensuality. However, death is also given eloquent attention. The following passage demonstrates how awareness of our mortality might provide the basis for a mature philosophy of life (Mathers, 1974):

> O sons of men,
> Turn quickly and you will see death
> Behind your shoulder.
> Adam saw him,
> Nimrod saw him
> Who wound his horn in the forest,
> The masters of Persia saw him.
> Alexander, who wrestled with the world
> And threw the world,
> Turned quickly and saw death
> Behind his shoulder....
> O sons of men,
> When you give yourselves to the sweet trap of life
> Leave one limb free for God.
> The fear of death is the beginning of wisdom
> And the fair things you do
> Shall blow and smell like flowers
> On the red and fiery day. (pp. 300–301)

Both the *Old Testament* and *The Arabian Nights* emphasize the brevity of life and the possibility of sudden death at any time. It would be foolish to allow ourselves to be carried away by our own triumphs and ambitions. Both documents con-trast the power of God with the powerlessness of the mortal person, but not with the same emotional tone. The troubled, fleeting shadow portrayed in the *Old Testament* finds neither pleasure nor solace. In contrast, the readers of Scheherazade's tales of one thousand and one nights are expected to give themselves to "the sweet trap of life." What are we to do, then? Should we spend our lives lamenting and "eating worms" before the worms eat us? Or should we enjoy the sweet trap while we can, knowing full well that our pleasures and triumphs will not endure because *we* will not endure?

It is worth keeping this divergence in mind. Death education and counseling today carry forward the awareness that death is a central fact of life. Once we have the basic facts in mind, however, we still have a choice of what attitudes we will take toward these facts and what lessons we intend to draw from them. At one extreme, we might crawl into a box and wait for the end; at the other, we might attempt to live in a feverish quest for thrills. Perhaps "the fear of death is the beginning of wisdom," but it is only the beginning. We still have the challenge of developing a coherent and meaningful life based on our awareness that "all flesh is as grass."

The *New Testament* introduced a radically different perspective: "Whoso eateth my flesh, and drinketh my blood, hath eternal life; and I will raise him up at the last day" (John 6:54). "And this is the promise that he hath promised us, even eternal life" (John 3:15). "And the sea gave up the dead which were in it; and death and hell delivered up the dead which were in them: and they were judged every man according to their works. And death and hell were cast into the lake of fire" (Revelation 20:13–14).

In centuries to come, Christians would differ among themselves on many death-related issues (e.g., is it faith, good works, or predestination that will ensure the triumph over death?). From the start, however, it was clear that at the core of Christianity was its bold contention that man had been redeemed from death through Jesus.

The Christian "death education lesson" differed markedly from those of the *Old Testament* and the *Arabian Nights*. We do not have to go through life in sorrow and lament, nor surrender to the "sweet trap" with the bittersweet knowledge that it will soon snap shut on us. Instead, we should feel joyful about the life to come after this brief and unsatisfactory sojourn on Earth is completed. This rousing lesson did not escape change through time, however. As the Christian faith grew larger and its membership became more diverse, other themes became increasingly significant. Three related themes remain influential today, although all have been challenged within as well as outside of the Christian orbit:

1. Death is punishment for all humans because of Adam and Eve's disobedience in seeking forbidden knowledge (original sin doctrine).
2. Death is a test that will separate the worthy from the unworthy—the final exam of all final exams.
3. Life on Earth is just something we must endure; its pleasures are insubstantial, if not deceptive. Death, therefore, is a blessed release.

Not all Christians subscribe to these views. However, they have the cumulative weight of centuries behind them and are still influential today. Death educators and counselors are usually well aware of this powerful and complex heritage. For example, the fact that the Christian tradition includes images of death both as punishment and as blessing should alert us to the many possible implications. "I am eager to fulfill myself through death" can be a compelling wish that competes with the equally compelling fear, "What if I am judged to have lived a sinful and unworthy life?" Consider another example: A born-again minister paid an unexpected visit to a woman hospitalized with a terminal illness. He burst into her room with these words: "God knows what a sinner you are! Prepare yourself for the moment of judgment!" The astonished woman quietly replied, "God and I have never given each other any trouble." Undeterred, he made repeated attempts to bully the exhausted woman into confessing her sins and placing her life into his hands. Upon learning of this incident, the official hospital chaplain was even more distressed than the woman who had fallen victim to this brutal "educational" or "counseling" intervention. Unfortunately, there is a potential for harming people at vulnerable points in their lives by attempting to impose one's own beliefs on them. Responsible death educators and counselors hold a variety of religious beliefs, but they are also aware and respectful of the traditions that influence their students and clients.

Nevertheless, traditional ways of communicating about death might not always be effective in the 21st century. These traditions developed in societies that differed from ours in many ways. In medieval times, for example, most people lived in small, agrarian communities. They had little education and little contact with people outside their own circle. The concepts of having "inalienable" human rights, holding one's own political and religious opinions, and being free to pursue unlimited personal interests and ambitions were unknown. People lived in low-technology societies that were fairly stable from generation to generation and that offered little protection against the forces of nature and the disasters encountered in everyday life. When darkness fell at night, few would venture out of doors where both real and fantasy terrors lurked. Little faith could be placed in the wrong-headed "medical" treatments of the time that frequently caused as much suffering as the diseases themselves. Many newborn babies failed to survive into adulthood. Infections associated with childbirth, wounds, and injuries often proved fatal to adults, and epidemics periodically decimated the population.

Some of the most vivid and forceful traditions reached their peak and faded away before our own era. The dance of death, for example, was a compelling image that was introduced by poets, artists, and performers in the 13th century, if not earlier. The living and the dead are portrayed as engaging in a slow and solemn dance together. The *danse macabre* theme often depicted Death as a skeletal figure who laid claim to all mortal souls, whether low or high born (Kastenbaum, 2002). "We all look the same to Death: kings, bishops or peasants, we are all mortal beings" was part of the core message. A powerful message this was—bearing in mind that society was highly stratified at the time, with a few "high and mighty" people lording over the masses. The zing of this message gradually decreased as the ruling classes became destabilized by social and technological changes that continue into our own time. Emphasis also shifted from contemplations of death to preventing and treating life-threatening disorders.

Death was often personified in medieval writings and illustrations. In this 15th-century invocation of the danse macabre, a pair of skeletal personifications of death are gentle in their approach to a monk and a nun.

Another significant tradition arose in the 15th century: Christian guidebooks for priests and others who might be in the position to help people in their last days and hours of life. This has become known to historians as the *Ars moriendi* tradition—literally, the art of dying well. These guidebooks differ in many ways from the writings on dying and death that have appeared in our own time. For example, most of the guidebooks limited themselves to describing rituals that should be performed as part of the deathbed scene. The themes of death as punishment and as a test of the soul's worthiness were often dominant. People were never more at risk than at the moment of death. The priest tried to help the dying person resist the assaults and temptations of the demons who hoped to consign the soul to the flames of

hell. As discussed later, there might be a subtle link between the priestly soul-saver and at least one image of the modern death educator/counselor.

Despite these differences, the *Ars moriendi* guidebooks were motivated by some of the same beliefs and concerns that have reappeared in our own death awareness movement. These include (a) the view that *how* a person dies is a significant matter; therefore, (b) some deaths are better than others; so (c) a "good death" is a real achievement and flows more readily from a life that has been lived in the recognition of mortality, with the support of caring people who have also prepared themselves properly for the encounter with death.

The capstone of the *Ars moriendi* tradition was reached in 1651 with the publication of Jeremy

Taylor's *Rules and Exercises of Holy Dying* (1651/ 1977). Reverend Taylor recommended that we all give ourselves a daily "refresher course" on life and death. Today, we might describe this kind of exercise as a life review. Taylor, however, would not have us wait until we are well up in years and reluctantly aware that this final act of life is not long in coming:

> For, if we make but one general account, and never reckon till we die…we shall only reckon by great sums, and remember nothing but clamorous and crying sins, and never consider concerning particulars, or forget very many.… But if we observe all the little passages of our life…see every day sins increase so fast, and virtues grow up so slow…we may see our evil and amend it.… *As therefore every night we must make our bed the memorial of our grave, so let our evening thoughts be an image of the day of judgment.* (pp. 48–49)

Death education and counseling had to begin anew after centuries of avoidance. What is the nature of death education and counseling today? We begin with death education.

DEATH EDUCATION AND COUNSELING: THE CURRENT SCENE

We can gain a quick view of the changed scene by becoming familiar with an organization known as the Association for Death Education and Counseling (ADEC). This nonprofit organization was incorporated in 1976 with the purpose of improving the quality of death education and death-related counseling (Wass, 2002). In pursuing these goals, ADEC introduced national training workshops and certification procedures for death educators and counselors. If you attend one of ADEC's national conferences you will probably be impressed with the combination of maturity and receptivity to new knowledge. What you will not see is the person who has read one book and attended one workshop and is ready to impose his or her ignorance on the world. The "pop death" people have pretty much come and gone.

Fortunately, the most valuable elements of the early death awareness movement have continued to flourish. The typical participant is a person who is well aware of his or her own death-related feelings and who has had direct experience in one or more areas of real-life concern (e.g., supporting families after the death of a child, counseling people who have tested positive for the AIDS virus, and training hospice volunteers). You will probably find this person to be compassionate, realistic, welcoming of newcomers, and blessed with a resilient sense of humor. For weird people who are committed to bizarre projects, we will have to look elsewhere.

Some people may still put themselves forward as death educators or counselors without possessing either the personal or the experiential qualifications. The minister who burst into the dying woman's hospital room was motivated by his personal gender, not by the expressed needs of a person he had never met. The teacher who does not even know the existence of scholarly and professional journals such as *Omega, Death Studies, Illness, Crisis and Loss,* and *Mortality* will be lecturing from assumptions and limited personal observations that are often at variance with the facts. (See Appendix for useful journal, book, and organizational sources.) There are still places where unqualified people can function in the role of death educators or counselors, but with increasing professional and public sophistication these opportunities are diminishing. Every year, more educators and counselors qualify themselves for certification by ADEC.

People come to this topic with a variety of needs and expectations. Students in my classes, for example, often enroll with the purpose of adding to their competencies as nurses, paramedics, social workers, counselors, or psychologists. Others have had personal experiences, such as the death of a parent or the serious illness of a spouse, that give the topic special urgency. Still others are keenly interested in working with the dying or the bereaved; others have become curious about some particular facet of death (e.g., funerals or the near-death experience). All these expectations can be addressed in a death education course, but it is difficult to give them all equal attention. Although the classroom situation is flexible enough to permit a mix of thought and feeling, structure and openness, it may not be able to meet all the students' needs.

Clinical skills are probably developed best in clinical situations. Classroom examples can be helpful, but case experience and supervision are also needed. "Deep learning"—an experience that is emotional as well as intellectual—can be achieved at times in the classroom, but this more often requires a series of in-depth and intimate discussions that are not always possible within academic constraints. It is useful for all participants to recognize what can and should be accomplished in a particular course, conference, or workshop and what must be achieved in other settings.

Richard Kalish (1980/1981) observes that the death educator came along at a time when two of society's most important traditional roles had undergone significant change. According to Kalish's analysis, the priest was once the dominant person who mediated our relationship to death. ("Priest" is used here in the generic sense.) The physician has gained increasing importance, however, as society shifted its orientation from hopes of a better life after death to a longer and healthier life on Earth. The death educator entered the scene when society was no longer as enthusiastic about accepting an afterlife as substitute for a long and fulfilling life on Earth, but also at a time when society had judged that the physician did not have the "magic" either. This situation led Kalish to portray death educators as "deacons who will never become priests." The priest and the physician both possess a kind of vested power and authority not shared by the death educator (who may, however, also *be* a priest or physician). Death educators or "deacons" can come into conflicts with priests and physicians by venturing into their turfs in ways that are considered unwelcome or competitive. Death educators can also seem to be promising too much and thereby set themselves up for failure: "Death educators and counselors are treading sacred ground, and must be expected to be attacked for their errors, their vanities, any signs of greed or lust or need of power" (p. 83).

Kalish's point that death educators and counselors must be aware of their role relationships with other professionals is well taken, as is the caution that they should refrain from creating unrealistic expectations on the part of students or clients. Furthermore, skill in teaching or learning about death does not fully equip a person for therapeutic interventions outside the classroom.

Social pressures may also encourage the death educator to deliver a "comforting product rather than a searching encounter." The result of sugar-coated superficialities in the name of death education can be an *illusion of understanding and control.* Death is not just one more fact of life to be placed alongside another. However, once a course number has been assigned and all the academic niceties have been observed, there may be the unearned assumption that "we covered death today" (Kastenbaum, 1977).

Effective death educators come from a variety of established fields, such as psychology, psychiatry, medical ethics, nursing, sociology, and the ministry. It is valuable to have a solid grounding in one or more substantive fields as well as particular competency in death-related topics.

The Expanding Scope of Death Education

The scope of death education is gradually expanding to include a greater variety of people who are responsible for human services. For example, many colleges of nursing offer courses or modules in dealing with end-of-life issues (Ferrell, 1999), and a "Peaceful Death" initiative for nursing care has been established by the American Association of Colleges of Nursing (www.aacn.nche.edu/Publications/deathfin.htm). Medical schools still lag behind both in course offerings and in dying/death content in textbooks (Dickinson & Mermann, 1996). Many school districts have established procedures for crisis intervention, but there is still relatively little death education being offered in the entire range from prekindergarten through the 12th grade (Wass, Miller, & Thornton, 1990). Only approximately 1 school in 10 reported having any kind of death education program. The possibility of providing occasional death education at the "teachable moment" by discussing recent death-related events is seldom utilized. It is possible that many teachers do not feel secure in opening discussions on such emotion-laden topics as the death of a teacher or student. Survey results show that teachers are being offered very few opportunities to develop their own expertise in this area. Suicide prevention/intervention programs are no longer quite as rare, though, with approximately

1 in every 4 schools reporting some kind of effort in this area. Wass et al. suggest that "public attitudes toward death may not have changed as dramatically as we would like, and the 'death avoidance' previously observed by social scientists may still be prevalent today" (p. 262).

Durlak (1994) reviewed studies on the effects of death education and observed that

> not everyone is afraid of or uncomfortable with death, and thus not every participant should be expected to show reduced negative feelings about death after a death education program. Even if all participants are highly anxious about death, one particular program might work more effectively for some than others. (p. 256)

As Durlak (1994) also notes, death education programs are complex interventions that offer information, modeling, support, and persuasive communications. We should also expect their effects to be complex and to vary with the personality and experience of the students. It would be simplistic to maintain that death education courses have the basic function of reducing death anxiety. As we have seen (Chapter 1), there is little solid information available on what constitutes the "right" level of death anxiety. Furthermore, most people express only a moderate level of death anxiety most of the time, if the most commonly used assessment techniques are to be trusted. In addition, the term "death anxiety" is often used in a vague way. Precisely what are we trying to reduce? Furthermore, anxiety is a valuable signal; it tells us that something is disturbing our peace of mind. Perhaps we should respond to death anxiety as a clue and see where it leads us rather than moving swiftly to dull or displace the symptom. There will be circumstances in which the reduction of death anxiety could be an appropriate and perhaps even an urgent goal of educational efforts. However, I do not think it would be wise to conceive of death education primarily as an instrument for reducing death anxiety.

Death education is not a standardized product that can be prescribed and administered in precise dosages. It is a complex process that depends much on the interacting personalities of instructor and students and on much else as well, such as the scholarly and professional qualifications of all participants, the specific purpose of the course,

and the amount of time that can be devoted to this enterprise. Furthermore, a more intense situation arises when death suddenly intrudes into the lives of students or instructors. It is during these challenging times that we all learn a good deal more about ourselves and have the opportunity to put what we think we know and believe into practice.

COUNSELING AND THE COUNSELORS

Not everybody has the sense of personal security and confidence to provide services to terminally ill or grieving people. Some health care professionals continue to avoid human contact with dying people and their families as much as possible. Sherman (1996) found that nurses who report higher levels of personal death anxiety are less willing to work with dying people, especially those with many symptoms to manage. However, Sherman also found that the willingness to work with terminally ill people could be influenced either positively or negatively by the quality of social support available from other health care providers. It is difficult to open oneself to the emotional challenges of interacting with a dying person if one feels alone and abandoned by colleagues for doing so.

Although our emphasis here is on counseling and psychotherapy, we also examine the experiences of other people who provide direct services to terminally ill patients, their families, the grieving, or the suicidal. These include the many nurses, social workers, clergy, and hospice volunteers who enter into close personal relationships with people who are confronting death. Counseling, like education, can occur in informal circumstances or as part of a systematic program. The boundary between counseling and education can also be crossed easily from either side. A classroom discussion, for example, may become transformed into an advice-sharing session to help a student decide whether or not to continue his or her practice of avoiding funerals. Similarly, a priest who is counseling the spouse of a dying person may be able to reduce anxiety by providing specific information about church beliefs and practices. In exploring counseling and the counselors, we are not entirely forgetting death education.

Characteristics of Professionals in the Death System

It is an article of faith that people who would help others must also be aware of their own personalities and in control of their own conflicts. This requirement seems applicable to all caregivers who accept responsibility in death-related situations, whether ministers or social workers, psychiatrists or hospice volunteers. A useful early study (Morrison, Vanderwyst, Cocozza, & Dowling, 1981/1982) found that professionals representing five different fields were neither more nor less anxious than a comparison population. However, those who had never been married and those with a serious medical illness expressed higher levels of death concern. It may be reassur-

ing to learn that mental health specialists are as "normal" as everybody else in their self-reported death attitudes. However, the unexpected finding that never-married mental health professionals express a higher level of death concern merits further investigation. Perhaps more attention should be given to the interaction between a caregiver's personal life and his or her orientation toward death.

Neimeyer, Behnke, and Reiss (1983), medical residents in pediatrics, were asked to provide autobiographical information, complete the Death Threat Index, and respond to a pair of case history vignettes. They were to imagine themselves as being the attending physician in each case and to make several ratings. Further information was obtained by asking a group of more advanced

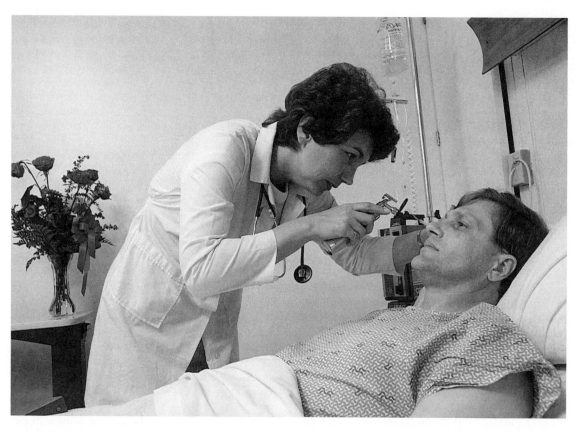

Ophthalamoscopes are used routinely to evaluate the health of our eyes, but also may be called on to determine signs of death.

medical residents to rate each of the study participants on their actual effectiveness in helping patients and their families cope with death. The medical residents who felt most strongly threatened by death were also those who most often used avoidance strategies when caring for a dying patient. These were the young physicians who busied themselves in reviewing charts and finding other things to do instead of meeting their patients' needs for personal contact, information, guidance, and emotional support. We might well expect similar findings among other health care specialists when personal death anxiety leads to the avoidance of meaningful interactions with patients and their families.

The most extensive study of caregivers' response to working with dying people was conducted by Mary Vachon (1987), who has extensive experience as a helping person. She interviewed approximately 600 professional caregivers from hospitals, palliative care facilities, chronic care institutions, and voluntary agencies. The caregivers included Australians and Europeans as well as Canadians and Americans. What was the basic source of stress for physicians, nurses, and others who care for dying patients? How did they cope with this stress?

Her answers might surprise those who have not worked in a health-care setting. The findings are expressed in one of her chapter titles, "Dying Patients Are Not the Real Problem." The caregivers reported they were most stressed by their work environment and occupational roles and not by their direct work with dying patients and their families. They had many specific stresses to report (e.g., poor communication within the health care facility, conflicts between one unit and another, and lack of continuity as employees come and go). Many of the specific stresses were continuous or recurring and showed through inadequate patterns of communication. As Vachon (1987) noted, it is possible that underlying death anxiety contributed to the stress and communication difficulties, but the overall evidence points to the significance of environmental variables.

Vachon's (1987) findings ring true. Tense, anxious, frustrated, and exhausted caregivers have difficulty bringing their best selves to dying patients and their families. For example, we do not have to assume that a nurse who withdraws from a dying person is motivated by her own excessive death anxieties. It is perhaps even more likely that she is caught in a role conflict (between technical expert and humane caregiver), a time bind, and an ambiguous situation created by poor interstaff communications. Professional caregivers who do have intense death-related fears are not likely to find much opportunity to reduce or resolve them on the job. This makes it tempting for them to "go with the flow" and perpetuate a brisk, distant, noninteractive strategy of making it through the day—in other words, reducing the profound to the ordinary and the routine, as we have already seen.

Whatever improves communication among caregivers is likely to reduce frustration and anxiety. Delving into the caregiver's personal anxieties may not always be the most useful place to begin. Instead, we might help caregivers to be more helpful with terminally ill people and their families by preventing or reducing the systematic stresses they encounter in their workplace. There is a growing research literature that identifies specific sources of stress (Riordan & Salzer, 1992). It has also been found that burnout and staff turnover are relatively low among hospice nurses (Turnipseed, 1987), suggesting that some of the principles and practices of a well-functioning hospice might be applied to other health care settings.

Careful selection, effective training, and a supportive work environment should be given high priority whether we are dealing with professional or volunteer caregivers in death-related situations. Caregivers are often well aware of their lack of preparation for communicating with terminally ill people and their families. McGrath, Vates, Clinton, and Hart (1999), for example, found that communication problems were a major source of stress for nurses who work with dying patients and their families. The nurses were strongly motivated to help but often felt "very uncomfortable and distressed as I really didn't know how to answer these questions." Their perceived failures in communicating with dying people stayed with them as a continuing source of stress: "But never did I talk to them about their feelings about death or dying. I wanted to, I knew I should, but I couldn't. I felt lost for words" (p. 24).

Fortunately, it is possible to improve our skills and thereby also reduce our anxieties in communicating with people in difficult situations.

Attention can be given to body language as well as verbal communication. People preparing for careers in nursing, medicine, social work, and other human service fields have often found it useful to take courses and workshops to improve their communication skills.

A related question has recently received a hint of an answer. Thanatologists are scholars, researchers, and clinicians who study death-related issues. How do they deal with death in their own lives? One of the first significant research conferences on dying and death was held in Berkeley, California, in 1973. All the participants agreed to complete a battery of measures assessing their attitudes toward death and dying. Fifteen years later, a partial follow-up study was done. The data were missing for a while, however, but were recently rediscovered and analyzed. Feifel and Strack (2001) note that these pioneering thanatologists

> reported real apprehensions and concerns about their own death and the consequences of death. At the same time, gazing steadily at death over long periods of time does not seem to cause morbid preoccupation or increase one's fear of mortality. Indeed, across the 15-year time interval of this survey, many participants reported a lessening fear of death, greater acceptance of death, and/or an increased appreciation of life accompanying their continued exposure to thanatology. (p. 108)

The self-reported death anxiety of thanatologists was similar to that of the population in general. Furthermore, their lessening fear and increased acceptance during the 15-year period are also consistent with an attitudinal shift that seems to occur with many other people as they move deeper into the adult years. I also add that many students after completing a course in death education have told me that they are still concerned but feel more competent and comfortable in dealing with death-related issues; also, above everything, their appreciation of life has been enhanced.

Counseling and Psychotherapy

People do not necessarily need counseling or psychotherapy when death enters their lives. Sometimes, the needed strength can be drawn from love, friendship, a familiar environment, and one's own beliefs, values, and coping resources. Financial security and competent nursing and medical care are also likely to help see the person through. Before considering counseling or therapy, it is usually wise to assess the total situation. Perhaps what this man needs is a more effective pain management regime; perhaps what this woman needs is the opportunity to spend some time with the sister or brother she has not seen for years. Counseling and therapy are options that may be worth considering, but not to the neglect of the many other factors that could provide comfort and peace of mind.

Many counselors believe that one of the most important goals is to help their clients summon their own inner strengths. A sense of helplessness can reduce an individual's ability to cope with illness not only physically but also psychologically. The counselor can help to restore self-confidence, relaxation, and a renewed sense of still being a valuable and lovable person. This more positive psychological state is thought to have a favorable effect on bodily response, for example, through improved cardiovascular circulation or more vigorous functioning of the immune system. The success of a healing-oriented approach depends as much on the caregiver's personality as on his or her "technique." It is difficult to imagine a nervous, time-conscious, and hard-driving personality achieving the same results as a firm but patient and gentle individual. Those who would provide counseling or psychotherapy in death-related situations would be wise to select an approach that is in harmony with their own personalities as well as one that is well grounded in the knowledge of human nature.

Two very different examples support this point. At one extreme is what might be termed the healing care approach, as represented by an entire team of therapists who have worked with severely impaired and terminally ill geriatric patients (Kastenbaum, Barber, Wilson, Ryder, & Hathaway, 1981). Therapeutic touch, singing together, and interpreting each other's dreams and fantasies are among the untraditional modalities that are used in addition to dialogue. Conveniences such as carefully scheduled sessions and a formal setting are put aside. The therapists make themselves available when needed at any hour of

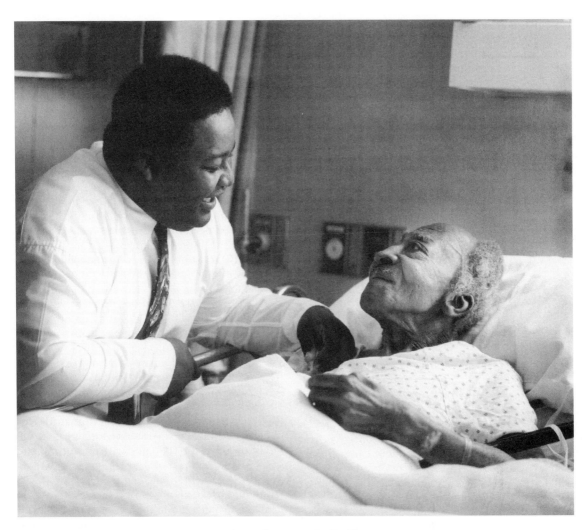

A caring relationship is often the best medicine for a terminally ill person.

the day or night. Not all caregivers would find this approach acceptable or possible, but it may be the treatment of choice when a person is at risk of dying alone and in despair. A recent study confirms that intentional touch can also reduce the distress of bereaved mothers (Kempson, 2000/2001). Other studies have found positive effects of intentional or therapeutic touching with people suffering from a variety of losses and trauma (Field, 1995; Westland, 1993).

Quite different from the cognitive-behavioral approach is the behavior modification approach

(Beck, 1995; Sobel, 1981). Some behavioral principles were used by the healing care therapists. However, when the overall approach is behavior modification there is more of a "rational" as contrasted with an emotion-intensive framework. One does not have to be an exceptionally intuitive person to conduct successful behavior modification. In fact, spontaneity at the wrong time might interfere with the treatment plan. The behavior modification approach may be taken not only with the dying patients but also with the professional and personal support network. For example, a systematic desensitization technique might help reduce some of the anxieties of the dying person's spouse and thereby also reduce the anxiety in their interactions.

Still another approach emphasizes "reconstructing the language of grief" (Hedtke, 2002). Attention is given to the way in which our habits of thought and speech influence the response to death and dying. For example, well-meaning friends

> often say "I am sorry" to someone whose loved one is dead. However,…these words bind the grievers to an unspoken agreement about how they will proceed with their grief. This process is both produced and sanctioned to not take too long, not be too messy, not dwell on our loved one's memory, and not include public displays of extreme emotion. A focused tacit conspiracy actively dismembers the stories and meanings and intimate connections of our loved one's life. The rules are say good-bye, move on, and resume life as soon as possible. (pp. 287–288)

Becoming more aware of such language-mediated "rules" can help to improve communication and relieve grieving people of unrealistic and burdensome expectations.

There is no definitive list of counseling and therapeutic approaches that can be effective in death-related situations, nor is there compelling evidence to demonstrate that one approach is generally superior to another. Furthermore, there is no reason to suppose that all dying people require such interventions. Counseling and therapy do have a place, however, in the total spectrum of services that should be available when appropriate. For people grieving over the death of loved ones, peer support groups are often very helpful (Lieberman, 1996). People who have already made strides toward recovery from grief seem to know when a newly bereaved person needs words of comfort, approval for anger, a hug, or companionable silence.

HOW WE ALL CAN HELP

We all can help by realizing that *prosocial action* is well within our capabilities. Even though we live in a world in which self-interest and competition are salient, we are also a species that has re-

peatedly demonstrated concern and compassion for others. In fact, some of our other fellow creatures have also shown this ability.

Perhaps you remember the following incident in the newspapers or saw it for yourself on television news on August 16, 1996. A 3-year-old had fallen into the outdoor gorilla exhibit at the Brookfield Zoo in Illinois. He landed 18 feet down in the rock-studded pit and was injured, unable to move, and probably unconscious. A gorilla saw what happened. Binti Jua rushed over to the injured boy, with Koola, her 16-month old daughter, clinging to her back. The gorilla gently took the boy in her arms and brought him to a gate where he could be rescued easily. The boy survived his injuries. It turns out that Binti had been raised by humans, but it is possible that, as a good mother, she would have saved the little boy's life anyway.

Binti Jua's prosocial action is a useful reminder that murder, suicide, loss, and indifference do not tell the entire story. An aging Sigmund Freud came to the conclusion that our journey through life revolves around our relationship to opposing instincts: *Eros,* the drive toward experience, stimulation, and love, and *Thanatos,* the drive toward self-destruction and death. According to Freud, the only hope for survival of the human race as well as a rewarding life for individuals is to moderate the force of Thanatos with the caring and joy of Eros (Freud, 1915, 1917). Later, Abraham Maslow (1954, 1968) made the cogent counterargument that we do not always have to transform instinctual dangers and conflicts into positive feelings, but that the healthy and creative side of our personalities comes directly from healthy and creative experiences. Either way, there is a caring and loving side to human nature that can be called on when we face peril and loss, as well as in our everyday interactions. Developing our own caring impulses should be a major priority for individual and society. Also, when we need a refresher course, perhaps we can call on that outstanding death educator and counselor, Binti Jua!

One way in which we can help is to recognize our potential for helping and, therefore, not feel obliged to leave everything to "experts." The experts will usually tell you that there is no substitute for the comforting presence of a family member or intimate friend. Another way in which we can help is to become more competent in communicating with each other about sudden, unexpected deaths. Communication is especially difficult because nobody really wants to break the bad news and nobody wants to hear it. There is no magic way to convert a tragic into a positive situation. Some approaches are better than others in helping people start the long and difficult process of acknowledging and coping with the unexpected loss. An excellent resource is Kenneth Iserson's book, *Grave Words: Notifying Survivors about Sudden, Unexpected Deaths* (1999). It provides useful suggestions not only to his fellow physicians but also to all of us who might find ourselves in the situation of telling—or listening to—the bad news. For example, we can learn how to deal with the explosive anger that a person may express upon learning of the unexpected death. Iserson provides guidelines for telephone notifications as well as direct conversations in a variety of circumstances. Iserson emphasizes the importance of clear and accurate communication to avoid adding confusion to grief:

> Although to some it may seem cruel and to others obvious, notifiers must use one of the "D" words when informing survivors about a death. "D" words include: "Died," "Death," and "Dead." For many reasons, including their own discomfort, many notifiers prefer to use euphemisms instead. The more common ones use such phrases as "passed away," "passed on," "left us," "checked out," "fatally injured," "gone," "deceased," or "expired." But it is better if you use a "D" word. (p. 43)

Iserson (1999) also offers a detailed guide to ways we can continue to be helpful during and after the funeral/memorial service. He reminds us, for example, how useful it can be to run errands, arrange child care schedules, arrange housekeeping chores, do grocery shopping or yard work, care for pets, and so forth. Here and elsewhere, Iserson provides abundant examples of things that all of us can do when the lives of people we care about are disrupted by sudden and unexpected death.

Another way we can help is to improve our awareness of the total family response to death. We respond to dying, grief, and loss as individuals but also as members of family constellations that often have their own style of coping with stress.

Elliott Rosen's *Families Facing Death* (1998) focuses not on the sudden death but on the sometimes lengthy period of time in which family life is under stress in the anticipation of death. His observations include some facts that have not been generally appreciated, for example, the early onset of family stress:

> A family actually begins to address the prospect of loss with the very first symptoms of disease. As incredible as this may seem, when any member of a family is stricken with illness, even the mildest of physical ailment, the family automatically begins a process of adaptation to preserved threatened homeostasis.... If little Mary Smith gets the sniffles, her parents may become overly solicitous, aware of every twitch of the youngster's nose. Mary may want to crawl into Mommy's lap, a behavior she had more or less abandoned, and Mommy will readily comply. (p. 76)

Families sense the threat quickly and do what they can, for as long as they can, to keep things seeming and feeling "normal." The more aware we are of such family dynamics, the more likely we are to provide intelligent and effective support.

These are but a few of the ways in which we—all of us—can help each other.

SUMMARY

Often, there is a feeling of helplessness when people close to us are dying or grieving. Perhaps we should just stand back and leave it all to the experts. This chapter proposes that there is much all of us can do, whether as professional careproviders, family members, friends, colleagues, or neighbors. Learning how to communicate effectively, both verbally and nonverbally, is a key.

We saw that death education and counseling have their roots in ancient times. In the past, the emphasis was often on guiding people safely from one life to the next. Much of the emphasis today is on the individual and family facing death or living with grief. Common to both past and current philosophies is the belief that death is a central fact of life and deserves our most serious and enlightened attention. We cannot simply repeat the approaches taken in the past, however, because conditions of life in ancient and medieval times differ so much from our own. Nevertheless, attention to the Arabian perspective on mortality and the Christian *Ars moriendi* guidebooks reminds us that we are not the first to face life-and-death issues.

The modern death awareness movement in the United States was established during the 1970s with such developments as the beginnings of the ADEC. Effective death educators come from a variety of fields, including anthropology, psychology, psychiatry, medical ethics, nursing, social work, sociology, and the ministry. The scope of death education continues to expand, now reaching more people who are preparing for professional caregiving careers. Nevertheless, many human service providers (teachers, in particular) still complete their studies without preparation for helping the dying, grieving, or suicidal people they will occasionally encounter. Professional caregivers often experience intense stress as they struggle not only to communicate with patients and families but also to cope with difficult work environments. It has become clear that improved communication among caregivers is needed to reduce their frustration and anxiety. People do not necessarily need counseling or psychotherapy when death enters their lives. Often, the needed strength can be drawn from love, friendship, a familiar environment, and one's own beliefs, values, and coping resources. Financial security and competent nursing and medical care are also important.

We can all help each other when facing death-related stress and loss. Specific examples were given in the areas of communicating in unexpected, sudden death situations and understanding family responses to life-threatening illness. Expert care providers often play a significant role, but there is no substitute for compassion and companionship from one person to another.

REFERENCES

Beck, J. (1995). *Cognitive therapy basics and beyond.* New York: Guilford.

Chambliss, D. F. (1996). *Beyond caring.* Chicago: University of Chicago Press.

Chethik, N. (2001). *FatherLoss.* New York: Hyperion.

Dickinson, G. E., & Mermann, A. C. (1996). Death education in U.S. medical schools. *Academic Medicine, 71,* 1348–1349.

Durlak, J. A. (1994). Changing death attitudes through death education. In R. A. Niemeyer (Ed.), *Death anxiety handbook* (pp. 243–262). Washington, DC: Taylor & Francis.

Feifel, H., & Strack, S. (2001). Thanatologists view death: A 15 year perspective. *Omega, Journal of Death and Dying, 43,* 97–112.

Field, T. (1995) Message therapy for infants and children. *Developmental and Behavioral Pediatrics, 16,* 105–111.

Freud, S. (1915). Thoughts for the times on war and death. In *Collected works of Sigmund Freud* (Vol. 14). London: Hogarth Press.

Freud, S. (1917). Mourning and melancholia. In *Collected works of Sigmund Freud* (Vol. 14). London: Hogarth Press.

Goldberg, C. (2002, November 6). Aging may affect visibility of feelings but not intensity. *Arizona Republic,* p. A-18.

Hedtke, L. (2002). Reconstructing the language of death and grief. *Illness, Crisis & Loss, 10,* 285–293.

Iserson, K. V. (1999). *Grave words. Notifying survivors about sudden, unexpected deaths.* Tucson, AZ: Galen.

Kalish, R. A. (1980/1981). Death educator as deacon. *Omega, Journal of Death and Dying, 11,* 75–85.

Kastenbaum, R. (1977). We covered death today. *Death Education, 1,* 85–92.

Kastenbaum, R. (2002). Danse macabre. In R. Kastenbaum (Ed.), *Macmillan encyclopedia of death and dying* (Vol. 1, pp. 201–202). New York: Macmillan.

Kastenbaum, R., Barber, T. X., Wilson, S. G., Ryder, B. L., & Hathaway, L. B. (1981). *Old, sick and helpless: Where therapy begins.* Cambridge, MA: Ballinger.

Kastenbaum, R., & Schneider, S. (1991). Does ADEC have a prayer? A survey report. *Forum Newsletter, 16*(5), 12–13.

Kempson, D. A. (2000/2001). Effects of intentional touch on complicated grief of bereaved mothers. *Omega, Journal of Death and Dying, 42,* 341–354.

Lieberman, M. (1996). *Doors close, doors open.* New York: Grosset/Putnam.

Maslow, A. H. (1954). *Motivation and personality.* New York: Harper & Row.

Maslow, A. H. (1968). *Toward a psychology of being.* New York: Van Nostrand Reinhold.

Mathers, P. (Trans.). (1974). *The book of the thousand and one nights* (Vol. 2). New York: St. Martin's.

McGrath, P., Yates, P., Clinton, M., & Hart, G. (1999). "What should I say?" Qualitative findings on dilemmas in palliative care nursing. *Hospice Journal, 14,* 17–34.

Morrison, J. K., Vanderwyst, D., Cocozza, J., & Dowling, S. (1981/1982). Death concerns among mental health workers. *Omega, Journal of Death and Dying, 12,* 179–190.

Neimeyer, C. J., Behnke, M., & Reiss, J. (1983). Constructs and coping: Physicians' responses to patient death. *Death Education, 7,* 245–266.

Neimeyer, C. J. (Ed.), *Death anxiety handbook* (pp. 243–262). Washington, DC: Taylor & Francis.

Powell, D. (2002, November 5). Presentation, Neuroscience Society annual meeting, Orlando, Florida.

Rosen, E. (1998). *Families facing death* (Rev. ed.). San Francisco: Jossey-Bass.

Rosenblatt, P. C. (2000). *Parent grief. Narratives of loss and relationship*. New York: Brunner/Mazel.

Schneider, S., & Kastenbaum, R. (1993). Patterns and meanings of prayer in hospice caregivers: An exploratory study. *Death Studies, 17,* 471–485.

Sherman, D. W. (1996). Nurses' willingness to care for AIDS patients. *Image, Journal of Nursing Scholarship, 28,* 205–214.

Smith, L. R. (1996). Gillian's journey. *Forum Newsletter 22*(1), 14–16.

Sobel, H. (Ed.). (1981). *Behavior therapy in terminal care.* Cambridge, MA: Ballinger.

Taylor, J. (1977). *The rules and exercises of holy dying.* New York: Arno. (Original work published 1651)

Turnipseed, D., Jr. (1987). Burnout among hospice nurses: An empirical assessment. *Hospice Journal, 3,* 105–119.

Vachon, M. L. S. (1987). *Occupational stress in the care of the critically ill, the dying, and the bereaved.* Washington, DC: Hemisphere.

Wass, H. (2002). Death education. In R. Kastenbaum (Ed.), *Macmillan encyclopedia of death and dying* (Vol. 1, pp. 211–218). New York: Macmillan.

Wass, H., Miller, M. D., & Thornton, G. (1990). Death education and grief/suicide intervention in the public schools. *Death Studies, 14,* 253–268.

Westland, G. (1993). Massage as therapeutic tool. Part I. *British Journal of Occupational Therapy, 56,* 129–134.

GLOSSARY

Ars Moriendi: The art of dying well. First presented in illustrated books of the 15th century.

Artificial Hydration: Providing fluids through an intervenous tube. ("Artificial nutrition" can also be provided in this way.)

Danse Macarbre: A visual image of personified Death leading people to their graves in a slow, dignified dance (first appearing in the 13th century).

Death Threat Index: A self-report measure of some aspects of death anxiety.

Prosocial: Thoughts, feelings, and actions that are motivated by the intention to help others.

Socrates, the gadfly of Athens, teaches his last lesson moments before he accepts the fatal cup of hemlock. The original 1787 painting by Jacques Louis David can be found in New York's Metropolitan Museum of Art.

chapter **16**

GOOD LIFE, GOOD DEATH?

Trying to make sense of it all

Good to begin well, better to end well.
—Advice from a fortune cookie

An analysis of e-mail, phone calls and voice mail messages from the World Trade Center shows that at least 353 of those who died in the towers were able to reach people outside, the New York Times *reported Sunday.*
—Associated Press (2002)

I am inclined to think that these muscles and bones of mine would have gone off long ago to Megara or Boeotia—by the dog they would, if they had been moved only by their own idea of what was best, and if I had not chosen the better and nobler part, instead of playing truant and running away, of enduring any punishment which the state inflicts.
—A prisoner awaiting execution in 399 B.C.

"My in-laws had started to treat us like outcasts and nobody would come near us or touch us," she said, adding that she can cope with the threat of death, but not with the stigma AIDS carries.
—Quoted in Hussain (2002)

As I walked into Dad's room I was struck by how small he looked. Above him an oscilloscope traced the electrical activity of his heart, and chrome IV poles framed the head of his bed. The IV in his left arm was attached to a bottle of saline, and a plastic bag of antibiotic solution was piggy-backed into the tubing at his wrist. Another IV, this one a large-bore catheter that entered the subclavian vein just below the mid-portion of his right collarbone, was attached to a three-way stopcock valve. Through it saline was flowing at a to-keep-open rate; also attached to the stopcock was a manometer that provided measurement of central venous pressure, a guide to his volume status. The third channel led to a dopamine drip with its own infusion pump that was standing by, just in case that medication was needed to raise his blood pressure. Oxygen tubing ran from his nose. A call button was pinned to his pillow. A urine bottle hung at his bedrail. On his bedside table was a cafeteria tray with his untouched breakfast, a pitcher of water, and a menu of the next day's meals.

"Hi, Dad." I managed to say. "How are you doing?"
—Byock (1997, p. 15)

"The party is still going on. I don't want to go."
—Billie S., a woman receiving hospice home care

I don't know if that computer play station deal is the best or the worse thing we ever bought for our kids. They're at the computer or, I should say, in the computer practically all the time, seems that way. Two worlds in our house and I don't know if I want to know which world they like best.
—Sharon T., mother of two boys

Kumui was brought immediately to the tent where her father lay. Avel spoke only once, saying, "Ah, now that you are here I can die easily." He then closed his eyes, and within two hours he was dead.
—Counts and Counts (1985, p. 42)

We have moved together through a territory both familiar and unfamiliar. The territory encompassed by this book has been familiar because much of what we have surveyed has its setting in our own society. It is also familiar because we have examined human interactions, children developing their ideas about the world, adults encountering challenge, the facts behind headlines, and, perhaps most significantly, the workings of our own minds. All these familiar landmarks have taken on unfamiliar aspects, however. The human interactions have included comforting or discomforting responses to dying people and grief when a relationship has ended in death. Our visit to the world of childhood re-

vealed curiosities and anxieties about death that adults have usually assumed are not of concern to the young. The headlines have often opened the way to discovering the extent of suicide, homicide, and other destructive patterns within our society. Our minds have revealed something of their struggle to acknowledge the reality of risk and death while at the same time trying to protect us against a keen awareness of mortality. Furthermore, we have repeatedly found a diversity of ideas and opinions on core issues, including the nature and meaning of death.

What does it all add up to? How *should* we think about death in all its forms? Death sometimes makes itself known to us as a thought that curls around the edges of our minds for a moment before it disappears again. Sometimes it is the invisible blow we feel when we see the marks of mortality in the appearance of a person we love. Sometimes it is the bodies trapped in the crushed automobile or scattered at the scene of a mass murder. All these aspects of death (along with so many others) are difficult to bring together within a simple and pleasingly rational framework. It is in our nature, however, to try to make sense of our experiences. Each of us will continue to integrate our thoughts and feelings about death in our own way.

This chapter explores several issues worth considering as you review your own perspective. Our unifying theme is the question: *Good life, good death?* A fortune cookie is perhaps not the soundest guide, but I have no quarrel with its message that both a good beginning and a good ending are desirable—and perhaps related. Many people believe that a "good life" prepares the way for a "good death." This has long been a component of religious beliefs as expressed, for example, by Jeremy Taylor (1665/1970) in *Rules and Exercises of Holy Dying*. Some have drawn the lesson that we should live each day as though it is our last. Buddhist philosophy emphasizes a continuous flow in which life and death move together in everything we do (Gyatso, 1985). A good death is intrinsically related to a good life because what we call "life" and what we call "death" have always been companions. Variations on this theme have developed in recent years. For example, Avery Weisman, a pioneering psychotherapist and researcher with terminally ill people, introduced the influential concept of an *appropriate death*—that is, the death people would choose for themselves if they really had a choice (Weisman, 1972). The "good death" might be very different from one person to another, the key factor being the "fit" between that person's unique life and the way that life comes to an end. Others focus on the importance of having lived a full and rewarding life. People who can accept their lives are more likely to experience a "good death." Partisans of this view include Erikson (1950) in his theory of life span development and Tomer

and Eliason (1996) in their regret theory of death anxiety.

That a good life leads to a good death is an appealing concept. At this point, however, let's keep it in mind as a possibility to be explored rather than a demonstrated fact. We will be in a better position to reflect on this idea as this chapter and book come to a close.

THREE PATHS TO DEATH

The people who sent messages to their loved ones from the World Trade Center (WTC) towers on September 11, 2001, the condemned prisoner in Athens, and AIDS victims in Gauhati, India, were in circumstances that raise difficult questions about a "good death."

The men and women who died in the twin WTC towers expected to put in a day's work, mingle with their colleagues, and then return home for an evening with family or friends. Neither they nor their loved ones had reason to expect that their lives would come to an abrupt end. They suffered what Leviton (1991) had previously identified as a "horrendous death." It would be difficult to find anything good about this kind of death:

• The victims had done nothing to provoke the savage attack.
• Their individuality had counted for nothing: The terrorist's goal was to compile a large body count.
• The sudden and unexpected catastrophe allowed no time for the victims to prepare themselves spiritually for the end of their lives or make practical arrangements for their families.
• Families were shattered, burdened with grief, deprived of companionship and support, and faced with the challenge of somehow going on with life despite this tremendous blow. The report of last-minute communications from victims to families raises a specific question, though: Is it better to die swiftly or to become aware that we will die in just a few moments? Research has consistently shown that most people say they would prefer to slip away from life, preferably from peaceful sleep. Awareness of imminent death (or even the *possibility* of imminent death) is regarded as a tormenting suspense. More than

one respondent has added in a Woody Alle-
nesque phrase, "I'd rather not be there when I
die." One can also imagine the shock and anxiety
of the family members who received that last call
from the WTC. Nevertheless, family members
have cherished that last communication and
used it as a transitional memory structure between the person they loved and the absence
they now experience. It is also obvious that the
victims were strongly motivated to make that final contact. They could still be part of the family
for another moment. Furthermore, the simple
act of placing the call was something that one
could still do—an expression of self against the
obliterating conflagration. Good to die at the
WTC on September 11, 2001? No. Resoundingly,
no. Good to have had that last moment, that last
opportunity to communicate with loved ones?
Probably so.

• Socrates is generally considered to be the father of philosophical thought, although other
resourceful and provocative thinkers preceded
him. He was respected in his own time as valiant
soldier, decent stone mason, and wise and witty
seeker of truth. It was clear both then and now
that his death sentence was the unexpected outcome of bogus charges brought against him as
payback for his independent thinking that had
bruised some Athenian egos (Ahrensdorf, 1995;
Kastenbaum, 2002). Socrates could have escaped
execution either by a few words of contrition or
by boarding a ship provided by his friends (the
authorities would have preferred that he make
off rather than embarrass them by actually being
executed). In the event, the last days and hours
of Socrates' life (as described second-hand by
his pupil and friend, Plato) became one of the
core documents and one of the most inspira-
tional episodes in the history of thought. Within
his prison walls, Socrates patiently reasoned with
his friends about the meaning of life and death
and sought to relieve their anxieties by his own
serenity. When he accepted the cup of hemlock
(if that is what it really was; see Ober, 1988) from
the reluctant hands of a jailer, Socrates offered
himself as a model for facing death with integrity,
equanimity, and his characteristic twist of humor. This was in several respects quite a bad
death: miscarriage of justice, silencing one of hu-

mankind's greatest thinkers, and depriving a
great but troubled city-nation of an invaluable
citizen. However, history also regards this unfortunate occasion as a sterling example of a very
good death: bringing a clear and calm philosophical mind to the end of life and facing death in
such a way as to affirm and fulfill all that has
gone before. Despite the injustice of the situation, here was a good death that flowed from a
good life.

• AIDS has been not only a lethal but also a
tainted pathway to death throughout the world.
Enlightened caregivers have had to contest with
negative attitudes toward both the disease and
its victims. This prejudice and its pattern of
avoidant behaviors exist both in developed nations such as the United States and in countries
that are struggling for stability and survival (such
as most of sub-Saharan Africa). Our example
comes from India, where the actual number of
people infected with HIV/AIDS is massively underestimated and where both the victims and
their families are often isolated and, in effect,
punished. This situation has ominous implications for the population at large because prevention and treatment measures are being restricted
by the pattern of denial. It is estimated that there
are approximately 4 million HIV/AIDS cases in
India, but this number could increase to 25 million by 2010. The human side is illustrated by
the woman quoted at the start of the chapter.
Her family was shunned while her husband suffered and then died from AIDS, and landlords
would boot them out when they learned of his
condition. The whole family was rejected by society not because the husband was dying but
because he was dying of AIDS. The symptoms
that accompany AIDS are stressful, painful, and
eventually debilitating (although controlled more
adequately today in societies with the resources
to do so). From a physical standpoint, the AIDS
pathway to death is one that most people would
characterize as definitely not good. It becomes
even more stressful when society denies its existence and/or punishes the victims. Rejection—
"social death" at the extreme—can be one of the
worst dimensions of a death that is an ordeal on
its own terms, but rejection is also something
that society can choose to reject.

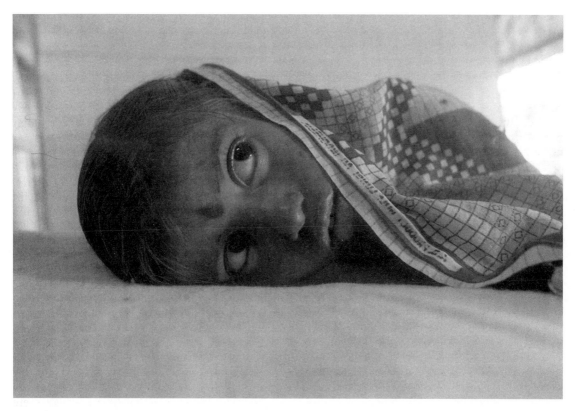

This young woman is among the many victims of AIDS in India, a nation that has been slow to recognize and respond to this disaster.

We now consider a more extended example from our own society that raises the good death/bad death issue in a different way.

A FATHER DIES: A MISSION BEGINS

Ira Byock, M.D., is president of the American Academy of Hospice and Palliative Medicine and a leading advocate for improved care of terminally ill people. Early in his medical career, his father was struck with a fatal illness. Byock was stunned, moved, and instructed by this experience. Consider just a few aspects of his experience:

• *He saw his father connected to a life-support system.* Byock (1997) describes this scene in the opening

quotation, and what a disturbing scene it was. As a physician, Byock recognized and understood the function of all the equipment that was connected to the small-looking man in the bed. As a son, he felt disoriented by the devices that surrounded his father and established a barrier between them. How do you relate to a person who has become a component of a life-support system; what do you say? "Hi, Dad," I managed to say, "How are you doing?" Here is a situation that has confronted an increasing number of people in recent years. From the standpoint of the family member, this situation presents daunting barriers to communication; one could hardly feel more awkward and unnatural. We know less from the standpoint of the person who is the centerpiece of the life-support system. Often, consciousness and responsiveness are impaired, but sometimes the person can hear and understand what is being said. A scene such as this would be difficult to describe as "good death" by either the patient or the family member.

But wait—the purpose of life-support systems is to support life. As it turned out, Byock's father recovered from this particular life-threatening episode with the assistance of these devices and competent nursing care. This made it possible for the family to have more time together with the father still an active participant. It might have been anything but a "good death" if he had died during this episode, but as it happened, persistent medical and nursing care gave him a little more time to live. Situations such as these caution us against sweeping and simplistic conclusions about the relationship between life-support systems and the "good death."

• *His father's death occurred later, peacefully, at home.* Byock (1997) noted,

> He appeared suddenly to be relaxed, as if the work, whatever it had been, was over. He was peaceful, no longer sweating, and his breathing was easy and deep, though irregular. Mom stood touching his foot, and Anita and I sat on each side of the bed touching his arms, as he drew his last breath and left. For the next hour we continued our vigil: hugging one another, crying intermittently, grieving openly and together. (p. 24)

Even without analyzing the concept of the "good death" in any detail, it is obvious that this final scene was much more positive than the in-hospital life-support system situation. Sy Byock seemed to experience the moment of death as a relief and release. There was no way of knowing whether or not he had any awareness of the situation, but if he did, it would have been the loving presence of his family. A sense of unity and completion was experienced by the family, much different from the alienating hospital situation. The same person and the same family had two very different experiences, one at the brink of death and one at the actual final moment.

• *A death changes a life.* Byock had been intensely involved with his father and other family members during the final illness. The death had been expected. Indeed, Byock may have been the first

to recognize the early symptoms as indications of a fatal condition. Even with all this knowledge and expectation, however, he was stunned by the death. It was so difficult to accept the fact that he would never see his father again. Furthermore, this personally significant loss broke through all that Byock had learned about managing terminal illness as a physician. He realized that the health care system was at war with death and, therefore, with dying people as well. Physicians and their emergency response teams would engage in dramatic attempts to prolong or restore life as, for example, by heart resuscitation. These were futile exercises. The patients would die anyway. Please excuse me if I must quote again, because Byock's (1997) observations here speak so strongly to my own experiences as a psychologist in geriatric care facilities:

> If death on the wards was macabre, in the emergency room it was ghastly. In the hands of the medical system, even passings that should have been peaceful turned gruesome. Nursing homes, for example, routinely sent patients only moments away from death to the hospital by ambulance, lights and sirens blazing. By transferring the almost-dead to the emergency room, nursing homes could claim a mortality rate of nearly zero, while providing evidence to families, and any interested attorneys, that "everything possible" had been done. This bizarre scenario extended not only to sudden deaths but also to people who were unconscious, in the final moments of dying, and expected to die. Even though the medical people knew that death had arrived and any efforts would be futile, the system and their training compelled them to attempt CPR before they could pronounce someone officially dead. (p. 27)

Byock is a physician who, touched by his father's death and appalled by the mismanagement of dying people in the health care system, has contributed much to medical education and improvement of terminal care. He transformed himself from a well-trained insider to a change agent dedicated to awakening the establishment to the need for more humane and effective care. Byock does not spell out his idea of the "good death" as such, but his observations clearly identify one of the major negatives and one of the major positives. Futile medical procedures perpetuate the health care system's unwillingness to face the reality of dying and death and can even constitute a kind of assault on the patient in which respect and dignity lose out. The opportunity for family and patient to have time together in familiar surroundings can encourage meaningful communication and the affirmation and demonstration of loving relationships. Whatever else the "good death" might be, it is more likely to occur within a supportive interpersonal framework and without medical interventions that are both futile and alienating. We will continue to work with the concept of the "good death" as we move along.

A Shift in the Meaning of Life and Death?

"Dying well" is perhaps a more accurate term than the "good death" because the emphasis is usually on what occurs while the person is still living. Nevertheless, our interpretations of death are likely to influence our attitudes toward end-of-life experiences. A person who regards death as destination and fulfillment may have a different set of expectations and priorities than a person who regards death as end or outcome. Five alternative interpretations were considered in Chapter 4. These were all what might be called structural or cognitive models. Each proposed its own version of the nature of death. We can refresh our memory with the help of Table 16-1.

Each of these interpretations has its distinctive implications for how we might think about life

TABLE 16-1

Meanings That Have Been Given to Death

- Death is an enfeebled form of life.
- Death is a continuation of life.
- Death is perpetual development.
- Death is waiting.
- Death is cycling and recycling.

and how we might prepare ourselves for death. We have also examined at our *feelings* about death, especially in Chapter 3 when we focused on anxiety, denial, and acceptance. Now we again consider our death-related thoughts and feelings because shifts will continue to occur as we move deeper into the 21st century. One of these developments is associated with the emergence of a cybernetic society and will be considered later. Here, we attend to the words of Billie S., the hospice patient who sighed, "The party is still going on. I don't want to go." She is not the only person who feels this way. It appears that a long life has become more attractive for many people. This has something to do with the fact that more people are living longer. By itself, though, a long life has not always been welcome. Throughout world history, many people have feared growing old because of possible infirmity, suffering, and abandonment. The psalmist of the Old Testament records the lament, "Cast me not off in the time of old age; forsake me not when my strength faileth. Now also when I am old and greyheaded, O God, forsake me not" (Psa. 71:9).

Death has often been regarded as a release from infirmity, suffering, and indignity. This attitude has not been restricted to elderly people because infirmity, suffering, and indignity can occur at any age. Suicide has been one way of acting on the feeling that life can be cured only by death. Another path to the release of death has been systematic degradation of health and heightened risk-taking, such as by the abuse of alcohol and drugs. Less obvious is the quiet withdrawal from life. Activities that once were attractive now seem either out of reach or only further sources of distress. Some seek but others avoid close relationships as a way of edging closer to escape from life. Read history at ground level—the lives of everyday people—and we repeatedly encounter the scourges of poverty, famine, illness, bereavement, oppression, and war. Life was difficult and dangerous. Many people had to ask themselves, "Why go on?" even as they struggled to go on.

Lullabies, those charming and comforting songs we sing to sleeping babies, actually have their origins in misery so deep and pervasive that the desire to live was strenuously challenged by

The celebration of life can not only continue, but also take on special meaning when "the days draw down to a precious few."

the temptation to get it all over with. Kalle Achte (1989) tell us that

> lullabies originated during the centuries that most people lived in agricultural communities, did hard work, and battled against the forces of nature. Famine was an ever-present threat, and epidemics killed many people, especially young children.... A woman's life was especially difficult at that time. Some mothers may have felt that death offered the only release from a joyless life and continuous labor. The mother's own depression and frustration may have been crucial factors in the origins of lullabies with death themes. Perhaps overworked and depressed mothers transferred their own death wishes to the child. (pp. 177–178)

The following is an example of a death-themed lullaby:

> Today Vanyushka will die
> the funeral will be held tomorrow
> we shall bury Vanya
> and toll the big bell. (p. 177)

Achte (1989) also tells us that death-ridden lullabies became much less common as the conditions of life improved for many people—and that is our very point here. Life has been looking better to people fortunate enough to receive such benefits as abundant food and improved health care and such perks as the automobile and the VCR. Traditional attitudes toward death were forged during lengthy stretches of history when for most people life was difficult, dangerous, and brief. These attitudes became somewhat less compelling as conditions of life improved.

The models identified here represent a variety of ways in which to respond to the sorrows and stresses of life. For example, we might contrast the ancient "death is an enfeebled form of life" with the once radically new Christian doctrine that "death is waiting" (for a spiritually enhanced afterlife). Believers in both models of death shared the same difficult life conditions. Their expectations and behaviors might have differed significantly, however. The person who maintained the older belief might regard death as not so dramatically different from life. One gets worn down from aging and hard times and so drifts from one

shade of enfeebled life to another. There is not that much to fear from death because one has already lost so much, and there is not much to expect from death because the decline continues to continue. In contrast, the Christian vision of death offered a transformation. The miseries and uncertainties of life can be exchanged for the blessings of heaven. Death therefore could seem a lot more appealing than the frustrations, disappointments, sorrows, and suffering of life. This positive outlook, however, was shadowed by the fear of damnation and punishment. Perhaps a stressful life would be followed by an even more stressful experience after death. The stakes were high for Christians: salvation or damnation?

Today, fewer people seem impelled to think of death as either a terrifying punishment or a release from a burdensome life. This life on Earth has attracted some of the attention formerly accorded to death. Many elderly men and women are active, vigorous, and strongly engaged with life. Attitude studies find that many elderly people are well satisfied with their lives. A retired public health officer, for example, told me that "I am finally discovering who I am after all these years, and having the time of my life. The absolute time of my life!"

We would not want to exaggerate the differences between past and present attitudes toward life and death. Many people treasured life and did all they could to survive in difficult circumstances. There were also people then as well as now who "had it made" and were more interested in having a pleasant life continue than in entering a promised land after death. Nevertheless, there seems to be a subtle shift in recent years. People may hold traditional beliefs about the nature and meaning of death and yet not give these beliefs quite so central a position. In other words, death may be becoming less *salient* in everyday life. We may still have our own individual mix of anxiety, denial, and acceptance and yet feel less intensely about death as either an overpowering catastrophe or a transcendent blessing.

The *regret theory* of death anxiety (Chapter 2) suggests that people who consider themselves to have full and satisfying lives are less anxious about death because they have already lived well. This is a plausible concept and has some supportive observations. Nevertheless, this view might be incomplete. I have known many people who have been well weathered by life. They have had their share of losses, sorrows, and disappointments. But regret? Not really. Willa T., a woman in her mid-80s, nearly blind for the past several years, offers her understanding of life in response to an open-ended interview question:

> You can't change the past. All the bad stuff was part of all the good stuff. You can't really pick and choose. All in all, I've had more in life than I had any right to expect. But, listen, I want more. More life. I don't want to hear about "them pearly gates." I don't want to see them pearly gates any time soon. It's not that I have any problem with death. I don't. Do you understand? It's that I'm used to living and I haven't used up living. Poor Razzi was the same way. She died last night, you know, or early in the morning. I am not afraid of that happening to me, but, oh, it would be a shame, wouldn't it, to have to leave when there's so much more in front of you every day!

Within this perspective, Death is not an awesome figure, terrifying or beatific. Instead, Death is more the spoil-sport who turns out the lights and says "The party's over" before we are ready to go. There has been little or no research on this subtle shift from strong attitudes, positive or negative, to the feeling that life is so rewarding and meaningful that it should just go on and on. What have you noticed, and what do you make of it?

HORRENDOUS DEATH

Death sometimes takes on a very different aspect, however. Millions of people continue to suffer deprivation, lack of opportunity, oppression, and high vulnerability to violence. There are places in the world, including the United States, in which poverty is widespread, hunger frequent, and health care inadequate. Furthermore, there are also societal practices that destroy lives—sometimes in direct and brutal ways and sometimes in less direct but nevertheless efficient ways.

Death educators, counselors, and researchers have usually focused their attention on individuals and families who are attempting to cope with terminal illness, grief, or suicidality. A few thana-

tologists, though, have been urging more attention to the deaths that some people impose on others, especially in cruel and degrading ways. Prominent among these advocates is the distinguished public health educator Dan Leviton, who has introduced the seminal concept of *horrendous death*. The following is an interview with Leviton:

1. *Precisely what is a horrendous death—how does it differ from other deaths?* Horrendous death (HD) is the label given to deaths that are caused by people, usually affecting large populations, and often torturous, violent, and preventable. HD sometimes is motivated by the intention to kill others. Examples are death resulting from war, terrorism, homicide, genocide, and intentional racism (e.g., lynching) as well as environmental assault. But HD may also result from accidents, drug misuse, suicide, environmental degradation, hunger, poverty, and indirect effects of racism. Another characteristic of HD is that it is premature. Most of us wish to die peacefully in our sleep in old age with minimal suffering. It is the rare person who envisions dying of HD. Exceptions are those who have had a close call with HD, or who have had loved ones or close friends die this way. Most of us are unable to think of our children, grandchildren, and mates dying this way. In this sense HD is always premature, "unnatural," and a surprise. The usual response of survivors is "I can't believe it." As a death educator since the late 1960s I am familiar with the concept of denial of death, but I never realized its depth until embarking on this Quixotian project to prevent HD. Nor did I realize how such denial prevents us from acting in our own interest simply because so few of us think about dying a HD—until it happens.

Can you think of yourself or the person most beloved to you—or, for that matter, your companion animal—burning to death as a result of a flame thrower, that almost universal military weapon, or burning to death in an explosion from a terrorist's bomb? These are characteristic forms of HD, and they happen to real people.

2. *What led or motivated you to come up with this concept?* By training I am a health educator who specializes in thanatology and gerontology. Thus, I am interested in improving individual and community health and well-being. Anything that

reduces unnecessary mortality, morbidity, and suffering is in my purview.

I read Herman Feifel's classic, *The Meaning of Death* (1959). His thesis was that our attitudes toward death—especially denial—affect individual and community behavior. He saw death in much the same way as Freud saw our repression of the sexual drive, that is, as a powerful factor affecting human behavior. My variation of Feifel's insight and that of other early leaders in thanatology was that the denial of death affected not only individual but global health and well-being. A second motivating factor was the commonsense observation that many deaths are caused by people. As a husband and father I vowed to do what I could to ensure that my kids and wife did not die a HD. It is deadly *not* to act. I know that if anyone can die a HD anywhere, my family can die similarly. So my actions, while altruistic, are also self-serving. They have survival value.

Another motivation was the realization that we do have research-based social policies that could prevent the various forms of HD—but are not implemented. They deal with underlying root causes and outcomes and include early warning and surveillance systems. Where are these policies? They languish on the shelves of the United Nations and World Health Organization, the Stockholm International Peace Research Institute, the Children's Defense League, the Sierra Club, and a variety of national and international think tanks, governmental, and nongovernmental agencies. What a waste! So I set about to develop a process that would integrate themes of thanatology and public health in order to implement existing social policies that could prevent HD. A second goal was to try to galvanize others to address this issue, the most important and profound of our time. Another approach is our advocacy work. For example, since 1972 I have directed the Adult Health and Development Program at the University of Maryland (see our web page at www.inform.umd.edu/HLPH/AHDP). We train students and volunteers to work on a one-to-one basis with institutionalized or noninstitutionalized older adults to improve the latter's health and well-being. One of the goals is to "contribute to world peace and global cooperation by integrating a variety of individuals into a mutually supportive and purposeful group" (Leviton, 1995; Leviton, Kennedy, Woodruff, & Like, 1998). Thanks to a variety of grants we have trained representatives from about 40 universities and colleges (including one in Beijing, China) to have their own Adult Health and Development Program.

3. *Is there anything that one person—such as the person reading this book—can do?* You bet! Here is a partial list, but every reader can add to it:

- Run for office with quality of health and prevention of HD as a priority.
- Demand the same of political candidates. I mean really demand! We need to take a proactive approach.
- Discover information from sources outside the mainstream media. They are owned and operated by wealthy corporations whose priorities and motives may not be entirely oriented toward public health and well-being. Learn of political power and economics. My personal preferences are scientific journals and magazines such as *The Nation, Z,* and *World Watch.*
- Speak out. Don't be afraid to make politically incorrect statements
- Ask questions.
- Share your concerns with others.
(*End of interview*)

As Leviton also implies, HD may be the outcome of something as commonplace as economic priorities (e.g., making more money more easily comes before safe housing). One recent study found a higher death rate for patients who are treated at for-profit dialysis centers compared with nonprofit facilities (Tanner, 2002). Another study (Schultz & Francis, 2002) found a widespread practice in which large companies take out life insurance policies on their employees and assign the death benefits to themselves; they also harvest significant tax breaks in the process. These are but a few examples of economic practices that show high regard for the "bottom line" and little regard for the intrinsic value of the individual. The possibilities of HD exist in many situations, perhaps even more so whenever protection of life seems to conflict with personal motives, corporate profit, or governmental power.

Perhaps we should also give more attention to the force of habit and inertia. An industry or a nation that has always done things in a certain way is likely to continue doing so even when there are unfortunate consequences. International concern for human rights, environmental protection, and public health and safety has gathered strength only in recent years, long after many societal units established their own way of doing things. Apart from everything else, it may be regarded as just plain "inconvenient" to consider the life-and-death implications of practices that have always seemed suitable for doing business as usual.

Two central issues await further attention: Does thanatology have any business concerning itself with death on the larger scale as distinguished from individual and family situations? How can people be helped to appreciate the reality of other people, those who are not flesh-and-blood companions, in their own lives?

The answer to the first question remains in doubt. Some death educators and other thanatologists believe we should focus attention on helping the dying, the grieving, and the suicidal. Supporting this view is the judgment that few thanatologists are qualified by training to make significant changes in social policy and practice. It is also feared that entering the arena of HD (including events such as those discussed in Chapter 9) might take away from the more traditional concerns related to dying and death. Others believe that we would be ignoring too important a reality by ignoring large-scale phenomena such as HD. How can we be so concerned about an individual here and a family there and not also be concerned about social forces that result in premature and sometimes barbaric forms of death for many other people? Advocates of a broader thanatology also recognize that few death educators, counselors, and therapists have backgrounds that favor large-scale social action. On the other hand, nothing would be accomplished unless the effort is made, and the educational dimension of an effective social movement may be well within the competency of death educators. People in both camps would be interested in learning what you think about this choice: focus attention on dying, grief, and suicide or also consider larger scale social phenomena that affect who dies when and how?

The Golden Rule Revisited

Suppose that we do consider our subject matter to include the objective of preventing deaths that result from human indifference or malice. Leviton has proposed a course of political action. Another approach also deserves consideration. Few guides to life are more familiar than what has sometimes been called the golden rule: *Do unto others as you would have done to yourself.* This simple guide has often proven difficult to follow even for those who accept it in principle. Perhaps you have come across a copy of this notorious sign that has found its way into some offices: *The beatings will continue until morale improves.* Beating, threats, and demands that we should be "nice" to each other have not proven spectacularly successful. Rational demonstrations that we are all better off if we respect and cooperate with each other have also had only occasional success.

World culture has long been faced with a discordant pair of propositions. One is the *should,* as in "we should treat each other with respect and compassion." The other is the *observational,* as in "every day I see self-interest, malice, and indifference in human interactions." This tension between ideal and reality courses through the spiritual teachings of world religions, critical decision making on the national and international level, and our own day-by-day interactions. This tension has its many twists and turns. For example, peacekeeping forces in Kosovo and East Timor had to use lethal weapons in order to prevent violence. In the domestic sphere, this kind of irony was not lost on the mother who saw her young son hit another child. "Don't hit!" she commanded, as she slapped her son. A moment later she was flushed with embarrassment. "Oh, my god—what have I done!" It can be difficult for the most well-meaning person to pursue the ideal of the golden rule when confronted with stress, complexity, and conflict.

Horrendous death can be regarded as the extreme case. Sometimes our failure to "do unto others" results in hurt feelings, strained relationships, missed opportunities, and the like. Sometimes a buildup of anger, distrust, or simply indifference to others becomes the bomb whose fuse is ignited by circumstances. If we can be impressed only by massive numbers, perhaps we should remind ourselves of the 11 million Russian peasants who were systematically killed by their own countrymen by either starvation or murder (Chapter 9). More than 6 million Jews, many of them loyal German citizens, were victims of the Nazi's "final solution." Both the Russian (Conquest, 1986) and the Nazi (Friedlander, 1995; Goldhagen, 1996) catastrophes had their origins in the most dangerous of all territories: the human mind. "Peasants" and "Jews" were not like us. They were subhuman and therefore meant to be exploited, ignored, or destroyed in accordance with our own plans and aspirations.

It is typical of HD practices that many of those responsible for the killing felt they had done nothing wrong. So powerful is this sense of emotional insulation from the killing that people may refuse to believe what happened even in the face of overwhelming evidence (Lifton, 1986; Lipstadt, 1994).

From so much suffering and death, what lesson stands out most clearly? *The golden rule is flagrantly disregarded and HD becomes a more imminent prospect when we do not feel a basic bond with other people.* The study of human development and its psychopathology has revealed that we cannot take such a bonding process for granted. Infants and children who are deprived of loving parents

Millions of television watchers witnessed the fall of Saddam Hussein's regime (April 9, 2003), which has been held responsible for thousands of horrendous deaths.

or parent-surrogates often do not show the ability to form intimate relationships with others. Children growing up within dysfunctional families often have mixed experiences of affection, neglect, and cruelty that interfere with their ability to create and maintain close relationships. Whatever contributes to a loving and supportive home environment in all likelihood also contributes to the development of human feeling and empathy.

There is another level of social influence, however, that can inhibit the development of emotional bonds with others. Division of the human race into *Us and Them* has been a common mindset throughout history. People who are regarded as belonging to the ingroup may be respected, cherished, and protected. There is little sense of human bonding, though, for those who are regarded as outsiders. The "rules of engagement" may be so different that outsiders are taken to be fair prey (as in slavery or crime) and to have no claim on human rights.

Often, a tradition has been passed from generation to generation that emphasizes how superior, moral, and entitled We are, and how inferior, untrustworthy, and illegitimate They are. People who are compassionate, helpful, and loyal to each other may consider it their right, or duty, to keep Them in their place or even, when sufficiently provoked, to wipe them off the face of the earth. Read or listen to the experiences of people who were either the perpetrators or the victims in mass violence. You are likely to encounter again and again the dehumanization of the victim. "They are not at all like us—they are stupid beasts, unworthy creatures, vermin to be destroyed" is the common refrain. Furthermore, belief in a radical difference between Us and Them has often been inculcated as a way of avoiding the moral misgivings and horror that one would otherwise feel in inflicting suffering and death.

It is much easier to treat others as less than human if we do not actually know them. We are no longer as free to act on images, assumptions, and stereotypes when we see for ourselves that the Others are, like us, real and unique persons. "Do unto others…" too often has had an escape clause. We may feel we should do right by others if they are not really Other, and Other may in-

clude a large proportion of the human race: people who speak a different language, come in a different color or gender, or simply live in the wrong side of town or even just across the symbolic turf border within the same neighborhood. Can group esteem exist without putting down other groups? Can we develop the willingness and ability to feel ourselves a part of the total human community? Positive answers to these questions would go a long way toward avoiding the buildup of distrust and contempt that has prepared the way for inflicting HD either by direct action or by callous indifference.

Positive signs already exist. Some people have learned from the difficult lessons of racial discrimination, the Holocaust, and other 20th century disasters. Furthermore, the far reaches of the world now seem more within personal range for people who interact regularly through e-mail and the Internet. Many industries and corporations involve multicultural partnerships; many campuses are enriched with students and faculty of the most varied backgrounds. Travel has also developed friendships that cross over national, racial, and ethnic lines. Disasters in Bosnia, Kosovo, Turkey, Taiwan, and East Timor, for example, all had personal meanings to some of my students, who in turn helped the rest of us to put a human face on the tragedies. Whatever enhances communication and personalization should help to develop human bonds that provide some protection against HD.

One powerful trend, however, has the potential for weakening our sense of deep connection with others. It also carries the potential for blurring our awareness of the difference between real and virtual life and, therefore, between real death and its electronic counterfeit. We must pay another brief visit to the compelling satellite world of so-called virtual reality.

Are We Live or on Tape? The Life-and-Death Challenges of Virtual Reality

Face-to-face encounters almost completely dominated human interactions until technological innovations offered supplements, enhancements, and replacements. Photography not only altered our sense of identity but also transformed our relationship to the past, especially loved ones who now could still be with us just as they were. The tiny framed oval photograph of grandmother or the portrait showing the entire family as it once was became among the most cherished of possessions. Photographs provided a powerful new way for the dead to speak to the living. This point is well made in the movie, *Dead Poets Society*, as a teacher (Robin Williams) directs his students to study a photograph of an earlier generation of students. The intense aliveness of this vanished generation becomes a unique lesson to the present student generation. The dead were once young and full of life, just as are the students of today. The lesson here: Seize the day! In this and in many other ways, the photograph has added an enduring visual context within which today's lives and deaths gain resonance.

The telephone had its own distinctive transformational effect. The human voice with all its subtle tones and inflections now could transcend distance. The pangs of separation and absence—so closely associated with bereavement—could be relieved by hearing the familiar reassuring voice. So the process has continued, with every significant new form of communication having its effects on our symbolic relationship with both life and death. Sound recording not only revolutionized the place of music in society but also rescued conversations and speeches from being carried away in the ever-flowing river of time. "Are we live or on tape?" became a question with philosophical as well as practical implications. Does it really matter if the voice we hear is that of a person who is speaking to us in "real time" (another new concept)? The voice and message are the same if taped, and even if the speaker is deceased. The ear processes the sound in the same way (given an accurate recording) whether the message is live, on tape, or from the living or the dead.

Another important dimension is the remarkable new ability to time-shift. Those who were born into the age of electronics might take time-shifting for granted as they program the VCR to record a show for later viewing. Nevertheless, time-shifting is among the features that most distinguish present times from the human past. The role of time in human life was well described by the Persian poet Omar Khayyam (1990) in the 11th century:

> The Moving Finger writes; and, having writ,
> Moves on: nor all your Piety nor Wit
> Shall lure it back to cancel half a Line,
> Nor all your Tears wash out a Word of it. (p. 42)

Time rules. Operating through time, life does not give us a second chance. Errors cannot be corrected; failures cannot be repaired. No matter how clever or religious we might be, time will take its own course and, with that course, all that we hold dear, including life. How should we come to terms with death, given this view of time? People differed, then as now. Some, for example, attempted to prove Khayyam wrong by delving into alchemy or magic to prolong youth and life. The quest for perpetual youth was a desperate and occasionally inspired effort to bend time to human desire (Kastenbaum, 1995). Others decided to burn their candles brightly and live as intensely as they could within a shortened frame of time. Still others sought to distract themselves from the disappearing sands of time by drink or other means. Time was not fragmented into stopwatch or nanosecond measures but was regarded as the long, slow, unopposable wave that swept away kingdoms as inexorably as it did the individual's youth and life.

Time's rule has now been challenged. We can convert immediate experience to the time-insensitive format of digital encoding. Essentially, time becomes number (or its electronic equivalent). Life remains perishable in the stream of time, but episodes within life can be stored "for later viewing at our convenience."

What are the implications of these changes on our views of life and death? Perhaps you can recall from earlier chapters how difficult it is for children to develop and for adults to face the basic facts of death. The popularity of the idea that death is a kind of sleep also reveals our reluctance to recognize it on its own terms. We are often grateful for any opportunity to escape the recognition of mortality even (or especially) when in jeopardy. Technology's very good tricks of recording and time-shifting can play right into our preference for keeping death out of awareness. Every time we take advantage of a time-eluding technology we might be making it that much easier to blur the difference between "virtual" and "real reality."

Consider a person who has had limited primary social interaction during infancy and childhood. Place a computer in front of that person and provide access to a vast universe of images and symbols. Give that person the opportunity to manipulate the images and symbols. Allow that person the power of trashing and deleting whatever does not please. Add the attraction of game playing. To this game playing add a personal impulse that has been stimulated by mass media society since childhood: the pleasures to be found not only in victory but also in destruction.

Some of the most popular computer-mediated games are variations on the shooting galleries that were long popular in carnivals and fairs. With the embellishments of vivid graphics one can zap the alien invaders or blast away at other life-form images. The most technologically updated aliens are the latest stand-ins for the Other: people who are not like us and therefore suitable as targets for our rage, pride, and entertainment. Competing to see who can get the highest score of targets destroyed in a computer game is an activity that comes painfully close to representing our society's aggressive edge. That the same group of people most attracted to zapping computer games also produces the most real-life killers is a connection that is as difficult to overlook as it is to interpret with any degree of confidence.

Do one more "favor" for this computer-linked person. Give this person the opportunity to interact through innumerable "chat rooms" (not rooms at all, of course, but electronic artifacts that can lull us into supposing we are interacting with real people in a real place). The people with whom this person interacts may or may not be the persons they represent themselves to be. More significantly, it is possible to carry on this attenuated form of interaction to the neglect of real-life relationships. Notoriously complex, shifting, and sometimes "messy" are real-life relationships. Furthermore, the real people in our lives are not always available when we need them. Computer-mediated interactions are always available, though, just a mouse click away. Real-life relationships also have a way of making demands on

us when we would rather not be bothered. One might often prefer the company of cybernetic-generated or -mediated spirits to that of flesh-and-blood mortals.

The crucial point, of course, is that the images and icons displayed on our monitors are not flesh-and-blood mortals. No heart stops beating when, with the touch of a finger, we trash or discard. Is it possible that our computer-bred, computer-linked person will fail to appreciate the crucial difference between the real death of real people and the pseudolethality that flourishes in virtual reality? Currently, we have no solid information on the effect of the computer lifestyle on our orientation toward life and death. Perhaps there is little basis for concern. However, perhaps the many hours spent linked to computers rather than engaged in direct interactions will make it even easier to evade the realization that death is a central fact of real life.

Perhaps it will become even easier with a few keystrokes to endanger the lives of people we have never met. There is less reluctance to harm people who are not known individually and whose suffering and death will not be seen. The 60 million (not a misprint) peasants who starved to death during China's catastrophic farm reform movement were not family, friends, or neighbors of the leadership. The planners and leaders did not have to see the effects of decisions they made at a distance. When bombs were first dropped on a civilian population (Guernica, Spain), there was a widespread reaction of shock and outrage. Aerial assault on civilian populations persisted and intensified, however, in part because those who unleashed their bombs with the push of a button or the slide of a lever could not see the faces and mangled bodies below. The same action involved in pushing a button (or clicking a mouse) can have the effect of playing a game, sending a communication, or destroying lives.

The law-abiding, peacefully occupied person who is engrossed in computer-mediated interactions might also have rich and deep connections with other real-life people. Perhaps most people are also able to switch back to human reality when they turn off the computer. The various forms taken by virtual reality might prove to be enhancements to understanding and apprecia-

tion of life and very little of a threat. On the other hand, the concerns expressed here might prove to be all too well-founded. We just do not know yet if future generations will have a firm grasp of both virtual reality and the kind of reality that is experienced by mortal beings.

"THE GOOD DEATH:" FANTASY OR REALITY?

What can we say now about the relationship between a life and its death? Does having lived a "good life" contribute to ending with a "good death?" What about the reverse: Can the way a person dies alter the meaning and quality of that person's entire life? "Good death" has been kept in quotation marks to remind us that there are many opinions to choose from, including views that dismiss the whole idea of a good death. Now we can dispense with the quotation marks and get right to the central issues. We will also con-

tinue to speak of the good death, the term that has come into general usage, even though what we are really concerned with here is the way in which a life comes to its end.

Some of the most important observations and ideas can be summarized in the following propositions. You are invited to bring your own experience and judgment to the evaluation of these propositions. In doing so, you will notice that some of the propositions seem to be at odds with each other, and that the propositions are difficult to compare because they draw on different realms of observation, evidence, and belief. And so—to the challenge!

Proposition 1. We can agree that some forms of death are terrible even if we cannot always agree on what constitutes a good death. People should be spared such deaths. The terrible death is dominated by suffering. There is physical pain to the point of agony. There may also be extreme mental pain, such as when a mother sees her child being killed while she herself is dying. Torture and humiliation, which were often part of HD in the 20th century, are aimed to destroy the person spiritually as well as physically.

Essentially, a terrible death is the kind of ending that most people would most desperately want to avoid for themselves and their loved ones. Because suffering is universal, it is not unreasonable to assume that people everywhere would fear a death marked by extreme physical, mental, and spiritual suffering. However, some people have believed that suffering is a valuable experience. We *should* suffer because this either helps to pay for our sins or promotes our spiritual growth. This belief can be held to a lesser or greater degree. In the past, the extreme position has been used to argue against providing pain relief to women in labor, a particularly cruel example of gender discrimination. There are also contemporary examples of withholding pain relief to terminally ill people for similar reasons. However, terminally ill people today rarely see any inherent value in suffering. It is an unfortunate situation when people in a position to provide care and the dying patient have very different ideas about the value of suffering.

Proposition 2: The good death should enact the highest values held by society. Both the individual and society benefit from such a death. The individual is seen as accomplishing something of exceptional merit. Society is strengthened by having one of its members demonstrate allegiance to its values with his or her last breath. Furthermore, each person's death is important as a possible test of both individual character and society's strength. This emphasis on how a person faces death contrasts sharply with the "failed machine" model that has often been implicit in medical management. The community and its health care professionals cannot turn away from a dying person if there is something important that all believe should be accomplished as life gives way to death.

However, *what* precisely is to be accomplished at the end of life? The answer to this question varies. One of the most dramatic models is the heroic death. The person is to die bravely. The Kamikaze pilot and the Sioux warrior were among the many men who accepted combat missions in which their deaths were almost assured. In Norse mythology, the Vikings who died as battlefield heroes were rewarded with an afterlife in Valhalla. Both women and men are included among the martyrs—people who chose death rather than renounce their religious faith. The type of suicide that Durkheim described as altruistic (Chapter 8) may also belong here. The heroic death usually involves choice. Loyalty to one's people or God takes precedence over staying alive.

Heroic deaths seem to always have been exceptional and, therefore, especially admired and remembered. Not everybody has the opportunity or the ability to end his or her life in a way that dramatically affirms core social values. Many more people, however, have been able to demonstrate their social conscience by facing death with resolute allegiance to the values they cherish. For example, some cultural traditions hold that one should bear suffering in silence. I have known people who did not speak of their pain nor seek comfort and relief during their final illness. They were determined to live up to what was expected of them by tradition.

Others have acted in accordance with cultural expectations, such as going off to a particular place or even assuming a particular physical position when death is near. Some traditions also expect the dying person to offer memorable last words. A striking example is that of the *jisei* or farewell verse written by Japanese Zen buddhists monks and Haiku poets. Although the tradition has varied over the centuries, it was often considered best to be sitting upright at the moment of death, using one's last words to offer a poem to those gathered around. In contrast to religious traditions in which last words are supposed to be pious, the *jisei* often is playful and surprising:

> My last breath chases the first
> Two whispers at play
> In the garden of lost boys

and

> Tell them whatever you like
> My *jisei* was perfect
> or I coughed up a green toad

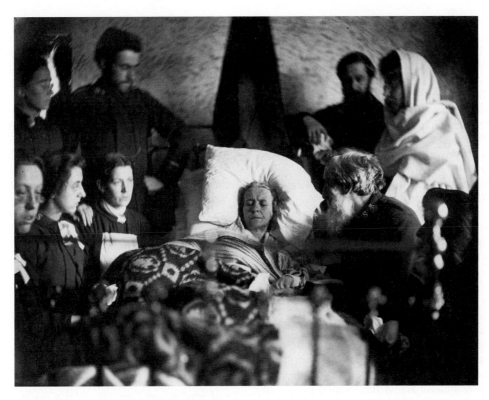

The celebration of life can not only continue, but also take on special meaning when "the days draw down to a precious few."

If we embrace Proposition 2, we should expect to discover a great many variations—as many ideas about the good death as there are societal values. One of the most striking variations is *oppositional death.* People who have become bitter or disillusioned may use their last words and energies in attacking society's values. For example, a hospice chaplain spoke to me soon after having left the bedside of a dying woman who had rejected him and cursed God. He was shaken by this encounter but already starting to make sense of it:

She couldn't have said anything that would have upset me more, and she knew it. Life had been a kind of poison to her for a long time, since her son, then her husband died. I think this was her getting the poison out and her using the strongest word she knew—that would be God. [A strange kind of prayer?] That's exactly what it was. A strange kind of prayer. I will go back to her—and she will take my hand.

It is likely that societal expectations influence the way we deal with the end of our lives even if we are not attempting to achieve a particular kind of death. Experienced caregivers have usually learned to suspend their own expectations and attend instead to the cultural values that are most cherished by terminally ill people and their families.

Proposition 3: The good death is one in which our most significant personal relationships are affirmed. These relationships may also embody societal and religious values, but it is their personal meanings that are especially cherished. Studies of deathbed scenes, actual (Kastenbaum, 1994, 2000) and imagined (Kastenbaum & Normand, 1990), find that relationships are usually the uppermost concern. People most often desire the companionship of those who have shared their lives through the years. This does not mean that dying people want to have all the people in their lives with them all the time. Sometimes it is enough to be with a person a time or two in order to achieve a sense of closure in the relationship.

Recall the last words of a dying father in Kaliai, a region of western New Britain, to his daughter: "Ah, now that you are here I can die easily. He then closed his eyes and within 2 hours he was dead" (Counts & Counts, 1985, p. 42).

There are also circumstances in which the dying person may feel more comfortable having only indirect interactions with some people because of certain tensions or concerns. Even when interpersonal contact is minimal or indirect, the quality of the interaction may help to affirm the value of the relationship. That one smile or hand clasp might be enough to let others know that they have been appreciated.

Effective palliative care has done much to provide opportunities for continuing and affirming relationships near life's end. Relief of pain without dulling consciousness has helped people to have many quality interactions that otherwise would not have occurred. Being able to spend more time at home has also enhanced the opportunity for natural interactions.

The good death as affirmation of our most meaningful personal relationships has many implications for the way in which we have shaped our lives. People whose interpersonal relationships have been prevailingly antagonistic, conflictful, or distant are less likely to have loving companions at their side near the end of life. Furthermore, nurses and other service providers may also find it difficult to establish caring relationships with people who have cultivated an abusive attitude toward others throughout their lives. Personal characteristics that earn the respect and affection of other people throughout the years often contribute to a warm and supportive interpersonal network at the end of life.

Proposition 4: The good death is one in which there is a transfiguring personal experience. As death approaches one feels a profound sense of beauty, love, or understanding. The moment of death is also the peak experience of life. This construction of the good

death has been with us in many forms throughout the centuries. The Moody-type near-death experience (Chapter 14) has brought renewed attention to this mystical state of being. The final pages of Tolstoy's *The Death of Ivan Ilych* (Chapter 2) provide a dramatic literary example, but there are also real-life people who seem to be having powerful and distinctive experiences near the end of their lives (Kastenbaum, 1994). Perhaps a subtle remote influence on the current interest in a transfiguring moment of death is the medieval fascination with deathbed conversions and miracles (Aries, 1981).

There are several frames of mind that can be associated with the good death as a transfiguring experience:

- *A sense of adventure:* "Life has been a series of adventures—why not death as well?
- *A sense of mystical awareness:* "I just know there is more to life than the everyday, so the moment of death may open these mysteries to me."
- *A sense of escaping from a disappointing life:* "This transfiguring moment will make up for the hurts and sorrows I have experienced in life."
- *A need to avoid the stressful realities of dying and separation:* "I will get myself to think only of the beauty and wonder of dying, not the physical side of it, and not the interpersonal issues."

At the end of their lives, some people seem to have a distinctive and powerful experience that we cannot share. The first person I observed in this situation was an old man close to death who was sitting up in bed with a surprising display of renewed strength. He gestured eloquently while engaging in an animated conversation with a visitor visible or audible only to himself. This was a serious interaction in which, apparently, important matters were being discussed and resolved. For whatever it means, all of us felt that he was not out of his mind but had taken his mind someplace else. However, we did not know. The next time I saw a dying person seeming to interact with a "spirit visitor," I still did not know what was happening.

Other people near death slip away as into a deeper sleep, and we may choose to interpret this also as the outer manifestation of a transfiguring state of being. However, do *most* people die with an exalted experience? That is quite a different question, and the answer is likely to depend on whether we rely primarily on faith and hope or on what can be learned through direct observation.

Proposition 4 remains a powerful model of the good death, but one that can distract us from the "ordinary" challenges that are faced by dying people and their families. There is a tendency to scrub dying and death clean before these anxiety-arousing topics can be acknowledged. "Healthy dying" (Kastenbaum, 1979) is a theme that attempts to sugarcoat the actual stress and loss experienced by many terminally ill people. The model of the good death as transfigured life is sometimes used to avoid dealing with disturbing realities. The idea of the good death as a peak experience is compelling enough on its own terms that it does not need an assist from denial.

Proposition 5: The good death is one in which people continue to be themselves as long as possible, preferably to the very end. This view is similar to Weisman's (1972) concept of an appropriate death: the death a person would choose for himself or herself. It is not identical, though, because some people would prefer to take a different turning at the end of their lives (e.g., an heroic or transfiguring death).

Most of the terminally ill people in the National Hospice Demonstration Study (Chapter 6) who were asked about the last 3 days of their lives expressed a preference for a familiar routine: a day like any other, at home, with the people who meant the most to them. In a recent study, elderly Israelis also emphasized the value they placed on continuity (Leichtentritt & Rettig, 2000). This value encompassed the funeral and memorial process as well. One respondent expressed his thoughts as follows:

My funeral should correspond with whom I am …[with] the way I lived my life. My family knows I do not want them to sit Shiva over me…. I do not wish people to mourn after me in this way—it is not who I am.

Another respondent had a different emphasis:

I am willing to suffer a lot. I am willing to tolerate pain, but I am *not* willing to tolerate a disrespect-

ful process…. I have seen funerals in my life that were disrespectful—that is exactly what I do not wish for…. When I said that I wish for a respectful process…it does not end the moment I close my eyes. (p. 237)

Many people seem comfortable with the idea of ending their lives much as they have lived. This model of the good death is usually consistent with the model that emphasizes affirming one's closest interpersonal relationship. Again, the hospice movement has proved valuable in helping many people to continue being themselves through the final phase of life.

EXTINCTION: DEATH OF LIFE OR DEATH OF DEATH?

Trying to understand and come to terms with death is difficult enough. But *extinction?* It would be sensible to avoid this subject because it involves cosmic and ecological considerations that seem a long way from our everyday lives. If we want to be honest about it, extinction might just be too large, inconceivable, and threatening a topic to add to the many concerns we have already encountered. Why be so sensible, though? We will be sensible enough, though, to call on some assistance in thinking about extinction.

St. Paul's Cathedral, 1623

The physicians were doing what they could. As his life continued to slip away they prepared draughts fortified with additional ingredients that are as well unmentioned. This failing, they next applied pigeons "to draw the vapours" from his head. Privately, he mused:

But what have I done, either to breed or to breathe these vapours? They tell me it is my melancholy; did I infuse, did I drink in melancholy Into myself? It is my thoughtfulness; was I not made to think?

He played resourcefully with the idea of vapours even as the pigeons performed their ministrations, suggesting that the most poisonous emanations come not from Nature's deadly creatures but from those people who specialize in deceitful and mean-spirited actions. This meditation is concluded with a simple message to the angel-surrogates who were gathered around him: "Be a good pigeon to draw this vapour from the head and from doing any damage there."

What history remembers occurred a few days after the wine and pigeon treatments. He was edging even closer to death but still able to record his thoughts. Lying abed so close to St. Paul's Cathedral (he was dean of this illustrious religious center), he could not help but hear the bells repeatedly tolling as one soul or another departed this earth. Who was it this time? Will he be the next?

> Who bends not his ear to any bell which upon any occasion rings? But who can remove it from that bell which is passing a piece of himself out of this world? No man is an island, entire of himself; every man is a piece of the continent, a part of the main. If a clod be washed away by the sea, Europe is the less…. Any man's death diminishes me, because I am involved in mankind, and therefore never send to know for whom the bell tolls; it tolls for thee.

This is an excerpt from the 17th of John Donne's *Devotions* (1963/1975), all of which are recommended to anybody who is ready to consider the human condition without blinking too much. Donne knew life and death better than almost anybody. He reveled in the passion that binds lovers together, affirmed the bonds that unite all humans everywhere, and meditated on the mysterious relationship between a mortal soul and God.

All that lives should have compassion toward all that lives. In a sense, we are each other. This is a facet of Donne's message that can prepare us to consider extinction. (Perhaps this message was affirmed by the pigeons without whose skilled efforts Donne might not have lived to and beyond Devotion 17.) Consider now one other implication from the same source. One of Donne's sonnets begins

> Death, be not proud, though some have called thee
> Mighty and dreadful, for thou are not so;
> For those whom thou think'st thou dost overthrow
> Die not, poor Death, nor yet canst thou kill me.

It concludes

> One short sleep past, we wake eternally,
> And Death shall be no more: Death, thou shalt die.

This is an expression of the faith in the Christian promise that Donne had labored to achieve through years of doubt. Whether or not one shares this faith, though, all can reflect on his confident dismissal: *"Death, thou shalt die."* Reflect, if you will, on the startling idea that death could die. Now introduce the idea of extinction. That death itself could perish becomes a less fantastic prospect. Death might die at its own hand. Every species extinguished perhaps reduces the power of death. Extinction of all life would be the supreme act of (let's call it) *thanatocide*. The Egyptians who honored the dung beetle by placing its likeness in the chest of dead pharoahs and queens were among the many who discerned that life needs death. However, death, though, also needs life.

Sigmund Freud (1920/1960) suggested that we have two basic instincts: one devoted to life *(Eros)* and the other to death *(Thanatos)*. This is the normal state of affairs. Eros and Thanatos scrimmage with each other throughout our lives, but the final outcome is never in doubt. The trick, thought Freud, was to keep the game going. Eros and only Eros would whirl us into a daze, and Thanatos, unrestrained, might suddenly destroy others as well as ourselves. Keep a little death in life and enough life to counterbalance death. This facet of Freudian theory is nearly extinct, but it is still another way of conveying the idea that impulses toward death are inherently self-destructive or thanatocidal. Total extinction would be game, set, and match.

The Death of Species

Extinction usually refers to the destruction of an entire species or life-form. Most famous perhaps is the termination of the dinosaur reign approximately 65 million years ago. Mass extinctions are known to have occurred at least five times in the distant past, and there is consensus that the sixth mass extinction is in progress right now. (Actually, scientists believe that there were a great many more extinctions in the past that have not left sufficient evident to analyze.) The five most documented mass extinctions are summarized in Table 16-2.

Pinpointing the causes of each mass extinction requires educated guesswork, but collisions with asteroids (and meteor showers) are suspected in most of the episodes, although with tumultuous changes in earth/sea formations and extreme climactic changes. At least one thing is clear: All these extinctions occurred without human contrivance or influence.

Many species have lost their struggle for life apart from the mass extinctions. This process was first brought to general attention by Charles Darwin (1869) in his landmark book, *On the Origin of Species by Means of Natural Selection, or the Preservation of Favoured Races in the Struggle for Life.* His observations led him to the conclusion that life-forms are related to each other in a complex web of circumstances. (Echoes of Donne? No nematod is an island entire to itself.) The circumstances include everything that make up the living environment or, as it came to be called later, the ecosphere (Broswimmer, 2002). Life-forms have to contend both with each other and with the resources, limitations, and hazards of their ecosphere. Over the course of years, some creatures are able to adapt to their environments and continue to flourish; others are displaced or left helpless when local circumstances change. Robust controversies about "survival of the fittest" and the "theory of evolution" still resound

today. Nevertheless, the general picture of nature now includes recognition of a continual effort to survive under a variety of pressures and changes.

Species appeared and disappeared for millions of years by natural selection (or luck) long before humans came along to lend our own distinctive contributions to the process. Today, though, it is our role in the continuing extinction of species that is arousing the most concern. Earlier in this book, a few examples were given, such as the frogs and vultures that are being decimated by pesticide and other agricultural or industrial residue. There are so many other examples, however, that one hardly knows where to start or stop. One example from the United States may serve to remind us of what the world has been losing in diversity of species and how our own kind has contributed (Kearl, 2002):

> Perhaps the most poignant of recent extinctions is the passenger pigeon, which was to be hunted into oblivion. At the beginning of the American Civil War, this was one of the most successful bird species in North America, comprising an estimated 49% of the entire bird population. In 1870, a single flock 1 mile wide and 320 miles long flew over Cincinnati. In 1974, the last surviving pigeon died in that city's zoo. As of 2001, conservationists estimated that one in every six species of birds is in decline on the continent and could wane by half by the Year 2030. (p. 278)

TABLE 16-2

Mass Extinctions

	When?	*Who Died?*	*Why?*
Ordivician–Silurian	439 million years ago	85% of all species	Shifts in earth layers
Late Devonian	365 million years ago	75% of all species (marine life even more)	Asteroids, one or more
Permian–Triassic	251 million years ago	90% of marine and land vertebrates and many trees	Asteroid, volcanoes, falling sea level
Late Triassic	200–214 million years ago	75% of all species; end of mammal-like reptiles	Asteroids, heavy rainfall
Cretacious	65 million years ago	Dinosaurs, 18% of land invertebrates; 47% of marine life	Asteroid near Yucatan and Siberian eruptions

Source: Adapted from Hallam and Wignall (1997) and Kearl (2002).

I have difficulty in trying to imagine that enormous flock of birds and even greater difficulty in accepting the fact that our species contrived to eliminate theirs (and a sorry return for their kins' banishing of John Donne's vapours). Extinction occurs on such a scale and in so many ways that it does challenge our ability to take it all in. Planet Earth continues to change, change rapidly, and change in a great many ways—most often in ways that are leading to the death of species that might otherwise remain our companions.

Is death of species good or bad, or does it occupy a moral zone beyond our usual ways of thinking? For the limited purposes of this book, perhaps all we can suggest is to remember that we are not alone on this planet and our own lives and deaths may be as truly connected to all life-forms as the dean of St. Paul's suggested while the bells continued to toll.

FROM GOOD LIFE TO GOOD DEATH: A PERSONAL STATEMENT

Welcome back, now, to our own lives. Obviously, we cannot simply choose or create a model of the good death and take it home until needed. Circumstances not completely in our control are likely to affect the conditions of our death. Furthermore, we might hesitate to shape our lives around the end of our days. There is a case to be made for enjoying each day as it comes and not burying ourselves prematurely. Perhaps there is a way of integrating a realization of death into our ongoing lives that does justice to both. Perhaps no two of us would do this in quite the same way.

Here, then, is one person's way of doing it or, rather, trying to do it, because intention does not always rule events or even one's own feelings. Here is what I try to do, based in unequal parts on what I have learned, what I do not know, and what I feel. This statement is offered only as an example that might be useful in reviewing your own approach:

• I hope to achieve an ongoing balance between awareness of risk and danger and a free and open attitude toward life. I do not want to put myself

or others in jeopardy by engaging over much in denial or related defensive strategies (Chapter 2). This awareness of possible threat to life encompasses physical, environmental, and man-made sources of danger. Yet I do not intend to crawl into a hole and pull the hole down with me. Like most other people who have been active in death-related studies, I enjoy life a lot and intend to keep doing so.

• I realize that I have a very limited ability to influence the large forces and events that in turn influence how long people live and how they die. Nevertheless, I also notice how surprisingly many opportunities there are to do something in a positive direction. Sometimes this is as simple as listening a little more intently or offering an alternative way to deal with a situation, perhaps just by demonstrating that alternative in my own behavior.

• I doubt that my death or anything associated with my death will be able to make up for the mistakes and shortcomings of my life. This means that I do not rely on a ninth inning rally, although that would be exciting. (While on the intensive care unit, I managed to stay alive by fouling off enough pitches from The Closer to stay in the game a while longer.) Instead, I feel that I have to try for a good at bat in every opportunity that comes along. That may or may not influence the final score, but nevertheless seems the best way to play the game within the decided limits of my ability.

• The Buddhist and Hindu perception of what we call life and what we call death as a coexisting flow makes a lot of sense to me. No—not to the point that I dismiss the idea of death as the end of life as I have come to know it. However, I do recognize at least some of the little births and little deaths that accompany us throughout life and from which we might be wise enough to learn.

• I know something of grief and loss and so I have some sensitivity to these feelings as they mark the faces, words, and lives of others as well. I try to be aware—at the right time, when it most counts—that this person with whom I am interacting may still be struggling with the pain of loss while trying to move on with life.

• I appreciate life the more. As a youth I went along pretty much assuming that life was both within and all about me and therefore could be taken for granted. Studies of dying and death, as well as personal experiences, have taught me to treasure life in all its forms. Yes, that does include the gigantic wolf spider that dropped down beside me one evening and decided I was OK while at the same time I was deciding he (she?) was OK; life in the trouble-making twinkle in an aged person's eyes; life in the open-eyed wonder of a young child; life in the here-right-now intensity of an athlete; and life in the who-cares-where-we-are engrossment of lovers. I can understand, I think, why encounters with death have soured some people on life. However, it happens that death has given me—and I think many other thanatologists—an ever-fresh appreciation for life.

SUMMARY

This chapter has given us an opportunity to reflect on some (certainly, not all) of the issues we have been encountering throughout the book. We were particularly interested in the meaning of the good death and how this might relate to the ways in which we live. Examples from WTC victims, people shunned because they have HIV/AIDS, and the way a great philosopher accepted his death introduced us to some of the dimensions and complexities of this issue.

A physician's response to the terminal illness of his father reminded us of how much both medical management and family support influence the outcome. Ira Byock, touched by his father's death and appalled by the mismanagement of dying people in the health care system, became an effective force for the improvement of terminal care. Eliminating futile medical procedures and providing opportunity for family and patient to have time together in natural surroundings could be seen as basic steps to prepare for the "good death."

We then noticed that the traditional meanings that have been given to death now face a new competitor or, more accurately, a newly strengthened competitor. More people today are enjoying long, healthy, and materially enhanced lives. Death is therefore less tempting as release from

the stresses and sorrows of life (as, for example, once a major factor in the lullabies sung to babies). We also noted that "not wanting to leave the party" is a trend that stands the regret theory of death anxiety on its head. According to regret theory, people who feel they have led satisfying lives are less anxious about death. However, more people may now regret (rather than fear) death just because life seems so pleasant that it should go on and on.

Horrendous death then demanded our attention as the extreme opposite of the good death. An interview with Dan Leviton, an expert on HD, called attention to the many ways in which people have either inflicted suffering, humiliation, and death on others or have achieved the same result through indifference and neglect. Leviton offered suggestions for preventing HD, and we also revisited the golden rule as a guide to protecting each other's lives. The harm done by perpetuating the Us versus Them distinction was given special consideration.

An influential new sociotechnological development also commanded our attention. Computer-generated and -mediated imagery is providing what amounts to an alternative universe of experience and interaction. We wondered about the possible impact of virtual reality on our conceptions of life and death and, therefore, on the meaning of a "good death." Photography, sound recording, and time-shifting technology have also contributed to a sense of mastery over the transience of the moment and the inexorable flow of time. Will people who are born with two umbilical cords—one connected to their mother and the other to a computer—have full appreciation for real life and real death? Questions such as these were raised in the hope of stimulating closer observation and thought.

Five propositions about the good death are identified. First, we can agree that some deaths are terrible even if we cannot always agree on what constitutes a good death. The terrible death is dominated by suffering. Second, the good death should enact the highest values held by society. Here, the heroic and the oppositional death were given particular attention. Third, the good death is one in which our most significant personal relationships are affirmed. Fourth, the good death is one in which there is a transfiguring personal experience. Finally, the good death is one in which people continue to be themselves as long as possible, preferably to the very end.

We were also encouraged to reflect on both the history and the future of extinction, a process that continues to destroy entire species and which human values and actions continue to influence.

In conclusion, I offered a personal statement about the good life and the good death.

REFERENCES

Achte, K. (1989). Lullabies of death. In R. Kastenbaum & B. K. Kastenbaum (Eds.), *Encyclopedia of death* (pp. 176–178). Phoenix, AZ: Arno.

Ahrensdorf, P. J. (1995). *The death of Socrates and the life of philosophy.* Albany: State University of New York Press.

Aries, P. (1981). *At the hour of our death.* New York: Knopf.

Associated Press. (2002, May 27). *At least 357 killed in terror attacks made phone calls.* New York: Author.

Broswimmer, F. J. (2002). *Ecocide: A short history of mass extinction of species.* New York: Pluto.

Byock, I. (1997). *Dying well.* New York: Riverhead.

Conquest, R. (1986). *The harvest of sorrow.* New York: Oxford University Press.

Counts, D., & Counts, D. (1985). *Aging and its transformations: Moving toward death in Pacific societies.* Lanham, MD: University Press of America.

Donne, J. (1975). *Devotions.* Ann Arbor: University of Michigan Press. (Original work published 1623).

Erikson, E. H. (1950). *Childhood and society.* New York: Norton.

Feifel, H. (Ed.). (1959). *The meaning of death.* New York: McGraw-Hill.

Freud, S. (1960). *Beyond the pleasure principle.* New York: Norton. (Original work published 1920).

Friedlander, H. (1995). *The origins of Nazi genocide.* Chapel Hill: University of North Carolina Press.

Goldhagen, D. J. (1996). *Hitler's willing executioners.* New York: Knopf.

Gyatso, Tenzin, the 14th Dali Lama. (1985). *Kindness, clarity, and insight* (J. Hopkins, Trans.). Ithaca, NY: Snow Lions.

Hallam, A., & Wignall, P. B. (1997). *Mass extinctions and their aftermath.* New York: Oxford University Press.

Hussain, W. (2002, December 1). *Activist gives face to disease. Wants to make people aware others live in secrecy in India.* New York: Associated Press.

Kastenbaum, R. (1979). "Healthy dying": A paradoxical quest continues. *Journal of Social Issues, 35,* 185–206.

Kastenbaum, R. (1994). Is there an ideal deathbed scene? In I. B. Corless, B. B. Germino, & M. Pittman (Eds.), *Dying, death, and bereavement* (pp. 109–122). Boston: Jones & Bartlett.

Kastenbaum, R. (1995). *Dorian, graying: Is youth the only thing worth having?* New York: Baywood.

Kastenbaum, R. (2000). *The psychology of death* (3rd ed.). New York: Springer.

Kastenbaum, R. (2002). Socrates. In R. Kastenbaum (Ed.), *Macmillan encyclopedia of death and dying* (Vol. 2, pp. 769–772). New York: Macmillan.

Kastenbaum, R., & Normand, C. (1990). Deathbed scenes as imagined by the young and experienced by the old. *Death Studies, 14,* 201–218.

Kearl, M. (2002). Extinction. In R. Kastenbaum (Ed.), *Macmillan encyclopedia of death and dying* (Vol. 2, pp. 275–283). New York: Macmillan.

Khayyam, O. (1990). *The Rubaiyat of Omar Khayyam* (E. Fitzgerald, Trans.) New York: Dover. (Original work published in the 12th century.)

Leichtentritt, R. D., & Rettig, K. D. (2000). The good death: Reaching an inductive understanding. *Omega, Journal of Death and Dying, 41,* 221–248.

Leviton, D. (Ed.). (1991). *Horrendous death and health: Toward action.* New York: Hemisphere.

Leviton, D. (1995). Horrendous death: Linking thanatology and public health. In J. Kauffman (Ed.), *Awareness of mortality* (pp. 185–213). Amityville, NY: Baywood.

Leviton, D., Kennedy, J., Woodruff, R., & Like, K. (1998). *ADHP Manual for staffers* (3rd ed.). College Park, MD: University of Maryland Press.

Lifton, R. J. (1986). *The Nazi doctors: Medical killing and the psychology of genocide.* New York: Basic Books.

Lipstadt, D. (1994). *Denying the Holocaust.* New York: Plume.

Ober, W. B. (1988). Did Socrates die of hemlock poisoning? In *Boswell's clap & other essays. Medical analyses of literary men's afflictions.* New York: Harper & Row.

Schultz, E. E., & Francis, T. (2002, April 23). Firms benefit from insuring workers' lives. *Wall Street Journal,* p. B1.

Tanner, L. (2002, November 20). *Higher death rate reported at for-profit dialysis centers.* New York: Associated Press.

Taylor, J. (1970). *The rules and exercises of holy dying.* New York: Arno. (Original work published 1665)

Tomer, A., & Eliason, G. (1996). Toward a comprehensive model of death anxiety. *Death Studies, 20,* 343–366.

Weisman, A. D. (1972). *On dying and denying: A psychiatric study of terminality.* New York: Behavioral Publications.

GLOSSARY

Appropriate Death: The way a person would choose to have his or her life come to an end.

Genocide: Killing people because of their nationality, religion, race, or any other group characteristic.

Horrendous Death: A premature and unexpected death caused by other people, often violent and painful.

Quixotian: A brave but misguided and futile attempt to do something great (see *Don Quixote*).

SELECTED LEARNING RESOURCES

There are many other organizations—national, international, and local—that might be able to provide you with useful information or services. Valuable articles on death-related issues also appear in a variety of scholarly and professional journals as well as in quality magazines and newspapers. The Internet, that cybernetic version of Pandora's Box, offers expert and reliable information but also unsubstantiated opinion, discredited assumptions, engaging or repulsive fantasies, barely disguised sales pitches, messages of faith, and cheap humor: Browser beware! This Appendix is limited to death-related issues as addressed by a sampling of responsible national organizations, scholarly and professional journals in the interdisciplinary field of thanatology, and some of the Internet-only resources that have been found most useful by students, teachers, and counselors. You have probably already discovered that Web sites do have a way of flashing into virtual existence and then disappearing, and some in fact are dead (no longer updated or linked to an ongoing operation). With all these preliminary words out of the way, please consider yourself invited to browse the following guide. Resources with a focus on children are italicized. Contact information varies by information provided by each organization.

NATIONAL ORGANIZATIONS

Alcor Life Extension Foundation (cryonics)
7895 E. Acoma Drive, #110
Scottsdale, AZ 85260-6916
(877) GO-ALCOR
info@alcor.org
www.alcor.org

American Academy of Hospice and Palliative Medicine
4700 W. Lake Avenue
Glenville, IL 60025-2485
(847) 375-4712
aahpm@aahpm.org
www.aapm.org

American Association of Suicidology
4201 Connecticut Avenue NW, Suite 310
Washington, DC 20008
(202) 237-2280
www.suicidology.org

American Cancer Society
1599 Clifton Road NE
Atlanta, GA 30329
www.cancer.org

American Cryonics Society
P.O. Box 1509
Cupertino, CA 95015
(800) 523-2001
cryonics@ips.net

American Heart Association
7272 Greenville Avenue
Dallas, TX 75231
(800) AHA-USA1
www.americanheart.org

American Hospice Foundation
2120 L Street NW, Suite 200
Washington, DC 20037
ahf@msn.com
www.americanhospice.org

American Sudden Infant Death Syndrome Institute
2480 Windy Hill Road, Suite 380
Marietta, GA 30067
(800) 232-SIDS
prevent@sids.org
www.sids.org

Association for Death Education and Counseling
342 North Main Street
West Hartford, CT 06117
(860) 586-7503
info@adec.org
www.adec.org

Befrienders International
26–27 Market Place,
Kingston upon Thames
Surrey KT1 1JH, England
admin@befrienders.org
www.befrienders.org

Brady Center to Prevent Gun Violence
1225 Eye Street NW, Suite 1100
Washington, DC 20005
(202) 289-7319
www.gunlawsuits.org

Canadian Association for Suicide Prevention
11456 Jasper Avenue
Edmonton, Alberta T4K OM1 Canada
casp@suicideprevention.ca
www.thesupportnetwork.com/CASP

Candlelighters Childhood Cancer Foundation
3910 Warner Street
Kensington, MD 20895
info@candlelighters.org
www.candlelighters.org

Center for Death Education and Bioethics
435NH, 1725 State Street
University of Wisconsin
La Crosse, WI 54601
cdeb@uwlax.edu
www.uwlax.edu/sociology/cde&b

Center to Improve Care of the Dying
1001 22nd Street, Suite 802
Washington, DC 20037
(202) 467-2222

Children's Hospice International
901 N. Pitt Street, Suite 230
Alexandria, VA 22314
(800) 24-CHILD
chiorg@aol.com

Compassionate Friends, Inc.
P.O. Box 3696
Oak Brook, IL 60522
TCFCanada@aol.com
www.compassionatefriends.org

Concerns of Police Survivors (COPS)
P.O. Box 3199
South Highway 5
Camdenton, MO 65020
Cops@nationalcops.org
www.nationalcops.org

Cremation Association of North America
401 North Michigan Avenue
Chicago, IL 60611
cana@sba.com
www.cremationassocation.org

Dougy Center for Grieving Children
3909 SE 52nd Avenue
Portland, OR 97286
help@dougy.org
www.dougy.org or
www.grievingchild.org

**Elizabeth Glaser Pediatric
AIDS Foundation**
2950 31st Street, #125
Santa Monica, CA 90405
(888) 499-HOPE
www.pedaids.org/index/html

European Association for Palliative Care
National Cancer Institute of Milan
Via Venezian 1
20133, Milan, Italy
Eapc@istitutotumori.m.it
www.eapcnet.org

Funeral Consumers Alliance
P.O. Box 10
Hinesburg, VT 05461
(800) 765-0107
www.funerals.org

Hemlock Society
P.O. Box 101810
Denver, CO 80250
Email@hemlock.org
www.hemlock.org

Hospice and Palliative Nurses Association
Penn Center W. One, Suite 209
Pittsburgh, PA 15276
Hpna@hpna.org
www.hpna.org

Hospice Association of America
228 Seventh Street, SE
Washington, DC 20003
(202) 546-4759
www.nahc.org

Hospice Foundation of America
2001 S Street NW, Suite 300
Washington, DC 20009
(800) 854-3402
www.hospicefoundation.org

Hospice Information
St. Christopher's Hospital
51 Lawrie Park Road

London SE26 6DZ, England
Info@hospiceinformation.info
www.hospiceinformation.info

**International Association
for Suicide Prevention**
Rush Center for Suicide Prevention
1725 W. Harrison St., Suite 955
Chicago, IL 60612
iasp@aol.com
www.who.int/ina-ngo

**International Association
of Pet Cemeteries**
5055 Route 11
Ellenburg Depot, NY 12935
(518) 549-3000
www.iaopc.com

Last Acts
The Robert Wood Johnson Foundation
P.O. Box 2316
Princeton, NJ 08542
www.lastacts.org

Leukemia and Lymphoma Society
1311 Mamoronek Avenue
White Plains, NY 10605
(800) 955-4572
www.leukemia.org

Living Bank International (organ donation)
P.O. Box 6725
Houston, TX 77265
Info@livingbank.org
www.livingbank.org

Make-A-Wish Foundation of America
3550 N. Central Avenue, Suite 300
Phoenix, AZ 85012
mawfa@wish.org

Mothers Against Drunk Driving (MADD)
P.O. Box 541688
Dallas, TX 75354
(800) GET-MADD
www.madd.org

**National Association of People
with AIDS**
1413 K Street NW, 7th Floor
Washington, DC 20005
napwa@napwa.org
www.napwa.org

National Center for Death Education
Mount Ida College
777 Dedham Street
Newton Centre, MA 02159
Ncde@mountida.edu
www.muntida.edu/shells/adm/
schools-programs

**National Coalition to Stop
Handgun Violence**
100 Maryland Avenue, Northeast
Washington, DC 20002
(202) 544-7190

**National Funeral Directors
and Morticians Association**
3951 Snapfinger Parkway, Suite 570
Omega World Center
Decatur, GA 30035
nfdma@nfdma.com
www.nfdma.com

National Hemophilia Foundation
116 W. 32nd Street, 11th Floor
New York, NY 10001
info@hemophilia.org
www.hemophilia.org

**National Hospice and Palliative
Care Organization**
1700 Diagonal Road, Suite 300
Alexandria, VA 22314
info@nhpco.org
www.nhpco.org

National Institute for Jewish Hospice
Cedars-Sinai Medical Center
444 S. San Vincente Blvd., Suite 101,
Los Angeles, CA 90048
(800) 446-4448

**National Native American AIDS
Prevention Center**
436 14th Street, Suite 1020
Oakland, CA 96412
information@nnaapc.org
www.nnaapc.org

**National Organization of Parents
of Murdered Children, Inc.**
100 E. 8th Street, B-41
Cincinnati, OH 45202
natlomc@aol.com
www.pomc.com

**National Organization
for Victims Assistance**
1730 Park Road, N.W.
Washington, DC 20010
nova@try-nova.org
www.try-nova.org

**National SIDS/Infant Death
Resource Center**
2070 Chain Bridge Road, Suite 450
Vienna, VA 22182
sids@circlesolutions.com
www.sidscenter.org

National Stroke Association
9707 E. Easter Lane
Englewood, CO 80112
(800) STROKES
www.stroke.org

**National Women's Health
Resource Center**
120 Albany Street, Suite 820
New Brunswick, NJ 089
nfo@healthywomen.org
www.healthywomen.org

Oncology Nursing Society
501 Holiday Drive
Pittsburgh, PA 15220-2749
Customer.service@ons.org.
www.ons.org

Partnership for Caring: America's Voices for the Dying (formerly, Choice in Dying)
1620 Eye Street NW, Suite 202
Washington, DC 20007
pfc@partnershipforcaring.org
www.partnershipforcaring.org

Project on Death in America
Open Society Institute
400 W. 59th Street
New York, NY 10019
(212) 548-1334
www.soros.org/death

SHARE Pregnancy and Infant Loss Support, Inc.
National SHARE Office
300 First Capitol Drive
St. Charles, MO 63301
Share@nationalshareoffice.com
www.nationalshareoffice.com

Society of Military Widows
5535 Hempstead Way
Springfield, VA 22151
benefits@militarywidows.org
www.militarywidows.org

Starlight Foundation International
12424 Wilshire Boulevard, Suite 1050
Los Angeles, CA 90025
(800) 274-7827
www.atk.Isi.ukas.edu/funding/resources/STARLIGHT

United Network for Organ Sharing
1100 Boulders Parkway, Suite 500
Richmond, VA 23225
www.unos.org

SCHOLARLY AND PROFESSIONAL JOURNALS

Death Studies
Taylor & Francis
1101 Vermont Ave, NW, Suite 200
Washington, DC 20005

(901) 678-4680
neimeyer@cc.memphis.edu
www.tandf.co.uk/journals

European Journal of Palliative Care
National Cancer Institute of Milan
Via Venezian 1, 20133
Milan, Italy
www.eapcnet.org

Hospice Journal
Haworth Press
10 Alice Street
Binghamton, NY 13904
getinfo@haworth.com
www.haworthpressinc.com

Illness, Crisis and Loss
Sage Publications
2455 Teller Road
Thousand Oaks, CA 91320
(800) 818-7243
www.sagepub.com

Journal of Near-Death Studies
Kluwer Academic Publishers
101 Philip Drive, Assinippi Park
Norwell, MA 02061
kluwer@wkap.com

Journal of Pain and Palliative Care
The Haworth Press
10 Alice Street
Binghamton, NY 13904-1580
getinfo@haworthpressinc.com
www.haworthpressinc.com

Mortality
Taylor & Francis
11 New Fetter Lane
London EC4P 4EE, United Kingdom
www.tandf.co.uk

Omega, Journal of Death and Dying
Baywood Publishing
26 Austin Avenue
Amityville, NY 11701

(800) 638-7819
info@baywood.com
www.baywood.com

Suicide and Life-Threatening Behavior
Guilford Publications
72 Spring Street
New York, NY 10012
(800) 365-7006
info@guilford.com
www.guilford.com

INTERNET RESOURCES

General Sites with Multiple Hotlinks

Bereavement Resources
www.funeral.net/info/brvres.

GriefNet
http://www.rivendell. org

Mental Health Net
http://www.cmhc.com

Yahoo's Death Page
www.yahoo.com/Society_and Culture/Death

WEBSTER
http://www.katsden.com/death/index.html

Funerals and Memorializations

Death Rituals & Funeral Customs
www.encarta.msn.com

Funeral and Memorial Societies of America
http://ubiweb.c.champlain.edu/famsa.directory.htm

Internet Cremation Society
www.cremation.org

Pet Grief Support Page
www.petloss.com

World Wide Cemetery
http://www.interlog.com/cemetery

Death Education Opportunities

Cultural Diversity
http://www.excepc.com/dboals/diversit.html

DeathNet
www.rights.org/deathnet/open.html

Interactive Bereavement Courses
http://bereavement.org/index.html

Sociology Online Library
http://www.fisk.edu/vl/Sociology/Overview.html

Humor

The Bones
http://www.thebones.com

Death Clock
www.deathclock.com

Professional and Caregiver Resources

AIDS Caregivers Support Network
www.wolfenet.com/acsn

American Association of Suicidology
www.cyberpsych.org

American Lung Association
www.lungusa.org

Association for Death Education and Counseling
http://www.adec.org

Canadian Palliative Care Association
www.cpca.net

Family Crisis
www.excite.com/family/family_in_crisis

Last Acts
http://www.lastacts.org

National Center for Posttraumatic Disorder
http://www.dartmouth.edu/dms/pts/dindex.html

Project on Death in America

http://www.soros.org/death.html

Suicide Information & Education

http://www.siec.ca

Trauma

http://www.ozemail.com.av/dwillsb/trauma.htm

INDEX